A HANDBOOK
on
DEUTERONOMY

The Handbooks in the **UBS Handbook Series** are detailed commentaries providing valuable exegetical, historical, cultural, and linguistic information on the books of the Bible. They are prepared primarily to assist Bible translators as they carry out the important task of putting God's Word into the many languages spoken in the world today. The text is discussed verse by verse and is accompanied by running text in two modern English translations.

Over the years church leaders and Bible readers have found the UBS Handbooks to be useful for their own study of the Scriptures. Many of the issues Bible translators must address when trying to communicate the Bible's message to modern readers are the ones Bible students must address when approaching the Bible text as part of their own private study and devotions.

The Handbooks will continue to be prepared primarily for translators, but we are confident that they will be useful to a wider audience, helping all who use them to gain a better understanding of the Bible message.

Helps for Translators

UBS Handbook Series:

A Handbook on . . .

Genesis
Exodus
Leviticus
Deuteronomy
The Book of Joshua
The Book of Ruth
The Books of First and Second
    Samuel
The Book of Esther
The Book of Job
Psalms
Proverbs
Ecclesiastes
Song of Songs
Lamentations
The Book of Daniel
The Book of Amos
The Books of Obadiah, Jonah,
    and Micah
The Books of Nahum, Habak-
    kuk, and Zephaniah
The Gospel of Matthew
The Gospel of Mark
The Gospel of Luke

The Gospel of John
The Acts of the Apostles
Paul's Letter to the Romans
Paul's First Letter to the
    Corinthians
Paul's Second Letter to the
    Corinthians
Paul's Letter to the Galatians
Paul's Letter to the Ephesians
Paul's Letter to the Philippians
Paul's Letters to the Colossians
    and to Philemon
Paul's Letters to the
    Thessalonians
Paul's Letters to Timothy and
    to Titus
The Letter to the Hebrews
The Letter from James
The First Letter from Peter
The Letter from Jude and the
    Second Letter from Peter
The Letters of John
The Revelation to John

Technical Helps:

Bible Index
Fauna and Flora of the Bible
Greek-English Lexicon of the
    New Testament
Hebrew Poetry in the Bible
Marginal Notes for the Old
    Testament
Marginal Notes for the New
    Testament

New Testament Index
Old Testament Quotations in
    the New Testament
The Practice of Translating
Short Bible Reference System
The Theory and Practice of
    Translation

A HANDBOOK ON

Deuteronomy

by Robert G. Bratcher
and Howard A. Hatton

UBS Handbook Series

UNITED
BIBLE
SOCIETIES

New York

Books in the series of **UBS Helps for Translators** may be ordered from a national Bible Society or from either of the following centers:

United Bible Societies
European Production Fund
P.O. Box 81 03 40
D-70520 Stuttgart
Germany

United Bible Societies
1865 Broadway
New York, NY 10023
U. S. A.

L. C. Cataloging-in-Publication Data

Bratcher, Robert G.
    A handbook on Deuteronomy / by Robert G. Bratcher and Howard
       A. Hatton.
    Includes bibliographical references (p.) and index.
    ISBN 0-8267-0104-3 (pbk.)
       1. Bible. O.T. Deuteronomy–Commentaries. I. Title: Deutero-
    nomy. II. Hatton, Howard, 1929- III. Title. IV. Series

    BS1275.3 .B72 2000
    222'.15077–dc21

                         00-048830
                               CIP

ABS-12/00-1,000-1,000-Y1-105921

Contents

Preface

This Handbook, like others in the series, concentrates on exegetical information important for translators, and it attempts to indicate possible solutions for translational problems related to language or culture. The authors do not consciously attempt to provide help that other theologians and scholars may seek but which is not directly related to the translation task. Such information is normally sought elsewhere. However, many church leaders and interested Bible readers have found these Handbooks useful and informative, and we hope that this volume will be no exception.

The format of A *Handbook on Deuteronomy* follows the general pattern of earlier volumes in the series. The Revised Standard Version (RSV) and Today's English Version (TEV) texts are presented in parallel columns, first in larger segments that will make possible an overview of each section of discourse, and then in bold print, normally verse by verse, followed by detailed comments and discussion. However, when lines of poetry appear in either RSV or TEV, the text in bold print appears across the page rather than in columns, so that the reader may easily identify the difference between individual lines of poetry, and whether a certain line has been printed with a primary or a secondary indentation. RSV serves as the base upon which the discussion takes place, and quotations from the verse under discussion are printed in **boldface**. Quotations from other verses of RSV and from other versions are printed between "quotation marks" and in normal typeface. TEV serves as a primary model of how a translation may take shape; however, many other versions are provided as well, especially where they offer models that may be more satisfactory than those of TEV.

Although the New Revised Standard Version (NRSV) is regarded as an update of RSV, the RSV remains the base for discussion. The reader should keep in mind that the Handbook attempts to explain the ancient Hebrew text to translators who have not learned that language. Since NRSV has succeeded in rendering the message of the ancient text in a form easily understood by today's reader, it reveals less correspondence with the form and shape of the ancient text than does RSV. The authors have therefore found it easier to discuss the ancient text by using RSV as the base.

A limited Bibliography is included for the benefit of those interested in further study. The Glossary explains technical terms according to their usage in this volume. The translator may find it useful to read through the Glossary in order to become aware of the specialized way in which certain terms are used. An Index gives the location by page number of some of the important words and subjects discussed in the Handbook, especially where the Handbook provides the translator with help in rendering these concepts into the receptor language.

The editor of the UBS Handbook Series continues to seek comments from translators and others who use these books, so that future volumes may benefit and may better serve the needs of the readers.

Abbreviations Used in This Volume

General Abbreviations, Bible Texts, Versions, and Other Works Cited

(For details see Bibliography)

A.D.	*Anno Domini* (date), "in the year of our Lord"	NIV	New International Version
		NJB	New Jerusalem Bible
B.C.	(date) Before Christ	NJPSV	New Jewish Publication
BRCL	Brazilian Portuguese common language version		Society version (TANAKH)
CEV	Contemporary English Version	NRSV	New Revised Standard Version
FFB	Fauna and Flora of the Bible	POCL	Portuguese common language version
FRCL	French common language version	REB	Revised English Bible
		RSV	Revised Standard Version
GECL	German common language version	SPCL	Spanish common language version
HOTTP	Hebrew Old Testament Text Project	TEV	Today's English Version
		TOB	*Traduccion œcuménique de la Bible*
JB	Jerusalem Bible		
Mft	Moffatt		
NEB	New English Bible		

Books of the Bible

Gen	Genesis	Lam	Lamentations
Exo	Exodus	Ezek	Ezekiel
Lev	Leviticus	Dan	Daniel
Num	Numbers	Hos	Hosea
Deut	Deuteronomy	Hab	Habakkuk
Josh	Joshua	Zeph	Zephaniah
1,2 Sam	1,2 Samuel	Hag	Haggai
1,2 Kgs	1,2 Kings	Zech	Zechariah
1,2 Chr	1,2 Chronicles	Mal	Malachi
Neh	Nehemiah	Matt	Matthew
Psa	Psalms	Rom	Romans
Pro	Proverbs	1,2 Cor	1,2 Corinthians
Eccl	Ecclesiastes	Gal	Galatians
Song	Song of Songs	Eph	Ephesians
Isa	Isaiah	Heb	Hebrews
Jer	Jeremiah	Rev	Revelation

Hebrew Transliteration Table

The following system of transliteration has been adopted in order to keep all references as simple as possible for those readers who are not trained in Hebrew.

The English vowels, *a, e, i, o,* and *u,* represent the nearest equivalent sounds of the corresponding Hebrew vowels. Gemination of consonants caused by *dagesh forte* will be represented by a single consonant unless the information being discussed requires the distinction. The presence of *dagesh lene* will not be reflected in the representation of *gimel, daleth,* and *kaf,* since the resulting difference in English pronunciation is negligible or nonexistent. Consonants are represented as follows:

א	ʾ	ט	t	פ, ף	f
ב	b	י	y	צ	ts
כ	v	כ, ך	k	ק	q
ג	g	ל	l	ר	r
ד	d	מ, ם	m	שׂ	s
ה	h	נ, ן	n	שׁ	sh
ו	w	ס	s	ת	t
ז	z	ע	ʾ	ת	th
ח	ch	פ	p		

Those who work with the Hebrew text will, of course, wish to consult their copies of the text directly.

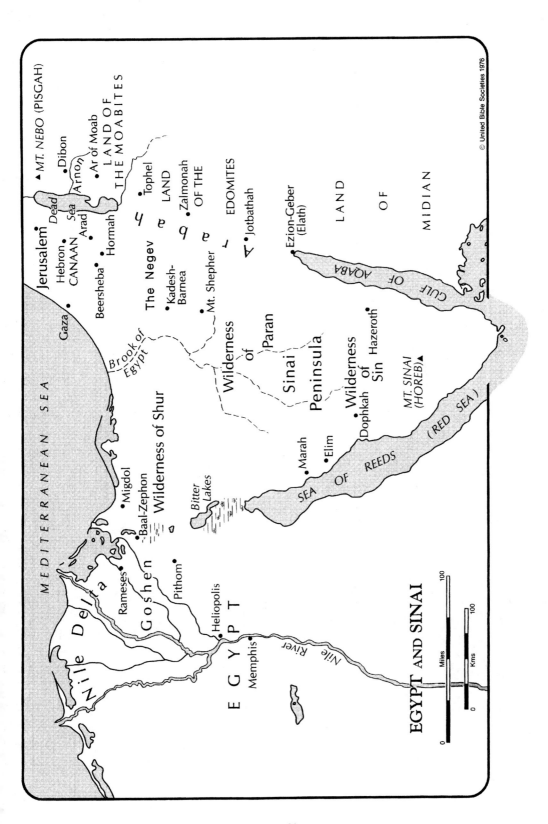

EGYPT AND SINAI

© United Bible Societies 1976

MEDITERRANEAN SEA

Nile Delta

Goshen

E G Y P T

Nile River

Memphis

Heliopolis

Pithom

Rameses

Migdol

Baal-Zephon

Wilderness of Shur

Bitter Lakes

Marah

Elim

SEA OF REEDS

(RED SEA)

Dophkah

Wilderness of Sin

MT. SINAI (HOREB)▲

Hazeroth

Wilderness Peninsula

Sinai

Wilderness of Paran

Gaza

Brook of Egypt

Beersheba

The Negev

Kadesh-Barnea

Mt. Shepher

Jerusalem

Hebron

CANAAN

Arad

Hormah

Dead Sea

▲MT. NEBO (PISGAH)

Dibon

Arnon

Ar of Moab

LAND OF THE MOABITES

Tophel

Zalmonah

LAND OF THE

EDOMITES

Jotbathah

Ezion-Geber (Elath)

GULF OF AQABA

LAND

OF

MIDIAN

Miles

0   100

Kms

0   100

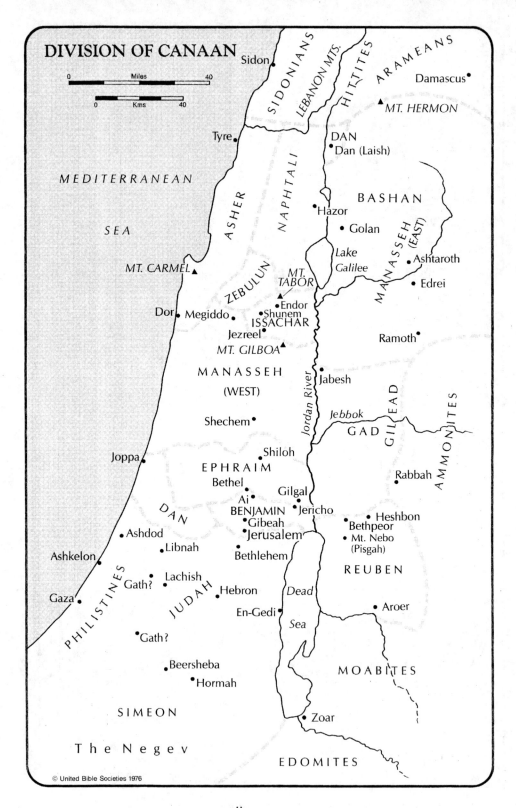

DIVISION OF CANAAN

Miles
0   40

Kms
0   40

MEDITERRANEAN

SEA

Sidon

SIDONIANS

LEBANON MTS.

HITTITES

ARAMEANS

Damascus

MT. HERMON

Tyre

DAN

Dan (Laish)

ASHER

NAPHTALI

BASHAN

Hazor

Golan

MANASSEH (EAST)

Ashtaroth

Lake Galilee

Edrei

MT. CARMEL

ZEBULUN

MT. TABOR

Endor

Dor

Megiddo

Shunem

ISSACHAR

Ramoth

Jezreel

MT. GILBOA

MANASSEH (WEST)

Jabesh

Jordan River

Jebbok

GILEAD

AMMONITES

Shechem

GAD

Shiloh

Joppa

EPHRAIM

Bethel

Gilgal

Rabbah

DAN

Ai

BENJAMIN

Jericho

Gibeah

Heshbon

Ashdod

Jerusalem

Bethpeor

Mt. Nebo (Pisgah)

Libnah

Bethlehem

REUBEN

Ashkelon

Lachish

Dead

Gath?

JUDAH

Hebron

Gaza

En-Gedi

Sea

Aroer

PHILISTINES

Gath?

Beersheba

MOABITES

Hormah

SIMEON

Zoar

The Negev

EDOMITES

© United Bible Societies 1976

xii

Translating Deuteronomy

Deuteronomy is the fifth book in the Bible, the last of the five "Books of Moses," as they are called. These books are also known as the Pentateuch ("five scrolls"). The name comes from the title of the book in the Septuagint, which is the Greek translation of the Hebrew Old Testament. The Greek word, which means "second law," appears in 17.18 as the translation of the Hebrew "copy of this law" (Greek *Deuteronomion*). The Hebrew title, which is simply "Words," comes from the opening words of the book, "These are the words."

More than any other book in the Old Testament, this book claims to have divine authority for the faith and practice of the Israelites. The book appears as an accurate and complete record of God's laws, given by God through Moses to the people of Israel. In the opening and closing sections, references are made to "this book" as a finished and identifiable whole (1.1; 28.58, 61; 29.20, 21, 27; 30.10; 31.24-26; see also Josh 1.7-8). Its text is complete and final, to which nothing is to be added and from which nothing is to be deleted (4.2; 12.32; 31.24). The book claims divine authority.

1. Structure and contents

The book is presented as a series of the speeches that Moses delivered to the Israelites while they were camped in the plains of Moab, on the east side of the Jordan River (1.5; 4.46), opposite the city of Jericho. On the first day of the eleventh month of the fortieth year after they had left Egypt, Moses began to tell the people everything the LORD had commanded him to tell them (1.3-5). Moses was then 120 years old (31.2).

The repeated use of the phrase "this day" 4.8; 30.2, 8, 11, 16; 32.45-46) creates the impression that all of Moses' speeches were delivered on the same day, the first day of the eleventh month (1.3; see 32.48).

In his first speech (1.5–4.40) Moses reviews the history of the people, beginning with their stay at Mount Sinai. In obedience to the LORD's command, they left Mount Sinai, and eleven days later they arrived at Kadesh Barnea (1.2, 19-21). A scouting party was sent into the land of Canaan, and it brought back reports of the strength of the fortified cities and the enormous size of the inhabitants of the land. The people were frightened and refused to enter the land; they then wandered some thirty-eight years in the wilderness (2.14) until they arrived in the territory of Moab, on the east side of the Jordan River. By defeating King Sihon of Moab and King Og of Bashan, the Israelites consolidated their hold on the territory east of the Jordan and were now ready to cross the river into Canaan. Moses ends this first speech with a fervent appeal to the people that they remain faithful to the covenant with their God, and renounce all pagan gods and idols. If they do this, God will be with them and they will live in peace and prosperity in Canaan, the Promised Land (4.15-40).

The second speech (5.1–26.19) consists of two parts: the first part (5.1–11.31) deals with the Ten Commandments, the covenant of God with Israel, and how they are to be applied in the people's lives. The second part (12.1–26.19) is a unit that sets forth the laws, rules, and regulations that will govern all aspects of life, private and communal, once the people are settled in the land of Canaan. This unit is considered by many to have been "the book of the Law" that was discovered in the Temple in Jerusalem by the High Priest Hilkiah, and which brought about the religious reform by King Josiah of Judah in 621 B.C. (2 Kgs 22.1–23.30). The second speech ends with another eloquent plea by Moses that the people obey faithfully all God's laws, and God will be with them and make them the greatest nation on earth (26.16-19).

Then come warnings and promises, blessings and curses (chapters 27–28), after which Moses gives his third speech (chapters 29–30), in which he renews the covenant (29.1, 10-15). This covenant in Moab is in addition to the original covenant at Mount Sinai. Again Moses ends the discourse with an eloquent appeal to the people, urging them to choose life, not death (30.19-20).

The book ends with the installation of Joshua as Moses' successor, followed by the LORD's last instructions to Moses, the song of Moses, Moses' final instructions to the people, Moses' blessing of the tribes, and a report of the death of Moses (chapters 31–34). The book's final words are a tribute to Moses, the greatest of all the prophets of Israel, the man who maintained an intimate relationship with God unmatched by any other prophet in Israel's history (34.10-12).

2. Outline of contents

3. Style and Vocabulary

(a) The greater part of the book consists of Moses' discourses. In most modern languages direct speech is identified either by the use of opening and closing quotation marks (so RSV and TEV), or else by the use of a dash at the beginning of the quoted material (see the Brazilian Portuguese common language version [BRCL] and the French common language version [FRCL]). More recently, however, some translations in English, such as the New International Version [NIV], the New Jewish Publication Society version, or "TANAKH" [NJPSV], The New Revised Standard Version [NRSV], and the Revised English Bible [REB], have not used quotation marks to set off the long discourses. Some translations, like the Contemporary English Version [CEV], are experimenting with the use of narrower columns to set off and identify lengthy quoted material.

Wherever the speech is interrupted by the end of a section or chapter, it is often helpful to include a transition statement such as "And Moses said," or "Moses went on to say," or "And Moses continued," to be placed at the beginning of the new section or chapter, so that the reader will know who is the speaker (so CEV).

Within the long discourses Moses often quotes instructions that the LORD had given him (3.2), or quotes what he had said to the LORD (3.24-25) or to the people (3.18-22), or the people's comments (1.41). In such cases most languages have devices to indicate a second level of quoted material, such as the single quotation marks in English. (In British English and in many countries, the single and double quotation marks are used in reverse order to that in American English and in other countries. Translators will need to determine which system of quotation marks is proper for their own language.)

Whatever the language's way of handling this, the translator must make sure that the reader will know exactly where a quotation begins and where it ends.

(b) Sometimes information is inserted that interrupts the direct discourse, and this material must be signaled, usually by the use of parentheses (1.2; 2.20-24; 10.6-9).

(c) The people are very often addressed in the second person singular; the verbs in the Ten Commandments (5.7-21), for example, are all in the second person masculine singular, but they are directed to all the Israelites: "You shall have no other gods before me" (5.7). In English the singular and the plural form of the second person are the same; but in languages where different forms are used, such as French, Spanish, Italian, Portuguese, and German, the translator must make sure that the reader knows that all the people are being addressed and not just an individual.

(d) The phrase "the LORD your God" appears very frequently, as Moses addresses the people. This is a way of emphasizing that Yahweh, and Yahweh alone, is their God, whom they must worship and obey. In languages that have different forms for the inclusive and the exclusive personal adjectives and pronouns, the translator must make sure not to have Moses say that the LORD is not his God, only the God of the Israelites.

The phrase is used so frequently as to become redundant sometimes. So in 30.3 Moses says: "then the LORD your God . . . will gather you again from all the peoples where the LORD your God has scattered you." A translator will determine whether such redundancy is effective or not in his or her language.

(e) A number of words are used for the commands that Moses transmits to the people: "statute" (4.1), "ordinance" (4.1), "commandment" (4.2), "testimony" (4.45). An unusual phrase is "all the commandment" (5.31). These various nouns are rarely mutually exclusive in meaning, but they serve as terms for God's commands which are very similar in sense. If a language has several terms that can be used, it will be well for the translator to be quite consistent in translating each one; for this the RSV will serve as a good model. Otherwise at least two different terms should be used, such as "law" and "instruction."

The translator must decide how to translate *torah*, which is usually rendered "Law," that is, the whole of all the commandments and laws that Moses gave the people (see 1.5; 4.44; 17.18, 19; 27.3, 8, 26). In many languages the word is capitalized, "the Law," and this may be a good model to follow. The phrase "the Law of God" may be even better.

(f) One theme appears time and again in the book: the land of Canaan is God's gift to the people of Israel. By force of arms they will defeat the Canaanites and possess the land, but it is always God who makes it possible for them to do so. The possession of the land is often described by the use of the verb "to inherit" and the noun "inheritance" (see 1.38, 4.21). In English and other modern languages, "inherit" and "inheritance" carry the meaning that it is because of the death of the original owner that someone becomes the owner of property or goods. This meaning, of course, must be avoided in translating these terms in Deuteronomy.

(g) Constant reference is made to "the place which the LORD will choose, to make his name dwell there" (see 12.5, 11, 21; 14.23-24; 16.2, 6, 11; 26.2). This is the way of speaking of the central place of worship for all the Israelites (eventually, Jerusalem).

This expression and other words and phrases are used quite frequently in the book, and a translator should take pains to render them in the same way, every time they appear.

(h) The frequent use of "you" having seen the plagues of the exodus and other marvelous events indicates that there were still some old people present who remembered those great events.

4. A Note on Yahweh

Although not used either by RSV or TEV, the divine name "Yahweh" appears often in this Handbook. "Yahweh" represents the Hebrew name for God, YHWH (four consonants without vowels), whose precise origin and meaning are disputed (see Exo 3.14-15; 6.2-3). Like most modern translations, RSV and TEV translate "the LORD," a practice that goes back to the Septuagint *ho Kurios* and the Vulgate *Dominus*, both of them meaning "Lord," which is a title, not a proper name.

This written practice of using the title "Lord" (written in capital letters "LORD") conforms to the oral tradition followed in the public reading of the Hebrew Scriptures in the synagogue. In the present, as in the past, whenever the divine name YHWH occurs in the text, the Jewish reader says *Adonai*, a Hebrew title meaning "(my) Lord." The name "Yahweh" itself is taboo: it is regarded by Jewish people today as too holy to be uttered.

Adonai YHWH appears in 3.24 and 9.26. RSV translates "O Lord GOD," and TEV "Sovereign LORD." Something like "LORD Almighty" or "The All-Powerful LORD" are other possibilities (see 3.24).

But there is an increasing number of translations that are breaking with this tradition. The Brazilian translation, *A Bíblia na Linguagem de Hoje* (1988), uses "o Deus Eterno" and "o Eterno" (as did Moffatt [Mft] and the French Segond). But *La Bible de Jérusalem* and its translations into a number of other languages use *Yahvé* and its equivalents. It is recommended that a fresh translation consider the possibility of doing the same.

5. Translation of Poetry

Translating Hebrew poetry is not an easy task, for if translators attempt to keep the poetic form of the Hebrew, the meaning will be often hard to understand. It is important, then, that translators try to introduce poetic features in their own languages that will produce the same or similar impact for the intended readers and not change the meaning of the original.

Before a translator can make a decision about how to translate poetry, he or she must first determine whether the receptor language uses poetry at all. If poetic forms do exist, then it will be necessary to determine whether a song recounting a nation's history and giving warnings about the folly of disobeying a deity (32.1-43), or a song of blessing (33.2-29), are used in that culture. If such poetic forms exist, translators should then consult with people in the community who are known to be competent poets.

If, after careful research, a translator and the translation committee decide to translate 32.1-43 and 33.2-29 into poetry, it must also be decided who will do this translation. This will often be someone different from the person who translates the prose passages of the book. To be successful, poetry must be translated by a person who is a skilled poet in the receptor language. The search for such a person may be difficult but will be rewarding.

In the translation the poem must express all the ideas and the purpose of the original poem; but often it cannot carry over all the poetic forms or rhetorical devices of the Hebrew poetic structure. The main rhetorical devices that appear in Hebrew poetry are various forms of semantic parallelism, where the second of two lines is related in meaning to the first. (Translators are advised to read the excellent discussion on semantic parallelism in *A Handbook on the Book of Psalms*, pages 3-9).

Examples of parallelism that we find in chapters 32 and 33 of Deuteronomy are:

1. Parallelism where the second line means practically the same thing as the first line. An example may be found in the third and fourth lines of 32.2:

> **May my teaching drop as the rain,**
> **my speech distil as the dew.**

or the first and second lines of 32.7:

> **Remember the days of old,**
> **consider the years of many generations;**

or the final two lines of 33.9:

> **For they observed thy word,**
> **and kept thy covenant.**

2. Parallelism where the second line heightens the effect of the previous line. An example is in 32.10:

> **He found them in a desert land,**
> **and in the howling waste of the wilderness;**

or the first two lines in 33.27:

> **The eternal God is your dwelling place,**
> **and underneath are the everlasting arms.**

3. Parallelism where one line has a general statement, and the following line uses terms that are narrower or more precise in meaning. Lines one and two in 32.33 provide a good example:

> **Their wine is the poison of serpents,**
> **and the cruel venom of asps.**

or the first and second lines of 33.17:

> **His firstling bull has majesty;** ·
> **and his horns are the horns of a wild ox;**

If semantic parallelism such as this will be unnatural style for poetry in a language, the parallel lines may be combined in some way. A good example is in 32.1, where the parallel lines in RSV,

> **Give ear, O heavens, and I will speak;**
> **and let the earth hear the words of my mouth.**

have been combined by BRCL to:

> Listen, heaven and earth,
> and pay attention to my words.

While translating the two poems in chapters 32 and 33, translators must be cautious in using English translations as models. RSV, of course, shows more clearly the poetic form of the Hebrew, but this form cannot easily be transferred into another language without losing much of the original emphasis and feeling. TEV and CEV have attempted to translate this poetry in a dynamic or functional way, but their translations do not represent true English poetry. Most English translations have simply used indented lines of varying length, often beginning with capital letters. But this is not true English poetry; it is simply showing readers that the original Hebrew is in poetic form.

In summary: translators must insure that the translated poem has the same meaning as the original Hebrew poem, and it should convey as much as possible the same feeling and emphasis displayed in the original. However, the words, the word pictures, and other rhetorical devices used in the Hebrew will often have to be quite different in the translator's language.

Translators are urged to follow the procedure that is suggested in *A Handbook on the Book of Amos*, page 19:

> The first step in translating into the poetry of any language is to make a simple translation of the ideas of the original into meaningful prose, without being concerned with the poetic form.
>
> As that is done, the translator should keep track of the kinds of images used, the kinds of emotion that he wants to reproduce . . . . This step is necessary in order to make sure that the meaning is preserved.
>
> After that, the same translator, or someone else who is more skilled in poetic style, can take this prose translation and restructure it into the poetic form of the language. We suggest this procedure because it

is easier for a poet to work with his or her own language as he or she tries to sense the feeling and rhythms that will make a suitable poem.

6. A Note on HOTTP

In discussing textual problems, this Handbook refers frequently to "HOTTP," which stands for *Preliminary and Interim Report on the Hebrew Old Testament Text Project* (Pentateuch, 1973).

The HOTTP committee identified four phases in the development of the Hebrew text: (1) the "oral or written literary products in forms as close as possible to those originally produced"; (2) the "earliest attested text," defined as "the earliest form or forms of the text which can be determined by the application of techniques of textual analysis to existing textual evidence"; (3) the "Proto-Masoretic text," the consonantal text as authorized by Jewish scholars shortly after A.D. 70; (4) the Masoretic text, "as determined by the Masoretes in the 9th and 10th centuries A.D."

The committee's goal was to discover the form or forms of the second phase of the text. Once it determined this phase of the text in Hebrew, the committee supplied a translation of it into English and French. Not always will the translator find that the committee's decision answers a translation problem, since the overriding concern of the committee was to deal with textual problems. The committee took pains to explain this matter, and its statement on page xvii should be read carefully. Not every HOTTP textual proposal commended itself to the writers of this Handbook, especially in decisions that are classified {C} (meaning that there is "considerable doubt" about the form of the text) and {D} (meaning that the form of the text is "highly doubtful").

Translators and translation consultants are urged to familiarize themselves with the principles employed by the HOTTP committee and to be especially well acquainted with the "Factors Involved in Textual Decisions" (pages ix-xvi), in order to gain the most profit from this valuable textual help.

Title

Deuteronomy, "second law," comes from the Greek Old Testament Translation (the Septuagint) of Deut 17.18, where the Hebrew means "a copy of the law." The Hebrew title consists of the first two words of the book, "These (are) the-words."

Most translations simply transliterate the English name "Deuteronomy," that is, they spell it in their own alphabet. However, some translators may wish to have a more meaningful title; for example, "Explanation of the Law" (Thai Common Language Bible). The important thing is to find a short meaningful title.

1. Moses' first speech

(1.1–4.43)

1A. Introduction (1.1-5)

REVISED STANDARD VERSION

TODAY'S ENGLISH VERSION

Introduction

1 These are the words that Moses spoke to all Israel beyond the Jordan in the wilderness, in the Arabah over against Suph, between Paran and Tophel, Laban, Hazeroth, and Dizahab. 2 It is eleven days' journey from Horeb by the way of Mount Seir to Kadesh-barnea. 3 And in the fortieth year, on the first day of the eleventh month, Moses spoke to the people of Israel according to all that the LORD had given him in commandment to them, 4 after he had defeated Sihon the king of the Amorites, who lived in Heshbon, and Og the king of Bashan, who lived in Ashtaroth and in Edrei. 5 Beyond the Jordan, in the land of Moab, Moses undertook to explain this law, saying,

1 In this book are the words that Moses spoke to the people of Israel when they were in the wilderness east of the Jordan River. They were in the Jordan Valley near Suph, between the town of Paran on one side and the towns of Tophel, Laban, Hazeroth, and Dizahab on the other. (2 It takes eleven days to travel from Mount Sinai to Kadesh Barnea by way of the hill country of Edom.) 3 On the first day of the eleventh month of the fortieth year after they had left Egypt, Moses told the people everything the LORD had commanded him to tell them. 4 This was after the LORD had defeated King Sihon of the Amorites, who ruled in the town of Heshbon, and King Og of Bashan, who ruled in the towns of Ashtaroth and Edrei. 5 It was while the people were east of the Jordan

> in the territory of Moab that Moses began to
> explain God's laws and teachings.
> He said,

Instead of ending this opening section at verse 8, as TEV does, there are other possibilities for translators: (1) end it at verse 5 (as New Jerusalem Bible [NJB], and French common language version [FRCL] do), since at verse 6 Moses begins to speak, or (2) end the section at verse 4 (as Contemporary English Version [CEV] does), since verse 5 tells where and when Moses began his speeches.

Section heading: there should be two headings here. The first one, "Moses' first speech," may also be expressed as "Moses begins to talk to the Israelites." The subheading, as the title of 1.1-4 or 1.1-5, may be "Introduction," "Moses' first words," "First words," or else something like NJB "Time and Place," or even "The time and place where Moses spoke his final words" may be more appropriate.

1.1	RSV	TEV

These are the words that Moses spoke to all Israel beyond the Jordan in the wilderness, in the Arabah over against Suph, between Paran and Tophel, Laban, Hazeroth, and Dizahab.	In this book are the words that Moses spoke to the people of Israel when they were in the wilderness east of the Jordan River. They were in the Jordan Valley near Suph, between the town of Paran on one side and the towns of Tophel, Laban, Hazeroth, and Dizahab on the other.

These are the words that Moses spoke to all Israel: this can be rendered "This is a [written] report [or, record] of what Moses said to all the people of Israel." The pronoun **These** must, of course, point forward, not backward. So the sentence may begin "What follows is . . . ," or even "In this book are the words . . ." (TEV, BRCL, German common language version [GECL]); FRCL has "This book reports . . . ," and CEV has "This book contains the speeches that Moses made . . . ." And instead of the literal **words**, it will be better for translators to have something similar to "the long speeches" (BRCL, FRCL), or even "the discourses."

To all Israel means, of course, "to all the people of Israel," "to all the Israelites." However, in some languages simply translating "to the Israelites" or "to the people of Israel" will mean that "all" are included.

Beyond the Jordan: the point of view of the writer is the land of Israel, so that "the other side of the Jordan River" means the east side, that is, Transjordan. More precisely Moses and the people of Israel are in the plains of Moab (Num 33.48; 36.13). CEV makes this clear with "while Israel was in the land of Moab." **Jordan** may be translated as "Jordan River" or "the river named Jordan."

In the wilderness: this was an area without permanent human habitation, usually dry and rocky, unfit for cultivation of crops, but with occasional patches of moisture and vegetation. Translations have often used the term "desert" for

wilderness, meaning that it had only sand; but this is not accurate, as this **wilderness** did have vegetation of various kinds. In cultures where very dry areas like this are unknown, we may translate **wilderness** with a descriptive phrase; for example, "rocky region with little vegetation," "place where people don't settle," "a place where no house is," and so on.

In the Arabah over against Suph: the **Arabah** is the deep depression that makes for the Jordan Valley, running to the Dead Sea and further south as far as the Gulf of Aqaba. TEV "the Jordan Valley" accurately names the part of the **Arabah** that is spoken of here. The phrase **against Suph** modifies **the Arabah**, that is, "that part of the Arabah that faces [or, is opposite] Suph." We do not know exactly what "opposite Suph" means, since the identity and location of **Suph** are unknown. The Hebrew preposition means "in front of"; in more general terms the phrase can be represented by "near a place named Suph." NJB has "facing Suph." In languages that will have difficulty expressing "Jordan Valley," it will be possible to combine the two phrases **beyond the Jordan in the wilderness** and **in the Arabah over against Suph**, and translate the first part of this verse as follows:

- This book contains the long speeches that Moses spoke to the Israelites while they were in the land of Moab. They were camped near the place called Suph in the wilderness east of the river named Jordan.

Between Paran and Tophel, Laban, Hazeroth, and Dizahab: TEV and the Revised English Bible (REB) make it clear that Paran is on one side, and the other four towns are on the other side of the Jordan. None of these localities has been identified. Since it is not clear whether Paran was to the west and the other towns to the east, translators should leave this ambiguous. Another way to express this is "The town of Paran was on one side of them and the towns of . . . on the other side." CEV resolves this problem with "The town of Paran was in one direction from their camp, and the towns of . . . were in the opposite direction." In cultures where the only large human settlements are villages surrounded by fences, translators will need to use descriptive phrases for "towns"; for example, "large villages with high fences around them," and in the case of "cities," when this term occurs later in Deuteronomy (see 1.22), we may say "very large villages . . ." or something similar.

1.2	RSV	TEV

It is eleven days' journey from Horeb by the way of Mount Seir to Kadesh-barnea.	(It takes eleven days to travel from Mount Sinai to Kadesh Barnea by way of the hill country of Edom.)

This verse is placed within parentheses by New Revised Standard Version (NRSV), REB, FRCL, TEV, GECL, since its relation to what comes before and what follows is unclear. See verse 19. A translator must be aware of what parentheses mean in a given language. In English (such as TEV) they mean that the statement inside them interrupts the flow of the discourse, which goes directly from what comes before them to what follows them. In some languages parentheses indicate that the material enclosed is not very important and can be overlooked.

It is eleven days' journey: this converts into something like 250-270 kilometers (160-170 miles). In some languages we may express this clause as "It takes only eleven days to walk from Mount Sinai . . . ," or "A person needs only eleven days to . . . ."

Horeb is the area in which Mount Sinai is located, and the word often functions as the name of the mountain itself (as TEV translates).

By the way of Mount Seir: this means the road that runs through the mountainous region of **Seir**, better known as Edom. Another way to express this phrase is "by way of [or, through] the area with many hills [or, hilly area] named Edom."

Kadesh-barnea is an oasis in the desert (that is, the Negev), some 80 kilometers (50 miles) south of Beersheba (see map, page xi).

An alternative translation model for this verse is:

- A person needs only eleven days to walk from Mount Sinai to Kadesh Barnea through the hilly area named Edom.

1.3 RSV TEV

And in the fortieth year, on the first day of the eleventh month, Moses spoke to the people of Israel according to all that the LORD had given him in commandment to them,

On the first day of the eleventh month of the fortieth year after they had left Egypt, Moses told the people everything the LORD had commanded him to tell them.

In the fortieth year: that is, forty years after leaving Egypt.

The eleventh month was named Shebat, the month beginning with the new moon in what now is usually January; but this can vary by as much as four weeks because their calendar was based upon the appearance of the new moon as the beginning of every month.

The people of Israel: this is more naturally represented in English by "the Israelites" (as NRSV has it).

According to all that the LORD had given him in commandment to them: the phrase **according to** (or, "just as") does not refer to the manner in which Moses delivered Yahweh's message to the people; it is simply saying that Moses told them everything that Yahweh had ordered him to tell them.

The translation of "Yahweh" (spelled YHWH in Hebrew), the name of the God of Israel, is a matter dealt with in most Bibles, and the Introduction to TEV explains why it happens that practically all major translations into English and other world languages have "the LORD" or its equivalent. Since the publication in English of the Jerusalem Bible, "Yahweh" has been shown to be an option for translators, and the translations of the Jerusalem Bible into other languages

(German, Spanish, Portuguese) have the same transliteration of the Hebrew name.

There is, however, another option for translators: substitute another personal name from the language and culture of the translation. *A Handbook on Leviticus*, page 10, has some helpful comments on this issue:

> . . . there may be a personal name for God which is distinct from the generic name for "god" but quite similar in usage to the biblical term . . . . In such cases it may be wise to adopt this name as the equivalent of YHWH. This possibility has often been overlooked in past translations of the Bible. But even though the commonly used name in the receptor language is not an exact equivalent of YHWH, it may be wise to use it in translation and give a full explanation of the Biblical name in the glossary.

However, translators who consider this option should be sensitive to the ideas and meanings associated with the name of a local deity. If these should contradict or even distort the biblical concept of God, then translators should follow one of the other options.

The solution to this problem requires serious study and research by the leaders of the Christian community for which the translation is intended. For other comments on the translation of "Yahweh," see "Translating Deuteronomy," pages 7 and following. Translators should also pay particular attention to comments in the prefaces of RSV and TEV, and discussions in other UBS Handbooks.

1.4 RSV	TEV
after he had defeated Sihon the king of the Amorites, who lived in Heshbon, and Og the king of Bashan, who lived in Ashtaroth and in Edrei.	**This was after the LORD[a] had defeated King Sihon of the Amorites, who ruled in the town of Heshbon, and King Og of Bashan, who ruled in the towns of Ashtaroth and Edrei.**

[a] the LORD; *or* Moses.

Verse 4 in Hebrew continues without a break from verse 3, but in many languages it is better to make a break, as TEV does (also NRSV). "This was after . . . ," or we may say "He spoke to the people after . . . ."

He had defeated: the Hebrew text is ambiguous, since the pronominal suffix "he" can mean either Moses or Yahweh. REB keeps the ambiguity by using the passive construction "after the defeat of . . ."; this, however, is not recommended. TEV has "the LORD," while CEV, FRCL, BRCL, GECL, and Spanish common language version (SPCL) have "Moses," which is the preferred interpretation and recommended for translators. This does not mean that Moses single-handedly defeated Sihon; it means that the Israelites, commanded

by Moses, defeated the Amorites commanded by Sihon. It is a fairly common
thing to credit victory (and defeat) to the commander of the fighting troops.

For the defeat of **Sihon the king of the Amorites**, see Num 21.21-32. These
Amorites were the people living in the hill country east of the Jordan (see Num
13.29). **Amorites** will be expressed in some languages as "people of Amor." **King**
in certain languages will be rendered as "high [or, great] chief" or just "the
great one." So **Sihon the king of the Amorites** may also be expressed as "Sihon,
the great chief in the town of Heshbon, who ruled over the people of Amor."

Heshbon was a town some fifteen kilometers (nine miles) east of the northern
tip of the Dead Sea. **Bashan** was the region to the northeast of Lake Galilee.
For the location of the towns of **Ashtaroth** and **Edrei**, see map, page xii.

Who lived . . . who lived: since the verbs have a king as subject, in both cases
the verb may be rendered "who ruled" (TEV, REB; NRSV "reigned"). The Hebrew
text says that Og had "lived [or, ruled] in Ashtaroth in Edrei"; the Greek
translation, the Septuagint, has "in Ashtaroth and in Edrei." Taking its clue
from the account in Num 21.33-35 (see also Deut 3.1), which reports the defeat
of Og in Edrei (verse 33), REB, FRCL, and others connect "in Edrei" with the verb
"he defeated" and translate "defeated Og . . . (who lived in Ashtaroth) in Edrei."
This is possible, but most, like TEV, NRSV, GECL, New Jewish Publication
Society version (NJPSV, or "TANAKH"), NJB, translate "lived [or, ruled] in
Ashtaroth and Edrei" (see Josh 12.4; 13.12, 31). SPCL takes Ashtaroth to be a
town and Edrei a region, but this does not seem very likely. It is recommended
that the translation say "who ruled in the towns of Ashtaroth and Edrei" or
"who ruled over the people in the towns of . . . ," and the first part of the verse
may be alternatively expressed as "He [Moses] spoke to the people after he had
defeated Sihon, who . . . ."

1.5	RSV	TEV

Beyond the Jordan, in the land of | It was while the people were east of
Moab, Moses undertook to explain | the Jordan in the territory of Moab
this law, saying, | that Moses began to explain God's
  | laws and teachings.
  | He said,

Beyond the Jordan: see verse 1.

Moses undertook to explain this law: the Hebrew verb translated **undertook**
can be taken to mean "decided," "resolved" (REB, NJB), or "began" (TEV, CEV, New
International Version [NIV], BRCL). The verb translated **explain** is found
elsewhere in the Bible only in Deut 27.8 and Hab 2.2, in both of which passages
it means "write." But no translation referred to in this Handbook has that
meaning here. It is usually rendered "explain" or "make plain." **This law** seems
to refer to what follows, perhaps what is found in chapters 5–26 (Mayes). It
seems probable that the reader would understand **this law** to mean the Torah,
as given in the three speeches of Moses. GECL has "the law of the Lord," and
FRCL "the law of God." This may be a good model to follow if the word **law**
carries the idea of legal enactments, in the modern sense of the word.

It is regrettable that the Hebrew *torah* is uniformly translated in English Bibles by "law" or "Law," which is due to the translation of the Hebrew word into *nomos* ("law") by the Greek of the Septuagint, and the use of the same Greek word in the New Testament to refer to the Old Testament *torah*. The Hebrew word means rather what would be called "instruction" or "teaching" (as NJPSV has it, "this Teaching"). Translators may consider the possibility of using something other than "law" or its equivalents and say something like "teaching" or "instruction" throughout the Bible. Notice that TEV translates as "God's laws and teachings," in an effort to include all the material that Moses talks about in his speeches.

Saying: this comes at the end of the verse and is the link to what follows. But since a new section will begin with the next verse (as was suggested in the introduction to this chapter), it is recommended that the translation of this word be placed at the beginning of verse 6, "Moses said" or its equivalent. However, if translators follow CEV and begin a new section at 1.5, the translation of **saying** may be placed at the end of this verse as in RSV; for example, "Moses began explaining those laws [or, instructions] by saying . . . ."

1B. The order to leave Mount Sinai (1.6-8)

RSV	TEV
6 "The LORD our God said to us in Horeb, 'You have stayed long enough at this mountain; 7 turn and take your journey, and go to the hill country of the Amorites, and to all their neighbors in the Arabah, in the hill country and in the lowland, and in the Negeb, and by the seacoast, the land of the Canaanites, and Lebanon, as far as the great river, the river Euphrates. 8 Behold, I have set the land before you; go in and take possession of the land which the LORD swore to your fathers, to Abraham, to Isaac, and to Jacob, to give to them and to their descendants after them.'	6 "When we were at Mount Sinai, the LORD our God said to us, 'You have stayed long enough at this mountain. 7 Break camp and move on. Go to the hill country of the Amorites and to all the surrounding regions—to the Jordan Valley, to the hill country and the lowlands, to the southern region, and to the Mediterranean coast. Go to the land of Canaan and on beyond the Lebanon Mountains as far as the great Euphrates River. 8 All of this is the land which I, the LORD, promised to give to your ancestors, Abraham, Isaac, and Jacob, and to their descendants. Go and occupy it.' "

Section heading: this section may be entitled "The order to leave Mount Sinai [or, Horeb]," or "God orders the Israelites to leave Sinai."

1.6 RSV	TEV
"The LORD our God said to us in Horeb, 'You have stayed long enough at this mountain;	"When we were at Mount Sinai, the LORD our God said to us, 'You have stayed long enough at this mountain.

As noted at the end of verse 5, this verse may begin "And Moses said" or "And Moses went on to say." RSV, TEV, BRCL, SPCL, NJB and others have a double set of quotation marks; but this can become rather cumbersome, and some disregard the first set, that is, Moses' words (see NRSV, REB). This may be better in some languages. Another possible model, though, is to end verse 5 with a colon (:); for example. "⁵ . . . Moses began to explain these laws saying: ⁶ When we were . . . ." We may also follow the CEV model and begin verse 6 with "People of Israel, when we were in . . . ."

Languages differ in the way they handle reported speech. In this verse and at other places in following verses, there will be two levels of reported speech. English versions use different typographical systems to show this; for example, RSV and TEV use double quotation marks (" and ") for Moses' words, and single quotation marks (' and ') for the LORD's words. CEV, however, prefers to use a colon at both levels:

> ⁵ Moses began explaining those laws by saying:
>   ⁶ People of Israel, . . . the LORD our God told us:
>   You have stayed . . . .

However, this is not recommended because it leaves unclear where the quotation ends.

Another typographical system is shown in the alternative translation model below. Translators should use a system that is the most natural way for reporting speech in their language.

Horeb: see verse 2.

The LORD our God: throughout this chapter various terms are used to refer to Yahweh; we find "the LORD" (verse 3), "the LORD our God" (verses 19, 20), "the LORD your God" (verses 10, 26, 30), "the LORD, the God of your fathers" (verses 11, 21). In some languages we must say something like "The LORD [or, Yahweh] who is our God." Care must be taken that "our God" does not mean "the God we own." In some languages it will be necessary to say "the God we serve" or "the God we worship."

You have stayed long enough at this mountain: they had been at Mount Sinai almost twelve months (see Exo 19.1 and Num 10.11-12). The verb translated **stayed** may carry the idea of lingering, resting, remaining inactive; it is related to the noun "sabbath" (day of rest). Instead of **at this mountain** the translation can be "at the foot of this mountain" (FRCL).

An alternative translation model for this verse is:

- And Moses said: People of Israel, when we were camping at the foot of Mount Sinai, Yahweh, the God we worship, said to us, "You have stayed here long enough.

1.7	RSV	TEV
	turn and take your journey, and go to the hill country of the Amorites, and to all their neighbors in the Arabah, in the hill country and in the lowland, and in the Negeb, and by the sea-	Break camp and move on. Go to the hill country of the Amorites and to all the surrounding regions—to the Jordan Valley, to the hill country and the lowlands, to the southern region,

coast, the land of the Canaanites, and Lebanon, as far as the great river, the river Euphrates.

and to the Mediterranean coast. Go to the land of Canaan and on beyond the Lebanon Mountains as far as the great Euphrates River.

This verse describes the extent of the territory that God tells the Israelites they are to conquer and possess. It includes practically all of modern day Israel, Lebanon, and Syria (see God's promise to Abraham in Gen 15.18).

Turn and take your journey, and go: NRSV is clearer in English, with "Resume your journey, and go" (see also TEV); NIV has "Break camp, and advance into." It is not necessary to have three verbs, as though every verb carries a distinct, separate meaning. The first two verbs "turn and start out" go together: "start marching again," "resume your journey."

The hill country of the Amorites: here the phrase may have the broader meaning of all the land of Canaan (as in verse 19), and not just a particular region, even though in verse 4 "the Amorites" are people living on the east side of the Jordan. (See also that verse for a comment on **Amorites**.)

Instead of following RSV **all their neighbors in the Arabah, in the hill country** . . . , it is better to imitate TEV, "and to all the surrounding regions—to the . . ." (also NRSV "as well as into the neighboring regions—the Arabah . . ."). Another possible model for the first part of this verse is "Break camp [or, Pack up your tents] and resume your journey. Go into the land that belongs to the Amorites and their neighbors. This includes: . . . ."

The Arabah: see verse 1.

The hill country and . . . the lowland: or "the hill country and the Shephelah" (NRSV; also REB). The Shefelah was the low hill country between the mountains of Judah and the plain of Philistia. Another way to express **hill country is** "an area with many hills."

The Negeb was the wilderness between the southern hill country and the desert to the south. For a comment on the translation of **wilderness**, see verse 1.

And by the seacoast: NRSV is more natural in English, "and the seacoast"; also TEV, "the Mediterranean coast." This was the plain along the coast. So we may express **by the seacoast** as "the flat area along the edge of the Mediterranean Sea."

The land of the Canaanites: or in more natural English, "the land of Canaan." This phrase may mean the whole country, in which case this is a summary statement, as REB translates: ". . . and on the coast; in short, all Canaan and the Lebanon . . . ." But the phrase may also be used in a more restricted sense to mean Phoenicia, on the coast (as in the NJPSV footnote). It seems better, however, to take it to mean the whole land of Canaan.

Lebanon: or "the Lebanon Mountains," since at that time there was no country known as Lebanon.

The great river, the river Euphrates: the Euphrates is sometimes called simply "the River" (Josh 24.3, 14-15). **Great** here means "large" or "wide." In some languages this phrase will be expressed as "the great [or, wide] river named Euphrates."

It may help to give the directions for the Lebanon Mountains and the Euphrates, as follows: "as far north as the Lebanon Mountains, and as far east as the great Euphrates River" (see BRCL).

The whole verse may be translated as follows:

- Get moving again, and advance into the land of the Amorites and all the nearby regions: the Jordan Valley, the hill country and the lowlands, the Negeb [or, the southern wilderness], and the Mediterranean coast. That is, move into the whole land of Canaan and the Lebanon Mountains, and advance as far as the mighty Euphrates River.

1.8   RSV   TEV

Behold, I have set the land before you; go in and take possession of the land which the LORD swore to your fathers, to Abraham, to Isaac, and to Jacob, to give to them and to their descendants after them.'

All of this is the land which I, the LORD, promised to give to your ancestors, Abraham, Isaac, and Jacob, and to their descendants. Go and occupy it.' "

Behold: in Hebrew the verb (literally, "See") is the second person singular; the people are addressed as a single being. The verb functions as an attention getter and may be translated "See," "Look," or even "Listen," "Pay attention." In certain African languages an ideophone will be a good attention getter here.

I have set the land before you: the Hebrew verb means "to present," "to offer," "to deliver" (see 2.31), and **before you** means that the Israelites will possess it, conquer it. NJPSV translates "I place this land at your disposal"; FRCL "I offer you this land"; BRCL "Here is the land that I am giving you," or we can say "I give this land to you."

Go in and take possession of the land: the verb translated "take possession of" does not say anything about whether force will have to be used to possess the land. In the context, however, the readers of the book knew that it was only by the use of force that the Israelites became the masters of the land of Canaan. If in a language there is a term for **take possession** that has the sense of using force, that term should be employed here.

Which the LORD swore to your fathers . . . to give to them: this may also be translated "that the LORD promised to give to your fathers [or, ancestors]." Since an important promise was always accompanied by a sacred vow, "to swear" means "to make a solemn promise," and in certain languages this will be expressed as "I, Yahweh, made a strong promise to your ancestors." In the case of Yahweh making a promise, he would "swear" by his own name that he would do what he promised to do. In many languages it will be better to use the term "ancestors" instead of **fathers**. Moses mentions the three great patriarchs of Hebrew history, Abraham, Isaac, and Jacob. Other ways of expressing **fathers** or "ancestors" are "those who lived long ago," "grandfathers in ancient times," "big [or, famous] grandfathers," and so on. In many languages translators will find it more natural style to place the clause **which the LORD swore . . .** immediately after the first sentence, **I have set this land before you**, as in TEV, CEV, and others.

Instead of "the LORD," NRSV, following the Samaritan Pentateuch text and the Septuagint, has "I." On translational grounds, however, in order to avoid the rather unnatural situation of Yahweh referring to himself in the third person, it is possible to translate "I, the LORD" (TEV, FRCL, SPCL, BRCL), or "I, Yahweh."

Your fathers: your includes Moses, of course, as Yahweh is speaking.

To give translates the same Hebrew verb translated "present" in the first part of the verse.

Their descendants after them: it is not necessary to represent the redundant "after them," since descendants always come after their ancestors. **Descendants** may be variously expressed as "grandchildren and great-grandchildren," or even "the people who follow after them [or, come down from them]."

1C. Moses appoints judges (1.9-18)

RSV

9 "At that time I said to you, 'I am not able alone to bear you; 10 the LORD your God has multiplied you, and behold, you are this day as the stars of heaven for multitude. 11 May the LORD, the God of your fathers, make you a thousand times as many as you are, and bless you, as he has promised you! 12 How can I bear alone the weight and burden of you and your strife? 13 Choose wise, understanding, and experienced men, according to your tribes, and I will appoint them as your heads.' 14 And you answered me, 'The thing that you have spoken is good for us to do.' 15 So I took the heads of your tribes, wise and experienced men, and set them as heads over you, commanders of thousands, commanders of hundreds, commanders of fifties, commanders of tens, and officers, throughout your tribes. 16 And I charged your judges at that time, 'Hear the cases between your brethren, and judge righteously between a man and his brother or the alien that is with him. 17 You shall not be partial in judgment; you shall hear the small and the great alike; you shall not be afraid of the face of man, for the judgment is God's; and the case that is too hard for you, you shall bring to me, and I will hear it.' 18 And I commanded you at that time all the things that you should do.

TEV
Moses Appoints Judges

9 Moses said to the people, "While we were still at Mount Sinai, I told you, 'The responsibility for leading you is too much for me. I can't do it alone. 10 The LORD your God has made you as numerous as the stars in the sky. 11 May the LORD, the God of your ancestors, make you increase a thousand times more and make you prosperous, as he promised! 12 But how can I alone bear the heavy responsibility for settling your disputes? 13 Choose some wise, understanding, and experienced men from each tribe, and I will put them in charge of you.' 14 And you agreed that this was a good thing to do. 15 So I took the wise and experienced leaders you chose from your tribes, and I placed them in charge of you. Some were responsible for a thousand people, some for a hundred, some for fifty, and some for ten. I also appointed other officials throughout the tribes.

16 "At that time I instructed them, 'Listen to the disputes that come up among your people. Judge every dispute fairly, whether it concerns only your own people or involves foreigners who live among you. 17 Show no partiality in your decisions; judge everyone on the same basis, no matter who they are. Do not be afraid of anyone, for the decisions you make come from God. If any case is too difficult for you, bring it to me, and I will decide it.' 18 At the same time I gave you instructions for everything else you were to do.

This account is somewhat difficult to understand. Moses speaks of choosing reputable, respected men as "leaders" (verse 13), and then he does so (verse 15); then he gives instructions to "your judges" (verse 16), who have not been mentioned before. In the parallel account (Exo 18.13-27) Moses follows Jethro's advice and chooses leaders (Exo 18.25), who serve as judges (18.26). See the comments at verse 16 on how the matter can be handled.

Section heading: instead of TEV "Moses Appoints Judges," it may be better to translate "Moses selects [or, appoints] leaders for the people." BRCL uses the word "Helpers."

1.9   RSV   TEV

"At that time I said to you, 'I am   Moses said to the people, "While
not able alone to bear you;   we were still at Mount Sinai, I told
          you, 'The responsibility for leading
          you is too much for me. I can't do it
          alone.

Since a new section begins here, it may be helpful to introduce Moses as the speaker; for example, TEV "Moses said to the people . . . ."

At that time: that is, while they were still at Mount Sinai. TEV brings this out clearly with "While we were still at Mount Sinai . . . ," and CEV has "Right after the LORD commanded us to leave Mount Sinai . . . ."

I am not able alone to bear you: Moses was saying that he couldn't bear the burden of governing the people by himself; he needed help. REB has "You are too heavy a burden for me to bear unaided," and NIV is very much like it, ". . . for me to carry alone." The verbal phrase "to bear you" may be rendered "to look after you," "to direct you," "to govern you," or even "being your leader" (CEV).

In some languages two levels of quotation marks as in RSV and TEV will be unnatural style. See verse 6 for further comments. CEV (using a colon) may be a helpful alternative model for this verse:

- *Moses said:*
  ⁹ Right after the LORD commanded us to leave Mount Sinai, I told you:
  Israel, being your leader is too big a job for one person.

Another possible model is:

- Moses said, "Right after the LORD commanded us to leave Mount Sinai, I told you that being your leader was too big a job for one person. . . .

1.10 RSV TEV

the LORD your God has multiplied
you, and behold, you are this day as
the stars of heaven for multitude.

The LORD your God has made you as
numerous as the stars in the sky.

The LORD your God has multiplied you: in some languages "your God" will
mistakenly mean that **the LORD** is not the God of Moses, but only of the people
he is addressing. Of course this is not what the text is implying. Rather **your
God** emphasizes that Yahweh is the God of the Hebrews, and they must always
be aware of that central fact of their existence as a people. So **your God** or its
equivalent should be used whenever possible. This will occur frequently in this
book. In some cases we may have to say, for example, "the LORD our God" (CEV)
or "Yahweh, the God [whom] we worship." The verb "multiply" means, of
course, to increase in numbers by making them a fertile people who had many
children (descendants). NJB has "increased your numbers." In certain languages
we may express this as "The LORD, the God whom you [plural] worship, has
caused you to have so many children and grandchildren that there are as many
of you as . . . ."

Behold: this translates a different Hebrew word from the one used in verse
8, but the meaning is the same. In some languages an attention-getting marker
will be appropriate here (see the discussion at 1.8), but in most languages this
word will not need to be translated, as it will sound unnatural (compare TEV,
CEV). Or we may say ". . . and so you are now as numerous . . . ."

As the stars of heaven for multitude: NRSV is more natural in English, "as
numerous as the stars of heaven." Where there are two words, as in English, for
"heaven" and "sky," here the word to be used should be "sky." If it should
happen that the phrase "stars *in the sky*" sounds ridiculous (where else are
there stars?), "in the sky" may be omitted.

The whole statement may be translated:

● The LORD our God [or, The God whom we worship] has given you
so many children [or, descendants], that now there are as many
of you as there are stars [in the sky].

1.11 RSV TEV

May the LORD, the God of your fathers, make you a thousand times as
many as you are, and bless you, as
he has promised you!

May the LORD, the God of your ancestors, make you increase a thousand times more and make you prosperous, as he promised!

This verse is in the form of a wish, or a prayer. NJB takes it to be a statement,
but this seems quite unlikely. FRCL translates "I hope that . . . ." We may also
say "I pray that . . . ."

The LORD, the God of your fathers: again, if **your** excludes Moses, the
translation must be "the God of our fathers"—that is, "of our ancestors." The

possessive "your [or, our]" must not be understood to mean that God belonged to the ancestors; therefore it may be necessary to translate "the God that your [or, our] ancestors worshiped." For a comment on **fathers** or "ancestors," see verse 8.

Make you a thousand times as many as you are: for languages that have a name for the quantity "one thousand," there is no great problem involved in translating this: "make you a thousand times more than you are now." But languages not having a numerical system that reaches to one thousand must be content to say the equivalent of "many, many more," and we may translate "cause you to have many, many more children and grandchildren." The figure is not meant literally; it is a typical hyperbole (exaggeration) expressing the desire that the Israelites become a very numerous people.

And bless you, as he has promised you: the verb "to bless" means "to do good things to," "to give good things to"; TEV "make prosperous."

An alternative translation model for this verse is:

• I pray that Yahweh, who is the God we worship, will cause you to have many, many more children and grandchildren, and also give lots of good things to you as he has promised.

1.12	RSV	TEV

How can I bear alone the weight and burden of you and your strife?	**But how can I alone bear the heavy responsibility for settling your disputes?**

How can I bear alone the weight . . . ? This is what is called a rhetorical question; that is, Moses does not want an answer to his question (as though someone could tell him how he could bear the weight alone), but he is declaring, emphatically, that it is not possible for him to bear the weight alone. So in languages that would not use a rhetorical question in this context, we may translate, for example, "But I cannot alone bear the heavy responsibility . . ." or "But I cannot take care of all your problems . . . alone" (CEV), or else "There is no way I could bear . . . ."

The weight and burden of you and your strife: this translates the Hebrew "the-load-of-you and the-burden-of-you and your-strife." The first two nouns have the same meaning, and it may be that they function as a phrase, "heavy burden" or "heavy load." The noun translated **strife** means more precisely "complaints" and here refers to the complaints the people made against Moses, accusing him of being a failure and of making them suffer (see Exo 17.7; Num 14.1-4). See REB "and put up with your complaints." This seems preferable to TEV "disputes" and RSV **strife**.

It is possible that all three nouns go together in one phrase: "the heavy load of your complaints" or "your continual [or incessant, or unending] complaining." And the entire verse may be alternatively expressed as:

- But I cannot alone bear [or, put up with] your unending complaints against me.

1.13   RSV   TEV

Choose wise, understanding, and experienced men, according to your tribes, and I will appoint them as your heads.'	Choose some wise, understanding, and experienced men from each tribe, and I will put them in charge of you.'

Choose wise, understanding, and experienced men: the men they are to select are to have characteristics designated by three words that are broadly similar, whose meanings overlap one another. The first two, **wise** and **understanding**, are words used many times in the Old Testament. If there is a difference in meaning, **wise** may be used to describe someone who considers every matter very carefully, and **understanding** describes someone with good judgment or discernment. If a language does not have a range of terms like the Hebrew, we may combine the two terms and say, for example, "People who consider every matter very carefully," or even idiomatically, "people with very big minds." The third word, **experienced**, is not used as often. It is a passive construction of the verb "to know," and so probably means "known," that is, "reputable," "respected." So NRSV has "reputable," and FRCL "having a good reputation." In a number of languages we may also say "have much face." REB translates "men of wisdom, understanding, and repute." The first part of this verse may thus be translated:

- You must choose some men who are known for their ability to consider every matter carefully and who also have a good reputation.

According to your tribes: this may mean "for your tribes" (NRSV, REB), but it most likely means "from your tribes" (TEV, FRCL, BRCL, SPCL). It is better to say "from each [or, every] tribe." If the possessive "your" excludes Moses (as though he did not belong to one of the tribes of Israel), it seems better to say "from every one of the twelve tribes." Traditionally **tribes** in English and its equivalent in other languages has been used to translate the Hebrew word; but in some languages something like "clans" or "family groups" will be more adequate, since the **tribes** of Israel were subgroups of the people as a whole.

I will appoint them as your heads: after the people have chosen these men, Moses will officially install, or commission, them as leaders of the people. The word **heads** (that is, leaders) probably involves military and executive (or, judicial) authority.

1.14   RSV   TEV

And you answered me, 'The thing   **And you agreed that this was a good**
that you have spoken is good for us **thing to do.**
to do.'

This verse offers no problems for translators. NRSV is clearer than RSV; it has
"The plan you have proposed is a good one." NJB is even more concise, "Your
plan is good." NJPSV and REB are alike: "What you propose to do is good." CEV
has "That's a good idea!"

1.15   RSV   TEV

So I took the heads of your tribes,   **So I took the wise and experienced**
wise and experienced men, and set   **leaders you chose from your tribes,**
them as heads over you, command-   **and I placed them in charge of you.**
ers of thousands, commanders of   **Some were responsible for a thou-**
hundreds, commanders of fifties,   **sand people, some for a hundred,**
commanders of tens, and officers,   **some for fifty, and some for ten. I**
throughout your tribes.   **also appointed other officials**
                                        throughout the tribes.

So I took the heads of your tribes: the text does not say that the people
picked these men out; this may be understood from the narrative, but there is
no account of it. It would not do for the translation to go beyond the Hebrew
text and say that the people picked out the leaders. By the verb took, the text
means that Moses summoned them to come to him.

Wise and experienced men: using two of the three terms in verse 13. We
assume that in verse 13 "men" refers to males, and here in verse 15 they are
also males. The "leaders" (TEV) of tribes would always have been men.

And set them as heads over you: this seems to suggest an installation
ceremony.

Commanders: since this is primarily a military position, the equivalent of
"captains" or "chiefs" may be used. In descending order of authority these men
were placed in charge of groups of one thousand men, one hundred men, fifty
men, and ten men. Languages lacking terms for these quantities will have to
use other means to display the difference in the number of men in each of the
four groups referred to.

Officers: it is difficult to determine what was the precise responsibility of
these men; they appear with the elders (Num 11.16) and with judges (Deut
16.18; Josh 8.33), and also in military contexts (Deut 20.5,8,9; Josh 1.10; 3.2).
Dhorme translates "scribes," but this does not seem appropriate here. The
English word "officers" will be understood by most readers in a military sense;
NRSV is better with "officials." It seems better to choose some more general
term; FRCL has "the task of overseeing." An alternative translation model for
this sentence is "I also appointed other officials as overseers of your people."

Throughout your tribes: this modifies all the actions in the earlier part of the verse. Again, the translator must be aware of the possible misunderstanding of the possessive "your." CEV avoids this problem with "your official leaders," also leaving **tribes** implicit.

1.16 RSV	TEV
And I charged your judges at that time, 'Hear the cases between your brethren, and judge righteously between a man and his brother or the alien that is with him.	"At that time I instructed them, 'Listen to the disputes that come up among your people. Judge every dispute fairly, whether it concerns only your own people or involves foreigners who live among you.

And I charged your judges at that time: unlike TEV, a translation should represent the Hebrew text and use the appropriate word for "judges," as distinct from "commanders" and "officers." The verb "charge" means to command, order, or instruct. The word translated **judges** is used elsewhere in the general sense of "leaders," but here it means those who settle legal disputes among the people. CEV makes it clear that those **judges** were not the same people as in the previous verse: "and others became judges." We may also express this as "and I appointed other men as judges. I gave them the following instructions . . . ."

At that time: as in verse 9.

Hear the cases between your brethren, and judge righteously between a man and his brother or the alien that is with him: the formal equivalence of the Hebrew text in RSV makes for very unnatural English. NRSV is much better: "Give the members of your community a fair hearing, and judge rightly between one person and another, whether citizen or resident alien." And REB has "Hear the cases that arise among your kinsmen and judge fairly between one person and another, whether fellow-countryman or resident alien." TEV likewise has reconstructed the text in order to make sense.

Hear the cases means to listen, as judge, to what two (or more) people claim about their dispute with each other; **your brethren** means "your fellow-Israelites" or more generally "your people" (TEV). To **judge righteously** means to judge in a fair and impartial way; **a man and his brother** in this context means a man (or, person) and another Israelite, or "between two Israelites" (CEV); while **the alien that is with him** means the non-Jew that the Israelite is having a legal dispute with. The Hebrew word translated **alien** (or, "resident alien") means a foreigner who lived permanently in an Israelite community; not being able to own land, he had little influence and could be the object of discrimination and exploitation. The Israelites knew what it was to live as resident aliens in a foreign land (see 10.29). NJPSV translates ". . . and decide justly between any man and a fellow Israelite or a stranger."

CEV has a radical reordering of the clauses of this verse. In some languages this will be a helpful model to follow:

● and others became judges. I gave these judges the following
instructions: When you settle legal cases, your decisions must be
fair. It doesn't matter if the case is between two Israelites, or
between an Israelite and a foreigner living in your community.

1.17	RSV	TEV

You shall not be partial in judgment; you shall hear the small and the great alike; you shall not be afraid of the face of man, for the judgment is God's; and the case that is too hard for you, you shall bring to me, and I will hear it.'

Show no partiality in your decisions; judge everyone on the same basis, no matter who they are. Do not be afraid of anyone, for the decisions you make come from God. If any case is too difficult for you, bring it to me, and I will decide it.'

This verse includes three separate instructions:

(1) **You shall not be partial in judgment; you shall hear the small and the great alike.** NRSV rightly places a colon instead of a semi-colon after "judgment," since what follows is a further elaboration of the first item. By **small and great** is meant the lowly, poor, powerless people, as opposed to the important, wealthy, influential members of the community. It is possible to reverse the order of these two clauses: "It doesn't matter if one person is poor [or, helpless] and the other is powerful [or, wealthy], you must judge impartially."

(2) **You shall not be afraid of the face of man, for the judgment is God's.** Again, NRSV is much clearer in English: "You shall not be intimidated by anyone"; this is more simply "Don't be afraid of anyone" (CEV). And the reason for this instruction is that judgment is given in God's name and with God's authority. In this community in which God's laws ruled the people, any enforcement of the law was an application of God's will. So TEV has "for the decision you make comes from God." Another way to express this is "For God will help you to make the right [or, correct] decision."

(3) **And the case that is too hard for you, you shall bring it to me, and I will hear it.** The meaning here is quite clear; Moses will **hear**—that is, decide, settle, judge—any dispute that is too difficult for the appointed judge to handle. The clause **you shall bring it to me** can be taken to mean "bring the people to me" (CEV), as it is two people who are having a dispute. And this final sentence may thus be expressed as "If any dispute is too difficult for you to decide, bring the people who are involved to me and I will make the decision."

1.18	RSV	TEV

And I commanded you at that time all the things that you should do.

At the same time I gave you instructions for everything else you were to do.

I commanded: as in verse 16. NJB has "I gave you instructions."

At that time: as in verse 9, at Mount Sinai.

All the things that you should do: Moses was talking to Israelites, giving them instructions about their duties and responsibilities as the people of God.

1D. The spies are sent out from Kadesh Barnea (1.19-33)

RSV

19 "And we set out from Horeb, and went through all that great and terrible wilderness which you saw, on the way to the hill country of the Amorites, as the LORD our God commanded us; and we came to Kadesh-barnea. 20 And I said to you, 'You have come to the hill country of the Amorites, which the LORD our God gives us. 21 Behold, the LORD your God has set the land before you; go up, take possession, as the LORD, the God of your fathers, has told you; do not fear or be dismayed.' 22 Then all of you came near me, and said, 'Let us send men before us, that they may explore the land for us, and bring us word again of the way by which we must go up and the cities into which we shall come.' 23 The thing seemed good to me, and I took twelve men of you, one man for each tribe; 24 and they turned and went up into the hill country, and came to the Valley of Eshcol and spied it out. 25 And they took in their hands some of the fruit of the land and brought it down to us, and brought us word again, and said, 'It is a good land which the LORD our God gives us.'

26 "Yet you would not go up, but rebelled against the command of the LORD your God; 27 and you murmured in your tents, and said, 'Because the LORD hated us he has brought us forth out of the land of Egypt, to give us into the hand of the Amorites, to destroy us. 28 Whither are we going up? Our brethren have made our hearts melt, saying, "The people are greater and taller than we; the cities are great and fortified up to heaven; and moreover we have seen the sons of the Anakim there.' " 29 Then I said to you, 'Do not be in dread or afraid of them. 30 The LORD your God who goes before you will himself fight for you, just as he did for you in Egypt before your eyes, 31 and in the wilderness, where you have seen how the LORD your God bore you, as a man bears his son, in all the way that you went until you came to this place.' 32 Yet in spite of this word you did not believe the LORD your God, 33 who went before you in the way to seek you out a place to pitch your tents, in

TEV

The Spies Are Sent Out from Kadesh Barnea

19 "We did what the LORD our God commanded us. We left Mount Sinai and went through that vast and fearful desert on the way to the hill country of the Amorites. When we reached Kadesh Barnea, 20-21 I told you, 'You have now come to the hill country of the Amorites, which the LORD our God, the God of our ancestors, is giving us. Look, there it is. Go and occupy it as he commanded. Do not hesitate or be afraid.'

22 "But you came to me and said, 'Let's send men ahead of us to spy out the land, so that they can tell us the best route to take and what kind of cities are there.'

23 "That seemed like a good thing to do, so I selected twelve men, one from each tribe. 24 They went into the hill country as far as Eshcol Valley and explored it. 25 They brought us back some fruit they found there, and reported that the land which the LORD our God was giving us was very fertile.

26 "But you rebelled against the command of the LORD your God, and you would not enter the land. 27 You grumbled to one another: 'The LORD hates us. He brought us out of Egypt just to hand us over to these Amorites, so that they could kill us. 28 Why should we go there? We are afraid. The men we sent tell us that the people there are stronger and taller than we are, and that they live in cities with walls that reach the sky. They saw giants there!'

29 "But I told you, 'Don't be afraid of those people. 30 The LORD your God will lead you, and he will fight for you, just as you saw him do in Egypt 31 and in the desert. You saw how he brought you safely all the way to this place, just as a father would carry his son.' 32 But in spite of what I said, you still would not trust the LORD, 33 even though he always went ahead of you to find a place for you to camp. To show you the way, he went in front of you in a pillar of fire by night and in a pillar of cloud by day.

fire by night, to show you by what way you
should go, and in the cloud by day.

Section heading: in languages that do not use the passive voice, we may
translate as "Moses sends out men to explore the land" (see TEV, CEV). However,
instead of the emphasis laid by TEV and CEV on the sending out of the spies,
some translations stress the Israelites' lack of faith. NJB has "Kadesh: the
Israelites lose faith," and FRCL "Israel's disobedience at the border of the
Promised Land."

It is possible to start a new section at verse 26 with a heading such as
"Rebellion Against the LORD" (NIV), or "Israel Refused to Obey the LORD" (CEV).
However, the Handbook prefers to follow TEV, which includes verses 26-33 as
part of a section ending at verse 33, where a new section begins (verses 34-45).

For a parallel account of this section, see Num 13.1-39.

1.19	RSV	TEV
	"And we set out from Horeb, and went through all that great and terrible wilderness which you saw, on the way to the hill country of the Amorites, as the LORD our God commanded us; and we came to Kadesh-barnea.	"We did what the LORD our God commanded us. We left Mount Sinai and went through that vast and fearful desert on the way to the hill country of the Amorites. When we reached Kadesh Barnea,

Since this begins a new section, Moses should be introduced again as the
speaker; for example, "Moses said to the Israelites."

And we set out from Horeb: see map, page xi. For **Horeb** (that is, Mount
Sinai), see 1.2. Another way to express this clause is "We left Mount Sinai."

And went through all that great and terrible wilderness which you saw: for
wilderness see 1.1. It is described as follows: "an almost waterless limestone
plateau . . . a journey of more than one hundred miles" (Craigie). The adjectives
great and terrible may be translated "large and fearful," "vast and dangerous."
The addition of **which you saw** is somewhat redundant, but it brings more
vividly to the minds of the hearers the hardships they suffered on their long
journey. CEV expresses **went through all that great and terrible wilderness
which you saw** as ". . . so we started out into the huge desert. You know how
frightening it was." It is also possible to translate this as "We walked through
that huge wilderness. It was a frightening place."

The hill country of the Amorites: here this phrase means the whole land of
Canaan and its people, not just one particular region, as it may be in verse 7.
It may also be rendered as "the country full of hills [or, hilly country] that
belonged to the people called Amorites."

The LORD our God: see in verse 10 "the LORD your God."

Instead of putting **as the LORD had commanded us** at the end, it is better in
English, with NRSV, TEV, and others, to place it at the start of the verse: "There,
just as the LORD our God had ordered us, we . . . ," or "The LORD had com-

manded us to leave Mount Sinai and go to the hill country that belonged to the Amorites, so we started out . . ." (CEV).

Came to Kadesh-barnea: see verse 2. **Came** is not natural in English, since the speaker Moses is not now at Kadesh Barnea, and a more general term, "we arrived at" or "reached," is better.

1.20-21	RSV	TEV
	20 And I said to you, 'You have come to the hill country of the Amorites, which the LORD our God gives us. 21 Behold, the LORD your God has set the land before you; go up, take possession, as the LORD, the God of your fathers, has told you; do not fear or be dismayed.'	20-21 I told you, 'You have now come to the hill country of the Amorites, which the LORD our God, the God of our ancestors, is giving us. Look, there it is. Go and occupy it as he commanded. Do not hesitate or be afraid.'

For **country of the Amorites** see verse 7 and elsewhere. **You have come** may also be expressed as "We have reached" (CEV), as Moses would have been including himself here.

Gives: this is better translated "is giving" (NRSV, TEV) or "is about to give."

What follows in the rest of the chapter describes what took place at Kadesh Barnea.

Behold: see verse 8.

Has set the land before you: see verse 8.

Go up: this verb does not always mean to go from a lower to a higher elevation, but may have the more general sense of "go," "go into," or "proceed." Here, however, **go up** makes sense, since Kadesh Barnea was at a lower level than the hill country.

Take possession: see verse 8.

The LORD, the God of your fathers: see verse 11.

Has told you: that is, "has ordered you," "has commanded you."

Do not fear or be dismayed: the use of two verbs that mean almost the same thing makes the command even stronger; the Israelites are to be completely fearless as they begin to invade the land that Yahweh, their God, is giving them. In some languages **do not fear or be dismayed** may be translated as "Don't have any fear in your hearts at all," or figuratively, for example, "Don't let your hearts fall [or, melt]."

1.22   RSV   TEV

Then all of you came near me, and   "But you came to me and said,
said, 'Let us send men before us,   'Let's send men ahead of us to spy
that they may explore the land for us, out the land, so that they can tell us
and bring us word again of the way   the best route to take and what kind
by which we must go up and the   of cities are there.'
cities into which we shall come.'

Then all of you came near me: or, "Then all of you came to me" (CEV). Instead
of the word **Then**, The New English Bible [NEB], REB, SPCL, and GECL begin with
"But," which better suits the context. Instead of immediately obeying the order
to invade the land and take possession of it, the Israelites propose a delaying
course of action; this may be seen as the first indication of their lack of faith.

Let us send men before us: in Num 13.1-2 it is God who orders that the
twelve spies be sent out. CEV prefaces this sentence with "Before we go into the
land, let's send . . . ." This may be helpful.

That they may explore the land for us, and bring us word again: NRSV "bring
back a report to us" is an improvement over the literal rendering "bring us
word again." A simpler way of expressing this is "and can tell us about . . . ."

Of the way by which we must go up: the purpose of the spies' exploration of
the land would be to decide which would be the best route to take in their
invasion of the land, and to find out how strong and heavily defended were the
cities that they would have to conquer. Again, **go up** does not necessarily mean
to go to a higher elevation (see verse 21).

The cities into which . . . : in today's world **cities** are usually much larger
than most of the communities named in the Bible, and "towns" (REB, NJB) is a
more accurate term. For a comment on the translation of "towns," see verse 1.

Into which we shall come: the translator must be aware of the point of view
of the narrative. As they attacked the cities, the Israelites were "going" into
them; from the point of view of the cities they would be "coming" into them. In
most languages "going" will be the more natural point of view. However, in
certain languages all directional information depends on where the speaker is
located. In such a case translators should generally place the writer of
Deuteronomy in the area of Canaan.

CEV has a helpful alternative model for this verse:

•   Then all of you came to me and said, "Before we go into the
         land, let's send some men to explore it. When they come back,
         they can tell us about the towns we will find and what roads we
         should take to get there."

1.23   RSV   TEV

The thing seemed good to me, and I   "That seemed like a good thing to
took twelve men of you, one man for   do, so I selected twelve men, one
each tribe;   from each tribe.

The thing seemed good to me: this is more clearly translated "I thought the plan was a good one," or even "I gave my approval to your plan." See verse 14.

And I took: see the same use of the verb in verse 15.

One man for each tribe: this is better rendered "one man from each tribe [or, from each of the twelve tribes]."

1.24	RSV	TEV

and they turned and went up into the hill country, and came to the Valley of Eshcol and spied it out.	They went into the hill country as far as Eshcol Valley and explored it.

And they turned and went up: as in verse 7, this means "They set out and went up" (NRSV). Since **the hill country** is where they go, "went up" is quite appropriate.

And came: or, "and arrived."

Valley of Eshcol: as commentators point out, "wadi" is a better translation of the Hebrew word than "valley," since this is not a valley in the normal sense of the word. Rather, it is a ravine or watercourse that is dry during the dry season but that can become a torrent in the rainy season. However, in cultures where dry ravines or wadis like this do not exist, it will be better to translate "the dry river valley named Eshcol," with a footnote explaining what a "wadi" is like. The name *Eshcol* means "cluster," a reflection of the fruit that grew there (next verse), especially the grapes (Num 13.22-24); CEV has "Bunch Valley." It was located in the region of Hebron, but its exact site is unknown.

Spied it out: or "explored it" (TEV).

As the verse stands, it seems to say that the twelve spies explored only the Valley of Eshcol. But it is more reasonable to assume that, as REB has it, "they reconnoitered as far as the wadi of Eshcol," or we may say "they explored as far as the dry river valley [or, wadi] named Eshcol." It is recommended that translators follow one of these models.

1.25	RSV	TEV

And they took in their hands some of the fruit of the land and brought it down to us, and brought us word again, and said, 'It is a good land which the LORD our God gives us.'	They brought us back some fruit they found there, and reported that the land which the LORD our God was giving us was very fertile.

And they took in their hands: this is better translated "They gathered [or, picked]." **The fruit** is not necessarily restricted to fruits as such but may have the broader sense of "produce" (NRSV).

The quaint **and brought us word again** should be "brought back a report to us" (NRSV). Some translators will prefer to use direct speech here as RSV does, and also combine the expression **and brought us word again** with the word **said** and translate: "They reported, The land that the LORD our God is giving us is a fertile land.' "

A good land may be rendered "a fine country" (NJB), "a rich land" (REB), or "a very fertile land" (see TEV), or even "a land that produces much fruit [or, produce]."

The LORD our God: see verse 19.

1.26   RSV   TEV

"Yet you would not go up, but   "But you rebelled against the com-
rebelled against the command of the   mand of the LORD your God, and you
LORD your God;   would not enter the land.

You would not go up, but rebelled: something stronger than "disobeyed" should be used here, and in English **rebelled** is the exact word to use. This was an open revolt, a mutiny, against God's order through Moses.

The LORD your God: see verse 10.

1.27   RSV   TEV

and you murmured in your tents, and   You grumbled to one another: 'The
said, 'Because the LORD hated us he   LORD hates us. He brought us out of
has brought us forth out of the land   Egypt just to hand us over to these
of Egypt, to give us into the hand of Amorites, so that they could kill us.
the Amorites, to destroy us.

You murmured in your tents: this was a rather passive revolt, not an active one in which people left their tents and hurled angry accusations against Moses. Instead of **murmured** the translation should be "grumbled" or "complained." A translation should be careful to use an appropriate word for a dwelling that can be taken down and carried (**tents**), not a permanent construction ("houses" or "homes"). Something like "You stayed in your tents and grumbled" (CEV) is a good model.

And said: the complaints were the exact opposite of the truth. It was out of love and compassion that Yahweh had delivered the Israelites from Egypt, the land of slavery, and he had promised to be with them and to assure them success as they took possession of the land of Canaan (see, for instance, 4.37-38). But they accused God of hating them and of bringing them out of Egypt in order to exterminate them.

Hate in certain languages is expressed as "being enemies of," so in this context we may say "The LORD [or, Yahweh] must consider us his enemies," or "In Yahweh's sight we must be his enemies."

To give us into the hand of the Amorites, to destroy us: the phrase "the hand of the Amorites" means that the Amorites would do the killing; God would allow the Israelites to be captured and killed by the Amorites. It is important to translate the whole statement in such a way that the clear subject of the verb "destroy" or "kill" is Yahweh, not the Amorites (as in TEV). NJB has ". . . and so destroy us" (with Yahweh as the subject). An alternative model is:

". . . he brought us out of Egypt, just so he could give us over to the Amorites, and in that way destroy us."

1.28	RSV	TEV

RSV	TEV
Whither are we going up? Our brethren have made our hearts melt, saying, "The people are greater and taller than we; the cities are great and fortified up to heaven; and moreover we have seen the sons of the Anakim there.' "	Why should we go there? We are afraid. The men we sent tell us that the people there are stronger and taller than we are, and that they live in cities with walls that reach the sky. They saw giants there!'

Whither are we going up? NRSV is more natural with "Where are we headed?" NJB brings out even better the intent of the question: "What kind of place are we going to?"

Our brethren have made our hearts melt: in the context these **brethren** are the twelve Israelites chosen to spy out the land, and a translation should make this clear. So TEV has "the men we sent," and CEV has "the men who explored the land." To "melt the heart" means to cause people to lose all courage, to fill them with fear with the report they brought back, that the people were bigger and stronger than the Israelites themselves, and their cities were fortified and heavily defended.

The people are greater and taller than we: instead of **taller than we**, as in the Masoretic text (the standard Hebrew text that translators normally follow), the Hebrew Old Testament Text Project (HOTTP) prefers "more numerous than we" (a {C} decision), which is found in a few Hebrew manuscripts. HOTTP says the Masoretic reading is due to assimilation to parallel passages (see 2.10, 21). However, no major modern translation has "more numerous," and a translator should feel free to follow the Masoretic text. **Greater** refers to physical strength. The order of the words **greater and taller** may be reversed in some languages to "taller and stronger."

The expression **fortified up to heaven** indicates the height of the walls that surrounded the **cities** ("towns," see verse 22); this is a typical exaggeration not to be taken literally. The translation may say "their towns are strongly defended, and the walls that surround them reach as high as the sky." A town with walls was considered a city even though it may have been very small. In languages that don't distinguish between cities, towns, and even villages, we may say "a very large place with walls [or, with a high fence] around it."

The sons of the Anakim: the Anakim and others (see 2.10-11, 20-21) were the legendary original inhabitants of the land, famous for their size. **Sons of the Anakim** will be expressed in many languages as "people who are descended from the giant Anak."

It is possible to reorder the clauses from **the people are greater** on as follows:

-    . . . the towns are strongly defended, and the walls that surround them reach up to the sky. The people who live there are taller and stronger than we are, and some of them are the descendants of the giant Anak.

1.29   RSV   TEV

Then I said to you, 'Do not be in dread or afraid of them.	**"But I told you, 'Don't be afraid of those people.**

There is no substantial difference between the two verbs translated **be in dread** and **be . . . afraid**. The verb for **be in dread** is used less frequently than the other verb and appears also at 7.21; 20.3; 21.6. Another way to express this is "Don't let your hearts fall [or, melt] when you think about these people."

1.30   RSV   TEV

The LORD your God who goes before you will himself fight for you, just as he did for you in Egypt before your eyes,	**The LORD your God will lead you, and he will fight for you, just as you saw him do in Egypt**

The LORD your God: see verse 10.

Who goes before you: or "who leads you," or "who is in charge of you" (since in a military campaign the officer in charge led his troops).

Will himself fight for you: this is quite emphatic, and the translation should be equally emphatic. Other ways to express this clause are "He will fight on your side" (CEV) or "He will help you as you fight."

As he did for you in Egypt before your eyes: few if any of the Israelites with Moses in Kadesh Barnea had been present in Egypt when the exodus took place, since all the adults who had left Egypt had died in the wilderness (Num 26.63-65). But the Israelites Moses was addressing had heard the story and knew what Yahweh had done for his people.

Before your eyes means "as you saw [him do it]" (see TEV), and this final sentence may be expressed as "just as he did when we saw him do all those things to the Egyptians" (CEV).

1.31   RSV   TEV

and in the wilderness, where you have seen how the LORD your God bore you, as a man bears his son, in all the way that you went until you came to this place.'	**and in the desert. You saw how he brought you safely all the way to this place, just as a father would carry his son.'**

The wilderness: see verse 19.

You have seen: the emphasis here is on the people's own experience. Moses is simply reminding them of what they themselves know, because all of this happened to them.

The LORD your God bore you, as a man bears his son: the verb "to bear" means to carry, so that **his son** refers to a young child. However, in many languages two different verbs will be used; for example, "how he brought you . . . just as a father will carry" (TEV) or "has taken care of you . . . just as you might carry" (CEV).

In all that way that you went until you came to this place: care must be taken with the two verbs **went** and **came** so that the proper perspective is maintained. "This place" is Kadesh Barnea (verse 19). It is possible to change the order of the clauses of this verse as follows: "and you know that the LORD has taken care of you [or, us] all the time you [or, we] have been in the wilderness, just as you [or, we] might carry one of your [or, our] children."

1.32	RSV	TEV

Yet in spite of this word you did not believe the LORD your God,

But in spite of what I said, you still would not trust the LORD,

Yet in spite of this word: that is, in spite of Moses' speech reminding them how Yahweh had led and protected them all the way from Egypt. Other ways to express this are "But in spite of what I said" (TEV) or "I said all these things, yet you still . . . ."

You did not believe: this verb means, basically, "to be firm," and means to trust in, to rely on, or to believe. NJB has "you put no faith in," and NJPSV "you have no faith in." Driver points out that the verb in Hebrew is a participle, suggesting a continuous attitude, "you continued not believing." Terms for **believe** in many languages are highly figurative; for example, "place one's heart in" (Thai), "to conform with the heart" (Timorese), and so on. Other examples may be found in *A Handbook on the Gospel of Mark*, pages 38-39.

1.33	RSV	TEV

who went before you in the way to seek you out a place to pitch your tents, in fire by night, to show you by what way you should go, and in the cloud by day.

even though he always went ahead of you to find a place for you to camp. To show you the way, he went in front of you in a pillar of fire by night and in a pillar of cloud by day.

The order of the phrases and clauses in RSV reflects the structure of the Hebrew text. The phrases **in fire by night** and **in the cloud by day** should be clearly connected to the verbal phrase "to show you the way you should go," as done in TEV.

Went before you in the way: that is, "went ahead of you on your journey," or "went ahead of you [or, us] as you [or, we] walked through the wilderness."

To seek out a place to pitch your tents can be translated "to find a place where you could camp"; but in some languages "to find a place where you could erect [or, put up] your tents" will be more natural. The reader must be able to understand what was involved in this kind of travel, where tents were set up and taken down as the Israelites traveled through the wilderness. Moses would have included himself as one of the Israelites, so it may be necessary to change the second person pronouns to first person inclusive throughout.

To show you by what way you should go: Yahweh went ahead of the people in a cloud by day and in a column of fire by night (Exo 13.21-22), to show them the direction they should take, and this may be shown in translation: "leading us in the right direction and showing us where to camp" (CEV). **In fire by night** (TEV "pillar of fire") may be also expressed as "in a flaming fire at night," or even "in a fire in the form of a column [or, pillar]." **In the cloud by day** may be rendered in a similar way. However, in cultures where "pillars" and "columns" are unknown, a general model like "in a thick cloud" or "in a flaming fire" is possible.

An alternative translation model for this verse is:

- even though he always went ahead of us in the wilderness. During the daytime the LORD was in a column of cloud, leading us in the right direction and showing us where to set up our tents. And at night he was present in a column of fire.

1E. The LORD punishes Israel (1.34-44)

RSV	TEV
	The LORD Punishes Israel

34 "And the LORD heard your words, and was angered, and he swore, 35 'Not one of these men of this evil generation shall see the good land which I swore to give to your fathers, 36 except Caleb the son of Jephunneh; he shall see it, and to him and to his children I will give the land upon which he has trodden, because he has wholly followed the LORD!' 37 The LORD was angry with me also on your account, and said, 'You also shall not go in there; 38 Joshua the son of Nun, who stands before you, he shall enter; encourage him, for he shall cause Israel to inherit it. 39 Moreover your little ones, who you said would become a prey, and your children, who this day have no knowledge of good or evil, shall go in there, and to them I will give it, and they shall possess it. 40 But as for you, turn, and journey into the wilderness in the direction of the Red Sea.'

41 "Then you answered me, 'We have sinned against the LORD; we will go up and fight, just

34 "The LORD heard your complaints and became angry, and so he solemnly declared, 35 'Not one of you from this evil generation will enter the fertile land that I promised to give your ancestors. 36 Only Caleb son of Jephunneh will enter it. He has remained faithful to me, and I will give him and his descendants the land that he has explored.' 37 Because of you the LORD also became angry with me and said, 'Not even you, Moses, will enter the land. 38 But strengthen the determination of your helper, Joshua son of Nun. He will lead Israel to occupy the land.'

39 "Then the LORD said to all of us, 'Your children, who are still too young to know right from wrong, will enter the land—the children you said would be seized by your enemies. I will give the land to them, and they will occupy it. 40 But as for you people, turn around and go back into the desert on the road to the Gulf of Aqaba.'

as the LORD our God commanded us.' And every man of you girded on his weapons of war, and thought it easy to go up into the hill country. 42 And the LORD said to me, 'Say to them, Do not go up or fight, for I am not in the midst of you; lest you be defeated before your enemies.' 43 So I spoke to you, and you would not hearken; but you rebelled against the command of the LORD, and were presumptuous and went up into the hill country. 44 Then the Amorites who lived in that hill country came out against you and chased you as bees do and beat you down in Seir as far as Hormah. 45 And you returned and wept before the LORD; but the LORD did not hearken to your voice or give ear to you.

41 "You replied, 'Moses, we have sinned against the LORD. But now we will attack, just as the LORD our God commanded us.' Then each one of you got ready to fight, thinking it would be easy to invade the hill country.
42 "But the LORD said to me, 'Warn them not to attack, for I will not be with them, and their enemies will defeat them.' 43 I told you what the LORD had said, but you paid no attention. You rebelled against him, and in your pride you marched into the hill country. 44 Then the Amorites who lived in those hills came out against you like a swarm of bees. They chased you as far as Hormah and defeated you there in the hill country of Edom. 45 So you cried out to the LORD for help, but he would not listen to you or pay any attention to you.

Section heading: as indicated at verse 19, CEV and NIV do not begin a separate section here but consider verses 19-45 as a single section. However, TEV begins a new section here with the heading "The LORD Punishes Israel." Other ways to express this are "The LORD punishes the Israelites [or, people of Israel]," or "Yahweh warns the Israelites not to attack the land."

1.34 RSV TEV

"And the LORD heard your words, and was angered, and he swore,

"The LORD heard your complaints and became angry, and so he solemnly declared,

The LORD heard your words: or "the LORD heard what you said" or "The LORD heard your complaints" (TEV; similarly REB, SPCL, FRCL, BRCL).

And was angered: the verb represents a strong emotion, and something like "he was angry" or even "he was furious" represents the meaning well. Many languages will have figurative expressions for "anger"; for example, "The LORD's heart [or, nose] became very hot" or "The LORD's heart [or, liver, or stomach] burned [or, pained] greatly." *A Handbook on the Gospel of Mark*, page 106, contains some other excellent examples.

And he swore: as RSV stands, a reader might suppose that Yahweh used bad language. The verb, of course, means "made a solemn promise" (as in verse 8).

1.35 RSV TEV

'Not one of these men of this evil generation shall see the good land which I swore to give to your fathers,

'Not one of you from this evil generation will enter the fertile land that I promised to give your ancestors.

Not one of these men of this evil generation: instead of the exclusive "men," something like "Not one person" or "No one" will be better. The meaning is that none of the Israelites who were adults when they left Egypt would live to enter the land of Canaan. They are all characterized as "evil," which here reflects mainly their lack of faith in God's promise and in Moses' leadership. In some languages it will be more natural style to begin with a statement; for example, "You people of this time [or, today] have evil hearts, so I will not let one of you . . . ."

The good land which I swore to give to your fathers: see verse 8. For **good land** see verse 25.

1.36   RSV   TEV

except Caleb the son of Jephunneh; he shall see it, and to him and to his children I will give the land upon which he has trodden, because he has wholly followed the LORD!'

Only Caleb son of Jephunneh will enter it. He has remained faithful to me, and I will give him and his descendants the land that he has explored.'

The only exception to the statement in verse 35 is Caleb; and in verse 38 Joshua is also named as another adult who will enter the land of Canaan. An alternative model is:

● 	Caleb, the son of Jephunneh, is the only person living today who . . . .

He shall see it: this means more than merely getting a look at the land from a distance, as Moses did; it means Caleb will enter the land and see it. So TEV has "will enter it," and CEV has "that I will allow to go in."

To him and to his children: "to him and to his descendants." Caleb and his descendants will become owners of that part of the land that he himself explored (**the land upon which he has trodden**). Care should be taken not to give the impression that Caleb would be given the whole land of Canaan. For the region that was eventually assigned to Caleb, see Josh 14.6-15. For "descendants" see verse 8.

Because he has wholly followed the LORD: the verbal expression may be translated "has been perfectly obedient to Yahweh" (NJB); "remained loyal to the LORD" (NJPSV); "he followed the LORD loyally" (REB). If there is a problem in having Yahweh refer to himself in the third person, a translation can say ". . . to me, the LORD." However, we may also translate "He has remained faithful to me" (TEV) or "He obeyed me completely" (CEV).

It may be better to change the order of the clauses and begin with the reason why Caleb will be given part of the land: "Because Caleb has always been loyal to me, I, the LORD, . . ." or "Caleb has always been faithful to me, and so I, the LORD . . . ."

1.37   RSV   TEV

The LORD was angry with me also on your account, and said, 'You also shall not go in there;	Because of you the LORD also became angry with me and said, 'Not even you, Moses, will enter the land.

The LORD was angry with me also on your account: the translation should be quite clear that the report of what Yahweh said to Moses ends at verse 36, and Moses himself begins speaking in verse 37. In some translations it may be useful to begin this verse "And Moses said to them: Because of you . . . ." Moses says that it was because of the people's disobedience that Yahweh became angry with him also. "It was because of what you did that the LORD became angry with me also." For a comment on **angry** see verse 34.

You shall not go in there: something like "You also will not set foot on that land" or "Neither will you enter the land of Canaan" will be better. It is also possible to say "I won't let you go into the land either."

1.38   RSV   TEV

Joshua the son of Nun, who stands before you, he shall enter; encourage him, for he shall cause Israel to inherit it.	But strengthen the determination of your helper, Joshua son of Nun. He will lead Israel to occupy the land.'

Here is God's statement that Joshua, not Moses, will lead the people into the land of Canaan.

Who stands before you: this is a way of referring to Joshua as Moses' assistant, or helper. He is not Moses' equal but is inferior to him. NJPSV "who attends you" and REB "who is in attendance on you" are somewhat old-fashioned. NRSV and CEV "your assistant" is better.

Encourage him: the verb means "to strengthen." Languages have various idioms for expressing the idea of instilling determination and courage in someone; for example, "give heart power to" (Thai), or "cause his heart [or, liver] to become strong."

He shall cause Israel to inherit it: a clearer way of expressing what this means is "He will lead the Israelites to conquer [or, possess] the land [of Canaan]." In such a context as this the verb "to inherit" is not an accurate translation of the Hebrew verb. In English, at least, "inherit" means to come into the possession of something following the death of its owner.

It is possible to change the order of the clauses in this verse as follows:

●   Instead, I will let Joshua, the son of Nun, who is your assistant, lead the Israelites to conquer [or, occupy] the land. So you must encourage him.

1.39   RSV   TEV

Moreover your little ones, who you   "Then the LORD said to all of us,
said would become a prey, and your   'Your children, who are still too
children, who this day have no   young to know right from wrong, will
knowledge of good or evil, shall go   enter the land—the children you said
in there, and to them I will give it,   would be seized by your enemies. I
and they shall possess it.   will give the land to them, and they
                                           will occupy it.

In the previous verse Yahweh was speaking to Moses directly. But now he
speaks to all the Israelites again. So it will be helpful for translators to begin
the verse with something like "Then the LORD said to all of us" (TEV), or "Then
the LORD spoke to you again" (CEV).

Moreover: here the meaning of the statement that none of that evil
generation would enter the land of Canaan (verse 35) becomes clear. In addition
to Joseph and Caleb, **your little ones . . . and your children** will enter the land.
There is no difference in meaning between "little ones" and "children": this is
a double way of referring to the younger generation. They are described as **who
this day have no knowledge of good or evil**, that is, they are not mature
enough to make moral decisions and so cannot be punished. TEV "too young to
know right from wrong" expresses the meaning well, or we may say "innocent
young children" (CEV).

Who you said would become a prey: that is, the Israelites said that their
children would be taken captive by their enemies (see Num 14.31). This seems
to be one of their excuses for not obeying Moses' command. In languages that
do not use the passive voice (as TEV does), we may say "your enemies would
capture . . . ." "Your enemies" in a number of languages will be expressed as
"those who hate you."

And to them I will give it, and they shall possess it: this states that the land
is both God's gift and the people's achievement. They will be able to conquer the
land because God will give it to them. Both RSV and TEV have a complicated
structure. It is possible to restructure the verse as follows:

• 	Then the LORD said to all of us, "You said that your enemies
	would capture your young children. But I will help these children
	go into the land and occupy it instead of you.

1.40   RSV   TEV

But as for you, turn, and journey into   But as for you people, turn around
the wilderness in the direction of the   and go back into the desert on the
Red Sea.'   road to the Gulf of Aqaba.'

But as for you, turn, and journey into: this order is very much like the one in
verse 7. The people are to turn back from Kadesh Barnea and return to the
wilderness; so NRSV "journey back."

For **wilderness** see 1.1.

In the direction of the Red Sea: or "on the road to the Red Sea" (compare TEV; see 2.1; Num 14.25). The literal meaning of the name of this body of water seems to be "Sea [or, Lake] of Reeds," and the TEV footnote at Exo 13.18 provides a brief statement of how it is used:

> RED SEA: *(in Hebrew literally "Sea of Reeds") evidently referred to (1) a series of lakes and marshes between the head of the Gulf of Suez and the Mediterranean, the region generally regarded as the site of the events described in Exodus 13, and was also used to designate (2) the Gulf of Suez, and (3) the Gulf of Aqaba.*

Most Bibles in English follow the traditional "Red Sea" in all occurrences of the name; TEV has "Red Sea" when the name appears in the context of the exodus from Egypt, and elsewhere "Gulf of Aqaba" (Exo 23.31; Num 14.25; 21.4; Deut 1.40; 2.1; Judges 11.16; 1 Kgs 9.26; 2 Chr 8.17; Jer 49.21) or "Gulf of Suez" (Exo 10.19; Num 33.10; Isa 11.15), as required by the context. Here Mft, TEV, BRCL, and *Traduction œcuménique de la Bible* [TOB] (footnote) have "Gulf of Aqaba"; FRCL, NJPSV, GECL have "Sea of Reeds." A translator must decide how this name is to be translated in each instance, whether to try to let the context determine the meaning assigned, or simply to translate by the traditional "Red Sea" in all passages.

1.41	RSV	TEV
	"Then you answered me, 'We have sinned against the LORD; we will go up and fight, just as the LORD our God commanded us.' And every man of you girded on his weapons of war, and thought it easy to go up into the hill country.	"You replied, 'Moses, we have sinned against the LORD. But now we will attack, just as the LORD our God commanded us.' Then each one of you got ready to fight, thinking it would be easy to invade the hill country.

The people's answer in the first part of the verse offers no difficulty. Moses is reporting what the people said to him at Kadesh Barnea.

We have sinned against the LORD: the verb "to sin" in a context like this means primarily to do something contrary to God's will, and something like "make a mistake" or "commit an error" is not strong enough; the general idea of "do something bad," that is, something that violates moral values and standards, will in places be an adequate translation. But when God is expressly mentioned, as here, the sense of disobeying God's command is required. So CEV has "We disobeyed the LORD our God."

We will go up and fight: the men are ready to set out at once and invade the land. In languages that require an object or goal for **fight**, we may translate, for example, "fight our [inclusive] enemies."

And every man of you girded on his weapons of war: the obsolete verb "to gird" means to put on or around, and here it means to put on a shield and perhaps a helmet, in addition to taking up a sword or spear. NRSV "strapped on your battle gear" is much clearer; or we may even say "put on all your weapons [for fighting]," or in languages spoken by people who do not strap on weapons, we may say something like "all of you carrying your weapons."

And thought it easy to go up into the hill country: the Hebrew verb translated **thought it easy** occurs only here in the Old Testament, and its meaning is not quite certain; most translate as do RSV and TEV.

The hill country is the land of Canaan itself, to the north of Kadesh Barnea, where they are. For **hill country** see verse 7.

1.42   RSV   TEV

And the LORD said to me, 'Say to   "But the LORD said to me, 'Warn
them, Do not go up or fight, for I am   them not to attack, for I will not be
not in the midst of you; lest you be   with them, and their enemies will
defeated before your enemies.'   defeat them.'

And the LORD said to me, 'Say to them, Do not go up: there are three levels of direct discourse here; TEV, CEV, REB, and others reduce them to two, by using indirect discourse for the last one. It is possible to reduce the three to one: "And the LORD ordered me to tell them not to attack . . . ." Translators must decide which makes for a more natural account in their language.

I am not in the midst of you: this may be translated "I will not be with you," "I will not go with you." If indirect discourse is used, the second plural "you" must be changed to "them": "I will not be with them."

Lest you be defeated before your enemies: this is unnatural language in English, and translators should say something like "or else you will be defeated by your enemies" or "otherwise your enemies will defeat you." This is what will happen if they attack the enemy on their own; since Yahweh will not be with them, they will be defeated. For **enemies** see verse 39.

An alternative model restructuring this verse is:

• But the LORD said, 'Do not go and fight. If you do, you will be
  defeated because I will not be with you.'

1.43   RSV   TEV

So I spoke to you, and you would not   I told you what the LORD had said,
hearken; but you rebelled against the   but you paid no attention. You re-
command of the LORD, and were   belled against him, and in your pride
presumptuous and went up into the   you marched into the hill country.
hill country.

The first part of the verse is better translated by NRSV: "Although I told you, you would not listen." TEV expresses it more clearly: "I told you what the LORD had said, but you paid no attention." Again the people show their lack of faith.

You rebelled against the command of the LORD: this is very much like verse 26.

Were presumptuous: this shows arrogance and pride on their part. NIV "in your arrogance"; NJPSV "willfully"; REB "defiantly." They would not obey God's command. Other ways to express **and were presumptuous** are "You thought you were big," "You thought you were so great" (CEV), or "You lifted yourselves up," and so on.

And went up into the hill country: for **hill country** see verse 7. CEV places this clause before **and were presumptuous**: "You disobeyed him and went into the hill country anyway. You thought you were so powerful . . . ."

1.44	RSV	TEV

Then the Amorites who lived in that hill country came out against you and chased you as bees do and beat you down in Seir as far as Hormah.	Then the Amorites who lived in those hills came out against you like a swarm of bees. They chased you as far as Hormah and defeated you there in the hill country of Edom.

The Amorites who lived in that hill country: the name **Amorites** stands here as a general term for the inhabitants of the land of Canaan; in Num 14.43, 45 these people are identified as Amalekites and Canaanites. See also 1.4, 7.

Came out against you and chased you as bees do: this figure is used also in Psa 118.12; Isa 7.18. It portrays not only the speed of the attack but also its persistence and fury; once bees start after someone, they do not turn back. **Came out against you** means "attacked you." **Bees** are found in most areas of the world. However, in a culture where **bees** are unknown, we may say, for example, "flying insects that sting" or "stinging insects that fly." The stress here is not on the type of insect, but on its speed and viciousness, and also its ability to attack in swarms.

Beat you down in Seir as far as Hormah: the verb means to strike, hit, or beat, and consequently to defeat, destroy, and even kill. The geographical note is oddly stated in RSV and will not be understood by readers who cannot identify Seir or Hormah. Seir is Edom, the region occupied by the descendants of Esau, and Hormah is a city southeast of Beersheba. The meaning is that the Amorites chased the Israelites into Edom, and at the town of Hormah they defeated them.

An alternative translation model for the final part of the verse may be:

- They chased your soldiers [or, fighting men] into the land of Edom and defeated them at the city of Hormah.

1.45	RSV	TEV

And you returned and wept before the LORD; but the LORD did not hearken to your voice or give ear to you.	So you cried out to the LORD for help, but he would not listen to you or pay any attention to you.

You returned: presumably to their camp at Kadesh Barnea. CEV has "Then you came back to the place of worship at Kadesh-Barnea."

And wept before the LORD: this seems to indicate a religious service in which the Israelites poured out to God their grief and anguish. TEV has "cried out to the LORD for help." A note of repentance or sorrow for their sin may be understood; but the statement that Yahweh did not respond indicates that they were asking for help, so we may say "wept asking the LORD for help" or "cried out to the LORD to help you."

· **The LORD did not hearken to your voice or give ear to you**: this literal translation is not current English. The two verbal expressions mean the same: "the LORD didn't listen to your cries, he paid no attention to you," or "but the LORD would not pay any attention to you."

1F. The years in the desert (1.46–2.25)

RSV

46 So you remained at Kadesh many days, the days that you remained there.
Chapter 2
1 "Then we turned, and journeyed into the wilderness in the direction of the Red Sea, as the LORD told me; and for many days we went about Mount Seir. 2 Then the LORD said to me, 3 'You have been going about this mountain country long enough; turn northward. 4 And command the people, You are about to pass through the territory of your brethren the sons of Esau, who live in Seir; and they will be afraid of you. So take good heed; 5 do not contend with them; for I will not give you any of their land, no, not so much as for the sole of the foot to tread on, because I have given Mount Seir to Esau as a possession. 6 You shall purchase food from them for money, that you may eat; and you shall also buy water of them for money, that you may drink. 7 For the LORD your God has blessed you in all the work of your hands; he knows your going through this great wilderness; these forty years the LORD your God has been with you; you have lacked nothing.' 8 So we went on, away from our brethren the sons of Esau who live in Seir, away from the Arabah road from Elath and Ezion-geber.
"And we turned and went in the direction of the wilderness of Moab. 9 And the LORD said to me, 'Do not harass Moab or contend with them in battle, for I will not give you any of their land for a possession, because I have given Ar to the sons of Lot for a possession.' 10 (The Emim formerly lived there, a people great and many, and tall as the Anakim; 11 like the Anakim they are also known as Rephaim, but the Moabites call them Emim.

TEV
The Years in the Desert

46 "So then, after we had stayed at Kadesh for a long time, 1 we finally turned and went into the desert, on the road to the Gulf of Aqaba, as the LORD had commanded, and we spent a long time wandering about in the hill country of Edom.
2 "Then the LORD told me 3 that we had spent enough time wandering about in those hills and that we should go north. 4 He told me to give you the following instructions: 'You are about to go through the hill country of Edom, the territory of your distant relatives, the descendants of Esau. They will be afraid of you, 5 but you must not start a war with them, because I am not going to give you so much as a square foot of their land. I have given Edom to Esau's descendants. 6 You may buy food and water from them.'
7 "Remember how the LORD your God has blessed you in everything that you have done. He has taken care of you as you wandered through this vast desert. He has been with you these forty years, and you have had everything you needed.
8 "So we moved on and left the road that goes from the towns of Elath and Eziongeber to the Dead Sea, and we turned northeast toward Moab. 9 The LORD said to me, 'Don't trouble the people of Moab, the descendants of Lot, or start a war against them. I have given them the city of Ar, and I am not going to give you any of their land.' "
(10 A mighty race of giants called the Emim used to live in Ar. They were as tall as the Anakim, another race of giants. 11 Like the Anakim they were also known as Rephaim; but the Moabites called them Emim. 12 The Horites used to live in Edom, but the descendants

12 The Horites also lived in Seir formerly, but the sons of Esau dispossessed them, and destroyed them from before them, and settled in their stead; as Israel did to the land of their possession, which the LORD gave to them.) 13 'Now rise up, and go over the brook Zered.' So we went over the brook Zered. 14 And the time from our leaving Kadesh-barnea until we crossed the brook Zered was thirty-eight years, until the entire generation, that is, the men of war, had perished from the camp, as the LORD had sworn to them. 15 For indeed the hand of the LORD was against them, to destroy them from the camp, until they had perished.

16 "So when all the men of war had perished and were dead from among the people, 17 the LORD said to me, 18 'This day you are to pass over the boundary of Moab at Ar; 19 and when you approach the frontier of the sons of Ammon, do not harass them or contend with them, for I will not give you any of the land of the sons of Ammon as a possession, because I have given it to the sons of Lot for a possession.' 20 (That also is known as a land of Rephaim; Rephaim formerly lived there, but the Ammonites call them Zamzummim, 21 a people great and many, and tall as the Anakim; but the LORD destroyed them before them; and they dispossessed them, and settled in their stead; 22 as he did for the sons of Esau, who live in Seir, when he destroyed the Horites before them, and they dispossessed them, and settled in their stead even to this day. 23 As for the Avvim, who lived in villages as far as Gaza, the Caphtorim, who came from Caphtor, destroyed them and settled in their stead.) 24 'Rise up, take your journey, and go over the valley of the Arnon; behold, I have given into your hand Sihon the Amorite, king of Heshbon, and his land; begin to take possession, and contend with him in battle. 25 This day I will begin to put the dread and fear of you upon the peoples that are under the whole heaven, who shall hear the report of you and shall tremble and be in anguish because of you.'

of Esau chased them out, destroyed their nation, and settled there themselves, just as the Israelites later chased their enemies out of the land that the LORD gave them.)

13 "Then we crossed the Zered River as the LORD told us to do. 14 This was thirty-eight years after we had left Kadesh Barnea. All the fighting men of that generation had died, as the LORD had said they would. 15 The LORD kept on opposing them until he had destroyed them all.

16 "After they had all died, 17 the LORD said to us, 18 'Today you are to pass through the territory of Moab by way of Ar. 19 You will then be near the land of the Ammonites, the descendants of Lot. Don't trouble them or start a war against them, because I am not going to give you any of the land that I have given them.'"

(20 This territory is also known as the land of the Rephaim, the name of the people who used to live there; the Ammonites called them Zamzummim. 21 They were as tall as the Anakim. There were many of them, and they were a mighty race. But the LORD destroyed them, so that the Ammonites took over their land and settled there. 22 The LORD had done the same thing for the Edomites, the descendants of Esau, who live in the hill country of Edom. He destroyed the Horites, so that the Edomites took over their land and settled there, where they still live. 23 The land along the Mediterranean coast had been settled by people from the island of Crete. They had destroyed the Avvim, the original inhabitants, and had taken over all their land as far south as the city of Gaza.)

24 "After we had passed through Moab, the LORD told us, 'Now, start out and cross the Arnon River. I am placing in your power Sihon, the Amorite king of Heshbon, along with his land. Attack him, and begin occupying his land. 25 From today on I will make people everywhere afraid of you. Everyone will tremble with fear at the mention of your name.'

Some translations make verse 46 the last verse of the paragraph, rendered as a complete sentence, and begin a new section at 2.1 (RSV, NIV, REB, NJB). The Handbook, however, follows other translations, including TEV, CEV, and NRSV, in making verse 46 the first verse of this section.

Section heading: instead of TEV "The Years in the Desert," a translation may imitate NJB "From Kadesh to the Arnon," or even "The Israelites travel from Kadesh to the Arnon River."

1.46   RSV   TEV

So you remained at Kadesh many   **"So then, after we had stayed at**
days, the days that you remained   **Kadesh for a long time,**
there.

With the beginning of a new section, Moses may need to be introduced again
as the speaker; for example, "Moses said to the Israelites, ..."
  You remained at Kadesh: Moses continues to address his fellow Israelites.
If the second person plural **you** excludes Moses, the translation should instead
say "We remained at Kadesh." In the next verse (2.1) the narrative in Hebrew
goes to the inclusive first person plural, "Then we turned, and went . . . ." If a
translation imitates RSV, "*You* stayed at Kadesh . . . ," and begins 2.1 "Then *we*
turned . . . ," it will be better to begin a new section at 2.1. But if, like TEV, a
translation uses the first person plural in both verses (which this Handbook
recommends), it will be better to start the section with 1.46.
  Many days, the days that you remained there: this is a rather odd phrase but
is intended to emphasize that the Israelites stayed in Kadesh Barnea for a very
long time before they started on their way back. Another way to express it is
"We remained at Kadesh for a long time."

2.1   RSV   TEV

"Then we turned, and journeyed   **we finally turned and went into the**
into the wilderness in the direction of   **desert, on the road to the Gulf of**
the Red Sea, as the LORD told me;   **Aqaba, as the LORD had commanded,**
and for many days we went about   **and we spent a long time wandering**
Mount Seir.   **about in the hill country of Edom.**

Some translators may decide to follow RSV and NIV and make this verse the
beginning of the section, rather than beginning it at verse 46 of chapter 1. In
this case the section heading should be placed here; and Moses should be
introduced again here as the speaker; for example, "Moses said to the
Israelites, ..."
  Then we turned, and journeyed: see 1.40, where the order to do this is given.
This clause may also be rendered as "We resumed our journey and went into
the wilderness." For **wilderness** see 1.1.
  In the direction of the Red Sea: TEV has "on the road to the Gulf of Aqaba,"
and CEV has "by way of the Red Sea Road." The TEV rendering is preferable (see
also 1.40).
  Went about Mount Seir: the verb may mean to wander rather aimlessly, to
walk around without a set goal, as RSV, TEV, CEV, and REB translate; or it may
mean to bypass, to avoid going through, to go around, as NJPSV, NRSV, NJB
"skirted" translate. This meaning is supported by Num 21.4, where the same
verb is used. It is not easy to decide which is the better translation, especially
in light of verse 4, which says they were to go through Edom, and also verse 8,
where the Hebrew text is not at all clear. On the basis of what the Hebrew of

verse 8 seems to mean, it is recommended that here the translation be "bypass" or "go around." CEV follows this interpretation, with "We spent many years wandering around outside the hill country of Seir," where "outside" means that they did not enter Edom but bypassed it. **Mount Seir** is not a particular mountain but the hill country of Seir (REB, NJPSV), that is, of Edom (see the comment at 1.2), the region south of the Dead Sea.

2.2-3 RSV	TEV
2 Then the LORD said to me, 3 'You have been going about this mountain country long enough; turn northward.	**2 "Then the LORD told me 3 that we had spent enough time wandering about in those hills and that we should go north.**

The LORD said to me, 'You have been going . . .': Yahweh is speaking to Moses, but in the statement **You have been going** the second person plural is used, referring to the Israelites. The necessary change must be made to avoid making it seem that Yahweh is giving instructions only to Moses and no one else. Ways to express this are: "The LORD said to me, 'The people of Israel had wandered [or, walked aimlessly] . . . ,' " or we may use indirect speech in verses 2-3 as follows: "The LORD told me that we had spent enough time wandering . . ." (TEV). Here the pronoun "we" is inclusive.

You have been going around: here the same verb is used that appears in verse 1, and it should be translated the same way; for example, "wandering around outside the hill country of Edom" or "skirting the hill country of Edom." Instead of using the direct form, as RSV does, TEV uses indirect discourse, which continues through verse 7.

Turn northward: "Go north," "Head north," "Start marching north."

2.4 RSV	TEV
And command the people, You are about to pass through the territory of your brethren the sons of Esau, who live in Seir; and they will be afraid of you. So take good heed;	**He told me to give you the following instructions: 'You are about to go through the hill country of Edom, the territory of your distant relatives, the descendants of Esau. They will be afraid of you,**

And command the people may be also expressed as "He told me to give you the following instructions: . . ." (TEV), or "And give the people these orders: . . ." (CEV).

You are about to pass through the territory of your brethren the sons of Esau: the Israelites, proceeding north, would go through Edom, where the descendants of Esau lived. These **sons of Esau** were a kindred race; in English "kindred" (NRSV) or "distant relatives" (TEV) is the best way to express the meaning. **Seir** is Edom (1.2). An alternative translation model for this sentence may be "You will very soon walk [or, travel] through the hill country of Edom. It is the land that belongs to your distant relatives, the descendants of Esau." For "descendants" see 1.8.

They will be afraid of you: the relation between this statement and what follows is not clear. If the Edomites were afraid of the Israelites, why should the Israelites be careful not to fight them? REB provides a good answer by translating "Although they are afraid of you, be very careful not to quarrel with them . . ." (also NJPSV). And the adversative "but" used in TEV, ". . . but you must not start a war with" (also BRCL), is another way to handle the matter. Either one makes for a good translation.

So take good heed: this means to be careful, to not act rashly, and goes with what follows: "so be careful not to attack them." NRSV has "be very careful not to engage in battle with them."

2.5   RSV   TEV

do not contend with them; for I will   but you must not start a war with
not give you any of their land, no, not   them, because I am not going to give
so much as for the sole of the foot to   you so much as a square foot of
tread on, because I have given   their land. I have given Edom to
Mount Seir to Esau as a possession.   Esau's descendants.

Do not contend with them: the Hebrew verb is different from the one used in 1.30, but in this context it has essentially the same meaning: wage war against, fight, attack.

For I will not . . . : the reason the Israelites are not to fight the Edomites—even though the Edomites are afraid of them—is that Yahweh will not allow the Israelites to win.

The exaggerated figure **not so much as for the sole of the foot to tread on** is better rendered in English by "not . . . so much as a square foot" (TEV) or, even more idiomatically, "not even an inch [of their land]." NIV has "not even enough to put your foot on."

I have given Mount Seir to Esau as a possession: another way to express this is "I have given the region [or, territory] of Edom to the descendants of Esau as their own land." **Mount Seir** is the hill-country region of Seir, better known as Edom. So it may be better here to say "Edom." (See Gen 36.6-8 for an account of Esau's separating from Jacob to settle in Edom.) To use simply the proper name **Esau** here (NRSV, REB, NJPSV, NJB) is to raise unnecessary difficulties for the reader. The active **I have given** must not be disregarded, as done by SPCL.

It should be noted that the same language is used of Edom being the God-given heritage of the Edomites as is used of Canaan being the heritage of the Israelites.

2.6   RSV   TEV

You shall purchase food from them for money, that you may eat; and you shall also buy water of them for money, that you may drink.	**You may buy food and water from them.'**

The Israelites are neither to antagonize the Edomites nor ask for their help.

Purchase food . . . for money . . . buy water . . . for money: the equivalent of this statement in natural English is given by TEV, where the common verb "buy" is used of the food and the water; most translations use two verbs, "to purchase" and "to buy," but this is not necessary if a single verb will be good style. The use in English of **for money** is unnecessarily repetitive, but in some languages this repetition may be quite natural and should be retained.

It will be helpful for many translators to express this verse as follows:

- As you walk through their land, you may buy food and water.

2.7   RSV   TEV

For the LORD your God has blessed you in all the work of your hands; he knows your going through this great wilderness; these forty years the LORD your God has been with you; you have lacked nothing.'	**"Remember how the LORD your God has blessed you in everything that you have done. He has taken care of you as you wandered through this vast desert. He has been with you these forty years, and you have had everything you needed.**

In this verse Yahweh reassures the people. Yahweh has never let the people go without food and water, or other basic necessities.

The LORD your God has blessed you: the second person pronoun in Hebrew is singular; the Israelites are addressed as though they are one person. But the **you** may be changed in translation to "us" (inclusive); for example, "Yahweh caused us to be successful [or, prosper] . . . ." **Blessed** in English has become a religious cliche with no precise meaning. Unfortunately many modern translations still use it (for example, TEV, CEV, NIV). Here the term means to "cause to prosper" or "make successful" (see also 1.11).

All the work of your hands: this is better as expressed by NRSV "all your undertakings," or TEV "everything you have done." The two clauses may be expressed as "Yahweh our [inclusive] God has caused us to be successful in everything that we have done."

He knows your going through this great wilderness: this is more naturally expressed "He knows what happened to you as you went through that vast wilderness." The following phrase, **these forty years**, may be included: "He knows what happened to you during the forty years you were wandering around in that vast wilderness." Again the **you** may be changed to "us" and "we." REB

51

"He has watched over your journey" is possible following "During all that time
. . . ," since the Hebrew verb "to know" means in places "to take an interest in,"
"to care for" (see Gen 39.6; Psa 1.6). So TEV has "He has taken care of you as you
wandered through this vast desert," and CEV has "The LORD has helped us and
taken care of us during the past forty years that we have been in this huge
desert."

The LORD your God has been with you: see "[not] in your midst" in 1.42.

You have lacked nothing: this can be expressed in a positive way, as in TEV,
"You have had everything you needed."

2.8	RSV	TEV

So we went on, away from our brethren the sons of Esau who live in Seir,
away from the Arabah road from
Elath and Ezion-geber.
"And we turned and went in the
direction of the wilderness of Moab.

"So we moved on and left the road
that goes from the towns of Elath
and Eziongeber to the Dead Sea, and
we turned northeast toward Moab.

So we went on, away from our brethren: this may mean that the Israelites
departed, leaving behind the Edomites (so NJPSV, TOB, NJB); or it may mean,
more precisely, "So we passed by our kin" (NRSV; also REB "So we went on past
our kinsmen"; also BRCL, FRCL). It is difficult to determine which meaning is
intended. The Hebrew text is not at all clear, and it appears to embody an
inconsistency. It seems to say that the Israelites bypassed Edom (see verse 1),
even though the verb used is one that means ordinarily "to go through" (as in
2.4); it is not the verb that normally means "to go around" (see 2.3). But with
the verb goes the preposition "from" (as in Num 20.21), which makes the
Hebrew say that the Israelites avoided going through Edom. So CEV has "We
went past the territory that belonged to our relatives, the descendants of Esau."
This is what the Hebrew seems to mean, and is recommended to the translator;
but the other meaning "went away from" is also possible.

Our brethren the sons of Esau who live in Seir: as in verse 4. It is difficult
to know why TEV has omitted this bit of information; perhaps it was regarded
as unnecessarily repetitive.

Away from the Arabah road from Elath and Ezion-geber: the Hebrew here
is also unclear, and the translations vary. NJPSV is quite literal but makes
sense: "away from the road of the Arabah, away from Elath and Ezion-geber."
FRCL is similar: "We also avoided the road of the Arabah and the sites of Elath
and Ezion-geber." TEV's "So we moved on and left the road that goes from the
towns of . . ." is a possible rendering of the Hebrew text. GECL is even freer: "So
we went northward through the territory of our kinspeople, the descendants of
Esau, but did not use the road that goes from Ezion-geber and Elath through
the Arabah to the Dead Sea."

We turned and went: this may be stated more naturally, "We resumed our
journey," "We kept on going." NJPSV has "We marched on in the direction of
. . . ." As TEV makes clear, Moab was to the north (see map, page xii).

2.9   RSV   TEV

And the LORD said to me, 'Do not harass Moab or contend with them in battle, for I will not give you any of their land for a possession, because I have given Ar to the sons of Lot for a possession.'	The LORD said to me, 'Don't trouble the people of Moab, the descendants of Lot, or start a war against them. I have given them the city of Ar, and I am not going to give you any of their land.' "

Do not harass Moab or contend with them in battle: the meaning is clear enough, but the English is not natural. REB is better, "Do not harass the Moabites or provoke them to battle," or we may say "Do not cause trouble for the people of Moab or make them fight you." In this context "to harass" means to bother or molest by unprovoked attacks, verbal or physical.

Ar was the capital of Moab (see verse 18; Num 22.36); here it stands for the whole country. This is why RSV and TEV translate as **Moab**.

The sons of Lot are Lot's descendants, the Moabites (Gen 19.37). This final sentence in some languages may seem to indicate that **the sons of Lot** are a different people from "the people of Moab." In such a case we may place this phrase immediately after **Moab**; for example, "Don't . . . with the people of Moab. They are the descendants of Lot, and I have given them . . . ," or even "The people of Moab are the descendants of Lot, so don't harass them or make them fight you."

2.10-11   RSV   TEV

10 (The Emim formerly lived there, a people great and many, and tall as the Anakim; 11 like the Anakim they are also known as Rephaim, but the Moabites call them Emim.	(10 A mighty race of giants called the Emim used to live in Ar. They were as tall as the Anakim, another race of giants. 11 Like the Anakim they were also known as Rephaim; but the Moabites called them Emim.

Verses 10-12 are an explanatory note that is not part of the narrative itself. For this reason RSV has placed them between parentheses, while TEV makes them a separate paragraph, also between parentheses. CEV makes them a separate section with the heading "Tribes that Lived near Canaan." This is also possible.

The Emim . . . a people great and many: it is better to follow TEV, identifying these people as "A mighty race of giants" or "A powerful tribe [or, clan] of giants." The various legendary giants, the original inhabitants of the land, went by several names. A translation must have a consistent system of transliterating proper names, taking care to avoid names that are suggestive or already have a distinct meaning in the language. **Emim** may also be expressed as "people of Emim." The origin of the name **Emim** is unknown; perhaps it is related to the Hebrew noun "terror," but this cannot be proved. The name

Rephaim is used to mean "giants"; but its origin is uncertain. It must be transliterated like any other personal name. The **Anakim** or "people descended from Anak" have already been mentioned (1.28). **Giants** may be expressed as "very tall people." **Mighty** means "powerful" or "strong."

CEV has a helpful model for these two verses:

•   [10] Before the LORD gave the Moabites their land, a large and powerful tribe lived there. They were the Emim, and they were as tall as the Anakim. [11] The Moabites called them Emim, though others sometimes used the name Rephaim for both the Anakim and the Emim.

2.12   RSV   TEV

The Horites also lived in Seir for-   The Horites used to live in Edom, but
merly, but the sons of Esau dispos-   the descendants of Esau chased
sessed them, and destroyed them   them out, destroyed their nation, and
from before them, and settled in their   settled there themselves, just as the
stead; as Israel did to the land of   Israelites later chased their enemies
their possession, which the LORD   out of the land that the LORD gave
gave to them.)   them.)

Horites: NRSV has "Horim," which is closer to the Hebrew form. The name probably means "cave dwellers," but this cannot be proved; it does not mean "people of Hor" or "descendants of Hor." The name should be transliterated: "the people called Horites . . . ."

Seir is Edom. **The sons of Esau** are Esau's descendants, that is, the Edomites (see verses 4-5).

Dispossessed them: that is, "drove them out of their country."

Destroyed them from before them, and settled in their stead: this means that the Edomites completely defeated and killed the Horites and took possession of their territory, making it their own country.

As Israel did to the land of their possession: the Edomites did what the Israelites were to do later in their conquest of Canaan. Even though the Israelites, like the Edomites, conquered the country by force, the point is always made that it was Yahweh who gave them the land for them to possess.

2.13   RSV   TEV

'Now rise up, and go over the brook   "Then we crossed the Zered River
Zered.' So we went over the brook   as the LORD told us to do.
Zered.

This verse returns to the main narrative, and it is good for a translation to make it clear that once more Yahweh is speaking to Moses. If translators have made verses 10-12 into a separate section as CEV does, it is even more important to begin verse 13 with something like "Moses said to the Israelites," or even "Moses continued to speak to the . . . ."

In obedience to the LORD's command, the Israelites cross **the brook Zered**. The initial command **rise up** means "Get going," "Go forward." Here NRSV has "the Wadi Zered," and CEV has "Zered Gorge." Its location is not certain; some identify it with the Wadi el-Hesa, which flows into the southeastern end of the Dead Sea. See 1.24 for ways to translate **valley** or "wadi."

2.14	RSV	TEV

And the time from our leaving Kadesh-barnea until we crossed the brook Zered was thirty-eight years, until the entire generation, that is, the men of war, had perished from the camp, as the LORD had sworn to them.	This was thirty-eight years after we had left Kadesh Barnea. All the fighting men of that generation had died, as the LORD had said they would.

This verse and the next one provide information about the length of time it took the Israelites to get to the land of Canaan.

The **thirty-eight years** is two years short of the standard "forty years" (1.2) from the time the Israelites left Egypt until they entered Canaan. It may be that the author is subtracting the two years it took for them to reach Sinai, as well as the time spent in Kadesh Barnea (Num 1.1; 9.1; 10.11-12). RSV is too complicated. The TEV rendering is a more natural one: "This was thirty-eight years after we left Kadesh Barnea."

The entire generation, that is, the men of war: this is better expressed by NRSV, "the entire generation of warriors," and REB, ". . . of fighting men."

As the LORD had sworn to them: for "swear" see 1.8.

2.15	RSV	TEV

For indeed the hand of the LORD was against them, to destroy them from the camp, until they had perished.	The LORD kept on opposing them until he had destroyed them all.

The hand of the LORD was against them: this is a vivid way of saying that Yahweh kept punishing them and killing them, until all who belonged to the adult generation that left Egypt had died.

To destroy them from the camp, until they had perished: here **the camp** stands for the people themselves, the community, and God is portrayed as rooting them out and killing them.

An alternative translation model for this verse is:

●   Yahweh kept punishing them until they were all dead.

2.16-17   RSV   TEV

16 "So when all the men of war   16 "After they had all died, 17 the
had perished and were dead from   LORD said to us,
among the people, 17 the LORD said
to me,

The RSV literal translation of verse 16 is strange English. There is no need
in English to say **had perished and were dead**, and the following **from among
the people** is simply a way of identifying them as people of Israel. TEV provides
all the information in modern English: "After they had all died." REB is more
wordy but still natural: "When the last of the fighting men among the people
had died."

The LORD **said to me**: Yahweh is still talking to Moses alone, yet in the
following verse the command is for all the people. TEV has therefore translated
"said to us." Translators should follow either model, depending upon what is
normal in their own language.

2.18   RSV   TEV

'This day you are to pass over the   'Today you are to pass through the
boundary of Moab at Ar;   territory of Moab by way of Ar.

Pass over the boundary of Moab at Ar: the word translated **boundary** can
also mean the region itself, and not only its frontier. TEV is clearer with "Today
you are to pass through," which can be followed as a good model for this verse.
Ar is a city some 25 kilometers (15 miles) east of the southern end of the Dead
Sea (see map, page xi).

Alternative translation models for this verse are:

● Today you must travel through the territory of Moab near the city of Ar.

● Today you must go past the city of Ar and cross Moab's northern border.

2.19   RSV   TEV

and when you approach the frontier   You will then be near the land of the
of the sons of Ammon, do not harass   Ammonites, the descendants of Lot.
them or contend with them, for I will   Don't trouble them or start a war
not give you any of the land of the   against them, because I am not go-
sons of Ammon as a possession,   ing to give you any of the land that I
because I have given it to the sons of   have given them.' "
Lot for a possession.'

The Hebrew word translated **frontier** here is different from the one translated
"boundary" in verse 18, and can be taken to mean "boundary" or "frontier." The

phrase **the sons of Ammon** means "the Ammonites," or "people of Ammon" who, like the Moabites, were descended from Lot (Gen 19.30-38).

For **do not harass them or contend with them**, see verse 9. The assignment of this region to the Ammonites is stated in the same way as the assignment made to the Moabites in verse 9.

2.20-22 RSV	TEV
20 (That also is known as a land of Rephaim; Rephaim formerly lived there, but the Ammonites call them Zamzummim, 21 a people great and many, and tall as the Anakim; but the LORD destroyed them before them; and they dispossessed them, and settled in their stead; 22 as he did for the sons of Esau, who live in Seir, when he destroyed the Horites before them, and they dispossessed them, and settled in their stead even to this day.	(20 This territory is also known as the land of the Rephaim, the name of the people who used to live there; the Ammonites called them Zamzummim. 21 They were as tall as the Anakim. There were many of them, and they were a mighty race. But the LORD destroyed them, so that the Ammonites took over their land and settled there. 22 The LORD had done the same thing for the Edomites, the descendants of Esau, who live in the hill country of Edom. He destroyed the Horites, so that the Edomites took over their land and settled there, where they still live.

Verses 20-23 are another explanatory note that disrupts the narrative. It is well to place these verses within parentheses, as RSV, NRSV, TEV, REB, and others do. The speech of Yahweh resumes at verse 24.

Verse 20 speaks of an ancient race of giants known by some as **Rephaim** and by others as **Zamzummim**. The suffix **-im** is the Hebrew pluralizer. For **Rephaim** see verse 11. The origin of **Zamzummim** is uncertain; some think it was an insulting term used by the Ammonites, but this cannot be proved. This name will have to be transliterated, like any other personal name.

In verse 21 **a people great and many, and tall as the Anakim** is exactly like the wording in verse 10. The rest of the verse is virtually like verse 12, except that here Yahweh is named as the one who destroys them. **Dispossessed them** means "to drive out" or "dislodge" the inhabitants. TEV has "took over their land."

Verse 22 describes the same kind of event with the same kind of language. At the end of the verse, **and settled in their stead even to this day** is better expressed by TEV "and settled there, where they still live."

To this day: some translations may wish to imitate BRCL, which here and elsewhere includes a footnote:

to this day: that is, until the time this account was written.

2.23	RSV	TEV

As for the Avvim, who lived in villages as far as Gaza, the Caphtorim, who came from Caphtor, destroyed them and settled in their stead.)

The land along the Mediterranean coast had been settled by people from the island of Crete. They had destroyed the Avvim, the original inhabitants, and had taken over all their land as far south as the city of Gaza.)

This verse speaks of another primitive race, the **Avvim**; they are not identified as giants, but this is suggested by the name being linked with the others in the context of the explanatory note.

Gaza was one of the five Philistine city-states, on the Mediterranean coast.

As for **the Caphtorim** and **Caphtor**, it is generally agreed that these are the Philistines, who came originally from Crete (see Amos 9.7). This migration took place about 1200 B.C. Translators are urged to say "Philistines" or "people from Philistia," rather than using the form **Caphtorim**.

Another possible model for this verse is:

• The same thing happened to the Avvim, who lived in the land along the Mediterranean coast as far south as Gaza. People who came from the island of Crete destroyed the Avvim and took over all their land.

2.24	RSV	TEV

'Rise up, take your journey, and go over the valley of the Arnon; behold, I have given into your hand Sihon the Amorite, king of Heshbon, and his land; begin to take possession, and contend with him in battle.

"After we had passed through Moab, the LORD told us, 'Now, start out and cross the Arnon River. I am placing in your power Sihon, the Amorite king of Heshbon, along with his land. Attack him, and begin occupying his land.

Moses continues speaking to the Israelites (recalling the words of Yahweh), and this should be stated clearly in translation; for example, "Moses said to the Israelites: After we had traveled through Moab, the LORD told us, ..."

CEV makes verses 24-25 a new section, but translators are advised to begin a new section at verse 26 (see TEV).

Rise up, take your journey, and go over: as in other similar instances, this can be expressed more naturally, as in NRSV: "Proceed on your journey and cross . . . ." CEV is even clearer, with "Pack up your belongings, take down your tents, and cross over . . . ."

The valley of the Arnon: the Arnon river flowed from east to west into the east side of the Dead Sea (see the map, page xii). So this phrase can be translated, as TEV does, "[cross] the Arnon River."

I have given into your hand: it is Yahweh who makes it possible for the Israelites to defeat their enemies. Yahweh, so to speak, hands the enemies over to the Israelites, who thus overpower them. **Have given into your hand** may also be expressed as "give into your power" or "let you have power over."

Sihon the Amorite, king of Heshbon: see 1.4, 7.

Begin to take possession, and contend with him: the order is given for the Israelites to begin their conquest of the land on the east side of the Jordan River. The language is similar to that in verse 9.

2.25	RSV	TEV

RSV	TEV
This day I will begin to put the dread and fear of you upon the peoples that are under the whole heaven, who shall hear the report of you and shall tremble and be in anguish because of you.'	From today on I will make people everywhere afraid of you. Everyone will tremble with fear at the mention of your name.'

I will begin to put the dread and fear of you upon the peoples that are under the whole heaven: this can be expressed in a more natural way: "I shall fill the peoples under all heaven with fear and terror of you" (NJPSV), or "I will make all the nations to be terribly afraid of you." For comments on "fill with fear" or "melt the heart," see 1.28, 29. The phrase "under the whole heaven" is a way of including all peoples everywhere and can be more simply stated as "all the nations in the world" (FRCL, BRCL, SPCL), or even "all people everywhere in the world."

Who shall hear the report of you and shall tremble and be in anguish because of you: this further emphasizes the fear that will possess the various peoples whose lands the Israelites will invade and conquer. It is not clear whether **the report of you**, that is, "the news about you," will be of the Israelites' successive victories as they advance, or refers to their miraculous escape from Egypt. In any case a translation should say no more than the Hebrew text. **Shall hear the report of you** may also be expressed as "when anyone mentions [or, talks about] you." The two verbs **shall tremble** and **be in anguish** may be combined as TEV has done: "will tremble with fear at the mention of your name"; or if there are vivid terms that are similar in meaning in a receptor language, we may translate in a way similar to CEV: "They will tremble with fear when anyone mentions you, and they will be terrified when you appear."

1G. Israel defeats King Sihon (2.26-37)

RSV

TEV
Israel Defeats King Sihon

26 "So I sent messengers from the wilderness of Kedemoth to Sihon the king of Heshbon, with words of peace, saying, 27 'Let me pass through your land; I will go only by the road, I will turn aside neither to the right nor to the left. 28 You shall sell me food for money, that I may eat, and give me water for money, that I may drink; only let me pass through on foot, 29 as the sons of Esau who live in Seir and the Moabites who live in Ar did for me, until I go over the Jordan into the land which the LORD our God gives to us.' 30 But Sihon the king of Heshbon would not let us pass by him; for the LORD your God hardened his spirit and made his heart obstinate, that he might give him into your hand, as at this day. 31 And the LORD said to me, 'Behold, I have begun to give Sihon and his land over to you; begin to take possession, that you may occupy his land.' 32 Then Sihon came out against us, he and all his people, to battle at Jahaz. 33 And the LORD our God gave him over to us; and we defeated him and his sons and all his people. 34 And we captured all his cities at that time and utterly destroyed every city, men, women, and children; we left none remaining; 35 only the cattle we took as spoil for ourselves, with the booty of the cities which we captured. 36 From Aroer, which is on the edge of the valley of the Arnon, and from the city that is in the valley, as far as Gilead, there was not a city too high for us; the LORD our God gave all into our hands. 37 Only to the land of the sons of Ammon you did not draw near, that is, to all the banks of the river Jabbok and the cities of the hill country, and wherever the LORD our God forbade us.

26 "Then I sent messengers from the desert of Kedemoth to King Sihon of Heshbon with the following offer of peace: 27 'Let us pass through your country. We will go straight through and not leave the road. 28 We will pay for the food we eat and the water we drink. All we want to do is to pass through your country, 29 until we cross the Jordan River into the land that the LORD our God is giving us. The descendants of Esau, who live in Edom, and the Moabites, who live in Ar, allowed us to pass through their territory.'
30 "But King Sihon would not let us pass through his country. The LORD your God had made him stubborn and rebellious, so that we could defeat him and take his territory, which we still occupy.
31 "Then the LORD said to me, 'Look, I have made King Sihon and his land helpless before you; take his land and occupy it.' 32 Sihon came out with all his men to fight us near the town of Jahaz, 33 but the LORD our God put him in our power, and we killed him, his sons, and all his men. 34 At the same time we captured and destroyed every town, and put everyone to death, men, women, and children. We left no survivors. 35 We took the livestock and plundered the towns. 36 The LORD our God let us capture all the towns from Aroer, on the edge of the Arnon Valley, and the city in the middle of that valley, all the way to Gilead. No town had walls too strong for us. 37 But we did not go near the territory of the Ammonites or to the banks of the Jabbok River or to the towns of the hill country or to any other place where the LORD our God had commanded us not to go.

Section heading: there are other options: "The Israelites Defeat King Sihon"; FRCL has "The Occupation of the Kingdom of Sihon," or "The Israelites occupy the land of King Sihon."

2.26   RSV

TEV

"So I sent messengers from the wilderness of Kedemoth to Sihon the king of Heshbon, with words of peace, saying,

"Then I sent messengers from the desert of Kedemoth to King Sihon of Heshbon with the following offer of peace:

At the beginning of this section Moses should be introduced again as the speaker; for example, "Moses said to the Israelites: 'After we had crossed the Arnon river . . . .'"

Messengers: in terms of military campaigns, these are variously known in English as "couriers," "emissaries," "envoys," or even "ambassadors." The location of **Kedemoth** is unknown.

With words of peace, saying: this is more naturally stated by NJPSV "with an offer of peace, as follows"; see also NJB "this peaceful message," and CEV "telling him that his nation and ours could be at peace." **Peace** in this context means "absence of war." So we may translate "I sent messengers to King Sihon, who ruled in the town of Heshbon, telling him that his people and ours need not have to fight with each other. I said: . . . ." Moses wanted to avoid war with Sihon.

2.27 RSV	TEV
'Let me pass through your land; I will go only by the road, I will turn aside neither to the right nor to the left.	'Let us pass through your country. We will go straight through and not leave the road.

Let me pass through: Moses, as leader, speaks for all the Israelites. In most languages it will be better to use the plural, "Let us [exclusive] pass through" (also in verses 48-49).

I will turn aside neither . . . : Moses promises that the Israelites will go straight through Sihon's country, staying on the main road and not stopping to plunder or pillage. It will be an entirely peaceful passage through his country. In some languages the last part of the verse may be expressed as "We will keep to the road, and we will go straight through."

2.28 RSV	TEV
You shall sell me food for money, that I may eat, and give me water for money, that I may drink; only let me pass through on foot,	We will pay for the food we eat and the water we drink. All we want to do is to pass through your country,

This verse is almost exactly like 2.6; here the two verbs are **sell** and **give**, both meaning the same, since the Israelites offer to pay for what they receive.

Only let me pass through on foot: this emphasizes the peaceful nature of the Israelites' passage through the land. The phrase **on foot** is not in contrast with other ways of passing through (on horses, or in chariots); rather, it means they will pass through peacefully, without bothering the people. So FRCL has "Allow us simply to pass through your country," and TEV "All we want to do is pass through your country."

2.29   RSV   TEV

as the sons of Esau who live in Seir and the Moabites who live in Ar did for me, until I go over the Jordan into the land which the LORD our God gives to us.'	until we cross the Jordan River into the land that the LORD our God is giving us. The descendants of Esau, who live in Edom, and the Moabites, who live in Ar, allowed us to pass through their territory.'

As the sons of . . . : The first part of the verse recalls how the Edomites and the Moabites gave free passage to the Israelites. For the Edomites see verse 4, and for the Moabites see verses 18-19.

Care should be taken to link the last part of the verse (**until I go over the Jordan into the land . . .**) with verse 28. NRSV uses dashes to make the proper connection: "Only allow me to pass through on foot—just as the descendants . . . who live in Ar—until I cross the Jordan." In most cases it will be better to restructure the verse in a way similar to TEV: "until we reach the Jordan River and cross over it into the land that the LORD our God is giving us. The descendants of Esau, who live in Edom, and the people of Moab, who live in Ar, allowed us to pass through their lands." The singular **I go over** means not only Moses himself but all the people.

The LORD our God: our is exclusive, since Yahweh is not the God of Sihon and his people.

2.30   RSV   TEV

But Sihon the king of Heshbon would not let us pass by him; for the LORD your God hardened his spirit and made his heart obstinate, that he might give him into your hand, as at this day.	"But King Sihon would not let us pass through his country. The LORD your God had made him stubborn and rebellious, so that we could defeat him and take his territory, which we still occupy.

The LORD your God: here Moses is addressing the Israelites; if the second person plural "your God" gives the meaning that Yahweh is not the God of Moses, the inclusive first plural should be used: "our God," or "Yahweh whom we worship."

Hardened his spirit and made his heart obstinate: by the use of two similar expressions, the fact is emphasized that it was Yahweh who caused Sihon to refuse peaceful passage to the Israelites. The language is similar to that of Exo 4.21, which speaks of the king of Egypt. Yahweh made Sihon obstinate, stubborn, defiant. A hard **heart** indicated a stubborn attitude. In many languages there will be similar figurative expressions for "stubbornness" using the "heart" or "liver"; for example, "Yahweh caused his heart [or, liver] to become hard."

That he might give him into your hand: see verse 24. Moses is speaking not only of Sihon but of Sihon and his people.

As at this day: see verse 22.

There are better ways of stating the last part of this verse: "in order to hand him over to you, as he has now done" (NRSV); "in order that he and his land might become subject to you, as it is to this day" (REB).

2.31 RSV	TEV
And the LORD said to me, 'Behold, I have begun to give Sihon and his land over to you; begin to take possession, that you may occupy his land.'	"Then the LORD said to me, 'Look, I have made King Sihon and his land helpless before you; take his land and occupy it.'

The language is familiar: see verse 24. For **Behold** see 1.8.

Begin to: for Yahweh's order, see REB, "Begin the conquest, occupy the land."

2.32-33 RSV	TEV
32 Then Sihon came out against us, he and all his people, to battle at Jahaz. 33 And the LORD our God gave him over to us; and we defeated him and his sons and all his people.	32 Sihon came out with all his men to fight us near the town of Jahaz, 33 but the LORD our God put him in our power, and we killed him, his sons, and all his men.

The fighting began at **Jahaz**, whose location is unknown. The victory of the Israelites was complete. Again it is stated that it was Yahweh who enabled them to win.

Then Sihon came out: in certain languages it will be necessary to indicate where Sihon came out of; for example, "Then Sihon came out of the town of Heshbon with all his soldiers."

And the LORD our God gave him over to us may be expressed as "And the LORD [or, Yahweh] our God helped us defeat him."

2.34 RSV	TEV
And we captured all his cities at that time and utterly destroyed every city, men, women, and children; we left none remaining;	At the same time we captured and destroyed every town, and put everyone to death, men, women, and children. We left no survivors.

As noticed before, instead of **cities** the word "towns" or its equivalent may be more appropriate (so NRSV).

Utterly destroyed every city, men, women, and children: some languages may require two different verbs to express the idea of destroying towns and killing people. In some languages we may say "Break down the towns and kill all the people." In others a figurative expression such as "wipe the towns and people from the face of the earth" may be employed. The Hebrew verb belongs to the vocabulary of what is called "holy war," in which the total slaughter of the people is portrayed as a religious act. Mayes' comment is worth recording: "the verb *charam* is the technical term used for the extermination of the enemy in a holy war as well as for the exclusive reservation of certain things to Yahweh. The common factor is that the things so designated are not available for common use . . ."—and so have to be destroyed (see 13.16-18). An alternative translation model for this sentence may be "At that time we captured and destroyed every town and killed every man, woman, and child."

We left none remaining: see NRSV "We left not a single survivor," or "not one person survived."

2.35   RSV   TEV

only the cattle we took as spoil for ourselves, with the booty of the cities which we captured.   **We took the livestock and plundered the towns.**

The two terms **spoil** and **booty** are the appropriate words to use of enemy possessions that are seized by victorious troops after a battle. The animals were taken from the fields, and all the valuable articles in the houses were seized. In English the two words in this kind of context are exact synonyms, like "pillage" and "plunder." **Only** indicates that this is an exception to the general statement in the previous verse. Whatever could not be carried away was usually destroyed, so that nothing was left.

Cattle or "livestock" (TEV, CEV) probably refers to not only cows and bulls (oxen), but sheep and goats (see also Exo 9.2-3). In cultures where **cattle** are unknown, we may employ a descriptive phrase such as "all domesticated animals." It will also be helpful to include an illustration of these animals. See a further discussion on **cattle** in *Fauna and Flora of the Bible* (FFB), pages 75-76.

We took: some other verb may be more appropriate for taking **the cattle**; something like "we drove away the cattle" will be better in some languages.

With the booty of the cities may be expressed as "everything else of value in the towns that we captured."

A possible alternative model is:

- We took all the domesticated animals and everything else of value in the towns we captured.

2.36   RSV   TEV

From Aroer, which is on the edge of the valley of the Arnon, and from the   **The LORD our God let us capture all the towns from Aroer, on the edge of**

city that is in the valley, as far as Gilead, there was not a city too high for us; the LORD our God gave all into our hands.	the Arnon Valley, and the city in the middle of that valley, all the way to Gilead. No town had walls too strong for us.

Aroer: for its location see map, page xii.

The valley of the Arnon: see verse 24.

And from the city that is in the valley: NRSV places this within parentheses: "(including the town that is in the wadi itself)" (see TEV). The identity of this town has not been established.

Gilead is the northern region of the territory on the east side of the Jordan River. So we may say "all the way north to the region of Gilead."

A city too high for us: that is, a fortified city (or, town) whose walls were too high and strong for the Israelites to break through. See in 1.28 the fear of the Israelites that those fortified towns could not be conquered.

Gave all into our hands: it was Yahweh who made it possible for the Israelites to defeat King Sihon and his people.

The reading **into our hands** follows the Samaritan Pentateuch and the Septuagint (also Vulgate "to us"); the Hebrew has "[gave all] before us," which HOTTP prefers (an {A} decision). In a translation which is concerned about meaning, there is no great difference between the two, since "before us" simply reinforces **all**, and the indirect object "us" is understood. So a translator may feel free to follow RSV, or NRSV "gave everything to us," or "let us capture every town."

2.37 RSV	TEV
Only to the land of the sons of Ammon you did not draw near, that is, to all the banks of the river Jabbok and the cities of the hill country, and wherever the LORD our God forbade us.	But we did not go near the territory of the Ammonites or to the banks of the Jabbok River or to the towns of the hill country or to any other place where the LORD our God had commanded us not to go.

This verse makes clear that the Israelites strictly obeyed Yahweh's commands and did not invade any region or attack any town unless Yahweh told them to. The translator should notice that the language switches from the first person plural of the previous verses to the second person plural; if such a change will cause difficulty for the readers, the first person plural forms should be maintained (so TEV and CEV).

The sons of Ammon: that is, the Ammonites, or "people of Ammon," or even "the descendants of Ammon" (see verse 19).

All the banks of the river Jabbok: for part of its way the river ran north to south, thus forming the western boundary of the Ammonite territory (see map, page xii). The Israelites did not invade Ammon. CEV interprets this to mean "We stayed away from all the Ammonite towns both in the hill country and near the Jabbok river."

And wherever the LORD our God forbade us: NRSV translates "just as the LORD our God had charged," with a textual note indicating that this follows the Septuagint and the (Jerusalem) Targum; the Hebrew text has "and all," instead of "just as." HOTTP prefers the Hebrew and gives the following translation: "and, generally, whatsoever the LORD our God commanded you." A translator who wishes to follow the HOTTP decision may take TOB as a model: "and all the places the LORD our God had forbidden us," or we may say "or to any other place where the LORD our God had commanded us not to go."

1H. Israel conquers King Og (3.1-11)

<table>
<tr><td align="center">RSV</td><td align="center">TEV
Israel Conquers King Og</td></tr>
<tr><td>

1 "Then we turned and went up the way to Bashan; and Og the king of Bashan came out against us, he and all his people, to battle at Edrei. 2 But the LORD said to me, 'Do not fear him; for I have given him and all his people and his land into your hand; and you shall do to him as you did to Sihon the king of the Amorites, who dwelt at Heshbon.' 3 So the LORD our God gave into our hand Og also, the king of Bashan, and all his people; and we smote him until no survivor was left to him. 4 And we took all his cities at that time—there was not a city which we did not take from them—sixty cities, the whole region of Argob, the kingdom of Og in Bashan. 5 All these were cities fortified with high walls, gates, and bars, besides very many unwalled villages. 6 And we utterly destroyed them, as we did to Sihon the king of Heshbon, destroying every city, men, women, and children. 7 But all the cattle and the spoil of the cities we took as our booty. 8 So we took the land at that time out of the hand of the two kings of the Amorites who were beyond the Jordan, from the valley of the Arnon to Mount Hermon 9 (the Sidonians call Hermon Sirion, while the Amorites call it Senir), 10 all the cities of the tableland and all Gilead and all Bashan, as far as Salecah and Edrei, cities of the kingdom of Og in Bashan. 11 (For only Og the king of Bashan was left of the remnant of the Rephaim; behold, his bedstead was a bedstead of iron; is it not in Rabbah of the Ammonites? Nine cubits was its length, and four cubits its breadth, according to the common cubit.)

</td><td>

1 "Next, we moved north toward the region of Bashan, and King Og came out with all his men to fight us near the town of Edrei. 2 But the LORD said to me, 'Don't be afraid of him. I am going to give him, his men, and all his territory to you. Do the same thing to him that you did to Sihon the Amorite king who ruled in Heshbon.'

3 "So the LORD also placed King Og and his people in our power, and we slaughtered them all. 4 At the same time we captured all his towns—there was not one that we did not take. In all we captured sixty towns—the whole region of Argob, where King Og of Bashan ruled. 5 All these towns were fortified with high walls, gates, and bars to lock the gates, and there were also many villages without walls. 6 We destroyed all the towns and put to death all the men, women, and children, just as we did in the towns that belonged to King Sihon of Heshbon. 7 We took the livestock and plundered the towns.

8 "At that time we took from those two Amorite kings the land east of the Jordan River, from the Arnon River to Mount Hermon. 9 Mount Hermon is called Sirion by the Sidonians, and Senir by the Amorites.) 10 We took all the territory of King Og of Bashan: the cities on the plateau, the regions of Gilead and of Bashan, as far east as the towns of Salecah and Edrei."

(11 King Og was the last of the Rephaim. His coffin, made of stone, was six feet wide and almost fourteen feet long, according to standard measurements. It can still be seen in the Ammonite city of Rabbah.)

</td></tr>
</table>

Section heading: beside the TEV heading "Israel Conquers King Og," or "Defeat of Og King of Bashan" (NIV), other headings are possible, such as "The

Israelites conquer the kingdom of Og," or "The Israelites kill Og the king of Bashan and occupy his land."

3.1 RSV	TEV
"Then we turned and went up the way to Bashan; and Og the king of Bashan came out against us, he and all his people, to battle at Edrei.	**"Next, we moved north toward the region of Bashan, and King Og came out with all his men to fight us near the town of Edrei.**

With the beginning of a new section, it is a good idea to introduce Moses again as the speaker, and to summarize briefly what leads up to this in chapter 2; for example, "Moses said to the people of Israel, After killing King Sihon we turned north . . . .' "

Then we turned and went up the way to Bashan: the Israelites headed north to the region of **Bashan**, which is elevated land that lies to the northeast of Lake Galilee. The name **Bashan** means "fertile land."

Og . . . and all his people: the text does not mean that all men, women, and children of Og's kingdom went to battle with him; rather it means "all his fighting men," or "all his soldiers." For a comment on **king** see 1.4.

Edrei was on the southern boundary of Bashan (see 1.4).

3.2 RSV	TEV
But the LORD said to me, 'Do not fear him; for I have given him and all his people and his land into your hand; and you shall do to him as you did to Sihon the king of the Amorites, who dwelt at Heshbon.'	**But the LORD said to me, 'Don't be afraid of him. I am going to give him, his men, and all his territory to you. Do the same thing to him that you did to Sihon the Amorite king who ruled in Heshbon.'**

Yahweh promises Moses that the same will happen in the fight against Og that happened against Sihon: Yahweh will hand Og and his army over to the Israelites, who will defeat them completely. For **the LORD** see 1.3, and for **Do not fear** see 1.21.

I have given him . . . into your hand: even more strongly than in 2.31, the future event is spoken of as having already taken place. This can be expressed by "I will certainly give . . . ." For the expression **given . . . into your hand**, see 2.36.

You shall do to him as you did to Sihon may also be expressed as "Destroy him just as you did Sihon . . . ." However, "and his people" is understood in the command to destroy, so we may translate "Destroy him and his people just as . . . ."

3.3   RSV   TEV

So the LORD our God gave into our   "So the LORD also placed King Og
hand Og also, the king of Bashan,   and his people in our power, and we
and all his people; and we smote him   slaughtered them all.
until no survivor was left to him.

The same thing happens in the Israelite conquest of King Og's territory that
happened in the conquest of Sihon's kingdom (2.32-36). BRCL has "So the LORD,
our God, enabled us to defeat King Og and all his army."
    We smote him until no survivor was left to him: "We kept on fighting him
until all of his men had been killed," or "We kept on . . . until we had killed him
and all his soldiers."

3.4   RSV   TEV

And we took all his cities at that   At the same time we captured all his
time—there was not a city which we   towns—there was not one that we
did not take from them—sixty cities,   did not take. In all we captured sixty
the whole region of Argob, the king-   towns—the whole region of Argob,
dom of Og in Bashan.   where King Og of Bashan ruled.

This verse, describing the complete conquest of Og's territory, is like 2.34.
    All his cities . . . not a city which we did not take from them: we should notice
the switch of pronouns, from **his [cities]** to **[from] them**. The second clause is
repetitive, and in many languages it will be more natural style to combine both
clauses and translate, for example, "We captured [or, conquered] all his towns."
City is really "town" (so TEV, and CEV; also see 1.4).
    Argob is identified as Og's domain in the territory of Bashan (1 Kgs 4.13).
It is possible to reorder the clauses of this verse as follows:

•   About that time we conquered the whole region of Argob in the
     territory of Bashan where King Og ruled. We captured all his
     towns. There were sixty of them.

3.5   RSV   TEV

All these were cities fortified with   All these towns were fortified with
high walls, gates, and bars, besides   high walls, gates, and bars to lock
very many unwalled villages.   the gates, and there were also many
                                            villages without walls.

All these were cities: for the sixty fortified towns, see 2.36.
    The Hebrew word translated **gates** appears in its dual form, which explains
NRSV "double gates," and the footnote in NJPSV "double-leaf doors." This is quite
possible, because the metal bars (usually bronze) were normally laid across the

inside of a pair of double gates to keep them from being pushed open by enemies. Most translations, though, have simply "gates." The phrase **gates and bars** means "gates with bars," "barred gates" (REB), and may be also rendered as "gates with metal bars across them on the inside," or even "double gates locked with bars."

Many unwalled villages: these were small farming villages not big enough or wealthy enough to have walls or strong fences around them. In case of war the villagers would go to the nearest fortified town. The Hebrew word translated **unwalled villages** appears in the Septuagint as a proper name, "the Perizzites," which is what NJB has. Other translations have "villages without walls" or the like; REB has "open settlements." This Handbook prefers the Hebrew text.

An alternative translation model for this verse is:

- They had protected these towns with high walls [or, fences] and double gates locked with bronze bars. There were also many villages with no walls [or, fences].

3.6-7   RSV   TEV

6 And we utterly destroyed them, as we did to Sihon the king of Heshbon, destroying every city, men, women, and children. 7 But all the cattle and the spoil of the cities we took as our booty.

6 We destroyed all the towns and put to death all the men, women, and children, just as we did in the towns that belonged to King Sihon of Heshbon. 7 We took the livestock and plundered the towns.

These two verses describe the outcome of the battle in the same words used in 2.34-35 to describe the defeat of Sihon. Care should be taken to use the same words in translating the two accounts. The verbal phrase **utterly destroyed** in verse 6 is the same as the one used in 2.34.

3.8   RSV   TEV

So we took the land at that time out of the hand of the two kings of the Amorites who were beyond the Jordan, from the valley of the Arnon to Mount Hermon

"At that time we took from those two Amorite kings the land east of the Jordan River, from the Arnon River to Mount Hermon.

This verse summarizes the two campaigns against Sihon and Og.

The Amorites is the general term used of the inhabitants of the land. See 1.27.

Beyond the Jordan: that is, on the east side of the river, the other side from the point of view of the writer in Israel.

The valley of the Arnon: see 2.24.

Mount Hermon: at the northern end of the land, near the Syrian border.

CEV has a helpful model for this verse:

- Sihon and Og had ruled Amorite kingdoms east of the Jordan River. Their land stretched from the Arnon gorge in the south to Mount Hermon in the north, and we captured it all.

3.9   RSV   TEV

(the Sidonians call Hermon Sirion, while the Amorites call it Senir),	(Mount Hermon is called Sirion by the Sidonians, and Senir by the Amorites.)

This verse is, so to speak, a footnote, added to the text by someone other than the original writer. It explains that Hermon was also called **Sirion** and **Senir**.

A translation should end verse 8 with a full stop, and have verse 9 in parentheses, as a complete sentence (see TEV). Verse 10 will then begin a new complete sentence. RSV and NRSV do not do this and so make it very difficult for public reading.

Sidonians: people of Sidon, a Phoenician city on the Mediterranean coast, north of Israel.

3.10   RSV   TEV

all the cities of the tableland and all Gilead and all Bashan, as far as Salecah and Edrei, cities of the kingdom of Og in Bashan.	We took all the territory of King Og of Bashan: the cities on the plateau, the regions of Gilead and of Bashan, as far east as the towns of Salecah and Edrei."

This verse is a summary of all the territory east of the Jordan that had been conquered by the Israelites.

The tableland is the southern plateau, going from Gilead, in the north, to the boundary of Moab at the Arnon River. Another way to express **tableland**, or "plateau," is "high, flat land." **Gilead** was the central area of east Jordan, divided into two by the Jabbok River (see map, page xii).

Salecah and **Edrei** (see 1.4) appear as two towns more or less in the same region. Both seem to have been at the southern boundary of the land (Josh 13.11-12).

3.11   RSV   TEV

(For only Og the king of Bashan was left of the remnant of the Rephaim; behold, his bedstead was a bedstead of iron; is it not in Rabbah of the	(King Og was the last of the Rephaim. His coffin,[b] made of stone,[c] was six feet wide and almost fourteen feet long, according to standard

Ammonites? Nine cubits was its
length, and four cubits its breadth,
according to the common cubit.[a])

measurements. It can still be seen in
the Ammonite city of Rabbah.)

[b] coffin; *or* bed.

[a] Heb *cubit of a man*

[c] stone; *or* iron.

Here is another footnote: a note about the iron (or, stone) bedstead (or, coffin) of King Og.

King **Og** is said to have been the last survivor of the **Rephaim** (see 2.11), the legendary race of giants. We may also render this as "King Og was the last of the people called Rephaim."

The Hebrew word translated **bedstead** by RSV and others is taken to mean "coffin," as TEV has it, or more precisely "sarcophagus," a stone burial container (so FRCL and REB). And the word understood to mean **iron** (RSV) is thought to mean "black basalt," the material out of which the sarcophagus was carved. The Septuagint translates "iron bed," and this is how most translations have it. Some commentators think that a sarcophagus is meant, but it is impossible to know for sure. In many cultures "sarcophagus" will be an unknown term, so it is recommended that the equivalent of "[stone] coffin" be used. However, in cultures where other forms of burial are used, we may say something like "They buried him in a large stone container that was six feet wide and . . . ."

Rabbah, the capital of ancient Ammon, is now Amman, the capital of Jordan.

A standard cubit (**common cubit**) was more or less forty-five centimeters (eighteen inches) in length. **Nine cubits** would be approximately four meters, or almost fourteen feet; and **four cubits** converts into one meter and eighty centimeters (1.8 meters), or six feet. Most translations give approximate round figures. TEV omits the information about "cubits" and says "according to standard measurements." Another way to express this is "according to what they considered the correct measurement."

1I. The tribes that settled east of the Jordan (3.12-22)

RSV

TEV

*The Tribes That Settled East of
the Jordan*

12 "When we took possession of this land at that time, I gave to the Reubenites and the Gadites the territory beginning at Aroer, which is on the edge of the valley of the Arnon, and half the hill country of Gilead with its cities; 13 the rest of Gilead, and all Bashan, the kingdom of Og, that is, all the region of Argob, I gave to the half-tribe of Manasseh. (The whole of that Bashan is called the land of Rephaim. 14 Jair the Manassite took all the region of Argob, that is, Bashan, as far as the border of the Geshurites and the Maacathites, and called the villages after his own name, Havvoth-jair, as it is to this day.) 15 To Machir I gave Gilead, 16 and to the Reubenites and the Gadites I gave the territory from Gilead as far as the valley of the Arnon, with the middle of the valley as a boundary, as far over as the river Jabbok, the boundary of the Ammonites; 17 the Arabah also, with the Jordan as the boundary, from Chinnereth as far as the sea of the Arabah, the Salt Sea, under the slopes of Pisgah on the east.
18 "And I commanded you at that time, saying, 'The LORD your God has given you this land to possess; all your men of valor shall pass over armed before your brethren the people of Israel. 19 But your wives, your little ones, and your cattle (I know that you have many cattle) shall remain in the cities which I have given you, 20 until the LORD gives rest to your brethren, as to you, and they also occupy the land which the LORD your God gives them beyond the Jordan; then you shall return every man to his possession which I have given you.'
21 And I commanded Joshua at that time, 'Your eyes have seen all that the LORD your God has done to these two kings; so will the LORD do to all the kingdoms into which you are going over. 22 You shall not fear them; for it is the LORD your God who fights for you.'

12 "When we took possession of the land, I assigned to the tribes of Reuben and Gad the territory north of the town of Aroer near the Arnon River and part of the hill country of Gilead, along with its towns. 13 To half the tribe of Manasseh I assigned the rest of Gilead and also all of Bashan, where Og had ruled, that is, the entire Argob region."
(Bashan was known as the land of the Rephaim. 14 Jair, from the tribe of Manasseh, took the entire region of Argob, that is, Bashan, as far as the border of Geshur and Maacah. He named the villages after himself, and they are still known as the villages of Jair.)
15 "I assigned Gilead to the clan of Machir of the tribe of Manasseh. 16 And to the tribes of Reuben and Gad I assigned the territory from Gilead to the Arnon River. The middle of the river was their southern boundary, and their northern boundary was the Jabbok River, part of which formed the Ammonite border. 17 On the west their territory extended to the Jordan River, from Lake Galilee in the north down to the Dead Sea in the south and to the foot of Mount Pisgah on the east.
18 "At the same time, I gave them the following instructions: 'The LORD our God has given you this land east of the Jordan to occupy. Now arm your fighting men and send them across the Jordan ahead of the other tribes of Israel, to help them occupy their land. 19 Only your wives, children, and livestock—I know you have a lot of livestock—will remain behind in the towns that I have assigned to you. 20 Help the other Israelites until they occupy the land that the LORD is giving them west of the Jordan and until the LORD lets them live there in peace, as he has already done here for you. After that, you may return to this land that I have assigned to you.'
21 "Then I instructed Joshua: 'You have seen all that the LORD your God did to those two kings, Sihon and Og; and he will do the same thing to everyone else whose land you invade. 22 Don't be afraid of them, for the LORD your God will fight for you.'

Verses 12-17 report the division of the land east of the Jordan River among the tribes of Reuben, Gad, and Manasseh, as well as the clan of Machir (verse 15) and a man named Jair (verse 14). The translator will notice that in several places TEV makes clear how the various limits of each region relate to one another in terms of direction, whereas RSV is quite unclear. The translator is encouraged to imitate TEV in this respect. In the discussion that follows, we will notice how this matter is handled by other translations, especially FRCL, REB, and SPCL. And attention should always be paid to the map, page xii.

Section heading: instead of the TEV heading, "The Tribes that Settled East of the Jordan," other possible headings are NJB "The Partitioning of Transjordan"; FRCL "The Partitioning of the Country of Gilead"; CEV "The Land East of the Jordan River is Divided," or "Moses divides the land east of the Jordan river," or even "The people from the tribes of Reuben and Gad receive land east of the Jordan River."

3.12	RSV	TEV
	"When we took possession of this land at that time, I gave to the Reubenites and the Gadites the territory beginning at Aroer, which is on the edge of the valley of the Arnon, and half the hill country of Gilead with its cities;	"When we took possession of the land, I assigned to the tribes of Reuben and Gad the territory north of the town of Aroer near the Arnon River and part of the hill country of Gilead, along with its towns.

At the beginning of this new section, Moses should be introduced once again as the speaker; for example, "Moses said to the people of Israel."

When we took possession of the land at that time: it may be a good idea to say "the land east of the Jordan" (BRCL). The phrase **at that time** is frequently used (2.34; 3.4, 8, 18, 21, 23), but in the context it is quite redundant; it simply repeats the opening **When**.

I gave to the Reubenites and Gadites: it is better to say something like "I assigned to the tribes of Reuben and Gad," or "I assigned to the people from the tribes of Reuben and Gad." For "tribe" see 1.13.

The territory beginning at Aroer: NRSV is clearer, "the territory north of Aroer"; TEV helps by saying "north of the town of Aroer."

Aroer, which is on the edge of the valley of the Arnon: so also 2.36; 4.48. Inasmuch as the Arnon is a river, it makes more sense in English, at least, to say "the Arnon River," as TEV does (also SPCL), rather than "the Wadi Arnon" (NRSV; also NJPSV, REB) or "the Arnon Gorge" (NIV). BRCL has "the valley of the Arnon River."

Instead of **on the edge of the valley**, HOTTP prefers "on the gorge" (so also CEV), since the phrase "the edge of" is not in the Hebrew text. But this phrase is present in 2.36 and 4.48, and on that basis a translator is justified in saying the same thing here; Aroer did not change location from one chapter to the next.

And half of the hill country of Gilead with its cities: NRSV and REB, like TEV, have "towns." This is a reference to the part of Gilead south of the Jabbok River. CEV has "and went far enough north to include the southern half of the Gilead region."

3.13   RSV   TEV

the rest of Gilead, and all Bashan,   To half the tribe of Manasseh I as-
the kingdom of Og, that is, all the   signed the rest of Gilead and also all
region of Argob, I gave to the half-   of Bashan, where Og had ruled, that
tribe of Manasseh. (The whole of that   is, the entire Argob region."
Bashan is called the land of   (Bashan was known as the land of
Rephaim.   the Rephaim.

It is good idea to begin a new sentence here, "To half the tribe of Manasseh
I assigned . . . ," or "I assigned to half the tribe of Manasseh the . . . ."

The rest of Gilead: or "the other half of Gilead," or "the northern half of
Gilead" (CEV).

And all of Bashan, the kingdom of Og, that is, all the region of Argob: the
writer includes all the names used for this region (see verse 4). TEV restructures
the items, for ease of understanding. It should be clear that Og is a person, not
the name of the country; so TEV "where Og had ruled."

For **the half-tribe of Manasseh** it may be useful to have a footnote explaining
that the other half of the tribe settled in the territory west of the Jordan River.
See Josh 13.29-31 for East Manasseh and 17.1-13 for West Manasseh.

The last sentence of the verse is placed within parentheses by RSV and TEV,
linking it with verse 14. NJPSV and SPCL join it to the first part of this verse, as
follows: "and all of Bashan under Og's rule—the whole Argob district, all that
part of Bashan which is called Rephaim country—I assigned to the half-tribe
of Manasseh."

Is called: TEV has "was known as," the meaning expressed by NRSV, REB, BRCL,
and which this Handbook recommends.

For **Rephaim** see 2.11,20.

Something like the following may serve as a model for this verse:

- And to the half-tribe of Manasseh I assigned the rest of Gilead
  and all of Bashan, that is, the entire region of Argob, the territory
  ruled by King Og, which used to be called the land of the Rephaim.

However, the CEV model using two sentences will be helpful in many languages:

- I gave the northern half of Gilead and all of the Bashan region to
  half of the tribe of Manasseh. Bashan had belonged to King Og,
  and the Argob region in Bashan used to be called the land of the
  Rephaim.

3.14   RSV   TEV

Jair the Manassite took all the region   Jair, from the tribe of Manasseh,
of Argob, that is, Bashan, as far as   took the entire region of Argob, that
the border of the Geshurites and the   is, Bashan, as far as the border of

Maacathites, and called the villages after his own name, Havvoth-jair, as it is to this day.)	Geshur and Maacah. He named the villages after himself, and they are still known as the villages of Jair.)

Jair the Manassite: this translates the Hebrew "Jair son of Manasseh," and that is how it is translated by NJPSV, NJB, REB, FRCL, TOB. But Jair does not appear to have been the son of Manasseh; 1 Chr 2.21-22 says that Segub, the son of Machir's daughter, was Jair's father (making Machir his great-grandfather and Manasseh his great-great-grandfather). So it is better to translate "Jair a descendant of Manasseh" (BRCL, SPCL, NIV) or "Jair, from the tribe of Manasseh" (TEV).

The border of the Geshurites and the Maacathites: it is better to translate "the border of Geshur and Maacah," or "the territories of Geshur and Maacah" (SPCL). They were small Aramean states south of Mount Hermon. An alternative translation model for the first part of this verse is "Jair, from the tribe of Manasseh, conquered the entire region of the Argob, which was also called Bashan. This region goes as far as the territories of Geshur and Maacah."

Called the villages after his own name, Havvoth-jair: the Hebrew name means "villages [or, settlements] of Jair."

As it is to this day: that is, at the time this account was written (see 2.22).

3.15 RSV TEV

To Machir I gave Gilead,	"I assigned Gilead to the clan of Machir of the tribe of Manasseh.

To Machir I gave Gilead: Machir was the son of Manasseh (Gen 50.23); here the name stands for "the clan of Machir of the tribe of Manasseh" (TEV), or "the descendants of Machir, son of Manasseh" (FRCL). See Num 32.39-40.

This refers to the northern part of Gilead; the southern part was assigned to the tribes of Reuben and Gad. So we may translate:

- I assigned the northern half of the territory of Gilead to the descendants of Machir, who was a son of Manasseh.

3.16 RSV TEV

and to the Reubenites and the Gadites I gave the territory from Gilead as far as the valley of the Arnon, with the middle of the valley as a boundary, as far over as the river Jabbok, the boundary of the Ammonites;	And to the tribes of Reuben and Gad I assigned the territory from Gilead to the Arnon River. The middle of the river was their southern boundary, and their northern boundary was the Jabbok River, part of which formed the Ammonite border.

To the Reubenites and Gadites: "To the tribes of Reuben and Gad," or "to the people of the tribes of Reuben and Gad."

The territory from Gilead as far as the valley of the Arnon: that is, from Gilead south to the Arnon River.

With the middle of the valley as a boundary, as far over as the river Jabbok, the boundary of the Ammonites: see TEV for clarity and precision. But it must be said that in Hebrew verse 16 is not all that clear. The Septuagint translates as follows: "And to Reuben and Gad I gave [the territory] from Gilead to the Wadi Arnon (the boundary was in the middle of the wadi) and as far as the Jabbok." Instead of **with the middle of the valley as a boundary, as far over as the river Jabbok**, HOTTP prefers "in the middle of the river and (its adjacent) territory, and unto the river Jabbok." The HOTTP Preliminary Report is not at all clear, and translators may stay with RSV, or translate in a similar way to NRSV, as follows: ". . . from Gilead as far as the Arnon River, with the middle of the river as a boundary, and up to the Jabbok River."

3.17	RSV	TEV
	the Arabah also, with the Jordan as the boundary, from Chinnereth as far as the sea of the Arabah, the Salt Sea, under the slopes of Pisgah on the east.	On the west their territory extended to the Jordan River, from Lake Galilee in the north down to the Dead Sea in the south and to the foot of Mount Pisgah on the east.

It is a good idea to make a break at the end of verse 16 and begin a new sentence here, as TEV does. And it should be made clear that this verse is a summary statement of the territory assigned to all three tribes: Reuben, Gad, and East Manasseh. So this verse may start with "On the west the territory of the three tribes extended to . . . ."

The Arabah: see 1.1.

Chinnereth: this is Lake Galilee (TEV) or the Sea of Galilee (most English translations). In areas where lakes are unknown, we may express "Lake Galilee" as "a small fresh water sea named Galilee."

The sea of the Arabah, the Salt Sea: today it is known as the Dead Sea.

Under the slopes of Pisgah on the east: this is not easy to understand. NJPSV makes "the slopes of Pisgah" the eastern boundary. Mount Pisgah is about 15 kilometers (9 miles) east of the northern end of the Dead Sea. Here the name may refer to the mountain itself, or more likely to the whole mountain range, of which Mount Nebo was the summit (32.49; 34.1). It is recommended that TEV be followed here: "and to the foot of Mount Pisgah on the east."

3.18	RSV	TEV
	"And I commanded you at that time, saying, 'The LORD your God has given you this land to possess;	"At the same time, I gave them the following instructions: 'The LORD our God has given you this land east of

| all your men of valor shall pass over armed before your brethren the people of Israel. | the Jordan to occupy. Now arm your fighting men and send them across the Jordan ahead of the other tribes of Israel, to help them occupy their land. |

I commanded you: as the context shows, Moses is speaking to the three tribes that settled east of the Jordan. CEV makes this clear with "At the same time I told the men of Reuben, Gad, and half of Manasseh."

The LORD your God: again, if the second person plural **your** makes it appear that Yahweh is not the God of Moses, the inclusive form of the first person plural should be used, namely, "The LORD our [inclusive] God." For a comment on LORD, or "Yahweh," see 1.3.

This land: that is, the land east of the Jordan River (compare TEV).

All your men of valor shall pass over armed before your brethren the people of Israel: the meaning is that the fighting men or soldiers of the three tribes east of the Jordan were to cross the Jordan River to the west side ahead of the fighting men from the other tribes and help them conquer the territory on the west side. When the conquest was completed, they were to return to their homes east of the Jordan. See Num 32.16-22. **Armed** suggests the act of "arming" them. TEV has "Now arm your fighting men"; or we may say "Now give weapons to your soldiers."

3.19	RSV	TEV

| But your wives, your little ones, and your cattle (I know that you have many cattle) shall remain in the cities which I have given you, | Only your wives, children, and livestock—I know you have a lot of livestock—will remain behind in the towns that I have assigned to you. |

These fighting men were to leave their families and cattle behind on the east side of the Jordan.

Your cattle (I know you have many cattle): Bashan was known for its fine cattle. For a comment on **cattle** or "livestock," see 2.35.

It is possible to combine verses 18 and 19 as follows:

- ¹⁸⁻¹⁹ At the same time I told the men from the tribes of Reuben, Gad, and half of Manasseh: "The LORD our [inclusive] God has let you occupy this land east of the Jordan river. Your wives and children can stay here with the large herds of cattle I know you have. Now give weapons to all your soldiers, and they must cross the Jordan river ahead of the soldiers from the other tribes of Israel, to help them occupy their land.

3.20   RSV   TEV

until the LORD gives rest to your brethren, as to you, and they also occupy the land which the LORD your God gives them beyond the Jordan; then you shall return every man to his possession which I have given you.'	Help the other Israelites until they occupy the land that the LORD is giving them west of the Jordan and until the LORD lets them live there in peace, as he has already done here for you. After that, you may return to this land that I have assigned to you.'

Until the LORD gives rest to your brethren, as to you: that is, until Yahweh gives them complete victory over their enemies, as he did to the eastern tribes. Then they will be able to settle down and live in peace, "secure from the threat of enemies, and from the threat of homelessness" (Mayes). So the first part of this verse may be rendered as:

● You must help the other Israelites to conquer their enemies and occupy the land that the LORD is giving them west of the Jordan river. Then they will be able to live there securely.

The LORD your God: again the second person is used.
The land . . . beyond the Jordan: here, verse 25, and 11.30 are the three passages in which "beyond the Jordan" means on the west side of the Jordan; elsewhere it means the east side. Here the point of view is that of Moses, who is on the east side of the river.
As elsewhere, verses 17-19 make it clear that the Israelites are able to conquer and possess the land because Yahweh is giving it to them. His gift comes first and is the cause of their conquest of the land.

3.21   RSV   TEV

And I commanded Joshua at that time, 'Your eyes have seen all that the LORD your God has done to these two kings; so will the LORD do to all the kingdoms into which you are going over.	"Then I instructed Joshua: 'You have seen all that the LORD your God did to those two kings, Sihon and Og; and he will do the same thing to everyone else whose land you invade.

Joshua has seen how Yahweh enabled the Israelites to defeat Kings Sihon and Og (**these two kings**—which TEV makes clear) and occupy their lands; and Yahweh will do the same in all the kingdoms the Israelites will invade in Canaan, west of the Jordan.
All that the LORD your God has done to these two kings may be alternatively expressed as "how the LORD our [inclusive] God has helped us to destroy King Sihon and King Og."

3.22   RSV   TEV

You shall not fear them; for it is the   **Don't be afraid of them, for the LORD**
LORD your God who fights for you.'   **your God will fight for you.'**

You shall not fear them: English translations make it appear that Moses is
addressing Joshua; but the plural forms in Hebrew make it clear that Moses is
speaking to all the people, and not only to Joshua. A translation should make
that clear if the target language, like English, does not have different forms for
the singular and the plural.

1J. Moses is not permitted to enter Canaan (3.23-29)

RSV   TEV
Moses Is Not Permitted to Enter Canaan

23 "And I besought the LORD at that time,   23 "At that time I earnestly prayed,
saying, 24 'O Lord GOD, thou hast only begun   24 'Sovereign LORD, I know that you have
to show thy servant thy greatness and thy   shown me only the beginning of the great and
mighty hand; for what god is there in heaven   wonderful things you are going to do. There is
or on earth who can do such works and mighty   no god in heaven or on earth who can do the
acts as thine? 25 Let me go over, I pray, and mighty things that you have done! 25 Let me
see the good land beyond the Jordan, that   cross the Jordan River, LORD, and see the
goodly hill country, and Lebanon.' 26 But the fertile land on the other side, the beautiful hill
LORD was angry with me on your account, and   country and the Lebanon Mountains.'
would not hearken to me; and the LORD said to 26 "But because of you people the LORD was
me, 'Let it suffice you; speak no more to me of angry with me and would not listen. Instead,
this matter. 27 Go up to the top of Pisgah, and he said, 'That's enough! Don't mention this
lift up your eyes westward and northward and   again! 27 Go to the peak of Mount Pisgah and
southward and eastward, and behold it with   look to the north and to the south, to the east
your eyes; for you shall not go over this Jor- and to the west. Look carefully at what you
dan. 28 But charge Joshua, and encourage and   see, because you will never go across the Jor-
strengthen him; for he shall go over at the   dan. 28 Give Joshua his instructions.
head of this people, and he shall put them in Strengthen his determination, because he will
possession of the land which you shall see.'   lead the people across to occupy the land that
29 So we remained in the valley opposite Beth- you see.'
peor.   29 "So we remained in the valley opposite
                                               the town of Bethpeor."

Section heading. Instead of the TEV heading, "Moses Is Not Permitted to
Enter Canaan," something like the following may be useful: "The LORD will not
let Moses enter the Promised Land," "The LORD tells Moses that he will not
enter the Promised Land," or "God Refuses to Let Moses Enter Canaan" (CEV).

3.23-24   RSV   TEV

23 "And I besought the LORD at   **23 "At that time I earnestly prayed,**
that time, saying, 24 'O Lord GOD,   **24 'Sovereign LORD, I know that you**
thou hast only begun to show thy   **have shown me only the beginning**
servant thy greatness and thy mighty **of the great and wonderful things**

79

hand; for what god is there in heaven or on earth who can do such works and mighty acts as thine?	you are going to do. There is no god in heaven or on earth who can do the mighty things that you have done!

O Lord GOD: in his prayer, Moses addresses God as *Adonai Yahweh*; only here and in 9.26 (also a prayer by Moses) is this title used in this book. Translators have the following options in translating "Adonai Yahweh." One option is to follow RSV; but the spelling GOD may seem strange to readers. Another option is to imitate TEV, or to say something like "Yahweh the All Powerful One," or "Yahweh, our Lord," or "Yahweh who is the Most Powerful." This Handbook recommends the second option (see "Translating Deuteronomy," page 7 and following).

Thou hast only begun to show thy servant: Moses is confident that Yahweh will still perform many miracles and mighty acts in the future. To make clear that "your servant" refers to Moses himself, it may be well to translate ". . . to show me, your servant . . ." or simply to follow TEV and CEV "me."

Thy greatness and thy mighty hand: here **hand** stands for power, might, force. So the translation can be "your greatness and your power." FRCL has "you have shown me the first signs of your greatness and of your irresistible power."

What god is there . . . ? This is a rhetorical question, a way of stating "There is no god in heaven or on earth," that is, no other god anywhere. The question does not deny the existence of other gods; it denies that any other god has the power that Yahweh, the God of Israel, has. **God** in small letters indicates a pagan deity. This term presents a difficult translation problem in many languages. *A Handbook on the Books of Nahum, Habakkuk, and Zephaniah*, page 20, discusses the problem of "God" versus "god":

> In English the supreme God is differentiated from lesser gods or deities by the use of a capital letter. In many other languages this device is not suitable, for the term for God is only used for the Christian God, so it will seem strange to refer to other gods. There are two possible solutions. Translators may use a term or terms which refer to supernatural beings which non-Christians in the culture worship, or they may use the term for the Christian God with an adjective; for example, "false gods" or "small gods." This will show that these are beings which are thought to be like God but are not really God.

The final sentence of this verse may be alternatively rendered as "No other god in the sky or on earth is able to do the mighty things that you do." However, if a translator uses a term such as "small god" or "false god," we may translate, for example, "If there are false gods in the sky or earth, they cannot do the mighty things that Yahweh has done."

3.25   RSV   TEV

Let me go over, I pray, and see the **Let me cross the Jordan River, LORD,**
good land beyond the Jordan, that **and see the fertile land on the other**
goodly hill country, and Lebanon.' **side, the beautiful hill country and**
                                        the Lebanon Mountains.'

Let me go over: that is, "Let me cross the Jordan River," or "Let me go to the
other side of the Jordan."

I pray: this represents in English the Hebrew particle of polite entreaty. In
many languages it will be necessary to use an equivalent polite formula here;
for example, "Please let me cross the Jordan River . . ." (CEV).

The good land: it is **good** as a place that will make a good country for the
Israelites, a fertile land. So we may say "a fertile land," or "a land that will
grow good crops."

Beyond the Jordan: on the west side of the river.

That goodly hill country: that is, that beautiful, or fine, hill country. For **hill
country** see 1.1.

Lebanon: the Lebanon Mountains, to the north.

In some languages Moses' quote (verses 24-25) will end with something like
"That is what I said to Yahweh."

3.26   RSV   TEV

But the LORD was angry with me on **"But because of you people the**
your account, and would not hearken **LORD was angry with me and would**
to me; and the LORD said to me, 'Let **not listen. Instead, he said, 'That's**
it suffice you; speak no more to me **enough! Don't mention this again!**
of this matter.

The LORD was angry with me on your account: the verb, different from the
two verbs used in 1.34, 37, is a strong one, picturing Yahweh as furious with
Moses. For a comment on **angry** see "angered," 1.24.

On your account: this refers to their lack of faith when Yahweh commanded
them to invade the land (2.26-33). It seems strange that Yahweh should be
angry with Moses because of the Israelites, but as their leader Moses must bear
responsibility for their behavior. "Because of you people" (TEV, CEV) is a good
model.

Would not hearken to me: that is, "would not listen to me," "would not pay
attention to my plea."

Let it suffice you: this very inadequate translation is improved in NRSV,
"Enough from you!"; see also REB "Enough!" TEV "That's enough!" and their
equivalents in Spanish, Portuguese, and French.

Speak no more to me about this matter: TEV has "Don't mention this again,"
but we may also express this as "I don't want to hear you talking about this any
more."

3.27   RSV   TEV

Go up to the top of Pisgah, and lift   Go to the peak of Mount Pisgah and
up your eyes westward and north-   look to the north and to the south, to
ward and southward and eastward,   the east and to the west. Look care-
and behold it with your eyes; for you   fully at what you see, because you
shall not go over this Jordan.   will never go across the Jordan.

Go to the top of Pisgah: in some languages the equivalent of "Climb [up] to
the top of Mount Pisgah" will be more natural style.

Lift up your eyes ... and behold it with your eyes: this literal word-for-word
equivalence of the Hebrew text is quaint and unnatural. Something like "take
a good look . . . look all around" is normal English. In certain languages this
will be expressed as "look out over . . . ."

Westward ... northward ... southward ... eastward: languages usually have
a standard order or pattern for referring to the four points of the compass. In
English and many other languages it is "north, south, east, and west." In some
languages something like "Look in all directions" or "Look all around you" will
be used. Translators should use the patterns followed in their languages.

You shall not go over this Jordan: the literal translation "this Jordan" makes
it sound like there is some other Jordan elsewhere. CEV has a good model: "but
you are not going to cross the Jordan River."

3.28   RSV   TEV

But charge Joshua, and encourage   Give Joshua his instructions.
and strengthen him; for he shall go   Strengthen his determination, be-
over at the head of this people, and   cause he will lead the people across
he shall put them in possession of   to occupy the land that you see.'
the land which you shall see.'

Charge Joshua: "Give Joshua instructions [or, orders]."

Encourage and strengthen: there are usually idiomatic phrases in a given
language, sometimes including bodily features, that serve as vivid equivalents
of the text; for example, "cause him to have a brave heart, and give strength to
his heart."

He shall go over at the head of this people: "he will lead the Israelites across
the river."

He shall put them in possession: by means of his leadership, Joshua will
enable the Israelites to conquer and occupy the land.

Which you shall see: that is, from the top of Mount Pisgah (34.1-3).

In some languages it will be helpful to restructure this verse as follows:

- It is Joshua who is going to lead the people of Israel across the
  Jordan river to occupy the land that you see before you. So help
  him be strong and brave, and tell him what he must do.

3.29   RSV   TEV

**So we remained in the valley oppo-   "So we remained in the valley
site Beth-peor.   opposite the town of Bethpeor."**

It is not certain where the town of Bethpeor was located, other than that it
was on the east side of the Jordan. It is probably the same as Baalpeor (4.3),
perhaps opposite Jericho.

1K. Moses urges Israel to be obedient (4.1-14)

               RSV   TEV
                                          Moses Urges Israel to Be Obedient

1 "And now, O Israel, give heed to the statutes and the ordinances which I teach you, and
do them; that you may live, and go in and take
possession of the land which the LORD, the
God of your fathers, gives you. 2 You shall not
add to the word which I command you, nor
take from it; that you may keep the commandments of the LORD your God which I command
you. 3 Your eyes have seen what the LORD did
at Baal-peor; for the LORD your God destroyed
from among you all the men who followed the
Baal of Peor; 4 but you who held fast to the
LORD your God are all alive this day. 5 Behold,
I have taught you statutes and ordinances, as
the LORD my God commanded me, that you
should do them in the land which you are
entering to take possession of it. 6 Keep them
and do them; for that will be your wisdom and
your understanding in the sight of the peoples,
who, when they hear all these statutes, will
say, 'Surely this great nation is a wise and
understanding people.' 7 For what great nation
is there that has a god so near to it as the
LORD our God is to us, whenever we call upon
him? 8 And what great nation is there, that
has statutes and ordinances so righteous as all
this law which I set before you this day?
9 "Only take heed, and keep your soul diligently, lest you forget the things which your
eyes have seen, and lest they depart from your
heart all the days of your life; make them
known to your children and your children's
children— 10 how on the day that you stood
before the LORD your God at Horeb, the LORD
said to me, 'Gather the people to me, that I
may let them hear my words, so that they may
learn to fear me all the days that they live
upon the earth, and that they may teach their
children so.' 11 And you came near and stood
at the foot of the mountain, while the moun-

1 Then Moses said to the people, "Obey all
the laws that I am teaching you, and you will
live and occupy the land which the LORD, the
God of your ancestors, is giving you. 2 Do not
add anything to what I command you, and do
not take anything away. Obey the commands
of the LORD your God that I have given you.
3 You yourselves saw what the LORD did at
Mount Peor. He destroyed everyone who worshiped Baal there, 4 but those of you who were
faithful to the LORD your God are still alive
today.
5 "I have taught you all the laws, as the
LORD my God told me to do. Obey them in the
land that you are about to invade and occupy.
6 Obey them faithfully, and this will show the
people of other nations how wise you are.
When they hear of all these laws, they will say,
'What wisdom and understanding this great
nation has!'
7 "No other nation, no matter how great,
has a god who is so near when they need him
as the LORD our God is to us. He answers us
whenever we call for help. 8 No other nation,
no matter how great, has laws so just as those
that I have taught you today. 9 Be on your
guard! Make certain that you do not forget, as
long as you live, what you have seen with your
own eyes. Tell your children and your grandchildren 10 about the day you stood in the
presence of the LORD your God at Mount Sinai,
when he said to me, 'Assemble the people. I
want them to hear what I have to say, so that
they will learn to obey me as long as they live
and so that they will teach their children to do
the same.'
11 "Tell your children how you went and
stood at the foot of the mountain which was
covered with thick clouds of dark smoke and
fire blazing up to the sky. 12 Tell them how the

tain burned with fire to the heart of heaven, wrapped in darkness, cloud, and gloom. 12 Then the LORD spoke to you out of the midst of the fire; you heard the sound of words, but saw no form; there was only a voice. 13 And he declared to you his covenant, which he commanded you to perform, that is, the ten commandments; and he wrote them upon two tables of stone. 14 And the LORD commanded me at that time to teach you statutes and ordinances, that you might do them in the land which you are going over to possess.

LORD spoke to you from the fire, how you heard him speaking but did not see him in any form at all. 13 He told you what you must do to keep the covenant he made with you—you must obey the Ten Commandments, which he wrote on two stone tablets. 14 The LORD told me to teach you all the laws that you are to obey in the land that you are about to invade and occupy.

With this exhortation to the people (verses 1-40), Moses' first discourse comes to an end. One commentator (Craigie) calls chapter 4 "a miniature sermon on the covenant and the laws."

Section heading: some translations may choose to make 4.1-40 one section, but it seems preferable to divide it into several sections, as TEV does (so also FRCL, SPCL, BRCL). For verses 1-14 FRCL has the heading "Put into Practice the Law of the Lord," TEV has "Moses Urges Israel to Be Obedient," and CEV has "Israel Must Obey God."

4.1	RSV	TEV

"And now, O Israel, give heed to the statutes and the ordinances which I teach you, and do them; that you may live, and go in and take possession of the land which the LORD, the God of your fathers, gives you.

Then Moses said to the people, "Obey all the laws that I am teaching you, and you will live and occupy the land which the LORD, the God of your ancestors, is giving you.

And now, O Israel, give heed to: since this begins a new section, it is a good idea to reintroduce Moses as the speaker, as TEV and CEV do. **And now** marks a turning point, a transition in the discourse. **O** is a marker in old English which RSV uses to indicate that someone is being addressed. It is routinely omitted in NRSV. **Israel** refers to "people of Israel," "Israelites," or even "fellow-Israelites." It is advisable to begin Moses' words with the vocative: "People of Israel! Obey . . . ." In this context **give heed to** means "obey," "follow," "put into practice."

The statutes and the ordinances: in this context the two Hebrew words mean much the same: "rules and regulations," "laws and commands," all the laws that regulated all aspects of the Israelites' lives. There are other Hebrew words used (see especially Psalm 119), and some languages will not have more than two or three different terms for "laws," in which case something like "all the laws," or "all the rules and regulations" may be used. However, in some languages **ordinances** and **statutes** will be described as "all the things that people must do or not do."

Which I teach you: "that I am telling [or, teaching] you," "that I am making known to you." This is a process of education and learning; the Israelites are not simply to obey the laws, but they are to know them, and in some cases even to memorize them.

And do them: NRSV "that I am teaching you to observe" is closer to the Hebrew. Here "to observe" means "to obey." An alternative translation model for the first part of this verse is "Then Moses said to the people of Israel, 'You must obey all the things that I am telling [or, teaching] you to do or not to do.'"

That you may live and . . . : that is, "so that you may survive to enter" (NJB). Moses has no idea how long it will be before the Israelites begin to invade (**go in**) and conquer (**take possession of**) the land of Canaan (see 1.8).

The LORD, the God of your fathers: if "your" means for readers that Yahweh is not the God of Moses, then the inclusive "our" should be used, "the God of our ancestors" (see 1.11). For **LORD** see 1.3. For **fathers** or "ancestors" see 1.8. CEV translates the phrase **God of your fathers** as "He is the God your ancestors worshiped."

Gives you: "is giving you," "is about to give you."

4.2	RSV	TEV
	You shall not add to the word which I command you, nor take from it; that you may keep the commandments of the LORD your God which I command you.	Do not add anything to what I command you, and do not take anything away. Obey the commands of the LORD your God that I have given you.

You shall not add . . . nor take from: the Law is regarded as a complete and perfect whole, and the Israelites are not to add any more rules to it nor take any out. So TEV has "Do not add anything to what I command you, and do not take anything away."

The Law is here called **the word** (**which I command you**). But the Hebrew word for **word** can have the more general sense of "matter," "subject," or even "thing," and that is how NRSV, NJB, NJPSV, NIV, and SPCL take it here: "You shall not add anything to what I am commanding you . . . ."

Which I command you: see "which I teach you" in verse 1.

Commandments translates the word most commonly used for the laws of Israel; it appears forty-three times in this book.

The LORD your God: see 1.10.

It is possible to reorder the clauses of this verse as follows:

- I have told you everything that Yahweh your [or, our] God has commanded you to do. Don't add anything or take anything away.

4.3   RSV   TEV

Your eyes have seen what the LORD did at Baal-peor; for the LORD your God destroyed from among you all the men who followed the Baal of Peor;	**You yourselves saw what the LORD did at Mount Peor. He destroyed everyone who worshiped Baal there,**

Your eyes have seen: this can be said more simply, "You have seen" or, more emphatically, "With your very own eyes you saw." NRSV "You have seen for yourselves" is good.

What the LORD did at Baal-peor: this refers to what is reported in Num 25.1-9. Baal, the Canaanite god of fertility, had a sanctuary at Mount Peor, in Moab, which may be the same as the town Bethpeor (3.29; see map, page xii). The TEV model is a good one: "You yourselves saw what the LORD did at Mount Peor."

Destroyed all the men who followed the Baal of Peor: here the verb "destroy" means "to kill," and "follow" means "to worship," "to become a devotee of." **The Baal of Peor** may also be expressed as "The god Baal at Mount Peor." For "god" see 3.4.

It is possible to rearrange the clauses of this verse as follows:

•   You yourselves saw how he killed everyone among you who worshiped the god Baal at Mount Peor.

4.4   RSV   TEV

but you who held fast to the LORD your God are all alive this day.	**but those of you who were faithful to the LORD your God are still alive today.**

You who held fast to: the verb means "to be loyal," "to be faithful." NRSV translates "who remained faithful to."

Are all alive this day: the lesson is clear. If the Israelites remain faithful to Yahweh, they will indeed live; if they reject Yahweh, they will die as did the 24,000 at Mount Peor.

4.5   RSV   TEV

Behold, I have taught you statutes and ordinances, as the LORD my God commanded me, that you should do them in the land which you are entering to take possession of it.	**"I have taught you all the laws, as the LORD my God told me to do. Obey them in the land that you are about to invade and occupy.**

All the constituent parts of this verse appear in 4.1, where they have been dealt with. Here Moses says he has already taught the Israelites the **statutes and ordinances** they are to obey.

As the LORD my God commanded me: the first singular pronoun **my** should be retained in translation, unless it means for readers that Moses' God is not the God of the people he is addressing. Some languages will express this as "As the LORD [or, Yahweh] whom I worship told me to do."

Do them: that is, "obey," "put into practice," "follow."

4.6   RSV   TEV

Keep them and do them; for that will   Obey them faithfully, and this will
be your wisdom and your under-   show the people of other nations
standing in the sight of the peoples,   how wise you are. When they hear of
who, when they hear all these stat-   all these laws, they will say, 'What
utes, will say, 'Surely this great na-   wisdom and understanding this
tion is a wise and understanding   great nation has!'
people.'

Keep them and do them: that is, "Obey them faithfully" (TEV, and similarly CEV), "Practice them carefully." NJPSV has "Observe them faithfully"; NIV and REB "Observe them carefully," and NRSV "Observe them diligently."

That will be your wisdom and understanding in the sight of the peoples: by carefully obeying God's laws, the Israelites will be regarded by their neighbors as a wise and intelligent people, as a people full of wisdom and good sense. Alternative ways of saying this are "Obey them faithfully, and this will show the people of other nations how wise you are" (TEV), or "If you faithfully obey the things that I have taught you to do, you will show the people of other nations that you are very wise."

When they hear all these statutes: this probably means "when they learn of" or "when they know about" (REB). NJB has "Once they know what all the laws are." It does not mean that all the laws would be read to the other nations. CEV has a good model: "In fact, everyone who hears about your laws will say . . . ."

Upon learning of these laws, the neighboring peoples will exclaim, **"Surely this great nation is a wise and understanding people"**—using the same two adjectives to describe them. Other ways to render this are "The people of this great nation must be very wise" or "The people of this large and powerful nation must be . . . ." **Great** here means both large in number and politically powerful.

4.7   RSV   TEV

For what great nation is there that   "No other nation, no matter how
has a god so near to it as the LORD   great, has a god who is so near when
our God is to us, whenever we call   they need him as the LORD our God
upon him?   is to us. He answers us whenever we
                                          call for help.

After the direct quotation in verse 6 of what people of other nations will say about the Israelites, in verse 7 Moses resumes his address to the people. To ensure that those who hear the text being read aloud understand this, it may be helpful to make verse 7 a separate paragraph and begin it with "And Moses continued . . . ."

Moses' words in verses 7-8 are in the form of two rhetorical questions, and in some languages it will be useful to render them as direct statements, as TEV does. The point of Moses' rhetorical questions is that Israel's God, Yahweh, always answers promptly and decisively whenever the people pray for his help.

A god: the Hebrew word is plural in form, but in most instances it is singular in meaning; here, however, some translations translate it as plural, "gods" (TOB, FRCL, SPCL, NJPSV, NIV). It seems preferable, however, to take it as singular. For **god** see 3.24.

So near to it as the LORD our God is to us: if the figure of physical nearness raises difficulties for the readers, it may be better to say "so quick [or, ready] to help it as the LORD our God is ready to help us." For another instance of this figure, see Psa 145.18; and see the story of Elijah and the prophets of Baal in 1 Kgs 18.20-40.

Whenever we call upon him: "every time we pray for him to help us."

In some languages it will be helpful to use at least three sentences for translating this verse:

* No other nation, no matter whether it is great or small, has a god like ours. The LORD our God [or, The God whom we worship] is quick to help us. He answers us whenever we call for him to help.

4.8	RSV	TEV
	And what great nation is there, that has statutes and ordinances so righteous as all this law which I set before you this day?	No other nation, no matter how great, has laws so just as those that I have taught you today.

This is another rhetorical question, whose answer is "None." It may be a good idea to translate it as an emphatic statement of fact: "And there is surely no other great nation . . . ."

Statutes and ordinances: see 4.1.

Righteous: applied to laws, "fair, right, just."

All this law: or "this entire Law." The Hebrew noun *torah* is related to the verb "to teach"; but the translation of the noun in the Septuagint by the Greek noun "law" has been carried over into the Latin Vulgate and major European languages, including English. Most standard translations still use "law," but SPCL here has "teaching," and NJPSV translates "as perfect as all this Teaching." REB has "code of laws," and NIV "this body of laws." Translators must determine whether the use of "law" is so deep-seated that another word such as "teaching" is not practical, and also whether the use of "law" gives the correct sense for readers in their language. Whatever the initial use and meaning of the Hebrew noun *torah*, at the time Deuteronomy was written the Torah was, in fact, Israel's code of laws. A translation like "has rules and regulations as fair as all this law" maintains the repetition of the Hebrew (see RSV) but will be too wordy in many languages. TEV reduces the repetition with "No other nation . . . has laws so just as those that I have taught you today," while CEV has ". . . has laws that are as fair as the ones I have given you." If their languages do not have a number of different terms for "rules and regulations" like the Hebrew, translators are advised to follow TEV or CEV.

Which I set before you this day: Moses is doing this orally, of course, not in writing, so the translation can be "this law [or, these laws] that I am giving you today" (so BRCL; also NJB, REB, NRSV).

4.9 RSV	TEV
"Only take heed, and keep your soul diligently, lest you forget the things which your eyes have seen, and lest they depart from your heart all the days of your life; make them known to your children and your children's children—	Be on your guard! Make certain that you do not forget, as long as you live, what you have seen with your own eyes. Tell your children and your grandchildren

It is a good idea to begin a new paragraph here, as RSV does. The word translated **Only** marks a transition, calling attention to what follows. It may be alternatively translated as "But this one thing," "Just be sure that," and so on.

Take heed and keep your soul diligently: literally "guard yourself and guard your soul earnestly." Israel is addressed in the second person singular, but in many languages it will be more natural style to use the second person plural here (see verse 14). NRSV provides a good model: "But take care and watch yourselves closely"; also NIV "Be careful and . . ." or CEV "be very careful."

Lest you forget the things that your eyes have seen: **lest you forget** means "so that you will not forget" or "in order not to forget" (NRSV). This clause should be bound closely with what comes before it: ". . . and make sure that you do not forget what you saw"—referring to God's appearance to the people at Mount Sinai (Exodus 19–20). An alternative translation model for the first part of this verse is "So you must be careful not to forget the things you have seen God do."

And lest they depart from your heart may also be expressed as "Keep on remembering them," "Keep on reminding yourselves" (CEV), or idiomatically as "Keep them always in your heart."

All the days of your life may be rendered as "as long as you live" (TEV). The whole sentence may be expressed as "For as long as you live, keep on reminding yourselves about them."

Make them known: "teach them." This theme recurs frequently in the book; see 6.7, 20; 11.19; 31.13; 32.46.

Your children and your children's children: "your children and grandchildren." No doubt great-grandchildren would be included also, should an Israelite live long enough to have them.

4.10 RSV	TEV
how on the day that you stood before the LORD your God at Horeb, the LORD said to me, 'Gather the people to me, that I may let them hear my words, so that they may learn to fear me all the days that they live upon the earth, and that they may teach their children so.'	about the day you stood in the presence of the LORD your God at Mount Sinai,[d] when he said to me, 'Assemble the people. I want them to hear what I have to say, so that they will learn to obey me as long as they live and so that they will teach their children to do the same.'

[d] Sinai; *or* Horeb.

Instead of continuing the long and complex sentence, as RSV does, it is better to follow TEV and begin a new sentence at the end of verse 9: "Tell your children and grandchildren [10] about the day . . . ," or we may bring verse 9 to a full stop and begin a new sentence at verse 10: "Tell them about the day . . . ."

On the day that you stood before the LORD your God at Horeb: this refers to Exo 19–20. Here **before** means "in the presence of" (TEV). TEV consistently uses "Sinai" as the name of the mountain, in keeping with its practice of using the better-known name when there are two names (or more) for the same person or place. Translators are urged to do the same.

Gather the people to me: "Bring all the people together in my presence," "Assemble all the people in front of me." In some languages this clause will be expressed as "Call the people of Israel to come and gather in front of me," or even "Bring the people here to . . . ."

That I may let them hear my words: "so that I can speak to them," "so that they will hear what I will say to them." The **words** are the Ten Commandments (see verse 13), but there is no reason for the translation to say that here.

So that they may learn to fear me: the translation of the phrase "to fear God" may be difficult (see also 5.29; 6.2, 13, 24). The basic idea is that of reverence or awe, as befits God's transcendence and holiness. A word that means simply "be afraid of" should not be used. NJPSV and NIV have "revere"; FRCL "respect"; "obey" (TEV, CEV) is not satisfactory here. Translators should, if possible, use a term that refers to "great respect" or "awe." In cultures that are ruled by kings or chiefs, such a term should be readily available. A possible solution in English is to use two words; for example, "respect and obey." If no suitable term is found, we may follow the solution of BRCL. It uses the normal verb "to fear" (*temer*) and marks it with an asterisk, with the following explanation in the Glossary: "*Fear God:* Show respect or reverence for God, in acknowledgment of his greatness and holiness. It does not mean simply to be afraid of God, but to show him respect, love, obedience, and worship."

All the days that they live upon the earth: "all their lives," "as long as they live."

And that they may teach their children so: that is, "teach their children to fear God."

An alternative translation model for this verse is:

● Tell them about the day when you all stood at the foot of Mount
   Sinai in the presence of Yahweh your [or, our] God. Yahweh said,
   "Moses, call the people of Israel to come here before me. I want to
   speak to them so that they will learn to respect and obey me as
   long as they live. I want them also to teach their children to
   respect and obey me."

4.11 RSV TEV

And you came near and stood at the foot of the mountain, while the mountain burned with fire to the heart of heaven, wrapped in darkness, cloud, and gloom.	"Tell your children how you went and stood at the foot of the mountain which was covered with thick clouds of dark smoke and fire blazing up to the sky."

Moses is speaking to the people.
You came near: that is, near to where Yahweh was.
Stood at the foot of the mountain: Mount Sinai (see Exo 19.17).
The mountain burned with fire to the heart of heaven: this sounds like the
description of a volcanic eruption, with the flames leaping high in the sky. NJB
has "the mountain flamed to the very sky," NRSV translates "the mountain was
blazing up to the very heavens," and CEV has "the fire went up to the sky."
   The mountain was **wrapped in darkness, cloud, and gloom** (see Exo 19.18);
the Hebrew text says ". . . the heart of heaven, darkness, cloud, and gloom"
(without a verb). Some translations do not take the three words to represent
three different phenomena, but a way of saying "dark cloud and thick mist"
(REB), "black clouds and deep darkness" (NIV), "deep dark clouds" (CEV). The
Hebrew word translated **gloom** is translated in the Septuagint by a Greek word
that means "storm," or "whirlwind" (see its use in Heb 12.18). The Septuagint
adds, at the end, "a loud voice" (see 5.22), but this should not appear in the
translation.

4.12 RSV TEV

Then the LORD spoke to you out of the midst of the fire; you heard the sound of words, but saw no form; there was only a voice.	Tell them how the LORD spoke to you from the fire, how you heard him speaking but did not see him in any form at all.

The people heard the sound of Yahweh's voice, as he spoke to them **out of the
midst of the fire** that blazed on top of Mount Sinai. The verse stresses the fact
that there was no visible manifestation of Yahweh; only the sound of his voice
was heard.
   TEV essentially combines this clause and the final one with "there was only
a voice"; but this is not emphatic enough. The text avoids saying "You did not
see Yahweh"; it says "you saw no form." (It is interesting to notice that in Num

12.8 Yahweh says that Moses does see "the form" of Yahweh when Yahweh talks to him.) The Hebrew noun (also verse 15) means here the "visible form" of a living being; in other contexts it means an artifact, the representation in wood or metal of a god (see 4.16, 23, 25; 5.8).

If in a given language there is no word to express the notion of "visible form," a translation may say "You saw nothing"; "You didn't see a thing [or, anyone]."

There was only a voice: "you only heard a voice"; "you only heard someone speaking."

An alternative translation model for this verse is:

- Tell them how the LORD spoke to you from the fire. You heard him speaking, but you didn't see anyone. All you heard was someone speaking.

4.13	RSV	TEV
	And he declared to you his covenant, which he commanded you to perform, that is, the ten commandments;[b] and he wrote them upon two tables of stone.	He told you what you must do to keep the covenant he made with you—you must obey the Ten Commandments, which he wrote on two stone tablets.

[b] Heb *words*

And he declared to you: "And he announced to you," "And he told you about . . . ," or "He told you what you must do to keep . . . ."

His covenant: "the covenant he was about to make with you." The very important word **covenant** appears first in Gen 6.18 and occurs twenty-nine times in Deuteronomy. A translation should use the same word to translate the Hebrew *berith* and the Greek *diathēkē* used in the New Testament; by the time Deuteronomy is translated in a given language, it is most likely that a satisfactory word will have been found that can be used throughout the Bible. **Covenant** means, generally, an alliance, agreement, pact, treaty, or often a contract in writing. The translator must be aware of the different senses of the word when used in a context of commercial enterprises or military alliances; these other senses may very well make an otherwise satisfactory word unsuitable for its use of the **covenant** that God describes and offers to his people, the focus being on God's promise.

In places where the Bible has already been translated, and the word for **covenant** is already part of the religious vocabulary of church people, it may be that a different word will not be accepted. In such a case it will be helpful to include a Glossary note, like the one in BRCL:

A treaty made by God with his people. This treaty (alliance, pact, contract) was the following: the Eternal was the God of Israel, and Israel was the people of the Eternal God. God blessed the people, and they, in turn, obeyed God.

Another way to render this clause is "He told you that he was making an agreement [or, contract] with you."

Which he commanded us to perform: the Hebrew verb "to do" governs both **his covenant** and **the ten commandments**, since "the ten words" are the covenant. But in many languages two different verbs will have to be used for the two objects: "keep the covenant" and "obey the ten words." It is also possible to express this as "He told you that in order for you to keep the agreement you must obey [or, follow] the Ten Commandments."

The ten commandments: as the RSV note indicates, the Hebrew noun normally means "words." But in this context translators are urged to use "Ten Commandments," as there were actually more than ten Hebrew words.

And he wrote them upon two tables of stone: better, ". . . two stone tablets" (NRSV), or even "two flat stones" (CEV). The verb **wrote** may have to be translated "carved," "cut into," or "inscribed." All the "ten words" were inscribed on each of the two tablets, in keeping with the customs of the time. (Each party to a treaty received one tablet, which would be kept in their sanctuary.) In the case of Israel, the sanctuary of Yahweh and that of the people was one and the same, so both tablets were kept there together in the sacred box. (Exo 40.20).

4.14   RSV   TEV

RSV	TEV
And the LORD commanded me at that time to teach you statutes and ordinances, that you might do them in the land which you are going over to possess.	The LORD told me to teach you all the laws that you are to obey in the land that you are about to invade and occupy.

All the words and phrases of this verse have been dealt with in 4.1, 5. The only difference here is the use of the verb "go over" (instead of "go in"). This means crossing the Jordan River into the land of Canaan. CEV brings this out with "the land that you will conquer west of the Jordan River."

1L. Moses warns the people not to worship idols (4.15-31)

RSV   TEV
                                     Warning against Idolatry

RSV	TEV
15 "Therefore take good heed to yourselves. Since you saw no form on the day that the LORD spoke to you at Horeb out of the midst of the fire, 16 beware lest you act corruptly by making a graven image for yourselves, in the form of any figure, the likeness of male or female, 17 the likeness of any beast that is on the earth, the likeness of any winged bird that flies in the air, 18 the likeness of anything that creeps on the ground, the likeness of any fish	15 "When the LORD spoke to you from the fire on Mount Sinai, you did not see any form. For your own good, then, make certain 16 that you do not sin by making for yourselves an idol in any form at all—whether man or woman, 17 animal or bird, 18 reptile or fish. 19 Do not be tempted to worship and serve what you see in the sky—the sun, the moon, and the stars. The LORD your God has given these to all other peoples for them to worship. 20 But you are

93

that is in the water under the earth. 19 And beware lest you lift up your eyes to heaven, and when you see the sun and the moon and the stars, all the host of heaven, you be drawn away and worship them and serve them, things which the LORD your God has allotted to all the peoples under the whole heaven. 20 But the LORD has taken you, and brought you forth out of the iron furnace, out of Egypt, to be a people of his own possession, as at this day. 21 Furthermore the LORD was angry with me on your account, and he swore that I should not cross the Jordan, and that I should not enter the good land which the LORD your God gives you for an inheritance. 22 For I must die in this land, I must not go over the Jordan; but you shall go over and take possession of that good land. 23 Take heed to yourselves, lest you forget the covenant of the LORD your God, which he made with you, and make a graven image in the form of anything which the LORD your God has forbidden you. 24 For the LORD your God is a devouring fire, a jealous God.

25 "When you beget children and children's children, and have grown old in the land, if you act corruptly by making a graven image in the form of anything, and by doing what is evil in the sight of the LORD your God, so as to provoke him to anger, 26 I call heaven and earth to witness against you this day, that you will soon utterly perish from the land which you are going over the Jordan to possess; you will not live long upon it, but will be utterly destroyed. 27 And the LORD will scatter you among the peoples, and you will be left few in number among the nations where the LORD will drive you. 28 And there you will serve gods of wood and stone, the work of men's hands, that neither see, nor hear, nor eat, nor smell. 29 But from there you will seek the LORD your God, and you will find him, if you search after him with all your heart and with all your soul. 30 When you are in tribulation, and all these things come upon you in the latter days, you will return to the LORD your God and obey his voice, 31 for the LORD your God is a merciful God; he will not fail you or destroy you or forget the covenant with your fathers which he swore to them.

the people he rescued from Egypt, that blazing furnace. He brought you out to make you his own people, as you are today. 21 Because of you the LORD your God was angry with me and solemnly declared that I would not cross the Jordan River to enter the fertile land which he is giving you. 22 I will die in this land and never cross the river, but you are about to go across and occupy that fertile land. 23 Be certain that you do not forget the covenant that the LORD your God made with you. Obey his command not to make yourselves any kind of idol, 24 because the LORD your God is like a flaming fire; he tolerates no rivals.

25 "Even when you have been in the land a long time and have children and grandchildren, do not sin by making for yourselves an idol in any form at all. This is evil in the LORD's sight, and it will make him angry. 26 I call heaven and earth as witnesses against you today that, if you disobey me, you will soon disappear from the land. You will not live very long in the land across the Jordan that you are about to occupy. You will be completely destroyed. 27 The LORD will scatter you among other nations, where only a few of you will survive. 28 There you will serve gods made by human hands, gods of wood and stone, gods that cannot see or hear, eat or smell. 29 There you will look for the LORD your God, and if you search for him with all your heart, you will find him. 30 When you are in trouble and all those things happen to you, then you will finally turn to the LORD and obey him. 31 He is a merciful God. He will not abandon you or destroy you, and he will not forget the covenant that he himself made with your ancestors.

This section is, in effect, an amplification of the commandment forbidding graven images (5.8-10).

Section heading: possible titles for the section 4.15-31 are "Moses warns the people not to worship idols," or a much shorter sentence following CEV, "Don't worship Idols."

4.15 RSV TEV

"Therefore take good heed to your- "When the LORD spoke to you from
selves. Since you saw no form on the fire on Mount Sinai, you did not
the day that the LORD spoke to you at see any form. For your own good,
Horeb out of the midst of the fire, then, make certain

Since this verse begins a new section, translators should indicate that Moses
is speaking; for example, "Moses said to the people of Israel."

Therefore take good heed to yourselves: this is like the second verbal phrase
in the opening words of verse 9, "guard yourself carefully." In verse 9 Israel is
addressed in the second person singular; here the second person plural is used.

TEV and CEV place this warning at the end of the verse, after the statement
of its basis, namely, the fact that at Mount Sinai the people had not seen any
form when Yahweh spoke to them. REB, NRSV, NIV do the same thing, and this
is a good model for the translator to follow.

Since you saw no form . . . : see verse 12. FRCL avoids using the word "form,"
saying instead "you did not see him himself" (using the emphatic *lui-même*).

On the day that . . . : as in verse 10.

Out of the midst of the fire: as in verse 12.

4.16 RSV TEV

beware lest you act corruptly by that you do not sin by making for
making a graven image for your- yourselves an idol in any form at
selves, in the form of any figure, the all—whether man or woman,
likeness of male or female,

Beware lest you act corruptly: RSV **beware** is required by the construction of
the English sentence, referring back to "take good heed to yourselves" in verse
15. As already mentioned, it is better to restructure verse 15-16, using TEV or
CEV as a model. The verb **act corruptly** means to sin, do wrong. This is a
religious or moral offense, not a crime as such. The Hebrew carries the idea of
going to ruin, rottenness, spoiling something that is good—in this case, the
sacred relationship between Yahweh and his people. **Beware lest you act
corruptly** may also be expressed as "Be careful that you do not disobey Yahweh
by . . . ," or ". . . that you do not ruin your relationship with Yahweh by . . . ," or
even ". . . that you do not defile yourselves by . . . ."

A graven image: this is essentially an image or an idol, made of stone (10.1,
3) or wood (1 Kgs 5.18) that was carved into the shape of an animal, human
being, or some object. In languages where there is no term for **graven image** or
"idol," it will be necessary to translate the underlying meaning and connect it
to the rest of the verse. For example, "that you do not disobey Yahweh by
carving out the likeness of any living thing, whether a person [or, people] or
. . . ." In this context "likeness" means "the image of" or "what looks like."

The form of any figure: as the rest of the verse shows, the prohibition is
against making such images, figures, or statues resembling a human being or

an animal as a representation of the God of Israel, to be used in worship. FRCL follows TOB by translating the Hebrew *semel* (RSV **figure**) by "divinity." The meaning of the word is uncertain; see its use in Ezek 8.3, 5, and in 2 Chr 33.7, where RSV renders "the image of the idol." It seems better not to use the word "divinity" or "god" here, but to follow RSV **figure** or **likeness**.

The likeness of a male or female: "that looks like a man or a woman."

An alternative translation model for verses 15-16 is:

● 15 Moses said to the people of Israel: "When Yahweh spoke to you from the fire on Mount Sinai, you didn't see him. 16 So make certain [or, be careful] that you do not disobey him by carving out the likeness of [or, what looks like] a man or a woman, ..."

4.17-18   RSV   TEV

17 the likeness of any beast that is on the earth, the likeness of any winged bird that flies in the air, 18 the likeness of anything that creeps on the ground, the likeness of any fish that is in the water under the earth.	17 animal or bird, 18 reptile or fish.

All living beings are here grouped under four headings (see Gen 1.26). TEV has kept the essential information by translating "animal or bird, reptile or fish" (also SPCL, FRCL). Some translations may prefer to use a fuller form, in keeping with the Hebrew style. Whatever is used, it should sound natural in that language.

Any beast that is on the earth: "any land animal."

Any winged bird that flies in the air: "any [wild] bird."

Anything that creeps on the ground: "any reptile or insect," "any of the smaller animals or insects."

Any fish that is in the water under the earth: this corresponds to the Hebrew concept of the universe as consisting of three parts: the heavens, the earth, and the water under the earth (see 5.8). This **water under the earth** was the vast subterranean ocean under the surface of the earth, not the lakes and seas on the surface of the earth. A literal translation here will require a note explaining what is meant by this strange phrase.

4.19   RSV   TEV

And beware lest you lift up your eyes to heaven, and when you see the sun and the moon and the stars, all the host of heaven, you be drawn away	Do not be tempted to worship and serve what you see in the sky—the sun, the moon, and the stars. The LORD your God has given these to all

96

and worship them and serve them, things which the LORD your God has allotted to all the peoples under the whole heaven.

other peoples for them to worship.

This verse prohibits the Israelites from worshiping any of the heavenly bodies; they were regarded by many peoples as representing various gods or being controlled by different gods. Only the other nations should worship them; and that is by the decision of Yahweh (see 32.8-9).

And beware lest: "and be careful not to . . . ."

You lift up your eyes to heaven, and when you see: this is not a prohibition against looking at the sun and the other heavenly bodies, but of worshiping them as gods.

All the host of heaven: a collective term including all heavenly bodies; that is, the sun, the moon, and the stars (Gen 1.16). It is possible to reorder the clauses at the beginning of this verse as follows: "when you look at the sun or moon or stars, don't be tempted to . . . ."

You be drawn away: the verb means "to lead astray," "to entice," "to tempt." This is spiritual apostasy, and we may express this as "Don't let your heart lead you astray to . . . ."

Worship and serve them: these are not two separate actions, but the one action of devoted worship. REB and CEV have "bow down and worship"; SPCL "don't fall into the temptation to worship."

Things which: this translates the Hebrew relative pronoun "that," "which."

For **the LORD your God** see 1.16.

Has allotted: "has assigned," "has designated"; FRCL "has reserved for," and CEV has "The LORD put them there for . . . ." God has reserved these heavenly bodies to be worshiped by **all the peoples under the whole heaven**, a wordy way of saying "all the other peoples on earth," "everybody else in the world." The text clearly states that Yahweh provided these heavenly bodies as objects of worship for all people, except his own people, Israel.

An alternative translation model reordering the clauses of this verse is:

- When you look at the sun or moon or stars, don't be tempted [or, let your heart cause you] to bow down and worship them. The LORD your God has designated them for everybody else in the world to worship.

4.20	RSV	TEV

But the LORD has taken you, and brought you forth out of the iron furnace, out of Egypt, to be a people of his own possession, as at this day.

But you are the people he rescued from Egypt, that blazing furnace. He brought you out to make you his own people, as you are today.

Has taken you and brought you forth: the two verbs describe two actions in sequence; God asserted his dominion over the Hebrews and then delivered

97

them from bondage in Egypt. In this way he made them his own people, exclusively his.

Out of the iron furnace, out of Egypt: see the same description of Egypt in 1 Kgs 8.51; Jer 11.4 (see also Isa 48.10). This is a figure of intolerable suffering; translations in general try to keep the figure, translating variously: REB "the smelting-furnace"; NRSV "the iron-smelter"; NJB "the iron-foundry"; NIV "iron-smelting furnace"; NJPSV "blast furnace." These all sound somewhat technical, and something more general like "a blazing furnace" or "a red-hot furnace" is surely more effective. However, in many languages it will be necessary to use a simile here; for example, "brought you out of Egypt, where you suffered terribly like being in a red-hot furnace."

To be a people of his own possession: this is the first time the phrase is used of the people as Yahweh's **possession**; elsewhere it has indicated the land of Canaan as Israel's possession (see 3.28). The fact that they are the LORD's people is shown by his rescuing them from Egypt. So we may translate "But today you are still the LORD's people, because he rescued you from Egypt, where you suffered terribly like . . . ."

As at this day: this sounds like a later addition to the text, but its use here does not disrupt the flow of the narrative too much. NJB has "as you still are today."

4.21   RSV   TEV

Furthermore the LORD was angry with me on your account, and he swore that I should not cross the Jordan, and that I should not enter the good land which the LORD your God gives you for an inheritance. | Because of you the LORD your God was angry with me and solemnly declared that I would not cross the Jordan River to enter the fertile land which he is giving you.

Furthermore: this is misleading, not justified by the text or context. It is better to start a new paragraph with this verse, as does NRSV. The restructuring of TEV can be imitated, "Because of you the LORD was angry with me," or that of CEV, "The LORD was angry with me because of what you said."

Angry with me: no attempt should be made to soften the vivid language used in the Bible of God's feelings. For **angry** or "angered" see 1.34, 37.

On your account: see 1.37; 3.26. In Num 20.12 and Deut 32.48-52 the fault is said to lie with Moses and Aaron.

He swore: see 1.8.

I should not cross the Jordan and I should not enter: this is essentially one action, not two: "I would not cross the Jordan River to enter . . ." (TEV), or "that he would not let me cross the River Jordan into the . . . ."

That good land: rich, fertile; NJB "the fine country." See also 1.25.

Gives you for an inheritance: this is the first occurrence of the noun (see the verb "inherit" in 1.38). The meaning is that the land of Canaan is a gift from God. Since **inheritance** usually assumes the death of the original owner, it is better not to use it; so TEV "he is giving you" (also BRCL, CEV); see also verse 38.

4.22   RSV   TEV

For I must die in this land, I must not   I will die in this land and never cross
go over the Jordan; but you shall go   the river, but you are about to go
over and take possession of that   across and occupy that fertile land.
good land.

I must die: NRSV "I am going to die," or TEV "I will die," expresses the Hebrew
better.

In this land: that is, Moab, on the east side of the Jordan.

I must not go over the Jordan: "I will not [get to] cross the Jordan River."

CEV has a helpful model for the first two clauses of this verse: "So I must stay
here and die on this side of the Jordan . . . ."

You shall go over and take possession: see 1.8.

For **that good land** see the previous verse.

4.23   RSV   TEV

Take heed to yourselves, lest you   Be certain that you do not forget the
forget the covenant of the LORD your   covenant that the LORD your God
God, which he made with you, and   made with you. Obey his command
make a graven image in the form of   not to make yourselves any kind of
anything which the LORD your God   idol,
has forbidden you.

This verse uses the same vocabulary, expressions, and constructions as are
used in verses 9 and 15.

The covenant of the LORD your God, which he made with you: this is a very
full expression. For **covenant** see 4.13.

A graven image in the form of anything: see verses 16-18.

4.24   RSV   TEV

For the LORD your God is a devour-   because the LORD your God is like a
ing fire, a jealous God.   flaming fire; he tolerates no rivals.

A devouring fire: perhaps a simile would be better; for example, "like a fire
that burns everything up," or "like a fire destroying everything in its path"
(CEV). So the whole sentence may be expressed as "Because Yahweh your God
will be like a fire that burns everything before it," or "Because if Yahweh gets
angry with you, he will be like a fire . . . ." This is a vivid representation of
Yahweh's anger.

A jealous God: the adjective **jealous** in modern English speech always carries
bad overtones and means "resentful about and envious of what belongs to
someone else"; this meaning is not appropriate when applied to God. Rather the

meaning should be "desiring to preserve what is rightly his." TEV expresses **a jealous God** as "he tolerates no rivals." In some languages it will be necessary to make the meaning of "rivals" clear by saying, for example, "Yahweh will not tolerate your worshiping [or, loving] other gods."

4.25

RSV	TEV
"When you beget children and children's children, and have grown old in the land, if you act corruptly by making a graven image in the form of anything, and by doing what is evil in the sight of the LORD your God, so as to provoke him to anger,	"Even when you have been in the land a long time and have children and grandchildren, do not sin by making for yourselves an idol in any form at all. This is evil in the LORD's sight, and it will make him angry.

Verses 25-26 are one sentence in RSV; it is better to divide the material into several sentences. This is a stern warning against idolatry and a threat that the Israelites will be completely destroyed if they worship other gods.

When you beget children and children's children and have grown old in the land: "when you have been [lived] in the land [of Canaan] for a long time, and have children and grandchildren" (TEV). This looks forward to a period of time some forty or fifty years in the future. The verb translated "grow old" need not necessarily refer to old age but more generally to an extended period of time: "after you have lived there many years" is a possible translation. In some languages **beget children and children's children** may be expressed as "have children and they give you grandchildren."

If you act corruptly by making a graven image in the form of anything: the clause **if you act corruptly** is better expressed as "if you sin" or "do not sin by . . ." (TEV), or even "do not disobey Yahweh by . . . ."

Doing what is evil in the sight of the LORD your God: "doing what the LORD your God considers wrong" or ". . . condemns as evil."

So as to provoke him to anger: "so that he becomes angry with you" (see verse 21, where a different Hebrew verb is used).

4.26

RSV	TEV
I call heaven and earth to witness against you this day, that you will soon utterly perish from the land which you are going over the Jordan to possess; you will not live long upon it, but will be utterly destroyed.	I call heaven and earth as witnesses against you today that, if you disobey me, you will soon disappear from the land. You will not live very long in the land across the Jordan that you are about to occupy. You will be completely destroyed.

I call heaven and earth to witness against you this day: the punishment that Moses is about to describe is so severe that he calls the whole universe to listen to what he is about to say. Among other peoples at that time it was common to call upon the gods to witness to what someone was about to say or do; here the whole world, as God's creation, is to be witness. There is hardly any alternative to using the biblical phrase **heaven and earth** or else "universe," "the whole world"; but it should not convey the idea that Moses is calling on all the inhabitants of the Earth to pay attention to what he is about to say, so as to serve as witnesses against the people of Israel. **To witness against you today** may also be expressed as "to take notice of what you are doing today." In some languages it will be necessary to supply the content of "what you are doing" as TEV does ('if you disobey me"), or else say "Today I am asking heaven and earth to watch what you do. If you ever make idols . . . ."

The two statements **you will soon utterly perish** and **you . . . will be utterly destroyed** sound like Moses is forecasting total annihilation of the Israelites, leaving no survivors. But as the next verse shows, this is typical exaggeration (hyperbole) and means that many will lose their lives. In languages that do not use the passive voice, we may say "I will cause you all to die"; it is not necessarily God himself who does the destroying.

The land you are going over the Jordan to possess: see verse 22.

You will not live long upon it: the next verse makes it clear that Moses is talking about their deportation or exile to a foreign country, after being conquered by enemy forces.

4.27	RSV	TEV

And the LORD will scatter you among the peoples, and you will be left few in number among the nations where the LORD will drive you.	The LORD will scatter you among other nations, where only a few of you will survive.	

The exile of Israelites to other countries is seen as God's punishment for their idolatry.

The LORD will scatter you among the peoples . . . the LORD will drive you: again, the repetition gives emphasis in Hebrew. For languages in which repetition does not produce emphasis, a translator may wish to reduce the repetition (see TEV, SPCL, BRCL). **The LORD will scatter you . . .** may also be expressed as "the LORD will make you go in all directions to where you will live among other peoples."

The verb translated **will drive you** may have the gentler sense of "lead you" (Septuagint; NRSV, REB). In this context, however, the harsher sense seems justified (NIV, NJPSV, NJB), namely "will force you to leave the land."

You will be left few in number: "only a few of you will survive" (TEV). In the context, the people's idolatry and their punishment is seen as happening within the next fifty years (see verse 25).

4.28   RSV   TEV

And there you will serve gods of   There you will serve gods made by
wood and stone, the work of men's   human hands, gods of wood and
hands, that neither see, nor hear, nor   stone, gods that cannot see or hear,
eat, nor smell.   eat or smell.

In those foreign countries, where they will live as exiles, the Israelites will
worship pagan gods, lifeless idols. There is no hint in the text that their
conquerors will force them to do this, it is rather that on their own they will
eventually worship the pagan deities.

Serve: that is, worship (see verse 19).

The **gods of wood and stone** are man-made idols, **the work of men's hands**;
therefore they cannot **see**, **hear**, **eat**, or **smell** (see Psa 115.4-6; 135.15-17). In
some languages this first sentence will be expressed as "There you will worship
idols made of wood and stone that represent gods . . ." or ". . . likenesses of gods
that they have made out of wood . . . ." See the comments on "graven image" in
4.16.

4.29   RSV   TEV

But from there you will seek the   There you will look for the LORD your
LORD your God, and you will find   God, and if you search for him with
him, if you search after him with all   all your heart, you will find him.
your heart and with all your soul.

But from there: "But while you are there," "But in that country." Yahweh is
not restricted to his own land, the land of Israel. He can be "found" anywhere.

You will seek the LORD your God and you will find him: the idea of looking
for God and finding him may not be easy to express without sounding ludicrous,
as though God were hiding or living in some place difficult to find. The
"seeking" consists of praying to God, and the "finding" of having the prayer answered. So we may translate "But in that country you will pray to the LORD
your God, and he will answer you."

If you search for him: here a different Hebrew verb is used; other models can
be "if you really look for him," "if you really try to find him," or "if you really try
to contact him . . . ." In some languages this **if** clause will come first. In such
cases translators must ensure that this verse fits with the flow of the
paragraph.

With all your heart and with all your soul: in general the **heart** stands for
intellect or will, and the **soul** for emotion, feelings. This phrase recurs
frequently (10.12; 11.13; 13.3; 26.16; 30.2, 6, 10); the triple phrase "heart, soul,
and might" is used in 6.5. Some possibilities are "whole-heartedly," "completely," "with all your being," "earnestly." Translators are urged to use descriptive
language similar to the Hebrew if it does not sound strange or unnatural.
Otherwise we may simply have to combine the two parts of the verse; for

example, "If you earnestly pray to the LORD your God in that country, he will listen to you."

4.30	RSV	TEV

When you are in tribulation, and all these things come upon you in the latter days, you will return to the LORD your God and obey his voice,

When you are in trouble and all those things happen to you, then you will finally turn to the LORD and obey him.

When you are in tribulation: "When you are in trouble," "When you are suffering [or, being mistreated]." This still refers to their exile.

All these things come upon you: these things are their deportation, their loss of freedom, and eventual idolatry.

In the latter days: in some contexts this phrase has the technical sense of the time when God will intervene forcibly into human affairs and establish his rule over the world (the Septuagint translation favors this interpretation). Here, however, it is more likely that the phrase refers to a decisive turning point in the future (see Ezek 38.8, 16; Hos 3.5). REB has "in days to come"; TEV, FRCL. and SPCL "finally." It should be noted that this phrase goes with what is before, not with what follows.

You will return to the LORD your God: they will once more acknowledge Yahweh as their God and worship and serve him alone. CEV has "you may finally decide that you want to worship only the LORD."

Obey his voice: the verb can be translated "hear" or "listen to"; here "hear" means to heed, or obey.

It is possible to combine verses 29 and 30 as follows:

●   ²⁹⁻³⁰ When you are there [or, in that land] and the time comes when you will endure all kinds of trouble, you may then decide to turn back to the LORD your God and obey him. If at that time you pray to him wholeheartedly, he will answer you [or, come and help you].

4.31	RSV	TEV

for the LORD your God is a merciful God; he will not fail you or destroy you or forget the covenant with your fathers which he swore to them.

He is a merciful God. He will not abandon you or destroy you, and he will not forget the covenant that he himself made with your ancestors.

A merciful God: compassionate, tenderhearted; the same God described so harshly in verse 24. In many languages there will be idiomatic expressions using the heart, liver, or even bowels (or, intestines) that mean **merciful**; for example, "He [God] cries in his heart for you," or "His bowels yearn for you."

He will not fail you: he will not abandon, leave, forsake, desert.

Destroy: a different verb is used in verses 3, 26, but the meaning is the same (the Septuagint translates both verbs with the same Greek verb).

Forget the covenant: see verse 23. In some languages it will be more natural style, or even obligatory, to state this positively; for example, "He will remember the agreement he made with . . . ."

With your fathers, which he swore to them: see 1.8. This covenant is the one that God made with the patriarchs, Abraham, Isaac, and Jacob.

1M. Israel's unique status (4.32-40)

RSV	TEV
32 "For ask now of the days that are past, which were before you, since the day that God created man upon the earth, and ask from one end of heaven to the other, whether such a great thing as this has ever happened or was ever heard of. 33 Did any people ever hear the voice of a god speaking out of the midst of the fire, as you have heard, and still live? 34 Or has any god ever attempted to go and take a nation for himself from the midst of another nation, by trials, by signs, by wonders, and by war, by a mighty hand and an outstretched arm, and by great terrors, according to all that the LORD your God did for you in Egypt before your eyes? 35 To you it was shown, that you might know that the LORD is God; there is no other besides him. 36 Out of heaven he let you hear his voice, that he might discipline you; and on earth he let you see his great fire, and you heard his words out of the midst of the fire. 37 And because he loved your fathers and chose their descendants after them, and brought you out of Egypt with his own presence, by his great power, 38 driving out before you nations greater and mightier than yourselves, to bring you in, to give you their land for an inheritance, as at this day; 39 know therefore this day, and lay it to your heart, that the LORD is God in heaven above and on the earth beneath; there is no other. 40 Therefore you shall keep his statutes and his commandments, which I command you this day, that it may go well with you, and with your children after you, and that you may prolong your days in the land which the LORD your God gives you for ever."	32 "Search the past, the time before you were born, all the way back to the time when God created human beings on the earth. Search the entire earth. Has anything as great as this ever happened before? Has anyone ever heard of anything like this? 33 Have any people ever lived after hearing a god speak to them from a fire, as you have? 34 Has any god ever dared to go and take a people from another nation and make them his own, as the LORD your God did for you in Egypt? Before your very eyes he used his great power and strength; he brought plagues and war, worked miracles and wonders, and caused terrifying things to happen. 35 The LORD has shown you this, to prove to you that he alone is God and that there is no other. 36 He let you hear his voice from heaven so that he could instruct you; and here on earth he let you see his holy fire, and he spoke to you from it. 37 Because he loved your ancestors, he chose you, and by his great power he himself brought you out of Egypt. 38 As you advanced, he drove out nations greater and more powerful than you, so that he might bring you in and give you their land, the land which still belongs to you. 39 So remember today and never forget: the LORD is God in heaven and on earth. There is no other god. 40 Obey all his laws that I have given you today, and all will go well with you and your descendants. You will continue to live in the land that the LORD your God is giving you to be yours forever."

Section heading: a heading for this section can be something like "Israel's unique status" (see FRCL "The privilege of Israel").

4.32   RSV   TEV

"For ask now of the days that are past, which were before you, since the day that God created man upon the earth, and ask from one end of heaven to the other, whether such a great thing as this has ever happened or was ever heard of.

"Search the past, the time before you were born, all the way back to the time when God created human beings on the earth. Search the entire earth. Has anything as great as this ever happened before? Has anyone ever heard of anything like this?

As a separate section, this should begin with something like "Moses said" or "Moses continued to speak to the people of Israel."

For ask now: the introductory **For** makes no sense in English and should not be imitated. In a general way verse 32 is a consequence of what has been said before. The verb **ask** does not have an indirect object, that is, whom they are to ask. It means either "talk about it [with one another]" or most likely "think about it." The subject they are to discuss or think about is the way in which God has dealt with Israel. The people are told to recall their history.

Ask now of the days that are past: "Think over your [or, our] past history"; "Talk [or, Think] about what has happened in the past" (see a similar command in 32.7).

Since the day God created man upon the earth: they are to go back to the beginning of the human race. The terminology of Gen 1.27 is used. Instead of **man** it is preferable in English to say "human beings" (NRSV), "the human race" (NJB). So we may say "Since the time God created human beings [or, people]."

Ask from one end of heaven to the other: RSV repeats the verb **ask** because of the sentence structure. Here the Israelites are told not only to study their own history but to include the whole earth in their inquiry into how God had dealt with them. The expression **from one end of heaven to the other** here does not mean that a search should be made in heaven but over all the earth (see its use in Psa 19.6).

Whether such a great thing as this has ever happened: in some languages it may be better to express this as a direct question: "Has anything as great as this ever happened before?" The phrase **great thing** includes what follows in verses 33-38: Yahweh's appearance at Sinai (verse 33, 36); the exodus from Egypt (verse 34, 37); the conquest of Canaan (verse 38).

Or was ever heard of: TEV provides a good model for making this a separate question, "Has anyone ever heard of anything like this?" CEV makes it into a statement, "No one has ever heard of another god trying to do such things."

4.33   RSV   TEV

Did any people ever hear the voice of a god speaking out of the midst of the fire, as you have heard, and still live?

Have any people ever lived after hearing a god speak to them from a fire, as you have?

Verses 33-34 are two rhetorical questions, each expecting a negative answer. It may be better to express them as emphatic statements, even though this may result in a loss of stylistic beauty. Verse 34 especially is much too long and complex to be read as a single question.

Did any people ever hear . . . ? Israel's experience with its God is unique; no other people had had Israel's experience of being chosen by a god to receive special treatment. The question has to do not only with the people hearing **a god speaking out of the midst of the fire**, but of their having lived after hearing that god speak. TEV provides a good model for restructuring the verse; see also FRCL: "Is there any other people who has heard a god speak to them out of the midst of the fire and has survived, as has happened with you?" This refers to Mount Sinai (see verse 12).

Translators must take care to translate the general term "a god," not "God" in particular. For **god** see 3.24.

4.34   RSV   TEV

Or has any god ever attempted to go and take a nation for himself from the midst of another nation, by trials, by signs, by wonders, and by war, by a mighty hand and an outstretched arm, and by great terrors, according to all that the Lᴏʀᴅ your God did for you in Egypt before your eyes?	Has any god ever dared to go and take a people from another nation and make them his own, as the Lᴏʀᴅ your God did for you in Egypt? Before your very eyes he used his great power and strength; he brought plagues and war, worked miracles and wonders, and caused terrifying things to happen.

This is another rhetorical question, whose answer is "No." Since it is so long and complex, it may be well to translate it as a statement; for example, "No other god ever dared [or, tried] to go and take a group of people . . . ."

Attempted to go and take a nation for himself from the midst of another nation: the verb **attempted** may be translated "dared" (see its use in 28.56, where RSV has "venture"). For **go and take a nation**, see verse 20. Here Yahweh is portrayed as forcibly going to Egypt and seizing the Israelites to be his own people. If **take a nation for himself . . .** is too difficult to translate, we may say "Yahweh your God dared to go and take you out of Egypt; no other god has ever done something like this."

Yahweh did this by using **trials, signs, wonders, war,** and **great terrors.** All these events refer to the plagues God sent on the Egyptians to force the king to let the Israelites leave the country (Exo 7.14–12.36). In a series like this the precise meaning of each term is not as important as the cumulative effect of all of them used together:

trials refer to the sufferings inflicted on the Egyptians;

signs were the plagues themselves, seen as demonstrations of God's power;

wonders means miraculous events in general; in this context they are bad, not good;

106

war seems to refer to what happened to the Egyptians as they chased the Israelites across the "Red Sea" (Exo 14.14; 15.3-4; Deut 11.4);

great terrors were terrifying events, unspecified.

TEV may serve as a good model for this list: "plagues and wars . . . miracles and wonders, and . . . terrifying things." See the similar list in 26.8.

By a mighty hand and an outstretched arm: a vivid metaphor for great power, mighty strength; so "used his great power and strength" (also 5.15; 7.19; 11.2; 26.8). An alternative translation model for **by trials . . . great terrors** may be:

- He used his great power and strength and caused the Egyptians to suffer terribly. He did amazing and dreadful things that terrified the Egyptians, and he fought against them for you.

According to all that the LORD your God did for you in Egypt: the initial **according to** is a poor rendering of the Hebrew in English; it should have been "as": "as the LORD your God did for you in Egypt" (NRSV).

Before your eyes: that is, "in your presence." These were public, not private, displays of Yahweh's power. Time is shortened, and Moses' addresses his audience, forty years after the exodus, as the very people who left Egypt. Another way of saying this is "You actually saw."

It is possible to combine verses 32-34, putting the order of events in a more logical sequence:

- [32-34] When the LORD your God brought you out of Egypt and made you his own people, you yourselves actually saw how he used his great power and strength and caused the Egyptians to suffer terribly. He did amazing and dreadful things that terrified them, and he fought against them for you. Later at Mount Sinai you heard him talking to you out of the fire. And yet you are still alive! Has anything like this ever happened since the time God created human beings? Even if you search the entire earth you will find that no one has heard of another god who did such things as the LORD your God has done for you.

4.35 RSV	TEV
To you it was shown, that you might know that the LORD is God; there is no other besides him.	**The LORD has shown you this, to prove to you that he alone is God and that there is no other.**

To you it was shown: "You saw [all these things] for yourselves," or "God showed you [all these things]." REB has "You have had sure proof."

That you might know that the LORD is God: "to prove to you that . . ." (TEV), "to convince you that . . . ." NRSV translates "so that you would acknowledge."

There is no other god besides him: "there is no other god," "Yahweh is the only god," "he alone is God" (TEV), or "he is the only true God" (CEV) (see 5.7; 32.39).

4.36   RSV   TEV

Out of heaven he let you hear his voice, that he might discipline you; and on earth he let you see his great fire, and you heard his words out of the midst of the fire.	He let you hear his voice from heaven so that he could instruct you; and here on earth he let you see his holy fire, and he spoke to you from it.

In this verse the point is made that, though Yahweh's voice was heard coming from Mount Sinai, Yahweh himself was not there but in heaven.

Out of heaven he let you hear his voice: "You heard him speak to you from heaven." See Exo 20.22.

That he might discipline you: the Hebrew verb might be translated "instruct" (NJB, REB), but here "discipline" is better (NIV, NJPSV); see its use in 8.5, of a father disciplining his son. The purpose of all these events was to make Israel an obedient people. An alternative model is "teach you to obey him."

And on earth he let you see his great fire: see verses 11-12.

You heard his words out of the midst of the fire: see verses 12, 15.

4.37   RSV   TEV

And because he loved your fathers and chose their descendants after them, and brought you out of Egypt with his own presence, by his great power,	Because he loved your ancestors, he chose you, and by his great power he himself brought you out of Egypt.

Verses 37-39 are one long sentence in Hebrew and in RSV. Most translators will need to divide the section into several shorter sentences (see the models in TEV and CEV).

He loved your fathers: this refers to their ancestors, particularly the patriarchs, Abraham, Isaac, and Jacob. "Love" is often described in a figurative fashion; for example, "his heart [or, liver] yearned for" or "his heart [or, liver] felt very warm towards." For **fathers** see 1.8.

Chose their descendants after them: the people of Israel, when Yahweh decided to make them his own. God's love for them and his choice of them are linked also in 7.7-8 and 10.15. The plurals **their** and **them** follow the Samaritan, Septuagint, Syriac, Targum, and Vulgate; the Hebrew Text has the singular "his descendants after him," which HOTTP prefers. The committee suggests two interpretations of the Hebrew: (1) "their posterity after each of them"; (2) "his posterity after him" (that is, the posterity of Jacob). A meaningful translation of the first interpretation will come out the same as the translation of the text

of the ancient versions. It will be helpful in certain languages to state directly
that Yahweh chose the Israelites; for example, "he chose you, their descendants,
to be his own people."

Brought you out of Egypt: the same verb that is used in verse 20.

With his own presence: literally "with his face," meaning that Yahweh did
this himself, without an intermediary. The Septuagint, like modern translations, has "he led you out himself." TEV has "he himself brought . . ." (and see
Exo 33.14).

By his great power: this probably goes with the previous words (REB, FRCL,
NJB, NJPSV); for example, "So the LORD used his great power and personally
brought you out of Egypt."

4.38 RSV	TEV
driving out before you nations grea-ter and mightier than yourselves, to bring you in, to give you their land for an inheritance, as at this day;	As you advanced, he drove out na-tions greater and more powerful than you, so that he might bring you in and give you their land, the land which still belongs to you.

Driving out before you nations . . . : this can be a reference to the conquest
of territories east of the Jordan ruled by King Sihon of Heshbon (2.26-37), and
by King Og of Bashan (3.1-7). The tribes of Reuben and Gad and half the tribe
of Manasseh settled in these regions. Versions like RSV, TEV, and NJB
("dispossessing . . .") put this conquest in the past, and therefore must refer in
this context to the territories east of Jordan. But it is also possible that Moses
is speaking of the conquest of the land of Canaan (see 7.1; 9.1; 11.23). NIV " to
drive out" and REB "so that he might drive out" are versions that allow the
conquest to be still in the future. Since the discourse context is Moses speaking
to the Israelites before they enter Canaan to conquer it, translators who choose
this option will need to express it as action that is still to happen.

Nations greater and mightier than yourselves: the translation of **nations** may
be a problem. These were large, organized racial and tribal groups, with laws
and some form of political structure, but not nation-states in the modern sense
of the word, with territorial boundaries strictly defined. A word such as "tribes"
should be avoided if possible. But if it must be used, we may say, for example,
"large tribes" or "big groups of people." By definition these were pagan peoples;
traditionally there were seven of them in Canaan (see 7.1). **Greater and mightier** means "larger in number and more powerful [militarily]."

To bring you in: in some languages care must be taken about the point of
view of the person who is speaking; here Moses and his audience are outside
Canaan, so "take you in" fits better than "bring you in."

To give you their land for an inheritance: very rarely will the noun "inheritance" or the verb "inherit" be suitable in a text like this (see verse 21 also),
since the words mean (at least in English) receiving something as the result of
the death of the former owner. What is meant is "to possess," "to own," "to
make it [permanently] yours."

As at this day: this clearly reflects the writer's point of view (see 2.22; 4.20). TEV has "the land which still belongs to you."

4.39   RSV   TEV

know therefore this day, and lay it to your heart, that the LORD is God in heaven above and on the earth beneath; there is no other.

So remember today and never forget: the LORD is God in heaven and on earth. There is no other god.

This verse is the conclusion of the long sentence beginning with verse 37 (see the comment there).

Know . . . lay it to your heart: this may be treated as the double expression of one action, or else as two separate actions: "Recognize . . . and reflect without ceasing" (FRCL); "Acknowledge . . . take to heart" (NRSV); "Hence grasp this . . . and meditate on it constantly" (NJB), "Remember today and never forget" (TEV).

In heaven above and on the earth beneath: in many languages this may be somewhat redundant, and something like "in heaven and on earth" (TEV) or "in the whole universe" may be more natural.

For the rest of the verse, see verse 35.

4.40   RSV   TEV

Therefore you shall keep his statutes and his commandments, which I command you this day, that it may go well with you, and with your children after you, and that you may prolong your days in the land which the LORD your God gives you for ever."

Obey all his laws that I have given you today, and all will go well with you and your descendants. You will continue to live in the land that the LORD your God is giving you to be yours forever."

For **keep** see 4.6; for **statutes**, 4.1; for **commandments**, 4.2.

That it may go well with you and your children after you: "that you and your descendants may prosper," "all will go well with you and your descendants" (TEV), or "that you and your descendants will be successful."

Prolong your days in the land: this is not primarily a matter of their living an unusually long time but of their keeping possession of the land of Canaan for many generations. TEV has "You will continue to live in the land." We may also say "that you and your descendants will live a long time in the land."

Gives you forever: the promise is made that the land of Canaan will belong to the Israelites for all time to come.

1N. The cities of refuge east of the Jordan River (4.41-43)

RSV

41 Then Moses set apart three cities in the east beyond the Jordan, 42 that the manslayer might flee there, who kills his neighbor unintentionally, without being at enmity with him in time past, and that by fleeing to one of these cities he might save his life: 43 Bezer in the wilderness on the tableland for the Reubenites, and Ramoth in Gilead for the Gadites, and Golan in Bashan for the Manassites.

TEV

The Cities of Refuge East of the Jordan

41 Then Moses set aside three cities east of the Jordan River 42 to which a man could escape and be safe if he had accidentally killed someone who had not been his enemy. He could escape to one of these cities and not be put to death. 43 For the tribe of Reuben there was the city of Bezer, on the desert plateau; for the tribe of Gad there was Ramoth, in the territory of Gilead; and for the tribe of Manasseh there was Golan, in the territory of Bashan.

In Hebrew the speech of Moses concludes at the end of verse 40. This new section is a narrative about choosing cities of refuge, and Moses is referred to in the third person. Instructions for choosing cities of refuge are given also in 19.1-13 and Num 35.9-34. In Josh 20.1-9 we read of the six cities that Joshua chose, three east of the Jordan and three west of the river.

Section heading: TEV has "The Cities of Refuge East of the Jordan River," NIV has "Cities of Refuge," and CEV has "Safe Towns." Other possibilities are "Towns where people can escape to" or "Towns where people will be safe."

4.41   RSV   TEV

Then Moses set apart three cities in the east beyond the Jordan,

Then Moses set aside three cities east of the Jordan River

Then Moses: since this new section is narration in the third person, translators may wish to express **Then** as a time connection that is appropriate in their language; for example, "Later Moses . . ." or "After he finished speaking to the people, Moses . . . ."

Set apart: chose, selected, or reserved these three towns. For **cities** or "towns" see 1.22.

In the east, beyond the Jordan: as stated in 1.1, **beyond the Jordan** is from the viewpoint of those who live in Canaan, west of the Jordan.

4.42   RSV   TEV

that the manslayer might flee there, who kills his neighbor unintentionally, without being at enmity with him in time past, and that by fleeing to one of these cities he might save his life:

to which a man could escape and be safe if he had accidentally killed someone who had not been his enemy. He could escape to one of these cities and not be put to death.

That the manslayer might flee there who kills his neighbor unintentionally: the meaning of the text is clear and should be expressed naturally: "so that anyone who accidentally kills another person can flee there and be safe [or, find safety]."

Another qualification is added, **without being at enmity with him in the past**, to make quite clear that this law has nothing to do with premeditated murder. NIV uses standard legal language: "unintentionally . . . without malice aforethought." TEV is simpler with "accidentally killed someone who had not been his enemy."

By fleeing to one of these cities he might save his life: the underlying assumption is that a member of the dead person's family would seek to kill the man, even though the killing had been accidental. In the city of refuge he would be safe. A fuller treatment is given in 19.1-13.

An alternative translation model for languages that do not have the passive voice is the following:

- He could escape to any of these towns and they [unknown agents] cannot execute him.

4.43   RSV   TEV

Bezer in the wilderness on the table-land for the Reubenites, and Ramoth in Gilead for the Gadites, and Golan in Bashan for the Manassites. | For the tribe of Reuben there was the city of Bezer, on the desert plateau; for the tribe of Gad there was Ramoth, in the territory of Gilead; and for the tribe of Manasseh there was Golan, in the territory of Bashan.

For the location of these cities, see the map, page xii. There is a city of refuge for each of the three tribes east of the Jordan, listed from south to north: For **cities** or "towns" see 1.22.

For the tribe of Reuben, **Bezer in the wilderness of the tableland**: for **wilderness** see 1.1; **tableland** is plateau, flat country (see 3.10). **Bezer** was not far from Heshbon, the capital city of King Sihon (2.26).

For the tribe of Gad, **Ramoth** in the territory of **Gilead**.

For the tribe of (East) Manasseh, **Golan** in the territory of **Bashan**: see 3.1-7.

2. Moses' second speech
(4.44–26.19)

2A. God's words from Mount Sinai (4.44–11.32)

2A-1. Introduction to the giving of God's Law (4.44-49)

RSV

44 This is the law which Moses set before the children of Israel; 45 these are the testimonies, the statutes, and the ordinances, which Moses spoke to the children of Israel when they came out of Egypt, 46 beyond the Jordan in the valley opposite Beth-peor, in the land of Sihon the king of the Amorites, who lived at Heshbon, whom Moses and the children of Israel defeated when they came out of Egypt. 47 And they took possession of his land and the land of Og the king of Bashan, the two kings of the Amorites, who lived to the east beyond the Jordan; 48 from Aroer, which is on the edge of the valley of the Arnon, as far as Mount Sirion (that is, Hermon), 49 together with all the Arabah on the east side of the Jordan as far as the Sea of the Arabah, under the slopes of Pisgah.

TEV

Introduction to the Giving of God's Law

44 Moses gave God's laws and teachings to the people of Israel. 45-46 It was after they had come out of Egypt and were in the valley east of the Jordan River, opposite the town of Bethpeor, that he gave them these laws. This was in the territory that had belonged to King Sihon of the Amorites, who had ruled in the town of Heshbon. Moses and the people of Israel defeated him when they came out of Egypt. 47 They occupied his land and the land of King Og of Bashan, the other Amorite king who lived east of the Jordan. 48 This land extended from the town of Aroer, on the edge of the Arnon River, all the way north to Mount Sirion, that is, Mount Hermon. 49 It also included all the region east of the Jordan River as far south as the Dead Sea and east to the foot of Mount Pisgah.

This section is the writer's introduction to Moses' second speech.

Section headings: translators should have a major heading here, "Moses' Second Speech," followed by the heading "God's Words from Mount Sinai" or "God Speaks from Mount Sinai." This should be followed by a subheading, "Introduction to the Giving of God's Laws" (TEV), which may also be expressed as "Moses begins to talk about God's Laws," or "Moses tells the people what the LORD wants them to do."

4.44   RSV

TEV

This is the law which Moses set before the children of Israel;

Moses gave God's laws and teachings to the people of Israel.

This whole section, from verse 44 to verse 49, is one long sentence in Hebrew and in RSV. In most languages it is desirable to break this into a number of separate sentences; see TEV.

The law: see 1.5. This is the Torah, which is set forth in chapters 5–26.
Set before: that is, "transmitted to," "delivered to," "gave to."
The children of Israel: the people of Israel, the Israelites.

4.45-46   RSV   TEV

45 these are the testimonies, the statutes, and the ordinances, which Moses spoke to the children of Israel when they came out of Egypt, 46 beyond the Jordan in the valley opposite Beth-peor, in the land of Sihon the king of the Amorites, who lived at Heshbon, whom Moses and the children of Israel defeated when they came out of Egypt.	45-46 It was after they had come out of Egypt and were in the valley east of the Jordan River, opposite the town of Bethpeor, that he gave them these laws. This was in the territory that had belonged to King Sihon of the Amorites, who had ruled in the town of Heshbon. Moses and the people of Israel defeated him when they came out of Egypt.

TEV has rearranged the material in verses 46-47 in a more orderly chronological sequence, to allow the reader to understand the meaning of the text.

Testimonies: this word appears here for the first time in this book (see also 6.17, 20). Something like "precepts," "stipulations" (NIV), or "instructions" can serve as a translation; there is no significant difference in meaning between this and the following two words.

The testimonies, the statutes, and the ordinances: see 4.1. TEV combines the three terms into "these laws," while CEV has "these laws and teachings." Some languages will have a number of suitable terms, while others will need to follow TEV or CEV.

Moses spoke them when they came out of Egypt: "Moses gave them [to the Israelites] after they had left [or, escaped from] Egypt."

Beyond the Jordan: see 1.1.

The valley opposite the town of Beth-peor: see 3.29.

For the rest of the verse, see 1.4; 2.26-36. It will not be necessary in many languages to include the final clause **when they came out of Egypt**, as this information is already in verse 45.

It is possible to restructure verses 45 and 46 as follows:

- 45-46 The Israelites had come from Egypt and were camped east of the Jordan River near to the town of Beth-Peor. There Moses gave them these laws and teachings. Their camp was in the territory that had formerly belonged to King Sihon, who ruled in the town of Heshbon over the Amorites. But Moses and the Israelites had defeated him,

4.47   RSV   TEV

And they took possession of his land and the land of Og the king of Bashan, the two kings of the Amorites, who lived to the east beyond the Jordan;	They occupied his land and the land of King Og of Bashan, the other Amorite king who lived east of the Jordan.

This is a summary statement of the conquest of these two territories (see 2.26–3.10). If translators have a comma at the end of verse 46, they may begin verse 47 with "and King Og who ruled in Bashan, and occupied their lands. These two Amorite kings had ruled the territory east of the Jordan River" (so also CEV).

4.48   RSV   TEV

from Aroer, which is on the edge of the valley of the Arnon, as far as Mount Sirion[c] (that is, Hermon),	This land extended from the town of Aroer, on the edge of the Arnon River, all the way north to Mount Sirion,[e] that is, Mount Hermon.
[c] Syr: Heb *Sion*	[e] *One ancient translation* Sirion; *Hebrew* Sion.

Aroer . . . on the edge of the valley of the Arnon: see 2.36; 3.12.

Mount Sirion (that is, Hermon): as the RSV note states, the Hebrew has "Sion"; Syriac reads "Sirion." HOTTP prefers the Hebrew text, and states " 'Sion' may be another name for 'Sirion.' " (It should be noted that "Sion" is not the same name as the Hebrew for "Zion.") In light of 3.8-9 translators may prefer "Sirion," perhaps with a footnote stating that the Hebrew text has another name for the same mountain, "Sion," with a reference to 3.8-9. The TEV model will be a helpful one for many translators.

4.49   RSV   TEV

together with all the Arabah on the east side of the Jordan as far as the Sea of the Arabah, under the slopes of Pisgah.	It also included all the region east of the Jordan River as far south as the Dead Sea and east to the foot of Mount Pisgah.

The Arabah: see 1.1.

The sea of the Arabah: the Dead Sea (see 3.17).

Under the slopes of Pisgah: TEV gives an understandable rendering of the text. FRCL has "the region that includes the eastern part of the Jordan Valley, as far as the Dead Sea, at the foot of Mount Pisgah." See map, page xii.

2A-2. The ten commandments (5.1-21)

RSV

1 And Moses summoned all Israel, and said to them, "Hear, O Israel, the statutes and the ordinances which I speak in your hearing this day, and you shall learn them and be careful to do them. 2 The LORD our God made a covenant with us in Horeb. 3 Not with our fathers did the LORD make this covenant, but with us, who are all of us here alive this day. 4 The LORD spoke with you face to face at the mountain, out of the midst of the fire, 5 while I stood between the LORD and you at that time, to declare to you the word of the LORD; for you were afraid because of the fire, and you did not go up into the mountain. He said:

6 " 'I am the LORD your God, who brought you out of the land of Egypt, out of the house of bondage.

7 " 'You shall have no other gods before me.

8 " 'You shall not make for yourself a graven image, or any likeness of anything that is in heaven above, or that is on the earth beneath, or that is in the water under the earth; 9 you shall not bow down to them or serve them; for I the LORD your God am a jealous God, visiting the iniquity of the fathers upon the children to the third and fourth generation of those who hate me, 10 but showing steadfast love to thousands of those who love me and keep my commandments.

11 " 'You shall not take the name of the LORD your God in vain: for the LORD will not hold him guiltless who takes his name in vain.

12 " 'Observe the sabbath day, to keep it holy, as the LORD your God commanded you. 13 Six days you shall labor, and do all your work; 14 but the seventh day is a sabbath to the LORD your God; in it you shall not do any work, you, or your son, or your daughter, or your manservant, or your maidservant, or your ox, or your ass, or any of your cattle, or the sojourner who is within your gates, that your manservant and your maidservant may rest as well as you. 15 You shall remember that you were a servant in the land of Egypt, and the LORD your God brought you out thence with a mighty hand and an outstretched arm; therefore the LORD your God commanded you to keep the sabbath day.

16 " 'Honor your father and your mother, as the LORD your God commanded you; that your days may be prolonged, and that it may go well with you, in the land which the LORD your God gives you.

TEV
The Ten Commandments

1 Moses called together all the people of Israel and said to them, "People of Israel, listen to all the laws that I am giving you today. Learn them and be sure that you obey them. 2 At Mount Sinai the LORD our God made a covenant, 3 not only with our fathers, but with all of us who are living today. 4 There on the mountain the LORD spoke to you face-to-face from the fire. 5 I stood between you and the LORD at that time to tell you what he said, because you were afraid of the fire and would not go up the mountain.

"The LORD said, 6 'I am the LORD your God, who rescued you from Egypt, where you were slaves.

7 " 'Worship no god but me.

8 " 'Do not make for yourselves images of anything in heaven or on earth or in the water under the earth. 9 Do not bow down to any idol or worship it, for I am the LORD your God and I tolerate no rivals. I bring punishment on those who hate me and on their descendants down to the third and fourth generation. 10 But I show my love to thousands of generations of those who love me and obey my laws.

11 " 'Do not use my name for evil purposes, for I, the LORD your God, will punish anyone who misuses my name.

12 " 'Observe the Sabbath and keep it holy, as I, the LORD your God, have commanded you. 13 You have six days in which to do your work, 14 but the seventh day is a day of rest dedicated to me. On that day no one is to work—neither you, your children, your slaves, your animals, nor the foreigners who live in your country. Your slaves must rest just as you do. 15 Remember that you were slaves in Egypt, and that I, the LORD your God, rescued you by my great power and strength. That is why I command you to observe the Sabbath.

16 " 'Respect your father and your mother, as I, the LORD your God, command you, so that all may go well with you and so that you may live a long time in the land that I am giving you.

17 " 'Do not commit murder.

18 " 'Do not commit adultery.

19 " 'Do not steal.

20 " 'Do not accuse anyone falsely.

21 " 'Do not desire another man's wife; do not desire his house, his land, his slaves, his cattle, his donkeys, or anything else that he owns.'

17 " 'You shall not kill.

18 " 'Neither shall you commit adultery.

19 " 'Neither shall you steal.

20 " 'Neither shall you bear false witness against your neighbor.

21 " 'Neither shall you covet your neighbor's wife; and you shall not desire your neighbor's house, his field, or his manservant, or his maidservant, his ox, or his ass, or anything that is your neighbor's.'

22 "These words the LORD spoke to all your assembly at the mountain out of the midst of the fire, the cloud, and the thick darkness, with a loud voice; and he added no more. And he wrote them upon two tables of stone, and gave them to me.

22 "These are the commandments the LORD gave to all of you when you were gathered at the mountain. When he spoke with a mighty voice from the fire and from the thick clouds, he gave these commandments and no others. Then he wrote them on two stone tablets and gave them to me.

The whole of chapter 5 is one section, and the division at the end of verse 22 (TEV, CEV, NJB, BRCL, FRCL) is somewhat artificial. However, if a division is made, it is better to have it at the end of verse 22 than of verse 21 (NRSV, SPCL).

In all the commandments the people of Israel are addressed in the second person singular. It may not be natural to do this in translation, as all the people are being addressed by Moses, and the appropriate form must be used. In verses 1-5 the "you" is plural; the singular pronoun begins to appear at verse 6.

There are two levels of direct speech in the text of this section. The first level is Moses' address, which goes to the end of chapter 26. When Moses quotes Yahweh's words, this is a second level. RSV and TEV use double quotation marks to mark the beginning of Moses' speech at 5.1 and its end at 26.19. But it should be noted that many major translations in English do not do this, using quotation marks only for the second level of direct speech (see CEV, NJPSV, NIV, NRSV, REB). A translation should indicate the levels of direct speech by expressions and devices that are natural in the language and that will be understood by the readers. One punctuation possibility for the first level is a colon [:] (as in CEV, NIV and others).

Yahweh is quoted in verses 6-21; the first person, **I the LORD your God**, is used in verses 6-10, but beginning at verse 11 the third person **the LORD your God** is used. TEV and FRCL retain the first person throughout. However, it seems better to follow the Hebrew and switch to the third person at verse 11 if this is natural style in the translator's language.

Section heading: for the section heading, the standard expression already used in the New Testament for **[the ten] commandments** should be used (see Mark 10.19, for example).

5.1	RSV	TEV

And Moses summoned all Israel, and said to them, "Hear, O Israel, the statutes and the ordinances which I

Moses called together all the people of Israel and said to them, "People of Israel, listen to all the laws that

speak in your hearing this day, and | I am giving you today. Learn them
you shall learn them and be careful | and be sure that you obey them.
to do them.

And Moses summoned all Israel: it is not necessary to preserve **And** in translation, unless it is a natural feature of the language. "Moses called all the people of Israel to meet with him."

"Hear, O Israel, all the statutes and ordinances . . .": this may be expressed as "People of Israel [or, Israelites], listen to . . . ." For **statutes and ordinances** see 4.1.

Which I speak in your hearing this day: that is, "that I am announcing [or, proclaiming] to you today [or, now]," "that I am giving you today" (TEV), or "Today I am telling you the laws that you . . ." (CEV). The phrase **in your hearing** is quite repetitive and unnatural in today's English, and perhaps in some other languages as well. The language should be natural and conform to normal style.

You shall learn them and be careful to do them: or "you must learn them and obey them faithfully" or "learn them and be sure that you obey them." (TEV). See similar commands in 4.2, 5, 6.

5.2	RSV	TEV

The LORD our God made a covenant | At Mount Sinai the LORD our God
with us in Horeb. | made a covenant,

The LORD our God may be "The LORD [or, Yahweh] whom we worship." For **The LORD** see 1.3.

Made a covenant with us: see 4.13, 23.

In Horeb: at Mount Sinai (see 1.6).

5.3	RSV	TEV

Not with our fathers did the LORD | not only with our fathers, but with all
make this covenant, but with us, who | of us who are living today.
are all of us here alive this day.

Not with our fathers . . . but with us: for **not with** TEV has "not only with," and CEV translates "that agreement wasn't only for." It is not clear who "our ancestors" (**our fathers**) are in this context. They could be the patriarchs, Abraham, Isaac, and Jacob (see 1.8; 4.31), but it seems more probable that they are the fathers and mothers of these people, who had gathered at Mount Sinai, where the covenant was made (4.10-14), forty years earlier, and who had subsequently died (1.35; 2.14-16). So we may translate "parents" or "mothers and fathers" here. This view is even more likely in light of what follows: **who are all of us here alive this day** (see 4.4), which contrasts with those who had died since the revelation at Mount Sinai. Israel is regarded as a corporate unity at all times, regardless of the generations of which it is made up.

An alternative translation model for this verse is:

●   Yahweh made this agreement [or, covenant] not only with our parents, but also with us who are here today.

5.4	RSV	TEV

The LORD spoke with you face to face at the mountain, out of the midst of the fire,	There on the mountain the LORD spoke to you face-to-face from the fire.

The LORD spoke with you face to face: the sense of **face to face** is "The LORD spoke to you personally [or, in person]."

At the mountain, out of the midst of the fire: that is, "from the fire on the mountain"; see 4.12, 15.

5.5	RSV	TEV

while I stood between the LORD and you at that time, to declare to you the word of the LORD; for you were afraid because of the fire, and you did not go up into the mountain. He said:	I stood between you and the LORD at that time to tell you what he said, because you were afraid of the fire and would not go up the mountain. "The LORD said,

While I stood between the LORD and you: Moses was the spokesman, the mediator who transmitted Yahweh's message to the people. As commentators point out, this differs from what is said in the previous verse (and see verse 22 also). NRSV places this verse within parentheses, but it is uncertain what readers will understand this device to mean, and translators are discouraged from doing this.

To declare to you the word of the LORD: this does not mean a single "word" but refers to Yahweh's message, the "ten words" of the covenant in particular. NJB translates, "to let you know what Yahweh was saying."

You were afraid because of the fire, and you did not go up: this may be expressed as "the fire [on the mountain] made you afraid to go up . . . ." See Exo 24.1-2. For **afraid** see 1.21, 29. TEV has a good model and translators are urged to follow it.

5.6	RSV	TEV

" 'I am the LORD your God, who brought you out of the land of Egypt, out of the house of bondage.	'I am the LORD your God, who rescued you from Egypt, where you were slaves.

In this verse Yahweh gives the reason why he is making this covenant with Israel. This statement also explains why he has the right to require that the Israelites obey the commandments of verses 7-21, which are the terms of the covenant. This historical prologue is like those found in treaties of that time between rulers and leaders of states.

I am the LORD your God: this standard phrase may be translated "I, Yahweh, am your God." Most translations, however, are the same as RSV.

Who brought you out: that is, "who led you out" or "who rescued you from."

The house of bondage means "the country where you were slaves." NIV has "the land of slavery," and REB "the land where you lived as slaves." The Israelites were not slaves in the sense of being forced to work without pay, and being the property of someone, but rather they were forced by the Egyptians to do heavy construction work. But at the same time they were provided with food and allowed to live in their homes in Goshen. So in languages where a distinction must be made between "slaves" as owned by someone, and people forced to do hard work, we may translate ". . . from Egypt where you were forced to do hard labor."

5.7	RSV	TEV
" 'You shall have no other gods before[d] me.		" 'Worship no god but me.

[d] Or *besides*

You shall have no other gods before [or, besides] **me**: this may be expressed "You shall [or, must] not worship any other god except me," or "Do not worship any god but me." NJB translates "You will have no gods other than me." It is better to use the verb "worship" or "obey," rather than "have."

This commandment does not deny the existence of other gods; it demands of the Israelites that they acknowledge only Yahweh as their god. Psa 81.9-10 has a good statement of this first commandment. The **you** is singular as mentioned in the introduction to this chapter. But many translators will wish to use a plural pronoun here and throughout the rest of the chapter.

See the comment on **gods** at 3.24.

5.8	RSV	TEV
" 'You shall not make for yourself a graven image, or any likeness of anything that is in heaven above, or that is on the earth beneath, or that is in the water under the earth;		" 'Do not make for yourselves images of anything in heaven or on earth or in the water under the earth.

For the words and phrases of this commandment, see 4.16-18.

The force of **make for yourself** is "make for your own use."

A graven image, or any likeness: there is a small problem in the Hebrew text here that HOTTP addresses. The standard (Masoretic) Hebrew text has "a [graven] image of any likeness," that is, an image that looks like any being (in the whole universe). RSV and some other versions follow the text found in many Hebrew manuscripts, a Qumran manuscript, the Samaritan, Septuagint, Syriac, Targum, and Vulgate (and see Exo 20.4). In this case a translation like TEV may be preferable, as the two phrases "an image" and "a likeness" mean the same thing. However, in some languages where there is no term for **graven image** or "idol," it will be necessary to translate the underlying meaning; for example, "You shall not carve out the likeness of anything living in . . . ," where "likeness" means "the image of."

Heaven will be translated as "sky" in many languages.

For **water under the earth** see 4.18.

5.9	RSV	TEV
	you shall not bow down to them or serve them; for I the LORD your God am a jealous God, visiting the iniquity of the fathers upon the children to the third and fourth generation of those who hate me,	Do not bow down to any idol or worship it, for I am the LORD your God and I tolerate no rivals. I bring punishment on those who hate me and on their descendants down to the third and fourth generation.

You shall not bow down to them or serve them: or "You must not . . . ." See 4.19. **Bow down** in some languages will be expressed as "prostrate yourself before." So we may also render this first sentence as "Do not prostrate yourselves before [or, bow down to] any likeness [or, image] of these gods."

I . . . am a jealous God: see 4.24; 6.14-15. There are better ways of translating the concept of **jealous** when applied to God. FRCL has "I demand to be your only God," and see TEV, "I tolerate no rivals"; or we may say "I demand that you love only me." For a further discussion see 4.24.

Visiting the iniquity of the fathers upon . . . : that is, extending the punishment for the sins of fathers onto their children, grandchildren, and great-grandchildren. This may require considerable restructuring (see below).

Instead of **the children to the third and fourth generation**, it is better to say "their children, grandchildren, and great-grandchildren."

Those who hate me refers back to **the fathers**, not to the future generations. The verb **hate** can be translated "oppose me" (FRCL), "are against me," or even "my enemies." TEV and CEV interpret **the iniquity** as being the sin of "hate" or "rejection." So TEV restructures the sentence, combining **fathers** and **those who hate me** to read "I bring punishment on those who hate me and on their descendants down to the third and fourth generations." CEV puts the clause **those who hate me** at the beginning of the sentence, making it conditional: "If you reject [the equivalent of "hate"] me, I will punish . . . ."

An alternative translation model for this verse is:

• Do not bow down to [or, prostrate yourselves before] and worship any likeness of these gods. I am Yahweh, the God you must worship. I will not tolerate your worshiping any other gods. If you hate me, I will punish you for that sin. I will punish not only you, but your children, grandchildren, and great-grandchildren.

5.10   RSV   TEV

| but showing steadfast love to thousands of those who love me and keep my commandments. | But I show my love to thousands of generations[f] of those who love me and obey my laws. |

[f] thousands of generations; *or* thousands.

Showing steadfast love: the Hebrew verb translated **showing** is literally "doing," better translated "acting with . . . ." This is the first occurrence in this book of the noun *chesed*, which appears frequently in the Hebrew Scriptures. When used of God it refers to God's covenant love, God's faithfulness in keeping his promise to the people of Israel, to be their God and to bless them. It is variously translated: NJPSV has "kindness," which does not seem adequate; something like "love" (TEV, NIV, SPCL), "faithful [or, loyal] love," or "unchanging love" is better. REB has "I keep faith with." See 7.9, 12. For a comment on **love** see 4.37.

To thousands: it is better to follow TEV "to thousands of generations," or NRSV and NJPSV "to the thousandth generation" (also FRCL, BRCL, SPCL). See 7.9.

Who love me and keep my commandments: see 4.2.

5.11   RSV   TEV

| " 'You shall not take the name of the LORD your God in vain: for the LORD will not hold him guiltless who takes his name in vain. | " 'Do not use my name for evil purposes, for I, the LORD your God, will punish anyone who misuses my name. |

Take the name . . . in vain: that is, to use the name in a manner not befitting God's holiness. The phrase **in vain** means essentially "for a worthless purpose." This could involve the use of magic, incantations, or curses. TEV has "for evil purposes," NIV and NJB "misuse the name," NRSV "make wrongful use of," REB "make wrong use of," NJPSV "swear falsely" (which is supported by Jer 7.9). Craigie defines it as "an attempt to manipulate God for personal ends."

Will not hold him guiltless: this is variously expressed as "will not leave unpunished" (NJB), "will not acquit" (NRSV), and "will punish" (TEV, CEV). It is better to avoid RSV's exclusive **him** and say instead "I will punish anyone [or, any person] who . . . ."

122

It must be noted that in this verse Yahweh refers to himself in the third person. In a number of languages it will be better to change this to the first person; for example, "I, the LORD your God" (TEV) or "I am the LORD your God, and I will . . ." (CEV).

5.12

RSV	TEV
" 'Observe the sabbath day, to keep it holy, as the LORD your God commanded you.	" 'Observe the Sabbath and keep it holy, as I, the LORD your God, have commanded you.

Observe the sabbath day to keep it holy: the verb **Observe** (Exo 20.8 has "Remember") means "Take care," "Be careful," or "Make sure" (see the same verb in 4.9, 15). FRCL has "Take care to consecrate to me . . ."; other possibilities are "Make sure that you treat the Sabbath as a holy day" or "Make sure that you treat the day of rest as belonging [or, dedicated] to me."

Sabbath is a word that in some places will have to be carefully translated so as to avoid misunderstandings. Most modern translations use the traditional word for "Sabbath"; SPCL, however, has "day of rest," and this may be a more meaningful translation. If, however, a translator transliterates the word **sabbath**, a footnote and a note in the Glossary should be included.

To keep it holy means to dedicate the day to God. Since God himself had made the seventh day a special day of rest (Gen 2.3; Exo 20.11), Israel was to do the same. Another way to express the first part of this verse is "Keep on observing the day of rest and dedicate it to me."

As the LORD your God commanded you: this refers back to the original giving of the commandments at Mount Sinai (Exo 20.8).

5.13

RSV	TEV
Six days you shall labor, and do all your work;	You have six days in which to do your work,

Six days you shall labor, and do all your work: this may be treated as a statement of fact, "There are six days in which to do your work," or as a command, "Do all your work in six days." What the Hebrew says is literally a command, but it is possible that it can be read as a statement, showing the special nature of the seventh day, the day of rest. **Work** here refers to work in general, such as daily business, the work one does to earn a living. Again the singular **you** may be changed to the plural if required.

5.14

RSV	TEV
but the seventh day is a sabbath to the LORD your God; in it you shall not	but the seventh day is a day of rest dedicated to me. On that day no one

do any work, you, or your son, or
your daughter, or your manservant,
or your maidservant, or your ox, or
your ass, or any of your cattle, or the
sojourner who is within your gates,
that your manservant and your maidservant may rest as well as you.

is to work—neither you, your children, your slaves, your animals, nor
the foreigners who live in your
country. Your slaves must rest just
as you do.

But the seventh day is a sabbath to the LORD your God: that is "The seventh
day is a day of rest that is to be dedicated to the LORD your God"; or we may say
"The seventh day is a day of rest that belongs to me, Yahweh your God." Notice
that the third person reference to God may be changed to first person.

The rest of the verse itemizes the people and the animals in the Israelite
household that are included in the prohibition. We may notice that the man's
wife is not listed, and one explanation is that this was done to allow normal
domestic activities to be carried on during the sabbath.

Your son or your daughter: in all instances plural forms should be used, "all
your sons and daughters," or "all your children." **Your manservant . . . your
maidservant** means "your male and female slaves."

Your ox . . . your ass . . . any of your cattle: the translation can give the
names of the animals, as in the Hebrew text. In cultures that have cattle, the
translation of **ox** usually presents no problem. Here the word applies to either
a male or a female member of a herd of cattle, not as in English, where "bull"
refers only to a male and "cow" refers only to a female. The **ass** or "donkey" is
smaller than the horse, with shorter legs and longer ears. It was the beast of
burden used for carrying supplies and also for agricultural work. It will be
helpful in cultures where "cows" and "donkeys" are unknown to include
illustrations of these animals and have a general translation such as "all your
[work] animals" (see also 2.35).

The sojourner who is within your gates: this means "the resident aliens [or,
foreigners] who live in your towns [or, country]." See 1.16.

That your manservant and your maidservant may rest as well as you: this
is said to emphasize the fact that the man's slaves were to have a day off from
work. In this final sentence **your manservant** and **your maidservant** may be
combined as "slaves" (see TEV, CEV). For "slaves" see verse 6.

5.15	RSV	TEV

You shall remember that you were a
servant in the land of Egypt, and the
LORD your God brought you out
thence with a mighty hand and an
outstretched arm; therefore the LORD
your God commanded you to keep
the sabbath day.

Remember that you were slaves in
Egypt, and that I, the LORD your God,
rescued you by my great power and
strength. That is why I command you
to observe the Sabbath.

The commandment is given emphasis by the reminder that the Israelites had been slaves in Egypt, where they got no day of rest. The sabbath commemorates freedom from forced labor; they are now not forced to work, but commanded to rest. The first part of the verse may be alternatively translated as "This day of rest will remind you that you did hard labor in Egypt, and that I, Yahweh, the God you worship . . . ."

Brought you out thence with a mighty hand and an outstretched arm: see 4.34. The TEV model "rescued you by my great power and strength" will be helpful for many translators. However, "used my great power and strength to rescue you" is also possible.

Therefore the LORD your God commanded you to keep the sabbath day will sound unnatural in some languages. Another model is "That is why I, Yahweh, command you to observe the sabbath [or, special day of rest]."

5.16　　　　RSV　　　　　　　　　　　　TEV

" 'Honor your father and your mother, as the LORD your God commanded you; that your days may be prolonged, and that it may go well with you, in the land which the LORD your God gives you.

" 'Respect your father and your mother, as I, the LORD your God, command you, so that all may go well with you and so that you may live a long time in the land that I am giving you.

Honor your father and your mother: to honor is to respect and obey.

As the LORD your God commanded you: see verse 12.

For the rest of the verse, see 4.40. The primary emphasis of **your days may be prolonged** here, as in 4.40, is that the Israelites, as a people, will live in the land of Canaan for many generations. This, of course, is not incompatible with an individual Israelite living to a ripe old age—which is the way the commandment is understood in Eph 6.2-3. In any case both clauses, **your days may be prolonged** and **it may go well with you**, go with the final part of the verse, **in the land which the LORD your God gives you**.

5.17　　　　RSV　　　　　　　　　　　　TEV

" 'You shall not kill.

" 'Do not commit murder.

You shall not kill: this does not include all killings (of people), such as killing in war or the execution of criminals. It is more narrowly restricted to murder, that is, the deliberate killing of a fellow human being. In English, at least, the proper translation is "You shall not murder" (TEV, NRSV, NJPSV, NIV, REB). This also is the proper translation of the citation of this commandment in the New Testament (Matt 5.21; 19.18; Mark 10.29; Luke 18.20; Rom 13.9; James 2.11). In languages where the various terms for killing are not clearly defined, it may be better to use the more general word for **kill** and say something like "kill from anger" or "kill deliberately." Translators should find a term that excludes

killing accidentally; it should be a term that means killing that society regards
as wrong.

5.18   RSV   TEV

" 'Neither shall you commit adul-   " 'Do not commit adultery.
tery.

Neither shall you commit adultery: it is not necessary to begin with **Neither**,
a literal translation of the common Hebrew conjunction *waw* that may be
translated "and," "but," "also," "neither," and so on, depending on the immediate context. However, in languages where using a conjunction will be natural
style, a translator may choose to include it. To **commit adultery** is for a married
individual to have sexual relations with some person who is not his or her
spouse. In the context the commandment is directed to men, and adultery was
to have relations with another man's wife or with a woman who was promised
in marriage to another man (see 22.22-25).
   In translation the prohibition should apply to both sexes. If an equivalent
term cannot be found in a language, it may be necessary to say, for example,
"You shall not sleep with someone else's spouse." Care must be taken not to use
a term that is considered crude or vulgar; euphemisms or polite ways of
referring to sexual intercourse can be readily found in most languages; and
many languages have their own standard idioms or euphemisms for adultery.

5.19   RSV   TEV

" 'Neither shall you steal.   " 'Do not steal.

Neither shall you steal: some commentators believe that the primary, if not
exclusive, force of this command had to do with kidnaping, that is, taking a
fellow Israelite by force. But this is contested, and the prohibition here has to
do with taking something belonging to someone else without their permission.

5.20   RSV   TEV

" 'Neither shall you bear false wit-   " 'Do not accuse anyone falsely.
ness against your neighbor.

Neither shall you bear false witness against your neighbor: this has to do
with giving false testimony against a fellow Israelite in a trial, a testimony that
hurts the other person's reputation (see 10.16-19; Exo 23.1). The commandment
should not be translated simply by "You shall not lie." However, we may say
something like "Do not tell lies about someone when you are giving evidence in
court."

5.21   RSV   TEV

" 'Neither shall you covet your   " 'Do not desire another man's
neighbor's wife; and you shall not   wife; do not desire his house, his
desire your neighbor's house, his   land, his slaves, his cattle, his don-
field, or his manservant, or his maid- keys, or anything else that he owns.'
servant, his ox, or his ass, or any-
thing that is your neighbor's.'

This commandment, unlike the others, deals with an inner motivation, not
with an action. By forbidding the motivation, the resultant action is also
forbidden. All the people and things included in the list belong to a person's
male fellow Israelite: they are his property, his cattle, and his slaves. In Exo
20.17 the all-inclusive "your neighbor's household" comes first, and then the
items belonging to that household.

You shall not covet your neighbor's wife: obviously what can be prohibited
and punished is not the desire as such but the attempt to satisfy that desire.
The verb **covet** here is different from the verb translated **desire** in the following
clause, but the two have almost the same meaning (the Septuagint translates
both by the same Greek verb). **Neighbor** here meant "a fellow Israelite," and as
applied to people today it means "a fellow human being," not just the person
living next door. So TEV has "Do not desire another man's wife."

After the list of particular items, **home, ox . . . ass** (see verse 14), comes the
final inclusive summary: **or anything that is your neighbor's**.

Here ends the direct quotation of Yahweh's words that began in verse 6.

5.22   RSV   TEV

"These words the LORD spoke to   "These are the commandments the
all your assembly at the mountain   LORD gave to all of you when you
out of the midst of the fire, the cloud, were gathered at the mountain.
and the thick darkness, with a loud   When he spoke with a mighty voice
voice; and he added no more. And   from the fire and from the thick
he wrote them upon two tables of   clouds, he gave these command-
stone, and gave them to me.   ments and no others. Then he wrote
                                      them on two stone tablets and gave
                                      them to me.

If translators begin a new section here, it will be a good idea to start the
verse with something like "Moses said to the people: . . . ." This Handbook,
however, recommends that a new section begin with verse 23.

All your assembly means "all of you who were together [or, gathered]." See
4.10-13 for this verse.

With a loud voice: Yahweh spoke loudly enough for everybody to hear him.

And he added no more: these are all the "words" (commandments) that
Yahweh gave directly to the people at Mount Sinai (see 4.13; 9.10; 10.4).

And then he wrote them upon two tables of stone: in modern English "tablets" is used (TEV, NRSV, and others) instead of **tables** (see also 4.13). In the nature of the case the verb "to write" may not be appropriate for what is engraved or inscribed on stone; so something like "carved" or "inscribed" may be better.

2A-3. Moses mediates between God and the people (5.23-33)

RSV	TEV
	The People's Fear

23 And when you heard the voice out of the midst of the darkness, while the mountain was burning with fire, you came near to me, all the heads of your tribes, and your elders; 24 and you said, 'Behold, the LORD our God has shown us his glory and greatness, and we have heard his voice out of the midst of the fire; we have this day seen God speak with man and man still live. 25 Now therefore why should we die? For this great fire will consume us; if we hear the voice of the LORD our God any more, we shall die. 26 For who is there of all flesh, that has heard the voice of the living God speaking out of the midst of fire, as we have, and has still lived? 27 Go near, and hear all that the LORD our God will say; and speak to us all that the LORD our God will speak to you; and we will hear and do it.'

28 "And the LORD heard your words, when you spoke to me; and the LORD said to me, 'I have heard the words of this people, which they have spoken to you; they have rightly said all that they have spoken. 29 Oh that they had such a mind as this always, to fear me and to keep all my commandments, that it might go well with them and with their children for ever! 30 Go and say to them, "Return to your tents." 31 But you, stand here by me, and I will tell you all the commandment and the statutes and the ordinances which you shall teach them, that they may do them in the land which I give them to possess.' 32 You shall be careful to do therefore as the LORD your God has commanded you; you shall not turn aside to the right hand or to the left. 33 You shall walk in all the way which the LORD your God has commanded you, that you may live, and that it may go well with you, and that you may live long in the land which you shall possess.

23 "When the whole mountain was on fire and you heard the voice from the darkness, your leaders and the chiefs of your tribes came to me 24 and said, 'The LORD our God showed us his greatness and his glory when we heard him speak from the fire! Today we have seen that it is possible for people to continue to live, even though God has spoken to them. 25 But why should we risk death again? That terrible fire will destroy us. We are sure to die if we hear the LORD our God speak again. 26 Has any human being ever lived after hearing the living God speak from a fire? 27 Go back, Moses, and listen to everything that the LORD our God says. Then return and tell us what he said to you. We will listen and obey.'

28 "When the LORD heard this, he said to me, 'I have heard what these people said, and they are right. 29 If only they would always feel this way! If only they would always honor me and obey all my commands, so that everything would go well with them and their descendants forever. 30 Go and tell them to return to their tents. 31 But you, Moses, stay here with me, and I will give you all my laws and commands. Teach them to the people, so that they will obey them in the land that I am giving them.'

32 "People of Israel, be sure that you do everything that the LORD your God has commanded you. Do not disobey any of his laws. 33 Obey them all, so that everything will go well with you and so that you will continue to live in the land that you are going to occupy.

Section heading. As noted at the beginning of this chapter, some versions begin a separate section at verse 22. However, a better choice is to follow the division of TEV at verse 23, using the heading "The People's Fear" or CEV "The

People Were Afraid." An alternative may be "Moses mediates between God and the people" or "Moses speaks to the people on behalf of God."

5.23 RSV	TEV
And when you heard the voice out of the midst of the darkness, while the mountain was burning with fire, you came near to me, all the heads of your tribes, and your elders;	**"When the whole mountain was on fire and you heard the voice from the darkness, your leaders and the chiefs of your tribes came to me**

If translators follow the recommendation of this Handbook, to begin the new section here instead of at verse 22, it may be useful to introduce Moses again as the speaker: "And Moses went on to say: 'When . . . . ' "

And when you heard: it is not necessary to begin the verse with **And** (see NRSV, NJPSV, and others).

For **the voice out of the midst of the darkness** and **while the mountain was burning with fire** see 4.11-12, 33.

You came near to me, all the heads of your tribes, and your elders: here the pronoun **you**, which refers in previous verses to all the Israelites, is limited by the following **heads of your tribes, and your elders**. To translate literally, as RSV does, may be natural style in some languages, but it is unnatural in most others. So the translation may be "You came near to me, that is, all the heads . . . ," or else it should imitate TEV and others and say "The chiefs of all your tribes and the elders came . . . ." For **heads of your tribes** see 1.15. **Elders** were respected elderly males, wielding considerable authority in their communities (see also 27.1; 29.10; 31.9, 28). They were recognized for their maturity and ability to lead. If in the translation the two ideas of leadership and authority can be combined in one term like "elders," then that term should be used. However, if such a term is not available, then TEV "your leaders," or CEV "the chiefs of your tribes," or even BRCL "[other] authorities" are possible models. FRCL provides a definition in its Vocabulary, "heads of families or clans," and adds "Those in a given town formed a council, responsible for governing the town and rendering justice."

5.24 RSV	TEV
and you said, 'Behold, the LORD our God has shown us his glory and greatness, and we have heard his voice out of the midst of the fire; we have this day seen God speak with man and man still live.	**and said, 'The LORD our God showed us his greatness and his glory when we heard him speak from the fire! Today we have seen that it is possible for people to continue to live, even though God has spoken to them.**

And you said: grammatically "you, the people of Israel," but actually it refers to the tribal leaders and the elders, who were representing the people; see the previous verse. A translation should make this clear (see TEV, CEV, NJB): [23]" . . . came to me [24] and said, ..."

Behold: for emphasis. The sense is "See," "Look," "Listen."

For **LORD our God** see 5.2.

Has shown us his glory and greatness: the Israelites had not seen any bodily form (4.15, 32-33, 36) but only "his majestic Presence" (NJPSV). God's **glory** is represented in terms of a bright light. Possible alternative translations are "dazzling light," "dazzling light of his presence," or even "dazzling light that shows that God is present [or, near]." God's **greatness** is an expression of how people react to the power and majesty of the Creator and sovereign Lord of the universe, particularly in his acts on behalf of the chosen people. So we may say "How powerful he is."

We have heard his voice out of the fire: see 4.32, 36.

We have this day seen God speak with man and man still live: see 4.33. NRSV avoids the exclusive **man**: "We have seen that God may speak to someone and the person may still live."

An alternative translation model for this verse is:

- and said: Today the LORD our God has shown us the dazzling light that shows that he is here. He has also shown us how powerful he is. We heard his voice coming from the fire, and we have learned that, even if God speaks to someone, that person may still live [or, continue to live].

5.25   RSV   TEV

Now therefore why should we die? | But why should we risk death again?
For this great fire will consume us; if | That terrible fire will destroy us. We
we hear the voice of the LORD our | are sure to die if we hear the LORD
God any more, we shall die. | our God speak again.

Now therefore why should we die?: they fear they run the risk of dying if Yahweh were to speak to them again, and so they ask Moses to act as their mediator (see Exo 20.19). Instead of **die** it is better to say "risk death" (TEV, REB), or "run the risk of dying," or "take a chance on being killed" (CEV).

This great fire will consume us: the fire was not a natural fire but a display of Yahweh's power, which might destroy them. And if Yahweh were to speak again, they would surely die, as the following verse makes clear.

5.26   RSV   TEV

For who is there of all flesh, that has   **Has any human being ever lived after**
heard the voice of the living God   **hearing the living God speak from a**
speaking out of the midst of fire, as   **fire?**
we have, and has still lived?

This verse seems to contradict verse 24, but in fact verse 24 provides only a
rare exception to the rule. Moses and the other Israelites did in fact survive,
after Yahweh had spoken to them on that occasion, but normally people could
hardly hope to escape death.

Who is there of all flesh: the literal translation of the Hebrew is not normal
English idiom; TEV is better, "Has any human being . . . ." The Hebrew phrase
translated **all flesh** means here the entire human race, all humanity (in some
other contexts it means all living creatures). Another possible translation is
"Was there ever any person who . . . ?" NJPSV has "What mortal . . . ?"

The form of the Hebrew is a rhetorical question, whose expected answer is
negative, "No one." It may be better in some languages to use a direct emphatic
statement: "Nobody ever . . . and has survived," "There has never been a person
who . . . and has survived."

The living God: this title contrasts Yahweh with the gods of other peoples,
gods who were powerless, dead, lifeless idols. A translation may bring this out
by translating "The only living God." This contrasts well with human "flesh,"
mortal humankind.

As we have indicates that the elders are saying that they and the other
Israelites are the only people in the world who have ever heard God speak and
survived. They are the exception to the rule, but they don't want to go through
the experience again.

5.27   RSV   TEV

Go near, and hear all that the LORD   **Go back, Moses, and listen to every-**
our God will say; and speak to us all   **thing that the LORD our God says.**
that the LORD our God will speak to   **Then return and tell us what he said**
you; and we will hear and do it.'   **to you. We will listen and obey.'**

Go near, and hear . . . and speak to us: they ask Moses to act as an
intermediary, believing, as they do, that he will not die from such a close
encounter with Yahweh. TEV has "Go back, Moses, and listen to everything . . .";
or we may say "Moses, you [singular] go up close and listen . . . ."

And speak to us: Moses must go up the mountain and listen to the LORD, and
then return to tell the people what he said. So it will be good for translators to
indicate this; for example, "Then return and tell us" (TEV).

We will hear and do it: the people's spokesmen pledge the people to obey
God's commands.

5.28   RSV   TEV

"And the LORD heard your words,   "When the LORD heard this, he
when you spoke to me; and the LORD   said to me, 'I have heard what these
said to me, 'I have heard the words   people said, and they are right.
of this people, which they have spo-
ken to you; they have rightly said all
that they have spoken.

Moses now recounts what Yahweh said to him (verses 28b-31). In RSV and TEV
Yahweh's words are enclosed within single quotes, since they are a second level
of direct speech. See the comments at the beginning of chapter 5.

Notice the redundancy in the Hebrew text: "your words, when you spoke to
me"; "I have heard the words . . . that they have spoken to you"; "all that they
have spoken." TEV has removed most of the redundancy: "When the LORD heard
this, he said to me." In some languages it will be desirable to keep the
redundancy as giving a feeling of solemnity to the text.

They have rightly said all that they have spoken: NJPSV has "They did well
to speak thus"; BRCL "Everything they have said is right"; NJB "Everything they
have said is well said."

5.29   RSV   TEV

Oh that they had such a mind as this   If only they would always feel this
always, to fear me and to keep all my   way! If only they would always honor
commandments, that it might go well   me and obey all my commands, so
with them and with their children for   that everything would go well with
ever!   them and their descendants forever.

Oh that they had such a mind in them always: the Hebrew expression is in
the form of a question: "Who will give . . . ?" (meaning "If only there were . . . !").
This expresses a wish: "May they always be of such a mind" (NJPSV); "If only
their heart were always so" (NJB); "Would that they may always be of a mind"
(REB); "I wish that their hearts [or, minds] were always like this"; or even "I
wish that they would always think like this." In this passage **mind** translates
the Hebrew word for "heart," meaning here the people's attitude or resolve.

To fear me: see 4.10.

Keep all my commandments: see 4.2.

That it might go well with them and their children forever: see 4.40; 5.16. We
should note that the initial **it** is used idiomatically and does not refer back to
anything earlier in the text. We can readily substitute "everything" (TEV) or
"things." Here **children** means "descendants." Another model for this final
sentence is "Then they and their descendants would always enjoy a successful
life."

5.30 RSV TEV

Go and say to them, "Return to your tents."

Go and tell them to return to their tents.

In this verse Yahweh tells Moses what to say to the people. If the order is given in direct speech, as it is in RSV, double quotes enclose the quotation; but an indirect statement may be used, as in TEV, in which case no quotation marks are necessary. Since the command is such a brief one (**Return to your tents**), TEV may well be followed in most languages. As a general rule, however, each language should do what is natural and easily understood, both by the reader and by those who hear the text being read.

Return to your tents: the people are ordered to disperse, each family going to its own tent (1.27). In some languages the more general "Go back home" may be better.

5.31 RSV TEV

But you, stand here by me, and I will tell you all the commandment and the statutes and the ordinances which you shall teach them, that they may do them in the land which I give them to possess.'

But you, Moses, stay here with me, and I will give you all my laws and commands. Teach them to the people, so that they will obey them in the land that I am giving them.'

Stand here by me: that is, "Stay with me," "Stay by my side." Such human language does not mean that Yahweh was a being with a (human) body.

All the commandment: this is a strange singular form, with the accompanying plural forms. NJPSV takes the singular to be inclusive, translating "the whole Instruction—the laws and the rules—" (see also 11.22). This is possible, and a translator may choose to do the same. Most translations, like TEV, translate **the commandment** (4.2) as plural, in conformity with the plurals **the statutes and the ordinances** (4.1): "all my laws or commands," or as CEV translates, "my laws and teachings."

Which you shall teach them: it will be helpful in many languages to begin a new sentence here as TEV does: "Teach them to the people, so that . . . ."

That they may do them: this may be understood to mean that God is giving the people permission to obey his laws. It is better to follow TEV: "so that they will obey them."

The land which I am giving them to possess: the land of Canaan; for the language see 1.8; 3.18; 4.1.

5.32 RSV TEV

You shall be careful to do therefore as the LORD your God has com-

"People of Israel, be sure that you do everything that the LORD your

manded you; you shall not turn aside to the right hand or to the left.	God has commanded you. Do not disobey any of his laws.

Yahweh's speech has ended and Moses is again speaking to the Israelites. This should be indicated in translation; for example, "Moses spoke to the Israelites again, saying . . . ."

Be careful to do: see 5.1. Strict obedience is demanded, without any deviation from Yahweh's commands.

Not turn aside to the right hand or to the left: the path to be followed is straight. The sense is "Never fail to do exactly what God commands" (BRCL), or "Be careful to obey all his laws," or even "Do not disobey any of his laws" (TEV). See the idiom also in 17.11, 20.

5.33	RSV	TEV

RSV	TEV
You shall walk in all the way which the LORD your God has commanded you, that you may live, and that it may go well with you, and that you may live long in the land which you shall possess.	Obey them all, so that everything will go well with you and so that you will continue to live in the land that you are going to occupy.

You shall walk in all the way: this is a biblical idiom, meaning to live as God requires, obeying the commandments, statutes, and ordinances as given through Moses. If the figure **walk in the way** or "walk your lives in the way" is kept, the verb that follows should be "that the LORD your God has shown [or indicated, or traced] for you." NJB has "has marked for you."

It may go well with you: see verse 29.

You may live long in the land: see 4.40; 5.16.

Which you shall possess: see 1.8.

2A-4. The great commandment (6.1-9)

RSV	TEV
	The Great Commandment
1 "Now this is the commandment, the statutes and the ordinances which the LORD your God commanded me to teach you, that you may do them in the land to which you are going over, to possess it; 2 that you may fear the LORD your God, you and your son and your son's son, by keeping all his statutes and his commandments, which I command you, all the days of your life; and that your days may be prolonged. 3 Hear therefore, O Israel, and be careful to do them; that it may go well with you, and that you may multiply greatly, as the	1 "These are all the laws that the LORD your God commanded me to teach you. Obey them in the land that you are about to enter and occupy. 2 As long as you live, you and your descendants are to honor the LORD your God and obey all his laws that I am giving you, so that you may live in that land a long time. 3 Listen to them, people of Israel, and obey them! Then all will go well with you, and you will become a mighty nation and live in that rich and fertile land, just as the LORD, the God of our ancestors, has promised.

LORD, the God of your fathers, has promised you, in a land flowing with milk and honey.

4 "Hear, O Israel: The LORD our God is one LORD; 5 and you shall love the LORD your God with all your heart, and with all your soul, and with all your might. 6 And these words which I command you this day shall be upon your heart; 7 and you shall teach them diligently to your children, and shall talk of them when you sit in your house, and when you walk by the way, and when you lie down, and when you rise. 8 And you shall bind them as a sign upon your hand, and they shall be as frontlets between your eyes. 9 And you shall write them on the doorposts of your house and on your gates.

4 "Israel, remember this! The LORD—and the LORD alone—is our God. 5 Love the LORD your God with all your heart, with all your soul, and with all your strength. 6 Never forget these commands that I am giving you today. 7 Teach them to your children. Repeat them when you are at home and when you are away, when you are resting and when you are working. 8 Tie them on your arms and wear them on your foreheads as a reminder. 9 Write them on the doorposts of your houses and on your gates.

In this section Moses explains and emphasizes the first commandment (5.6-7). Verses 4-5, known as the **Shema** (from the opening word in Hebrew, *shema'*, "Hear"), are a summary of the very essence of Israel's faith and were cited by Jesus as the greatest of all commandments in the Torah (Matt 22.37; Mark 12.29-30; see Luke 10.27).

Section heading: here Moses states what TEV calls "The Great Commandment," which can be better represented by "The Greatest Commandment" or "The Most Important Commandment."

6.1 RSV	TEV
"Now this is the commandment, the statutes and the ordinances which the LORD your God commanded me to teach you, that you may do them in the land to which you are going over, to possess it;	"These are all the laws that the LORD your God commanded me to teach you. Obey them in the land that you are about to enter and occupy.

Moses continues speaking. Since most translations will have a break here, with a title for the section 6.1-9, as in TEV, it may be good to start anew (with closing quotes at the end of 5.33 if necessary), as follows: "Moses continued to speak to the Israelites: . . . ."

Now this is the commandment, the statutes and the ordinances: this construction is like the one in 5.31, and here the translator may follow the same procedure as there; see FRCL: "These are the commandments, the laws, and the rules" (similarly NJB, NIV). NJPSV has "And this is the Instruction—the laws and the rules—that the LORD . . ." (similarly NRSV), taking the first word **commandment** to be general, including the two terms **statutes** and **ordinances** that follow. The Handbook recommends that translators follow FRCL. However, if there are insufficient suitable terms in a language, we may say, for example, "These are the laws and teachings" (CEV), or even "These are all the laws" (TEV). For **commandment** see 4.2; **statutes and ordinances**, 4.1.

The LORD your God commanded me to teach you: Yahweh gave the Law to Moses and ordered him to teach it to the Israelites; **your** and **you** are plural in the Hebrew text. The verb for **teach** should be a general one if possible, and not make the reader think of a classroom with a teacher and students; Moses was to announce these laws in the hearing of the people. For **the LORD your God** see 1.6.

That you may do them: instead of **that**, meaning "in order that," it is often better to join this closely with the previous verb, as NRSV does: ". . . that the LORD your God charged me to teach you to follow." To **do** a commandment is to obey it, put it into practice. Something like the following may serve as a model: "These are the commandments, the laws and the rules that the LORD your God ordered me to teach you to obey."

In the land to which you are going over, to possess it: this wordy and awkward English is a formal equivalent of the Hebrew; TEV is more natural and simple. The phrase **going over** refers to the crossing of the Jordan River (see 4.14). For **to possess** see 1.8.

6.2	RSV	TEV
	that you may fear the LORD your God, you and your son and your son's son, by keeping all his statutes and his commandments, which I command you, all the days of your life; and that your days may be prolonged.	As long as you live, you and your descendants are to honor the LORD your God and obey all his laws that I am giving you, so that you may live in that land a long time.

That you may fear the LORD your God: this is the purpose of Moses' teaching the Law to the Israelites, to **fear** God, that is, to honor, respect, and obey him (see 4.10; 5.29).

You and your son and your son's son: although singular in form, these are all plural in meaning: "all of you, and your children and your grandchildren," that is, "for all future generations." Translators may follow the Hebrew pattern if this is natural style in their language and if it means "descendants."

By keeping all his statutes and commandments: this is what "to fear God" means: obedience to his laws. TEV has "obey all his laws."

The singular second person pronoun is used in Hebrew in **all the days of your life** and **your days may be prolonged**. The people of Israel are addressed as though they were one person (as in 5.6-21); but translators may continue to use the plural if this is more natural style.

That your days may be prolonged: this is not long life as such but permanent residence in the Promised Land (4.40; 5.16); see TEV.

6.3   RSV   TEV

Hear therefore, O Israel, and be careful to do them; that it may go well with you, and that you may multiply greatly, as the LORD, the God of your fathers, has promised you, in a land flowing with milk and honey.	Listen to them, people of Israel, and obey them! Then all will go well with you, and you will become a mighty nation and live in that rich and fertile land, just as the LORD, the God of our ancestors, has promised.

Moses continues addressing Israel in the second singular, except for **you may multiply greatly**, which is plural.

Hear therefore, O Israel: **Hear** is an attention-getter: "Listen to me, people of Israel!"; "Pay attention, Israelites!" This vocative addresses all the people as one individual. "Listen to them" (TEV) departs needlessly from the meaning of the Hebrew text.

Be careful to do them: this is a way of saying "Do your best to obey them" (see 5.1).

That it may go well with you: obedience will bring blessings of prosperity and peace (see the same language in 5.29).

That you may multiply greatly: this means to have many descendants. Both TEV "a mighty nation" and CEV "a successful and powerful nation" emphasize the consequence of being a nation with a large population; it is better to stay close to the immediate meaning of the Hebrew text (see 1.10).

The God of your fathers: **fathers** refers to their ancestors, especially Abraham, Isaac, and Jacob (see 1.8 and 6.10).

A land flowing with milk and honey: this is traditional language (see Exo 3.8), meaning "a rich and fertile land" (11.9; 26.9, 15; 27.3; 31.20). Many modern translations still keep the biblical figure (NRSV, REB). The meaning is that the land is a good one for large herds and flocks (**milk**), and for crops and fruit trees (**honey** is probably the thick syrup produced from dates, not wild honey made by bees). In some languages this phrase has been deeply established in the Christian vocabulary and may need to be retained, but in many other languages a literal translation will be meaningless. In such a case "rich and fertile land" (TEV) will be a suitable alternative model. We may also say something like "a land full of cattle and many crops (or, much fruit)."

6.4-5   RSV   TEV

4 "Hear, O Israel: The LORD our God is one LORD;[e] 5 and you shall love the LORD your God with all your heart, and with all your soul, and with all your might. [e] Or *the* LORD *our God, the* LORD *is one*; Or *the* LORD *is our God, the* LORD *is one*; Or *the* LORD *is our God, the* LORD *alone*	4 "Israel, remember this! The LORD—and the LORD alone—is our God.[g] 5 Love the LORD your God with all your heart, with all your soul, and with all your strength. [g] The LORD . . . is our God; *or* The LORD, our God, is the only God; *or* The LORD our God is one.

These two verses are the **Shema**, a basic statement of the Israelite faith. This command is called by Jesus the greatest in the Law (Matt 22.37; Mark 12.30; see also Luke 10.27). In verse 4 of the Hebrew text the last letter of the first word **Hear** and the last letter of the last word **one** are in bold type and raised above the line, thus emphasizing the importance of the confession.

Hear, O Israel: see verse 3.

The LORD our God is one LORD: RSV provides three alternative translations of this four-word statement in Hebrew; TEV has two alternatives. The Hebrew text says: "YHWH our-God YHWH one" (or "alone"). This has been understood in three different ways:

(1) Yahweh alone is Israel's God; Israel serves and worships only Yahweh. See TEV, NJPSV, FRCL, NRSV, REB, the Portuguese common language version [POCL], BRCL.

(2) Yahweh is the one and only God; there are no other gods. See CEV; Psa 96.5; 115.4-7; 135.15-18.

(3) Yahweh, the God of Israel, is one, in contrast with the many local manifestations of pagan gods such as Baal (see Joel 2.11-13). See NIV, TOB ("The LORD our God is the one LORD"), NJB ("Yahweh our God is the one, the only Yahweh").

The Handbook recommends that the first meaning be given in the text, with alternatives in a footnote.

You shall love the LORD your God with all your heart . . . soul . . . might: this is a way of commanding the people to love God completely, wholeheartedly, without any reservations; it is a love that includes emotion, intellect, will. So **love** here contains not only the elements of liking and affection but also devotion and commitment to God. Translators should attempt to find a term that contains both of these ideas. Cultures differ in their ideas about the psychological makeup of people. For the Hebrews the **heart** generally refers to the activities of the mind rather than to emotions. The **soul** refers to the emotions (see also 4.29). In some languages, however, the functions of **heart** and **soul** will be thought of as identical. **Might** refers to physical strength. In some languages it will be necessary to dispense with the figurative language completely and say, for example, "You must love the LORD your God in all that you think and with all your strength," or ". . . with all your strength and thinking," or even ". . . completely." The quote in Mark 12.30 adds "with all your mind," which is not in the Hebrew or the Septuagint. However, the meaning is the same as "heart," and in many modern languages "heart and mind" will be identical. In summary, this command means that the people should love God completely—with their whole being.

6.6	RSV	TEV

And these words which I command you this day shall be upon your heart;	**Never forget these commands that I am giving you today.**

These words which I command you this day: Moses is talking about the laws that, on that day, he is ordering the Israelites to obey. In verses 6-9 the second person "you" and "your" are singular in the Hebrew text; the people are addressed as a whole, and every individual is included. However, in some languages the plural will be more natural style.

Shall be upon your heart: in Hebrew thought the **heart** was the center of thought, of intellectual activity, as was noted under verse 5 and 4.29. This command means they are to remember and never forget these commandments. REB has "are to be remembered and taken to heart"; NJPSV translates "take to heart." Another model is "Memorize these laws that I am giving you today."

6.7 RSV	TEV
and you shall teach them diligently to your children, and shall talk of them when you sit in your house, and when you walk by the way, and when you lie down, and when you rise.	Teach them to your children. Repeat them when you are at home and when you are away, when you are resting and when you are working.

Teach . . . diligently: this translates a Hebrew word that seems to mean "repeat," or "say again and again"; this meaning is reinforced by the following **shall talk of them**. NRSV translates "Recite them . . . and talk about them"; REB has "repeat them . . . and speak of them," NJPSV "tell them . . . and keep on telling them." Any of these is a good model for the translator to follow.

When you sit in your house, and when you walk by the way: this means while at home or away from home, which includes, of course, the whole time. The following **when you lie down and when you rise** is also a way of including the whole day, either "when you are asleep and when you are awake" or TEV "when you are resting and when you are working." (These two constructions are a figure of speech called "merism," in which the two opposites include the whole subject.) Provided that such repetition is good style in a language, the translator should certainly follow the Hebrew.

6.8 RSV	TEV
And you shall bind them as a sign upon your hand, and they shall be as frontlets between your eyes.	Tie them on your arms and wear them on your foreheads as a reminder.

And you shall bind them as a sign upon your hand and as frontlets between your eyes: see 11.18-20. This command was later kept by writing scripture verses on pieces of parchment and placing them in small leather pouches, called *tefilin* ("phylacteries"), on the forehead and the left forearm (see Matt 23.5). CEV has "Write down copies and tie them . . . ." This will be a good model for many translators. However, in languages that must indicate the kind of material that these laws were to be written on, we may say, for example, "Write these laws on parchment and . . . ."

The word **frontlets**, which means a band or ornament on the forehead, has a meaning parallel to **sign** here. The two terms have the sense of "sign and symbol," a public demonstration of the person's commitment to God's Law. TEV uses only one phrase, "as a reminder"; NJPSV has "as a sign . . . as a symbol"; NRSV "as a sign . . . as an emblem." The literal **between your eyes** means on the forehead.

An alternative translation model for this verse is:

- Write down copies of these laws and tie them on your wrists and foreheads to help you remember them.

6.9   RSV   TEV

And you shall write them on the doorposts of your house and on your gates.

Write them on the doorposts of your houses and on your gates.

The doorposts of your house and . . . your gates: in later times *mezuzoth*, small containers holding scripture verses, were fastened to the right-hand doorpost of the house. In this context **gates** means the city gates (homes were not surrounded by fences, so they had no gates); TOB and FRCL make this clear, and the translator is urged to do the same; for example, "the gates [in the walls] of your towns."

2A-5. Warnings against disobedience (6.10-25)

RSV   TEV
Warnings against Disobedience

10 "And when the LORD your God brings you into the land which he swore to your fathers, to Abraham, to Isaac, and to Jacob, to give you, with great and goodly cities, which you did not build, 11 and houses full of all good things, which you did not fill, and cisterns hewn out, which you did not hew, and vineyards and olive trees, which you did not plant, and when you eat and are full, 12 then take heed lest you forget the LORD, who brought you out of the land of Egypt, out of the house of bondage. 13 You shall fear the LORD your God; you shall serve him, and swear by his name. 14 You shall not go after other gods, of the gods of the peoples who are round about you; 15 for the LORD your God in the midst of you is a jealous God; lest the anger of the LORD your God be kindled against you, and he destroy you from off the face of the earth.

10 "Just as the LORD your God promised your ancestors, Abraham, Isaac, and Jacob, he will give you a land with large and prosperous cities which you did not build. 11 The houses will be full of good things which you did not put in them, and there will be wells that you did not dig, and vineyards and olive orchards that you did not plant. When the LORD brings you into this land and you have all you want to eat, 12 make certain that you do not forget the LORD who rescued you from Egypt, where you were slaves. 13 Honor the LORD your God, worship only him, and make your promises in his name alone. 14 Do not worship other gods, any of the gods of the peoples around you. 15 If you do worship other gods, the LORD's anger will come against you like fire and will destroy you completely, because the LORD your God, who is present with you, tolerates no rivals.

16 "You shall not put the LORD your God to the test, as you tested him at Massah. 17 You shall diligently keep the commandments of the LORD your God, and his testimonies, and his statutes, which he has commanded you. 18 And you shall do what is right and good in the sight of the LORD, that it may go well with you, and that you may go in and take possession of the good land which the LORD swore to give to your fathers 19 by thrusting out all your enemies from before you, as the LORD has promised.

20 "When your son asks you in time to come, 'What is the meaning of the testimonies and the statutes and the ordinances which the LORD our God has commanded you?' 21 then you shall say to your son, 'We were Pharaoh's slaves in Egypt; and the LORD brought us out of Egypt with a mighty hand; 22 and the LORD showed signs and wonders, great and grievous, against Egypt and against Pharaoh and all his household, before our eyes; 23 and he brought us out from there, that he might bring us in and give us the land which he swore to give to our fathers. 24 And the LORD commanded us to do all these statutes, to fear the LORD our God, for our good always, that he might preserve us alive, as at this day. 25 And it will be righteousness for us, if we are careful to do all this commandment before the LORD our God, as he has commanded us.'

16 "Do not put the LORD your God to the test, as you did at Massah. 17 Be sure that you obey all the laws that he has given you. 18 Do what the LORD says is right and good, and all will go well with you. You will be able to take possession of the fertile land that the LORD promised your ancestors, 19 and you will drive out your enemies, as he promised.

20 "In times to come your children will ask you, 'Why did the LORD our God command us to obey all these laws?' 21 Then tell them, 'We were slaves of the king of Egypt, and the LORD rescued us by his great power. 22 With our own eyes we saw him work miracles and do terrifying things to the Egyptians and to their king and to all his officials. 23 He freed us from Egypt to bring us here and give us this land, as he had promised our ancestors he would. 24 Then the LORD our God commanded us to obey all these laws and to honor him. If we do, he will always watch over our nation and keep it prosperous. 25 If we faithfully obey everything that God has commanded us, he will be pleased with us.'

This section, following the previous section without a break, consists of warnings and instructions, impressing on the people that they need to always obey the LORD's commands without hesitation, and making clear what will happen to them if they disobey, once they are settled in the Promised Land.

Section heading: TEV has the heading "Warnings Against Disobedience." This may also be rendered as "Moses warns the people not to disobey God."

6.10   RSV   TEV

"And when the LORD your God brings you into the land which he swore to your fathers, to Abraham, to Isaac, and to Jacob, to give you, with great and goodly cities, which you did not build,

"Just as the LORD your God promised your ancestors, Abraham, Isaac, and Jacob, he will give you a land with large and prosperous cities which you did not build.

Verses 10-12 are one sentence in Hebrew, long but not complex. TEV restructures so as to avoid the long time clause at the beginning of verse 10 (**And when the LORD . . .**), before the main verb in verse 12 ("then take heed . . ."). Another way to restructure the passage is as follows:

¹⁰ The LORD your God promised your ancestors, Abraham, Isaac, and
Jacob, that he would give you the land into which he is taking you.
This land has large and prosperous towns that you did not build; ¹¹ it
has houses full of good things that you did not put in them; and it has
wells that you did not dig, and vineyards and olive orchards that you
did not plant. When the LORD takes you into this land, and you have
all the food you want, ¹² be sure that you do not forget the LORD, who
rescued you from Egypt, where you were slaves.

With the beginning of this new section, Moses may again be introduced as the
speaker.

And when the LORD your God brings you: the point of view here (**brings**) is
from within the land itself; since in this story Moses and the Israelites are not
yet in the land, it is better in English to translate "takes." So CEV has "Now he
will take you there."

Which he swore to your fathers . . . : for the promise that God made, "with
an oath," to give them the land, and for **your fathers**, see 1.8.

Great and goodly cities: Moses is talking about the "large and prosperous"
towns in Canaan.

6.11   RSV   TEV

and houses full of all good things, which you did not fill, and cisterns hewn out, which you did not hew, and vineyards and olive trees, which you did not plant, and when you eat and are full,	The houses will be full of good things which you did not put in them, and there will be wells that you did not dig, and vineyards and olive orchards that you did not plant. When the LORD brings you into this land and you have all you want to eat,

Good things: in the nature of the case, these are family possessions,
furniture, tools, food, cooking utensils, and perhaps animals.

Which you did not fill means "which you did not put in them" (CEV).

Cisterns hewn out, which you did not hew: it is not clear whether the
Hebrew word here means "cisterns" or "wells" (see Pro 5.15, where the two are
parallel in meaning). Cisterns are cavities, hollow places, or pits **hewn** (cut) out
of rock, to collect rainwater; new techniques were developed, perhaps during
the time the Israelites invaded Canaan, of plastering the sides of the bell-
shaped holes in the rock, to make them watertight. The porous limestone of the
country was not ideal for cisterns. But the word may mean "wells," which are
holes dug to find underground water. A translator should feel free to use the
word most easily understood by readers of the language.

Vineyards and olive orchards refer to pieces of land set aside for growing
grapes or olives. In cultures where grapes or olives are unknown, we may
borrow terms from the prestige language in the area, and for this first
occurrence of the terms in Deuteronomy say something like "a garden for

growing fruit called 'grape [or, olive].' " It will also be helpful to have a description of these fruits in a footnote or in the Glossary.

When you eat and are full: this refers to having enough food stored up to keep from going hungry. An alternative model may be "But when you have enough food to satisfy your hunger . . . ."

6.12   RSV   TEV

then take heed lest you forget the   make certain that you do not forget
LORD, who brought you out of the   the LORD who rescued you from
land of Egypt, out of the house of   Egypt, where you were slaves.
bondage.

Take heed lest you forget the LORD: that is, "Make sure that you do not forget the LORD." For **take heed** see 2.4; 4.1, 9, 15, 23. Here **forget** means "to neglect," "to disregard," "to disobey" (see 4.9, 23).

Egypt . . . the house of bondage: see 5.16.

6.13   RSV   TEV

You shall fear the LORD your God;   Honor the LORD your God, worship
you shall serve him, and swear by   only him, and make your promises in
his name.   his name alone.

This verse was quoted by Jesus in his encounter with the Devil (Matt 4.10; Luke 4.8).

You shall fear the LORD your God: see 4.10; 10.20.

You shall serve him: the Hebrew verb is the same one translated "bondage" in verse 12.

Swear by his name: this means to use Yahweh's name alone when making a promise or taking a vow. The person calls upon God to punish the one swearing if the promise is not kept. Another way to express this is "make strong [or, solemn] promises using his name" or "make strong promises and speak [or, utter] God's name."

6.14   RSV   TEV

You shall not go after other gods, of   Do not worship other gods, any of
the gods of the peoples who are   the gods of the peoples around you.
round about you;

Verses 14-15 are one sentence, with the prohibition first ("don't worship other gods"), followed by the consequences if the Israelites disobey the command. This combination of command and threat appears often in this book (see 4.23-26; 8.19-20; 11.16-17).

From this verse to verse 17, **you** and **your** are plural in Hebrew.

Go after other gods: this means to pledge allegiance to them, or to worship them. For **gods** see 3.24.

The gods of the peoples who are round about you refers to the gods worshiped by the Canaanites, the Moabites, the Edomites, and other neighboring peoples.

The Hebrew of this verse is repetitive, and both RSV and TEV maintain the redundancy. Another model of this strong command may be:

- You must not worship any of the gods that the other nations [or, people] worship.

6.15	RSV	TEV

RSV	TEV
for the LORD your God in the midst of you is a jealous God; lest the anger of the LORD your God be kindled against you, and he destroy you from off the face of the earth.	If you do worship other gods, the LORD's anger will come against you like fire and will destroy you completely, because the LORD your God, who is present with you, tolerates no rivals.

The LORD your God in the midst of you: Yahweh was present with them, in the Sacred Tent in particular. TEV has "who is present with you." We may also express this as "who lives among you."

A jealous God: see 4.24.

The anger of the LORD your God will be kindled against you: God's anger is likened to fire, which will blaze out and destroy the people (see Num 11.1-3). An alternative translation model using figurative language may be "The LORD's heart [or, liver] will burn against you like fire" (see also 1.34).

Destroy you from off the face of the earth: this is biblical language, literally translated. It means to destroy completely, to wipe out. In English "wipe you off the face of the earth" (NJPSV, NJB) is more natural, and this will be a natural expression in many languages. A literal translation of **the face of the earth** will not be understood in many languages; the phrase means simply "the earth."

An alternative translation model for verses 14-15 is:

- You must not worship any of the gods that the nations around you worship. If you do, the LORD's heart [or, liver] will become hot just like fire, and he will wipe you off the face of the earth. The LORD your God is present with you and will not tolerate your worshiping other gods.

6.16	RSV	TEV

RSV	TEV
"You shall not put the LORD your God to the test, as you tested him at Massah.	"Do not put the LORD your God to the test, as you did at Massah.

Put the LORD your God to the test: this means to try to make God do something extraordinary in order to prove that he cares for his people (see Isa 7.10-12; and see in Matt 4.5-7; Luke 4.9-12, the context in which Jesus cited this text). CEV brings this idea out, with "so don't try to make the LORD prove that he can help you," or we may say "so don't try to make the LORD your God do a marvelous thing to prove that he cares for you." For **the LORD your God** see 1.6.

As you treated him at Massah: see Exo 17.1-7.

6.17	RSV	TEV

You shall diligently keep the commandments of the LORD your God, and his testimonies, and his statutes, which he has commanded you.	Be sure that you obey all the laws that he has given you.

You shall diligently keep means to obey strictly (see also 4.2; 5.32). An alternative model, slightly changing TEV, is the following: "Be sure that you always obey all the laws."

For **commandments** see 4.2; **testimonies**, 4.45; **statutes**, 4.1.

6.18-19	RSV	TEV

18 And you shall do what is right and good in the sight of the LORD, that it may go well with you, and that you may go in and take possession of the good land which the LORD swore to give to your fathers 19 by thrusting out all your enemies from before you, as the LORD has promised.	18 Do what the LORD says is right and good, and all will go well with you. You will be able to take possession of the fertile land that the LORD promised your ancestors, 19 and you will drive out your enemies, as he promised.

You shall do what is right and good in the sight of the LORD: this means to do the things that Yahweh considers **right and good**, as defined in the laws that Yahweh is giving to the people.

That it may go well with you: that is, "that you may prosper [or, be successful]." See 5.29; 6.3.

Go in and take possession of the good land: see 1.8. The adjective **good** here means primarily fertile (see "flowing with milk and honey" in verse 3).

Which the LORD swore to give to your fathers: see 1.8. Although this clause follows literally the wording of the Hebrew text, it seems likely that it really means "that Yahweh promised your fathers that he would give," that is, ". . . give *to you*," as the following verse makes clear; so NRSV. The translator is encouraged to follow NRSV. An alternative model, then, is "that Yahweh promised your ancestors that he would give to you."

By thrusting out all your enemies before you: although the Hebrew text may be understood to mean that the Israelites are the subject of the verb "to thrust out" (so TEV and others), it seems more likely that Yahweh is the subject (so RSV, NRSV, NJB, NIV, REB). See the similar statement in Exo 34.11-12. This sentence reveals the way that Yahweh will help Israel to possess the land: their enemies must be thrown out first. For **enemies** see 1.42.

We may combine verses 18 and 19 as follows:

- ^18-19 ... then you will be able to take possession of this fertile land because the LORD will drive out your enemies, just as he promised your ancestors [that he would do]."

6.20   RSV   TEV

"When your son asks you in time to come, 'What is the meaning of the testimonies and the statutes and the ordinances which the LORD our God has commanded you?'

"In times to come your children will ask you, 'Why did the LORD our God command us to obey all these laws?'

Verses 20-25 are a confession of God's mighty acts of salvation on behalf of his people. This is in the form of a creed which fathers are to repeat to their children for all generations to come.

In the interests of inclusiveness, TEV (second edition), CEV, NRSV, NJPSV have "your children," instead of the exclusive masculine **your son**. NJB uses the singular, "your child asks ... tell your child." It could be, however, that in the context of the writing of the book this actually refers to a ceremony in which the (older) son would ask his father this question, and the father would answer. But it seems better to make the text inclusive.

In time to come (TEV, "In times to come") may also be rendered as "some day" or "sometime," or "in the future."

The question **What is the meaning of . . . ?** means "Why did God give you these . . . ?" or "For what reason did God give you . . . ?"

The testimonies: see 4.45; **the statutes and the ordinances**: 4.21.

6.21   RSV   TEV

then you shall say to your son, 'We were Pharaoh's slaves in Egypt; and the LORD brought us out of Egypt with a mighty hand;

Then tell them, 'We were slaves of the king of Egypt, and the LORD rescued us by his great power.

Then you shall say to your son: TEV has "Then tell them," or more simply "Then you will answer" (CEV).

We were Pharaoh's slaves in Egypt: **Pharaoh** is not a proper name but a title, which is why TEV has "the king of Egypt." For **slaves** see 5.6, and for "king" see 1.4.

The LORD brought us out of Egypt: for the verb "bring out" see 4.20.

With a mighty hand: this means by force, by means of great strength (as in 4.34). (The Septuagint has "a mighty hand and an outstretched arm," as the Hebrew text has in 4.34.)

The final part of the verse may also be rendered as "Yahweh used his great power to bring us out of Egypt."

6.22-23 RSV	TEV
22 and the LORD showed signs and wonders, great and grievous, against Egypt and against Pharaoh and all his household, before our eyes; 23 and he brought us out from there, that he might bring us in and give us the land which he swore to give to our fathers.	22 With our own eyes we saw him work miracles and do terrifying things to the Egyptians and to their king and to all his officials. 23 He freed us from Egypt to bring us here and give us this land, as he had promised our ancestors he would.

The LORD showed signs and wonders: this refers to the great miracles, that is, the plagues that God sent on Egypt (Exo 7.14–10.29). The Hebrew verb "to give" (RSV **showed**) in this context means "to do" or "to perform." For **signs and wonders** see 4.34 (also 7.19).

Great and grievous: this emphasizes the extraordinary nature of the plagues and their destructive effect. NRSV has "great and awesome." These adjectives describe **signs** and **wonders**. So it is possible to translate, for example, "performed marvelous things [or, things that make people astonished] and did horrible [or, horrifying] things to the Egyptians."

Pharaoh and all his household: this means, as TEV has it, the king and all his officials (not just his family); none of them escaped Yahweh's fury.

Before our eyes: the Israelites were eyewitnesses of the plagues that God sent on Egypt; and generations later, in the land of Canaan, an Israelite father would think of himself as part of the generation that was set free from Egypt (see the similar creedal confession in 26.5-10). Some translators will wish to place this clause at the beginning of the verse; for example, "With our own eyes we saw him [Yahweh] do . . ." (TEV).

In verse 23, as in verse 18, the sense is that Yahweh **swore** to the ancestors, that is, the patriarchs, that he would give the land of Canaan to the people who are now about to take possession of it (so TEV, CEV, NRSV, NJB, REB). It will be helpful to begin a new sentence at verse 23; for example, "The LORD rescued us from Egypt . . . ."

6.24   RSV   TEV

And the LORD commanded us to do   Then the LORD our God commanded
all these statutes, to fear the LORD   us to obey all these laws and to
our God, for our good always, that   honor him. If we do, he will always
he might preserve us alive, as at this   watch over our nation and keep it
day.   prosperous.

For **statutes** see 4.1; **fear**, 4.10.

For our good always: this is the purpose of strict obedience to God's
commands; **good** here includes material prosperity and security. This clause
can be joined to the next, **that he might preserve us alive**, as NIV has done: "that
we might always prosper and be kept alive"; see also NJPSV "for our lasting good
and for our survival," and CEV "If we do, the LORD will always protect us and
help us to be successful."

As at this day: the security and prosperity they now enjoy will last forever—if
they obey Yahweh's commands.

6.25   RSV   TEV

And it will be righteousness for us, if   If we faithfully obey everything that
we are careful to do all this com-   God has commanded us, he will be
mandment before the LORD our God,   pleased with us.'ʰ
as he has commanded us.'

                                            ʰ If we faithfully . . . with us; *or* The
                                            right thing for us to do is to obey
                                            faithfully everything that God has
                                            commanded us.

It will be righteousness for us: the noun **righteousness** here can be
understood in two different ways (note the alternative translation given in TEV):
  (1) The people's merit, God's approval of them. So TEV has "God will be
      pleased with us," NJPSV "it will be to our merit before the LORD our God,"
      BRCL "our lives will be pleasing to him," and NRSV "we will be in the right."
  (2) The people's conduct. NJB has "For us, right living will mean this," FRCL
      "our conduct will be according to God's will," and TOB "We will be righteous
      if we . . ." (with a footnote indicating that this is the kind of conduct that
      leads God to approve the person and receive that person as his friend).
It is hard to decide which of these is the better rendering; a translator should
feel free to choose either one, and perhaps include an alternative rendering in
a footnote.

All this commandment: see 5.31.

For the rest of the verse, see 6.1.

Alternative models illustrating interpretation (2) are as follows:

• We will live [or, walk] our lives according to God's will, if we
   faithfully obey everything that he has commanded us.

● 	If we faithfully obey everything that God has commanded us, we will be living our lives as he wants us to.

2A-6. The LORD's own people (7.1-11)

RSV

1 "When the LORD your God brings you into the land which you are entering to take possession of it, and clears away many nations before you, the Hittites, the Girgashites, the Amorites, the Canaanites, the Perizzites, the Hivites, and the Jebusites, seven nations greater and mightier than yourselves, 2 and when the LORD your God gives them over to you, and you defeat them; then you must utterly destroy them; you shall make no covenant with them, and show no mercy to them. 3 You shall not make marriages with them, giving your daughters to their sons or taking their daughters for your sons. 4 For they would turn away your sons from following me, to serve other gods; then the anger of the LORD would be kindled against you, and he would destroy you quickly. 5 But thus shall you deal with them: you shall break down their altars, and dash in pieces their pillars, and hew down their Asherim, and burn their graven images with fire.

6 "For you are a people holy to the LORD your God; the LORD your God has chosen you to be a people for his own possession, out of all the peoples that are on the face of the earth. 7 It was not because you were more in number than any other people that the LORD set his love upon you and chose you, for you were the fewest of all peoples; 8 but it is because the LORD loves you, and is keeping the oath which he swore to your fathers, that the LORD has brought you out with a mighty hand, and redeemed you from the house of bondage, from the hand of Pharaoh king of Egypt. 9 Know therefore that the LORD your God is God, the faithful God who keeps covenant and steadfast love with those who love him and keep his commandments, to a thousand generations, 10 and requites to their face those who hate him, by destroying them; he will not be slack with him who hates him, he will requite him to his face. 11 You shall therefore be careful to do the commandment, and the statutes, and the ordinances, which I command you this day.

TEV
The LORD's Own People

1 "The LORD your God will bring you into the land that you are going to occupy, and he will drive many nations out of it. As you advance, he will drive out seven nations larger and more powerful than you: the Hittites, the Girgashites, the Amorites, the Canaanites, the Perizzites, the Hivites, and the Jebusites. 2 When the LORD your God places these people in your power and you defeat them, you must put them all to death. Do not make an alliance with them or show them any mercy. 3 Do not marry any of them, and do not let your children marry any of them, 4 because then they would lead your children away from the LORD to worship other gods. If that happens, the LORD will be angry with you and destroy you at once. 5 So then, tear down their altars, break their sacred stone pillars in pieces, cut down their symbols of the goddess Asherah, and burn their idols. 6 Do this because you belong to the LORD your God. From all the peoples on earth he chose you to be his own special people.

7 "The LORD did not love you and choose you because you outnumbered other peoples; you were the smallest nation on earth. 8 But the LORD loved you and wanted to keep the promise that he made to your ancestors. That is why he saved you by his great might and set you free from slavery to the king of Egypt. 9 Remember that the LORD your God is the only God and that he is faithful. He will keep his covenant and show his constant love to a thousand generations of those who love him and obey his commands, 10 but he will not hesitate to punish those who hate him. 11 Now then, obey what you have been taught; obey all the laws that I have given you today.

In this section Moses reminds the people of the obligations imposed on them by the covenant that Yahweh had made with them. If they faithfully obey the laws that God is giving them that very day through Moses (verse 11), then God will bless them. When they enter the Promised Land they must do away with the people living there and destroy their altars and idols. Israel is uniquely the people of Yahweh (verse 6) and must serve and worship him alone.

Section heading: translators may choose to have a separate section heading for verses 1-11; for example, "The LORD's Own People" (TEV) or "Israel belongs to Yahweh." However, they may have just one heading for the whole chapter; for example, "Israel and the People of Canaan" (NRSV) or "Driving Out the Nations" (NIV). This Handbook follows the first option.

7.1   RSV   TEV

"When the LORD your God brings you into the land which you are entering to take possession of it, and clears away many nations before you, the Hittites, the Girgashites, the Amorites, the Canaanites, the Perizzites, the Hivites, and the Jebusites, seven nations greater and mightier than yourselves,

"The LORD your God will bring you into the land that you are going to occupy, and he will drive many nations out of it. As you advance, he will drive out seven nations larger and more powerful than you: the Hittites, the Girgashites, the Amorites, the Canaanites, the Perizzites, the Hivites, and the Jebusites.

With the beginning of a new chapter and section, Moses may need to be reintroduced as the speaker; for example, "Moses said to the people of Israel: . . . ."

Verses 1-2 are one sentence, and some restructuring may be required, such as TEV has done.

Brings: or "takes" (see 6.10).

Take possession: see 2.12.

Clears away many nations before you: see 4.38. The verb means "expel," "drive out" (REB, TEV, NIV). For **before you** TEV has "as you advance." The **many nations** are seven in number; the list here is complete.

Seven nations greater and mightier than yourselves: **greater** means larger in number of population, and **mightier** (Note Exo 1.9) refers to the combined strength of a large population rather than the physical strength of each individual.

The meaning and origin of the names of these **seven nations** are matters of dispute among scholars. Some of these groups are said to have been descended from Noah's son Ham (Gen 10.6, 15-19), but the Handbook does not recommend that they appear as "the descendants of . . . ." The **Jebusites** are identified as the inhabitants of Jebus, that is, Jerusalem (Josh 15.8, 63), and so can be called "the people who lived in [the city of] Jebus." The **Canaanites** can also be called "a people who lived in [the land of] Canaan." It seems, however, that the best translation of all seven of these names is "the people called 'Hittites' " and so on, transliterating the proper names in accordance with the rules of the target language.

In restructuring the text, the information about the **seven nations** may be placed nearer to the beginning of the verse, as follows:

- The LORD your God is going to take you into the land that you will possess. Seven nations that have more people and are stronger than you live in that land: the Hittites, the Girgashites, the Amorites, the Canaanites, the Perizzites, the Hivites, and the Jebusites. As you advance [into the land] God will drive them all out.

7.2   RSV   TEV

and when the LORD your God gives them over to you, and you defeat them; then you must utterly destroy them; you shall make no covenant with them, and show no mercy to them.

When the LORD your God places these people in your power and you defeat them, you must put them all to death. Do not make an alliance with them or show them any mercy.

The LORD your God gives them over to you: the meaning is better expressed by "delivers them into your power" (REB), or "lets you have power over them." The Israelites will fight those nations, but it is God who will give them the victory.

Gives them . . . and you defeat them: the two events are one action. Instead of the time clause **When . . .** , it may be better to restructure as follows: "The LORD your God will deliver them into your power and you will defeat them. When this happens . . . ."

Utterly destroy them: this is the word appropriate to a holy war; see its use in 2.34.

Make no covenant with them: the Israelites are forbidden to make any kind of alliances or treaties with these pagan peoples. CEV has "Don't make any peace treaties with them."

Show no mercy to them: and the Israelites are to be completely ruthless as they kill off these people. The book of Deuteronomy is rich in the vocabulary of slaughter and destruction. This clause may be combined with the clause **you must utterly destroy them**; for example, "you must show them no mercy, but destroy them completely," or "Then you must destroy them without mercy" (CEV).

7.3   RSV   TEV

You shall not make marriages with them, giving your daughters to their sons or taking their daughters for your sons.

Do not marry any of them, and do not let your children marry any of them,

Marriages were arranged by the parents. The bride was the passive partner: she was "given" by her father to the groom, and was "taken" from her own father. RSV here is a better representation of the Hebrew than TEV: the **giving** and **taking** clauses are an explanation of the main verb, **make marriages**. In some cultures it may be impossible to represent this cultural element, and a general statement forbidding intermarriage will have to be satisfactory; for example, "and don't let your sons and daughters marry any of them."

7.4 RSV	TEV
For they would turn away your sons from following me, to serve other gods; then the anger of the LORD would be kindled against you, and he would destroy you quickly.	because then they would lead your children away from the LORD to worship other gods. If that happens, the LORD will be angry with you and destroy you at once.

They would turn away your sons from following me: the reason for the ban on intermarrying with these pagans is that the Israelite husband would be led by his pagan wife and her family to worship their god, thus forsaking Yahweh. To "follow" means to worship and to be faithful to. Since verse 3 refers to both sons and daughters, an alternative model is "If you do, these people will lead your children away from the LORD to worship . . ." (similarly TEV).

From following me: even though the text does not indicate that this is a quotation of Yahweh's words, **me** is not Moses here, but Yahweh (see TEV).

To serve other gods: in this context it means not only worship but also obedience to the laws and rules of the pagan religion. So it may be expressed as "worship and serve other gods." For **gods** see 3.24.

The anger of the LORD would be kindled against you: see 6.15.

Destroy: this translates a verb different from the one in 6.15 and the one in 7.10; but the meaning is the same. The Septuagint uses the same Greek verb to translate all three different Hebrew verbs.

Quickly: God would destroy them at once, without delay.

7.5 RSV	TEV
But thus shall you deal with them: you shall break down their altars, and dash in pieces their pillars, and hew down their Asherim, and burn their graven images with fire.	So then, tear down their altars, break their sacred stone pillars in pieces, cut down their symbols of the goddess Asherah, and burn their idols.

Following the prohibition to intermarry comes the command to destroy the idols and places of worship of the peoples of Canaan.

AN ALTAR FOR SACRIFICE

Break down their altars: **altars**, on which sacrifices were offered, were made of stone and dirt. Many modern cultures have similar elevated structures for sacrificing animals and offering gifts to a deity. Sometimes this is a stone or wood platform or table. Terms for such structures may be used here. However, in cultures where **altars** are unknown, we may say, for example, "place [or, platform] for sacrificing animals."

Dash in pieces their pillars: these **pillars** were made of stone, erected near the shrines of Baal, the chief god of the Canaanites. Such **pillars** were symbols of this god. TEV has "sacred stone pillars." An alternative model may be "stone pillars dedicated to the male god Baal."

Hew down their Asherim: these were wooden poles, dedicated to Asherah, the goddess of fertility and the partner or female counterpart of Baal. TEV has "cut down their symbols of the goddess Asherah"; but CEV is clearer, with "cut down the poles that they use in worshiping the goddess Asherah." "Goddess" may also be rendered as "female god."

Burn their graven images: these were wooden idols. For **graven images** see also 4.16.

7.6	RSV	TEV

"For you are a people holy to the LORD your God; the LORD your God has chosen you to be a people for his own possession, out of all the peoples that are on the face of the earth.

Do this because you belong to the LORD your God. From all the peoples on earth he chose you to be his own special people.

This verse offers the reason for Yahweh's commands. It is better to keep it in the same paragraph with verses 1-5, as TEV and NRSV do.

Here the Hebrew text switches from the second person plural of address to the second singular, but in some languages translators may need to keep the plural pronoun.

You are a people holy to the LORD your God: the adjective **holy** means being the exclusive possession of Yahweh their God, and thus complete dedication to him. Holiness is not primarily moral and spiritual purity; it is total commitment to the exclusive worship and service of God. So TEV has "Do this because you belong to the LORD your God," and CEV has "Israel, you are the chosen people of the LORD your God."

God has chosen you: the initiative is God's, not Israel's. The verb has the sense of choosing from among several options: **out of all the peoples**.

For his own possession: this is the meaning of holiness, "belonging exclusively to God."

On the face of the earth: it is not necessary to reproduce the Hebrew figure "face of the earth"; it is enough to say "all the world," or "the whole earth" (see 6.15).

NJPSV offers a good model for this verse:

• You are a people consecrated to the LORD your God; of all the peoples on earth the LORD your God chose you to be His treasured people.

However, in languages that do not use the passive voice, we may translate

• Israel, you belong to the LORD your God. There are many nations [or, peoples] in the world, but he chose only you to be his special people.

7.7   RSV   TEV

It was not because you were more in number than any other people that the LORD set his love upon you and chose you, for you were the fewest of all peoples;

"The LORD did not love you and choose you because you outnumbered other peoples; you were the smallest nation on earth.

The Israelites were not chosen because they were **more in number** than other peoples; on the contrary, they were **the fewest** in number. This may not literally have been the case; it is a way of pointing out that they were an insignificant people, of little power and no prestige.

The LORD set his love on you: NJPSV and NRSV have "set his heart on you," which is a more natural expression in English. The verb means "desire" or "want." The Septuagint translates with a verb that means "prefer," "choose."

And chose you: this additional verbal phrase may be joined to the previous one, as follows: "he decided you were the people he wanted, and so he chose you," and the whole verse may be restructured as follows:

- The LORD [or, Yahweh] decided that you were the people he wanted, and chose you. This was not because you had more people [or, were more numerous] than any other nation. Actually you were the smallest nation on earth.

7.8	RSV	TEV

but it is because the LORD loves you, and is keeping the oath which he swore to your fathers, that the LORD has brought you out with a mighty hand, and redeemed you from the house of bondage, from the hand of Pharaoh king of Egypt.

But the LORD loved you and wanted to keep the promise that he made to your ancestors. That is why he saved you by his great might and set you free from slavery to the king of Egypt.

The LORD loves you: the Hebrew verb here is different from the one in verse 7. For **love** in this sense see 4.37.

Is keeping the oath which he swore to your fathers: see this language in 1.8. To "swear an oath" is to make a solemn promise, that is, to make a promise and bind it with a vow or pledge. **Your fathers** are the ancestors, particularly the patriarchs Abraham, Isaac, and Jacob. For **fathers** or "ancestors" see 1.8. An alternative translation model for the first part of this verse is "The LORD loves you and wants to keep the solemn promise that he made to your ancestors."

Brought you out with a mighty hand: see 4.34. This contrasts well with **from the hand of Pharaoh** at the end of the verse.

For **the house of bondage** see 5.6.

Pharaoh king of Egypt: here the title **Pharaoh** is used as a proper name (see also 11.3). For **king** see 1.4.

7.9	RSV	TEV

Know therefore that the LORD your God is God, the faithful God who keeps covenant and steadfast love with those who love him and keep his commandments, to a thousand generations,

Remember that the LORD your God is the only God and that he is faithful. He will keep his covenant and show his constant love to a thousand generations of those who love him and obey his commands,

Know therefore: the force of the Hebrew verb is "Keep in mind," "Do not forget," and this is what TEV "Remember" is intended to mean. Other possible translations are "You must think about this carefully," "You must understand," or even "Be sure in your minds."

The LORD your God is God: this seems to mean that only Yahweh, the God of the Israelites, is God; none of the deities worshiped by the pagans is God. NJB translates "the true God" (similarly CEV); TEV "the only God"; NJPSV "only the LORD your God is God."

The faithful God: this stresses the fact that Yahweh keeps his promises; he does not abandon his people if they remain faithful to him. An alternative way to render this is "You can trust him to keep . . . ."

Keeps his covenant and steadfast love: for **covenant** see 4.13; **steadfast love**, 5.10. NRSV joins the two terms, "maintains covenant loyalty," but the phrase "covenant loyalty" is not simple or easy to translate. An alternative model is the following: "He will keep his covenant [or, agreement] and always loves those . . . ."

Those who love him and keep his commandments: Israel's love for Yahweh is shown by faithful obedience to his laws. Since this is referring to Yahweh's love for Israel, translators may change **those** to "you [plural]" (see CEV).

For a thousand generations: this modifies the expression of God's faithful love for his people. It is an expansion of 5.10 "thousands." In practical terms it means "forever," "for all time." The translation of **generations** may be difficult, as well as the representation of the number **a thousand**. It may be necessary to say, simply, "God does not change, and he keeps on loving his people forever."

An alternative translation model for this verse is:

- I want you [plural] to understand that Yahweh the God you worship is the true God. If you love him and obey his commands, you can trust him always to keep his covenant with you and to love you.

7.10   RSV   TEV

| and requites to their face those who hate him, by destroying them; he will not be slack with him who hates him, he will requite him to his face. | but he will not hesitate to punish those who hate him. |

And requites to their face . . . by destroying them: this is not natural English. NRSV "repays in their own person" is better, but REB is even better: "he repays with destruction." We can say something like "pays them back by destroying them," "punishes them with destruction," or "punishes them by destroying them."

Those who hate him: see the same expression, with the same meaning, in 5.9. Here NRSV has "reject," and REB "defy and reject," which may serve as good models.

The second part of the verse is practically redundant, but it is better to keep the redundancy, if it is emphatic, as in Hebrew. The Hebrew text switches from the plural to the singular person of address.

He will not be slack: this means he will not hesitate (TEV), he will not be slow, he will not delay. CEV has "He will quickly destroy you."

7.11 RSV TEV

You shall therefore be careful to do the commandment, and the statutes, and the ordinances, which I command you this day.

Now then, obey what you have been taught; obey all the laws that I have given you today.

Therefore refers to the statement about God in verses 9-10.
Be careful to do: see 6.3.
For **the commandment, and the statutes, and the ordinances**, see 6.1.

2A-7. The blessings of obedience (7.12-26)

RSV

TEV
The Blessings of Obedience

12 "And because you hearken to these ordinances, and keep and do them, the LORD your God will keep with you the covenant and the steadfast love which he swore to your fathers to keep; 13 he will love you, bless you, and multiply you; he will also bless the fruit of your body and the fruit of your ground, your grain and your wine and your oil, the increase of your cattle and the young of your flock, in the land which he swore to your fathers to give you. 14 You shall be blessed above all peoples; there shall not be male or female barren among you, or among your cattle. 15 And the LORD will take away from you all sickness; and none of the evil diseases of Egypt, which you knew, will he inflict upon you, but he will lay them upon all who hate you. 16 And you shall destroy all the peoples that the LORD your God will give over to you, your eye shall not pity them; neither shall you serve their gods, for that would be a snare to you.

17 "If you say in your heart, 'These nations are greater than I; how can I dispossess them?' 18 you shall not be afraid of them, but you shall remember what the LORD your God did to Pharaoh and to all Egypt, 19 the great trials which your eyes saw, the signs, the wonders, the mighty hand, and the outstretched arm, by which the LORD your God brought you out; so will the LORD your God do to all the peoples of whom you are afraid. 20 Moreover the LORD your God will send hornets among them, until those who are left and hide themselves from you are destroyed. 21 You shall not be in dread of them; for the LORD your God is in the midst of you, a great and terrible God. 22 The LORD your God will clear away these nations before you little by little; you may not make an end of them at once, lest the wild beasts grow too

12 "If you listen to these commands and obey them faithfully, then the LORD your God will continue to keep his covenant with you and will show you his constant love, as he promised your ancestors. 13 He will love you and bless you, so that you will increase in number and have many children; he will bless your fields, so that you will have grain, wine, and olive oil; and he will bless you by giving you many cattle and sheep. He will give you all these blessings in the land that he promised your ancestors he would give to you. 14 No people in the world will be as richly blessed as you. None of you nor any of your livestock will be sterile. 15 The LORD will protect you from all sickness, and he will not bring on you any of the dreadful diseases that you experienced in Egypt, but he will bring them on all your enemies. 16 Destroy every nation that the LORD your God places in your power, and do not show them any mercy. Do not worship their gods, for that would be fatal.

17 "Do not tell yourselves that these peoples outnumber you and that you cannot drive them out. 18 Do not be afraid of them; remember what the LORD your God did to the king of Egypt and to all his people. 19 Remember the terrible plagues that you saw with your own eyes, the miracles and wonders, and the great power and strength by which the LORD your God set you free. In the same way that he destroyed the Egyptians, he will destroy all these people that you now fear. 20 He will even cause panic among them and will destroy those who escape and go into hiding. 21 So do not be afraid of these people. The LORD your God is with you; he is a great God and one to be feared. 22 Little by little he will drive out these nations as you advance. You will not be able to

numerous for you. 23 But the LORD your God will give them over to you, and throw them into great confusion, until they are destroyed. 24 And he will give their kings into your hand, and you shall make their name perish from under heaven; not a man shall be able to stand against you, until you have destroyed them. 25 The graven images of their gods you shall burn with fire; you shall not covet the silver or the gold that is on them, or take it for yourselves, lest you be ensnared by it; for it is an abomination to the LORD your God. 26 And you shall not bring an abominable thing into your house, and become accursed like it; you shall utterly detest and abhor it; for it is an accursed thing.

destroy them all at once, for, if you did, the number of wild animals would increase and be a threat to you. 23 The LORD will put your enemies in your power and make them panic until they are destroyed. 24 He will put their kings in your power. You will kill them, and they will be forgotten. No one will be able to stop you; you will destroy everyone. 25 Burn their idols. Do not desire the silver or gold that is on them, and do not take it for yourselves. If you do, that will be fatal, because the LORD hates idolatry. 26 Do not bring any of these idols into your homes, or the same curse will be on you that is on them. You must hate and despise these idols, because they are under the LORD's curse.

The blessings that will follow strict obedience to Yahweh's commands are great: fertile people and flocks, rich soil, health, prosperity, complete victory over their enemies. This will all come if they, the Israelites, kill their enemies, so that all memory of them will disappear; and they must also destroy their shrines and idols.

Section heading: TEV has the heading "The Blessings of Obedience," and CEV has "The LORD Will Bless You if You Obey." Another model may be "If you obey Yahweh he will cause you to prosper."

7.12 RSV	TEV
"And because you hearken to these ordinances, and keep and do them, the LORD your God will keep with you the covenant and the steadfast love which he swore to your fathers to keep;	"If you listen to these commands and obey them faithfully, then the LORD your God will continue to keep his covenant with you and will show you his constant love, as he promised your ancestors.

With the beginning of this new section, it may be good to introduce Moses again as the speaker; for example, "Moses continued to speak to the Israelites." Verses 12-13 are one sentence in Hebrew; in translation it is better to split up into two sentences at least.

Because you hearken: it is better to translate "If you pay attention to . . . ."
For **ordinances** see 4.1.

Keep and do them: this is redundant, for emphasis. The sense is "faithfully obey them," "always put them into practice."

Will keep with you the covenant and the steadfast love: see verse 9. In this context, however, the idea of continuity is present: "Then the LORD your God will continue to keep his covenant . . . and will always love you" (TEV).

Which he swore to your fathers: see verse 8.

7.13   RSV   TEV

he will love you, bless you, and mul-   He will love you and bless you, so
tiply you; he will also bless the fruit   that you will increase in number and
of your body and the fruit of your   have many children; he will bless
ground, your grain and your wine   your fields, so that you will have
and your oil, the increase of your   grain, wine, and olive oil; and he will
cattle and the young of your flock, in   bless you by giving you many cattle
the land which he swore to your   and sheep. He will give you all these
fathers to give you.   blessings in the land that he prom-
                                          ised your ancestors he would give to
                                          you.

The statement **love you, bless you, and multiply you** is fairly simple and
easy to understand. To **bless** is to cause good things to happen, to bestow
benefits on, or "cause you to prosper"; **multiply** means to cause to increase in
number.

The fruit of your body: here **body** represents the ability to have children, and
fruit means offspring or children. **Multiply you** and **bless the fruit of your body**
have the same meaning, so we may combine the two clauses and say, for
example, "He will cause you to prosper by giving you many children."

The fruit of your ground: this is a promise of abundant crops, as follows:
grain (wheat and barley), **wine** (grapevines, vineyards), **oil** (olive trees, the oil
being derived from olives). **Wine** is a fermented drink made from grapes (see
also 6.1 for **wine** and "olives").

Your cattle and the young of your flock: in this context **cattle** refers to bulls
and cows, and **flock** to goats and sheep. See similar lists in 11.14; 12.17; 14.23.
In some languages this sentence will be expressed something like "Your herds
of animals named 'cow' will have many babies [offspring]. So also will your
animals named 'sheep' and 'goat.'"

For **in the land which he swore . . .**, see 1.8.

7.14   RSV   TEV

You shall be blessed above all peo-   No people in the world will be as
ples; there shall not be male or fe-   richly blessed as you. None of you
male barren among you, or among   nor any of your livestock will be
your cattle.   sterile.

You shall be blessed above . . . : this may be expressed by the active voice,
"The LORD your God will bless you more than any other people," or "The LORD
your God will make you more prosperous [or, have more things] than . . . ."

There shall not be male or female barren among you: **barren** means inability
for a **male** to beget, or for a **female** to bear children. In some languages two
different words may be required. NRSV has "neither sterility nor barrenness,"
REB "an impotent male or a barren female."

Your cattle: this is livestock in general (see 2.35), not only cows as in the previous verse. In some languages, speaking about animals being **barren** may require different words from those used for people.

An alternative translation model for this verse is:

- God will cause you to prosper more than any other people. No male among you or your animals will be impotent and no female will be sterile.

7.15   RSV   TEV

And the LORD will take away from you all sickness; and none of the evil diseases of Egypt, which you knew, will he inflict upon you, but he will lay them upon all who hate you.	The LORD will protect you from all sickness, and he will not bring on you any of the dreadful diseases that you experienced in Egypt, but he will bring them on all your enemies.

Take away from you all sickness: this does not only mean that God will heal them from their illnesses, but that he will not allow them to get sick. REB "will keep you free from all sickness" or TEV "will protect you from all sicknesses" are better than RSV.

None of the evil diseases of Egypt: this is the negative counterpart of the blessings: "he will not inflict on you any of the evil diseases of Egypt." These **diseases** are probably the plagues (so NJB "evil plagues"); most translations use the more general "dreadful diseases" (NJPSV, TEV) or "terrible diseases" (NIV). Some of the most common diseases in Egypt included skin diseases, boils, eye infections, bowel dysfunctions. God will keep his people free from such diseases and will inflict them (**lay them**) upon their enemies.

Which you knew: this does not mean that the Israelites themselves had experienced these diseases (as TEV translates), but that they knew about them ("about which you know," NJPSV). The Septuagint has "which you saw and knew."

7.16   RSV   TEV

And you shall destroy all the peoples that the LORD your God will give over to you, your eye shall not pity them; neither shall you serve their gods, for that would be a snare to you.	Destroy every nation that the LORD your God places in your power, and do not show them any mercy. Do not worship their gods, for that would be fatal.

You shall destroy all: the Israelites are commanded, again, to wipe out their enemies. The Hebrew verb here is "to eat," meaning here to consume, to destroy. God will deliver the enemy into their power (see verse 2).

Your eye shall not pity them: they are to show no mercy as they exterminate them.

There follows a final warning against idolatry: **neither shall you serve their gods**.

A snare to you: this trap into which they will be caught, like a wild animal, will deprive them of their freedom and eventually kill them. So we may translate "Don't worship their gods; it would be like letting yourselves be caught in a trap." The two clauses may also be combined; for example, "Don't get trapped into worshiping other gods" or "Don't let your hearts deceive you into worshiping and serving other gods."

7.17   RSV   TEV

"**If you say in your heart, 'These   "Do not tell yourselves that these
nations are greater than I; how can I   peoples outnumber you and that you
dispossess them?'   cannot drive them out.**

Verses 17-19 are one long sentence, which should be broken up into shorter ones, as TEV does.

Besides TEV, REB offers a good model for verse 17: "You may say to yourselves, 'These nations outnumber us; how can we drive them out?' "

If you say in your heart: that is, "say to yourself" or "think." Hebrew here is singular, but most languages will use plural, referring to all the people. Other ways to express this are "Do not tell yourselves" (TEV), or "You may be thinking . . . [18] But stop worrying!" (CEV).

Greater than I: this means more numerous, more powerful (see 1.28).

Dispossess: this means to expel or drive out.

CEV has a helpful model for this verse:

● You may be thinking, "How can we destroy these nations? They are more powerful than we are." [18] But stop worrying!

7.18   RSV   TEV

**you shall not be afraid of them, but   Do not be afraid of them; remember
you shall remember what the LORD   what the LORD your God did to the
your God did to Pharaoh and to all   king of Egypt and to all his people.
Egypt,**

The people are told that they must recall what God had done to the king of Egypt and all the other Egyptians when he took the Israelites out of there.

The verb form of **you shall remember** is emphatic: "you must always remember and never forget." Such remembrance will cause the Israelites to lose their fear of the peoples of Canaan, as they invade the land. **Remember** may also be expressed as "bring to mind," "recall," and so on.

Pharaoh: see 6.22.

All Egypt: this could mean the land, but more likely it means the people, "all the Egyptians." So TEV has "to the king of Egypt and all his people." We may also say "to all the people of Egypt and their king."

7.19   RSV   TEV

the great trials which your eyes saw, the signs, the wonders, the mighty hand, and the outstretched arm, by which the LORD your God brought you out; so will the LORD your God do to all the peoples of whom you are afraid.	Remember the terrible plagues that you saw with your own eyes, the miracles and wonders, and the great power and strength by which the LORD your God set you free. In the same way that he destroyed the Egyptians, he will destroy all these people that you now fear.

This verse lists the events the Israelites witnessed in Egypt, all of them referring to the plagues God sent on the land and the people.

The great trials: here **trials** means "sufferings" or "ordeals," referring to the plagues (see TEV).

Which your eyes saw: TEV has "that you saw with your own eyes." They had been eyewitnesses of all the plagues.

The signs, the wonders: see 4.24.

The mighty hand, and the outstretched arm: see 4.34.

So will the LORD your God do: God will send on the peoples of Canaan the same disasters he sent on the Egyptians. So TEV has "In the same way that he destroyed the Egyptians" (see NRSV "The LORD your God will do the same . . . .").

All the peoples of whom you are afraid: see the list in verse 1.

7.20   RSV   TEV

Moreover the LORD your God will send hornets among them, until those who are left and hide themselves from you are destroyed.	He will even cause panic[i] among them and will destroy those who escape and go into hiding.
	[i] cause panic; *or* send hornets, *or* send plagues.

Hornets: it is not certain what this means. The word appears also in Exo 23.28 (where it is parallel with "my terror" in verse 27) and in Josh 24.12. TEV has "send panic" (similarly CEV) with alternative renderings. "Panic" suggests a sudden fear or desire to run away because of being terrified. POCL has "a great terror"; NJPSV "a plague"; the New Jewish Version, "a plague," with a footnote: "meaning of Heb uncertain"; REB "will spread panic." NRSV "the pestilence" is hard to understand. Whatever the disaster, the people who had been able to hide and escape being slaughtered by the Israelites will be killed by it.

Translators are urged to follow TEV, giving alternatives in a footnote. It is also possible to restructure the verse as follows:

● They may try to escape from you by hiding, but Yahweh will cause them to be filled with terror [panic] and will kill them all.

7.21 RSV TEV

You shall not be in dread of them; for the LORD your God is in the midst of you, a great and terrible God. So do not be afraid of these people. The LORD your God is with you; he is a great God and one to be feared.

You shall not be in dread of them: the same verb is used in 1.29 (see the comment there). **Them** refers to the peoples of Canaan, the enemies of the Israelites.

In the midst of you: see 6.15.

A great and terrible God: great can mean many things, depending on the context. In this verse it means that God is all powerful, and no other god can compare with him. In cultures where kings or high chiefs still rule, there will be natural expressions meaning "majestic," "above the heads of all," and so on. These will fit this context very well. However, in other languages it will often be necessary to use two or more terms; for example, "God is all-powerful and above every other god." The word **terrible** means here "awesome" (NRSV, NJPSV, NIV); it is derived from the Hebrew verb "to fear," and the meaning of this passive form is "one who is to be feared" or "one whom you should fear [or, be afraid of]."

7.22 RSV TEV

The LORD your God will clear away these nations before you little by little; you may not make an end of them at once,[f] **lest the wild beasts grow too numerous for you.** Little by little he will drive out these nations as you advance. You will not be able to destroy them all at once, for, if you did, the number of wild animals would increase and be a threat to you.

[f] Or *quickly*

Will clear away these nations before you: God will drive them out as the Israelites advance (see verse 1).

Little by little: this means God will do this gradually, not all at once. The reason for this strategy is given in the following statement.

You may not make an end of them at once: that is, ". . . not finish them off immediately." This would upset the balance of nature (the ecological balance). Exo 23.29-30 has a fuller statement of the matter. If all the native peoples of Canaan were killed, there would be an unusual increase in the number of wild animals, which would be a danger for the Israelites. Instead of **at once** here, Exo 23.30 has "in one year."

Wild beasts may be expressed as "forest [or, jungle] animals" in many languages, or "nondomestic animals" in others.

TEV is a helpful translation model for this verse, as is CEV:

● As you attack these nations, the LORD will force them out little by little. He won't let you get rid of them all at once—if he did, there wouldn't be enough people living in the land to keep down the number of wild animals.

7.23   RSV   TEV

But the LORD your God will give them over to you, and throw them into great confusion, until they are destroyed.	The LORD will put your enemies in your power and make them panic until they are destroyed.

This verse repeats the essence of verses 21-22.

Give them over to you: see verse 2.

Throw them into great confusion: exactly what God will do is not stated; whatever it is, it will cause the enemies to be afraid. NJPSV has "throw them into utter panic," NRSV "great panic." See verse 20 and similar expressions in Exo 14.24; 23.27.

Until they are destroyed: see verse 7.

7.24   RSV   TEV

And he will give their kings into your hand, and you shall make their name perish from under heaven; not a man shall be able to stand against you, until you have destroyed them.	He will put their kings in your power. You will kill them, and they will be forgotten. No one will be able to stop you; you will destroy everyone.

Give . . . into your hand means the same as "give over to you" in verses 2, 16. For **kings** see 1.4.

Make their name perish from under heaven: once the people are killed they will not have any descendants to carry on the family name. Or else the meaning of this statement may be that they will be completely forgotten; no one will remember them or their deeds. TEV has "and they will be forgotten," and CEV has "No one will remember they ever lived." **From under heaven** means simply "on earth."

Stand against you: that is, "resist you successfully" or "stop you" (TEV).

Destroyed: the same verb that is used in verse 23.

7.25 RSV TEV

The graven images of their gods you shall burn with fire; you shall not covet the silver or the gold that is on them, or take it for yourselves, lest you be ensnared by it; for it is an abomination to the LORD your God.

Burn their idols. Do not desire the silver or gold that is on them, and do not take it for yourselves. If you do, that will be fatal, because the LORD hates idolatry.

All objects of worship of pagan gods are to be destroyed, to avoid the possibility of the Israelites being drawn to worship them.

Graven images: these are idols of wood and metal (see 4.16; 5.8).

Burn with fire: see a similar phrase at 7.5.

Covet the silver or the gold: for **covet** see 5.21. Even **the silver** and **the gold** that was on the idols must be destroyed. These were wooden idols overlaid with silver or gold; the Israelites were to melt the metal off them and throw it away.

Lest you be ensnared by it: see the same idea (but not the same Hebrew word) in verse 16. CEV has "Don't get trapped into wanting the silver or gold on an idol." Another way to express this is "Don't let your hearts lead you into wanting the silver . . . ."

An abomination: this is something so hateful, so terrible, that it produces the strongest dislike. It may be expressed as "detestable" (NJB, NIV) or "abhorrent" (NJPSV, NRSV). POCL has "is horrified with these things"; BRCL "to worship idols is a disgusting thing"; TEV "because the LORD hates idolatry"; CEV "is disgusting to the LORD." We may also say "makes the LORD's insides turn over."

7.26 RSV TEV

And you shall not bring an abominable thing into your house, and become accursed like it; you shall utterly detest and abhor it; for it is an accursed thing.

Do not bring any of these idols into your homes, or the same curse will be on you that is on them. You must hate and despise these idols, because they are under the LORD's curse.

An abominable thing: this is the same word as "abomination" in verse 25. Here it has the particular meaning of a pagan idol. TEV has "Do not bring any of these idols into your homes"; but it is also possible to express this as "Do not bring any of these disgusting things into . . . ."

Become accursed like it: the verb here is the same one used in 2.34, and means to come under God's "curse," that is, God's condemnation and punishment. A person who comes into contact with an object devoted to destruction will suffer the same punishment (see Josh 6.18; 7.12). In languages that do not use the passive voice, we may say, for example, "Because God will destroy you as he destroyed . . . ."

Utterly detest and abhor: these terms have the same meaning; the structure of the Hebrew is very emphatic, using each verb twice in two different forms.

RSV tries to represent this by using the adverb **utterly**. The verb for **abhor** is the same verb root used for the noun **abomination** (verse 25). TEV has "You must hate and despise these idols."

2A-8. A good land to be possessed (8.1-10)

RSV	TEV
	A Good Land to Be Possessed

RSV	TEV
1 "All the commandment which I command you this day you shall be careful to do, that you may live and multiply, and go in and possess the land which the LORD swore to give to your fathers. 2 And you shall remember all the way which the LORD your God has led you these forty years in the wilderness, that he might humble you, testing you to know what was in your heart, whether you would keep his commandments, or not. 3 And he humbled you and let you hunger and fed you with manna, which you did not know, nor did your fathers know; that he might make you know that man does not live by bread alone, but that man lives by everything that proceeds out of the mouth of the LORD. 4 Your clothing did not wear out upon you, and your foot did not swell, these forty years. 5 Know then in your heart that, as a man disciplines his son, the LORD your God disciplines you. 6 So you shall keep the commandments of the LORD your God, by walking in his ways and by fearing him. 7 For the LORD your God is bringing you into a good land, a land of brooks of water, of fountains and springs, flowing forth in valleys and hills, 8 a land of wheat and barley, of vines and fig trees and pomegranates, a land of olive trees and honey, 9 a land in which you will eat bread without scarcity, in which you will lack nothing, a land whose stones are iron, and out of whose hills you can dig copper. 10 And you shall eat and be full, and you shall bless the LORD your God for the good land he has given you.	1 "Obey faithfully all the laws that I have given you today, so that you may live, increase in number, and occupy the land that the LORD promised to your ancestors. 2 Remember how the LORD your God led you on this long journey through the desert these past forty years, sending hardships to test you, so that he might know what you intended to do and whether you would obey his commands. 3 He made you go hungry, and then he gave you manna to eat, food that you and your ancestors had never eaten before. He did this to teach you that you must not depend on bread alone to sustain you, but on everything that the LORD says. 4 During these forty years your clothes have not worn out, nor have your feet swollen up. 5 Remember that the LORD your God corrects and punishes you just as parents discipline their children. 6 So then, do as the LORD has commanded you: live according to his laws and obey him. 7 The LORD your God is bringing you into a fertile land—a land that has rivers and springs, and underground streams gushing out into the valleys and hills; 8 a land that produces wheat and barley, grapes, figs, pomegranates, olives, and honey. 9 There you will never go hungry or ever be in need. Its rocks have iron in them, and from its hills you can mine copper. 10 You will have all you want to eat, and you will give thanks to the LORD your God for the fertile land that he has given you.

In this section Moses reminds the Israelites of what had happened to them during the forty years they had been wandering in the wilderness. The lessons they had learned should not be forgotten as they prepare to enter the good land that Yahweh is giving them.

Section heading: the TEV section heading "A Good Land to be Possessed" covers only verses 1-10, as does FRCL "The LORD has disciplined Israel in the desert" (see verse 5). NRSV "The LORD provides" and NIV "Do Not Forget the LORD" cover the entire chapter. Translators are urged to follow TEV and FRCL.

8.1 RSV TEV

"All the commandment which I command you this day you shall be careful to do, that you may live and multiply, and go in and possess the land which the LORD swore to give to your fathers.

"Obey faithfully all the laws that I have given you today, so that you may live, increase in number, and occupy the land that the LORD promised to your ancestors.

With the beginning of a new chapter and a new section, translators may need to indicate that Moses is still speaking to the people of Israel. The second person singular of address is used in the Hebrew text, but many translators will prefer to use the plural form.

All the commandment: see 6.25. This includes all the laws. For **commandment** see 4.2.

Be careful to do: that is, "Do your best to obey," "Obey faithfully" (TEV), or "Be sure that you obey" (CEV).

Live and multiply: this means to continue living in the land and to increase in number (see 7.13).

Swore to give to your fathers: see 1.8.

8.2 RSV TEV

And you shall remember all the way which the LORD your God has led you these forty years in the wilderness, that he might humble you, testing you to know what was in your heart, whether you would keep his commandments, or not.

Remember how the LORD your God led you on this long journey through the desert these past forty years, sending hardships to test you, so that he might know what you intended to do and whether you would obey his commands.

You shall remember all the way . . . in the wilderness: the forty years they have spent traveling through the wilderness is not something they will soon forget. The command **remember** is for them to recall and ponder the meaning of their forty years' experience. In some languages the negative "Don't forget" will be more natural style. For **wilderness** see 1.1.

That he might humble you: the structure of the Hebrew expresses the purpose of God through a conjunction and a sequence of three verbs, "in order to humble . . . testing . . . to know" (NRSV). This can also be expressed as "because he wanted to humble you . . ." or "because he wanted to make you submissive to him." **Humble** is not in the sense of "humiliate" but means to make the people submissive and teachable, to get rid of their proud sense of self-sufficiency by making them endure all sorts of hardships.

Testing you: they endured trying experiences because God wanted to learn their motives and their loyalty to him. "Test" here does not mean "tempt." NJPSV joins the two verbs "humble" and "test" into one phrase, "test you by hardships" (similarly TEV). An alternative model may be "causing you to endure hardships to test you."

To know what was in your heart: the purpose of the hardships was to reveal their disposition and will (TEV "what you intended"), especially to find out whether or not they would obey God's **commandments** (see 4.2). CEV "He wanted to find out . . ." may be a useful model for some translators.

8.3   RSV   TEV

And he humbled you and let you hunger and fed you with manna, which you did not know, nor did your fathers know; that he might make you know that man does not live by bread alone, but that man lives by everything that proceeds out of the mouth of the LORD.	He made you go hungry, and then he gave you manna to eat, food that you and your ancestors had never eaten before. He did this to teach you that you must not depend on bread alone to sustain you, but on everything that the LORD says.

He humbled you: as in verse 2.

Let you hunger: God did not always provide food for them. TEV has "made you go hungry," where "made" is the equivalent of **humbled**, referring back to "sending hardships" in verse 2. This is a possible model.

Fed you with manna: or "gave you manna to eat" (TEV). See Exo 16; Num 11.7-8.

Which you did not know, nor did your fathers know: this can be joined into one statement, as TEV has done; or else we can say "food that neither you nor your ancestors had ever heard about" (or, eaten). For **fathers** see 1.8.

He might make you know: they were meant to learn from these experiences. So TEV "He did this to teach you."

Man does not live by bread alone, but that man lives by everything that proceeds out of the mouth of the LORD: in English this is needlessly wordy; see TEV. In avoiding the exclusive "man," NRSV uses the impersonal "one does not live by bread alone," which doesn't sound right in the context. "People" is a better alternative. Instead of **bread** the word "food" should be used. The main lesson here is that it is not what a person can acquire by his or her own power that keeps that person alive and healthy, but obedience to God's commands. And this does not apply only to individuals; it applies to the people as a whole, as God's people.

An alternative model for the final part of this verse can be:

● God wanted to teach you that food alone is not enough to keep us [or, people] alive; to stay alive we need [or, everyone needs] everything that the LORD commands.

This statement is quoted by Jesus in Matt 4.4; Luke 4.4.

8.4   RSV   TEV

Your clothing did not wear out upon you, and your foot did not swell, these forty years.	During these forty years your clothes have not worn out, nor have your feet swollen up.

The Hebrew text uses the second singular form of address, but translators are urged to use the plural form, unless the singular is more natural style in their language. We may say something like the following: "Your [plural] clothes haven't worn out and your [plural] feet haven't swollen up."

Your clothing did not wear out and your foot did not swell: from walking through the wilderness all those years. This is an exaggerated way of saying that they had come through those difficult forty years in good shape (see also 29.5; Neh 9.21).

For **these forty years** see verse 2.

8.5   RSV   TEV

Know then in your heart that, as a man disciplines his son, the LORD your God disciplines you.	Remember that the LORD your God corrects and punishes you just as parents discipline their children.

Know then in your heart: to "know in the heart" means to be aware of, to realize, or to be convinced about. See the comment on a similar word at 4.39 and 7.9.

As a man disciplines his son: the inclusive plural may be adopted; see TEV "Remember that the LORD your God corrects and punishes you . . . just as parents discipline their children"; NRSV has "as a parent disciplines a child." Given the culture of the time, however, the exclusive "father" and "son" may be more appropriate in certain languages.

The verb **discipline** may mean to correct or punish, or to train or teach. The second option seems preferable here (see 4.36).

For **the LORD your God** see 1.6.

8.6   RSV   TEV

So you shall keep the command-ments of the LORD your God, by walking in his ways and by fearing him.	So then, do as the LORD has com-manded you: live according to his laws and obey him.

The way to obey Yahweh's **commandments** is **by walking in his ways**, that is, with conduct that conforms to God's laws. God's paths (**his ways**) are not the paths he walks in but the paths God lays down for his people. In some languages this will be expressed figuratively as "walk your lives according to God's laws" or even "walk along the path that God has set down for you."

Fearing him: as in 4.10.

8.7   RSV   TEV

For the LORD your God is bringing   The LORD your God is bringing you
you into a good land, a land of   into a fertile land—a land that has
brooks of water, of fountains and   rivers and springs, and underground
springs, flowing forth in valleys and streams gushing out into the valleys
hills,   and hills;

Verses 7-9 are one sentence in Hebrew, long but not complex, that describes the excellencies of the Promised Land.

Is bringing you: in some languages this will be expressed as "is taking you."
A good land: see 1.25.

Brooks of water, fountains, and springs: some languages may not have three different words for free-running **springs** and **brooks**. NRSV is better than RSV: "a land with flowing springs, with springs and underground waters welling up in valleys and hills" (REB is similar; see also TEV). Streams are normally formed from the water produced by springs up in the mountains. This seems to be what this passage is speaking about. CEV brings this idea out, with "streams that flow from springs in the valleys and hills." In dry areas or small flat islands in the ocean, "springs" may not exist. In such a case translators will need to use a descriptive phrase; for example, "places where water flows out of the ground [or, rock]."

We may translate this verse as:

● The LORD your God is bringing [or, taking] you into a fertile land. It's a land that has streams that are formed by water pouring out of places in the mountains.

8.8   RSV   TEV

a land of wheat and barley, of vines   a land that produces wheat and bar-
and fig trees and pomegranates, a   ley, grapes, figs, pomegranates,
land of olive trees and honey,   olives, and honey.

Here agricultural items are listed; these are all cultivated, not wild, except possibly the **honey** (see 32.13).

Wheat and **barley** were grain crops from which bread was made. In cultures where they are unknown, and a general term for "grain" is available, that term should be used here; for example, "grains named 'wheat' and 'barley.' " If such a general term is not available, we may use a phrase suggesting a similarity to grains that are known; for example, "rice-like plants named 'wheat' and 'barley.' " In some areas a general word for "fruit' may be employed for crops that have grains and must be threshed; for example, "fruits called 'wheat' and 'barley.' "

For **vines** see **vineyards** at 6.11. **Figs** may be rendered as "a sweet fruit named fig." **Pomegranates** are the fruit of a small tree of the same name found in west Asia and north Africa. They are red and shiny, about the size of a small apple. In cultures where this fruit is unknown, we may say "a fruit named pomegranate." After these first instances of "fig" and "pomegranate," translators may simply use the borrowed word without saying "a fruit named . . . ." For **olives** see 6.11. It will be helpful to include notes in the glossary describing these various types of fruit. Further information may be found in FFB.

For **milk and honey** see 6.3.

8.9 RSV	TEV
a land in which you will eat bread without scarcity, in which you will lack nothing, a land whose stones are iron, and out of whose hills you can dig copper.	There you will never go hungry or ever be in need. Its rocks have iron in them, and from its hills you can mine copper.

Eat bread without scarcity: or "never go hungry" (TEV). They will always have plenty of food to eat.

You will lack nothing: all their needs will be supplied.

Stones are iron: there will be plentiful iron ore in Canaan, and this may be expressed as "the rocks are full of iron ore."

Dig copper: in English, at least, "to mine copper" is more natural (so NRSV, TEV).

8.10 RSV	TEV
And you shall eat and be full, and you shall bless the LORD your God for the good land he has given you.	You will have all you want to eat, and you will give thanks to the LORD your God for the fertile land that he has given you.

Eat and be full repeats the thought of "without scarcity" in the previous verse.

You shall bless the LORD your God: here the verb "to bless" means to praise, to speak well of God for his goodness. In certain languages this will be expressed with direct speech; for example, "You shall say to God, 'You are wonderful [or, good] for giving us . . . .' "

2A-9. Warnings against forgetting the LORD (8.11-20)

RSV

TEV

Warnings against Forgetting the LORD

11 "Take heed lest you forget the LORD your God, by not keeping his commandments and his ordinances and his statutes, which I command you this day: 12 lest, when you have eaten and are full, and have built goodly houses and live in them, 13 and when your herds and flocks multiply, and your silver and gold is multiplied, and all that you have is multiplied, 14 then your heart be lifted up, and you forget the LORD your God, who brought you out of the land of Egypt, out of the house of bondage, 15 who led you through the great and terrible wilderness, with its fiery serpents and scorpions and thirsty ground where there was no water, who brought you water out of the flinty rock, 16 who fed you in the wilderness with manna which your fathers did not know, that he might humble you and test you, to do you good in the end. 17 Beware lest you say in your heart, 'My power and the might of my hand have gotten me this wealth.' 18 You shall remember the LORD your God, for it is he who gives you power to get wealth; that he may confirm his covenant which he swore to your fathers, as at this day. 19 And if you forget the LORD your God and go after other gods and serve them and worship them, I solemnly warn you this day that you shall surely perish. 20 Like the nations that the LORD makes to perish before you, so shall you perish, because you would not obey the voice of the LORD your God.

11 "Make certain that you do not forget the LORD your God; do not fail to obey any of his laws that I am giving you today. 12 When you have all you want to eat and have built good houses to live in 13 and when your cattle and sheep, your silver and gold, and all your other possessions have increased, 14 be sure that you do not become proud and forget the LORD your God who rescued you from Egypt, where you were slaves. 15 He led you through that vast and terrifying desert where there were poisonous snakes and scorpions. In that dry and waterless land he made water flow out of solid rock for you. 16 In the desert he gave you manna to eat, food that your ancestors had never eaten. He sent hardships on you to test you, so that in the end he could bless you with good things. 17 So then, you must never think that you have made yourselves wealthy by your own power and strength. 18 Remember that it is the LORD your God who gives you the power to become rich. He does this because he is still faithful today to the covenant that he made with your ancestors. 19 Never forget the LORD your God or turn to other gods to worship and serve them. If you do, then I warn you today that you will certainly be destroyed. 20 If you do not obey the LORD, then you will be destroyed just like those nations that he is going to destroy as you advance.

The major theme in this section is the warning against forgetting (verses 11, 14, 19) and the command to remember (verse 18). The section ends with a severe threat of complete destruction, if the Israelites do not obey the LORD their God.

Section heading: TEV has "Warnings against Forgetting the LORD," and CEV has "Don't Forget the LORD." Either of these models may be followed.

8.11   RSV   TEV

"Take heed lest you forget the LORD your God, by not keeping his commandments and his ordinances and his statutes, which I command you this day:

"Make certain that you do not forget the LORD your God; do not fail to obey any of his laws that I am giving you today.

With the beginning of this new section, it may be helpful to show that Moses is still speaking; for example, "Moses said to the people of Israel: . . . ."

Verses 11-16 are one long sentence in Hebrew, which can be easily broken up in translation. Even in TEV verses 12-14 are one sentence, which may be too long for some languages. CEV breaks this up into four sentences.

Take heed lest you forget: see 4.9, 15, 23.

By not keeping: that is, "by disregarding," "by disobeying."

Commandments . . . ordinances . . . statutes: see 4.1, 2.

Which I command you this day: see 4.2.

8.12	RSV	TEV

lest, when you have eaten and are full, and have built goodly houses and live in them,	**When you have all you want to eat and have built good houses to live in**

Lest refers back to "Take heed lest . . ." at the beginning of verse 11, and also connects with the beginning of verse 14 ". . . then your hearts be lifted up." This calls for restructuring, and translations such as TEV, FRCL, SPCL, and BRCL can serve as good models. TEV, for example, doesn't use the archaic **lest** but begins verse 14 with "be sure," echoing "Make certain" at the beginning of verse 11. See the alternative model at the end of verse 14.

When you have eaten points forward to the clause "then your heart be lifted up" (beginning of verse 14). For **eaten and are full** TEV has "You have all you want to eat," and CEV has "have plenty to eat."

Goodly houses: "fine houses" (NRSV) is today's English; "beautiful" or "magnificent" are other possibilities.

8.13	RSV	TEV

and when your herds and flocks multiply, and your silver and gold is multiplied, and all that you have is multiplied,	**and when your cattle and sheep, your silver and gold, and all your other possessions have increased,**

Your herds and flocks multiply: see 2.35 and 7.13. **Herds** are cattle, **flocks** are goats and sheep. CEV has "You will get more and more cattle, sheep . . ."; or we may say "You will get more and more cows, sheep, and goats."

Your silver and gold is multiplied: essentially, this means that they will get richer. If translators choose to not use **silver** and **gold**, the word "money" should not be used, but the general term "wealth," or the adjective "rich": "you will get richer."

All you have: this is a summary statement for all their possessions.

8.14   RSV   TEV

| then your heart be lifted up, and you forget the LORD your God, who brought you out of the land of Egypt, out of the house of bondage, | be sure that you do not become proud and forget the LORD your God who rescued you from Egypt, where you were slaves. |

Your heart be lifted up: this means pride. It can be expressed as "you become proud," or figuratively "you have a high heart [or, liver]." In at least one other language it is expressed as "you have become aggressive and fatter."

You forget the LORD your God: see verse 11.

The house of bondage: see 5.6.

An alternative translation model for verses 11-14 is the following:

- ¹¹ Make sure [or, certain] that you do not forget the LORD your God or disobey his laws and teachings that I am giving you today. ¹² You will have all you want to eat, you will build beautiful houses and live in them. ¹³ Your herds and flocks will keep growing larger, and you will acquire more and more silver and gold. All your possessions will increase. ¹⁴ Be very careful, then, that when all this happens you don't become proud. Don't forget that you once worked like slaves in Egypt, and that it was the LORD your God who set you free.

8.15   RSV   TEV

| who led you through the great and terrible wilderness, with its fiery serpents and scorpions and thirsty ground where there was no water, who brought you water out of the flinty rock, | He led you through that vast and terrifying desert where there were poisonous snakes and scorpions. In that dry and waterless land he made water flow out of solid rock for you. |

The great and terrible wilderness: the **wilderness** (see 1.1) was vast and filled with dangers (also 1.19 for **great and terrible**).

Fiery serpents: NRSV "poisonous snakes" is like TEV (CEV, REB, NIV "venomous snakes"). It is uncertain whether or not this refers to a fabulous creature, that is, a product of myths and legends, such as a dragon (see "flying serpent" in Isa 30.6). All in all it is better to follow TEV and NRSV. In some languages there will be different words for snakes, depending on whether they are poisonous or not. The poisonous variety should be chosen here.

Thirsty ground where there was no water: this is a description of desert wastes, "dry country without any water." TEV "dry and waterless land" is another good model. However, in some languages "dry and waterless" will be redundant; in such a case we may say, for example, "a land where people can find no water."

Brought you water out of the flinty rock: see Num 20.2-13. **Flinty rock** means solid rock, not soft or loose rock. It is possible to make the action of the LORD clearer by saying, for example, "In that land where there is no water, he [Yahweh] split open a rock, and water poured out so that you could drink" (very similar to CEV).

8.16 RSV	TEV
who fed you in the wilderness with manna which your fathers did not know, that he might humble you and test you, to do you good in the end.	In the desert he gave you manna to eat, food that your ancestors had never eaten. He sent hardships on you to test you, so that in the end he could bless you with good things.

Fed you in the wilderness with manna which your fathers did not know: see verse 8.

He might humble you and test you: see verse 2.

To do you good in the end: the testing was followed by blessings. At the end of it all God rewarded them with good things. TEV has "so that in the end he could bless you with good things"; we may also say "so that in the end he could give you all kinds of good things."

8.17 RSV	TEV
Beware lest you say in your heart, 'My power and the might of my hand have gotten me this wealth.'	So then, you must never think that you have made yourselves wealthy by your own power and strength.

Beware lest you say in your heart: that is, "Be careful not to say to yourself [or, yourselves]," or even "Be careful that you never think."

My power and the might of my hand: the Israelites might be tempted to think that they had prospered because of their own efforts, their own skill and strength. Many languages require direct speech here, although TEV has indirect speech. A model using direct speech is "Don't think, 'My own skill and hard work have made me rich.' " CEV has "don't say, 'I'm rich, I have earned it all myself.' " In some languages **wealth** is defined by possessions (cattle and so on) rather than silver and gold. So we may translate "that gives you the strength to get many possessions."

8.18 RSV	TEV
You shall remember the LORD your God, for it is he who gives you power to get wealth; that he may confirm	Remember that it is the LORD your God who gives you the power to become rich. He does this because

his covenant which he swore to your fathers, as at this day.	he is still faithful today to the covenant that he made with your ancestors.

You shall remember the LORD your God . . . it is he who gives you power to get wealth: it is God who makes them wealthy. We may say "gives you the power to become rich" (TEV) or "gives you the strength to get many possessions."

That he may confirm his covenant: God does this because he is faithful to the **covenant** (4.13) that he had made with them, and keeps his promises. We may also express this as "In this way he keeps [or, is faithful to] the covenant he made with . . . ." The phrase **as at this day** goes with **confirm his covenant**: "as he is doing today."

He swore to your fathers: see 1.8.

8.19   RSV   TEV

And if you forget the LORD your God and go after other gods and serve them and worship them, I solemnly warn you this day that you shall surely perish.	Never forget the LORD your God or turn to other gods to worship and serve them. If you do, then I warn you today that you will certainly be destroyed.

Now comes the solemn warning. Here and at the end of verse 20 **you** is plural in Hebrew, not singular.

Go after other gods to serve them: see 6.14; 7.4. The additional **and worship them** is essentially redundant, and a translation can use the one word for "worship," unless there are two words that are natural in this kind of context.

I solemnly warn you: that is, "I say very firmly," or "I want you to listen carefully to what I am saying." The verb **warn** in some languages will require direct speech; for example, "I solemnly warn you today, 'You will certainly die.' "

You shall surely perish: this is very strong in Hebrew. If the Israelites forsake Yahweh and worship pagan gods, he will destroy them all (see verse 20).

8.20   RSV   TEV

Like the nations that the LORD makes to perish before you, so shall you perish, because you would not obey the voice of the LORD your God.	If you do not obey the LORD, then you will be destroyed just like those nations that he is going to destroy as you advance.

Obey the voice means "obey the commands."

It is possible to restructure and combine verses 19 and 20 as follows:

176

● ¹⁹⁻²⁰ I am warning you today that, if you forget the LORD your God and worship other gods, the LORD will destroy you, just as he will destroy all the other nations you will fight against.

2A-10. The reason Yahweh will help Israel (9.1-6)

RSV

1 "Hear, O Israel; you are to pass over the Jordan this day, to go in to dispossess nations greater and mightier than yourselves, cities great and fortified up to heaven, 2 a people great and tall, the sons of the Anakim, whom you know, and of whom you have heard it said, 'Who can stand before the sons of Anak?' 3 Know therefore this day that he who goes over before you as a devouring fire is the LORD your God; he will destroy them and subdue them before you; so you shall drive them out, and make them perish quickly, as the LORD has promised you.
4 "Do not say in your heart, after the LORD your God has thrust them out before you, 'It is because of my righteousness that the LORD has brought me in to possess this land'; whereas it is because of the wickedness of these nations that the LORD is driving them out before you. 5 Not because of your righteousness or the uprightness of your heart are you going in to possess their land; but because of the wickedness of these nations the LORD your God is driving them out from before you, and that he may confirm the word which the LORD swore to your fathers, to Abraham, to Isaac, and to Jacob.
6 "Know therefore, that the LORD your God is not giving you this good land to possess because of your righteousness; for you are a stubborn people.

TEV

The People's Disobedience

1 "Listen, people of Israel! Today you are about to cross the Jordan River and occupy the land belonging to nations greater and more powerful than you. Their cities are large, with walls that reach the sky. 2 The people themselves are tall and strong; they are giants, and you have heard it said that no one can stand against them. 3 But now you will see for yourselves that the LORD your God will go ahead of you like a raging fire. He will defeat them as you advance, so that you will drive them out and destroy them quickly, as he promised.
4 "After the LORD your God has driven them out for you, do not say to yourselves that he brought you in to possess this land because you deserved it. No, the LORD is going to drive these people out for you because they are wicked. 5 It is not because you are good and do what is right that the LORD is letting you take their land. He will drive them out because they are wicked and because he intends to keep the promise that he made to your ancestors, Abraham, Isaac, and Jacob. 6 You can be sure that the LORD is not giving you this fertile land because you deserve it. No, you are a stubborn people.

Moses continues addressing the people, using the second person singular of address until verse 7. The translator should be consistent in the use of singular or plural form of the verb. The main thing is that the reader knows that Moses is addressing all the people. Moses reviews their history of unfaithfulness to God, especially the golden calf they had made to worship at Mount Sinai (Exo 21), and other acts of rebellion (verses 21-22; see Num 11.1-3, chapters 13–14; Exo 17.1-7). Nevertheless the people will possess the Promised Land because of God's love and faithfulness, not because of their own merits.

Section heading: the TEV title "The People's Disobedience" covers the whole chapter. It may be better to follow the example of FRCL (and TOB) and divide the chapter into three sections: (1) verses 1-6, "The reason Yahweh will help Israel"; (2) verses 7-17, "The Israelites make a golden calf"; (3) verses 18-29,

"Moses intercedes for the Israelites." An alternative title for verses 1-6 is "God will help the people of Israel even though they are stubborn."

9.1   RSV   TEV

"Hear, O Israel; you are to pass over the Jordan this day, to go in to dispossess nations greater and mightier than yourselves, cities great and fortified up to heaven,

"Listen, people of Israel! Today you are about to cross the Jordan River and occupy the land belonging to nations greater and more powerful than you. Their cities are large, with walls that reach the sky.

Verses 1-2 are one sentence in Hebrew, which in translation should be broken up into several sentences (see TEV, CEV). In verses 1-3 several matters are dealt with that have appeared before: for verse 1, see 1.28; 2.18; 4.38; 5.1; 6.4; 7.1; for verse 2, see 1.28; 7.15; for verse 3, see 4.24; 7.21-24.

Hear, O Israel: see 6.4.

You are to pass over the Jordan this day: the perspective given by RSV is that of Moses addressing the people on the day they are to begin crossing the Jordan River into the land of Canaan; note also TEV, "Today you are about to cross . . . ." But some other versions do not take **this day** so literally; see, for example, NIV "You are now about to cross," and CEV "You will soon cross." It has now been forty years since they departed from Egypt. For **Jordan** see 1.1; 4.21.

Dispossess: this means to drive away or dislodge. The object is **nations** (not "land"), and so something like "drive out" is best. See also 2.21.

Nations greater and mightier than yourselves: see 7.1.

Cities great and fortified up to heaven: these are large towns surrounded by high, strong walls. The expression **fortified up to heaven** is a colorful exaggeration that no reader would understand literally; even TEV and CEV "reach to the sky" should not be read as a factual truth. A translator is encouraged to use similar exaggeration if it is understood as such, or we may use a simile or other expression; for example, "and the walls around their towns seem to reach to the sky." For **cities** see 1.1, 22.

9.2   RSV   TEV

a people great and tall, the sons of the Anakim, whom you know, and of whom you have heard it said, 'Who can stand before the sons of Anak?'

The people themselves are tall and strong; they are giants, and you have heard it said that no one can stand against them.

A people great and tall: the **Anakim** had the reputation of being giants (TEV, see also 2.1-11), descendants of the legendary giant Anak. They also were said to be undefeatable, as Moses quotes what people in general say about them, "Who can stand up to the Anakim?" The sense is "Who can defeat them in

178

battle?" or "Who can fight them and defeat them?" or even "No one can defeat them in battle" (CEV).

Whom you know: this does not mean personal acquaintance of them, but hearsay: **of whom you have heard**, "you have heard it said" (TEV), or "People have told you."

Sons of Anak: it is better to say "the descendants of the giant Anak" (POCL), or "the Anakim." **Anak** is their ancestor, whose name they use as their group name. For a further discussion on **sons of Anak**, see 1.28.

9.3　　　RSV　　　　　　　　　　TEV

Know therefore this day that he who goes over before you as a devouring fire is the LORD your God; he will destroy them and subdue them before you; so you shall drive them out, and make them perish quickly, as the LORD has promised you.	But now you will see for yourselves that the LORD your God will go ahead of you like a raging fire. He will defeat them as you advance, so that you will drive them out and destroy them quickly, as he promised.

Know therefore . . . : now comes the assurance. Yahweh will enable the Israelites to defeat and drive out these giants.

For God as **a devouring fire**, see 4.24. For **the LORD your God** see 1.6.

He will destroy them: see 2.12. There is a series of four verbs, the first two about God: **destroy them and subdue them**, that is, "conquer them," "defeat them." It may be more natural to reverse the two verbs: "will defeat and destroy them" (see REB); TEV combines the two verbs into one, but it is better to use two, if it is not unnatural style in the language.

Before you: this is better translated by TEV "as you advance."

You shall drive them out: this translates the same Hebrew verb used in verse 1, "dispossess." We may also translate as "cause them to leave [the land]."

Make them perish quickly: see the verb in 8.19.

As the LORD has promised you: it is better to shift this nearer to the beginning of the sentence: ". . . as the LORD has promised you, he will go ahead of you like a raging fire burning everything in its path. He will defeat and destroy them . . . ."

9.4　　　RSV　　　　　　　　　　TEV

"Do not say in your heart, after the LORD your God has thrust them out before you, 'It is because of my righteousness that the LORD has brought me in to possess this land'; whereas it is because of the wickedness of these nations that the LORD is driving them out before you.	"After the LORD your God has driven them out for you, do not say to yourselves that he brought you in to possess this land because you deserved it. No, the LORD is going to drive these people out for you because they are wicked.

Do not say in your heart: see 8.17.

After the LORD your God has thrust them out before you: the verb here means "expel," "drive out," the same as in verse 3. TEV "driven them out *for you*" is not quite right; it should be "as you advance."

It is because of my righteousness: see 6.25. Here the plural form would be more natural, since this is the statement of the people, not of an individual. The word **righteousness** here means "good conduct" and is well translated by TEV "because we deserve it" (also FRCL); NJPSV "because of our virtues" is possible; REB "because of our merits" is better, or even "because we are such good people."

The LORD has brought me in to possess this land: this statement occurs over and over again. Here the point of view is the land of Canaan itself, so that **brought . . . in** is correct; for **possess** see 1.8; 2.12.

The wickedness of these nations: Yahweh is enabling the Israelites to conquer the land of Canaan because the pagan peoples who live there are wicked; we may say "they do wrong" (NJB), or "are evil people."

Driving them out before you: this is a phrase that occurs often and is repeated in the next verse.

9.5   RSV   TEV

Not because of your righteousness   It is not because you are good and
or the uprightness of your heart are   do what is right that the LORD is let-
you going in to possess their land;   ting you take their land. He will drive
but because of the wickedness of   them out because they are wicked
these nations the LORD your God is   and because he intends to keep the
driving them out from before you,   promise that he made to your ances-
and that he may confirm the word   tors, Abraham, Isaac, and Jacob.
which the LORD swore to your fa-
thers, to Abraham, to Isaac, and to
Jacob.

Not because of your righteousness (as in verse 4) **or the uprightness of your heart**: this second qualification has to do with right moral and spiritual attitudes, as contrasted with right conduct. REB and NIV use "integrity"; something like "It is not because you are a good [or, moral] people" gives the meaning of the phrase.

Confirm the word: this refers to God's promise (see 8.18).

The LORD swore to your fathers: see 1.8.

9.6   RSV   TEV

"Know therefore, that the LORD   You can be sure that the LORD is not
your God is not giving you this good   giving you this fertile land because
land to possess because of your   you deserve it. No, you are a stub-
righteousness; for you are a stub-   born people.
born people.

Verse 6 summarizes what is said in verse 4-5, and adds the final comment: **you are a stubborn people**. The Hebrew phrase rendered **stubborn** is "stiff-necked," used always of people (see 9.13; 10.16; 31.27; also Acts 7.51). It indicates their unwillingness to obey God's commands. In some languages this will be rendered with figurative expressions; for example, "hard-necked," "hard-hearted," or "bone-hearted."

2A-11. The Israelites make a golden calf (9.7-17)

RSV	TEV
7 Remember and do not forget how you provoked the LORD your God to wrath in the wilderness; from the day you came out of the land of Egypt, until you came to this place, you have been rebellious against the LORD. 8 Even at Horeb you provoked the LORD to wrath, and the LORD was so angry with you that he was ready to destroy you. 9 When I went up the mountain to receive the tables of stone, the tables of the covenant which the LORD made with you, I remained on the mountain forty days and forty nights; I neither ate bread nor drank water. 10 And the LORD gave me the two tables of stone written with the finger of God; and on them were all the words which the LORD had spoken with you on the mountain out of the midst of the fire on the day of the assembly. 11 And at the end of forty days and forty nights the LORD gave me the two tables of stone, the tables of the covenant. 12 Then the LORD said to me, 'Arise, go down quickly from here; for your people whom you have brought from Egypt have acted corruptly; they have turned aside quickly out of the way which I commanded them; they have made themselves a molten image.'	7 "Never forget how you made the Lord your God angry in the desert. From the day that you left Egypt until the day you arrived here, you have rebelled against him. 8 Even at Mount Sinai you made the LORD angry—angry enough to destroy you. 9 I went up the mountain to receive the stone tablets on which was written the covenant that the LORD had made with you. I stayed there forty days and nights and did not eat or drink anything. 10 Then the LORD gave me the two stone tablets on which he had written with his own hand what he had said to you from the fire on the day that you were gathered there at the mountain. 11 Yes, after those forty days and nights the LORD gave me the two stone tablets on which he had written the covenant.
13 "Furthermore the LORD said to me, 'I have seen this people, and behold, it is a stubborn people; 14 let me alone, that I may destroy them and blot out their name from under heaven; and I will make of you a nation mightier and greater than they.' 15 So I turned and came down from the mountain, and the mountain was burning with fire; and the two tables of the covenant were in my two hands. 16 And I looked, and behold, you had sinned against the LORD your God; you had made yourselves a molten calf; you had turned aside quickly from the way which the LORD had commanded you. 17 So I took hold of the two tables, and cast them out of my two hands, and broke them before your eyes.	12 "Then the LORD said to me, 'Go down the mountain at once, because your people, whom you led out of Egypt, have become corrupt and have done evil. They have already turned away from what I commanded them to do, and they have made an idol for themselves.' 13 "The LORD also said to me, 'I know how stubborn these people are. 14 Don't try to stop me. I intend to destroy them so that no one will remember them any longer. Then I will make you the father of a nation larger and more powerful than they are.' 15 "So I turned and went down the mountain, carrying the two stone tablets on which the covenant was written. Flames of fire were coming from the mountain. 16 I saw that you had already disobeyed the command that the LORD your God had given you, and that you had sinned against him by making yourselves a metal idol in the form of a bull-calf. 17 So there in front of you I threw the stone tablets down and broke them to pieces.

Moses reminds the people of their terrible sin at Mount Sinai of making a gold bull-calf and worshiping it (Exo 32.1-21). He does this in order to show the Israelites that they will enter the Promised Land only because Yahweh will take them there, not because they deserve to go there.

Section heading: some translators will wish to begin a new section here. Possible headings are "The Golden Calf" (FRCL) or "The Israelites make a golden calf."

9.7	RSV	TEV

Remember and do not forget how you provoked the LORD your God to wrath in the wilderness; from the day you came out of the land of Egypt, until you came to this place, you have been rebellious against the LORD.

"Never forget how you made the LORD your God angry in the desert. From the day that you left Egypt until the day you arrived here, you have rebelled against him.

If translators begin a new section here with a separate heading, it should be indicated that Moses is still speaking; for example, "Moses said to the Israelites, ..."

Remember and do not forget: see similar language in 8.2, 11, 18.

You provoked the LORD your God to wrath: the conduct of the Israelites made God angry; that is, "you caused Yahweh your God to get angry with you." For "angry" see 1.34.

For **wilderness** see 1.1.

From the day you came out of the land of Egypt, until you came to this place: Moses says that during the whole forty years the conduct of the Israelites has made God angry with them. In Hebrew **you came out** continues the second person plural; but **you came** is second person singular, which continues to be used. Translators may continue to use the second person plural, however, if that is more natural style in their language.

You have been rebellious: this means their unwillingness to obey God's commands, and may be expressed as "You were unwilling to obey his [Yahweh's] commands from the day that . . . ." This charge is made in a stronger form in 31.27.

9.8	RSV	TEV

Even at Horeb you provoked the LORD to wrath, and the LORD was so angry with you that he was ready to destroy you.

Even at Mount Sinai you made the LORD angry—angry enough to destroy you.

Even at Horeb: this refers to their experiences at Mount Sinai (see 1.2). So we may express this as "Even when we [inclusive] were at Mount Sinai you . . . ."

You provoked the LORD to wrath: as in verse 7.

For **so angry** see 1.34 and 1.37.

The LORD was . . . ready to destroy you: the same as in verse 3.

9.9 RSV TEV

When I went up the mountain to receive the tables of stone, the tables of the covenant which the LORD made with you, I remained on the mountain forty days and forty nights; I neither ate bread nor drank water.

I went up the mountain to receive the stone tablets on which was written the covenant that the LORD had made with you. I stayed there forty days and nights and did not eat or drink anything.

Here Moses recounts what is found in Exo 24.12-18; 31.18.

The tables of stone, the tables of the covenant: NRSV and all other modern translations use today's English, "stone tablets" (and see 4.13). **The tables of the covenant** may be expanded to say "the tablets on which the covenant was written." If it is natural in the translator's language, it is good to keep the author's style, repeating the two phrases, and not collapse the two into one, "the stone tablets on which the covenant had been written." FRCL uses the expression "the document of the covenant." For **covenant** see 4.13. The ten commandments were the terms of the covenant.

I neither ate bread nor drank water: something like "I went without food or water [during those forty days]" or "I didn't eat or drink a thing" expresses the meaning in a natural form. The reader should understand that Moses willingly did without food or water, not that he was in a situation where food and water were not available.

9.10-11 RSV TEV

10 And the LORD gave me the two tables of stone written with the finger of God; and on them were all the words which the LORD had spoken with you on the mountain out of the midst of the fire on the day of the assembly. 11 And at the end of forty days and forty nights the LORD gave me the two tables of stone, the tables of the covenant.

10 Then the LORD gave me the two stone tablets on which he had written with his own hand what he had said to you from the fire on the day that you were gathered there at the mountain. 11 Yes, after those forty days and nights the LORD gave me the two stone tablets on which he had written the covenant.

For the description of the scene in verse 10, see 5.22.

The LORD gave me . . . written with the finger of God: a literal translation might be understood to refer to two different divine beings. It may be best to combine the two names as follows: "The LORD your God gave me . . . on which he himself had inscribed . . . ." For **written** see 5.22. **With the finger** pictures God as having a human hand; the important sense is that God himself, and not Moses, did the writing.

On them were all the words: these **words** are the ten commandments, which Yahweh had inscribed himself ("with his own hand").

On the mountain out of the midst of the fire: see 5.22.

The day of the assembly: the gathering of the Israelites at Mount Sinai was the day they became a nation, a people belonging to Yahweh. TEV has "on the day that you were gathered there at the mountain." See also 5.22.

At the end: verse 11 is a summary conclusion of the events at Mount Sinai. See TEV for a helpful model.

9.12	RSV	TEV

Then the LORD said to me, 'Arise, go down quickly from here; for your people whom you have brought from Egypt have acted corruptly; they have turned aside quickly out of the way which I commanded them; they have made themselves a molten image.'	"Then the LORD said to me, 'Go down the mountain at once, because your people, whom you led out of Egypt, have become corrupt and have done evil. They have already turned away from what I commanded them to do, and they have made an idol for themselves.'

Arise, go down quickly from here: Moses had been lying down on his face (in a prone position), not doing a thing during the forty days. An alternative model is "Get up and hurry down the mountain."

Your people whom you have brought out of Egypt: here Yahweh is saying that Moses is responsible for the people. The sense of **your people** is that Moses was their leader, he was in charge of them.

Have acted corruptly: this accuses the people of committing a terrible sin, that is, building a metal idol in the shape of a calf. See the comment at 4.16.

Turned aside quickly out of the way which I commanded them: the Israelites had quickly disobeyed God and acted contrary to his commands. Other ways to express this are "they have already disobeyed what I commanded them" or "they have already stopped obeying me." But we may also keep the figurative language; for example, "They have quickly left the path that I commanded them to walk on."

A molten image: in most languages the phrase "metal image" will be the one to use. To indicate that it was made by the process of smelting metal ore and shaping the metal into the figure of a calf may be difficult; "cast metal" is the normal phrase in English (NIV "a cast idol").

9.13   RSV   TEV

"Furthermore the LORD said to me,   "The LORD also said to me, 'I know
'I have seen this people, and behold,   how stubborn these people are.
it is a stubborn people;

I have seen this people: God is saying that he has been watching how the
people acted during the forty years. **This people** uses the singular **this**, since
the word **people** is singular in form, but "these people" (TEV) sounds better in
English. Translators need to use the form that is the most natural in their
language. We may avoid this problem, however, by saying something like "I
have been watching the Israelites" (CEV).
    And behold: see 1.10. Something like "and it is clear that" or "and I know
that" would be good ways of translating the phrase.
    A stubborn people: as in verse 6.

9.14   RSV   TEV

let me alone, that I may destroy them   Don't try to stop me. I intend to de-
and blot out their name from under   stroy them so that no one will re-
heaven; and I will make of you a   member them any longer. Then I will
nation mightier and greater than   make you the father of a nation
they.'   larger and more powerful than they
                                           are.'

Let me alone: God is telling Moses to stand back or step aside, not to get in
his way; "Don't try to stop me . . ." (TEV). Apparently Yahweh regards Moses as
a person with considerable authority.
    That I may destroy them: the whole statement could be rephrased: "Step
aside and let me wipe them out" or "Don't interfere while I get rid of them."
    Blot out their name from under heaven: see similar language in 7.24.
    I will make of you a nation mightier and greater than they: God proposes to
exterminate the Israelites and make Moses the ancestor of a people that
eventually will outnumber the Israelites and be more powerful than they are.
This should be spelled out clearly in translation. The contrast between **them** in
the first sentence and **you** (Moses) in this sentence should be emphasized if
possible; a possible model is "I will make a larger and more powerful nation out
of you instead [of them]." TEV "the father of a nation" may not be the best way
of saying **of you a nation** in some languages. BRCL has "Of you and your
descendants I will make . . . ."

9.15   RSV   TEV

So I turned and came down from the   "So I turned and went down the
mountain, and the mountain was   mountain, carrying the two stone
burning with fire; and the two tables   tablets on which the covenant was

of the covenant were in my two   written. Flames of fire were coming
hands.   from the mountain.

I turned and came down: or "I got up [see verse 12] and went down . . . ."
Yahweh is the center of focus, so in many languages Moses will "go" down the
mountain away from Yahweh.

The mountain was burning with fire: that is, "The mountain was in flames"
or "There was fire on the mountain." This is possibly a way of describing a
volcanic eruption (see 4.11).

The two tables of the covenant: see verse 11.

It is not necessary to say literally **my two hands** unless that is the natural
way of referring to the hands. In some languages "both hands" will be the most
natural way to say this. TEV expresses the meaning well: "carrying the two
stone tablets on which the covenant was written." In languages that do not use
the passive voice, we may say, for example, "carrying the two stone tablets on
which Yahweh had written the covenant [or, Ten Commandments]."

9.16 RSV	TEV
And I looked, and behold, you had sinned against the LORD your God; you had made yourselves a molten calf; you had turned aside quickly from the way which the LORD had commanded you.	I saw that you had already disobeyed the command that the LORD your God had given you, and that you had sinned against him by making yourselves a metal idol in the form of a bull-calf.

I looked, and behold: see verse 13.

You had sinned against the LORD your God: the verb normally translated "to
sin" is used in this passage. In the Bible its basic meaning is to do something
that is contrary to God's will. It is a religious concept, not a legal one. The
verbal phrase "to sin against God" means to disobey God; it is an offense that
is an affront or an insult to God. So "sinned and disobeyed the LORD" will catch
the meaning better.

You had made yourselves: that means "you had made for yourselves," that
is, "to bow down to," "to worship" (as in verse 12).

A molten calf: a metal statue, or figure, in the shape of a calf. Both TEV and
REB have "bull-calf." It is not certain whether this idol is to be understood as a
fertility symbol, as was true of some religions at that time. It could have been
an image honoring some pagan god, or even one that was designed to honor
Yahweh. Whatever the intention of those who made it, it was clearly an idol, so
"they have taken metal and made an idol in the shape of a calf" may serve as
a model.

You had turned aside quickly: see verse 12.

So I took hold of the two tables, and cast them out of my two hands, and broke them before your eyes.

So there in front of you I threw the stone tablets down and broke them to pieces.

I took hold ... and cast them: this sounds as though Moses had laid the stone tablets down and then picked them up again. Or else it means that he took a firm grip on the tablets and threw them violently to the ground. This was a deliberate action, not an impulsive act. If translators have a word in their language that means using great force, that term should be used here. It was a way of showing that the covenant between Yahweh and Israel was no longer in existence; by building the idol the Israelites had canceled the covenant, and Moses, representing Yahweh, breaks the tablets of the covenant. No longer is there a covenant between Yahweh and Israel.

And cast them ... and broke them: that is, "I threw them down and broke them" This does not describe two separate actions but one—the act of throwing them to the ground broke them into pieces.

Before your eyes: Moses did this as a public gesture, so that all the Israelites could see that the covenant with Yahweh had been canceled. Other ways of saying this are "There right in front of you" or "right before your eyes" (CEV). In some languages this phrase may be placed at the beginning of the verse, as in TEV.

2A-12. Moses intercedes for the Israelites (9.18-29)

RSV TEV

18 Then I lay prostrate before the LORD as before, forty days and forty nights; I neither ate bread nor drank water, because of all the sin which you had committed, in doing what was evil in the sight of the LORD, to provoke him to anger. 19 For I was afraid of the anger and hot displeasure which the LORD bore against you, so that he was ready to destroy you. But the LORD hearkened to me that time also. 20 And the LORD was so angry with Aaron that he was ready to destroy him; and I prayed for Aaron also at the same time. 21 Then I took the sinful thing, the calf which you had made, and burned it with fire and crushed it, grinding it very small, until it was as fine as dust; and I threw the dust of it into the brook that descended out of the mountain. 22 "At Taberah also, and at Massah, and at Kibroth-hattaavah, you provoked the LORD to wrath. 23 And when the LORD sent you from Kadesh-barnea, saying, 'Go up and take possession of the land which I have given you,' then you rebelled against the commandment of the LORD your God, and did not believe him or

18 Then once again I lay face downward in the LORD's presence for forty days and nights and did not eat or drink anything. I did this because you had sinned against the LORD and had made him angry. 19 I was afraid of the LORD's fierce anger, because he was furious enough to destroy you; but once again the LORD listened to me. 20 The LORD was also angry enough with Aaron to kill him, so I prayed for Aaron at the same time. 21 I took that sinful thing that you had made—that metal bull-calf—and threw it into the fire. Then I broke it in pieces, ground it to dust, and threw the dust into the stream that flowed down the mountain.

22 "You also made the LORD your God angry when you were at Taberah, Massah, and Kibroth Hattaavah. 23 And when he sent you from Kadesh Barnea with orders to go and take possession of the land that he was giving you, you rebelled against him; you did not trust him or obey him. 24 Ever since I have known you, you have rebelled against the LORD.

obey his voice. 24 You have been rebellious against the LORD from the day that I knew you.

25 "So I lay prostrate before the LORD for these forty days and forty nights, because the LORD had said he would destroy you. 26 And I prayed to the LORD, 'O Lord GOD, destroy not thy people and thy heritage, whom thou hast redeemed through thy greatness, whom thou hast brought out of Egypt with a mighty hand. 27 Remember thy servants, Abraham, Isaac, and Jacob; do not regard the stubbornness of this people, or their wickedness, or their sin, 28 lest the land from which thou didst bring us say, "Because the LORD was not able to bring them into the land which he promised them, and because he hated them, he has brought them out to slay them in the wilderness." 29 For they are thy people and thy heritage, whom thou didst bring out by thy great power and by thy outstretched arm.'

25 "So I lay face downward in the LORD's presence those forty days and nights, because I knew that he was determined to destroy you. 26 And I prayed, 'Sovereign LORD, don't destroy your own people, the people you rescued and brought out of Egypt by your great strength and power. 27 Remember your servants, Abraham, Isaac, and Jacob, and do not pay any attention to the stubbornness, wickedness, and sin of this people. 28 Otherwise, the Egyptians will say that you were unable to take your people into the land that you had promised them. They will say that you took your people out into the desert to kill them, because you hated them. 29 After all, these are the people whom you chose to be your own and whom you brought out of Egypt by your great power and might.'

Section heading: some translators will choose to make verses 18-29 a new section with its own heading. Possible headings are "Moses intercedes for the Israelites" or "Moses pleads with Yahweh not to destroy the Israelites."

9.18   RSV   TEV

Then I lay prostrate before the LORD as before, forty days and forty nights; I neither ate bread nor drank water, because of all the sin which you had committed, in doing what was evil in the sight of the LORD, to provoke him to anger.

Then once again I lay face downward in the LORD's presence for forty days and nights and did not eat or drink anything. I did this because you had sinned against the LORD and had made him angry.

With the beginning of a new section, Moses may need to be reintroduced as the speaker.

Then I lay prostrate: Moses does at the foot of the mountain what he had done on top of it (verse 9).

Before the LORD: this is to indicate that what Moses was doing was a religious act. It could be that he lay down in front of the Covenant Tent for the forty days. TEV has "in the LORD's presence" and CEV has "at the place of worship." Verse 20 indicates that Moses prayed to Yahweh while lying prostrate before him. This may be included in the translation here; for example, ". . . at the place of worship and prayed to him [Yahweh] for you [plural]."

As before: see verse 9.

I neither ate bread nor drank water: see verse 9.

Doing what was evil in the sight of the LORD: see 4.25.

To provoke him to anger: see verse 7. The text does not mean they did this in order to provoke God, but that by doing this they did in fact provoke God.

188

Some restructuring will be needed in the last part of this verse. TEV offers a good model: "I did this because you had sinned against the LORD and made him angry."

9.19	RSV	TEV

For I was afraid of the anger and hot displeasure which the LORD bore against you, so that he was ready to destroy you. But the LORD hearkened to me that time also.	I was afraid of the LORD's fierce anger, because he was furious enough to destroy you; but once again the LORD listened to me.

I was afraid of the anger and the hot displeasure: God's anger is described in terms of fire and heat, a common enough way of talking about anger.

Which the LORD bore against you: to "bear anger" means to have it, to feel it, to nurture it. We may restructure the first sentence as follows: "The LORD was terribly angry with [or, his heart, or nose, burned fiercely against] you and I was afraid of him. He was so angry with you that he wanted to . . . ."

The LORD hearkened to me that time also: this probably refers back to 5.23-28, where Moses interceded successfully with Yahweh. TEV has "but once again the LORD listened to me."

9.20	RSV	TEV

And the LORD was so angry with Aaron that he was ready to destroy him; and I prayed for Aaron also at the same time.	The LORD was also angry enough with Aaron to kill him, so I prayed for Aaron at the same time.

The LORD was so angry with Aaron: for God's anger against Aaron see Exo 32.1-16, 21-25, 35. But nothing is said there of Moses' intervention on Aaron's behalf. TEV is a good model.

It is possible to combine verses 18-20 as follows:

● 18-20 I lay prostrate on the ground before the LORD [or, at the place of worship] and prayed to him for you [plural] as I did before. I didn't eat or drink for forty days and nights. You had committed a terrible sin by making that idol, and I was afraid that the LORD was angry enough with you and Aaron to destroy you. So I prayed for you and Aaron as I did before, and the LORD again answered my prayers.

9.21	RSV	TEV

Then I took the sinful thing, the calf which you had made, and burned it	I took that sinful thing that you had made—that metal bull-calf—and

189

with fire and crushed it, grinding it
very small, until it was as fine as
dust; and I threw the dust of it into
the brook that descended out of the
mountain.

threw it into the fire. Then I broke it
in pieces, ground it to dust, and
threw the dust into the stream that
flowed down the mountain.

I took the sinful thing: the idol itself was the result of the people's sin, and so
was a sinful object. But **the sinful thing** will be difficult to translate in some
languages. In such a case we may say, for example, "It was a sin for you to
make that idol [or, metal calf]," or "You sinned against God by making that
idol."

Burned it with fire and crushed it: after throwing it in the fire and presumably melting it (see Exo 32.30), Moses took the metal that had been melted
down and crushed it into pieces.

Grinding it very small, until it was as fine as dust: by whatever means (the
text doesn't say how), Moses reduced the material to the smallest particles
possible.

I threw the dust of it into the brook that descended out of the mountain: the
account in Exo 32.20 states that Moses threw the small bits or powder into
"water" and made the people drink the water. All of this took place at Mount
Sinai.

9.22   RSV   TEV

"At Taberah also, and at Massah,
and at Kibroth-hattaavah, you provoked the LORD to wrath.

"You also made the LORD your
God angry when you were at Taberah, Massah, and Kibroth Hattaavah.

On three other occasions, at **Taberah** (Num 11.1-3), **Massah** (Exo 17.1-7), and
Kibroth-hattaavah (Num 11.31-34), the Israelites had provoked the LORD's
anger (see verse 7).

9.23   RSV   TEV

And when the LORD sent you from
Kadesh-barnea, saying, 'Go up and
take possession of the land which I
have given you,' then you rebelled
against the commandment of the
LORD your God, and did not believe
him or obey his voice.

And when he sent you from Kadesh
Barnea with orders to go and take
possession of the land that he was
giving you, you rebelled against him;
you did not trust him or obey him.

This is another time when the Israelites did not obey Yahweh's command (see
1.19-26; Numbers 13–14). All the words used in this verse are the usual ones
in describing these matters.

Go up: this may mean to go up into the mountainous region; but it may simply be a way of saying "Get going" (see note at 1.19).

Take possession of the land: see 1.8.

Which I have given you: again, the two actions, one on the part of the Israelites and the other on the part of God, go together.

Rebelled against the commandment: to "rebel" means to disobey. "You refused to obey the commandment" (see verse 7).

Did not believe him or obey his voice: their lack of faith in Yahweh led to their act of rebellion, of disobedience. TEV has "you rebelled against him; you did not trust him or obey him." However, in some languages the repetition of "rebelled" and "did not . . . obey" will be unnatural style. In such a case we may say, for example, "You did not trust him and refused to obey him."

9.24	RSV	TEV
	You have been rebellious against the LORD from the day that I knew you.	Ever since I have known you, you have rebelled against the LORD.

You have been rebellious: this verbal phrase in Hebrew is from the same root as the verb **rebelled** in verse 23. Another way of saying this is "In fact, you have refused to obey Yahweh ever since . . . ."

From the day I knew you: this presumably means from the time Moses led the Israelites out of Egypt, forty years before. There is some textual evidence that the Hebrew text should be "he knew you," referring to God. It could be that this was seen as a criticism of God for not knowing beforehand how the Israelites would act, so that the text was changed in transmission. The HOTTP committee prefers "he knew you," as do CEV, NRSV, REB, and NJB; and a translator should feel free to translate it in this way.

9.25	RSV	TEV
	"So I lay prostrate before the LORD for these forty days and forty nights, because the LORD had said he would destroy you.	"So I lay face downward in the LORD's presence those forty days and nights, because I knew that he was determined to destroy you.

This refers back to what he had already said (verse 18). Moses lay face down on the ground in the LORD's presence for forty days.

Because the LORD had said he would destroy you: God threatened to do to the Israelites what he had promised them he would do to the peoples of Canaan.

9.26   RSV   TEV

And I prayed to the LORD, 'O Lord   And I prayed, 'Sovereign LORD, don't
GOD, destroy not thy people and thy   destroy your own people, the people
heritage, whom thou hast redeemed   you rescued and brought out of
through thy greatness, whom thou   Egypt by your great strength and
hast brought out of Egypt with a   power.
mighty hand.

O Lord GOD: this translates the Hebrew "Lord Yahweh" (the title and the
name). The Septuagint has "O Lord, Lord, King of the gods." For a comment on
the translation of **O Lord GOD**, see 3.24.

Thy heritage: this translates a noun related to a verb that means "to take
possession of" (1.38; 3.28; 4.21; see the noun at 4.20, "the people of the LORD,"
and 4.38, "the land of the Israelites"). So **thy people and thy heritage** means
"your very own people" (TEV).

Whom thou hast redeemed through thy greatness: here **greatness** refers to
God's might, his power; **redeemed** means "set free" (see 7.8). There is no idea
here of paying a price to someone to obtain that freedom.

A mighty hand: see 4.34. The Septuagint adds "and an outstretched arm" (as
in the Hebrew text of 4.34). The two sentences may be combined as follows:
"These are the people you rescued and brought out of Egypt by your great
strength and power" (TEV), or "You used your great strength and power to set
them free and bring them out of Egypt."

9.27   RSV   TEV

Remember thy servants, Abraham,   Remember your servants, Abraham,
Isaac, and Jacob; do not regard the   Isaac, and Jacob, and do not pay any
stubbornness of this people, or their   attention   to   the   stubbornness,
wickedness, or their sin,   wickedness, and sin of this people.

Remember thy servants: the verb **Remember** is used in the sense of recalling
how faithfully God's servants (the patriarchs) had obeyed God, and the
promises that God had made to them. Here **servants**, as elsewhere, means
people who willingly do what God commands, and who obey his laws. So we
may translate "Remember [or, Think about] how Abraham, Isaac, and Jacob
obeyed you faithfully."

Do not regard: here Moses is asking God not to keep thinking about the
stubbornness (see verse 6), the **wickedness** (see verse 4), and the **sin** (see verse
16) of the people of Israel. Note TEV "do not pay any attention to . . . ."

9.28   RSV   TEV

lest the land from which thou didst   Otherwise, the Egyptians will say
bring us say, "Because the LORD was   that you were unable to take your

192

not able to bring them into the land which he promised them, and because he hated them, he has brought them out to slay them in the wilderness."

people into the land that you had promised them. They will say that you took your people out into the desert to kill them, because you hated them.

Moses argues that, if God does not keep his promise to take the people into the Promised Land, then the Egyptians will say that God hated the Israelites and led them out of Egypt in order to kill them in the wilderness.

Lest the land from which thou didst bring us: here **bring** is correct, from the point of view of Moses in the land of Moab. **Lest** may be expressed as "Otherwise" (TEV), or even expanded to "If you destroy your people" (CEV), pointing back to verse 25.

The land . . . say: preferably "the people of the land say" (as in the Septuagint, "the inhabitants of the land say"); the Hebrew text has "the land say" (using a plural form of the verb). But it will be helpful to identify the people as "Egyptians"; for example, "If you destroy your people, the Egyptians will say . . . ."

Bring them into the land . . . brought them out: since these are the Egyptians speaking, it is better to say "take them" and "took them out."

An alternative translation model for the final part of this verse is:

● Yahweh was unable [or, wasn't powerful enough] to take them into the land that he had promised to give to them. In fact, he hated them so much that he took them into the wilderness in order to kill them.

Translators in some languages may prefer to use indirect speech; in this case the model of TEV will be helpful.

9.29   RSV   TEV

For they are thy people and thy heritage, whom thou didst bring out by thy great power and by thy outstretched arm.'

After all, these are the people whom you chose to be your own and whom you brought out of Egypt by your great power and might.'

For the structure and vocabulary of this verse, see 4.26; 9.26.

2A-13. Moses receives the commandments again (10.1-5)

RSV

TEV
Moses Receives the Commandments Again

1 "At that time the LORD said to me, 'Hew two tables of stone like the first, and come up

1 "Then the LORD said to me, 'Cut two stone tablets like the first ones and make a wooden

193

to me on the mountain, and make an ark of wood. 2 And I will write on the tables the words that were on the first tables which you broke, and you shall put them in the ark.' 3 So I made an ark of acacia wood, and hewed two tables of stone like the first, and went up the mountain with the two tables in my hand. 4 And he wrote on the tables, as at the first writing, the ten commandments which the LORD had spoken to you on the mountain out of the midst of the fire on the day of the assembly; and the LORD gave them to me. 5 Then I turned and came down from the mountain, and put the tables in the ark which I had made; and there they are, as the LORD commanded me.

Box to put them in. Come up to me on the mountain, 2 and I will write on those tablets what I wrote on the tablets that you broke, and then you are to put them in the Box.'
3 "So I made a Box of acacia wood and cut two stone tablets like the first ones and took them up the mountain. 4 Then the LORD wrote on those tablets the same words that he had written the first time, the Ten Commandments that he gave you when he spoke from the fire on the day you were gathered at the mountain. The LORD gave me the tablets, 5 and I turned and went down the mountain. Then, just as the LORD had commanded, I put them in the Box that I had made—and they have been there ever since."

In this section Moses tells the people that, in obedience to God's command, he carved two stone tablets, built a box to put them in, and went up the mountain with the stone tablets. On top of the mountain God inscribed on them the ten commandments, as before (Exo 34.1-9). The covenant, which had been canceled when Moses broke the first two stone tablets, was thus renewed.

Verses 6-9 are an unrelated narrative that interrupts the flow of Moses' speech, which goes from verse 5 directly to verse 10.

Section heading: the TEV section heading, "Moses Receives the Commandments Again" may be a good model to follow; or else we may use something like BRCL, "The New Tablets of the Law."

10.1	RSV	TEV

"At that time the LORD said to me, 'Hew two tables of stone like the first, and come up to me on the mountain, and make an ark of wood.

"Then the LORD said to me, 'Cut two stone tablets like the first ones and make a wooden Box to put them in. Come up to me on the mountain,

With the beginning of a new section it may be helpful to begin with something like "Moses said to the Israelites."

At that time: that is, at the end of the forty days during which Moses lay prostrate before the LORD (9.25). This may be made clear in translation: "Moses said to the people, 'When the forty days and nights had ended, the LORD told me . . . . ' "

Hew two tables of stone like the first: the English verbs "to cut," "to carve," or "to chisel" are appropriate for working with stone, and a translation should use the normal verb for this kind of work. The first two stone tablets had been carved out by God (9.10-11); these two are to be exactly like the original two.

Come up to me on the mountain: God is still on top of Mount Sinai (see 9.9).

Make an ark of wood: in the nature of the case, this is a box, a container for the two stone tablets. NIV has "a wooden chest," REB "a wooden chest, an ark." This box is later referred to as "the ark of the covenant" (verse 8). However, in the present context the translation should be simply "a chest" or "a box," or something similar.

RSV and TOB give the exact order of the Hebrew text, which seems to say that Yahweh tells Moses to make an ark after he goes back up the mountain with the stone tablets. This seems highly improbable, and most translations are like TEV (CEV, REB, FRCL, and others), which the translator is encouraged to follow.

10.2   RSV   TEV

And I will write on the tables the words that were on the first tables which you broke, and you shall put them in the ark.'	**and I will write on those tablets what I wrote on the tablets that you broke, and then you are to put them in the Box.'**

I will write: see 5.22.

The words that were on the first tables: **the words** are the ten commandments (see verse 4), as they were on the earlier occasion (see 9.10). However, translators are urged to use a more general translation here, such as "the same words" (CEV), or "what I wrote" (TEV).

Which you broke: see 9.17.

Put them in the ark: "put them in the Box" (TEV), or "put these stones in the chest" (CEV).

10.3   RSV   TEV

So I made an ark of acacia wood, and hewed two tables of stone like the first, and went up the mountain with the two tables in my hand.	**"So I made a Box of acacia wood and cut two stone tablets like the first ones and took them up the mountain.**

Acacia wood: the Hebrew is "*shittim* [wood]," a word that appears in the place-name "Abel-shittim" (Num 33.49), which, for obvious reasons, TEV translates "Acacia Valley." It was a durable wood, brownish orange in color, and these trees are still found in that part of the world. Where the **acacia** tree is unknown, we may say, for example, "wood from the tree called 'acacia,' " and then, when the term appears again, leave out the phrase "tree called." It will also be helpful to include a note in the Glossary describing this tree. See FFB for further information.

Like the first: exactly like the first two stone tablets, which God had made.

In my hand: the normal way of saying this in English is "in my hands" (NIV, REB); or else we may use the verb "holding . . ." or "carrying [the two tablets]."

10.4   RSV   TEV

And he wrote on the tables, as at the   Then the LORD wrote on those tablets
first writing, the ten commandments⁹   the same words that he had written
which the LORD had spoken to you   the first time, the Ten Command-
on the mountain out of the midst of   ments that he gave you when he
the fire on the day of the assembly;   spoke from the fire on the day you
and the LORD gave them to me.   were gathered at the mountain. The
                                             LORD gave me the tablets,

ᵍ Heb *words*

  And he wrote . . . , as at the first writing: an alternative model is "There [on
the mountain] the LORD wrote the Ten Commandments on them, just as he had
done the first time."
  On the mountain out of the midst of the fire on the day of the assembly: see
the same language in 9.10.
  The LORD gave them to me: that is, the two stone tablets, not the ten
commandments.

10.5   RSV   TEV

Then I turned and came down from   and I turned and went down the
the mountain, and put the tables in   mountain. Then, just as the LORD had
the ark which I had made; and there   commanded, I put them in the Box
they are, as the LORD commanded   that I had made—and they have been
me.   there ever since."

  I turned and came down from the mountain: this can be expressed more
naturally, "I came back down" (NIV, REB), or even "I took them down the
mountainside" (CEV).
  And there they are: Moses is saying that the two stone tablets are still in the
Box, where he had placed them some forty years earlier. TEV has "and they have
been there ever since"; CEV has "and they are still there."
  As the LORD commanded me: this could go at the beginning of the sentence,
"As the LORD commanded me, I placed the tablets . . . ." For **the LORD** see 1.6.

2A-14. The death of Aaron (10.6-7)

                    RSV   TEV

  6 (The people of Israel journeyed from   (6 The Israelites set out from the wells that
Beeroth Bene-jaakan to Moserah. There Aaron   belonged to the people of Jaakan, and went to
died, and there he was buried; and his son   Moserah. There Aaron died and was buried,
Eleazar ministered as priest in his stead.   and his son Eleazar succeeded him as priest.
7 From there they journeyed to Gudgodah, and   7 From there they went to Gudgodah and then
from Gudgodah to Jotbathah, a land with   on to Jotbathah, a well-watered place.
brooks of water.

It is not clear why the two separate notes (verses 6-7 and verses 8-9) are inserted here. Some device must be used in the translation to let the reader know that verses 6-9 are not part of what Moses was saying to the people at this time. One device is to enclose the section with parentheses, as RSV and TEV have done. Another device is to have two separate sections; in this case, no parentheses are needed.

Section heading: this short section can have the heading "The death of Aaron" or "Aaron dies."

10.6	RSV	TEV

(The people of Israel journeyed from Beeroth Bene-jaakan[h] to Moserah. There Aaron died, and there he was buried; and his son Eleazar ministered as priest in his stead.

(The Israelites set out from the wells that belonged to the people of Jaakan, and went to Moserah. There Aaron died and was buried, and his son Eleazar succeeded him as priest.

[h] Or *the wells of the Bene-jaakan*

In this section Moses is not the speaker.

The place-name **Beeroth Bene-jaakan** is explained in part in the RSV footnote. **Bene-jaakan** means "the sons [or, the people] of Jaakan"; see NIV "the wells of the Jaakanites." For this place see Num 33.31-32. TEV translates the name: "the wells that belonged to the people of Jaakan" (so also CEV).

There Aaron died: for the death and burial of Aaron, see Num 20.22-29, 33-38.

His son Eleazar ministered as priest in his stead: the Hebrew verb is simply "to priest," and the text is saying that Eleazar succeeded his father Aaron as (the chief) priest. In some languages there are different ways of speaking of a son, depending on his age in relation to his brothers. Eleazar was the third of Aaron's four sons Nadab, Abihu, Eleazar, and Ithamar (Num 3.1-4), and at the time of Aaron's death, he was the older of the two surviving sons. (The two older sons had been killed for disobeying the rules for the proper worship of Yahweh.) **Priest** will be difficult to translate in some languages, especially for translators who have not yet translated the New Testament. *A Handbook on Leviticus*, page 16, has an excellent discussion on the Levitical priests:

> . . . The primary duty of the priest was to serve as an intermediary between the LORD and his people. The means by which this was done was by sacrifice. Thus in some languages this word has been translated "sacrificer" or "intermediary." But care should be taken to avoid negative connotations of a word like "sacrifice" if it evokes ideas of pagan sacrifice quite different from those of the people of Israel.

A Handbook on the Gospel of Mark, page 69, lists terms that a number of cultures have used; for example, "one who presents man's sacrifice to God," "one who takes the name of the sacrifice," and "spokesman of the people before God."

10.7 RSV TEV

From there they journeyed to Gudgodah, and from Gudgodah to Jotbathah, a land with brooks of water.	From there they went to Gudgodah and then on to Jotbathah, a well-watered place.

They journeyed: it is better to make it clear that "the Israelites journeyed [or, traveled]." The itinerary in Num 33.32-33 does not mention **Gudgodah**; perhaps it is the same as "Hor-haggidgad." However, **Gudgodah** should be used here.

A land with brooks of water: that is, "a land with many streams," "a land with much water," or "a well-watered place" (TEV).

2A-15. The duties of the Levites (10.8-9)

RSV TEV

8 At that time the LORD set apart the tribe of Levi to carry the ark of the covenant of the LORD, to stand before the LORD to minister to him and to bless in his name, to this day. 9 Therefore Levi has no portion or inheritance with his brothers; the LORD is his inheritance, as the LORD your God said to him.)

8 At the mountain the LORD appointed the men of the tribe of Levi to be in charge of the Covenant Box, to serve him as priests, and to pronounce blessings in his name. And these are still their duties. 9 That is why the tribe of Levi received no land as the other tribes did; what they received was the privilege of being the LORD's priests, as the LORD your God promised.)

Verses 8-9 are a separate note, giving additional information about the Levites. The words **the LORD your God** at the end of verse 9 seem to show that Moses is the speaker.

Section heading: as a separate section these two verses can have a heading such as "The duties of the Levites" or "The duties of the men of the tribe of Levi."

10.8 RSV TEV

At that time the LORD set apart the tribe of Levi to carry the ark of the covenant of the LORD, to stand before the LORD to minister to him and to bless in his name, to this day.	At the mountain[j] the LORD appointed the men of the tribe of Levi to be in charge of the Covenant Box, to serve him as priests, and to pronounce blessings in his name. And these are still their duties.

[j] the mountain; or that time.

Here Moses' speech is continued from verse 5. Depending on how they have handled verses 6-7, translators may wish to show that Moses is again the speaker here; for example, "Moses spoke to the people again."

At that time: this can refer to verses 6-7, but it seems more likely that it refers back to verses 1-5, which speak of the Covenant Box.

Set apart the tribe of Levi: for the setting apart of the people of the tribe of Levi to serve as priests, see Exo 32.25-39. The TEV translation "appointed the men of the tribe . . ." will be a good model. For **tribe** see 1.13.

The Levites had three responsibilities: (1) **to carry the ark of the covenant** (Num 3.5-8); (2) **to stand before the LORD to minister to him**, that is, to "offer the prescribed sacrifices at the place of worship" or "to serve him [Yahweh] as priests" (TEV); (3) **to bless in his name**, that is, to pray the LORD's blessings for the people (see the priestly blessing in Num 6.22-27). In many languages **to bless** . . . may be expressed as "to ask Yahweh to be kind to his people and give them prosperity [or, cause them to be prosperous]."

Instead of **the ark of the covenant**, a translation may choose to imitate TEV "the Covenant Box." But a more comprehensive description may be necessary: "the Box that contained the two tablets of the covenant."

To this day: if Moses is the speaker of verses 8-9, this may be understood to refer to the time when Moses is speaking to the Israelites. But it may refer to the time of the writing of this account. If this is correct, a footnote should be added to inform the reader (see 2.22).

10.9	RSV	TEV

RSV	TEV
Therefore Levi has no portion or inheritance with his brothers; the LORD is his inheritance, as the LORD your God said to him.)	That is why the tribe of Levi received no land as the other tribes did; what they received was the privilege of being the LORD's priests, as the LORD your God promised.)

Levi . . . his brothers: this is a way of speaking of the tribe of Levi, the people of the tribe of Levi, as compared with the people of the other tribes. So TEV "That is why the tribe of Levi . . . ."

No portion or inheritance: these two nouns mean the same thing. They are variously translated; for example, NJPSV "no hereditary portion," and REB "no holding of ancestral land." This refers to the area of land assigned to each tribe; only the tribe of Levi was not assigned any land. In cultures where tribes or clans still exist, the idea of "ancestral land" will translate naturally. In other languages, however, we must say something like "received no land as the other tribes did" (TEV).

The LORD is his inheritance: instead of supporting themselves from the land that would have been assigned to them, the Levites' support came from their work as priests of Yahweh (see TEV). FRCL has "the privilege of serving the LORD"; BRCL "the right of the men of the tribe of Levi to serve as priests of God."

As the LORD your God said to him: see Num 18.20, where God said this to Aaron. Here **him**, meaning Levi, should be translated as a plural pronoun, since it does not mean that God said this to Levi, son of Jacob, but to the Levites as a tribe. For **the LORD your God** see 1.6.

If verses 6-9 are not treated as two separate sections (see note at verse 6), then this verse should be closed with a parenthesis, and a new paragraph should begin with verse 10.

2A-16. The LORD answers the prayer of Moses (10.10-11)

RSV

10 "I stayed on the mountain, as at the first time, forty days and forty nights, and the LORD hearkened to me that time also; the LORD was unwilling to destroy you. 11 And the LORD said to me, 'Arise, go on your journey at the head of the people, that they may go in and possess the land, which I swore to their fathers to give them.'

TEV

10 "I stayed on the mountain forty days and nights, as I did the first time. The LORD listened to me once more and agreed not to destroy you. 11 Then he told me to go and lead you, so that you could take possession of the land that he had promised to give to your ancestors.

Section heading: if translators make verses 6-9 into two separate sections, it will be good to have another heading here, such as "The LORD Answers the Prayer of Moses" (CEV).

10.10   RSV

"I stayed on the mountain, as at the first time, forty days and forty nights, and the LORD hearkened to me that time also; the LORD was unwilling to destroy you.

TEV

"I stayed on the mountain forty days and nights, as I did the first time. The LORD listened to me once more and agreed not to destroy you.

It may be helpful to start verse 10 with something like "Moses continued to speak to the Israelites."

Moses tells of another **forty days and forty nights** he stayed on the mountain (see 9.9).

The LORD hearkened to me at that time also: again the LORD answered his prayer. And as a consequence of Moses' prayer, the LORD **was unwilling to destroy you** (see 9.26 and similar passages). This can be rendered "the LORD agreed not to destroy you," or "the LORD decided not to . . . ."

10.11   RSV

And the LORD said to me, 'Arise, go on your journey at the head of the people, that they may go in and possess the land, which I swore to their fathers to give them.'

TEV

Then he told me to go and lead you, so that you could take possession of the land that he had promised to give to your ancestors.

Now comes the command to cross the Jordan River and take possession of the land of Canaan, which the LORD had promised the patriarchs he would give to their descendants (see 1.8).

Go on your journey at the head of the people: this makes it sound like Moses will lead the Israelites into the Promised Land, whereas he died in Moab without crossing the Jordan into the land of Canaan. TEV has "Then he told me to go and lead you . . ."; and CEV has, "Instead he told me, 'Moses, get ready to lead the people . . . .'" These are both possible alternatives to RSV.

For **possess the land** and **fathers**, see 1.8.

2A-17. What God demands (10.12-22)

RSV	TEV
	What God Demands

RSV	TEV
12 "And now, Israel, what does the LORD your God require of you, but to fear the LORD your God, to walk in all his ways, to love him, to serve the LORD your God with all your heart and with all your soul, 13 and to keep the commandments and statutes of the LORD, which I command you this day for your good? 14 Behold, to the LORD your God belong heaven and the heaven of heavens, the earth with all that is in it; 15 yet the LORD set his heart in love upon your fathers and chose their descendants after them, you above all peoples, as at this day. 16 Circumcise therefore the foreskin of your heart, and be no longer stubborn. 17 For the LORD your God is God of gods and Lord of lords, the great, the mighty, and the terrible God, who is not partial and takes no bribe. 18 He executes justice for the fatherless and the widow, and loves the sojourner, giving him food and clothing. 19 Love the sojourner therefore; for you were sojourners in the land of Egypt. 20 You shall fear the LORD your God; you shall serve him and cleave to him, and by his name you shall swear. 21 He is your praise; he is your God, who has done for you these great and terrible things which your eyes have seen. 22 Your fathers went down to Egypt seventy persons; and now the LORD your God has made you as the stars of heaven for multitude.	12 "Now, people of Israel, listen to what the LORD your God demands of you: Worship the LORD and do all that he commands. Love him, serve him with all your heart, 13 and obey all his laws. I am giving them to you today for your benefit. 14 To the LORD belong even the highest heavens; the earth is his also, and everything on it. 15 But the LORD's love for your ancestors was so strong that he chose you instead of any other people, and you are still his chosen people. 16 So then, from now on be obedient to the LORD and stop being stubborn. 17 The LORD your God is supreme over all gods and over all powers. He is great and mighty, and he is to be obeyed. He does not show partiality, and he does not accept bribes. 18 He makes sure that orphans and widows are treated fairly; he loves the foreigners who live with our people, and gives them food and clothes. 19 So then, show love for those foreigners, because you were once foreigners in Egypt. 20 Have reverence for the LORD your God and worship only him. Be faithful to him and make your promises in his name alone. 21 Praise him—he is your God, and you have seen with your own eyes the great and astounding things that he has done for you. 22 When your ancestors went to Egypt, there were only seventy of them. But now the LORD your God has made you as numerous as the stars in the sky.

Moses once again exhorts the people to obey God's commands when they have settled in the Promised Land. They must always be mindful of God's love for them and show the same kind of love for one another. In all things they must be faithful in their allegiance to Yahweh alone (verse 20).

Section heading: the TEV section heading, "What God Demands," may be too indefinite for some translations; "Worship and honor the LORD" or "Respect and obey Yahweh" may be better.

10.12	RSV	TEV

"And now, Israel, what does the LORD your God require of you, but to fear the LORD your God, to walk in all his ways, to love him, to serve the LORD your God with all your heart and with all your soul,

"Now, people of Israel, listen to what the LORD your God demands of you: Worship the LORD and do all that he commands. Love him, serve him with all your heart,

As with the beginning of other sections, it will be good to show that Moses is still speaking; for example, "Moses spoke to the people of Israel."

Verses 12-13 are a long, rhetorical question, which few translations will want to imitate. The question is a way of saying "This is what the LORD your God requires [or, demands] of you: . . . ," or "Listen to what . . . demands" (TEV), or even ". . . what the LORD your God wants you to do." A similar question is found in Micah 6.8. The verse can begin: "People of Israel, this is all that the LORD your God asks you to do."

To fear the LORD your God: see 4.10.

To walk in all his ways: see 5.33.

To love him . . . with all your heart and with all your soul: see 6.5. For **to serve him** see 6.13.

10.13	RSV	TEV

and to keep the commandments and statutes of the LORD, which I command you this day for your good?

and obey all his laws. I am giving them to you today for your benefit.

To keep the commandments and the statutes of the LORD: see 4.40.

This day: again the time signal is given; all this is taking place just before they are to cross the Jordan into the Promised Land.

For your good: meaning the same as "it may go well with you" in 4.40.

10.14	RSV	TEV

Behold, to the LORD your God belong heaven and the heaven of heavens, the earth with all that is in it;

To the LORD belong even the highest heavens; the earth is his also, and everything on it.

Verses 14 and 15 go together, emphasizing Yahweh's goodness in choosing the Israelites to be his people. The connection between the two verses should be quite clear.

Behold: a way of calling their attention; see 1.10.

To the LORD your God belong heaven and the heaven of heavens: this is a normal Hebrew way of making a superlative, which may not be natural in some languages (as it is not natural in English). The whole phrase means "all the heavens above," "even the highest heavens." REB has "heaven itself, the highest heaven," NJPSV "the heavens to their uttermost reaches," NIV "the heavens, even the highest heavens." Some repetition or other form of emphasis seems advisable; but the translator must decide whether a phrase like "even the highest heavens" (TEV) will lead the reader to think that there are a number of heavens, varying in height. POCL has "the heavens and all they contain." In many languages "sky" and "heaven" will be the same term; so "the sky and all it contains" or "everything in the sky" will be natural ways to express this. For **the LORD your God** see 1.6.

The earth with all that is in it: primarily this refers to all the living beings on earth. So we may translate "the earth and all the living things in it."

10.15	RSV	TEV

yet the LORD set his heart in love upon your fathers and chose their descendants after them, you above all peoples, as at this day.	But the LORD's love for your ancestors was so strong that he chose you instead of any other people, and you are still his chosen people.

The greatness of Yahweh's love for Israel is shown by the fact that God, the lord and owner of all creation, chose such an insignificant people as the Israelites to be his own people.

The LORD set his heart in love upon your fathers: see 4.37; 7.7. In Hebrew there are two verbs, "fix your desire on" and "love," which are combined into the one verbal phrase. SPCL has "He preferred your ancestors [over all other peoples] and loved them," which may be a good model to follow.

And chose their descendants after them, you . . . : this is unnatural and unnecessarily wordy. Something like "and he chose you, their descendants" may be better. In some languages it will be better to make a new sentence and say, for example, "He chose you. You are their descendants . . . ."

You above all peoples: of all the peoples on earth, Yahweh chose the Israelites to be his own people.

As at this day: again Moses reminds his hearers of their present situation. BRCL offers a good model to follow for this verse:

- But his love for your ancestors was so great that of all peoples on earth he chose you, and to this very day you are his chosen people.

10.16	RSV	TEV

Circumcise therefore the foreskin of your heart, and be no longer stubborn.

So then, from now on be obedient to the LORD and stop being stubborn.

Circumcise . . . the foreskin of your heart: this figure of speech reflects the rite of circumcision, by which a Jewish male became a member of the chosen race, bound to God by the covenant which God had made with Abraham, of which circumcision was the sign (Gen 17.1-14). To **circumcise . . . the . . . heart**" is to make your disposition and desire obedient to the terms of the covenant, that is, to obey God's laws (Jer 4.3-4). The meaning is clarified by what follows, **and be no longer stubborn** (see 9.6, 13).

In very few languages will this figure of speech mean very much; in fact in some languages such figurative language will be vulgar and offensive. Some translations provide a footnote explaining the figure. It is better to abandon the figure altogether and give the meaning in a straightforward manner, as TEV does with "be obedient to the LORD." See FRCL "be completely consecrated to the LORD your God." But SPCL "Put in your heart the sign of the covenant" (similarly POCL) is not very clear.

10.17	RSV	TEV

For the LORD your God is God of gods and Lord of lords, the great, the mighty, and the terrible God, who is not partial and takes no bribe.

The LORD your God is supreme over all gods and over all powers. He is great and mighty, and he is to be obeyed. He does not show partiality, and he does not accept bribes.

God of gods and Lord of lords: this is another instance of a superlative (see verse 14). It means "the greatest of all gods, the mightiest of all lords" (see Psa 136.2-3) or "The LORD your God is supreme over all gods and over all powers" (TEV). **Lord** means "ruler," or "one who has the power to rule." We may combine the two phrases and say "Yahweh your God is more powerful than all other gods and rulers." For **gods** see 3.24.

The great, the mighty, and the terrible God: the adjectives **great** (see 7.21) and **mighty** have almost the same meaning, and their equivalents should be easy to find; CEV combines the two terms with "tremendous power." **Terrible** means "awesome," one who is to be feared (see 7.21). The whole sentence may be also expressed as "and people should be afraid of his tremendous power."

Is not partial: God does not have favorites; he treats everyone alike (see 1.17, where the same is said of human judges). CEV has "his decisions are always fair," or we may say "He always judges people fairly."

Takes no bribes: as a judge God always gives a just and fair decision; he cannot be paid to render an unjust decision. If the figure of God's (not) accepting a bribe is too strange or difficult for readers to accept, the figure must be abandoned and the meaning expressed clearly; for example, "he always renders a right decision," "all his judgments are right," or "when God judges people he is always just."

10.18   RSV   TEV

He executes justice for the fatherless and the widow, and loves the sojourner, giving him food and clothing.

He makes sure that orphans and widows are treated fairly; he loves the foreigners who live with our people, and gives them food and clothes.

Executes justice for the fatherless and widows: this does not only mean that God is impartial in applying the law to orphans and widows, but that God actively takes their side. Another way to express this is "Makes sure that . . . are treated fairly" (TEV). Orphans and widows were the people with the least power in that society, and they were easily exploited by unscrupulous people. FRCL has "He defends the rights of orphans and widows" (see also CEV). The Hebrew word translated as **fatherless** by RSV and "orphan" by many other translations refers to "a child without a father." In languages that distinguish between "orphan," a child who has lost both parents, and "fatherless," a child who has lost only the father, the translator should choose "fatherless." Otherwise "orphan" may be used.

The sojourner: this means "resident aliens," foreigners who lived with the Israelites. BRCL has "the foreigners who live among us," and TEV "the foreigners who live with our people." We may note that this reference makes more sense in a context where the people are already settled in the land of Canaan.

Giving him food and clothing: it is better to use the plural form, "the foreigners who live in our land; he gives them food and clothing."

10.19   RSV   TEV

Love the sojourner therefore; for you were sojourners in the land of Egypt.

So then, show love for those foreigners, because you were once foreigners in Egypt.

For an almost exact parallel to this verse, see Lev 19.34 (see also Exo 22.21; 23.9). **Love** here refers to showing concern and care for these foreigners. Thus the translation may be "So you should show care and concern for . . . ," or even "So you should care for . . . ."

10.20   RSV   TEV

You shall fear the Lord your God; you shall serve him and cleave to

Have reverence for the Lord your God and worship only him. Be faith-

him, and by his name you shall swear.	ful to him and make your promises in his name alone.

This verse repeats almost word for word statements found elsewhere in the book (see 6.13). But the verb **cleave to** is used here for the first time. It means to maintain a close relationship with someone, to cling to them or stay close to them (also 11.22; 13.4; 30.20). It is the verb used of the relationship between husband and wife (Gen 2.24). TEV has "be faithful to." This is also possible.

By his name you shall swear: see 6.13.

10.21

RSV	TEV
He is your praise; he is your God, who has done for you these great and terrible things which your eyes have seen.	Praise him—he is your God, and you have seen with your own eyes the great and astounding things that he has done for you.

He is your praise: this can mean either (1) God is the one you must praise, or (2) God is the reason why other peoples praise you. Although the second is possible, it seems that the first meaning is to be preferred. FRCL translates "It is he to whom you must direct your praise." CEV has "Offer your praise to him." However, in languages where the idea of **praise** will require direct speech, we may say, for example, "You must say to him, 'You are wonderful [or, great].' " REB takes **your praise** in another way, "your proud boast"—that is, God is the one that you (the people of Israel) boast about.

Done for you these great and terrible things: see 7.21. This refers in a general way to all that God had done for the people during their forty years' wandering in the wilderness.

Which your eyes have seen: they themselves had seen the great and awesome things that God had done for them (see 3.21).

10.22

RSV	TEV
Your fathers went down to Egypt seventy persons; and now the LORD your God has made you as the stars of heaven for multitude.	When your ancestors went to Egypt, there were only seventy of them. But now the LORD your God has made you as numerous as the stars in the sky.

Your fathers went down to Egypt: this refers to the time when Jacob and his whole family went from the land of Canaan to Egypt, to join Joseph there (see Gen 46.26-27; Exo 1.5). CEV has a good model: "When your ancestors went to live in Egypt, there were only seventy of them."

The stars in heaven for multitude: see the same expression in 1.10.

2A-18. The LORD's greatness (11.1-7)

RSV

TEV
The LORD's Greatness

1 "You shall therefore love the LORD your God, and keep his charge, his statutes, his ordinances, and his commandments always. 2 And consider this day (since I am not speaking to your children who have not known or seen it), consider the discipline of the LORD your God, his greatness, his mighty hand and his outstretched arm, 3 his signs and his deeds which he did in Egypt to Pharaoh the king of Egypt and to all his land; 4 and what he did to the army of Egypt, to their horses and to their chariots; how he made the water of the Red Sea overflow them as they pursued after you, and how the LORD has destroyed them to this day; 5 and what he did to you in the wilderness, until you came to this place; 6 and what he did to Dathan and Abiram the sons of Eliab, son of Reuben; how the earth opened its mouth and swallowed them up, with their households, their tents, and every living thing that followed them, in the midst of all Israel; 7 for your eyes have seen all the great work of the LORD which he did.

1 "Love the LORD your God and always obey all his laws. 2 Remember today what you have learned about the LORD through your experiences with him. It was you, not your children, who had these experiences. You saw the LORD's greatness, his power, his might, 3 and his miracles. You saw what he did to the king of Egypt and to his entire country. 4 You saw how the LORD completely wiped out the Egyptian army, along with their horses and chariots, by drowning them in the Red Sea when they were pursuing you. 5 You know what the LORD did for you in the desert before you arrived here. 6 You recall what he did to Dathan and Abiram, the sons of Eliab of the tribe of Reuben. In the sight of everyone the earth opened up and swallowed them, along with their families, their tents, and all their servants and animals. 7 Yes, you are the ones who have seen all these great things that the LORD has done.

Chapter 11 serves as an introduction to the long section that deals mainly with the rules and regulations the people are to obey after settling in the land of Canaan (chapters 12–26). In this introduction Moses urges the people of Israel to obey all of God's laws so that they will receive his blessings in the Promised Land (verses 8-9, 31-32).

This section, verses 1-7, recalls God's great deeds on behalf of his people, from the exodus from Egypt to the present day. Verses 2-7 form one long complex sentence in Hebrew; it should be broken up into smaller sentences in translation.

Section heading: instead of the abstract "The LORD's Greatness" (TEV) as the section heading, it may be better to have "The great things the LORD has done for his people" or "The LORD does great things for his people." Or the heading (for verses 1-9) of FRCL may serve as a model: "A reminder of what God has done for Israel."

11.1 RSV

TEV

"You shall therefore love the LORD your God, and keep his charge, his statutes, his ordinances, and his commandments always.

"Love the LORD your God and always obey all his laws.

207

A new section begins here, so translators are advised to start the verse with something like "Moses said to the Israelites."

Love the LORD your God: for this command see the similar command in 6.5.

Keep his charge: as in the other passages, **keep** means "obey," "follow," "put into practice." The word **charge**, used here for the first time in this book, means "things commanded" or "obligation." Another way to express this is "do everything that he has required you to do." In the phrase **keep his charge**, the verb and the noun are from the same root, both in Hebrew and in Greek.

For **statutes** and **ordinances** see 4.1; for **commandments** see 4.2.

TEV combines all four Hebrew nouns in this verse in the one phrase, "all his laws." This is alright, since there are no strict differences in meaning among the four words, but TEV does lose some of the emphasis found in the use of three or more words. A translation should not give the impression that the words apply to different kinds of rules. And it may be that some languages do not have four different words for rules and regulations. CEV uses two words: "laws and teachings." **Charge** may also be taken as a general term, with the three following words giving particular types of rules. So an alternative model using three terms of similar meaning is the following: "Follow everything that he requires you to do: his statutes, ordinances, and commandments."

11.2   RSV   TEV

And consider this day (since I am not speaking to your children who have not known or seen it), consider the discipline[i] of the LORD your God, his greatness, his mighty hand and his outstretched arm,	Remember today what you have learned about the LORD through your experiences with him. It was you, not your children, who had these experiences. You saw the LORD's greatness, his power, his might,

[i] Or *instruction*

Consider this day: the verb means "think about," "ponder," "remember" (TEV, CEV, NRSV), "take thought" (NJPSV). **This day** is constantly emphasized (see 10.8, 15).

Since I am not speaking to your children . . . : RSV places this within parentheses, since the direct object of the verb **consider** is **the discipline of the LORD your God**. There are other, better ways of handling this; TEV has "Remember today what you have learned . . . . It was you, not your children, who had these experiences," and CEV has a slightly different model: "Remember, he corrected you and not your children." The emphasis is on the fact that the people who are there in Moab with Moses, and not their children, are the ones who experienced all those events. Then Moses lists the very things they saw (see verses 3, 7). For **the LORD your God** see 1.6.

The discipline of the LORD your God: the Hebrew noun can mean the act of disciplining, or "training," as NRSV, REB, NIV have it (see the verb in 8.5); or it can mean "lesson," "instruction" (so TEV "what you have learned"; see also

NJPSV, TOB). Either meaning fits well in the context, but it may be that the meaning "lesson" or "instruction" is to be preferred.

His greatness: instead of an abstract noun, a verbal phrase may be better: "how great [or mighty, or powerful] he is." CEV has "You are the ones who saw the LORD use his great power."

Mighty hand . . . outstretched arm: see 4.34. In some languages translators may need to combine **greatness**, **mighty hand**, and **outstretched arm** by using one expression such as "mighty power."

11.3   RSV   TEV

his signs and his deeds which he did in Egypt to Pharaoh the king of Egypt and to all his land;	and his miracles. You saw what he did to the king of Egypt and to his entire country.

His signs: see 4.34. Instead of the noun phrase **his deeds**, it may be better to say "the [great, or terrible] things [or, miracles] he did." These are the plagues God sent upon the land of Egypt (in 4.34 the plagues are referred to as "signs and wonders").

Pharaoh the king of Egypt: here the title "Pharaoh" is used as a proper name (see 6.21). For **king** see 1.4.

All his land: the sense is either "all his people" or "the entire country" (TEV), probably the latter.

An alternative translation model for verses 2 and 3 is:

- ² Think today about what the LORD taught you through your experiences with him. It was you, not your children, who experienced these things. You are the ones who saw the LORD use his great power, ³ when he did great miracles in Egypt and caused Pharaoh the king of Egypt and his whole land to suffer terribly.

11.4   RSV   TEV

and what he did to the army of Egypt, to their horses and to their chariots; how he made the water of the Red Sea overflow them as they pursued after you, and how the LORD has destroyed them to this day;	You saw how the LORD completely wiped out the Egyptian army, along with their horses and chariots, by drowning them in the Red Sea[k] when they were pursuing you.

[k] RED SEA: *See Word List.*

Here Moses recalls the destruction of the Egyptian army at the **Red Sea** (Exo 14.23-29).

WAR CHARIOTS

The army . . . their horses . . . their chariots: all these words are also found in Exo 14.23. **Army** refers to the Egyptian soldiers or fighting men, and in many languages it will be expressed as "all the Egyptian soldiers." The Egyptian war **chariots** were pulled by two horses. In many languages translators will need to use a descriptive phrase for **chariots**; for example, "horse-drawn war carts" or "war carts pulled by two horses." It will be helpful in cultures where **horses** are unknown to use a descriptive phrase, for example, "animal called 'horse,'" and include an illustration of this animal, preferably pulling a chariot. Also see FFB, pages 43-45.

He made the water of the Red Sea overflow them: that is, as explained in the account in Exodus, God allowed the waters of the Sea to fall back in place and drown the Egyptians. For **Red Sea** see 1.40.

As they pursued after you: the Egyptian soldiers rode in their chariots as they pursued the Israelites. It will therefore be helpful to place this clause at the beginning of the verse as follows: "When the Egyptian soldiers chased you in their war carts pulled by horses, you saw the LORD drown them in the Red Sea and destroy them completely [or, decisively]."

To this day: this means "and so things remain to this day" (REB). NIV has "the LORD brought lasting ruin on them."

11.5   RSV   TEV

and what he did to you in the wilder-   You know what the LORD did for you
ness, until you came to this place;   in the desert before you arrived here.

What he did to you in the wilderness: in English, at least, **did to you** is mostly used to refer to something bad; here it is better to follow TEV, CEV, REB, NIV, "did for you," referring to the many things God did for the people during the forty years in the wilderness. For **wilderness** see 1.1.

Until you came to this place: that is, "right up to the time you arrived here" (CEV), meaning Moab, across the Jordan River from Canaan.

11.6 RSV TEV

and what he did to Dathan and Abiram the sons of Eliab, son of Reuben; how the earth opened its mouth and swallowed them up, with their households, their tents, and every living thing that followed them, in the midst of all Israel;	You recall what he did to Dathan and Abiram, the sons of Eliab of the tribe of Reuben. In the sight of everyone the earth opened up and swallowed them, along with their families, their tents, and all their servants and animals.

For this incident see Numbers 16; Korah, the leader of the rebellion, is not mentioned here. See the TEV model.

The earth opened its mouth and swallowed them up: in many languages the idea of the earth opening its mouth will be an acceptable poetic metaphor. In others, however, it may not be natural to use this kind of language, in which the earth is pictured as a huge monster devouring its victims. The reader should not find the language unnatural or ridiculous. In such a case it will be helpful to show that Yahweh caused this event to occur; for example, "You saw how Yahweh caused the earth to open up underneath the tents of Dathan and Abiram the sons of Eliab from the tribe of Reuben. They, their families, their . . . fell down into the earth [or, this hole] and disappeared."

Their households: this means all the members of their families (the heads of families are being referred to).

Every living thing that followed them: this includes servants and animals (see the same term in Gen 4.7, 23). TEV makes this clear with "and all their servants and animals."

In the midst of all Israel: the disaster took place right there in the camp, where all the other Israelites saw it happen. So TEV has "In the sight of everyone."

11.7 RSV TEV

for your eyes have seen all the great work of the LORD which he did.	Yes, you are the ones who have seen all these great things that the LORD has done.

This conclusion ties in with verse 2.

All the great work: this includes all the extraordinary things God did as he led the people those forty years in the wilderness. CEV has a helpful model: "with your own eyes, you saw the LORD's mighty power do all these things." But we may also express this as ". . . you saw the LORD use his mighty power to do all these things."

2A-19. The blessings of the Promised Land (11.8-32)

RSV	TEV
	The Blessings of the Promised Land

8 "You shall therefore keep all the commandment which I command you this day, that you may be strong, and go in and take possession of the land which you are going over to possess, 9 and that you may live long in the land which the LORD swore to your fathers to give to them and to their descendants, a land flowing with milk and honey. 10 For the land which you are entering to take possession of it is not like the land of Egypt, from which you have come, where you sowed your seed and watered it with your feet, like a garden of vegetables; 11 but the land which you are going over to possess is a land of hills and valleys, which drinks water by the rain from heaven, 12 a land which the LORD your God cares for; the eyes of the LORD your God are always upon it, from the beginning of the year to the end of the year.

13 "And if you will obey my commandments which I command you this day, to love the LORD your God, and to serve him with all your heart and with all your soul, 14 he will give the rain for your land in its season, the early rain and the later rain, that you may gather in your grain and your wine and your oil. 15 And he will give grass in your fields for your cattle, and you shall eat and be full. 16 Take heed lest your heart be deceived, and you turn aside and serve other gods and worship them, 17 and the anger of the LORD be kindled against you, and he shut up the heavens, so that there be no rain, and the land yield no fruit, and you perish quickly off the good land which the LORD gives you.

18 "You shall therefore lay up these words of mine in your heart and in your soul; and you shall bind them as a sign upon your hand, and they shall be as frontlets between your eyes. 19 And you shall teach them to your children, talking of them when you are sitting in your house, and when you are walking by the way, and when you lie down, and when you rise. 20 And you shall write them upon the doorposts of your house and upon your gates, 21 that your days and the days of your children may be multiplied in the land which the LORD swore to your fathers to give them, as long as the heavens are above the earth. 22 For if you will be careful to do all this commandment which I command you to do, loving the LORD your God, walking in all his ways, and cleaving to him, 23 then the LORD will drive out all these nations before you, and you

8 "Obey everything that I have commanded you today. Then you will be able to cross the river and occupy the land that you are about to enter. 9 And you will live a long time in the rich and fertile land that the LORD promised to give your ancestors and their descendants. 10 The land that you are about to occupy is not like the land of Egypt, where you lived before. There, when you planted grain, you had to work hard to irrigate the fields; 11 but the land that you are about to enter is a land of mountains and valleys, a land watered by rain. 12 The LORD your God takes care of this land and watches over it throughout the year.

13 "So then, obey the commands that I have given you today; love the LORD your God and serve him with all your heart. 14 If you do, he will send rain on your land when it is needed, in the autumn and in the spring, so that there will be grain, wine, and olive oil for you, 15 and grass for your livestock. You will have all the food you want. 16 Do not let yourselves be led away from the LORD to worship and serve other gods. 17 If you do, the LORD will become angry with you. He will hold back the rain, and your ground will become too dry for crops to grow. Then you will soon die there, even though it is a good land that he is giving you.

18 "Remember these commands and cherish them. Tie them on your arms and wear them on your foreheads as a reminder. 19 Teach them to your children. Talk about them when you are at home and when you are away, when you are resting and when you are working. 20 Write them on the doorposts of your houses and on your gates. 21 Then you and your children will live a long time in the land that the LORD your God promised to give to your ancestors. You will live there as long as there is a sky above the earth.

22 "Obey faithfully everything that I have commanded you: Love the LORD your God, do everything he commands, and be faithful to him. 23 Then he will drive out all those nations as you advance, and you will occupy the land belonging to nations greater and more powerful than you. 24 All the ground that you march over will be yours. Your territory will extend from the desert in the south to the Lebanon Mountains in the north, and from the Euphrates River in the east to the Mediterranean Sea in the west. 25 Wherever you go in that land, the LORD your God will make the

will dispossess nations greater and mightier than yourselves. 24 Every place on which the sole of your foot treads shall be yours; your territory shall be from the wilderness and Lebanon and from the River, the river Euphrates, to the western sea. 25 No man shall be able to stand against you; the LORD your God will lay the fear of you and the dread of you upon all the land that you shall tread, as he promised you.

26 "Behold, I set before you this day a blessing and a curse: 27 the blessing, if you obey the commandments of the LORD your God, which I command you this day, 28 and the curse, if you do not obey the commandments of the LORD your God, but turn aside from the way which I command you this day, to go after other gods which you have not known. 29 And when the LORD your God brings you into the land which you are entering to take possession of it, you shall set the blessing on Mount Gerizim and the curse on Mount Ebal. 30 Are they not beyond the Jordan, west of the road, toward the going down of the sun, in the land of the Canaanites who live in the Arabah, over against Gilgal, beside the oak of Moreh? 31 For you are to pass over the Jordan to go in to take possession of the land which the LORD your God gives you; and when you possess it and live in it, 32 you shall be careful to do all the statutes and the ordinances which I set before you this day.

people fear you, as he has promised, and no one will be able to stop you.

26 "Today I am giving you the choice between a blessing and a curse— 27 a blessing, if you obey the commands of the LORD your God that I am giving you today; 28 but a curse, if you disobey these commands and turn away to worship other gods that you have never worshiped before. 29 When the LORD brings you into the land that you are going to occupy, you are to proclaim the blessing from Mount Gerizim and the curse from Mount Ebal. (30 These two mountains are west of the Jordan River in the territory of the Canaanites who live in the Jordan Valley. They are toward the west, not far from the sacred trees of Moreh near the town of Gilgal.) 31 You are about to cross the Jordan River and occupy the land that the LORD your God is giving you. When you take it and settle there, 32 be sure to obey all the laws that I am giving you today.

Moses continues exhorting the people to obey all of God's commands (verses 8, 11, 18, 22), so that God will bless them in the Promised Land. They have a choice: God's blessing if they obey, and God's curse if they disobey (verses 26-28).

Section heading: the TEV section heading, "The Blessings of the Promised Land," may be better expressed in other languages by the use of a verb: "The good things the LORD will do for his people in the Promised Land," or "The LORD promises to do good things for his people." NJB has "Promises and Warnings," FRCL "The land that the LORD cares for" (see verse 12).

11.8 RSV	TEV
"You shall therefore keep all the commandment which I command you this day, that you may be strong, and go in and take possession of the land which you are going over to possess,	"Obey everything that I have commanded you today. Then you will be able to cross the river and occupy the land that you are about to enter.

With the beginning of a new section, Moses should be reintroduced as the speaker.

Keep all the commandment: see 5.31.

That you may be strong: this strength is in terms of the power and might they will need as they invade and **take possession of the land** (see 1.8; 4.1). Another way to express this is "You will be strong enough to conquer . . . ."

You are going over to possess: as in 4.14. Translators should make it clear in the translation that the people had to cross the Jordan River in order to **go in and take possession of the land**.

CEV has an excellent model for this verse:

●   Soon you will cross the Jordan River, and if you obey the commands that I am giving you today, you will be strong enough to conquer the land.

11.9 RSV	TEV
and that you may live long in the land which the LORD swore to your fathers to give to them and to their descendants, a land flowing with milk and honey.	And you will live a long time in the rich and fertile land that the LORD promised to give your ancestors and their descendants.

Live long in the land: see 4.40; 5.16.
The LORD swore to your fathers to give them: see 1.8.
A land flowing with milk and honey: see 6.3.

11.10-11 RSV	TEV
10 For the land which you are entering to take possession of it is not like the land of Egypt, from which you have come, where you sowed your seed and watered it with your feet, like a garden of vegetables; 11 but the land which you are going over to possess is a land of hills and valleys, which drinks water by the rain from heaven,	10 The land that you are about to occupy is not like the land of Egypt, where you lived before. There, when you planted grain, you had to work hard to irrigate the fields; 11 but the land that you are about to enter is a land of mountains and valleys, a land watered by rain.

Verses 10-13 are one sentence, with some repetition: **you are entering to take possession of it** (verse 10) and **you are going over to possess** (verse 11), as in verse 8. In some languages the use of this kind of repetition may have a negative effect, leaving the reader bored with the narrative. A translator should use the style that will include all the information of the biblical text and at the same time keep the reader's interest.

Not like the land of Egypt: the main difference is the source of water needed to grow crops. In Canaan the seasonal rains supplied the water; in Egypt the water was made to flow in irrigation canals by a series of water wheels, turned by foot. This seems to be the most reasonable explanation of the expression **and watered it with your feet**; some believe it is simply a way of saying "by means of hard work" (TEV "work hard to irrigate the fields"). Some have suggested this means urinating, but this does not seem very likely. Alternative translation models are "you had to work hard to water your fields," or "you had to struggle just to water your crops" (CEV).

A land . . . which drinks water by the rain from heaven: in some languages there may be a problem in talking about the land "drinking" rain water; in such cases something like the following can be said: "a land with hills and valleys, which is watered by the rain" (or "which gets its water from the rains"); see verse 14 for more statements about the rains.

See TEV for a good alternative model for verse 11.

11.12 RSV	TEV
a land which the LORD your God cares for; the eyes of the LORD your God are always upon it, from the beginning of the year to the end of the year.	The LORD your God takes care of this land and watches over it throughout the year.

A land which the LORD your God cares for: here the verb translated **cares for** means "takes care of," "oversees," or "superintends."

The eyes of the LORD your God are always upon it: this is a picturesque way of saying that the LORD always watches over the land, to protect it. CEV says "the LORD your God keeps his eyes on this land." For **the LORD your God** see 1.6.

From the beginning of the year to the end of the year: an emphatic way of saying "always," "all the time," "through all seasons."

11.13 RSV	TEV
"And if you will obey my commandments which I command you this day, to love the LORD your God, and to serve him with all your heart and with all your soul,	"So then, obey the commands that I have given you today; love the LORD your God and serve him with all your heart.

My commandments: these are God's commandments, which Moses is passing on to the people. For **commandments** see 4.2.

This day: as in verse 8.

To love . . . and to serve: see 10.12.

With all your heart and with all your soul: see 4.29.

11.14 RSV	TEV
he^j will give the rain for your land in its season, the early rain and the later rain, that you may gather in your grain and your wine and your oil.	If you do, he will send rain on your land when it is needed, in the autumn and in the spring, so that there will be grain, wine, and olive oil for you,

^j Sam Gk Vg: Heb *I*

He will give the rain: Yahweh is the source of all that the people need (verses 14-15). In a number of languages this will be expressed as "He will cause the rain to fall."

The rain . . . in its season: that is, the rain comes at the right times of the year, in the fall (October), ending the summer drought, preparing the fields for sowing, and in the spring (April), the last rain before the dry season (see Jer 5.24). In some languages these are referred to as "autumn rains" and "spring rains" respectively. In cultures where rains normally fall during a monsoon season, we may say "He will cause the seasonal rains to fall" or "he will send rain on your land when it is needed" (TEV).

Grain . . . wine . . . oil: this includes all cereals, especially wheat and barley, the grape orchards, and the olive trees. For comments on these three terms, see 7.13.

11.15 RSV	TEV
And he will give grass in your fields for your cattle, and you shall eat and be full.	and grass for your livestock. You will have all the food you want.

Grass in your fields for your cattle: the animals include cows, goats, and sheep. See 2.35.

You shall eat and be full: they will always have enough, and more than enough, to eat. They will never go hungry.

11.16 RSV	TEV
Take heed lest your heart be deceived, and you turn aside and serve other gods and worship them,	Do not let yourselves be led away from the Lord to worship and serve other gods.

For this verse see the same language in 4.19; 8.19.

The passive form of the verb, **your heart be deceived**, may be difficult to imitate, since the question may be raised, "Who or what deceives?" (TEV "be led away" poses the same problem.) If a passive construction with no actor named is impossible, it may be necessary to make "your thoughts" or "your desires" the subject of the verb: "your desires lead you astray," "your thoughts make you do what is wrong."

11.17	RSV	TEV

RSV	TEV
and the anger of the LORD be kindled against you, and he shut up the heavens, so that there be no rain, and the land yield no fruit, and you perish quickly off the good land which the LORD gives you.	If you do, the LORD will become angry with you. He will hold back the rain, and your ground will become too dry for crops to grow. Then you will soon die there, even though it is a good land that he is giving you.

The anger of the LORD is kindled against you: see 6.15.

Shut up the heaven: this kind of poetic language may not make sense in some languages, so it may be easier to say "and he doesn't send you rain," "he does not let the rains come," "he will keep the rain from falling" (CEV) or "He will hold back the rain" (TEV).

The land yield no fruit: in more general terms, "your fields will not grow crops," or "you won't be able to grow crops in your fields." However, there will be many languages that will use an expression similar to the Hebrew; for example, "the land will become too dry and won't produce fruit."

You perish quickly: see 4.26.

11.18	RSV	TEV

RSV	TEV
"You shall therefore lay up these words of mine in your heart and in your soul; and you shall bind them as a sign upon your hand, and they shall be as frontlets between your eyes.	"Remember these commands and cherish them. Tie them on your arms and wear them on your foreheads as a reminder.

The first part of verse 18 is similar to 6.6; the second part is exactly the same as 6.8.

Lay up ... in your heart and in your soul: this includes both the mind and the feelings; so TEV says "Remember these commands and cherish them." CEV has "Memorize these laws and think about them."

11.19	RSV	TEV

RSV	TEV
And you shall teach them to your children, talking of them when you are sitting in your house, and when	Teach them to your children. Talk about them when you are at home and when you are away, when you

217

you are walking by the way, and   are resting and when you are work-
when you lie down, and when you   ing.
rise.

This verse is exactly like 6.7, except that here the opening verb is simply
teach.

11.20   RSV   TEV

And you shall write them upon the   Write them on the doorposts of your
doorposts of your house and upon   houses and on your gates.
your gates,

This verse is exactly like 6.9.

11.21   RSV   TEV

that your days and the days of your   Then you and your children will live
children may be multiplied in the   a long time in the land that the LORD
land which the LORD swore to your   your God promised to give to your
fathers to give them, as long as the   ancestors. You will live there as long
heavens are above the earth.   as there is a sky above the earth.

In RSV this verse is joined to verse 20 as a purpose clause. It may be better
to make this a complete sentence, beginning "Do this so that . . ." as a
statement of result, as TEV does: "Then you and your children . . ." (similarly
CEV).

Days . . . may be multiplied: again, as the final clause shows, this means
"that you and your descendants may live forever in this land." Moses is not
talking about each one of them living a long time, but about the Israelites'
permanent possession of the Promised Land.

Which the LORD swore to your fathers to give them: see 1.8.

As long as the heavens are above the earth: that is, forever, for all time to
come. The Promised Land is to belong to the people of Israel forever. Many
languages will use "sky" instead of **heavens** (see also TEV and CEV).

11.22   RSV   TEV

For if you will be careful to do all this   "Obey faithfully everything that I
commandment which I command   have commanded you: Love the
you to do, loving the LORD your God,   LORD your God, do everything he
walking in all his ways, and cleaving   commands, and be faithful to him.
to him,

Be careful to do: a command to obey, to put into practice; see 5.32.
All this commandment: see 5.31.
Walking in all his ways: see 8.6; 10.12
Cleaving to him: see 10.20.

11.23   RSV   TEV

then the LORD will drive out all these   Then he will drive out all those na-
nations before you, and you will   tions as you advance, and you will
dispossess nations greater and   occupy the land belonging to nations
mightier than yourselves.   greater and more powerful than you.

The LORD will drive out all these nations before you: see 9.5.
You will dispossess nations greater and mightier than yourselves: see 9.1.

11.24   RSV   TEV

Every place on which the sole of   All the ground that you march over
your foot treads shall be yours; your   will be yours. Your territory will ex-
territory shall be from the wilderness   tend from the desert in the south to
and Lebanon and from the River, the   the Lebanon Mountains in the north,
river Euphrates, to the western sea.   and from the Euphrates River in the
                                               east to the Mediterranean Sea in the
                                               west.

Every place on which the sole of your foot treads: this is a literal translation
of the Hebrew text and means simply "everywhere you go," "all the territory you
walk over," or "all the ground that you march over" (TEV).
The wilderness: the desert in the south.
And Lebanon: that is, as far as the Lebanon Mountains, in the north (see
TEV), since at that time there was no country known as Lebanon.
From the River, the river Euphrates: the eastern border. See 1.7.
The western Sea: that is, the Mediterranean, the western border.
The directions here are: south, north, east, and west. In some languages there
is a fixed order, such as north, south, east, and west in English. Translators
should feel free to follow the normal order used in their own languages.

11.25   RSV   TEV

No man shall be able to stand   Wherever you go in that land, the
against you; the LORD your God will   LORD your God will make the people
lay the fear of you and the dread of   fear you, as he has promised, and no
you upon all the land that you shall   one will be able to stop you.
tread, as he promised you.

Stand against you: as in 7.24.

Will lay the fear of you and the dread of you upon all the land: see 2.25. Here **land** is used in the sense of the peoples who live in Canaan. These two words, **fear** and **dread**, do not refer to ordinary fear, but rather to extreme terror. In a number of languages they will be expressed as "will make everyone tremble with terror" or ". . . be so terrified that their bodies shake."

That you shall tread: as in verse 24.

11.26 RSV	TEV
"Behold, I set before you this day a blessing and a curse:	"Today I am giving you the choice between a blessing and a curse—

BRCL begins a new section here that goes to the end of the chapter, with the heading "A Blessing and a Curse." Translators in other languages may want to do this also. If so, other possible models for a heading are "God will either bless or curse" or "God will either do good things for you or punish you." As with other new sections, it will be helpful to reintroduce Moses as the speaker.

The exhortation (chapter 11) closes with the choice that is given to the people: blessing or curse, good fortune or misfortune, success or failure. All of this comes from God, who will act in accordance with the people's willingness to obey him. It is not difficult to find a good translation for **blessing** (see 1.11), but one for **curse**, in which God is the actor, may prove somewhat difficult, since in many languages the term "curse" is associated with the profanity and vulgarity that accompany a loss of temper. In this context **a curse** is God's solemn resolve to punish the people as they deserve for disobeying him. It may be necessary to use the verb "to punish" or the noun "punishment."

But this **curse** is also binding. Once Yahweh has uttered blessings or cursings they cannot be taken back. Translators should study the way blessings and cursings function in their cultures. How do these curses by Yahweh compare to those of, for example, the Shaman or the "medicine man"? Will the vocabulary used in similar situations apply to Yahweh's curses?

I set before you this day: God is giving the people a choice; BRCL translates "And now I will let you choose whether you want a blessing or a curse." Again **this day** is emphasized.

An alternative translation model for this verse is:

• Today you must choose between two things: Do you want the LORD to do good things for you or to punish you?

11.27 RSV	TEV
the blessing, if you obey the commandments of the LORD your God, which I command you this day,	a blessing, if you obey the commands of the LORD your God that I am giving you today;

The subject and the vocabulary of this verse have occurred several times already. For **commandments** see 4.2.

11.28 RSV	TEV
and the curse, if you do not obey the commandments of the LORD your God, but turn aside from the way which I command you this day, to go after other gods which you have not known.	but a curse, if you disobey these commands and turn away to worship other gods that you have never worshiped before.

If you do not obey: this is the exact opposite of verse 27.

Turn aside from the way which I command you this day: see 9.12. This is a deliberate act of disobedience. Here **the way** refers to the rules and regulations that will be given in chapters 12–26, a section which is often called "The Deuteronomic Code."

To go after other gods which you have not known: this means to forsake Yahweh as their God and serve and worship other gods which they had never known before, that is, the gods of Canaan (see verse 16). For **gods** see 3.24.

11.29 RSV	TEV
And when the LORD your God brings you into the land which you are entering to take possession of it, you shall set the blessing on Mount Gerizim and the curse on Mount Ebal.	When the LORD brings you into the land that you are going to occupy, you are to proclaim the blessing from Mount Gerizim and the curse from Mount Ebal.

And when the LORD your God brings you: this is better expressed as "And after the LORD your God takes you . . . ." For **take possession** see 1.8 and elsewhere.

You shall set the blessing . . . and the curse: that is, on the two mountains whose names are given, they would "proclaim" (TEV, NIV, FRCL), or "announce" (BRCL, CEV, NJPSV, REB, BRCL), the rewards and punishments that would accompany obedience and disobedience (see chapter 27; also Josh 8.30-35). TEV has a good model: "You are to proclaim the blessing from Mount Gerizim and the curse from Mount Ebal." An alternative model may be "You are to proclaim from Mount Gerizim how Yahweh will reward you and announce from Mount Ebal how he will punish you."

11.30   RSV   TEV

Are they not beyond the Jordan, west of the road, toward the going down of the sun, in the land of the Canaanites who live in the Arabah, over against Gilgal, beside the oak[k] of Moreh?	**(These two mountains are west of the Jordan River in the territory of the Canaanites who live in the Jordan Valley. They are toward the west, not far from the sacred trees of Moreh near the town of Gilgal.)**

[k] Gk Syr: See Gen 12.6. Heb *oaks* or *terebinths*

The RSV form is that of a rhetorical question, "Are they not . . . ?" to which the answer is "Yes, they are." This is better translated as a statement of fact, as in NRSV, "As you know . . . ." TEV, NJPSV, and REB use parentheses around this verse, to show that it is not part of Moses' speech but a comment inserted later by the writer. NJPSV is a good model to follow: "(These mountains, as everyone knows, ...)"

Beyond the Jordan: that is, on the west side of the Jordan River; the point of view here is Moab.

MOUNT GERIZIM AND MOUNT EBAL

West of the road, toward the going down of the sun: this is a rather wordy way of saying "west"; it is not known what **road** is meant. NRSV translates "some distance to the west," and TEV has "They are toward the west."

The Arabah: the Jordan Valley (see 1.1).

Over against Gilgal "Near the town of Gilgal" (TEV). This town is near Jericho (see Josh 4.5).

Beside the oak of Moreh: see Gen 12.6; this is near Shechem, close to Gerizim, which is some 25-30 miles distant from Gilgal. The text as it stands is not very clear, unless **Gilgal** is another town, not the one known from the book of Joshua. It is not clear what is meant by **the oak of Moreh**. The tree could be a terebinth, but most translators have **oak**. The Hebrew word *moreh* may mean "teaching' or "divining"; it is not the name of a place or a person. It seems to have been a sacred tree or grove of trees where it was believed people would receive a revelation from God, or also where a sacrifice would be offered. TEV and CEV attempt to bring out the special nature of the place by saying "sacred trees"; it would be better to say "sacred tree" (as TEV has in Gen 6.12). It is possible that this is the same tree that in Judges 9.37 is called "the Diviners' oak" (RSV; see TEV "the oak of the fortunetellers").

11.31-32 RSV	TEV
31 For you are to pass over the Jordan to go in to take possession of the land which the LORD your God gives you; and when you possess it and live in it, 32 you shall be careful to do all the statutes and the ordinances which I set before you this day.	31 You are about to cross the Jordan River and occupy the land that the LORD your God is giving you. When you take it and settle there, 32 be sure to obey all the laws that I am giving you today.

All the words and phrases in this verse have appeared several times before. **Pass over the Jordan**: this means to cross over to the west side of the river. For **statutes and ordinances** see 4.1.
Which I set before you this day: this refers to what follows (chapters 12–26).

2B. Laws governing life in Canaan (12.1–23.14)

This is the beginning of the major part of the book (chapters 12–26), which contains the laws, rules, and regulations for the corporate life of Israel in the land of Canaan. The Handbook suggests making a major section here, with a heading such as "Laws governing life in Canaan." FRCL (following TOB) has a similar heading, "The Laws of the Lord."

Some editions of NRSV begin this section at 12.2, making 12.1 the last verse of the previous section. The Handbook recommends that in this matter TEV should be followed (along with most other versions), that is, making 12.1 part of what follows, not of what comes before.

2B-1. The one place of worship (12.1-28)

RSV

1 "These are the statutes and ordinances which you shall be careful to do in the land which the LORD, the God of your fathers, has given you to possess, all the days that you live upon the earth. 2 You shall surely destroy all the places where the nations whom you shall dispossess served their gods, upon the high mountains and upon the hills and under every green tree; 3 you shall tear down their altars, and dash in pieces their pillars, and burn their Asherim with fire; you shall hew down the graven images of their gods, and destroy their name out of that place. 4 You shall not do so to the LORD your God. 5 But you shall seek the place which the LORD your God will choose out of all your tribes to put his name and make his habitation there; thither you shall go, 6 and thither you shall bring your burnt offerings and your sacrifices, your tithes and the offering that you present, your votive offerings, your freewill offerings, and the firstlings of your herd and of your flock; 7 and there you shall eat before the LORD your God, and you shall rejoice, you and your households, in all that you undertake, in which the LORD your God has blessed you. 8 You shall not do according to all that we are doing here this day, every man doing whatever is right in his own eyes; 9 for you have not as yet come to the rest and to the inheritance which the LORD your God gives you. 10 But when you go over the Jordan, and live in the land which the LORD

TEV
The One Place for Worship

1 "Here are the laws that you are to obey as long as you live in the land that the LORD, the God of your ancestors, is giving you. Listen to them! 2 In the land that you are taking, destroy all the places where the people worship their gods on high mountains, on hills, and under green trees. 3 Tear down their altars and smash their sacred stone pillars to pieces. Burn their symbols of the goddess Asherah and chop down their idols, so that they will never again be worshiped at those places.

4 "Do not worship the LORD your God in the way that these people worship their gods. 5 Out of the territory of all your tribes the LORD will choose the one place where the people are to come into his presence and worship him. 6 There you are to offer your sacrifices that are to be burned and your other sacrifices, your tithes and your offerings, the gifts that you promise to the LORD, your freewill offerings, and the first-born of your cattle and sheep. 7 There, in the presence of the LORD your God, who has blessed you, you and your families will eat and enjoy the good things that you have worked for.

8 "When that time comes, you must not do as you have been doing. Until now you have all been worshiping as you please, 9 because you have not yet entered the land that the LORD your God is giving you, where you can live in peace. 10 When you cross the Jordan River, the LORD will let you occupy the land and live

your God gives you to inherit, and when he gives you rest from all your enemies round about, so that you live in safety, 11 then to the place which the LORD your God will choose, to make his name dwell there, thither you shall bring all that I command you: your burnt offerings and your sacrifices, your tithes and the offering that you present, and all your votive offerings which you vow to the LORD. 12 And you shall rejoice before the LORD your God, you and your sons and your daughters, your menservants and your maidservants, and the Levite that is within your towns, since he has no portion or inheritance with you. 13 Take heed that you do not offer your burnt offerings at every place that you see; 14 but at the place which the LORD will choose in one of your tribes, there you shall offer your burnt offerings, and there you shall do all that I am commanding you.

15 "However, you may slaughter and eat flesh within any of your towns, as much as you desire, according to the blessing of the LORD your God which he has given you; the unclean and the clean may eat of it, as of the gazelle and as of the hart. 16 Only you shall not eat the blood; you shall pour it out upon the earth like water. 17 You may not eat within your towns the tithe of your grain or of your wine or of your oil, or the firstlings of your herd or of your flock, or any of your votive offerings which you vow, or your freewill offerings, or the offering that you present; 18 but you shall eat them before the LORD your God in the place which the LORD your God will choose, you and your son and your daughter, your manservant and your maidservant, and the Levite who is within your towns; and you shall rejoice before the LORD your God in all that you undertake. 19 Take heed that you do not forsake the Levite as long as you live in your land.

20 "When the LORD your God enlarges your territory, as he has promised you, and you say, 'I will eat flesh,' because you crave flesh, you may eat as much flesh as you desire. 21 If the place which the LORD your God will choose to put his name there is too far from you, then you may kill any of your herd or your flock, which the LORD has given you, as I have commanded you; and you may eat within your towns as much as you desire. 22 Just as the gazelle or the hart is eaten, so you may eat of it; the unclean and the clean alike may eat of it. 23 Only be sure that you do not eat the blood; for the blood is the life, and you shall not eat the life with the flesh. 24 You shall not eat it; you shall pour it out upon the earth like water. 25 You shall not eat it; that all may go well with you and with your children after you,

there. He will keep you safe from all your enemies, and you will live in peace. 11 The LORD will choose a single place where he is to be worshiped, and there you must bring to him everything that I have commanded: your sacrifices that are to be burned and your other sacrifices, your tithes and your offerings, and those special gifts that you have promised to the LORD. 12 Be joyful there in his presence, together with your children, your servants, and the Levites who live in your towns; remember that the Levites will have no land of their own. 13 You are not to offer your sacrifices wherever you choose; 14 you must offer them only in the one place that the LORD will choose in the territory of one of your tribes. Only there are you to offer your sacrifices that are to be burned and do all the other things that I have commanded you.

15 "But you are free to kill and eat your animals wherever you live. You may eat as many as the LORD gives you. All of you, whether ritually clean or unclean, may eat them, just as you would eat the meat of deer or antelope. 16 But you must not eat their blood; you must pour it out on the ground like water. 17 Nothing that you offer to the LORD is to be eaten in the places where you live: neither the tithes of your grain, your wine, or your olive oil, nor the first-born of your cattle and sheep, the gifts that you promise to the LORD, your freewill offerings, or any other offerings. 18 You and your children, together with your servants and the Levites who live in your towns, are to eat these offerings only in the presence of the LORD your God, in the one place of worship chosen by the LORD your God. And you are to be happy there over everything that you have done. 19 Be sure, also, not to neglect the Levites, as long as you live in your land.

20 "When the LORD your God enlarges your territory, as he has promised, you may eat meat whenever you want to. 21 If the one place of worship is too far away, then, whenever you wish, you may kill any of the cattle or sheep that the LORD has given you, and you may eat the meat at home, as I have told you. 22 Anyone, ritually clean or unclean, may eat that meat, just as he would eat the meat of deer or antelope. 23 Only do not eat meat with blood still in it, for the life is in the blood, and you must not eat the life with the meat. 24 Do not use the blood for food; instead, pour it out on the ground like water. 25 If you obey this command, the LORD will be pleased, and all will go well for you and your descendants. 26 Take to the one place of worship your offerings and the gifts that you have promised the LORD. 27 Offer there the sacrifices which are to be

when you do what is right in the sight of the LORD. 26 But the holy things which are due from you, and your votive offerings, you shall take, and you shall go to the place which the LORD will choose, 27 and offer your burnt offerings, the flesh and the blood, on the altar of the LORD your God; the blood of your sacrifices shall be poured out on the altar of the LORD your God, but the flesh you may eat. 28 Be careful to heed all these words which I command you, that it may go well with you and with your children after you for ever, when you do what is good and right in the sight of the LORD your God.

completely burned on the LORD's altar. Also offer those sacrifices in which you eat the meat and pour the blood out on the altar. 28 Obey faithfully everything that I have commanded you, and all will go well for you and your descendants forever, because you will be doing what is right and what pleases the LORD your God.

Section heading: TEV has a heading for 12.1-28 "The One Place of Worship," which the Handbook also recommends to translators.

12.1	RSV	TEV

"These are the statutes and ordinances which you shall be careful to do in the land which the LORD, the God of your fathers, has given you to possess, all the days that you live upon the earth.

"Here are the laws that you are to obey as long as you live in the land that the LORD, the God of your ancestors, is giving you. Listen to them!

With the beginning of a new section, it will be helpful to start with something like "Moses said to the Israelites" or "Moses continued to speak to the Israelites, saying, ..."

Statutes and ordinances: see 4.1.

Be careful to do: this expression occurs frequently (5.1, 21; 6.3, 25; 7.11; 8.1; 11.22, 32).

The language of this verse is like that of other passages (see especially 1.8; 6.1, 18). The last clause, **all the days that you live upon the earth,** may go with the command **you shall be careful to do** (so TEV, CEV, FRCL, SPCL) or with the verb **to possess** (so, apparently, RSV, NRSV, REB). It is better to link it quite clearly with the command **be careful to do.**

Live upon the earth: TEV, NIV, NJB, BRCL, and POCL take the Hebrew noun *'adamah* in this expression to mean "the land," that is, the land of Canaan, and not **the earth**. In the first part of the verse the Hebrew word translated **land** is a different word, *'erets*. It seems better to take the word *'adamah* here to mean **the earth**, meaning, of course, "as long as you live" (see CEV).

The God of your fathers means "the God whom our [inclusive] ancestors worshiped." For **fathers** see 1.8.

The following model for this verse may be useful:

● These are the rules and regulations that you must obey in the land that the LORD, the God of our ancestors, is giving you. You must obey them as long as you live [or, always].

12.2 RSV | TEV

You shall surely destroy all the places where the nations whom you shall dispossess served their gods, upon the high mountains and upon the hills and under every green tree; | In the land that you are taking, destroy all the places where the people worship their gods on high mountains, on hills, and under green trees.

Verses 2-3 are a command for the Israelites to destroy all places of worship and all idols and images of the Canaanites.

You shall surely destroy: this compound form (literally, "destroying you shall destroy") uses the same verb used in 11.4. **Destroy** in this context means to completely get rid of something, either by tearing it down, smashing it into pieces, or burning it (see verse 3).

The nations whom you shall dispossess: see 9.1; 11.23.

Served their gods: see 4.28 and 6.13. On the translation of **gods** see 3.24.

High mountains . . . hills: where there are not two different words for "mountain" and "hill," the expression "big hills and small hills" can be used.

Green tree: this is rather "leafy tree" (NRSV), "spreading tree" (REB, NIV), or "luxuriant tree" (NJPSV), that is, a large tree with many leaves, providing shade. So CEV has "in the shade of large trees," and TEV "under green trees."

The structure of verse 2 is somewhat complex, and a translation should make the sentence flow naturally. One way to restructure the verse is the following:

- But the peoples [or, nations] that live there worship other gods. So after you capture the land, you must completely destroy the likenesses [or, images] of these gods, whether they are on mountains, hills, or in the shade of large leafy trees.

12.3 RSV | TEV

you shall tear down their altars, and dash in pieces their pillars, and burn their Asherim with fire; you shall hew down the graven images of their gods, and destroy their name out of that place. | Tear down their altars and smash their sacred stone pillars to pieces. Burn their symbols of the goddess Asherah and chop down their idols, so that they will never again be worshiped at those places.

For this command to destroy **their altars, their pillars, their Asherim**, and **graven images of their gods**, see 7.5. The only differences between the two verses is that here the fuller expression **the graven images of their gods** is used, whereas in 7.5 it is simply "their graven images"; and the last two verbs **burn** and **hew down** are reversed in 7.5.

Destroy their name out of that place: this summarizes the whole process of doing away completely with Canaanite religion and worship. **Their name** means "the names of their gods" (see similar use of "the name" in 7.24). BRCL translates "They will be completely forgotten"; POCL has "cause to vanish from that land anything that will bring those gods to mind." We may also translate as "Destroy the images of these gods so completely that no one will ever worship them in these places again."

12.4   RSV   TEV

You shall not do so to the LORD your   **"Do not worship the LORD your**
God.   **God in the way that these people**
                                                  worship their gods.

You shall not do so: the opposite applies to Yahweh. The Israelites are not to follow Canaanite rites and customs in the worship of their God; so NRSV "You shall not worship the LORD your God in such ways." TEV has "Do not worship the LORD your God in the way that these people worship their gods" (similarly CEV).

12.5   RSV   TEV

But you shall seek the place which   **Out of the territory of all your tribes**
the LORD your God will choose out of   **the LORD will choose the one place**
all your tribes to put his name and   **where the people are to come into**
make his habitation there; thither   **his presence and worship him.**
you shall go,

This verse has the first statement about "the one place of worship" (see also verses 14, 18, 21, 26). By the time this book was written, Jerusalem was the place that had been chosen by Yahweh where he was to be worshiped, in the Temple on Mount Zion.

You shall seek the place: this is from the point of view of Moses and the Israelites in Moab. God will choose the exact **place**, and the Israelites are to **seek** it. This is not in the sense that God will keep his choice a secret, which they will have to discover, but that they are to go directly to the place God chooses, since he would make his choice known. So REB has "you are to resort to the place," FRCL "you will go to worship him at the place," and BRCL "the LORD will choose . . . you will go there." In many languages it will be more natural style to use the pronoun "you" rather than "the people" as TEV does.

The place . . . out of all your tribes: the place will be, of course, within the territorial limits of the land of Israel. So we may say, for example, "a place somewhere in Israel" or "a place somewhere in the land."

To put his name and make his habitation there: this is a way of saying that a place of worship, a temple, will be built there for the worship of Yahweh. TEV offers a good model: "come into his presence and worship him." FRCL has "to live there and manifest his presence," BRCL "the place where he will live and where people will go to worship him."

An alternative translation model for this verse is:

• The LORD will choose a place somewhere in Israel [or, the land] where he will live and reveal his presence. You must find that place and go to worship the LORD there.

12.6 RSV	TEV
and thither you shall bring your burnt offerings and your sacrifices, your tithes and the offering that you present, your votive offerings, your freewill offerings, and the firstlings of your herd and of your flock;	There you are to offer your sacrifices that are to be burned and your other sacrifices, your tithes and your offerings, the gifts that you promise to the LORD, your freewill offerings, and the first-born of your cattle and sheep.

There are seven different offerings listed here.

(1) **Burnt offerings**: animals completely burned, except for the hide, as an offering to God. TEV calls them "sacrifices to be burned," and many other translations term them "whole burnt offerings."

(2) **Sacrifices**: the most general term possible; it usually means animal sacrifices whose meat is shared by the deity and the worshiper (or the priest).

(3) **Tithes**: this refers to giving the LORD one tenth of a person's gross income—in most instances, agricultural products such as grain, wine, and olive oil (see 14.22-23). In some languages the idea of **tithes** in this context may have to be translated by a phrase; for example, "one tenth of all the produce . . ." or "one part of . . . out of any ten."

(4) **The offering that you present**: a voluntary offering of whatever nature (REB "contributions"; NRSV "donations"), which the worshiper presented with his hands (see Exo 25.2-3).

(5) **Votive offerings**: any offering made as payment of a vow or promise. TEV has "the gifts that you promise to the LORD."

(6) **Freewill offerings**: offerings not required by law, which could include sacrifices of any kind. Another way to express this is "things you voluntarily give to him."

(7) **The firstlings of your herd and of your flock**: or, as TEV has it, "the first-born of your cattle and sheep." On "cattle" see 2.35 and 5.14.

If it is impossible to come up with different terms or expressions for these various offerings, a general term will have to be used that will include any and all kinds of sacrifices; for example, "There you must offer all your sacrifices to Yahweh" or "There you must slaughter your animals and offer them and your other gifts to Yahweh."

12.7 RSV	TEV
and there you shall eat before the LORD your God, and you shall rejoice, you and your households, in	There, in the presence of the LORD your God, who has blessed you, you and your families will eat and enjoy

all that you undertake, in which the   **the good things that you have**
LORD your God has blessed you.   **worked for.**

RSV follows the form and order of the Hebrew text; the last part of the verse is especially difficult to read. TEV uses a more natural style, which makes for easier understanding.

You shall eat before the LORD your God: Moses is talking about the sanctuary, or temple, in which the Israelites will offer their sacrifices. So FRCL has "at the sanctuary of the Lord." We may also use something like "And there, in the place where the LORD your God is present, ..." The meal is a sacred meal; in some sacrifices part of the animal offered in sacrifice was eaten by the worshipers. This should be made clear, as BRCL has it: "You and your families will eat of the meat of the sacrifices." Or we may say, for example, "You and your families will eat the meat of the animals you have slaughtered and offered to the LORD."

For **the LORD your God** see 1.6.

And you shall rejoice: or "and your hearts will be full of joy."

You and your households: the word "household" includes everyone in the one home, not only family members but servants and slaves also. So CEV has "You and your family and your servants."

All that you undertake: this includes all the work they have done, especially in cultivating their fields and tending their herds and flocks.

Blessed you means "made you prosper" or "caused you to be successful."

FRCL offers a good model for the whole verse:

●   It is there, also, at the sanctuary of the Lord, that you and your
        families will eat together the sacred meals; you will be full of joy
        because of the success that the Lord your God has given you in all
        that you have worked for.

12.8   RSV   TEV

You shall not do according to all that   "When that time comes, you must
we are doing here this day, every   not do as you have been doing. Until
man doing whatever is right in his   now you have all been worshiping as
own eyes;   you please,

This verse states that at the time of Moses' speech, before the people had entered the land of Canaan, there was lack of order in their worship rites and sacrifices, especially the lack of a single place where the sacrifices are to be offered. This is not a statement about the lack of political and social order, as in the similar text, Judges 21.25.

You shall not do according to all that we are doing here this day: the change in person from "you" to "we" may prove difficult, but it is a matter of fact. Moses, the speaker, will not be with the people in the land of Canaan. The command is that the people of Israel are to act differently in the Promised Land from the way they are acting **here this day** (again there is emphasis on "this day"). TEV keeps the "you" in both instances, with "you must not do as you have been doing. Until now you have . . . ." Translators in certain languages will find this a helpful model.

Every man doing whatever is right in his own eyes: as the whole context shows, this refers to sacrifices and worship. TEV offers a good model. "Until now you have been worshiping as you please." An alternative model may be "Until now [or, today] you have been offering sacrifices to Yahweh anywhere you want to."

12.9   RSV   TEV

for you have not as yet come to the   because you have not yet entered
rest and to the inheritance which the   the land that the LORD your God is
LORD your God gives you.   giving you, where you can live in
                                            peace.

This verse explains why at the present time, in Moab, the Israelites are not following God's laws for worship. Only after they have settled in Canaan will they be able to obey those laws.

You have not as yet come to: this is better expressed as "you have not yet arrived at," or, to make it plainer, "you have not yet entered the land where . . . ."

To the rest and to the inheritance: see 3.20. The two nouns are a compound phrase meaning "the inheritance where you will rest." The land of Canaan is spoken of as an **inheritance**, meaning that it is God's gift to the people. It is nearly always connected with the statement that the Israelites themselves will defeat the peoples of Canaan and take possession of their territory. In 1.39 the related verb is used, "(cause) to inherit"; in 3.28 the same verb, with Joshua as subject, is translated by RSV "Joshua . . . shall put them in possession of the land" (see also 4.21, 28). A translation should not give the idea that "inherit" means that the people are going to receive the land after God dies. TEV makes this clear, with "the land that the LORD your God is giving you."

The noun **rest** means primarily security, safety from enemies (as the next verse makes plain). FRCL has "the territory that the Lord your God will give you to possess so that you may have a peaceful life there"; BRCL "the land that the Eternal, our God, is giving you, a land where you will live in peace."

12.10   RSV   TEV

But when you go over the Jordan,   When you cross the Jordan River,
and live in the land which the LORD   the LORD will let you occupy the land
your God gives you to inherit, and   and live there. He will keep you safe
when he gives you rest from all your   from all your enemies, and you will
enemies round about, so that you   live in peace.
live in safety,

This verse amplifies and expands on verse 9. In Hebrew verses 10-11 are one long, complex sentence; RSV faithfully reproduces the vocabulary and structure of the original. However, in many languages translators should divide these verses into three or more sentences (see TEV).

Go over the Jordan: see 4.14.

The land which the LORD your God gives you to inherit: see previous verse, and 1.8.

The meaning of **rest** is here explained as **live in safety**; their enemies will not pose a threat to them. FRCL offers a good model: "He will keep you secure from all the enemies that surround you, and you will live in safety."

12.11   RSV   TEV

then to the place which the LORD your God will choose, to make his name dwell there, thither you shall bring all that I command you: your burnt offerings and your sacrifices, your tithes and the offering that you present, and all your votive offerings which you vow to the LORD.	The LORD will choose a single place where he is to be worshiped, and there you must bring to him everything that I have commanded: your sacrifices that are to be burned and your other sacrifices, your tithes and your offerings, and those special gifts that you have promised to the LORD.

Notice that RSV, following the Hebrew text, places the main verb **you shall bring** in the middle of the sentence. A more normal and intelligible ordering of the sentence is found in TEV: "The LORD will choose a single place where he is to be worshiped." However, in languages that do not use the passive voice, we may say, for example, ". . . where you must worship him." This verse repeats essentially verses 5-6. Here the verb **make . . . dwell** is used with **his name**, whereas in verse 5 the verb is "put." The figure of speech is different, but the action is the same.

All that I command you: Moses is the speaker.

The list of sacrifices and offerings here is the same as in verse 6, except that here "freewill offerings" are not included. And where verse 6 has simply "your votive offerings," here a fuller phrase is used: **all your votive offerings which you vow to the LORD**. The phrase is redundant, since a votive offering is something that is vowed. The verb "to vow" means to promise or to dedicate. The Hebrew is literally "your choice votive offerings." NRSV has "all your choice votive gifts which you vow to the LORD." TEV has "those special gifts that you have promised to the LORD." RSV fails to represent the adjective "choice" (TEV "special").

12.12   RSV   TEV

And you shall rejoice before the LORD your God, you and your sons	Be joyful there in his presence, together with your children, your

and your daughters, your menservants and your maidservants, and
the Levite that is within your towns,
since he has no portion or inheritance with you.

servants, and the Levites who live in
your towns; remember that the Levites will have no land of their own.

You shall rejoice before the LORD: or "You shall celebrate there at the place
for worshiping the LORD."

Instead of the all-inclusive "your households" of verse 3, here the fuller
statement appears: **your sons and your daughters, your menservants and your
maidservants**.

The Levite: that is, "the Levites," "members of the tribe of Levi," or
"descendants of the great ancestor Levi" (see 10.8-9; 18.1-2, for further
statements).

Has no portion or inheritance with you: that is, the tribe of Levi, unlike the
other tribes, will not be given its own territory (see 10.8-9 for **no portion or
inheritance**). Other ways to express this are "The descendants of Levi will have
no land of their own," or ". . . will not be given their own territory [in which to
live]."

12.13	RSV	TEV

Take heed that you do not offer your
burnt offerings at every place that
you see;

You are not to offer your sacrifices
wherever you choose;

The command is repeated in verses 13-14 and expressed in a very precise
way. There will be one place where the people are to offer their sacrifices to
Yahweh; they must not offer them anywhere else.

Every place that you see: this means "any place you might choose."

Here, and in verse 14, only **your burnt offerings** are mentioned; the others
are not named, but they are understood to be included. So we may translate
"You must not offer sacrifices just anywhere you want to," or even "You must
not slaughter animals and offer them to Yahweh just . . . ."

12.14	RSV	TEV

but at the place which the LORD will
choose in one of your tribes, there
you shall offer your burnt offerings,
and there you shall do all that I am
commanding you.

you must offer them only in the one
place that the LORD will choose in the
territory of one of your tribes. Only
there are you to offer your sacrifices
that are to be burned and do all the
other things that I have commanded
you.

For the content of this verse, see verse 7.

You shall do all that I am commanding you: Moses is speaking. TEV restructures in a helpful way.

12.15 RSV	TEV
"However, you may slaughter and eat flesh within any of your towns, as much as you desire, according to the blessing of the LORD your God which he has given you; the unclean and the clean may eat of it, as of the gazelle and as of the hart.	"But you are free to kill and eat your animals wherever you live. You may eat as many as the LORD gives you. All of you, whether ritually clean or unclean, may eat them, just as you would eat the meat of deer or antelope.

The thought or presupposition underlying this command is that the act of slaughtering animals at home, and not at the central sanctuary, is not a religious act, but a purely secular act. So the ritual rules do not apply. Everyone, whether ritually pure or impure, is free to eat the meat of these animals.

You may slaughter and eat flesh within any of your towns: this refers to domestic animals, not wild game. TEV is very clear: "But you are to kill and eat your animals wherever you live."

As of the gazelle . . . the hart: being wild animals, deers and antelopes (TEV) were not subject to the ritual rules that applied to sacrificial animals, and everyone could eat their meat. In cultures where these animals are unknown, we may use a more general translation, as the actual animals are unimportant: "just as you would eat the meat of wild animals [or, animals of the forest, or jungle]."

As much as you desire: this is meant to say "as often as you wish" (NRSV "whenever you desire").

According to the blessing of the LORD your God which he has given you: this means, depending on the number of animals that God has blessed them with. Their prosperity is due to God's blessing. TEV has "as many as the LORD gives you." For **the LORD your God** see 1.6.

The unclean and the clean: this means people who are ritually impure and pure; it does not mean actual bodily filth. The main effect on a person who became ritually impure was that such a person could not take part in community worship until the proper ritual had been performed to remove that person's impurity. This was ritual impurity, not a moral lapse. In some languages a lot of information understood by the original readers of the text must be included in order to allow the reader to understand the meaning of these terms. For **unclean** TEV has "ritually impure," while CEV has "all those people who are unclean and unfit for worship." Another way to express **unclean** is "religiously impure [or, unacceptable]." Some languages will render **the unclean and the clean** as "people with bad taboo and those with good taboo." Most translators will need to provide a detailed note in the Glossary on these terms.

The gazelle . . . the hart: in more modern terms, "the meat of deer or antelope" (TEV).

12.16   RSV   TEV

Only you shall not eat the blood; you   But you must not eat their blood;
shall pour it out upon the earth like   you must pour it out on the ground
water.   like water.

You shall not eat the blood: for the prohibition against eating blood, see verse 23 (also Gen 9.3-4; Lev 17.10-14). The Israelites devised a method of draining the blood out of the animal, a ritual still practiced by Jews today. Another way to render this sentence is "But you must not eat the blood of any animals" (CEV).

Pour it out upon the earth like water: as NRSV and TEV have it, "on the ground." To make it clearer, "Pour it out on the ground as you would pour out water."

12.17   RSV   TEV

You may not eat within your towns   Nothing that you offer to the LORD is
the tithe of your grain or of your wine   to be eaten in the places where you
or of your oil, or the firstlings of your   live: neither the tithes of your grain,
herd or of your flock, or any of your   your wine, or your olive oil, nor the
votive offerings which you vow, or   first-born of your cattle and sheep,
your freewill offerings, or the offer-   the gifts that you promise to the
ing that you present;   LORD, your freewill offerings, or any
                                                 other offerings.

Verses 17-18 are one sentence. As distinct from eating meat wherever they lived, the Israelites could not eat at home any of the offerings listed; all these had to be eaten at the central sanctuary. In many languages it will be necessary to divide this long sentence into at least three sentences (see TEV).

You may not eat within your towns: as in verse 15, this is equivalent to saying "You may not eat at home." For the sacrificial slaughter of their animals, the Israelites will have to leave home and go to the one sanctuary.

The tithe of your grain or of your wine or of your oil: see 7.13. These were the three main agricultural products. For the law of the **tithe** (verses 6 and 11), see Lev 27.30-32. Alternative translation models are "one-tenth of your grain or . . . ," or even "One kilogram [or whatever measure is commonly used] for every ten that you produce, or one liter [or gallon] of wine or olive oil for every ten that you produce."

The firstlings of your herd or of your flock: see verse 6.

Votive offerings . . . freewill offerings . . . the offering that you present: see verse 6.

12.18   RSV   TEV

but you shall eat them before the LORD your God in the place which the LORD your God will choose, you and your son and your daughter, your manservant and your maidservant, and the Levite who is within your towns; and you shall rejoice before the LORD your God in all that you undertake.	You and your children, together with your servants and the Levites who live in your towns, are to eat these offerings only in the presence of the LORD your God, in the one place of worship chosen by the LORD your God. And you are to be happy there over everything that you have done.

Eat them before the LORD your God in the place which the LORD your God will choose: as in verses 5, 11, 14.

For the rest of the verse, see verse 12. And for **you shall rejoice . . .** , see verse 7.

12.19   RSV   TEV

Take heed that you do not forsake the Levite as long as you live in your land.	Be sure, also, not to neglect the Levites, as long as you live in your land.

This verse emphasizes the duty of providing for the needs of the Levites (see verse 12).

Take heed that you do not forsake . . . : in some languages a positive command will be more natural style; for example, "Be sure, also, that you take care of the Levites, as long . . . ."

As long as you live in your land: see verse 1.

12.20   RSV   TEV

"When the LORD your God enlarges your territory, as he has promised you, and you say, 'I will eat flesh,' because you crave flesh, you may eat as much flesh as you desire.	"When the LORD your God enlarges your territory, as he has promised, you may eat meat whenever you want to.

Verses 20-25 repeat and expand what is said in verses 15-19. Here the rules are repeated for the benefit of a much later time, when the land of Israel will have grown considerably larger than it was at the time of the conquest.

When the LORD your God enlarges your territory, as he has promised you: here RSV and TEV are the same (except for the final **you**, missing in TEV). In some languages it will be helpful to place the clause **as he has promised you** at the beginning of the verse; for example, "The LORD has promised that later on he will give you [plural] more land." For **the LORD your God** see 1.6.

And you say, 'I will eat flesh,' because you crave flesh: in Hebrew the second person singular is directed to Israel as a whole, and so to every individual. As TEV shows, it is not necessary to keep the direct quotation " 'I will eat meat' "; rather we can say simply "and you want to eat meat" or "and you get hungry for meat." Then what follows comes naturally: "You may eat as much as you wish, any time you want to."

12.21 RSV	TEV
If the place which the LORD your God will choose to put his name there is too far from you, then you may kill any of your herd or your flock, which the LORD has given you, as I have commanded you; and you may eat within your towns as much as you desire.	If the one place of worship is too far away, then, whenever you wish, you may kill any of the cattle or sheep that the LORD has given you, and you may eat the meat at home, as I have told you.

Since, in the enlarged territory, some Israelites would be living a great distance from the one place of worship, permission is given them to eat at home. This repeats essentially verse 15.

The place . . . put his name there: see verses 5, 11.

Any of your herd or your flock: that is, "any of your cattle or sheep" (see TEV). God has given these animals to the Israelites (see verse 15).

As I have commanded you: Moses is the speaker, and he is setting forth these rules and regulations.

You may eat within your towns as much as you desire: as in verse 15.

12.22 RSV	TEV
Just as the gazelle or the hart is eaten, so you may eat of it; the unclean and the clean alike may eat of it.	Anyone, ritually clean or unclean, may eat that meat, just as he would eat the meat of deer or antelope.

See the second half of verse 15.

12.23 RSV	TEV
Only be sure that you do not eat the blood; for the blood is the life, and you shall not eat the life with the flesh.	Only do not eat meat with blood still in it, for the life is in the blood, and you must not eat the life with the meat.

The prohibition to eat blood (verse 16) is here justified by the statement **the blood is the life**. This may have to be expressed as "it is the blood that gives life to a living being."

12.24   RSV   TEV

You shall not eat it; you shall pour it out upon the earth like water.

Do not use the blood for food; instead, pour it out on the ground like water.

See the last part of verse 16.

12.25   RSV   TEV

You shall not eat it; that all may go well with you and with your children after you, when you do what is right in the sight of the LORD.

If you obey this command, the LORD will be pleased, and all will go well for you and your descendants.

You shall not eat it: this is the third time the prohibition is given. In many languages we may avoid the repetition by saying "If you obey this command" (TEV).

All may go well with you and your children after you: see 4.40; 6.18.

When you do what is right in the sight of the LORD: see 6.18, where the fuller phrase "what is right and good" is used (as in verse 26).

12.26   RSV   TEV

But the holy things which are due from you, and your votive offerings, you shall take, and you shall go to the place which the LORD will choose,

Take to the one place of worship your offerings and the gifts that you have promised the LORD.

The holy things which are due from you: this refers to the sacrifices and offerings made to God. The word **holy** here does not have a moral sense but means "sacred," "offered or dedicated to God." So TEV has "your offerings and gifts that you have promised to the LORD," and CEV "all sacrifices and offerings to the LORD."

Votive offerings: see verse 6.

The place which the LORD will choose: see verses 5, 11, 14, 18, 21.

12.27   RSV   TEV

and offer your burnt offerings, the flesh and the blood, on the altar of the LORD your God; the blood of your sacrifices shall be poured out on the altar of the LORD your God, but the flesh you may eat.	Offer there the sacrifices which are to be completely burned on the LORD's altar. Also offer those sacrifices in which you eat the meat and pour the blood out on the altar.

Here directions are given for the **burnt offerings** (see also verse 6).

Offer the flesh and blood upon the altar: the whole animal is to be burned on the altar.

The blood of your sacrifices: in RSV **sacrifices** appears to refer to the same **burnt offerings**. Actually this is another kind of sacrifice, mentioned in 27.7 and elsewhere, and which in Hebrew is there called an "offering of *shalom*" (TEV "fellowship offerings," RSV "peace offerings," and NRSV "offerings of well-being"; see also Lev 3; 7.11-36). These were offerings to affirm *shalom* or "fellowship" with a fellow Israelite and with God. This should be made clear in translation. So FRCL has "If they are complete sacrifices . . . ; if they are fellowship sacrifices . . . ." Another way to express **sacrifices** here is "Offerings to restore fellowship with people." For the different types of sacrifice, see verse 6.

12.28   RSV   TEV

Be careful to heed all these words which I command you, that it may go well with you and with your children after you for ever, when you do what is good and right in the sight of the LORD your God.	Obey faithfully everything that I have commanded you, and all will go well for you and your descendants forever, because you will be doing what is right and what pleases the LORD your God.

This is almost the same as verse 25. See also 5.16, 29; 6.18. Here the adverb **for ever** is added.

The verse may be restructured in the following way:

• If you carefully obey everything [the words] that I have commanded you, you will be doing what the LORD your God says is right and good. Then all will go well with you and your descendants forever [or, you and your descendants will prosper forever].

2B-2. Warning against idolatry (12.29–13.18)

RSV

TEV
Warning against Idolatry

29 "When the LORD your God cuts off before you the nations whom you go in to dispossess, and you dispossess them and dwell in their land, 30 take heed that you be not ensnared to follow them, after they have been destroyed before you, and that you do not inquire about their gods, saying, 'How did these nations serve their gods?—that I also may do likewise.' 31 You shall not do so to the LORD your God; for every abominable thing which the LORD hates they have done for their gods; for they even burn their sons and their daughters in the fire to their gods.

32 "Everything that I command you you shall be careful to do; you shall not add to it or take from it.

Chapter 13

1 "If a prophet arises among you, or a dreamer of dreams, and gives you a sign or a wonder, 2 and the sign or wonder which he tells you comes to pass, and if he says, 'Let us go after other gods,' which you have not known, 'and let us serve them,' 3 you shall not listen to the words of that prophet or to that dreamer of dreams; for the LORD your God is testing you, to know whether you love the LORD your God with all your heart and with all your soul. 4 You shall walk after the LORD your God and fear him, and keep his commandments and obey his voice, and you shall serve him and cleave to him. 5 But that prophet or that dreamer of dreams shall be put to death, because he has taught rebellion against the LORD your God, who brought you out of the land of Egypt and redeemed you out of the house of bondage, to make you leave the way in which the LORD your God commanded you to walk. So you shall purge the evil from the midst of you.

6 "If your brother, the son of your mother, or your son, or your daughter, or the wife of your bosom, or your friend who is as your own soul, entices you secretly, saying, 'Let us go and serve other gods,' which neither you nor your fathers have known, 7 some of the gods of the peoples that are round about you, whether near you or far off from you, from the one end of the earth to the other, 8 you shall not yield to him or listen to him, nor shall your eye pity him, nor shall you spare him, nor shall you conceal him; 9 but you shall kill him; your hand shall be first against him to put him to death, and afterwards the hand of all the people. 10 You shall stone him to death with

29 "The LORD your God will destroy the nations as you invade their land, and you will occupy it and settle there. 30 After the LORD destroys those nations, make sure that you don't follow their religious practices, because that would be fatal. Don't try to find out how they worship their gods, so that you can worship in the same way. 31 Do not worship the LORD your God in the way they worship their gods, for in the worship of their gods they do all the disgusting things that the LORD hates. They even sacrifice their children in the fires on their altars.

32 "Do everything that I have commanded you; do not add anything to it or take anything from it.

Chapter 13

1 "Prophets or interpreters of dreams may promise a miracle or a wonder, 2 in order to lead you to worship and serve gods that you have not worshiped before. Even if what they promise comes true, 3 do not pay any attention to them. The LORD your God is using them to test you, to see if you love the LORD with all your heart. 4 Follow the LORD and honor him; obey him and keep his commands; worship him and be faithful to him. 5 But put to death any interpreters of dreams or prophets that tell you to rebel against the LORD, who rescued you from Egypt, where you were slaves. Such people are evil and are trying to lead you away from the life that the LORD has commanded you to live. They must be put to death, in order to rid yourselves of this evil.

6 "Even your brother or your son or your daughter or the wife you love or your closest friend may secretly encourage you to worship other gods, gods that you and your ancestors have never worshiped. 7 Some of them may encourage you to worship the gods of the people who live near you or the gods of those who live far away. 8 But do not let any of them persuade you; do not even listen to them. Show them no mercy or pity, and do not protect them. 9 Kill them! Be the first to stone them, and then let everyone else stone them too. 10 Stone them to death! They tried to lead you away from the LORD your God, who rescued you from Egypt, where you were slaves. 11 Then all the people of Israel will hear what happened; they will be afraid, and no one will ever again do such an evil thing.

12 "When you are living in the towns that the LORD your God gives you, you may hear

stones, because he sought to draw you away from the LORD your God, who brought you out of the land of Egypt, out of the house of bondage. 11 And all Israel shall hear, and fear, and never again do any such wickedness as this among you.

12 "If you hear in one of your cities, which the LORD your God gives you to dwell there, 13 that certain base fellows have gone out among you and have drawn away the inhabitants of the city, saying, 'Let us go and serve other gods,' which you have not known, 14 then you shall inquire and make search and ask diligently; and behold, if it be true and certain that such an abominable thing has been done among you, 15 you shall surely put the inhabitants of that city to the sword, destroying it utterly, all who are in it and its cattle, with the edge of the sword. 16 You shall gather all its spoil into the midst of its open square, and burn the city and all its spoil with fire, as a whole burnt offering to the LORD your God; it shall be a heap for ever, it shall not be built again. 17 None of the devoted things shall cleave to your hand; that the LORD may turn from the fierceness of his anger, and show you mercy, and have compassion on you, and multiply you, as he swore to your fathers, 18 if you obey the voice of the LORD your God, keeping all his commandments which I command you this day, and doing what is right in the sight of the LORD your God.

13 that some worthless people of your nation have misled the people of their town to worship gods that you have never worshiped before. 14 If you hear such a rumor, investigate it thoroughly; and if it is true that this evil thing did happen, 15 then kill all the people in that town and all their livestock too. Destroy that town completely. 16 Bring together all the possessions of the people who live there and pile them up in the town square. Then burn the town and everything in it as an offering to the LORD your God. It must be left in ruins forever and never again be rebuilt. 17 Do not keep for yourselves anything that was condemned to destruction, and then the LORD will turn from his fierce anger and show you mercy. He will be merciful to you and make you a numerous people, as he promised your ancestors, 18 if you obey all his commands that I have given you today, and do what he requires.

This section deals with the various ways the people of Israel, after having settled in Canaan, might be tempted to abandon the LORD and worship pagan deities. Such a temptation might come from a prophet or an interpreter of dreams (13.1-5), from a family member (13.6-11), or from corrupt individuals attempting to subvert a whole community (13.12-18). There could be no compromise between the two: allegiance to Yahweh demanded the most severe punishment—destruction and death—for anyone who might try to lead the Israelites into idolatry (13.5, 8-10, 15-16).

Section heading: the TEV heading "Warning against Idolatry" may be stated in the form of a complete sentence: "Moses warns the people against worshiping foreign gods." We may also express this as "Don't worship false gods."

12.29-30   RSV   TEV

29 "When the LORD your God cuts off before you the nations whom you go in to dispossess, and you dispossess them and dwell in their land, 30 take heed that you be not ensnared to follow them, after they have been destroyed before you, and

29 "The LORD your God will destroy the nations as you invade their land, and you will occupy it and settle there. 30 After the LORD destroys those nations, make sure that you don't follow their religious practices, because that would be fatal. Don't try

that you do not inquire about their   **to find out how they worship their**
gods, saying, 'How did these nations   **gods, so that you can worship in the**
serve their gods?—that I also may   **same way.**
do likewise.'

Verses 29-30 are one long sentence, with verse 29 as a dependent time clause, modifying the main verb of the sentence **take heed** (verse 30). It will be necessary in many languages to restructure, as TEV has done, and make verse 29 a statement of fact, followed by the command in verse 30. With the beginning of a new section, it will be good to preface it with something like "Moses said to the people of Israel."

Cuts off before you the nations: **cuts off** is another verb in the rich vocabulary of destruction and extermination (see also 19.1). The phrase **before you** means "as you advance" (REB), "as you invade their land" (TEV).

Whom you go in to dispossess, and you dispossess them: this is a wordy literal equivalent of the Hebrew text, which can be expressed in a more natural and economical way. We may say something like the following: "As you invade the land of Canaan, the LORD your God will destroy the nations that are there. You will take their place and live in the land." For the verb **dispossess** see 12.2.

In verse 30 the warning begins **take heed . . .** , that is, "be careful," or "take care." NJPSV has "beware," TEV "make sure," CEV "be especially careful."

Ensnared: this verb, in this form, is found only here; it means "to be entangled" (as in a trap), "to be caught" (see the active "to trap" in 1 Sam 28.9). Here it is used figuratively, "lure," "seduce," "lead astray." The passive form of the verb may have to be transformed into the active, "be careful that no one will lure [or, entice] you . . . ."

To follow them, after they have been destroyed before you: even though the Canaanites will be defeated, there will be survivors who will try to get the Israelites to worship their gods. TEV "for that would be fatal" is a way of completing the idea of the verb "be ensnared," which means here that they will actually be trapped, not merely be lured or seduced.

And that you do not inquire about their gods: TEV offers a good translation: "Don't try to find out how they worship their gods." Or we may say "Don't show an interest in their religion."

'How did . . . ?' In RSV the question within single quotes is unnecessarily complicated, and a translation need not preserve the direct order, with the quoted question and the explanatory statement. It is possible to render it as an indirect quotation: ". . . don't try to learn about their gods by asking how those people worship them; if you do, you may do the same thing." However, the direct quotation will be more natural style in a number of languages. CEV offers a good model: "You must be especially careful not to ask 'How did these nations worship their gods? Shouldn't we worship the LORD in the same way?' "

To **serve** gods means to worship them, obey their commandments (see 6.13).

12.31   RSV   TEV

You shall not do so to the LORD your God; for every abominable thing which the LORD hates they have done for their gods; for they even burn their sons and their daughters in the fire to their gods.	Do not worship the LORD your God in the way they worship their gods, for in the worship of their gods they do all the disgusting things that the LORD hates. They even sacrifice their children in the fires on their altars.

You shall not do so to the LORD your God: this means "You are not to act that way in your worship of Yahweh, your God," or "Do not worship the LORD your God in the way they worship their gods."

Abominable thing which the LORD hates: this refers to pagan practices. For **abominable** see 7.25-26. The passion and strength of the verb **hates** should not be watered down in translation. The worst of those "abominations" was the offering as sacrifice, by fire, of children to their idols (see Lev 18.21; 2 Kgs 3.27).

12.32   RSV   TEV
[13.1]

¹"Everything that I command you you shall be careful to do; you shall not add to it or take from it.	"Do everything that I have commanded you; do not add anything to it or take anything from it.

¹ Ch 13.1 in Heb

This states, in a briefer form, the command in 4.2.

In the Hebrew text, and in the Septuagint, this verse is chapter 13, verse 1. The Hebrew chapter and verse numbers will be shown in square brackets, for those who need to use that chapter and verse system.

13.1   RSV   TEV
[13.2]

"If a prophet arises among you, or a dreamer of dreams, and gives you a sign or a wonder,	"Prophets or interpreters of dreams may promise a miracle or a wonder,

The one long sentence, verses 1-4, should be broken up into several sentences. TEV and CEV do that; but see another model at the end of the comments on verse 4.

A **prophet** is a person who announces (or, claims to announce) God's message to the people. If the usual word for **prophet** that has been employed in a language means only someone who foretells the future, it will be helpful in this context to say something like the following: "Suppose a person appears who claims to speak God's message . . . ."

A **dreamer of dreams** is someone who has dreams that are regarded as messages from God. Some people had the ability to interpret them; for example,

Joseph (Genesis 40–41), and Daniel (Daniel 2 and 4); see also Num 12.6 and Joel 2.28.

Gives you a sign or a wonder: it is not certain whether in this context the Hebrew verb **gives** means "performs [for you]" or "tells [you]." NIV and TOB have "announces to you"; TEV has "promises." The latter idea of "saying" or "announcing" is recommended by this Handbook. The meaning is that the prophet has proof that a miracle will occur.

A sign or a wonder: any extraordinary event that is seen as a miracle, a demonstration of God's power (see 4.34; 6.22).

An alternative translation model for this verse is:

- Suppose a prophet or an interpreter of dreams appears and says that he has proof that a miracle is going to happen.

13.2   RSV   TEV
[13.3]

| **and the sign or wonder which he tells you comes to pass, and if he says, 'Let us go after other gods,' which you have not known, 'and let us serve them,'** | **in order to lead you to worship and serve gods that you have not worshiped before. Even if what they promise comes true,** |

Comes to pass: that is, "actually happens" or "takes place."

"Let us go after other gods . . . and let us serve them": notice that RSV breaks up the prophet's message with Moses' own words, **which you have not known**. This may be acceptable for someone who is reading the text, but the hearer will find it hard to understand. It will be better in a number of languages to combine the two direct quotations, with Moses' comment following them; for example, " 'Let us worship and serve other gods.' These are gods that you have not served before." Or we may use indirect speech as TEV does: "in order to lead you to worship and serve gods that you have not worshiped before."

Go after . . . serve: this means simply to follow or pledge allegiance to, and worship; it does not mean to search for, or to try to find.

Other gods: this can be rendered "foreign [or, pagan] gods." For **gods** see 4.28.

Which you have not known: see 11.28.

13.3   RSV   TEV
[13.4]

| **you shall not listen to the words of that prophet or to that dreamer of dreams; for the LORD your God is testing you, to know whether you love the LORD your God with all your heart and with all your soul.** | **do not pay any attention to them. The LORD your God is using them to test you, to see if you love the LORD with all your heart.** |

You shall not listen to . . .: the Israelites are to refuse any appeal to abandon their God, Yahweh, and worship other gods. Other ways to express this are "do not pay any attention to them" (TEV) or "If the prophet says this, don't listen!" (CEV).

The LORD your God is testing you: the same verb occurs in Gen 22.1; it refers to an experience that reveals a person's character, motives, or integrity.

To know: the meaning of this is that God has to test them before knowing whether they love him. The translation should not try to disguise or modify the vivid human way of speaking about God. **The LORD your God is testing you, to know . . .** may also be expressed as "the LORD your God is using him [that prophet] to test you, to find out if . . . ."

You love the LORD your God with all your heart and with all your soul: see 6.5.

13.4 [13.5] RSV	TEV
You shall walk after the LORD your God and fear him, and keep his commandments and obey his voice, and you shall serve him and cleave to him.	Follow the LORD and honor him; obey him and keep his commands; worship him and be faithful to him.

This one verse has six verbs to express the relationship of the Israelites to their God.

Walk after: to follow, as people follow a leader.

Fear: to honor, respect, show reverence for (see 4.10).

Keep (his commands): to obey.

Obey his voice has the same sense, meaning to follow his directions, obey his orders.

Serve: as a worshiper "serves" his or her god.

Cleave to him: be loyal or dedicated to him (10.20).

For **the LORD your God** see 1.6.

An alternative translation model for verses 1-4 may be:

●   [1] A person who claims to announce God's message, or an interpreter of dreams [or, someone who receives messages from God in dreams], may appear among you and announce that he has proof that a miracle will happen. [2] If what he predicts does happen, he will try to lead you to worship and serve other gods, which you have not worshiped before. [3] But don't pay any attention to such a person. The LORD your God is using him to test you to find out if you love the LORD with all your heart and soul [or, completely]. [4] Follow the LORD and respect him; obey his commands; serve him and be faithful to him.

13.5   RSV   TEV
[13.6]
But that prophet or that dreamer of   But put to death any interpreters of
dreams shall be put to death, be-   dreams or prophets that tell you to
cause he has taught rebellion   rebel against the LORD, who rescued
against the LORD your God, who   you from Egypt, where you were
brought you out of the land of Egypt   slaves. Such people are evil and are
and redeemed you out of the house   trying to lead you away from the life
of bondage, to make you leave the   that the LORD has commanded you to
way in which the LORD your God   live. They must be put to death, in
commanded you to walk. So you   order to rid yourselves of this evil.
shall purge the evil from the midst of
you.

A careless reading of this verse as it appears in RSV could connect the verbal
phrase **to make you leave the way** to the words immediately before it, **the LORD
your God . . . redeemed you out of the house of bondage**. Actually it goes with
the description of the person who **has taught rebellion against the LORD your
God**. TEV attempts to solve this problem by making the clause **to make you
leave the way** part of a new sentence. However, another possibility is to place
the clause **who brought you out of the land . . .** at the beginning of the verse, as
follows:

> [4] . . . be faithful to him. [5] He rescued you from working like slaves in
> Egypt. So you must put to death any prophet or interpreter of dreams
> who tells you to rebel against the LORD.

Shall be put to death: such a person is a traitor and must be executed at once.
In some languages the passive voice must be transformed to the active; for
example, "But you must execute [or, kill] such a prophet or . . . ."
He has taught rebellion against the LORD your God: in the religious realm
this is called apostasy; in the political realm it is rebellion or sedition. Here
taught rebellion means "urged you to rebel"; REB has "preached rebellion"; or
we may say "tells you to disobey the LORD."
Who brought you out of the land of Egypt: see 5.6; 6.12.
Redeemed you out of the house of bondage: see 7.8.
To make you leave the way: the life of obedience to God is often pictured as
a journey, a path a person must walk. In a number of languages this figurative
language may be retained; for example, "to cause you to stop walking on the
path on which the LORD your God commanded you to walk."
You shall purge the evil: see 17.7, 12. The would-be leader of a rebellion
against Yahweh is seen as an impurity or an uncleanness that must be gotten
rid of in order to keep the people healthy and clean. Alternative translation
models for this final sentence are "You shall put this person to death in order
to get rid of this evil thing from among you"; or in languages where it will be
difficult to talk about evil apart from the person who does it, "That person is
evil, so you must put him to death."

13.6   RSV   TEV
[13.7]

"If your brother, the son of your mother, or your son, or your daughter, or the wife of your bosom, or your friend who is as your own soul, entices you secretly, saying, 'Let us go and serve other gods,' which neither you nor your fathers have known,

"Even your brother or your son or your daughter or the wife you love or your closest friend may secretly encourage you to worship other gods, gods that you and your ancestors have never worshiped.

Verses 6-9 are another long sentence that must be broken into several shorter and simpler sentences; TEV has six sentences and is a good model to follow. Translators should also study the model of CEV, which combines verses 6-10, omitting a number of repetitious phrases that are unnatural style in English.

Your brother, the son of your mother: there is a textual problem here; the Samaritan and the Septuagint have ". . . the son of your father or the son of your mother." The Hebrew, as it stands, seems to mean only a brother by your mother, but not by your father. There are several possibilities for the translator: (1) translate the Hebrew (as in NJPSV, TOB, and as recommended by HOTTP); (2) follow the Samaritan and Septuagint (as in NRSV, REB, NJB); (3) just say "your [own] brother" (as TEV, NIV, BRCL, POCL, SPCL, FRCL do). The best procedure to follow seems to be (3).

The wife of your bosom: NRSV "the wife you embrace" or TEV "the wife you love" could be taken to mean that there is also a wife you don't embrace or love; NJB "the spouse whom you embrace" is worse. Something like "your dear wife" is the most natural way to say this in English.

Your friend who is as your own soul: that is, "your dearest [or closest, or best] friend."

Entices you secretly: playing the part of the traitor, the wife or friend comes to the Israelite in private and tries to persuade him to commit idolatry. TEV has "secretly encourage you." In a number of languages direct speech will be natural style; for example, "Your own brother . . . may come to you secretly and say, 'Let's worship other gods!' "

Let us go and serve other gods: see verse 2.

Which neither you nor your fathers have known: see verse 2. **Your fathers** means "your ancestors."

13.7   RSV   TEV
[13.8]

some of the gods of the peoples that are round about you, whether near you or far off from you, from the one end of the earth to the other,

Some of them may encourage you to worship the gods of the people who live near you or the gods of those who live far away.

This verse continues the description of the pagan gods referred to in verse 6.

From one end of the earth to the other: all pagan gods are included. TEV does not formally represent these words, which simply emphasize **gods of the peoples that are . . . far off from you**. Instead of **earth** some translations have "from one end of the land . . ." (REB, TOB, NIV); but it seems that "earth" is to be preferred (RSV, NJB, NJPSV, and others). It means "anywhere on earth."

13.8 RSV	TEV
[13.9]	
you shall not yield to him or listen to him, nor shall your eye pity him, nor shall you spare him, nor shall you conceal him;	But do not let any of them persuade you; do not even listen to them. Show them no mercy or pity, and do not protect them.

There are five verbs in this verse to emphasize the need to reject any such inducement to idol worship.

Yield to him: that is, agree to do what he wants.

Listen to him: pay attention to what he says.

Your eye pity him: show no mercy, be pitiless (see also 7.16). In many languages there will be suitable figurative expressions; for example, "Do not have warm insides towards him" or "Don't let your heart [or, liver] feel towards him."

Spare him: this means the same as the previous verb; the two can be combined: "show him no pity or mercy."

Conceal: this means to cover up what was done, not to tell others about it. NJB renders it "conceal his guilt." It does not mean to physically hide the person, but to keep secret what he has done. This is wrong; that person's evil deed must be exposed and punished.

13.9 RSV	TEV
[13.10]	
but you shall kill him; your hand shall be first against him to put him to death, and afterwards the hand of all the people.	Kill them! Be the first to stone them, and then let everyone else stone them too.

You shall kill him: the Hebrew uses a compound verbal phrase, "killing you shall kill him." This is a way of being emphatic: "You must certainly kill him." How this is to be done follows.

Your hand shall be first: this is to be a public execution, with the person who was enticed taking the lead. He will be the first to throw the stones, and then the others will do the same. It may be necessary to make it clear in verse 9 itself that public execution by stoning is meant, as TEV does with "Kill him! Be the first to stone him, and then let everyone else stone him too."

13.10 RSV	TEV
[13.11]	
You shall stone him to death with stones, because he sought to draw you away from the LORD your God, who brought you out of the land of Egypt, out of the house of bondage.	Stone them to death! They tried to lead you away from the LORD your God, who rescued you from Egypt, where you were slaves.

You shall stone him to death: the verb is still the second person singular (as in verse 9). **Stone him to death** may also be rendered as "You shall take stones and throw them at him till he dies."

He sought to draw you away from the LORD your God: this is the worst of all sins, apostasy, faithlessness, rebellion against Yahweh. **Draw you away** means "lead you away," or even "cause you to rebel against."

Who brought you out of the land of Egypt, out of the house of bondage: see verse 5.

13.11 RSV	TEV
[13.12]	
And all Israel shall hear, and fear, and never again do any such wickedness as this among you.	Then all the people of Israel will hear what happened; they will be afraid, and no one will ever again do such an evil thing.

This verse describes the result of the execution of a would-be traitor.
All Israel: that is, all the people of Israel, all the Israelites.
Such wickedness: a most evil thing.
An alternative translation model for this verse is:

- When the rest of the people of Israel hear what happened to the prophet [or, that person], they will be afraid, and no one else will ever do such an evil thing again.

13.12-13 RSV	TEV
[13,13-14]	
12 "If you hear in one of your cities, which the LORD your God gives you to dwell there, 13 that certain base fellows have gone out among you and have drawn away the inhabitants of the city, saying, 'Let us go and serve other gods,' which you have not known,	12 "When you are living in the towns that the LORD your God gives you, you may hear 13 that some worthless people of your nation have misled the people of their town to worship gods that you have never worshiped before.

Verses 12-18 deal with another possibility, this one involving the attempt to lead astray a whole community (city or town). The punishment will fit the crime.

The section begins with a long sentence (verses 12-15), which must be broken up into smaller sentences. Here it is quite difficult to make verse 12 a complete sentence. The most logical way to begin is the way TEV restructures the sentence: "When you are living in the towns . . . ."

You hear in one of your cities is wrongly placed by RSV. **One of your cities** is the scene of the attempted revolt against God, not the place where it becomes known. NRSV has got it right: "If you hear it said about one of your towns . . ." (see also REB). CEV has "You may hear a rumor about one of the towns." However, we may also say "People may tell you about one of the towns."

One of your cities, which the LORD your God gives you to dwell there: in most languages "towns" or its equivalent will be better than **cities** (see 1.22). The point is that the Israelites, after conquering the land of Canaan, will be living in cities or towns already built by the Canaanites.

Base fellows is literally "sons of Belial"—worthless people, of no account. A modern equivalent in some dialects of English would be "bums." Most languages will have a good equivalent to describe such people, as they normally exist in every society.

Have drawn away the inhabitants of the city: as in verse 10, this is apostasy.

'Let us go and serve other gods,' which you have not known: see verses 2, 6.

13.14 RSV [13.15]	TEV
then you shall inquire and make search and ask diligently; and behold, if it be true and certain that such an abominable thing has been done among you,	If you hear such a rumor, investigate it thoroughly; and if it is true that this evil thing did happen,

Again, a group of verbs of similar meaning is used in order to emphasize the importance of the investigation that is to take place.

You shall inquire and make search and ask diligently: this is a complete and thorough investigation of the matter (see TEV, CEV).

Such an abominable thing: see 7.25; 12.31.

13.15 RSV [13.16]	TEV
you shall surely put the inhabitants of that city to the sword, destroying it utterly, all who are in it and its cattle, with the edge of the sword.	then kill all the people in that town and all their livestock too. Destroy that town completely.

The punishment is severe: the towns are to be put under a ban, that is, completely destroyed. (See in 2.33-36 how the towns ruled by Sihon were dealt with; see also 7.26.)

Put . . . to the sword . . . with the edge of the sword: if possible the translation should keep the word **sword**; for example, "you must take your swords and kill every one" (CEV). But if the word that is used means a dagger, or hatchet, or bolo, or knife, it will probably be better to use the general verb "to kill" (so TEV, FRCL, BRCL, and others).

13.16 RSV	TEV
[13.17]	
You shall gather all its spoil into the midst of its open square, and burn the city and all its spoil with fire, as a whole burnt offering to the LORD your God; it shall be a heap for ever, it shall not be built again.	Bring together all the possessions of the people who live there and pile them up in the town square. Then burn the town and everything in it as an offering to the LORD your God. It must be left in ruins forever and never again be rebuilt.

Spoil: this means the people's possessions, their valuables, which would normally be kept by the victors as a prize of war. REB has "goods," NJB "loot," NIV "plunder." An alternative translation model for this first sentence may be "Bring [or, Gather] all the possessions of the people who live there and pile them up . . . ."

The midst of its open square: this is the public square or large flat open area, near the town gate. If such a feature is not part of a given culture, something like "the main street" or "a large flat open area in the center of town" can be used.

A whole burnt offering: this is the sacrifice that is completely burned (see Exo 29.18; Lev 6.22-23; 8.21; 1 Sam 7.9).

It shall be a heap for ever . . . not be built again: never again will a town or city be built on that place; never again will people live there. It will be a desolate ruin forever. An alternative translation model for this sentence is "It must be left in ruins forever and never again rebuilt." However, **it shall not be built again** contains the idea that it must be left in ruins. So we may translate simply as "Don't ever rebuild that town."

13.17 RSV	TEV
[13.18]	
None of the devoted things shall cleave to your hand; that the LORD may turn from the fierceness of his anger, and show you mercy, and have compassion on you, and multiply you, as he swore to your fathers,	Do not keep for yourselves anything that was condemned to destruction, and then the LORD will turn from his fierce anger and show you mercy. He will be merciful to you and make you a numerous people, as he promised your ancestors,

The devoted things: these are the things that are under the ban, that is, that are dedicated to God and so must be destroyed completely (see verse 15; 2.34).

None . . . shall cleave to your hand: you are not to save any of those objects that must be destroyed. All of this is to be done in order to placate Yahweh's furious anger. TEV has a good model: "Do not keep for yourselves anything that was condemned to destruction." However, in languages that do not use the passive voice, we may express this as "Do not keep any of the things that belong to Yahweh. You must destroy them."

Show you mercy, and have compassion on you: these have very similar meanings, "be kind and merciful," "be forgiving and compassionate." Here NRSV (also REB) is more literal: "show you compassion, and in his compassion [multiply you]."

Multiply you: see 7.13.

An alternative translation model combining verses 16 and 17 may be:

- ^16-17 Gather all the possessions of the people who lived there, and pile them up in the open flat area near the town gate. Don't keep anything that belongs to Yahweh. You must burn all these things and the whole town. Don't ever rebuild the town. Then Yahweh will not be angry with you any more. He will be merciful to you and will cause you to prosper by giving you many children, as he promised your ancestors.

13.18   RSV   TEV
[13.19]

if you obey the voice of the LORD   if you obey all his commands that I
your God, keeping all his command-   have given you today, and do what
ments which I command you this   he requires.
day, and doing what is right in the
sight of the LORD your God.

There is a similar exhortation to this in 12.28.

It is a good idea to put a full stop at the end of verse 17 and begin verse 18 as a new sentence: "The LORD will do this if . . . ."

Obey the voice . . . keeping all his commandments: the Hebrew structure is again the use of a main verb and a participial subordinate clause, for emphasis. For **commandments** see 4.2.

Which I command you this day: again the emphasis is on "today" (see 11.26, 28, 32).

2B-3. A forbidden mourning practice (14.1-2)

RSV   TEV
                                               A Forbidden Mourning Practice

1 "You are the sons of the LORD your God;   1 "You are the people of the LORD your God.
you shall not cut yourselves or make any   So when you mourn for the dead, don't gash
baldness on your foreheads for the dead. 2 For   yourselves or shave the front of your head, as

252

you are a people holy to the LORD your God, and the LORD has chosen you to be a people for his own possession, out of all the peoples that are on the face of the earth.

other people do. 2 You belong to the LORD your God; he has chosen you to be his own people from among all the peoples who live on earth.

This is a short section, dealing with a pagan mourning practice, which does not relate to what comes before or after it (see Lev 19.28; 21.5).

Section heading: TEV has "A Forbidden Mourning Practice," and CEV has "Don't Mourn Like Other Nations." Another way to express this is "Don't show your sorrow for the dead the way other people do."

14.1	RSV	TEV

"You are the sons of the LORD your God; you shall not cut yourselves or make any baldness on your fore-heads for the dead.

"You are the people of the LORD your God. So when you mourn for the dead, don't gash yourselves or shave the front of your head, as other people do.

Since this seems to be a separate matter, it is recommended that translators start with something like "Moses said to the people of Israel."

You are the sons of the LORD your God: that is, ". . . the children [or, sons and daughters] of Yahweh," the covenant community. For **the Lord your God** see 1.6.

The last phrase of the verse, **for the dead**, modifies the two verbs **cut** and **make**. So it is better to place it first, as TEV does: "So when you mourn for the dead . . . ," or "when you show sorrow for the dead [or, people who have died]."

Cut yourselves: this refers to gashes and cuts that were made by followers of some religions and cults as part of mourning for the dead.

Make any baldness on your forehead: NRSV is somewhat better, "shave your forelocks." NJPSV, however, is best: "shave the front of your heads" (as also TEV).

14.2	RSV	TEV

For you are a people holy to the LORD your God, and the LORD has chosen you to be a people for his own possession, out of all the peo-ples that are on the face of the earth.

You belong to the LORD your God; he has chosen you to be his own people from among all the peoples who live on earth.

You are a people holy to the LORD your God: the Israelites were not allowed to do the things mentioned in the previous verse because they were dedicated to Yahweh alone; they belonged to him and served and worshiped only him. So TEV has "You belong to the LORD your God"; in order to connect this verse logically with verse 1, we may say "Because you belong to Yahweh the God you worship."

The LORD has chosen you to be a people of his own possession: this again emphasizes the fact that they are exclusively his.

Out of all the peoples that are on the face of the earth: of all the human race, Yahweh chose the Israelites to be his special people. It is possible to place this phrase at the beginning of the verse, as follows:

•   Because out of all the people who live on this earth, the LORD
      your God chose you to be his own people. You belong to him.

2B-4. Clean and unclean animals (14.3-10)

RSV	TEV
	Clean and Unclean Animals
3 "You shall not eat any abominable thing. 4 These are the animals you may eat: the ox, the sheep, the goat, 5 the hart, the gazelle, the roebuck, the wild goat, the ibex, the antelope, and the mountain-sheep. 6 Every animal that parts the hoof and has the hoof cloven in two, and chews the cud, among the animals, you may eat. 7 Yet of those that chew the cud or have the hoof cloven you shall not eat these: the camel, the hare, and the rock badger, because they chew the cud but do not part the hoof, are unclean for you. 8 And the swine, because it parts the hoof but does not chew the cud, is unclean for you. Their flesh you shall not eat, and their carcasses you shall not touch. 9 Of all that are in the waters you may eat these: whatever has fins and scales you may eat. 10 And whatever does not have fins and scales you shall not eat; it is unclean for you.	3 "Do not eat anything that the LORD has declared unclean. 4 You may eat these animals: cattle, sheep, goats, 5 deer, wild sheep, wild goats, or antelopes—6 any animals that have divided hoofs and that also chew the cud. 7 But no animals may be eaten unless they have divided hoofs and also chew the cud. You may not eat camels, rabbits, or rock badgers. They must be considered unclean; they chew the cud but do not have divided hoofs. 8 Do not eat pigs. They must be considered unclean; they have divided hoofs but do not chew the cud. Do not eat any of these animals or even touch their dead bodies. 9 "You may eat any kind of fish that has fins and scales, 10 but anything living in the water that does not have fins and scales may not be eaten; it must be considered unclean.

As nearly all translations indicate, the identity of some of the animals listed in this section is impossible to determine exactly. Many languages will not have individual names for some of the animals included in this list, and it will be necessary to include three or four different animals in one general group (see also the list in Lev 11.1-47, and the comments in *A Handbook on Leviticus*, pages 155-165, are useful).

In general it is recommended that the RSV names be followed.

In each case the Handbook will give a list of passages in the Old Testament where these animals appear (except for the more common ones: ox, sheep, goat, camel, and eagle).

The UBS Help for Translators, FFB, should be consulted for every one of the lesser-known species.

Section heading: the TEV heading "Clean and Unclean Animals" uses the adjectives "clean" and "unclean" as they appear in the text (verses 8, 10, 19, 20). Another possibility is to say "Animals that may be eaten, and animals that may not be eaten."

14.3 RSV TEV

"You shall not eat any abominable thing. **"Do not eat anything that the LORD has declared unclean.**

With the beginning of a new section, it is recommended that translators reintroduce Moses as the speaker.

Any abominable thing: see 7.25, 26.

In the list of animals which follows (verses 3-8), NRSV differs from RSV only at verse 5 (where it has "deer" instead of **hart**). NJPSV differs only at verse 7, where instead of **rock badger** it has "damian" (which is defined in the dictionary as "hyrax: the con[e]y of the Bible").

The only way to ensure an accurate translation of the RSV terminology would be to find the scientific designation of each of the species, and then to check the name in the language of the translation, to make sure it represents the proper scientific name.

14.4 RSV TEV

These are the animals you may eat: the ox, the sheep, the goat, **You may eat these animals: cattle, sheep, goats,**

The animals in this verse should offer no difficulty. These are the domesticated animals. Instead of **ox**, however, as in RSV (and others), it is better to say "cattle" (TEV) or something similar. See the comment on "cattle" at 2.35.

14.5 RSV TEV

the hart, the gazelle, the roebuck, the wild goat, the ibex, the antelope, and the mountain-sheep. **deer, wild sheep, wild goats, or antelopes—**

Hart: NRSV and NJB have "deer." The name occurs also in 12.22; 15.22; 1 Kgs 4.23; Psa 42.1; Isa 35.6; Lam 1.6.

Gazelle: see 12.22; 15.22 (and 12 more times in the Old Testament).

Roebuck: NIV has "roe deer." See also 1 Kgs 4.23.

In parts of the world where only one type of deer is found (or none), we may combine the first three types in this list and translate "all kinds of deer" or "all kinds of animals named 'deer.' "

Wild goat: NJB has "ibex"; see also Psa 104.18 (and see "Wildgoats' Rocks" in 1 Sam 24.2).

Ibex: NJB has "antelope." This name does not occur elsewhere in the Old Testament.

Antelope: NJB has "oryx" (an African antelope). See also Isa 51.20. If the **ibex** and **antelope** are unknown in a language or culture, we may simply say "all animals named 'antelope.' "

Mountain-sheep: this name does not occur elsewhere in the Old Testament. It is possible to combine this with **wild goat** and translate "wild sheep and goats" or "sheep and goats that live in the mountains."

14.6   RSV   TEV

Every animal that parts the hoof and   any animals that have divided hoofs
has the hoof cloven in two, and   and that also chew the cud.
chews the cud, among the animals,
you may eat.

Parts the hoof and has the hoof cloven: this is a double description of the same feature; it means simply "[any animal that] has cloven [or, divided] hoofs." In cultures where animals like this are unknown, we may use a descriptive phrase; for example, "having feet that are separated [or, split] in the middle," or "with feet that have two parts."

And chews the cud: in order to be considered clean, that is, fit to be eaten, an animal had to fit both of these descriptions: it had to have cloven hoofs and had to chew the cud. As verses 7 and 8 show, if an animal displayed only one of these characteristics, then it could not be eaten. Chewing the cud is part of the digestion process in certain animals that have more than one stomach. Such animals can bring up the food from their stomachs in order to chew it again. Some languages will have technical terms for this activity, but in others a descriptive phrase may be used; for example, "animals who chew their food a second

AN IBEX-GOAT WITH CLOVEN HOOFS

time" or "animals that bring up their food and chew it again."

14.7   RSV   TEV

Yet of those that chew the cud or have the hoof cloven you shall not eat these: the camel, the hare, and the rock badger, because they chew the cud but do not part the hoof, are unclean for you.

But no animals may be eaten unless they have divided hoofs and also chew the cud. You may not eat camels, rabbits, or rock badgers. They must be considered unclean; they chew the cud but do not have divided hoofs.

Camel: this animal is referred to many times in the Bible. If a language distinguishes between the two main types of camels, the one referred to here is the "dromedary," which has only one hump on its back. Otherwise translators may borrow the general term "camel" and explain it in a footnote or glossary.

ROCK HYRAX, PIG, CAMEL, AND RABBIT

Hare: TEV says "rabbit"; see Lev 11.6. Hares and rabbits don't really chew the cud, but their jaws move in such a way that they appear to be doing this. But in any case they were considered unclean by the Hebrews because they do not have cloven hoofs, and thus were not to be eaten.

Rock badger: as noted above, NJPSV has "damian"; NIV and NJB have "coney" (NIV footnote, "hyrax or rock badger"). It appears also in Lev 11.5 (and see **badger** in Psa 104.18; Pro 30.26; see also FFB, pages 69-70). This animal is about the same size as a rabbit and normally lives in rocky areas. It also does not chew the cud, but like the rabbit it appears to.

14.8   RSV   TEV

And the swine, because it parts the hoof but does not chew the cud, is unclean for you. Their flesh you shall not eat, and their carcasses you shall not touch.

Do not eat pigs. They must be considered unclean; they have divided hoofs but do not chew the cud. Do not eat any of these animals or even touch their dead bodies.

Swine: or, more familiarly, "pigs." See also Lev 11.7; Pro 11.27; Isa 65.4; 66.3, 17 (also in the New Testament).

RSV	TEV
9 "Of all that are in the waters you may eat these: whatever has fins and scales you may eat. 10 And whatever does not have fins and scales you shall not eat; it is unclean for you.	9 "You may eat any kind of fish that has fins and scales, 10 but anything living in the water that does not have fins and scales may not be eaten; it must be considered unclean.

Of the animals that live in the water, only those that have fins and scales are considered clean, that is, can be eaten; all others are unclean and cannot be eaten.

These two verses may be introduced by the statement "These are the sea creatures that you are allowed to eat: . . . ."

Fins and scales: since fish are known in almost every culture in the world, most languages will have suitable terms for these words. However, in the case of a culture where fish are unknown, it will be helpful to borrow terms from some other language and add a footnote or glossary item explaining these words.

2B-5. Birds and other creatures with wings (14.11-21)

RSV	TEV
11 "You may eat all clean birds. 12 But these are the ones which you shall not eat: the eagle, the vulture, the osprey, 13 the buzzard, the kite, after their kinds; 14 every raven after its kind; 15 the ostrich, the nighthawk, the sea gull, the hawk, after their kinds; 16 the little owl and the great owl, the water hen 17 and the pelican, the carrion vulture and the cormorant, 18 the stork, the heron, after their kinds; the hoopoe and the bat. 19 And all winged insects are unclean for you; they shall not be eaten. 20 All clean winged things you may eat. 21 "You shall not eat anything that dies of itself; you may give it to the alien who is within your towns, that he may eat it, or you may sell it to a foreigner; for you are a people holy to the LORD your God. "You shall not boil a kid in its mother's milk.	11 "You may eat any clean bird. 12-18 But these are the kinds of birds you are not to eat: eagles, owls, hawks, falcons; buzzards, vultures, crows; ostriches; seagulls, storks, herons, pelicans, cormorants;[j] hoopoes; and bats. 19 "All winged insects are unclean; do not eat them. 20 You may eat any clean insect. 21 "Do not eat any animal that dies a natural death. You may let the foreigners who live among you eat it, or you may sell it to other foreigners. But you belong to the LORD your God; you are his people. "Do not cook a young sheep or goat in its mother's milk.

This section deals mainly with birds and flying insects (verses 11-20). Two related comments are added in verse 21.

There are many differences among translations in the names of the birds that cannot be eaten. NRSV differs from RSV only at verse 17, where instead of **pelican** it has "desert owl." *A Handbook on Leviticus*, pages 162-163, has a chart giving the Hebrew word for each of these birds, a reference to FFB, and the names in RSV and other versions. The following advice is given:

In some languages it may be necessary to translate several terms by a single word in the receptor language. For example, there may be only one word for the various kinds of owls mentioned in the list [verse 16]. Translators may then have to say "the different kinds of owls" or something similar. In other languages there may be no word for certain of the birds in the list. If this is the case, it may be necessary to resort to a borrowing which is explained in a footnote or glossary entry. And although the final term in the list [bat] may not be considered a bird in the receptor language, it must be remembered that it was apparently included in this category in Jewish thinking .... Even though the receptor language classification may be entirely different from the Old Testament system, the translator must respect what is found in the text. But an explanatory footnote will certainly be acceptable.

In this Handbook we will note the places where NJPSV, NJB, NIV, and REB differ from RSV/NRSV; and we will note in most cases other passages in the Old Testament where these same creatures are mentioned.

Section heading: the suggested heading "Birds and other creatures with wings" may also be expressed as "Birds and flying insects" or "Birds and all insects with wings."

14.11-18   RSV   TEV

11 "You may eat all clean birds. 12 But these are the ones which you shall not eat: the eagle, the vulture, the osprey, 13 the buzzard, the kite, after their kinds; 14 every raven after its kind; 15 the ostrich, the nighthawk, the sea gull, the hawk, after their kinds; 16 the little owl and the great owl, the water hen 17 and the pelican, the carrion vulture and the cormorant, 18 the stork, the heron, after their kinds; the hoopoe and the bat.

11 "You may eat any clean bird. 12-18 But these are the kinds of birds you are not to eat: eagles, owls, hawks, falcons; buzzards, vultures, crows; ostriches; seagulls, storks, herons, pelicans, cormorants;[1] hoopoes; and bats.

[1] *The identification of some of these birds is uncertain.*

Eagle: this bird is quite common in the Old Testament.

Vulture: see also Lev 11.18; Psa 102.6; Pro 30.17; Lam 4.19; Hos 8.1; Zeph 2.14.

Osprey: NJPSV has "black vulture." See also Lev 11.13.

For the birds in verse 12 REB has "griffon-vulture, black vulture, bearded vulture."

In verse 13 the translations go their various ways: NJPSV, NIV, TOB, and FRCL have three different kinds of birds instead of the two in RSV. This is due to a problem in the Hebrew text, which does have three separate words. S.R. Driver

EAGLE   VULTURE

and others maintain that the first word (*ra'ah*) is a mistake; it is not found elsewhere in the Bible, and the third word (*da'yah*) is a correction of the first one (see also Mayes, *New Century Bible Commentary*, pages 241-42). NJPSV, however, has three birds, "the kite, the falcon, and the buzzard"; and NIV has "the red kite, the black kite, the falcon."

HOTTP recommends that two birds be listed, "the black kite and the red kite"; translators should feel free to follow the RSV wording, **the buzzard, the kite, after their kinds**, if this is appropriate in their language.

Buzzard: this bird does not appear elsewhere in the Old Testament.

Kite: see also Lev 11.14; Isa 34.15.

After their kinds: this means "of all varieties," "of every kind there is."

For **raven** in verse 14 REB has "every kind of crow," and TEV has simply "crows." See also Gen 8.7; Lev 11.15; 1 Kgs 17.4, 6; Psa 147.9; Pro 30.17; Job 38.41; Song 5.11; Isa 34.11; Zeph 2.14.

For the first three birds in verse 15, NIV has "horned owl, screech owl, gull"; REB has "desert owl, short-eared owl, long-eared owl"; and NJB has for the second and third birds "screech owl, seagull."

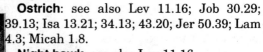

Ostrich: see also Lev 11.16; Job 30.29; 39.13; Isa 13.21; 34.13; 43.20; Jer 50.39; Lam 4.3; Micah 1.8.

Night hawk: see also Lev 11.16.

Sea gull: see also Lev 11.16.

Hawk: see Lev 11.18; Job 39.26; Isa 34.11.

For the three birds in verse 16, REB has "tawny owl, screech owl, little owl"; NJB has "owl, barn owl, ibis"; for the third bird NIV and NJPSV have "white owl."

OWL

The terms **little owl** and **great owl** do not appear elsewhere in the Old Testament; "owl" is found in Lev 11.17; Psa 102.6; Isa 34.11, 15; Zeph 2.14.

Water hen: see also Lev 11.18. NJPSV has "white owl."

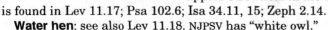

260

As suggested above, it may be necessary in certain languages to combine all the birds in this verse as "all kinds of owls."

Translations differ widely in the identification of the three birds in verse 17. For **pelican** NRSV and NIV have "desert owl," and REB "horned owl"; for **carrion vulture** NJPSV has "bustard," NJB "white vulture," and REB and NIV "osprey"; for **cormorant** REB has "fisher owl."

Pelican: see Lev 11.18.

Carrion vulture appears nowhere else in the Old Testament;

Cormorant appears also in Lev 11.17.

The translations being cited all agree on the four birds of verse 18, with the exception of REB, which

BATS AND A HOOPOE

instead of **heron** has "cormorant." (Of course the **bat** is not a bird, but it was considered one by the Hebrews.)

Stork: see also Lev 11.19; Psa 104.17; Jer 8.7; Zech 5.9.

Heron . . . hoopoe . . . bat: see also Lev 11.19.

14.19-20   RSV   TEV

19 And all winged insects are un-   19 "All winged insects are unclean for you; they shall not be   clean; do not eat them. 20 You may
eaten. 20 All clean winged things you eat any clean insect.
may eat.

All winged insects . . . winged things: both verses deal with flying insects (see also Lev 11.21-23). The Hebrew word in verse 20 appears some seventy times in the Old Testament and is a collective term for "flying creatures," which includes both insects and birds. In this context, however, it is highly unlikely that birds should suddenly appear in verse 20, and it is recommended that "winged [or, flying] insects" be used in both verses.

14.21   RSV   TEV

"You shall not eat anything that   "Do not eat any animal that dies a
dies of itself; you may give it to the natural death. You may let the for-
alien who is within your towns, that   eigners who live among you eat it, or
he may eat it, or you may sell it to a you may sell it to other foreigners.
foreigner; for you are a people holy   But you belong to the LORD your
to the LORD your God.   God; you are his people.

"You shall not boil a kid in its   "Do not cook a young sheep or
mother's milk.   goat in its mother's milk.

Anything that dies of itself: the reason for this law, forbidding the eating of any animal that "dies a natural death" (TEV), is that the animal's blood had not been properly drained out, so that anyone who ate such an animal would be eating blood, which was strictly forbidden (see 12.15, 22-27; Exo 22.31). Such an animal was ritually unclean.

In this case, however, the dead animal could be eaten by **the alien who is within your towns,** that is, a foreigner who lived permanently among the Israelites (see 1.16). Or it could be sold **to a foreigner,** that is, some foreigner who might be traveling through the Israelite community. CEV expresses this quite clearly with "You may give it to foreigners who live in your town, or sell it to foreigners who are visiting your town."

A people holy to the LORD your God: see 7.6; 14.2.

You shall not boil a kid in its mother's milk: for this law see also Exo 23.19; 34.26. Here **a kid** is the young either of a sheep or a goat; consequently TEV has "a young sheep or goat." It is thought by some that this was a Canaanite custom and thus abhorrent to the Israelites; but the evidence for such a Canaanite rite is far from conclusive.

2B-6. The law of the tithe (14.22-29)

RSV

22 "You shall tithe all the yield of your seed, which comes forth from the field year by year. 23 And before the LORD your God, in the place which he will choose, to make his name dwell there, you shall eat the tithe of your grain, of your wine, and of your oil, and the firstlings of your herd and flock; that you may learn to fear the LORD your God always. 24 And if the way is too long for you, so that you are not able to bring the tithe, when the LORD your God blesses you, because the place is too far from you, which the LORD your God chooses, to set his name there, 25 then you shall turn it into money, and bind up the money in your hand, and go to the place which the LORD your God chooses, 26 and spend the money for whatever you desire, oxen, or sheep, or wine or strong drink, whatever your appetite craves; and you shall eat there before the LORD your God and rejoice, you and your household. 27 And you shall not forsake the Levite who is within your towns, for he has no portion or inheritance with you.

28 "At the end of every three years you shall bring forth all the tithe of your produce in the same year, and lay it up within your towns; 29 and the Levite, because he has no portion or inheritance with you, and the sojourner, the fatherless, and the widow, who are within your towns, shall come and eat and be filled; that the LORD your God may bless you in all the work of your hands that you do.

TEV
The Law of the Tithe

22 "Set aside a tithe—a tenth of all that your fields produce each year. 23 Then go to the one place where the LORD your God has chosen to be worshiped; and there in his presence eat the tithes of your grain, wine, and olive oil, and the first-born of your cattle and sheep. Do this so that you may learn to honor the LORD your God always. 24 If the place of worship is too far from your home for you to carry there the tithe of the produce that the LORD has blessed you with, then do this: 25 Sell your produce and take the money with you to the one place of worship. 26 Spend it on whatever you want—beef, lamb, wine, beer— and there, in the presence of the LORD your God, you and your families are to eat and enjoy yourselves.

27 "Do not neglect the Levites who live in your towns; they have no property of their own. 28 At the end of every third year bring the tithe of all your crops and store it in your towns. 29 This food is for the Levites, since they own no property, and for the foreigners, orphans, and widows who live in your towns. They are to come and get all they need. Do this, and the LORD your God will bless you in everything you do.

This section deals with two different payments of the tithe, that is, the annual payment of one tenth of each Israelite's agricultural produce. Each year for two years out of every three the tithe was to be taken to the central place of worship (verses 22-26; see 12.6-7, 11); every third year it was to be deposited in the town in which or near which the Israelite lived (verses 27-29).

Section heading: the section heading in TEV, "The Law of the Tithe," is expressed in other ways in different translations; for example, "The Annual Tithe" (NJB) and "Tithes" (NIV, NRSV). In many languages there will not be one word that adequately expresses the meaning of the word "tithe," so that a phrase may be needed; "Give one-tenth [or, ten percent] of your produce to the LORD."

14.22	RSV	TEV
	"You shall tithe all the yield of your seed, which comes forth from the field year by year.	"Set aside a tithe—a tenth of all that your fields produce each year.

With the beginning of a new section, it is recommended that translators reintroduce Moses as the speaker. It may also be helpful to reintroduce the audience, the people of Israel (see alternative translation).

You shall tithe: in Hebrew this is an emphatic command, the compound verb form "tithing you shall tithe." To **tithe** means to give to God one tenth of a person's gross income—in this instance, agricultural produce (see verse 23 and also 12.6). In dealing with this, the most natural way of expressing the command is to say "Put aside one tenth," "set aside ten percent" (CEV), or "save up . . ." or "store away . . . ."

All the yield of your seed: this concept is more naturally expressed by "everything you grow in your fields," or "all your crops."

Which comes forth from the field year by year: a more natural way of saying this is "[all] that your fields produce [or, grow] each year" (TEV, NIV).

Although duplication and redundancy are common and effective in Hebrew, translators must constantly determine whether they are natural and effective in their language, and then act accordingly.

An alternative translation model for this verse is:

- People of Israel, every year you must set aside one part out of every ten parts of all that your fields produce.

14.23	RSV	TEV
	And before the LORD your God, in the place which he will choose, to make his name dwell there, you shall eat the tithe of your grain, of your wine, and of your oil, and the firstlings of	Then go to the one place where the LORD your God has chosen to be worshiped; and there in his presence eat the tithes of your grain, wine, and olive oil, and the firstborn of your

| your herd and flock; that you may learn to fear the LORD your God always. | cattle and sheep. Do this so that you may learn to honor the LORD your God always. |

Before the LORD your God: that is, in the place of worship, "In the presence of the LORD your God" (see 9.18 and elsewhere).

In the place he will choose to make his name dwell there: this refers to the central sanctuary. See 12.5, 11, 14, 21.

You shall eat the tithe of your grain, of your wine, and of your oil: these are the three principal agricultural products: wheat and barley, grapes for making wine, and olives for making olive oil.

The firstlings of your herd and flock: TEV "the first-born of your cattle and sheep" is more natural English; but "goats" should also be included. These animals are not included in the tithe of verse 21, but they were eaten by the Israelites as they feasted in the central sanctuary. These animals belonged to Yahweh and so were eaten in the sanctuary as an act of worship (see 12.6, 17; 15.19-23).

That you may learn to fear the LORD your God always: the payment of the tithe to God was to acknowledge God as the owner of the land and as the one who blessed the people with abundant crops. The people's prosperity was God's gift, not the result of their hard work. For **to fear**, in the sense of "honor" and "respect," see 4.10. For **the LORD your God** see 1.6.

An alternative translation model for this verse is:

- Take ten percent of your grain, wine, and olive oil, and the first-born of every cow, sheep, and goat, to the place where the LORD has chosen for you to worship him. Eat this food and the meat of these animals there. This will teach you to always respect the LORD your God.

14.24   RSV   TEV

| And if the way is too long for you, so that you are not able to bring the tithe, when the LORD your God blesses you, because the place is too far from you, which the LORD your God chooses, to set his name there, | If the place of worship is too far from your home for you to carry there the tithe of the produce that the LORD has blessed you with, then do this: |

Verses 24-26 are one long sentence with much repetition. TEV offers one model for breaking it up into more manageable units; but even shorter units may be attempted.

And if the way is too long for you ... because the place is too far from you: this repetition need not be reproduced literally in translation. These two segments, together with the following **which the LORD your God chooses to set his name there**, may be brought together in one sentence (see models below).

When the LORD your God blesses you: this refers to the abundant crops that
God has provided.

Alternative translation models for this verse are:

- If you live so far away from the one place of worship chosen by
  God that you cannot carry there the one-tenth of your produce,
  this is what you should do: . . .

- It may be that the one place that God has chosen for you to worship him is so far away from your home that you cannot carry
  there the one-tenth of your produce. If such is the case, then do
  this: . . .

14.25 RSV TEV

then you shall turn it into money, and bind up the money in your hand, and go to the place which the LORD your God chooses,	Sell your produce and take the money with you to the one place of worship.

Then you shall turn it into money: this simply means "Sell your crop [or,
produce]," that is, sell the one tenth of the crops that is to be taken to the
sanctuary. The **it** refers back to **the tithe** in verse 24. CEV has "then sell this
part."

Bind up the money in your hand: NRSV is better in English, "With the money
secure in hand." But the simpler and more natural "take your money with you"
(NIV, TEV) is better again. What is indicated is that the silver pieces would be
tied securely in a cloth, or napkin, for easy and safe carrying. **Money** here does
not refer to coins but to pieces of silver, of varying sizes.

14.26 RSV TEV

and spend the money for whatever you desire, oxen, or sheep, or wine or strong drink, whatever your appetite craves; and you shall eat there before the LORD your God and rejoice, you and your household.	Spend it on whatever you want— beef, lamb, wine, beer—and there, in the presence of the LORD your God, you and your families are to eat and enjoy yourselves.

At the central sanctuary the Israelite would buy what he was unable to bring
with him, and would celebrate with his family.

Oxen . . . sheep . . . wine . . . strong drink: instead of **oxen** and **sheep** the
translation may prefer words for their meat, such as "beef" and "lamb" (TEV),
since it is the eating of the animals that is in focus; otherwise we can say "cattle
and sheep" (NIV, REB).

Wine and strong drink: **wine** is a fermented drink made from grapes (see 7.13). **Strong drink** is an alcoholic beverage such as beer; it is a fermented drink, not distilled liquor (such as "scotch" and "bourbon"). NIV has "other fermented drink," NJB "fermented liquor," NJPSV "other intoxicant," NRSV and REB "strong drink." The Hebrew word is defined as "intoxicating drink, evidently a kind of beer." It is often paired with wine (Lev 10.9; 1 Sam 1.15; Luke 1.15). So both TEV and CEV translate it as "beer." In some languages readers have understood a literal translation of **strong drink** to mean "drink that makes you strong"; that is certainly not the sense of the Hebrew term.

Whatever you desire . . . whatever your appetite craves: this repetition may be effective in Hebrew, but it is not necessarily natural and effective in other languages. In both clauses the same Hebrew noun *nefesh* ("soul, appetite") is used, with two different verbs for "crave, desire, want."

You shall eat there . . . and rejoice: this can be more naturally rendered "feast with rejoicing" (REB), or "eat and enjoy yourselves" (TEV).

You and your household: as usual, the father of the family is the one being addressed, and here his family and the servants and attendants are included; thus "you, your family, and your servants" is a natural translation. In some languages there is a term that includes both family and servants; if so, that should be used here.

14.27	RSV	TEV

And you shall not forsake the Levite who is within your towns, for he has no portion or inheritance with you.

"Do not neglect the Levites who live in your towns; they have no property of their own.

TEV and REB join this verse to the following two verses; RSV and NJPSV join it to the verses that come before it. It is a linking verse; but everything considered, it seems better to join it to what follows, not to what comes before.

The verse is a reminder of the constant need to provide for Levites, who had no territory of their own and were thus dependent on the generosity of their fellow Israelites (see 12.19; 18.1-2; Num 18.20; 26.62).

You shall not forsake: that is, "Do not neglect [or, disregard]," "Do not fail to help."

The Levite who is within your towns: in most languages it is much better to use the plural form, "the Levites who live in your communities [or, towns]."

No portion or inheritance: this is a typical doublet, showing emphasis—"they have no land," "they were not allotted any territory" (see the comment at 12.2).

14.28	RSV	TEV

"At the end of every three years you shall bring forth all the tithe of your produce in the same year, and lay it up within your towns;

At the end of every third year bring the tithe of all your crops and store it in your towns.

The **tithe** every third year is not in addition to the annual one of verses 22-26, but a different use of the tithe in that year, given for the support of the Levites and other needy people in the community. For a more elaborate statement of this tithe, see 26.12-15.

At the end of every three years: stated more succinctly and naturally this is "every third year" (TEV, NRSV). The time would be after all the crops had been harvested.

You shall bring forth all the tithe of your produce: see the similar language in verse 22. **Bring forth** is completed by **lay it up**, that is, "take and deposit [or, store]."

In the same year: NRSV is better, "You shall bring out the full tithe of your produce for that year."

Lay it up within your towns: it is probable that there was a central deposit of some kind where all the produce was stored for distribution to the needy people in the community.

CEV has a helpful model for this verse:

● 　　Every third year, instead of using the ten percent of your harvest
　　　for a big celebration, bring it into town and put it in a community
　　　storehouse.

14.29　　　　RSV	TEV
and the Levite, because he has no portion or inheritance with you, and the sojourner, the fatherless, and the widow, who are within your towns, shall come and eat and be filled; that the LORD your God may bless you in all the work of your hands that you do.	This food is for the Levites, since they own no property, and for the foreigners, orphans, and widows who live in your towns. They are to come and get all they need. Do this, and the LORD your God will bless you in everything you do.

For other statements about providing for the needs of the poor and needy in Israel, see 16.11; 24.19-21; 26.12-15.

The Levite . . . has no portion or inheritance with you: as in verse 27 and 12.12.

The sojourner: these are the foreigners who lived permanently in Israel (see 1.16; 5.14; 10.18-19).

The fatherless, and the widow: see 10.18.

The LORD your God may bless you: this is the reward for compassion and generosity. On **bless** see also 2.7.

All the work of your hands that you do: a rather wordy way of saying "everything you do."

2B-7. The year for canceling debts (15.1-11)

RSV

TEV
The Seventh Year

1 "At the end of every seven years you shall grant a release. 2 And this is the manner of the release: every creditor shall release what he has lent to his neighbor; he shall not exact it of his neighbor, his brother, because the LORD's release has been proclaimed. 3 Of a foreigner you may exact it; but whatever of yours is with your brother your hand shall release. 4 But there will be no poor among you (for the LORD will bless you in the land which the LORD your God gives you for an inheritance to possess), 5 if only you will obey the voice of the LORD your God, being careful to do all this commandment which I command you this day. 6 For the LORD your God will bless you, as he promised you, and you shall lend to many nations, but you shall not borrow; and you shall rule over many nations, but they shall not rule over you.

7 "If there is among you a poor man, one of your brethren, in any of your towns within your land which the LORD your God gives you, you shall not harden your heart or shut your hand against your poor brother, 8 but you shall open your hand to him, and lend him sufficient for his need, whatever it may be. 9 Take heed lest there be a base thought in your heart, and you say, 'The seventh year, the year of release is near,' and your eye be hostile to your poor brother, and you give him nothing, and he cry to the LORD against you, and it be sin in you. 10 You shall give to him freely, and your heart shall not be grudging when you give to him; because for this the LORD your God will bless you in all your work and in all that you undertake. 11 For the poor will never cease out of the land; therefore I command you, You shall open wide your hand to your brother, to the needy and to the poor, in the land.

1 "At the end of every seventh year you are to cancel the debts of those who owe you money. 2 This is how it is to be done. Each of you who has lent money to any Israelite is to cancel the debt; you must not try to collect the money; the LORD himself has declared the debt canceled. 3 You may collect what a foreigner owes you, but you must not collect what any of your own people owe you.

4 "The LORD your God will bless you in the land that he is giving you. Not one of your people will be poor 5 if you obey him and carefully observe everything that I command you today. 6 The LORD will bless you, as he has promised. You will lend money to many nations, but you will not have to borrow from any; you will have control over many nations, but no nation will have control over you.

7 "If in any of the towns in the land that the LORD your God is giving you there are Israelites in need, then do not be selfish and refuse to help them. 8 Instead, be generous and lend them as much as they need. 9 Do not refuse to lend them something, just because the year when debts are canceled is near. Do not let such an evil thought enter your mind. If you refuse to make the loan, they will cry out to the LORD against you, and you will be held guilty. 10 Give to them freely and unselfishly, and the LORD will bless you in everything you do. 11 There will always be some Israelites who are poor and in need, and so I command you to be generous to them.

The first two sections in this chapter deal with a major provision in the life of the community, "The year of release," "The sabbatical year" (NJB), "The Sabbatical Year of Release" (NRSV). It includes the "release" of debts owed by fellow Israelites (verses 1-11) and of Israelite slaves owned by Israelites (verses 12-18).

Section heading: the first section may be entitled "The Year for Canceling Debts" (NIV) or "Cancel your debts in the seventh year."

15.1 RSV TEV

"At the end of every seven years you shall grant a release.

"At the end of every seventh year you are to cancel the debts of those who owe you money.

With the beginning of a new section, translators are advised to reintroduce Moses as the speaker; for example, "Moses said to the people of Israel: . . . ."

At the end of every seven years: this same form is used in 14.28; NRSV has "Every seventh year." This provision for the seventh year matches the older legislation of not cultivating the land every seventh year (see Exo 23.10-11; Lev 25.2-7).

You shall grant a release: the Hebrew noun translated **release** appears here, in verse 2, and in 31.10, and nowhere else in the Old Testament. Since this **release** means canceling debts, it is better to say, with NRSV, "you shall grant a remission of debts." NIV is better still, "you must cancel debts." CEV has "that loans do not need to be paid back." TEV "the debts of those who owe you money" seems needlessly wordy in English. However, in some languages it will be expressed in a similar way; for example, "lift the debts of those people who have borrowed money from you," or even "do not require that people who have borrowed money from you should pay it back."

15.2 RSV TEV

And this is the manner of the release: every creditor shall release what he has lent to his neighbor; he shall not exact it of his neighbor, his brother, because the LORD's release has been proclaimed.

This is how it is to be done. Each of you who has lent money to any Israelite is to cancel the debt; you must not try to collect the money; the LORD himself has declared the debt canceled.

The **release** is here defined in clear terms: the debt of every fellow Israelite is to be canceled.

And this is the manner of the release: simply, "This is what you must do," or "This is how it is to be done" (TEV, NIV).

From the second person singular in verse 1 the Hebrew text switches to the third person singular in verse 2, then back to the second singular in the rest of the section. In translation it is recommended that the second singular be kept in verse 2; or else we may follow the TEV, "Each of you . . . ."

Every creditor shall release what he has lent to his neighbor: since a **creditor** is a person who lends money to someone else, the word itself is redundant; see TEV, "Each of you who has lent money . . . ."

His neighbor: this is a way of speaking of a "fellow-Israelite" (TEV), which should be made clear in translation.

He shall not exact it: this is the negative form of the previous **shall release**; thus "don't try to collect the debt," or "don't ask him to pay it back."

His neighbor, his brother: the second term defines more exactly the first one. Some think that it is a later addition to the text. (The Hebrew text as we have it is "his neighbor and his brother," which seems to indicate additional editorial work. NJPSV has "his fellow or kinsman.") The best way to translate this is to say "his fellow-Israelite," or even "another Israelite."

The LORD's release has been proclaimed: this introduces a new element. **The LORD's release** means the release required by the LORD; the passive **has been proclaimed** suggests that there may have been a formal public proclamation of the beginning of the seventh year. But this is only a conjecture, and if the passive form of the verb cannot be used, we may say something like the following: "it is the year the LORD has ordered cancellation of all debts" or ". . . has ordered you to cancel [or, forgive] all debts."

15.3	RSV	TEV

Of a foreigner you may exact it; but whatever of yours is with your brother your hand shall release.	**You may collect what a foreigner owes you, but you must not collect what any of your own people owe you.**

This verse makes it clear that the law applies only to Israelites; foreigners must pay their debts, as usual (see similar discrimination in 23.20). Another way to say this is "You may collect money that a foreigner owes you."

Whatever of yours is with your brother: that is, whatever a fellow-Israelite owes you; that debt must be forgiven.

Your brother: your fellow-Israelite.

Your hand shall release: this is an idiomatic way of saying "you must cancel [or, forgive]." The most common verb used for the cancellation of debts should be chosen.

15.4	RSV	TEV

But there will be no poor among you (for the LORD will bless you in the land which the LORD your God gives you for an inheritance to possess),	**"The LORD your God will bless you in the land that he is giving you. Not one of your people will be poor**

Notice that verses 4-5 are one sentence. However, there are better ways of rearranging the material than the one followed by RSV (which is difficult to read aloud effectively); see TEV. It is also possible to combine verses 4 and 5 (see the alternative translation model at the end of verse 6).

But there will be no poor among you: this initial statement is explained by two further comments. These are that (1) the LORD will bless the people, and (2) the people must obey the LORD's commands (verse 3).

There will be no poor among you: in light of the contradictory statement in verse 11, the affirmation here is not absolute, but dependent on the people's faithful obedience to Yahweh's commands. **Poor** will be expressed in a number of languages as "a person with few possessions."

The LORD will bless you in the land which the LORD your God gives you for an inheritance to possess: this is frequently stressed, and these terms appear many times in this book. The verb **will bless** is in a compound form, which makes for an emphatic statement: "he will surely bless you." For a comment on the translation of **bless**, see 1.11. For **the LORD your God** see 1.6. For the terms **inheritance** and **possess**, see 1.8, 35. This sentence may be placed at the end of verse 5 (see the alternative model at the end of the comments on verse 6).

15.5   RSV   TEV

if only you will obey the voice of the LORD your God, being careful to do all this commandment which I command you this day.	if you obey him and carefully observe everything that I command you today.

If only you obey: this is the condition for the promise that there will be no poor people in the land. Again the emphatic form is used; the Hebrew verb is actually "hear," meaning "listen to," "pay heed to," that is, **obey**.

The voice of the LORD your God: that is, "what the LORD your God orders [or, tells] you to do."

Being careful to do: the sense is "doing your best to obey," or "carefully observing" (TEV).

All this commandment: see 5.31.

Again the emphasis is laid on **this day** (see 11.26, 28, 32; 13.18).

15.6   RSV   TEV

For the LORD your God will bless you, as he promised you, and you shall lend to many nations, but you shall not borrow; and you shall rule over many nations, but they shall not rule over you.	The LORD will bless you, as he has promised. You will lend money to many nations, but you will not have to borrow from any; you will have control over many nations, but no nation will have control over you.

God will bless the people so that they will prosper and thrive and dominate other nations. Israel will become a major economic power in the region, and thus able to exert influence over other nations (see also 28.12-13, 44).

Lend . . . borrow: these are financial terms, and the unstated object is "money." TEV has "You will lend money to many nations, but you will not have to borrow from any." It is also possible to say "You will let the people from other countries borrow money from you, but you will not have to borrow money from them."

271

Rule . . . not rule: this kind of rule seems to be economic supremacy, not necessarily domination achieved through force of arms. But a general word for "control" or "domination" will do.

An alternative translation model for verses 4-6 is as follows:

•   ⁴⁻⁶ No one in Israel will ever be poor, if you obey the LORD your God and carefully observe all his commands that I am giving you today. The LORD your God is giving you this land, and he has promised to make you successful in all that you do. He will do what he has promised. You will lend money to the people of other nations, but you will not have to borrow money from any of them. You will have control over other nations, but no nation will have control over you.

15.7

RSV	TEV
"If there is among you a poor man, one of your brethren, in any of your towns within your land which the LORD your God gives you, you shall not harden your heart or shut your hand against your poor brother,	"If in any of the towns in the land that the LORD your God is giving you there are Israelites in need, then do not be selfish and refuse to help them.

In verses 7-9 Moses commands the people to be generous toward their needy fellow-Israelites, and always be willing to help them. Wherever possible, exclusive language such as **poor man** or **one of your brethren** should be avoided. One way of doing this is to use plural forms, which generally include both males and females, or express this as "fellow Israelites" (TEV), or "poor Israelites" (CEV), or else "poor person."

A poor man, one of your brethren: that is, "a poor fellow-Israelite," "fellow-Israelites who are poor [or, in need]." For **poor** see verse 4.

In any of your towns within your land: this is a rather wordy way of saying "in any town in your country" or even "in the town where you live" (CEV).

You shall not harden your heart or shut your hand: these are two vivid idioms for lack of compassion and for stinginess. In English "hardhearted and tightfisted" (NRSV, NIV) match the Hebrew idioms. Other languages will have their own vivid idioms to express this; for example, "black-hearted" (Thai).

Your poor brother: "your needy fellow-Israelite" or "another Israelite, who has few possessions."

15.8

RSV	TEV
but you shall open your hand to him, and lend him sufficient for his need, whatever it may be.	Instead, be generous and lend them as much as they need.

Open your hand: a way of saying "be generous" (TEV) or "be kind" (CEV). In some languages this will be expressed as "having an open heart toward."

Lend him sufficient for his need, whatever it may be: simply "lend him as much as he needs." Again "money" is the unstated object of the verb **lend**.

15.9 RSV	TEV
Take heed lest there be a base thought in your heart, and you say, 'The seventh year, the year of release is near,' and your eye be hostile to your poor brother, and you give him nothing, and he cry to the LORD against you, and it be sin in you.	Do not refuse to lend them something, just because the year when debts are canceled is near. Do not let such an evil thought enter your mind. If you refuse to make the loan, they will cry out to the LORD against you, and you will be held guilty.

This verse warns the people not to be calculating in the help they give to needy fellow-Israelites. The closer the year for canceling all debts was, the less the borrower would have to repay the amount he or she had been lent. Consequently a person might be inclined not to lend money to anyone, since the debt would soon be canceled.

Some restructuring may be required in translating this verse. See TEV and CEV, and also the alternative model below.

Take heed lest there be a base thought in your heart: that is, "Be careful not to let a mean [or, selfish] thought enter your mind," or "Do not let such an evil thought enter your mind," or even "Don't think about doing such an evil thing."

And you say may also be expressed as "And you think."

The seventh year, the year of release is near: see verses 1-2 for these terms. It will be helpful to supply the information that is understood in the text, as CEV does: "then, I won't be able to get my money back."

Your eye be hostile toward your poor brother: here **hostile** means to show an unfriendly attitude. A possible translation is "you give him an unfriendly look"; NJPSV translates "you are mean"; NJB "scowl at your poor brother." Both TEV and CEV take **hostile** to mean a "refusal" or "unwillingness" to lend money to a poor person. This interpretation is also possible.

And he cry to the LORD against you: the Israelite who was refused help will complain to Yahweh about such a mean attitude, and Yahweh will condemn the hardhearted Israelite.

And it be sin in you: "God will judge you guilty of sin."

An alternative translation model for this verse is:

●   Be careful that you don't think "Soon it will be the seventh year when I must cancel debts, and I won't be able to get my money back." It would be evil to think that way and to be so selfish that you refuse to lend any money to your poor fellow Israelite. He may complain to Yahweh and Yahweh will decide that you have sinned.

15.10   RSV   TEV

You shall give to him freely, and | **Give to them freely and unselfishly,**
your heart shall not be grudging | **and the LORD will bless you in ev-**
when you give to him; because for | **erything you do.**
this the LORD your God will bless you
in all your work and in all that you
undertake.

This verse is the reverse of the previous verse.

You shall give to him freely: literally "giving you shall give," the emphatic construction. TEV has "Give to them freely and unselfishly."

Your heart shall not be grudging: this is a figure of speech for not being stingy, not showing an ungenerous spirit. See the expression "open your hand" with a similar meaning in verse 8.

The LORD your God will bless you in all your work and in all that you undertake: an emphatic statement, achieved by repetition (see 12.7). God will prosper the compassionate Israelites who are generous toward their needy fellow citizens.

15.11   RSV   TEV

For the poor will never cease out of | **There will always be some Israelites**
the land; therefore I command you, | **who are poor and in need, and so I**
You shall open wide your hand to | **command you to be generous to**
your brother, to the needy and to the | **them.**
poor, in the land.

The closing command is based on the fact that there would always be Israelites in need of help.

The poor will never cease out of the land: that is, "There will always be some Israelites who are poor or in need" (TEV; similarly CEV). This is simply a statement of fact, not an expression of God's will for his people. Jesus has this verse in mind as he rebukes his disciples (John 12.8).

You shall open wide your hand: another use of the compound form for emphasis (see verse 8 for the figure of an open hand).

To the needy and to the poor: these two phrases modify **to your brother**. They may mean exactly the same, or they may indicate temporary and permanent impoverishment. An alternative translation model may be "to those who have few possessions and need help."

2B-8. The treatment of slaves (15.12-18)

RSV

TEV

The Treatment of Slaves

12 "If your brother, a Hebrew man, or a Hebrew woman, is sold to you, he shall serve you six years, and in the seventh year you shall let him go free from you. 13 And when you let him go free from you, you shall not let him go empty-handed; 14 you shall furnish him liberally out of your flock, out of your threshing floor, and out of your wine press; as the LORD your God has blessed you, you shall give to him. 15 You shall remember that you were a slave in the land of Egypt, and the LORD your God redeemed you; therefore I command you this today. 16 But if he says to you, 'I will not go out from you,' because he loves you and your household, since he fares well with you, 17 then you shall take an awl, and thrust it through his ear into the door, and he shall be your bondman for ever. And to your bondwoman you shall do likewise. 18 It shall not seem hard to you, when you let him go free from you; for at half the cost of a hired servant he has served you six years. So the LORD your God will bless you in all that you do.

12 "If any Israelites, male or female, sell themselves to you as slaves, you are to release them after they have served you for six years. When the seventh year comes, you must let them go free. 13 When you set them free, do not send them away empty-handed. 14 Give to them generously from what the LORD has blessed you with—sheep, grain, and wine. 15 Remember that you were slaves in Egypt and the LORD your God set you free; that is why I am now giving you this command. 16 "But your slave may not want to leave; he may love you and your family and be content to stay. 17 Then take him to the door of your house and there pierce his ear; he will then be your slave for life. Treat your female slave in the same way. 18 Do not be resentful when you set slaves free; after all, they have served you for six years at half the cost of hired servants. Do this, and the LORD your God will bless you in all that you do.

Another "release" to be effected was the freeing of Israelite slaves after six years of servitude (see Exo 21.2-6; see also Lev 25.39-46). These were Israelite men and women who became slaves because they were unable to pay their debts (see references to this practice in 2 Kgs 4.1; Neh 5.5; Pro 22.7; Isa 50.1; Amos 2.6).

Section heading: instead of the TEV title "The Treatment of Slaves," a title that includes the key element of "release" such as "Setting Slaves Free" (CEV) may be better.

15.12 RSV

TEV

"If your brother, a Hebrew man, or a Hebrew woman, is sold to you, he shall serve you six years, and in the seventh year you shall let him go free from you.

"If any Israelites, male or female, sell themselves[m] to you as slaves, you are to release them after they have served you for six years. When the seventh year comes, you must let them go free.

[m] sell themselves; *or* are sold.

With the beginning of a new section, translators are advised to reintroduce Moses as the speaker.

Your brother: a fellow Israelite, male or female.

Hebrew: this word is not used very often, so translators are urged to use it here rather than "Israelite." In general "Hebrew" refers to a person's race; "Israelite" refers to nationality.

Is sold to you: TEV translates "sell themselves" (with the alternative "are sold" in footnote). Both translations are possible, based on the form of the Hebrew verb and the context. Translations vary: the reflexive form "sell themselves" is the choice of NIV, NJB, REB, FRCL, SPCL; the passive is used in NRSV (with alternative in footnote), NJB, TOB, BRCL. The context favors the reflexive sense, and it is recommended that it be followed. TEV follows this option, with "sell themselves to you as slaves."

As noted by commentaries "slave" (which appears in verse 15) may in some cultures not be appropriate for this kind of servitude; in English, at least, the only option is "indentured servant," which is rarely used and would be inappropriate in a common language translation. In verse 17 RSV "bondman" and "bondwoman" translate two different words (not simply the masculine and feminine forms of the same noun). Something more than "servant" is required, and "slave" may be the only option. Perhaps we may express this as "sell themselves to you as their masters and work for no pay," meaning that they had no freedom to seek work elsewhere.

Shall serve you: the verb should mean more than the work done by modern domestic helpers, as noted above. They would be the property of their masters and receive no pay.

In the seventh year: the text does not give the exact time, but it is assumed that it would happen at the beginning of the seventh year.

15.13   RSV   TEV

And when you let him go free from you, you shall not let him go empty-handed;	When you set them free, do not send them away empty-handed.

The beginning of verse 13 repeats the end of verse 12.

You shall not let him go empty-handed: to send them away without giving them something would only worsen their situation, since they had not earned any money during their time of servitude.

15.14   RSV   TEV

you shall furnish him liberally out of your flock, out of your threshing floor, and out of your wine press; as the LORD your God has blessed you, you shall give to him.	Give to them generously from what the LORD has blessed you with— sheep, grain, and wine.

The master was to give the freed slave, man or woman, many sheep (**out of your flock**), plenty of grain, wheat or barley or both (**out of your threshing** floor), and much wine (**out of your wine press**). It will rarely be of any value to translate the terms **threshing floor** and **wine press** literally, unless it happens that in a given language these two terms can be used to refer to the produce, grain and wine.

Furnish: the Hebrew verb means "put a necklace on" and is used only here and at Psa ·73.6. It can be taken as a figure of speech here and be translated "give" (TEV, CEV) or "supply" (NIV).

The Hebrew text is quite emphatic, with **shall furnish him** at the beginning of the verse, and **shall give to him** at the end. This emphasis should be carried over in translation.

TEV has a good model for this verse, but we may also restructure the clauses in a way similar to CEV and say:

- Give them sheep and a good supply of grain and wine. The more the LORD has given you, the more you should give them.

15.15 RSV TEV

You shall remember that you were a slave in the land of Egypt, and the LORD your God redeemed you; therefore I command you this today.	**Remember that you were slaves in Egypt and the LORD your God set you free; that is why I am now giving you this command.**

This verse furnishes the basis or motivation for freeing slaves. The Israelites themselves had been slaves in Egypt, and they would know what it means to be set free.

Remember: Israelites were never to forget the great act of liberation that made them the people of Yahweh.

Redeemed: see 7.8; see also 4.34; 9.26; 16.12; 24.18.

I command you this today: again "today" is stressed (see verse 5).

15.16 RSV TEV

But if he says to you, 'I will not go out from you,' because he loves you and your household, since he fares well with you,	**"But your slave may not want to leave; he may love you and your family and be content to stay.**

Verses 16-17 are one sentence, with verse 16 providing the setting for the action described in verse 17. TEV offers one model of how this long sentence may be broken into more manageable units.

If he says . . . because he loves . . . since: these circumstantial clauses may be placed first, in the order in which they happen; for example, "But the slave who has been well-treated by you may love you and your family. So he may say to you, 'I don't want to leave you.' "

I will not go out from you: that is, "I don't want to leave you."

He loves you and your household: see 14.26.

He fares well with you: this can be represented by "he is well-off with you" (NJPSV, NJB) or "you have treated him well."

15.17   RSV   TEV

then you shall take an awl, and   Then take him to the door of your
thrust it through his ear into the   house and there pierce his ear; he
door, and he shall be your bondman   will then be your slave for life. Treat
for ever. And to your bondwoman   your female slave in the same way.
you shall do likewise.

An awl: the word appears only here and in Exo 21.6. It is a sharp, pointed tool, made of wood, bone, flint, or metal. Some conjecture that a metal tag was affixed to the pierced ear lobe of the slave.

Ear: the actual part referred to is the ear lobe.

Into the door: apparently the door of the master's house (TEV, CEV). In some languages it will be necessary to make it clear that the slave must stand against or beside the door to provide a hard flat area for the owner to punch a clear hole through the ear (see a similar passage in Exo 21.6). So the first part of this verse may be expressed as follows:

- Then make him stand against [or, beside] the door of your house, and punch a hole through one of his ear lobes with an awl [or, a sharp piece of metal].

Bondman . . . bondwoman: better "male slave . . . female slave."

CEV combines the final two clauses in the following way: "such slaves will belong to you for life, whether they are men or women."

15.18   RSV   TEV

It shall not seem hard to you, when   Do not be resentful when you set
you let him go free from you; for at slaves free; after all, they have
half the cost of a hired servant he   served you for six years at half the
has served you six years. So the   cost of hired servants.[n] Do this, and
LORD your God will bless you in all   the LORD your God will bless you in
that you do.   all that you do.

                                      [n] at half . . . servants; *or* and have
                                      worked twice as hard as hired ser-
                                      vants.

This verse refers to the other case, of the slave who did leave the household, and is now a free person. TEV shows this, with "when you set slaves free." We may also say something like "In the case of slaves you set free, do not be resentful [or, complain]."

It shall not seem hard to you: this is not a statement of fact but an exhortation: "Do not feel aggrieved" (NJPSV), "Do not think it hard on you" (NJB), "Do not consider it a hardship" (NRSV). TEV has "Do not be resentful . . . ." The phrase **to you** translates what is literally "in your eyes," meaning from your point of view.

At half the cost of a hired servant: the meaning of the text, as translated by RSV, TEV, and CEV, is that the cost of maintaining a slave was half the cost of paying a hired servant. But there are other ways in which this text is understood: (1) "He has given you double the service of a hired man" (NJPSV, TOB; Dhorme and Driver); (2) "The six years of service was equivalent to the wages of a hired man" (Craigie). It is recommended that the RSV, TEV, and CEV understanding of the text be followed.

So the LORD your God will bless you in all that you do: see verse 10.

2B-9. The first-born cattle and sheep (15.19-23)

RSV	TEV
	The First-Born Cattle and Sheep

19 "All the firstling males that are born of your herd and flock you shall consecrate to the LORD your God; you shall do no work with the firstling of your herd, nor shear the firstling of your flock. 20 You shall eat it, you and your household, before the LORD your God year by year at the place which the LORD will choose. 21 But if it has any blemish, if it is lame or blind, or has any serious blemish whatever, you shall not sacrifice it to the LORD your God. 22 You shall eat it within your towns; the unclean and the clean alike may eat it, as though it were a gazelle or a hart. 23 Only you shall not eat its blood; you shall pour it out on the ground like water.	19 "Set aside for the LORD your God all the first-born males of your cattle and sheep; don't use any of these cattle for work and don't shear any of these sheep. 20 Each year you and your family are to eat them in the LORD's presence at the one place of worship. 21 But if there is anything wrong with the animals, if they are crippled or blind or have any other serious defect, you must not sacrifice them to the LORD your God. 22 You may eat such animals at home. All of you, whether ritually clean or unclean, may eat them, just as you eat deer or antelope. 23 But do not use their blood for food; instead, you must pour it out on the ground like water.

This section deals with first-born male livestock, which includes cattle, sheep, and goats (see Exo 13.2, 12). They are to be offered to God, and instructions are given about defective animals.

Section heading: in the title it may be better to use a collective term for livestock; or else TEV can be imitated, with the addition of "goats" (see 12.6, 17; 14.23): "The first-born males of cattle, sheep, and goats," or more simply "First-born domesticated animals."

15.19	RSV	TEV
	"All the firstling males that are born of your herd and flock you shall	**"Set aside for the LORD your God all the first-born males of your cattle**

consecrate to the LORD your God; you shall do no work with the first-ling of your herd, nor shear the first-ling of your flock.

and sheep; don't use any of these cattle for work and don't shear any of these sheep.

With the beginning of a new section, Moses should be reintroduced as the speaker.

Firstling males that are born of your herd and flock: for modern English style the TEV is to be preferred, with the addition of "goats."

Consecrate: in this context it means to treat the animal as belonging to Yahweh, not to the human owner. Something like "Set aside" (TEV) or "Set apart" (NIV) is a good translation; or else, "dedicate" (REB), or even "give it to the LORD." The first part of this verse may be also rendered as "Set aside for the LORD your God all the first-born males of your cows, sheep, and goats."

Do no work with: in this context the work was primarily that of pulling the plow. So REB, "You must not plough with the firstborn of your cattle," or we may say "You must not use any of the first-born males of your cows to plow your fields."

Shear: where there are sheep and the sheep grow wool, there will be no difficulty translating this passage. But where sheep and wool are unknown, a translator may be forced to use a long, descriptive statement; for example, "Don't cut off the hair of any of your first-born sheep." The use of sheep and their wool was a basic part of ancient Israelite culture, and no cultural equivalent should be attempted in translating this verse.

15.20	RSV	TEV

You shall eat it, you and your house-hold, before the LORD your God year by year at the place which the LORD will choose.

Each year you and your family are to eat them in the LORD's presence at the one place of worship.

These animals were to be eaten in the central sanctuary, perhaps during the Festival of Booths, when the tithes were offered (see 14.23).

It will be helpful to begin this verse with a word such as "Instead"; for example, "Instead, each year you must eat the first-born . . . ."

You and your household: see 14.26.

Before the LORD your God: in the sanctuary (see 14.26).

At the place which the LORD will choose: see 14.23.

15.21	RSV	TEV

But if it has any blemish, if it is lame or blind, or has any serious blemish

But if there is anything wrong with the animals, if they are crippled or

| whatever, you shall not sacrifice it to the LORD your God. | blind or have any other serious defect, you must not sacrifice them to the LORD your God. |

No defective animal could be offered to God (see 17.1).

Any blemish: any serious "defect" (NRSV), such as blindness or lameness, disqualified the animal from being offered to God.

An alternative translation model for this verse is:

- But if the animal is lame or blind, or has some other physical defect, you must not slaughter it and offer it to the LORD your God.

15.22   RSV   TEV

| You shall eat it within your towns; the unclean and the clean alike may eat it, as though it were a gazelle or a hart. | You may eat such animals at home. All of you, whether ritually clean or unclean, may eat them, just as you eat deer or antelope. |

Defective first-born males would be eaten in the homes of the owners (see similar instructions in 12.15-16).

The unclean and the clean: both ritually clean and unclean people could share in the meal (see 12.15).

A gazelle or a hart: see 12.15.

15.23   RSV   TEV

| Only you shall not eat its blood; you shall pour it out on the ground like water. | But do not use their blood for food; instead, you must pour it out on the ground like water. |

See 12.16.

2B-10. The Passover (16.1-8)

RSV   TEV
The Passover

1 "Observe the month of Abib, and keep the passover to the LORD your God; for in the month of Abib the LORD your God brought you out of Egypt by night. 2 And you shall offer the passover sacrifice to the LORD your God, from the flock or the herd, at the place which the LORD will choose, to make his name dwell there. 3 You shall eat no leavened bread with

1 "Honor the LORD your God by celebrating Passover in the month of Abib; it was on a night in that month that he rescued you from Egypt. 2 Go to the one place of worship and slaughter there one of your sheep or cattle for the Passover meal to honor the LORD your God. 3 When you eat this meal, do not eat bread prepared with yeast. For seven days you are to

it; seven days you shall eat it with unleavened bread, the bread of affliction—for you came out of the land of Egypt in hurried flight—that all the days of your life you may remember the day when you came out of the land of Egypt. 4 No leaven shall be seen with you in all your territory for seven days; nor shall any of the flesh which you sacrifice on the evening of the first day remain all night until morning. 5 You may not offer the passover sacrifice within any of your towns which the LORD your God gives you; 6 but at the place which the LORD your God will choose, to make his name dwell in it, there you shall offer the passover sacrifice, in the evening at the going down of the sun, at the time you came out of Egypt. 7 And you shall boil it and eat it at the place which the LORD your God will choose; and in the morning you shall turn and go to your tents. 8 For six days you shall eat unleavened bread; and on the seventh day there shall be a solemn assembly to the LORD your God; you shall do no work on it.

eat bread prepared without yeast, as you did when you had to leave Egypt in such a hurry. Eat this bread—it will be called the bread of suffering—so that as long as you live you will remember the day you came out of Egypt, that place of suffering. 4 For seven days no one in your land is to have any yeast in the house; and the meat of the animal killed on the evening of the first day must be eaten that same night.

5-6 "Slaughter the Passover animals at the one place of worship—and nowhere else in the land that the LORD your God will give you. Do it at sunset, the time of day when you left Egypt. 7 Boil the meat and eat it at the one place of worship; and the next morning return home. 8 For the next six days you are to eat bread prepared without yeast, and on the seventh day assemble to worship the LORD your God, and do no work on that day.

In 16.1-17 the three great festivals of ancient Israel are dealt with: Passover and Unleavened Bread (verses 1-8), the Harvest Festival (verses 9-12), and the Festival of Shelters (verses 13-15). These festivals are to be celebrated in the central sanctuary (verses 2, 11, 15). All Jewish males twenty years and older are to be present there on these occasions (verses 16-17; see Exo 23.4-17; 34.22-23).

It may be helpful to recall here a couple of matters that have already been discussed, but which a translator should always be aware of.

(1) "The LORD *your* God" is what Moses says constantly to the people of Israel; where exclusive and inclusive distinctions are important, it may be necessary to avoid the sense that Yahweh is the God only of the people of Israel, not the God of Moses. So we may say "the LORD [or, Yahweh], whom we [inclusive] worship."

(2) "The LORD . . . brought *you* out of Egypt": this may appear to say that Moses was not among those Yahweh delivered from Egypt. If there is any problem, we may translate "The LORD we [inclusive] worship brought us [inclusive] out . . . ."

Section heading: TEV, CEV, and NIV have either "Passover" or "The Passover." But we may also say "The Festival of Deliverance" or "The Festival to Remember the Passing Over."

16.1   RSV   TEV

"Observe the month of Abib, and keep the passover to the LORD your God; for in the month of Abib the LORD your God brought you out of Egypt by night.

"Honor the LORD your God by celebrating Passover in the month of Abib; it was on a night in that month that he rescued you from Egypt.

With the beginning of a new section, translators are advised to reintroduce Moses as the speaker.

Abib was the first month of the year in the Hebrew calendar, equivalent to modern March-April. It was later called "Nisan."

Keep the Passover to the LORD your God: the whole command may be stated "Celebrate the Passover Festival in honor of the LORD your God" (as in BRCL). The origin of the name **Passover** is given in Exo 12.13, 27, where it is derived from the verb "to pass over," in the statement that the angel of the LORD "passed over" the homes of the Hebrews in the destruction and death he brought to the land of Egypt. Alternative ways to translate this term are "The Festival [or, Fiesta] of Deliverance [or, Redemption]," "The Festival of Passing Over," or even "The Festival Celebrating when the Angel Passed Over." For **the LORD your God** see 1.6.

CEV has a helpful alternative model for this verse:

- *Moses said:* People of Israel, you must celebrate Passover in the month of Abib, because one night in that month years ago, the LORD your God rescued you from Egypt.

16.2   RSV   TEV

And you shall offer the passover sacrifice to the LORD your God, from the flock or the herd, at the place which the LORD will choose, to make his name dwell there.

Go to the one place of worship and slaughter there one of your sheep or cattle for the Passover meal to honor the LORD your God.

Instructions are given on how to celebrate Passover.

The passover sacrifice: that is, the animal offered in sacrifice, to celebrate the Passover Festival. For alternative ways to translate **passover**, see the previous verse.

From the flock or the herd: see 15.19.

The place which the LORD will choose, to make his name dwell there: see 12.5; 14.23. Originally Passover was a family festival, celebrated in the home.

An alternative translation model for this verse is:

- Go to the one place where Yahweh your [or, inclusive "our"] God chooses for you to worship him, and slaughter there one of your sheep or cattle while you are celebrating the Passover Festival. In this way you will honor Yahweh.

16.3   RSV   TEV

You shall eat no leavened bread with it; seven days you shall eat it with unleavened bread, the bread of

When you eat this meal, do not eat bread prepared with yeast. For seven days you are to eat bread prepared

283

affliction—for you came out of the
land of Egypt in hurried flight—that
all the days of your life you may
remember the day when you came
out of the land of Egypt.

without yeast, as you did when you
had to leave Egypt in such a hurry.
Eat this bread—it will be called the
bread of suffering—so that as long
as you live you will remember the
day you came out of Egypt, that
place of suffering.

The six-day Festival of Unleavened Bread was originally separate from the
one-day Passover Festival (see Exo 23.14-15; 34.18).

Unleavened bread: that is, bread made without leaven, or yeast (see Exo
12.15). The leaven, or yeast, was a piece of leavened dough saved over from the
previous baking of bread, and was normally added to the fresh dough to make
it rise. **Unleavened bread** may also be expressed as "bread with no yeast," or
"bread without anything added to make it rise," or even ". . . anything added to
make it soft to eat."

With it: that is, with the animal offered in sacrifice, which would be eaten by
the worshiper(s). We may also express this first sentence as "When you eat this
animal do not eat bread prepared with yeast."

The bread of affliction: NJPSV has "bread of distress," TEV, BRCL, SPCL "bread
of suffering," FRCL, TOB "bread of misery [or, sadness]." For the word itself, used
in connection with the conditions in Egypt, see Exo 3.7. The Israelites left
Egypt "in such a hurry" (TEV) that they didn't have time to prepare regular
leavened bread (Exo 12.33-34, 39).

The second part of the verse is rather repetitious, and translators should try
to arrange the clauses and phrases in such a way as to avoid the use of dashes,
such as those that appear in RSV and TEV.

TEV "that place of suffering" seems to add something that isn't in the text.
However, it was probably added in order to make clear the meaning of "bread
of suffering." A better way to do this is to add the words "that place where you
worked like slaves" after the word **Egypt**.

You may remember: this is the reason for the Passover Festival. It is to keep
alive the memory of that event which brought the Israelite nation into being as
the people of Yahweh. We may also translate "the bread without yeast will
remind you of the day . . . ."

An alternative translation model for this verse is:

• When you eat [the flesh of] this animal, do not eat bread that you
have made with yeast. For seven days you must eat bread
without yeast as you did when you had to quickly leave Egypt,
where you had been treated like slaves. As long as you live, this
will remind you of the day when you came out of Egypt.

16.4   RSV   TEV

No leaven shall be seen with you in   For seven days no one in your land
all your territory for seven days; nor   is to have any yeast in the house;

shall any of the flesh which you sac-	and the meat of the animal killed on
rifice on the evening of the first day	the evening of the first day must be
remain all night until morning.	eaten that same night.

No leaven shall be seen with you: this simply means that all leaven (or yeast) was to be removed from every household. **Leaven** was seen as an impure substance, and the word was sometimes used as a figure of evil.

The second part of the verse requires that the whole animal offered in sacrifice be eaten the first night, which seems to conflict with the instructions in verse 3. It may be, however, that we are to understand that a fresh animal was slaughtered each night of the seven-day festival.

The flesh which you sacrifice: more naturally, "the meat of the animal that you offered in sacrifice." The meaning of **nor shall any of the flesh . . . remain** is that the whole animal had to be eaten that very same evening.

16.5-6 RSV	TEV
5 You may not offer the passover sacrifice within any of your towns which the LORD your God gives you; 6 but at the place which the LORD your God will choose, to make his name dwell in it, there you shall offer the passover sacrifice, in the evening at the going down of the sun, at the time you came out of Egypt.	5-6 "Slaughter the Passover animals at the one place of worship— and nowhere else in the land that the LORD your God will give you. Do it at sunset, the time of day when you left Egypt.

These two verses remind the Israelites that the Passover is to be celebrated only in the one central place of worship. TEV has combined the two verses into one, eliminating some of the redundancy. Another translation model may be "Don't slaughter the Passover animals in your own town. You must offer them at the one place where Yahweh chooses for you to worship him."

The passover sacrifice: that is, the animal offered in sacrifice at the Passover Festival. For **passover** see verse 1.

Any of your towns which the LORD your God gives you: the Israelites conquered the Canaanite towns and villages and settled there. **Your towns** is literally "your gates" (also 5.14; 12.12; 14.21, 27).

At the place which the LORD your God will choose, to make his name dwell in it: see 12.5.

In the evening at the going down of the sun: this can be expressed by "at sunset," or "at the time when the sun goes down."

At the time you came out of Egypt: TEV and CEV have "the time of day when you left Egypt" (Exo 12.31, 42).

16.7 RSV	TEV
And you shall boil it and eat it at the place which the LORD your God will choose; and in the morning you shall turn and go to your tents.	Boil the meat and eat it at the one place of worship; and the next morning return home.

This verse refers only to the one-day Passover Festival.

Boil it and eat it: that is, the animal offered in sacrifice (verse 2). The verb translated **boil** may have the more general meaning "cook" (NRSV); in 2 Sam 13.8 it means "bake [cakes]." It may be better to use the more general term "cook."

The place: that is, the central sanctuary or central place for worshiping Yahweh.

In the morning you shall turn and go to your tents: after spending the night in the central sanctuary, they were to return to their tents the following morning. The Israelites, present by the thousands at the sanctuary for the week-long festival, set up tents in which to spend their days. TEV mistakenly has "return home"; CEV is better with "return to your tents the next morning."

16.8 RSV	TEV
For six days you shall eat unleavened bread; and on the seventh day there shall be a solemn assembly to the LORD your God; you shall do no work on it.	For the next six days you are to eat bread prepared without yeast, and on the seventh day assemble to worship the LORD your God, and do no work on that day.

The command to **eat unleavened bread** (see verse 3) for six days is repeated.

A solemn assembly: NJPSV has "a solemn gathering," NIV, NJB "an assembly." This was a formal worship, bringing the festival to a close. The purpose was to worship Yahweh. So TEV has "assemble to worship the LORD . . . ," and CEV has "come together to worship the LORD." A similar gathering in Exo 12.6 is called "a holy assembly."

To the LORD your God: "in honor of the LORD your God," or "to worship the LORD your God" (see TEV).

You shall do no work on it: on the closing day of the Festival, no work was to be done; the day would be equivalent to a sabbath.

2B-11. The Harvest Festival (16.9-12)

RSV	TEV
	The Harvest Festival
9 "You shall count seven weeks; begin to count the seven weeks from the time you first put the sickle to the standing grain. 10 Then	9 "Count seven weeks from the time that you begin to harvest the grain, 10 and then celebrate the Harvest Festival, to honor the

you shall keep the feast of weeks to the LORD your God with the tribute of a freewill offering from your hand, which you shall give as the LORD your God blesses you; 11 and you shall rejoice before the LORD your God, you and your son and your daughter, your manservant and your maidservant, the Levite who is within your towns, the sojourner, the fatherless, and the widow who are among you, at the place which the LORD your God will choose, to make his name dwell there. 12 You shall remember that you were a slave in Egypt; and you shall be careful to observe these statutes.

LORD your God, by bringing him a freewill offering in proportion to the blessing he has given you. 11 Be joyful in the LORD's presence, together with your children, your servants, and the Levites, foreigners, orphans, and widows who live in your towns. Do this at the one place of worship. 12 Be sure that you obey these commands; do not forget that you were slaves in Egypt.

The date for the Harvest Festival was carefully determined: it came the day after seven full weeks following the earliest harvest of grain (see Lev 23.16; see also Num 28.28-31). It was also known as "Festival of Weeks" (verse 10), "feast of harvest" (Exo 23.16), and "Pentecost" ("fiftieth day"; see Acts 2.1; 20.16; 1 Cor 16.8). It was celebrated on the sixth day of the month Sivan, equivalent to late May or early June (see Lev 23.15-21).

Section heading: both TEV and CEV have "The Harvest Festival." Another way to express this is "The Festival for harvesting [or, reaping] grain."

16.9	RSV	TEV

"You shall count seven weeks; begin to count the seven weeks from the time you first put the sickle to the standing grain.

"Count seven weeks from the time that you begin to harvest the grain,

With the beginning of a new section, Moses should be reintroduced as the speaker.

You shall count . . . begin to count: the instructions are clear and precise.

From the time you first put the sickle to the standing grain: this can be expressed more simply, "From the day you begin to harvest [or, reap] your grain." The translation of **put the sickle to** need not refer to the method of reaping the grain; the phrase is used here in order to mark the day of the Harvest Festival.

16.10	RSV	TEV

Then you shall keep the feast of weeks to the LORD your God with the tribute of a freewill offering from your hand, which you shall give as the LORD your God blesses you;

and then celebrate the Harvest Festival, to honor the LORD your God, by bringing him a freewill offering in proportion to the blessing he has given you.

You shall keep the feast of weeks to the Lord your God: to **keep** means to celebrate. A translator is free to translate literally **the feast of weeks** but may prefer the more meaningful "Harvest Festival" (TEV). **To the Lord your God** means "in honor of the Lord your God," or "to honor the Lord your God."

With the tribute of a freewill offering from your hand: in this rather unwieldy clause the Hebrew word translated **the tribute** occurs only here in the Old Testament, and its precise form and meaning are in doubt. The rendering of NRSV is supported by other translations and commentaries and should be followed: "contributing a freewill offering in proportion to the blessing that you have received from the Lord your God"; so NJPSV has "offering your freewill contribution according as the Lord your God has blessed you," and NIV "giving a freewill offering in proportion to the blessing the Lord your God has given you" (and see TEV). Some translators will wish to make the meaning of **as . . . blesses you** clear; for example, "Bring him [Yahweh] a freewill offering [or, offering from the heart], depending upon how much grain he has given you."

16.11	RSV	TEV
	and you shall rejoice before the Lord your God, you and your son and your daughter, your manservant and your maidservant, the Levite who is within your towns, the sojourner, the fatherless, and the widow who are among you, at the place which the Lord your God will choose, to make his name dwell there.	Be joyful in the Lord's presence, together with your children, your servants, and the Levites, foreigners, orphans, and widows who live in your towns. Do this at the one place of worship.

It will be better to start a separate sentence here, and not run on from verse 10 as RSV does.

And you shall rejoice before the Lord may also be expressed as "Your hearts will be full of joy as you celebrate the festival in the presence of Yahweh." **Before the Lord** may be rendered as "in the place where Yahweh dwells."

You shall rejoice: the festive gathering is to include everyone, starting with the man and his sons and daughters (the mother is not mentioned).

Manservant and . . . maidservant: the same two words used in 15.17.

The Levite who is within your towns: see 14.27.

The sojourner: see 5.14; 10.18-19.

The fatherless and the widow: see 14.29.

The place which the Lord your God will choose, to make his name dwell there: see 14.23.

16.12   RSV   TEV

You shall remember that you were a slave in Egypt; and you shall be careful to observe these statutes.

Be sure that you obey these commands; do not forget that you were slaves in Egypt.

This verse is almost the same as 15.15.

These statutes: see 4.1.

2B-12. The Festival of Shelters (16.13-17)

RSV

TEV
The Festival of Shelters

13 "You shall keep the feast of booths seven days, when you make your ingathering from your threshing floor and your wine press; 14 you shall rejoice in your feast, you and your son and your daughter, your manservant and your maidservant, the Levite, the sojourner, the fatherless, and the widow who are within your towns. 15 For seven days you shall keep the feast to the LORD your God at the place which the LORD will choose; because the LORD your God will bless you in all your produce and in all the work of your hands, so that you will be altogether joyful.

16 "Three times a year all your males shall appear before the LORD your God at the place which he will choose: at the feast of unleavened bread, at the feast of weeks, and at the feast of booths. They shall not appear before the LORD empty-handed; 17 every man shall give as he is able, according to the blessing of the LORD your God which he has given you.

13 "After you have threshed all your grain and pressed all your grapes, celebrate the Festival of Shelters for seven days. 14 Enjoy it with your children, your servants, and the Levites, foreigners, orphans, and widows who live in your towns. 15 Honor the LORD your God by celebrating this festival for seven days at the one place of worship. Be joyful, because the LORD has blessed your harvest and your work.

16 "All the men of your nation are to come to worship the LORD three times a year at the one place of worship: at Passover, Harvest Festival, and the Festival of Shelters. Each man is to bring a gift 17 as he is able, in proportion to the blessings that the LORD your God has given him.

The Festival of Shelters (NJB) is also known as "Tabernacles" (NIV) and as "Booths" (RSV, NJPSV). The name "booths" is probably derived from the custom of the farmers living in temporary shelters or huts set up in the fields during the time of harvest (see Lev 23.42; Neh 8.14,17). This was the festival of ingathering at the end of the agricultural year (see Exo 23.16; 34.22), and fell on days 15-22 of the month Tishri, usually the equivalent of the first half of October. Later the booths were associated with the forty years in the wilderness, as the Israelites traveled from Egypt to Canaan.

Section heading: TEV and CEV have "The Festival of Shelters," and NIV has "The Feast of Tabernacles." Another way to express this is "The festival for living in temporary shelters [or, huts]."

16.13   RSV   TEV

"You shall keep the feast of booths seven days, when you make your in-gathering from your threshing floor and your wine press;

"After you have threshed all your grain and pressed all your grapes, celebrate the Festival of Shelters for seven days.

OXEN THRESHING GRAIN

Since this is the beginning of a new section, translators should reintroduce Moses as the speaker.

You shall keep the feast of booths seven days: it is better to say something like "You will celebrate for seven days the Festival of Shelters." For comments on the translation of this Festival, see the **Section heading** paragraph above.

When you make your ingathering from your threshing floor and your wine press: TEV puts this at the beginning of the verse, making for a better style. It has "After you have threshed all your grain and pressed all your grapes." The **threshing floor** is the flat ground or wooden platform on which the grain is removed from the harvested plants by beating or dragging a heavy object such as a sledge over them (see the illustration). The farmer then tosses the grain into the air so that the chaff is blown away from the grain. Another way to express **ingathering from your threshing floor** is "After you have beaten the grain to separate it from the chaff." In cultures where a general term for "grain" is unavailable, we may use "seed" or even "fruit"; but it must be clear that this refers to "seed" or "fruit" from some sort of grass-like plant. The **wine press** was "a large wooden or stone vat or container which was connected to a lower container by a pipe or channel. As the grapes were mashed in the upper vat, the juice ran into the lower one" (*A Handbook on the Book of Job*, page 451). **Ingathering from . . . your wine press** may also be expressed as "the juice that you press [or, tread out] from your grapes."

An alternative translation model for this verse is:

290

BRINGING GRAPES TO A WINE PRESS

•   After you have beaten your grain out and separated it from the chaff, and have treaded out all your grapes, you must celebrate the Festival of Shelters for seven days.

16.14   RSV   TEV

you shall rejoice in your feast, you and your son and your daughter, your manservant and your maidservant, the Levite, the sojourner, the fatherless, and the widow who are within your towns.

Enjoy it with your children, your servants, and the Levites, foreigners, orphans, and widows who live in your towns.

    The list of those who are to be included in the joyful celebration is the same as in verse 11.

    Here the verse ends with **who are within your towns**, whereas in verse 11 it is **who are among you**; the slight difference should be respected in translation.

16.15   RSV   TEV

For seven days you shall keep the feast to the LORD your God at the

Honor the LORD your God by celebrating this festival for seven days at

place which the LORD will choose; the one place of worship. Be joyful, because the LORD your God will bless you in all your produce and in all the work of your hands, so that you will be altogether joyful. the one place of worship. Be joyful, because the LORD has blessed your harvest and your work.

The week-long festival in honor of **the LORD** was celebrated at the central sanctuary.

Because the LORD your God will bless you: this gives the reason for celebrating the festival as such. It may be better to place this at the beginning of the verse.

All your produce: this includes all kinds of agricultural produce: grains, wine, olive oil, figs, and so on.

All the work of your hands: see 14.29. An alternative translation model for this first part of this verse is:

●   · Because the LORD your God has helped you to have much produce
       [or, fruit] and be successful in all you do . . . .

You will be altogether joyful: again the note of thanksgiving and joy is struck (see verse 11).

16.16   RSV   TEV

"Three times a year all your males shall appear before the LORD your God at the place which he will choose: at the feast of unleavened bread, at the feast of weeks, and at the feast of booths. They shall not appear before the LORD empty-handed; "All the men of your nation are to come to worship the LORD three times a year at the one place of worship: at Passover, Harvest Festival, and the Festival of Shelters. Each man is to bring a gift

Verses 16-17 are a summary statement about these three major festivals (see Exo 23.17; 34.23), making it clear that all Jewish males (twenty years and older) had to be present at the central sanctuary.

Appear before the LORD your God: be present at the place of worship.

At the place which he will choose: the central sanctuary. For this first sentence TEV has "All the men of your nation are to come to worship the LORD three times a year at the one place of worship." As indicated at the beginning of this chapter, "your" may be also rendered as "our [inclusive]." However, another possibility is "all Israelite men." So CEV has "Each year there are three festivals when all Israelite men must go to the place where the LORD chooses to be worshiped."

They shall not appear . . . empty-handed: see 15.13. This can be stated in a positive form: "Everyone shall take something to offer to the LORD."

292

16.17	RSV	TEV

RSV	TEV
every man shall give as he is able, according to the blessing of the LORD your God which he has given you.	as he is able, in proportion to the blessings that the LORD your God has given him.

Every man shall give as he is able: this verse is like verse 10.

2B-13. The administration of justice (16.18-22)

RSV	TEV
	The Administration of Justice
18 "You shall appoint judges and officers in all your towns which the LORD your God gives you, according to your tribes; and they shall judge the people with righteous judgment. 19 You shall not pervert justice; you shall not show partiality; and you shall not take a bribe, for a bribe blinds the eyes of the wise and subverts the cause of the righteous. 20 Justice, and only justice, you shall follow, that you may live and inherit the land which the LORD your God gives you.	18 "Appoint judges and other officials in every town that the LORD your God gives you. These men are to judge the people impartially. 19 They are not to be unjust or show partiality in their judgments; and they are not to accept bribes, for gifts blind the eyes even of wise and honest men, and cause them to give wrong decisions. 20 Always be fair and just, so that you will occupy the land that the LORD your God is giving you and so that you will continue to live there.
21 "You shall not plant any tree as an Asherah beside the altar of the LORD your God which you shall make. 22 And you shall not set up a pillar, which the LORD your God hates.	21 "When you make an altar for the LORD your God, do not put beside it a wooden symbol of the goddess Asherah. 22 And do not set up any stone pillar for idol worship; the LORD hates them.

This section on "The Administration of Justice" (TEV title) is part of a larger section, 16.18–18.22, which deals with the offices of judge, king, priest, and prophet. There are five different matters addressed in this large section on judges:

(1) appointment of judges (16.18-20);

(2) forbidden pagan practices (16.21-22);

(3) animals offered in sacrifice (17.1);

(4) judging and executing anyone who tries to lead the people to idolatry (17.2-7);

(5) a central place of judgment for matters too difficult to be settled in local courts (17.8-13).

Section heading: the TEV title can be recast in the form of a complete sentence: "Moses tells the people how justice is to be administered," "Moses tells the Israelites how they must administer justice," or even "When you judge people, do it fairly." CEV stresses this aspect with the title "Treat Everyone with Justice."

16.18   RSV   TEV

"You shall appoint judges and offi-   "Appoint judges and other officials
cers in all your towns which the   in every town that the LORD your God
LORD your God gives you, according   gives you. These men are to judge
to your tribes; and they shall judge   the people impartially.
the people with righteous judgment.

As with previous new sections, Moses should be reintroduced as the speaker.

Appoint judges and officers: it is not clear how these officials were to be chosen. In English the verb **appoint** assumes that there is a higher authority who selects and installs such officers. The Hebrew verb is the one normally translated "give." BRCL "Choose" may be easier for many translators to imitate.

Judges: perhaps the word is used here in a more general sense of "governors" or "leaders" (see 1.16).

Officers: see 1.16. Here the **officers** are probably administrative assistants to the judges. TEV has "other officials," and CEV has "other officers." The first part of the verse may be alternatively expressed as "You must choose governors [or, leaders] and other officers [or, officials] in every town that Yahweh your God gives you."

All your towns which the LORD your God gives you: see verse 5.

According to your tribes: there was to be an even distribution of local judges and officers, so that every one of the twelve tribes had its fair share. NRSV restructures this part of the verse: "You shall appoint judges and officials throughout your tribes, in all your towns." Translators should keep the phrase **according to your tribes**, even though TEV and CEV omit it. For **tribes** see 1.13.

They shall judge the people: perhaps not just in the limited sense of settling legal disputes, but of administering all matters in the local communities; so NJPSV has "they shall govern the people."

Righteous judgment: TEV "impartially" expresses the meaning well, as the following instructions make clear; NIV has "fairly." See also 1.17 for a similar expression, "perfect in judgment."

16.19   RSV   TEV

You shall not pervert justice; you   They are not to be unjust or show
shall not show partiality; and you   partiality in their judgments; and
shall not take a bribe, for a bribe   they are not to accept bribes, for
blinds the eyes of the wise and sub-   gifts blind the eyes even of wise and
verts the cause of the righteous.   honest men, and cause them to give
                                         wrong decisions.

From the third person at the end of verse 18, referring to judges and officers, the narrative switches to the second person (singular), addressing the people as a whole. It may be better to keep in this verse the third person plural of verse 18b, as BRCL does, since it deals with the duties of the judges and officers in particular. However, CEV offers the alternative "Those of you that become judges."

You shall not pervert justice: there are various ways to speak of the miscarriage of justice. This is a general rule that can be expressed in a positive way: "Justice is to be administered fairly and equitably"; or "Justice is to be administered without fear or favor"; or even "They must judge [or, rule] fairly."

You shall not show partiality: this is one particular form of miscarriage of justice; it is not being impartial, but favoring one person over the other. See "righteous judgment" in the previous verse.

You shall not take a bribe: there are many vivid expressions for bribery; for example, Spanish *mordida*, "bite."

A bribe blinds the eyes of the wise: this expression is used in a figurative sense; it has to do with moral judgment. "A bribe makes it difficult for a wise judge to hand down the right decision." Another possible translation is "A bribe makes a wise judge close his eyes to what is right."

Subverts the cause of the righteous: that is, the cause (or, case) of an innocent person on trial is subverted when judges accept bribes. **Subverts** means to undermine or weaken (the cause of justice). So TEV has "and cause them to give wrong decisions."

16.20	RSV	TEV
	Justice, and only justice, you shall follow, that you may live and inherit the land which the LORD your God gives you.	Always be fair and just, so that you will occupy the land that the LORD your God is giving you and so that you will continue to live there.

Here it is possible to go back to the second person of the text, addressing the people as a whole.

Justice, and only justice, you shall follow: the Hebrew text says simply "Justice, justice [you must pursue]." True, fair, impartial justice must be the sole aim of the Israelites. TEV has "Always be fair and just."

That you may live and inherit the land: this does not mean "live long enough to inherit the land"; rather, it means that if they pursue justice they will go on living in the land of Canaan (see 5.16; 11.31). And here the verb **inherit** is an inappropriate translation of the Hebrew verb, which is used many times in the sense of "take possession of" (see 11.8, 10, 29; 12.1). NJPSV and NRSV translate "occupy"; NIV has "possess."

An alternative translation model for this verse is:

• People of Israel, if you want to occupy the land that the LORD your God is giving you, and continue to live there, you must always treat people fairly and justly.

16.21-22   RSV   TEV

21 "You shall not plant any tree as   21 "When you make an altar for
an Asherah beside the altar of the   the LORD your God, do not put be-
LORD your God which you shall   side it a wooden symbol of the god-
make. 22 And you shall not set up a   dess Asherah. 22 And do not set up
pillar, which the LORD your God   any stone pillar for idol worship; the
hates.   LORD hates them.

Plant any tree as an Asherah: this is not a good translation. The Hebrew
noun here does not mean a tree but a pole; in relation to **Asherah** (see 7.5) the
meaning is that a sacred pole should not be erected, or fixed into the ground,
next to the altar used in the worship of Yahweh. So NJPSV has "You shall not set
up a sacred post"; BRCL uses the compound "a post-idol."

The altar of the LORD your God: the altar used in the worship of Yahweh, on
which animals were offered in sacrifice. For **altar** see 7.5, and for **LORD your
God** see 1.6.

Set up a pillar: this is a stone pillar (see 7.5).

The LORD your God hates: see 12.31.

An alternative translation model for verses 21-22 is:

- 21 When you make an altar for offering sacrifices to the LORD
  your God, don't set up near it a sacred pole for worshiping the
  female god [or, goddess] Asherah. 22 And don't set up a sacred
  stone pillar. The LORD hates these things.

2B-14. Sacrifices that have something wrong with them (17.1)

            RSV   TEV

1 "You shall not sacrifice to the LORD your   1 "Do not sacrifice to the LORD your God
God an ox or a sheep in which is a blemish,   cattle or sheep that have any defects; the LORD
any defect whatever; for that is an abomina-   hates this.
tion to the LORD your God.

Section heading: as indicated in the previous chapter, TEV includes 17.1-13
in the section beginning with 16.18. However, CEV begins a new section here
with the title "Sacrifices that have something wrong with them" (17.1), and
begins 17.2-7 with the title "Put to Death People Who Worship Idols." The title
"Difficult Cases" is used for 17.8-13. The Handbook follows the CEV outline, and
translators are advised to do the same.

17.1   RSV   TEV

"You shall not sacrifice to the   "Do not sacrifice to the LORD your
LORD your God an ox or a sheep in   God cattle or sheep that have any
which is a blemish, any defect what-   defects; the LORD hates this.

**ever; for that is an abomination to
the LORD your God.**

With the beginning of a new section, translators are advised to begin the first
verse with something like "Moses said to the Israelites . . . ."

The same prohibition **You shall not sacrifice . . .** , using almost exactly the
same words, appears in 15.21. For **sacrifice** see 12.6.

An ox or a sheep: rather, "cattle or sheep" (see 5.14).

Blemish: see 15.21. The two words, **blemish** and **defect**, are close synonyms
in this context. If a distinction is needed in a language, the first term can refer
to a physical defect, while the second can be more general, "anything bad."

For **abomination** see 7.25.

2B-15. False gods (17.2-7)

RSV	TEV
2 "If there is found among you, within any of your towns which the LORD your God gives you, a man or woman who does what is evil in the sight of the LORD your God, in transgressing his covenant, 3 and has gone and served other gods and worshiped them, or the sun or the moon or any of the host of heaven, which I have forbidden, 4 and it is told you and you hear of it; then you shall inquire diligently, and if it is true and certain that such an abominable thing has been done in Israel, 5 then you shall bring forth to your gates that man or woman who has done this evil thing, and you shall stone that man or woman to death with stones. 6 On the evidence of two witnesses or of three witnesses he that is to die shall be put to death; a person shall not be put to death on the evidence of one witness. 7 The hand of the witnesses shall be first against him to put him to death, and afterward the hand of all the people. So you shall purge the evil from the midst of you.	2 "Suppose you hear that in one of your towns some men or women have sinned against the LORD and broken his covenant 3 by worshiping and serving other gods or the sun or the moon or the stars, contrary to the LORD's command. 4 If you hear such a report, then investigate it thoroughly. If it is true that this evil thing has happened in Israel, 5 then take them outside the town and stone them to death. 6 However, they may be put to death only if two or more witnesses testify against them; they are not to be put to death if there is only one witness. 7 The witnesses are to throw the first stones, and then the rest of the people are to stone them; in this way you will get rid of this evil.

Section heading: as indicated above, translators are advised to follow the CEV
outline for this chapter. Its title for this section is "Put to Death People Who
Worship Idols." "Idols" may be translated as "false gods," if that is more
meaningful in a language. For "gods" see 4.28.

17.2 RSV TEV

**"If there is found among you,
within any of your towns which the
LORD your God gives you, a man or**

**"Suppose you hear that in one of
your towns some men or women**

woman who does what is evil in the   **have sinned against the LORD and**
sight of the LORD your God, in trans-   **broken his covenant**
gressing his covenant,

Verses 2-5 are one sentence, which must be broken up into smaller units. The
passage has to do with what should be done to a person who leads a fellow-
Israelite to worship idols. This is an example of what is called "casuistic law,"
in which a possible criminal activity is described, and instructions are given on
what to do should such a thing occur. For this reason TEV begins with "Suppose
you hear . . ."; REB has "Should there be found . . . ," BRCL "It is possible that . . .
," FRCL "Perhaps some day . . . ."

If there is found among you: the passive verb may be difficult to represent
in translation; the clause means "Should it happen that . . . ," or "Suppose it
happens that . . . ," and it introduces a hypothetical situation (a situation that
may not have happened yet, but may come about in the future). The clause may
be rendered as a conditional clause, "If any Israelite man or woman living in
any of the towns that the LORD your God is going to give you does . . . ." TEV
"Suppose you hear that . . ." or BRCL "It is possible that . . ." are other possible
models.

Does what is evil in the sight of the LORD your God: this is basically a way
of saying "breaks God's law," "disobeys God," or else "sins against the LORD
your God" (see TEV; see 4.25; 9.18). For **the LORD your God** see 1.6.

In transgressing his covenant: this is the sin the person has actually
committed. For **covenant** see 4.13. Since by definition a covenant is an
agreement between two or more parties, it may be necessary to say "breaking
[or, violating] the covenant that God has made with you."

17.3   RSV   TEV

and has gone and served other gods   **by worshiping and serving other**
and worshiped them, or the sun or   **gods or the sun or the moon or the**
the moon or any of the host of   **stars, contrary to the LORD's com-**
heaven, which I have forbidden,   **mand.**

Has gone and served other gods and worshiped them: this is the sin that
breaks the covenant, of which the Ten Commandments are the basic stipulations or requirements (see 4.13). Idolatry is prohibited at the very beginning of
the commandments (5.7-8; see also 4.19; 8.19). The verbal form **has gone** does
not necessarily indicate travel to a pagan shrine; the verb here is used as an
auxiliary (like the frequent use of the verb "to rise"). CEV uses the word "start,"
as in ". . . may start worshiping."

It may be difficult to establish a difference between **served** and **worshiped**
pagan deities (see 4.19). "Bow down and worship" may be an alternative model.

Or the sun or the moon or any of the host of heaven: see 4.19.

Which I have forbidden: as it stands, the first person "I" of the text is Moses
himself, who is the speaker. But it seems fairly clear that the text means to say
that Yahweh, the God of Israel, was the one who had prohibited idol worship.

FRCL follows the Septuagint, "a thing he did not command," and translates "the LORD never ordered you to do such a thing." It is on the grounds of context, not text, that TEV has made Yahweh the subject: "contrary to the LORD's command." SPCL and BRCL have done the same, and the translator is encouraged to follow this example.

An alternative translation model combining verses 2 and 3 is the following:

- ² Moses said to the Israelites, "When you are living in the towns that the LORD your God is giving you, you may hear that a man or woman in your town has disobeyed the LORD's command ³ and has begun to bow down and worship other gods, or even the sun, moon, or stars. By doing this that person has sinned against the LORD and broken his covenant.

17.4	RSV	TEV

and it is told you and you hear of it; then you shall inquire diligently, and if it is true and certain that such an abominable thing has been done in Israel,		**If you hear such a report, then investigate it thoroughly. If it is true that this evil thing has happened in Israel,**

It is told you and you hear of it: this may be a typical double way of saying one thing (so NIV "this has been brought to your attention"; NJB "and this person is denounced to you"; also FRCL; and see TEV). Some take it as an either-or proposition (NJPSV, NRSV, REB), but this does not seem very likely.

You shall inquire diligently: or "make a thorough investigation." NIV has "you must investigate it thoroughly"; and see TEV. CEV has "You must carefully find out if . . . ." See the same kind of language in 13.14.

An abominable thing: see verse 1; 13.14.

Has been done in Israel: it may be that **Israel** here is not the country as such but a way of speaking of the people. But most take it as the country itself.

17.5	RSV	TEV

then you shall bring forth to your gates that man or woman who has done this evil thing, and you shall stone that man or woman to death with stones.		**then take them outside the town and stone them to death.**

This is apostasy. It is idolatry, forsaking Yahweh for other gods. Its punishment is death (see 13.6-11).

Bring forth to your gates: the open square in front of the city gate was the place where business and legal matters were settled (see Josh 20.6; Ruth 4.1). TEV, on the basis that the actual execution, by stoning, would be done outside the town, translates "outside the town." CEV is similar with "outside your town gates." It is interesting that the Septuagint omits "to your gates": "You shall take out [from their home] that man or woman and stone them . . . ." On the basis of Lev 24.14 and Num 15.36, some commentators hold that the execution itself would be outside the town, after the person had been condemned in the public square inside the gates. Deut 22.24 seems to support this (see also 21.19-21). A translator should feel free to make it clear that the stoning was done outside the town. For "town" see 1.1.

This evil thing: some word like "crime" or "terrible sin," may serve.

You shall stone that man or woman to death with stones: see 13.10.

An alternative translation model for this verse is:

- Then take the man or woman who has done this crime outside the town gates and throw stones at that person until that person dies.

17.6   RSV   TEV

| On the evidence of two witnesses or of three witnesses he that is to die shall be put to death; a person shall not be put to death on the evidence of one witness. | However, they may be put to death only if two or more witnesses testify against them; they are not to be put to death if there is only one witness. |

On the evidence of two witnesses or of three witnesses: as the second part of the verse shows, this means simply "two or more witnesses" (NJPSV, TEV). NIV and NRSV "of two or three witnesses" is not good, since in current English this expression actually means "[just] a few." See 19.15. Alternative translation models for the first part of this verse are "However, you may put that person to death only if two or more people give evidence against him," or ". . . two or more people say, 'I saw that person worshiping idols.' "

17.7   RSV   TEV

| The hand of the witnesses shall be first against him to put him to death, and afterward the hand of all the people. So you shall purge the evil from the midst of you. | The witnesses are to throw the first stones, and then the rest of the people are to stone them; in this way you will get rid of this evil. |

The hand of the witnesses shall be first against him: the witnesses, whose testimony led to the person's condemnation, were to be the first to throw stones at the condemned person.

Afterward the hand of all the people: for both groups, normal English usage is "The witnesses will be the first to throw stones at the condemned person, and after that all the other people are to do the same" (see also TEV).

For the rest of the verse, see 13.5.

2B-16. Difficult cases (17.8-13)

<table>
<tr><th>RSV</th><th>TEV</th></tr>
<tr><td>

8 "If any case arises requiring decision between one kind of homicide and another, one kind of legal right and another, or one kind of assault and another, any case within your towns which is too difficult for you, then you shall arise and go up to the place which the LORD your God will choose, 9 and coming to the Levitical priests, and to the judge who is in office in those days, you shall consult them, and they shall declare to you the decision. 10 Then you shall do according to what they declare to you from that place which the LORD will choose; and you shall be careful to do according to all that they direct you; 11 according to the instructions which they give you, and according to the decision which they pronounce to you, you shall do; you shall not turn aside from the verdict which they declare to you, either to the right hand or to the left. 12 The man who acts presumptuously, by not obeying the priest who stands to minister there before the LORD your God, or the judge, that man shall die; so you shall purge the evil from Israel. 13 And all the people shall hear, and fear, and not act presumptuously again.

</td><td>

8 "It may be that some cases will be too difficult for the local judges to decide, such as certain cases of property rights or of bodily injury or those cases that involve a distinction between murder and manslaughter. When this happens, go to the one place of worship chosen by the LORD your God, 9 and present your case to the levitical priests and to the judge who is in office at that time, and let them decide the case. 10 They will give their decision, and you are to do exactly as they tell you. 11 Accept their verdict and follow their instructions in every detail. 12 Anyone who dares to disobey either the judge or the priest on duty is to be put to death; in this way you will remove this evil from Israel. 13 Then everyone will hear of it and be afraid, and no one else will dare to act in such a way.

</td></tr>
</table>

Verses 8-13 speak of a central place of judgment for matters too complex to be handled in the local courts. Verses 8-11 are one long, complex sentence, which must be broken into smaller units.

The different cases to come up in the court may not fit precisely the normal categories and may require greater knowledge on the part of the judge. Under today's laws, for example, a person who kills another person has committed homicide. But it may have been an accident, for which the dead person may have been to blame; so the killer is not punished. Or the killer may have been careless, or did not follow usual procedure, in which case he is guilty of negligent homicide. Or else the person did it in a fit of anger and is guilty of unpremeditated murder. But if he planned the killing and deliberately carried it out, he is guilty of premeditated murder.

Section heading: as suggested at the beginning of this chapter, translators may make verses 8-13 a separate section with the heading "Difficult cases." Another way to express this is "Priests must decide difficult cases."

17.8   RSV   TEV

"If any case arises requiring deci-   "It may be that some cases will be
sion between one kind of homicide   too difficult for the local judges to
and another, one kind of legal right   decide, such as certain cases of
and another, or one kind of assault   property rights or of bodily injury or
and another, any case within your   those cases that involve a distinction
towns which is too difficult for you,   between murder and manslaughter.
then you shall arise and go up to the   When this happens, go to the one
place which the LORD your God will   place of worship chosen by the LORD
choose,   your God,

With the beginning of a new section, Moses should be reintroduced as the
speaker.

One kind of homicide and another: see Exo 21.12-14. In many languages it
will be necessary to define the two types: "kill someone on purpose [murder],"
or "kill someone accidentally" (similar to CEV).

One kind of legal right and another: in the broadest sense of the term,
"lawsuits" (NIV).

One kind of assault and another: this may be bodily assault, or else damage
to property.

Most modern translations reduce the wordiness considerably; see NIV, for
example, "bloodshed, lawsuits, or assaults." However, some translators will
need to expand; for example, "certain cases of property rights or bodily injury"
(TEV), or "whether injury or property damage was done by accident or on
purpose" (CEV).

Any case within your towns which is too difficult for you: this includes the
different cases cited and any others that may arise. **Too difficult for you** means
too difficult for the local magistrates to settle; consequently TEV has "the local
judges," and BRCL "the judge in that town." It will be helpful to place this clause
at the beginning of the verse; for example, TEV "It may be that some cases will
be too difficult for the local judges to decide." CEV repeats the phrase **too
difficult**: "It may be difficult to find out the truth in some legal cases in your
town . . . . If the case is too difficult, take it to . . . ."

Arise and go up: this means simply "go"; the verb **arise** functions as an
auxiliary. The **up** may be significant if the writer had Jerusalem in mind; for
example, "go up to the . . . ."

The place which the LORD your God will choose: the central sanctuary (see
16.16).

17.9   RSV   TEV

and coming to the Levitical priests,   and present your case to the levitical
and to the judge who is in office in   priests and to the judge who is in
those days, you shall consult them,   office at that time, and let them de-
and they shall declare to you the   cide the case.
decision.

Coming to the Levitical priests: a break should be made at the end of verse 8, and this verse should begin a new sentence, "Go to . . . ." **The Levitical priests**, or "the priests, the descendants of Levi," were Levites serving in the central sanctuary. All priests were descendants of Aaron, hence, Levites. For "Levite" see 12.12, and for **priests** see 10.6.

The judge who is in office in those days: it appears that judges took turns. It is not clear how the Levitical priests and the presiding judge worked together on these cases. CEV translates the first part of the verse as "this court will be made up of one judge and several priests who serve at the LORD's altar."

You shall consult them: that is, lay (or, present) your case before them.

They shall declare to you the decision: they will hand down the verdict, or give their decision about the case.

17.10   RSV   TEV

Then you shall do according to what they declare to you from that place which the LORD will choose; and you shall be careful to do according to all that they direct you;	They will give their decision, and you are to do exactly as they tell you.

What they declare to you from that place which the LORD will choose: this is wordy and awkward, involving quite a bit of repetition. It may be shortened as follows:

- There, in the place that the LORD will choose, they will hand down their verdict and tell you what you are to do; and you must do exactly what they tell you to do.

They declare: the same verb that is used in verse 9.
They direct you: that is, they tell you what you must do.

17.11   RSV   TEV

according to the instructions which they give you, and according to the decision which they pronounce to you, you shall do; you shall not turn aside from the verdict which they declare to you, either to the right hand or to the left.	Accept their verdict and follow their instructions in every detail.

Again the verse repeats what has already been said.

According to the instructions which they give you: this matches "they declare" in verse 10.

According to the decrees which they pronounce to you: this matches "they direct you" in verse 10. It means the decision the judge makes in any given case. The Hebrew is rather wordy and repetitive. Translators must decide whether such repetition is acceptable in their language, or whether to summarize as some translations have done; for example, TEV has "accept their verdict and follow their instructions in every detail," and CEV is more concise, with "Do exactly what they tell you."

You shall not turn aside, either to the right hand or to the left: see 5.32. The meaning of this figure of speech is quite clear; it means to carry out all instructions strictly, to the last detail, without neglecting anything.

17.12	RSV	TEV

RSV	TEV
The man who acts presumptuously, by not obeying the priest who stands to minister there before the LORD your God, or the judge, that man shall die; so you shall purge the evil from Israel.	Anyone who dares to disobey either the judge or the priest on duty is to be put to death; in this way you will remove this evil from Israel.

Acts presumptuously: see 1.43. This means to act from pride and self-will, with an arrogant attitude. NRSV is good: "presumes to disobey the priest"; also TEV "Anyone who dares to disobey either the judge or the priest on duty."

Stands to minister there before the LORD your God: that is, in the central sanctuary.

That man shall die: the sentence of death is to be passed on that person. In languages that do not use the passive voice as TEV does, we may say, for example, "they must put to death [or, execute] that man."

You shall purge the evil from Israel: see verse 7.

17.13	RSV	TEV

RSV	TEV
And all the people shall hear, and fear, and not act presumptuously again.	Then everyone will hear of it and be afraid, and no one else will dare to act in such a way.

The death sentence will be a most impressive object lesson.

Hear, and fear: when the people hear what has happened, they will be afraid (see 13.11).

And not act presumptuously again: that is, will not dare disobey the Law. TEV has "and no one else will dare to act in such a way." However, we may use a positive statement as CEV does: "they will be afraid and obey the decisions of the court."

2B-17. Instructions concerning a king (17.14-20)

RSV

TEV
Instructions concerning a King

14 "When you come to the land which the LORD your God gives you, and you possess it and dwell in it, and then say, 'I will set a king over me, like all the nations that are round about me'; 15 you may indeed set as king over you him whom the LORD your God will choose. One from among your brethren you shall set as king over you; you may not put a foreigner over you, who is not your brother. 16 Only he must not multiply horses for himself, or cause the people to return to Egypt in order to multiply horses, since the LORD has said to you, 'You shall never return that way again.' 17 And he shall not multiply wives for himself, lest his heart turn away; nor shall he greatly multiply for himself silver and gold.

18 "And when he sits on the throne of his kingdom, he shall write for himself in a book a copy of this law, from that which is in the charge of the Levitical priests; 19 and it shall be with him, and he shall read in it all the days of his life, that he may learn to fear the LORD his God, by keeping all the words of this law and these statutes, and doing them; 20 that his heart may not be lifted up above his brethren, and that he may not turn aside from the commandment, either to the right hand or to the left; so that he may continue long in his kingdom, he and his children, in Israel.

14 "After you have taken possession of the land that the LORD your God is going to give you and have settled there, then you will decide you need a king like all the nations around you. 15 Be sure that the man you choose to be king is the one whom the LORD has chosen. He must be one of your own people; do not make a foreigner your king. 16 The king is not to have a large number of horses for his army, and he is not to send people to Egypt to buy horses, because the LORD has said that his people are never to return there. 17 The king is not to have many wives, because this would make him turn away from the LORD; and he is not to make himself rich with silver and gold. 18 When he becomes king, he is to have a copy of the book of God's laws and teachings made from the original copy kept by the levitical priests. 19 He is to keep this book near him and read from it all his life, so that he will learn to honor the LORD and to obey faithfully everything that is commanded in it. 20 This will keep him from thinking that he is better than other Israelites and from disobeying the LORD's commands in any way. Then he will reign for many years, and his descendants will rule Israel for many generations.

In this section Moses gives instructions on how the people, once they have settled in the land of Canaan, are to select a king. It is taken for granted that they will want to be ruled by a king, as the surrounding nations are. This desire, as such, is not condemned here (see, by contrast, 1 Sam 8.5, 19-20; 10.19), but certain limitations are set, the most important of which is that God is the one who will choose their king.

Section heading: in many languages there will be no title that corresponds exactly to the status and role of "king," as understood in English. Any title for a chief of state is suitable, as long as it does not indicate a leader who has been elected to office by popular vote, such as "President" or "Prime Minister." Instead of the TEV title "Instructions concerning a King," it may be better to use a sentence such as "Moses tells the people how they are to choose a king." See the comment on "king" at 1.4.

17.14   RSV   TEV

"When you come to the land which   "After you have taken possession
the LORD your God gives you, and   of the land that the LORD your God is
you possess it and dwell in it, and   going to give you and have settled
then say, 'I will set a king over me,   there, then you will decide you need
like all the nations that are round   a king like all the nations around
about me';   you.

As at the beginning of other sections, it will be helpful to start this section
with something like "Moses said to the people of Israel."

The Hebrew sentence extends into the next verse, and in many instances it
will have to be divided into two or more sentences. These are instructions on
how the people are to proceed, should the time come when they want a king. So
FRCL has "Perhaps you will want to have a king . . . ."

Come to the land . . . possess it and dwell in it: these are three distinct
stages in the process of crossing the Jordan River, conquering the land, and
settling down in the Canaanite towns and villages.

The land which the LORD your God gives you: everything the Israelites do is
a consequence of God's action. This is the note that is always struck. They are
constantly reminded of the fact that the land of Canaan is God's gift to them.

And then say, 'I will set a king . . .': if the direct quotation is awkward or
unnatural in a given language, it may be better to go to indirect discourse, "and
then you decide that you want a king to rule you" (see TEV). For **king** see 1.4.

As always, the Hebrew text for **you** and **I** is singular for both pronouns; the
people are addressed as though they were an individual. It will be necessary in
most cases to use the plural: "say, 'We want a king' " (if direct discourse is
used), or "decide that you [plural] want a king" (if indirect discourse is
preferred).

I will set a king over me: the verb **set** means "to place"; in this context "to
choose" seems better than "to appoint" (NJB, REB). Or else we may say "You will
want to have a king to rule over you" (BRCL, POCL), or, more simply, "you will
want to have a king" (FRCL).

All the nations that are round about me: this is more simply and clearly
expressed as "all the surrounding [or, neighboring] nations."

17.15   RSV   TEV

you may indeed set as king over you   Be sure that the man you choose to
him whom the LORD your God will   be king is the one whom the LORD
choose. One from among your breth-   has chosen. He must be one of your
ren you shall set as king over you;   own people; do not make a foreigner
you may not put a foreigner over   your king.
you, who is not your brother.

**You may indeed set as king over you him whom the LORD your God will
choose**: this is the first and most important condition; the choice will be God's.

Nothing is said here as to how God will make his decision known to the people. TEV has a good model.

One from among your brothers: this is simply a way of saying "He must be an Israelite."

A foreigner, who is not your brother: the repetition is for emphasis, a device that may not work in some languages. The Hebrew verb in verses 14 and 15 that is translated **set** (three times) by RSV is different from the one translated **put**, but in this context the meaning is the same. For the translation of **foreigner** see the comment on "alien" at 1.16. The TEV model for the verse is a good alternative one.

17.16	RSV	TEV
	Only he must not multiply horses for himself, or cause the people to return to Egypt in order to multiply horses, since the LORD has said to you, 'You shall never return that way again.'	The king is not to have a large number of horses for his army, and he is not to send people to Egypt to buy horses,° because the LORD has said that his people are never to return there.

° to buy horses; *or* in exchange for horses.

He must not multiply horses for himself: this is a most unnatural use of the English language. NIV has "The king, moreover, must not acquire great numbers of horses for himself." These are **horses** used in war; the king is not to have a huge cavalry, as Solomon subsequently had (see 1 Kgs 10.26-29; 2 Chr 1.16; 9.28). In cultures where **horses** are unknown, we may say something like "animals named 'horse'" at this first occurrence of the term. An illustration of this animal should also be included. See also FFB, pages 43-45.

Cause the people to return to Egypt in order to multiply horses: the Hebrew text is not completely clear. Most translations, like TEV, take this to mean that the king is not to send people to Egypt to buy horses; but in a footnote TEV gives an alternative rendering, "send people to Egypt in exchange for horses." This rendering, which is favored by some, seems to mean sending slaves to Egypt in exchange for horses; or it can mean sending mercenary soldiers. The Hebrew says "on account of [or, for] horses." It is suggested that the rendering chosen by TEV and most other modern translations be followed.

The LORD has said to you, 'You shall never return that way again': this same statement is made in 28.58, but there is no record of Yahweh having made this promise. In some languages indirect speech will be preferable, as in TEV.

17.17	RSV	TEV
	And he shall not multiply wives for himself, lest his heart turn away; nor	The king is not to have many wives, because this would make him turn

shall he greatly multiply for himself silver and gold.	away from the LORD; and he is not to make himself rich with silver and gold.

He shall not multiply wives for himself: the same verb is used as in the previous verse, meaning "acquire many wives." This same instruction is given to the Israelite men as a whole (7.3-4).

Lest his heart turn away: these many wives include foreign women who might lead the king to worship pagan gods and thus forsake his loyalty to Yahweh. CEV makes this clear with "they might tempt him to be unfaithful to the LORD."

Greatly multiply for himself silver and gold: the same verb is used again, with the adverb "exceedingly," "excessively." In cultures where the precious metals **silver and gold** are not recognized as a symbol of wealth, a more general expression may be used: "The king must not become very wealthy," or even "The king must not acquire a great many possessions."

17.18   RSV   TEV

"And when he sits on the throne of his kingdom, he shall write for himself in a book a copy of this law, from that which is in the charge of the Levitical priests;	When he becomes king, he is to have a copy of the book of God's laws and teachings made from the original copy kept by the levitical priests.

When he sits on the throne of his kingdom: this seems to refer to the day the man God has chosen is installed as king. REB has "When he has ascended the throne of his kingdom"; or we may translate more generally, "when he begins to rule [or, reign]," or even "When he becomes king" (TEV, CEV). In cultures where chiefs rule, it may be necessary to talk about "sitting on his chair [or, stool]."

He shall write for himself in a book a copy of this law: the meaning of this part of the sentence is not completely clear. RSV takes it to mean that the king himself is to make a copy of **this law**; but the text may mean "he is to have a copy made for him." So NRSV has "he shall have a copy of this law written for him" (also NJPSV, TEV, FRCL, BRCL, POCL).

A book: here, more precisely, a scroll. If neither of these terms is available in a local language, the more general "he is to have a copy of this law made for him" may be used, without indicating the precise form the copy is to take.

There is much difference of opinion over the precise meaning of **this law**. The Hebrew noun is *torah*, which can mean:
   (1) the complete Torah; this is most unlikely, but TEV "the book of God's laws and teachings" can be taken to mean this;
   (2) the book of Deuteronomy, as we know it (see the use of **this law** in 1.5); this is the interpretation favored by most;
   (3) a section of the book of Deuteronomy, especially chapters 12-26; while possible, this would be very difficult to indicate in translation.

Probably the best translation is to say "this book of the law," without saying exactly what "this book" means; most readers will probably assume it means the book of Deuteronomy. However, if "book" is difficult to translate, we may simply say "a copy of these [or, God's] laws."

It is from the Septuagint translation of this verse that the book Deuteronomy gets its name. The Hebrew is "a copy of this law" (also Josh 8.32); the Septuagint translates "this second record of the law" (a similar translation in Josh 8.32).

From that which is in charge of the Levitical priests: the meaning of the Hebrew text here is disputed.

(1) Many take it as do RSV and TEV (and NIV, FRCL, BRCL, POCL, SPCL), that the copy is to be made from the original, which is kept by the Levitical priests (in the sanctuary); this seems to be the meaning of the Septuagint.

(2) NJB and REB translate "at the dictation of the Levitical priests."

(3) NRSV has "in the presence of the Levitical priests."

(4) NJB has "written . . . by the Levitical priests," with a footnote: "Nuance of Heb *milliphne* uncertain."

It is recommended that the translation favored by TEV and others be followed, namely, "from the original copy kept by the Levitical priests." For **Levitical priests** see 17.9.

17.19	RSV	TEV
	and it shall be with him, and he shall read in it all the days of his life, that he may learn to fear the LORD his God, by keeping all the words of this law and these statutes, and doing them;	He is to keep this book near him and read from it all his life, so that he will learn to honor the LORD and to obey faithfully everything that is commanded in it.

It shall be with him: it is the copy that has been made; "He will keep the copy . . . ."

He shall read in it all the days of his life: the king is to read some portion of the book every day. So we may translate "every day he must read [from] it."

He may learn to fear the LORD his God: **learn** may also be rendered as "teach himself to . . ." or "cause himself to . . . ." For **fear** see 4.10.

By keeping . . . and doing: again, a repetition for emphasis; "by learning and obeying," "by putting into practice."

All the words of this law and these statutes: these are not two separate sets of laws, but the same *torah*, that is, all the **laws and . . . statutes** (see 4.1) in this *torah*. To obey the Torah is to fear God. TEV has "obey faithfully everything that is commanded in it."

17.20   RSV   TEV

that his heart may not be lifted up | This will keep him from thinking that
above his brethren, and that he may | he is better than other Israelites and
not turn aside from the command- | from disobeying the LORD's com-
ment, either to the right hand or to | mands in any way. Then he will reign
the left; so that he may continue long | for many years, and his descendants
in his kingdom, he and his children, | will rule Israel for many generations.
in Israel.

That his heart may not be lifted up above his brethren: the king is not to be conceited or arrogant; he must not think of himself as superior to his fellow-Israelites (NIV "consider himself better than his brothers"). The word used to translate **his brethren** should not mean only his blood brothers, that is, sons (and daughters) of his own parents.

Turn aside from the commandment: that is, disregard, pay no attention to, or disobey. For **commandment** see 4.2.

To the right hand or to the left: see this idiom in 5.32.

That he may continue long in his kingdom, he and his children: this means that his royal line is to last a very long time. The Davidic dynasty, in Judah, lasted from about 1010 to 586 B.C., a total of some 424 years. This same kind of promise is made to Israelites as a whole in 5.32–6.2. Instead of **children** the word "descendants" is preferable. TEV has a helpful translation: "then he will reign for many years, and his descendants will rule Israel for many generations." CEV is shorter, with "he and his descendants will rule Israel for many years."

2B-18. The share of the priests (18.1-8)

                RSV   TEV
                                                The Share of the Priests

1 "The Levitical priests, that is, all the tribe of Levi, shall have no portion or inheritance with Israel; they shall eat the offerings by fire to the LORD, and his rightful dues. 2 They shall have no inheritance among their brethren; the LORD is their inheritance, as he promised them. 3 And this shall be the priests' due from the people, from those offering a sacrifice, whether it be ox or sheep: they shall give to the priest the shoulder and the two cheeks and the stomach. 4 The first fruits of your grain, of your wine and of your oil, and the first of the fleece of your sheep, you shall give him. 5 For the LORD your God has chosen him out of all your tribes, to stand and minister in the name of the LORD, him and his sons for ever.

6 "And if a Levite comes from any of your towns out of all Israel, where he lives—and he

1 "The priestly tribe of Levi is not to receive any share of land in Israel; instead, they are to live on the offerings and other sacrifices given to the LORD. 2 They are to own no land, as the other tribes do; their share is the privilege of being the LORD's priests, as the LORD has promised.

3 "Whenever cattle or sheep are sacrificed, the priests are to be given the shoulder, the jaw, and the stomach. 4 They are to receive the first share of the grain, wine, olive oil, and wool. 5 The LORD chose from all your tribes the tribe of Levi to serve him as priests forever.

6 "Any Levite who wants to may come from any town in Israel to the one place of worship 7 and may serve there as a priest of the LORD his God, like the other Levites who are serving there. 8 He is to receive the same amount of

may come when he desires—to the place which the LORD will choose, 7 then he may minister in the name of the LORD his God, like all his fellow-Levites who stand to minister there before the LORD. 8 They shall have equal portions to eat, besides what he receives from the sale of his patrimony.

food as the other priests, and he may keep whatever his family sends him.

In this section Moses deals with the priesthood, and in particular with the question of what the priests (Levites who serve at the sanctuary) are to receive for their services. The people are to give them a share of the animals offered in sacrifice, as well as the first harvests of the fields and the wool from the first shearing of the sheep. These are necessary because the priests have no other source of income.

Section heading: instead of the TEV title "The Share of the Priests," a sentence may be better: "Moses tells the people what they are to give to the priests," or "Moses tells the people what the priests are to receive."

18.1 RSV TEV

"The Levitical priests, that is, all the tribe of Levi, shall have no portion or inheritance with Israel; they shall eat the offerings by fire to the LORD, and his rightful dues.

"The priestly tribe of Levi is not to receive any share of land in Israel; instead, they are to live on the offerings and other sacrifices given to the LORD.

At the beginning of this new section, it will be helpful to have something like "Moses said to the people of Israel: . . . ."

The Levitical priests, that is, all the tribe of Levi: the redundant expression **that is, all the tribe of Levi** seems to be an explanatory note added later in the text to clarify what is meant by **the Levitical priests**. The Hebrew text says simply "to the priests the Levites all the tribe of Levi." For **Levitical priests** see 10.6, 8; 17.9.

Shall have no portion or inheritance: see these same two words together in 10.9. The added words **with Israel** mean "with the other Israelites." Some, however, take **Israel** here to mean the land (see TEV), but it seems better to take it to mean the people, as in the parallel case "his brothers" in 10.9. The sense is "They will not receive any territory of their own as the other tribes have received."

They shall eat the offerings by fire to the LORD: the phrase **the offerings by fire** is a general term for different sacrifices, including animal sacrifices burned whole (see Lev 1.1-17). Here NRSV offers a good model for translators, "they may eat the sacrifices that are the LORD's portion"; see also CEV, "they shall receive part of the sacrifices that are offered to the LORD."

And his rightful dues: the **his** here may refer to the tribe of Levi; see NJPSV "[the LORD's offering by fire] as their portion" (also NIV, REB). NRSV has "that are the LORD's portion," with a footnote: "Meaning of Heb uncertain." And TEV "and

311

other sacrifices given to the LORD" takes **his** to refer to Yahweh. The interpretation of NJPSV, NIV, and REB seems preferable.

The English phrase **his rightful dues** means the things that should be given, or assigned, to him. In this context these things are other sacrifices that are given to the priest. An alternative model is "that will be their inheritance," and the final part of the verse may be expressed as "They are to receive [or, be given] as their share parts of the animals that people burn on the altar and offer to Yahweh, along with other sacrifices assigned to them."

18.2   RSV   TEV

They shall have no inheritance   They are to own no land, as the other
among their brethren; the LORD is   tribes do; their share is the privilege
their inheritance, as he promised   of being the LORD's priests, as the
them.   LORD has promised.

This verse repeats what the first part of verse 1 says.

No inheritance among their brethren: it is strange that RSV here has **brethren**, whereas in 10.9 it has "brothers." Unlike the other tribes of Israel, the tribe of Levi was not assigned any territory. For **inheritance** see "inherit" in 1.38.

The LORD is their inheritance, as he promised them: see 10.9. This is more clearly expressed by TEV: "their share is the privilege of being the LORD's priests." The CEV model is also helpful: "because he has promised to provide for them in this way."

18.3   RSV   TEV

And this shall be the priests' due   "Whenever cattle or sheep are
from the people, from those offering   sacrificed, the priests are to be given
a sacrifice, whether it be ox or   the shoulder, the jaw, and the stom-
sheep: they shall give to the priest   ach.
the shoulder and the two cheeks and
the stomach.

And this shall be the priests' due: in verses 3-4 Moses says what the priests, the Levites, are to receive (their **due**) from the other Israelites.

From the people, from those offering a sacrifice: the second phrase defines more precisely the first one.

Ox or sheep: this is more accurately "cattle or sheep" (TEV). The Hebrew term does not mean only a castrated bull, as **ox** often does in English; it means any member of the bovine (cattle) family. The first part of the verse may thus be expressed as "Whenever you sacrifice a cow or sheep, you must give the priests
. . . . "

The shoulder and the two cheeks and the stomach: the parts mentioned are fairly clear. **The two cheeks** are the jowls (or, more simply, TEV "the jaw"); **the stomach** is more generally "the inner parts" (NIV), that is, the internal organs.

18.4	RSV	TEV
	The first fruits of your grain, of your wine and of your oil, and the first of the fleece of your sheep, you shall give him.	They are to receive the first share of the grain, wine, olive oil, and wool.

The first fruits of your grain, and of your wine and of your oil refers to the "first share" (TEV), or "first part" (CEV), of the grain harvest and the other products. See the same agricultural products in 7.13.

The first of the fleece of your sheep: this is the only place where the wool from the first shearing of the sheep is included as part of the priests' dues. In some languages this will be rendered as "the first part of the hair that you cut from your sheep."

18.5	RSV	TEV
	For the LORD your God has chosen him out of all your tribes, to stand and minister in the name of the LORD, him and his sons for ever.	The LORD chose from all your tribes the tribe of Levi to serve him as priests forever.

See the closely similar statement in 10.8.

Chosen him . . . him and his sons: the singular pronoun is here used in a collective sense, meaning all the male Levites.

In the name of the LORD: the Levites act as the LORD's authorized representatives. TEV has "to serve him as priests," and CEV has "to be his special servants."

Him and his sons for ever: the male Levites and their male descendants for all time to come.

CEV provides a good alternative model:

- Give these gifts to the priests, because the LORD has chosen them and their descendants out of all the tribes of Israel to be his special servants at the place of worship.

18.6	RSV	TEV
	"And if a Levite comes from any of your towns out of all Israel, where he lives—and he may come when he de-	"Any Levite who wants to may come from any town in Israel to the one place of worship

**sires—to the place which the LORD
will choose,**

In verses 6-8 instructions are given for Levites who may go to the sanctuary
and there serve for a while as priests. They are to be given the same as their
fellow Levites who serve there permanently.

In verse 6 the words **and he may come when he desires** stresses the strong
desire that motivates a Levite to go to the sanctuary. The Hebrew phrase is,
literally, "all the desire of his being"; so REB has "if he comes in the eagerness
of his heart." The text says more than the simple "if he wants to go" or "if he
decides to go." Something like "any Levite who sets his heart on going" will be
a better alternative. Notice should be taken of the point of view of the writer
(and reader) in the use of the verb **come**; a translator should be aware of what
the text implies, and may decide that "go" is better. For a comment on **Levite**
see 12.12.

The place which the LORD shall choose: as always, the central sanctuary (see
17.10).

An alternative translation model for this verse is:

•   If a Levite sets his heart [or, desires] to leave his home town
        and go [or, come] to the place where the LORD chooses to be wor-
        shiped, he may do this.

18.7	RSV	TEV

then he may minister in the name of the LORD his God, like all his fellow--Levites who stand to minister there before the LORD.		**and may serve there as a priest of the LORD his God, like the other Levites who are serving there.**

For the instruction as such and the terms used in this verse, see verse 5. **The
LORD his God** may also be expressed as "Yahweh, the God he serves."

Before the LORD: in the central sanctuary.

18.8	RSV	TEV

They shall have equal portions to eat, besides what he receives from the sale of his patrimony.[m]		**He is to receive the same amount of food as the other priests, and he may keep whatever his family sends him.**[p]

[m] Heb obscure

[p] *Probable text* and he may keep
. . . sends him; *Hebrew unclear*.

The Levite who spends some time at the sanctuary is to receive the same as
his fellow Levites.

Besides what he receives from the sale of his patrimony: the exact meaning of this clause is not altogether clear. Most translations agree with RSV, and REB phrases it nicely: "besides what he may inherit from his father's family." NJPSV "without regard to personal gifts or patrimonies" is a bit technical; NIV is more natural: "received money from the sale of family possessions" (similarly CEV). What is involved here is not land, that is, real estate, since the Levites had no land, but houses and other belongings.

An alternative translation model for this verse is:

- He is to receive the same amount of food as the other priests and may keep whatever money his family sends him from the sale of their possessions.

2B-19. Warnings against pagan practices (18.9-13)

RSV	TEV
	Warning against Pagan Practices
9 "When you come into the land which the LORD your God gives you, you shall not learn to follow the abominable practices of those nations. 10 There shall not be found among you any one who burns his son or his daughter as an offering, any one who practices divination, a soothsayer, or an augur, or a sorcerer, 11 or a charmer, or a medium, or a wizard, or a necromancer. 12 For whoever does these things is an abomination to the LORD; and because of these abominable practices the LORD your God is driving them out before you. 13 You shall be blameless before the LORD your God.	9 "When you come into the land that the LORD your God is giving you, don't follow the disgusting practices of the nations that are there. 10 Don't sacrifice your children in the fires on your altars; and don't let your people practice divination or look for omens or use spells 11 or charms, and don't let them consult the spirits of the dead. 12 The LORD your God hates people who do these disgusting things, and that is why he is driving those nations out of the land as you advance. 13 Be completely faithful to the LORD."

This section comes as a sort of parenthesis between the instructions about priests (18.1-8) and about prophets (18.14-22).

Section heading: the section is entitled "Warning against Pagan Practices" (TEV) or "Don't Do Disgusting Things" (CEV). As usual, a complete sentence may be better as a title: "Moses warns the people against following some pagan practices," or ". . . following practices that Yahweh hates."

18.9

RSV	TEV
"When you come into the land which the LORD your God gives you, you shall not learn to follow the abominable practices of those nations.	**"When you come into the land that the LORD your God is giving you, don't follow the disgusting practices of the nations that are there.**

With the beginning of a new section, Moses should be reintroduced as the speaker.

The land which the LORD your God gives you: see 17.14.

You shall not learn to follow: literally the Hebrew says "not learn to do," that is, "not imitate," "not copy," "not engage in" the same practices.

Abominable practices: see 7.25; 12.31.

A list of these detestable, hateful practices follows. If it is necessary to restructure **abominable**, God is the subject; it is God who hates these pagan practices.

18.10   RSV   TEV

There shall not be found among you any one who burns his son or his daughter as an offering," any one who practices divination, a soothsayer, or an augur, or a sorcerer,	Don't sacrifice your children in the fires on your altars; and don't let your people practice divination or look for omens or use spells

ⁿ Heb *makes his son or his daughter pass through the fire*

There shall not be found among you: this is a way of saying that what follows is prohibited, that no Israelite is to do any of these things. See the similar warning in 12.30-31. Alternative translation models for **There shall not be found . . .** may be "Don't . . ." or "You must not . . . ."

One who burns his son or daughter as an offering: the meaning here is that the person offers his child as a sacrifice to a pagan god. The RSV footnote gives the literal form of the Hebrew text, which some understand to mean a method of divination, of predicting the future. But this is highly doubtful, and it is recommended that the idea of sacrifice by fire be expressed. TEV "Don't sacrifice your children in the fire on your altars" is a good model.

There are four more forbidden practices in this verse, and an additional four in verse 11. Some of them seem to refer to the same thing, and today we do not know the precise distinction between the various terms—if such ever existed. Most of them have to do with the various means of predicting future events, and certain kinds of magic or witchcraft.

As usual the Handbook will cite RSV terms and note different terms used in other translations. In this verse NRSV and NJB are exactly the same as RSV. NJPSV and REB have "augur, soothsayer, diviner, sorcerer."

Practice divination: this involves the use of supernatural powers to reveal the future.

Soothsayer: the verb means to foretell future events, to predict the future, whether or not by use of magic or spiritual powers.

Augur: this involves interpreting various signs and omens, such as the pattern of birds in flight, the disposition of sticks or arrows flung on the ground, or the examination of an animal's entrails. NIV translates "interprets omens."

Sorcery: to gain control over someone through the help of spirits. NIV has "engages in witchcraft."

Some cultures may have all these practices, and translators can find precise terms to match the Hebrew. However, in other languages translators may need to follow TEV and use three different terms, and not four, on the assumption that the Hebrew terms are so closely related that precise distinctions between the various activities are not possible.

18.11	RSV	TEV
	or a charmer, or a medium, or a wizard, or a necromancer.	or charms, and don't let them consult the spirits of the dead.

NRSV has the following: "casts spells . . . consults ghosts or spirits . . . seeks oracles from the dead." TEV uses two different terms to cover the four Hebrew words. NRSV is a good model to follow.

A charmer: this activity means to cast a spell on a person, to "bewitch" that person. An alternative model is "one who sings his magic." Many languages will have similar expressions for this type of person.

A medium: a person who is able to communicate with the spirit world, in particular, with the spirits of the dead.

Wizard: someone who practices magic. "Magic," whether harmful or beneficial, occurs in most cultures, and there will be terms for it and the people who perform it. "Magic" may also be expressed as "secret [or, supernatural] powers," so **a wizard** can be translated "one who has secret [or, supernatural] powers."

Necromancer: someone who consults the dead. In many languages **medium** and **necromancer** will be combined; for example, "those who talk with spirits of the dead" (CEV).

In a number of cultures there will be different terms for all eight types of people in verses 10 and 11. However, in those languages that do not have equivalents for all the types of forbidden practices, the model below, from CEV, will be helpful. The underlying assumption is that all of them require magic or witchcraft, and they can be grouped into three basic types:

- 10-11 . . . And don't try to use any kind of magic or witchcraft to tell fortunes, or to cast spells, or to talk with spirits of the dead.

18.12	RSV	TEV
	For whoever does these things is an abomination to the LORD; and because of these abominable practices the LORD your God is driving them out before you.	The LORD your God hates people who do these disgusting things, and that is why he is driving those nations out of the land as you advance.

Is an abomination to the LORD: the LORD hates or detests people who indulge in those pagan practices. See 7.25.

Because of their abominable practices: that is, the things that the Canaanites do. For **abominable practices** see 7.26.

The LORD your God is driving them out before you: TEV uniformly translates **before you** by "as you advance" (see 4.38; 7.1, 22; 8.20; 9.3; 11.23).

18.13	RSV	TEV

You shall be blameless before the LORD your God.	Be completely faithful to the LORD."

Blameless: the Hebrew word (used also in God's command to Abraham in Gen 17.1) is understood in different ways. Some take it to mean "without moral fault" (see its use in Psa 18.23, 25). Many, like TEV "Be completely faithful," take it to indicate the degree of loyalty, or devotion, to God. So NRSV has "remain completely loyal to the LORD your God," REB "undivided in your service of the LORD your God," and NJB "faultless in your relationship with the LORD your God." (The Greek word used by the Septuagint to translate this Hebrew term appears in Matt 5.48.) It is recommended that the latter meaning be expressed in translation. So another way to render this verse is "Do everything that the LORD orders you to do." However, in the context of avoiding the **abominable practices** (verse 13), we may also translate "Don't ever do any of these disgusting [or, abominable] things."

2B-20. The promise to send a prophet (18.14-22)

RSV	TEV
	The Promise to Send a Prophet

| 14 For these nations, which you are about to dispossess, give heed to soothsayers and to diviners; but as for you, the LORD your God has not allowed you so to do. 15 "The LORD your God will raise up for you a prophet like me from among you, from your brethren—him you shall heed—16 just as you desired of the LORD your God at Horeb on the day of the assembly, when you said, 'Let me not hear again the voice of the LORD my God, or see this great fire any more, lest I die.' 17 And the LORD said to me, 'They have rightly said all that they have spoken. 18 I will raise up for them a prophet like you from among their brethren; and I will put my words in his mouth, and he shall speak to them all that I command him. 19 And whoever will not give heed to my words which he shall speak in my name, I myself will require it of him. 20 But the prophet who presumes to speak a word in | 14 Then Moses said, "In the land you are about to occupy, people follow the advice of those who practice divination and look for omens, but the LORD your God does not allow you to do this. 15 Instead, he will send you a prophet like me from among your own people, and you are to obey him. 16 "On the day that you were gathered at Mount Sinai, you begged not to hear the LORD speak again or to see his fiery presence any more, because you were afraid you would die. 17 So the LORD said to me, 'They have made a wise request. 18 I will send them a prophet like you from among their own people; I will tell him what to say, and he will tell the people everything I command. 19 He will speak in my name, and I will punish anyone who refuses to obey him. 20 But if any prophet dares to speak a message in my name when I did not command him to do so, he must die for it, and so |

my name which I have not commanded him to speak, or who speaks in the name of other gods, that same prophet shall die.' 21 And if you say in your heart, 'How may we know the word which the LORD has not spoken?'—22 when a prophet speaks in the name of the LORD, if the word does not come to pass or come true, that is a word which the LORD has not spoken; the prophet has spoken it presumptuously, you need not be afraid of him.

must any prophet who speaks in the name of other gods.'

21 "You may wonder how you can tell when a prophet's message does not come from the LORD. 22 If a prophet speaks in the name of the LORD and what he says does not come true, then it is not the LORD's message. That prophet has spoken on his own authority, and you are not to fear him.

This section deals with prophets. Verse 14 serves as a transition, and RSV connects it with the verses before it (also NRSV, REB, NJPSV); TEV, NIV, FRCL and others connect it with what follows. It seems better to connect it with what follows. For a discussion on "prophet" see 13.1.

Section heading: instead of the TEV title "The Promise to Send a Prophet," something like "Concerning prophets" may be used; or else "God promises to send a prophet to the people," or even "God promises to send a prophet like Moses."

18.14 RSV	TEV
For these nations, which you are about to dispossess, give heed to soothsayers and to diviners; but as for you, the LORD your God has not allowed you so to do.	Then Moses said, "In the land you are about to occupy, people follow the advice of those who practice divination and look for omens, but the LORD your God does not allow you to do this.

With the beginning of a new section, translators are advised to reintroduce Moses as the speaker.

These nations, which you are about to dispossess: see 9.1; 11.23; 12.2, 29.

Give heed to: this means "pay attention to," that is, "consult," "go to them for advice."

To soothsayers and to diviners: see 18.11.

The LORD your God has not allowed you so to do: God has forbidden the people of Israel to engage in these pagan practices. TEV has "The LORD your God does not allow you to do this," and CEV has ". . . won't allow you to do those things."

18.15 RSV	TEV
"The LORD your God will raise up for you a prophet like me from among you, from your brethren— him you shall heed—	Instead, he will send you a prophet like me from among your own people, and you are to obey him.^q

^q a prophet . . . him; *or* prophets . . . them. |

319

Raise up for you a prophet: the verb **raise up** in this context means "to cause to appear." More simply it means to send: "The LORD your God will send you a prophet." For **prophet** see 13.1. The noun is singular in the Hebrew text, and most translations take it to refer to a particular prophet who will appear in the future. But as the alternative rendering in TEV shows, the singular here may be understood as a collective, meaning "God will send you [from time to time] prophets"; NRSV provides the same alternative in a footnote. However, translations do not give this meaning in the text. The promise (in the singular) is used in the New Testament as a reference to Jesus (see Acts 3.22; 7.37).

Like me: this can be understood to mean "as he sent me," but most take it to mean that the coming prophet will be like Moses.

From among you, from your brethren: another case of duplication, for clarity. It means the coming prophet will be an Israelite, "one of your own people" (TEV, CEV).

To repeat what we have said earlier in the Handbook, the translator should be aware of what the second person pronouns **you** and **your** may mean in some languages; that is, the person (Moses) who says this is not an Israelite. Such a wrong meaning should be avoided. See, for example, 1.6.

Him you shall heed: the people are to listen to him and do as he commands. TEV is a suitable model for this verse, as is CEV:

*   Instead, he will choose one of your own people to be a prophet just like me, and you must do what that prophet says.

18.16	RSV	TEV
	just as you desired of the LORD your God at Horeb on the day of the assembly, when you said, 'Let me not hear again the voice of the LORD my God, or see this great fire any more, lest I die.'	"On the day that you were gathered at Mount Sinai, you begged not to hear the LORD speak again or to see his fiery presence any more, because you were afraid you would die.

Here Moses refers back to what happened at Mount Sinai (see 5.23-31).

Horeb: Mount Sinai (see 1.2).

The day of the assembly: see 9.10. NJPSV uses a capital letter, "the Assembly," a way of emphasizing its importance in the life of Israel. But in many languages it will be simpler to follow TEV and CEV with "you were gathered at Mount Sinai."

Let me not hear again the voice of the LORD my God: as usual the first person singular is used of the people as a whole. So it is possible to express this as ". . . and said to the LORD, 'Please don't let us hear your voice.' " However, instead of the direct quotation of what they said at that time, it may be better in some languages to use indirect speech, as TEV does: "you begged not to hear the LORD speak again."

See the great fire any more: this refers to the fire that burned on top of Mount Sinai, indicating the presence of Yahweh. CEV has "this terrible fire again."

Lest I die: continued exposure to God's fiery presence would kill them all. Another way to express this is "If we do [see the fire] we will die."

18.17 RSV	TEV
And the LORD said to me, 'They have rightly said all that they have spoken.	So the LORD said to me, 'They have made a wise request.

The LORD said to me: notice that here the usual formula "the LORD your God" is not used.

They have rightly said all that they have spoken: this is an unnatural and wordy way of saying "Everything they say is true." See the exact same statement in 5.28.

18.18 RSV	TEV
I will raise up for them a prophet like you from among their brethren; and I will put my words in his mouth, and he shall speak to them all that I command him.	I will send them a prophet like you from among their own people; I will tell him what to say, and he^r will tell the people everything I command.
	^{r} a prophet . . . him . . . he; *or* prophets . . . them . . . they.

The first part of this verse repeats verse 15.

I will put my words in his mouth: the literal equivalent in many languages will be natural and vivid; in English it is better to say something like "I will give him the message he is to deliver," or "I will tell him what to say" (TEV).

He shall speak to them: **them** is the people of Israel. So we may say "He will tell the people of Israel everything that I command" (similarly TEV).

18.19 RSV	TEV
And whoever will not give heed to my words which he shall speak in my name, I myself will require it of him.	He will speak in my name, and I^s will punish anyone who refuses to obey him.
	^{s} He will speak . . . and I; *or* When a prophet speaks in my name, I.

Whoever will not give heed to my words which he shall speak in my name: CEV expresses the sense better with "Since the message comes from me, anyone who doesn't obey the message will . . . ."

I myself will require it of him: see similar statements in Gen 9.5; Ezek 33.6; 34.10. It means that God will hold that person responsible. NJB has "will have to render an account to me," NJPSV "I myself will call him to account," and REB "I shall call that person to account." This "calling to account," of course, means punishment (see TEV).

18.20   RSV   TEV

But the prophet who presumes to   But if any prophet dares to speak a
speak a word in my name which I   message in my name when I did not
have not commanded him to speak,   command him to do so, he must die
or who speaks in the name of other   for it, and so must any prophet who
gods, that same prophet shall die.'   speaks in the name of other gods.'

This verse instructs the people on how they are to deal with a false prophet, that is, a person who claims to be speaking for Yahweh but who in fact is not. Any Israelite who spoke **in the name of other gods** would not be simply a false prophet but an apostate, a betrayer of the faith.

Presumes to speak: the verb is equivalent to the adjective "presumptuous" (see 1.43; 17.13), meaning to be "arrogant," "conceited." TEV has "dares to speak."

A word in my name: or "a message from me" (CEV).

That same prophet shall die: this means that such a person must be executed. So "he must die for it" (TEV), or "You must kill that person."

18.21   RSV   TEV

And if you say in your heart, 'How   "You may wonder how you can tell
may we know the word which the   when a prophet's message does not
LORD has not spoken?'—   come from the LORD.

How are the people to be sure that what the prophet says is truly a message from Yahweh? This question follows naturally from the previous verse.

If you say in your heart: this is equivalent to "If you say to yourself," "If you think." Again the second singular is used for the people as a whole, but a plural pronoun is permissible; for example, "You [plural] may ask yourselves [or, think]."

How may we know . . . ? Here, not like elsewhere, the first person plural is used.

. . . we know the word which the LORD has not spoken: this statement is nonsense in English. Strictly speaking we cannot "know" a word that has not been spoken. In the context, however, what it intends to say seems clear enough, that is, the people want to know how they can tell whether or not the prophet's message was actually given to him by God. So CEV says "How can we tell if a prophet's message really comes from the LORD?"

This verse connects closely and logically with the following verse, and the connection should be clear and natural in translation.

18.22 RSV	TEV
when a prophet speaks in the name of the LORD, if the word does not come to pass or come true, that is a word which the LORD has not spoken; the prophet has spoken it presumptuously, you need not be afraid of him.	If a prophet speaks in the name of the LORD and what he says does not come true, then it is not the LORD's message. That prophet has spoken on his own authority, and you are not to fear him.

This verse gives the answer to the question of the previous verse. To connect the two verses, a translator may say, for example, "You will know [if a prophet's message . . .], if . . . ."

Does not come to pass or come true: again, there is some redundancy here; the two verbal expressions mean the same. Some translations, however, use two separate expressions; for example, NRSV "the thing does not take place or prove true," and NJB "the thing does not happen and the word is not fulfilled." It seems better to imitate TEV and use one verbal expression: "and what he says does not come true." See also NJPSV "and the oracle does not come true."

That is a word which the LORD has not spoken: more naturally, "that message did not come from the LORD."

Has spoken it presumptuously: see the adjective "presumptuous" in 1.43; 17.13. An alternative model is "he has falsely claimed to speak for the LORD."

Not be afraid of him: here the verb "be afraid" means not to be intimidated, not to treat the presumed prophet with respect, not to be in awe of him. The object, rendered "of him" by most translations, may mean "of it," that is, the prophet's message (so NRSV). This is a possibility and translators should feel free to adopt it if it is possible to speak in their language of being afraid of a message.

An alternative translation model for verses 21 and 22 is:

- ²¹ You [plural] may think, "How can we know if a prophet's message really comes from the LORD?" ²² You will know, because if the LORD says something will happen, it will happen. But if it doesn't, you will know that the person has falsely claimed to speak for the LORD. Don't be afraid of such a person.

2B-21. The cities of refuge (19.1-13)

<table>
<tr><td align="center">RSV</td><td align="center">TEV
The Cities of Refuge</td></tr>
<tr><td>

1 "When the LORD your God cuts off the nations whose land the LORD your God gives you, and you dispossess them and dwell in their cities and in their houses, 2 you shall set apart three cities for you in the land which the LORD your God gives you to possess. 3 You shall prepare the roads, and divide into three parts the area of the land which the LORD your God gives you as a possession, so that any manslayer can flee to them.

4 "This is the provision for the manslayer, who by fleeing there may save his life. If any one kills his neighbor unintentionally without having been at enmity with him in time past— 5 as when a man goes into the forest with his neighbor to cut wood, and his hand swings the axe to cut down a tree, and the head slips from the handle and strikes his neighbor so that he dies—he may flee to one of these cities and save his life; 6 lest the avenger of blood in hot anger pursue the manslayer and overtake him, because the way is long, and wound him mortally, though the man did not deserve to die, since he was not at enmity with his neighbor in time past. 7 Therefore I command you, You shall set apart three cities. 8 And if the LORD your God enlarges your border, as he has sworn to your fathers, and gives you all the land which he promised to give to your fathers—9 provided you are careful to keep all this commandment, which I command you this day, by loving the LORD your God and by walking ever in his ways—then you shall add three other cities to these three, 10 lest innocent blood be shed in your land which the LORD your God gives you for an inheritance, and so the guilt of bloodshed be upon you.

11 "But if any man hates his neighbor, and lies in wait for him, and attacks him, and wounds him mortally so that he dies, and the man flees into one of these cities, 12 then the elders of his city shall send and fetch him from there, and hand him over to the avenger of blood, so that he may die. 13 Your eye shall not pity him, but you shall purge the guilt of innocent blood from Israel, so that it may be well with you.

</td><td>

1 "After the LORD your God has destroyed the people whose land he is giving you and after you have taken their cities and houses and settled there, 2-3 divide the territory into three parts, each with a city that can be easily reached. Then any of you that kill will be able to escape to one of them for protection. 4 If you accidentally kill someone who is not your enemy, you may escape to any of these cities and be safe. 5 For example, if two of you go into the forest together to cut wood and if, as one of you is chopping down a tree, the ax head comes off the handle and kills the other, you can run to one of those three cities and be safe. 6 If there were only one city, the distance to it might be too great, and the relative who is responsible for taking revenge for the killing might catch you and angrily kill an innocent person. After all, it was by accident that you killed someone who was not your enemy. 7 This is why I order you to set aside three cities.

8 "When the LORD your God enlarges your territory, as he told your ancestors he would, and gives you all the land he has promised, 9 then you are to select three more cities. (He will give you this land if you do everything that I command you today and if you love the LORD your God and live according to his teachings.) 10 Do this, so that innocent people will not die and so that you will not be guilty of putting them to death in the land that the LORD is giving you.

11 "But suppose you deliberately murder your enemy in cold blood and then escape to one of those cities for protection. 12 In that case, the leaders of your own town are to send for you and hand you over to the relative responsible for taking revenge for the murder, so that you may be put to death. 13 No mercy will be shown to you. Israel must rid itself of murderers, so that all will go well.

</td></tr>
</table>

Moses ordered the Israelites to establish what are called cities (or towns) of refuge, so as to avoid people taking the law into their own hands. Whatever the circumstances of the crime, the conviction and punishment of the criminal would conform to certain rules aimed to protect the innocent. The subject is dealt with earlier in the book (4.41-43) and also in Num 35.9-34 and Josh 20.1-9.

Section heading: the noun title, "The Cities of Refuge" or "Safe Towns" (CEV) may have to be expanded into a longer statement, "Cities where people can go to in order to be safe." See also the Section heading for 4.41-43 for further models.

19.1 RSV	TEV
"When the LORD your God cuts off the nations whose land the LORD your God gives you, and you dispossess them and dwell in their cities and in their houses,	"After the LORD your God has destroyed the people whose land he is giving you and after you have taken their cities and houses and settled there,

This is the beginning of a new chapter, so translators should begin with something like "Moses said to the Israelites: . . . ."

Verses 1-2 are a single long sentence, and it is possible to divide it into two or more sentences by making verse 1 a complete sentence:

> [1] The LORD your God will destroy . . . and you will live in their towns and houses. [2] After this [has happened], you must . . . .

Cuts off: here this means to "destroy" (NIV, TEV), "exterminate" (REB), "wipe from the earth," or whatever other verb suits the context.

Whose land the LORD your God gives you: again the point is made that the land of Canaan is God's gift to the people of Israel.

Dispossess them: this means to drive them out of their towns and homes. For further comments, see 12.1.

19.2-3 RSV	TEV
2 you shall set apart three cities for you in the land which the LORD your God gives you to possess. 3 You shall prepare the roads, and divide into three parts the area of the land which the LORD your God gives you as a possession, so that any manslayer can flee to them.	2-3 divide the territory into three parts, each with a city that can be easily reached. Then any of you that kill will be able to escape to one of them for protection.

TEV has combined verses 2-3 in order to make the text easier to understand, with the various events following a logical order. It is easy to see the logic of the TEV rearrangement: the division of the land into three areas must come before the selection of the three cities, one city in each area, after which the roads would be built.

Set apart three cities: that is, choose these cities (or towns) for this purpose. For **cities** see 1.22. It will be helpful to indicate again that these will be safe cities or towns that people can go to for safety.

The land which the LORD your God gives you to possess: repeating a statement that is made many times.

You shall prepare the roads: the text as we have it means that the Israelites are ordered to build good roads to each of these towns so that fugitives will be able to reach the town nearest to them without too much trouble. The meaning of the Hebrew text that RSV translates as **You shall prepare the roads** is in doubt, however, and NJPSV translates "survey the distances" (this is also an alternative rendering in NRSV, TOB, FRCL). The phrase is discussed at length in A.D. Hulst, *Old Testament Translation Problems*, and this meaning is found to be possible but not certain. A translator should feel free to give this meaning in a footnote, but it is recommended that the text follow RSV. Neither TEV nor CEV mentions **the roads**, but it seems best to do so. An alternative translation model is the following: "You shall build roads to these towns so that people can reach them easily."

Divide into three parts the area: actually this division was to come before the choice of the cities and the building of the roads. TEV has "divide the territory into three parts," and CEV has "Divide the land into three regions."

The land which the LORD your God gives you as a possession: a further repetition of this constant theme.

So that any manslayer can flee to them: it is important to use a general term for **manslayer** that means only that a person has killed another person, without indicating whether it was intentional (murder) or not (homicide). NRSV has "homicide," which is normally used of the act of killing, not of the killer. "A man who kills someone" (TEV) is a good model.

To them: that is, to any one of the three cities.

An alternative translation model for verses 2-3 is:

- 2-3 Divide the land into three parts [or, territories]. Choose a town in each part where people can go in order to be safe. Build roads to these towns so that people can reach them easily. Then a person who kills someone will be able to escape to any of these towns and be safe.

19.4   RSV   TEV

"This is the provision for the manslayer, who by fleeing there may save his life. If any one kills his neighbor unintentionally without having been at enmity with him in time past—

If you accidentally kill someone who is not your enemy, you may escape to any of these cities and be safe.

The provision: the same noun is used at the beginning of 15.2. It indicates what is to be done. So we may translate "This is what you must do [or, This is the rule] in the case of someone who . . . ."

The manslayer, who by fleeing there may save his life: this is rather complex. NIV has "This is the rule concerning the man who kills another and flees there to save his life," and NJPSV "Here is an example of how someone may save his life by fleeing to them." Another possibility is "This is the rule about a person who kills another person and flees to one of these towns in order to save his [or her] life." What follows deals with the case of the person who is legally allowed to flee to one of these towns and thus avoid being killed.

If any one kills his neighbor unintentionally: here **neighbor** means simply "another person" (NRSV), or, more precisely, a fellow-Israelite; it does not indicate someone who lives next door. The Hebrew verb is literally "to strike" or "to hit," here meaning to kill.

Unintentionally: that is, accidentally, without meaning to.

Without having been at enmity with him in the past: this is stated in order to further remove the possibility of murder.

19.5 RSV	TEV
as when a man goes into the forest with his neighbor to cut wood, and his hand swings the axe to cut down a tree, and the head slips from the handle and strikes his neighbor so that he dies—he may flee to one of these cities and save his life;	For example, if two of you go into the forest together to cut wood and if, as one of you is chopping down a tree, the ax head comes off the handle and kills the other, you can run to one of those three cities and be safe.

In verses 5-6 one particular example of accidental killing is given. A good way to start verse 5 is to say "For example" (TEV), "For instance" (NIV, NJPSV, REB), or "Suppose that . . ." (NRSV).

A man . . . with his neighbor: as in verse 4, this means "with his friend," or "with someone else." Or else, even more simply, "For instance, two men go to the woods . . . ."

The forest: or "the woods." An equivalent of "the jungle" may be used if there is no other word to designate an area where trees grow plentifully.

To cut wood: either firewood or else for carpentry.

His hand swings the axe to cut down a tree: that is, "While he is cutting down a tree with his ax," or else, like NIV, "As he swings his ax to fell a tree."

The head slips from the handle: the **head** is the heavy metal blade fixed to the wooden handle of an ax. **Slips** may not give the right sense in English, since it may not mean it happens with enough speed and force to kill a person; TEV has "comes off," but perhaps "flies off" is more appropriate in this context.

And strikes his neighbor so that he dies: "And the head hits the other man and he dies."

He may flee to one of these cities and save his life: this refers to the nearest town of refuge, where he can be safe from the dead man's relative who would go after him in order to kill him.

19.6	RSV	TEV
	lest the avenger of blood in hot anger pursue the manslayer and overtake him, because the way is long, and wound him mortally, though the man did not deserve to die, since he was not at enmity with his neighbor in time past.	If there were only one city, the distance to it might be too great, and the relative who is responsible for taking revenge for the killing might catch you and angrily kill an innocent person. After all, it was by accident that you killed someone who was not your enemy.

This verse gives the reason why there had to be three towns of refuge; if there were only one, it might be so far away from where an accidental death had occurred that the dead man's relative would overtake the killer before he reached the town of refuge. TEV emphasizes the need for three cities over one, with "If there were only one city, the distance to it might be too great, ..."

The avenger of blood: traditionally this has been taken to mean the dead man's nearest relative, whose duty it would be to avenge the death. But some believe that the designated avenger would be named by the local authorities. There is not enough evidence to determine which is correct; it is recommended that the idea of a relative be the one expressed by the translation. TEV has "the relative who is responsible to take revenge for the killing," and REB translates "the dead man's next-of-kin on whom lies the duty of vengeance" (see Num 25.12). "Avenge" or "revenge" means to "pay back" or "punish" someone in a way that fits the crime. So **avenger of blood** may also be expressed as "the relative who is responsible for punishing the murderer [or, killer]."

In hot anger: in Hebrew this is a verbal form meaning "to boil over." Alternative ways of expressing this are "be very angry" or "have a very hot heart," and so on.

Pursue the manslayer and overtake him, because the way is long: the meaning is clear enough, but the order of the clauses may be a problem. BRCL has "If there were only one city of refuge, it might be so far away that the relative responsible for avenging the death might have time to catch the man who killed his friend." (In Portuguese "his friend" is not ambiguous; it is the "friend" of the killer.)

Wound him mortally: more simply, "kill him."

The man did not deserve to die: this is why the three towns of refuge are needed. TEV translates this as "an innocent man." In some languages this will be expressed as "a pure [or, clean] person."

He was not at enmity with his neighbor in time past: as in verse 4.

19.7 RSV TEV

Therefore I command you, You shall set apart three cities.

This is why I order you to set aside three cities.

For this verse see verse 2.

19.8 RSV TEV

And if the LORD your God enlarges your border, as he has sworn to your fathers, and gives you all the land which he promised to give to your fathers—

"When the LORD your God enlarges your territory, as he told your ancestors he would, and gives you all the land he has promised,

In verses 8-10 instructions are given about three more towns, following the expansion of Israelite domination into other territories. It is not certain what the relation is between these three additional towns and those listed in 4.41-43; probably the three towns west of the Jordan River were selected first, and only later the three on the east side.

And if: in this context, "When" (NJPSV, TEV, CEV).

Enlarges your border: that is, "enlarges your territory" (TEV), or "gives you even more land" (see 12.20). For a description of the territory Israel would eventually occupy, see 11.22-25.

As he has sworn to your fathers: see 1.8.

The rest of the promise means "give you all the land that he promised your ancestors he would give you" (TEV, NRSV); see 6.18, 23.

19.9 RSV TEV

provided you are careful to keep all this commandment, which I command you this day, by loving the LORD your God and by walking ever in his ways—then you shall add three other cities to these three,

then you are to select three more cities. (He will give you this land if you do everything that I command you today and if you love the LORD your God and live according to his teachings.)

This verse continues without a break from verse 8. In many languages it will be better to put a full stop at the end of verse 8 and begin this verse "He will do this if . . . ."

Careful to keep all this commandment: see 4.2; 5.31.

I command you this day: again **this day** is emphasized (see 15.5).

Loving the LORD your God: see 6.5.

Walking ever in his ways: see 8.6; 10.12; 11.22.

You shall add three other cities to these three: "You will choose three more towns of refuge."

We should notice that TEV has placed part of this verse in parentheses. These are a useful device but may cause trouble for some readers.

It is also possible to combine verses 8 and 9 as follows:

- ⁸⁻⁹ The LORD your God has promised that if you obey all his commands that I am giving you today, and if you continue to love him and live [or, walk] according to his teachings, then he will give you the land that he promised to your ancestors. When that happens you must choose three other towns in addition to these three.

19.10   RSV   TEV

lest innocent blood be shed in your land which the LORD your God gives you for an inheritance, and so the guilt of bloodshed be upon you.

Do this, so that innocent people will not die and so that you will not be guilty of putting them to death in the land that the LORD is giving you.

This verse continues from the previous verse; but see TEV as an example of beginning a new sentence here: "Do this, so that innocent people . . . ."

Lest innocent blood be shed: that is, "so that innocent people will not be put to death." If the phrase **innocent blood** is normally used in a language to indicate an innocent person who has been killed, it may be used; otherwise the meaning should be made clear. The killing here is an execution; that is why "be put to death" or its equivalent should be used.

The guilt of bloodshed be upon you: the whole nation would be guilty of having put to death an innocent person. CEV makes this clear with "You will be guilty of murder if innocent people lose their lives."

19.11   RSV   TEV

"But if any man hates his neighbor, and lies in wait for him, and attacks him, and wounds him mortally so that he dies, and the man flees into one of these cities,

"But suppose you deliberately murder your enemy in cold blood and then escape to one of those cities for protection.

Verses 11-13 take up the case of murder.

Hates his neighbor: again **neighbor** stands here for "someone," "another person," or "a fellow-Israelite." In certain languages **hates his neighbor** will be expressed as "considers someone his enemy" (see also TEV).

Lies in wait . . . attacks . . . wounds him mortally so that he dies: this is a graphic description of a deliberate, premeditated, wilful act of murder.

Flees into one of these cities: see verse 5.

19.12   RSV   TEV

then the elders of his city shall send   In that case, the leaders of your own
and fetch him from there, and hand   town are to send for you and hand
him over to the avenger of blood, so   you over to the relative responsible
that he may die.   for taking revenge for the murder, so
                                             that you may be put to death.

The elders of his city: see 5.23. These are the town leaders, the authorities
of the community where the killer lives.

Send and fetch him . . . and hand him over: again there are various stages in
the process. The word **send** suggests that the elders commission some men to
go and find and bring back the killer. In a more general sense **send and fetch
him** can mean "shall have him brought back."

The avenger of blood: see verse 6.

So that he may die: so that he may be put to death, be executed.

19.13   RSV   TEV

Your eye shall not pity him, but you   No mercy will be shown to you. Isra-
shall purge the guilt of innocent   el must rid itself of murderers, so
blood° from Israel, so that it may be   that all will go well.
well with you.

° Or *the blood of the innocent*

Your eye shall not pity him: this is a vivid way of expressing lack of pity.
Where there is a good idiomatic phrase for such a feeling, it should be used. See
its use in 13.8.

Purge the guilt of innocent blood from Israel: a deliberate murder defiled the
land, and it had to be cleansed. This could be achieved only by executing the
murderer (see Num 35.33-34). For the verb **purge** see 13.5. Since the idea of
"cleansing" may not be natural in this context, something like "get rid of,"
"remove," "take away" can be used. Some translations, like TEV, FRCL, BRCL,
have "get rid of murderers," but this does not really represent the meaning of
the text, which is speaking not about murderers but about the land as such,
which had been defiled or soiled by the spilling of innocent blood (see Gen
4.10-11). In languages where the idea of **guilt of innocent blood** will be difficult
to translate, we may say something like "rid [or, remove from] the land of the
blood of innocent people who have been murdered," or "clear the name [or, face;
or, reputation] of the people of Israel for the innocent people who . . . ."

That it may be well with you: see 4.40.

2B-22. Ancient property lines (19.14)

<table>
<tr><td align="center">RSV</td><td align="center">TEV
Ancient Property Lines</td></tr>
<tr><td>14 "In the inheritance which you will hold in the land that the LORD your God gives you to possess, you shall not remove your neighbor's landmark, which the men of old have set.</td><td>14 "Do not move your neighbor's property line, established long ago in the land that the LORD your God is giving you.</td></tr>
</table>

This one-verse section may be joined to the next one (verses 15-21), with the title "Theft of land, and false witnesses." However, it is recommended that TEV and CEV be followed, making this a separate section.

Section heading: TEV has the title "Ancient Property Lines," (similarly CEV). Other titles may be "The command to not remove property border markers" or even ". . . stones that mark property lines."

<table>
<tr><td>**19.14**</td><td align="center">RSV</td><td align="center">TEV</td></tr>
<tr><td></td><td>**"In the inheritance which you will hold in the land that the LORD your God gives you to possess, you shall not remove your neighbor's landmark, which the men of old have set.**</td><td>**"Do not move your neighbor's property line, established long ago in the land that the LORD your God is giving you.**</td></tr>
</table>

This command is an ancient one and appears also in 27.17; Job 24.2; Pro 22.28; 23.10; Hos 5.10.

In the inheritance which you will hold in the land that the LORD your God gives you to possess: RSV has reversed the order of the Hebrew. NRSV, which is exactly the same as NJPSV, is more natural: ". . . the property that will be allotted to you in the land that the LORD your God is giving you to possess." TEV has condensed the text considerably but retains the essence of the command: "established long ago in the land that the LORD your God is giving you." For "inherit" (used twice in Hebrew) see 1.38, and for **possess** see 1.8.

You shall not remove your neighbor's landmark: the landmarks were stones, or piles of stones, marking the place where one person's property ended and another person's began. This was a matter not of "removing" but of "moving" (TEV, NRSV, NIV, NJPSV) the boundary markers, in order to increase your own property by diminishing someone else's. Since different types of boundary markers are used in some parts of the world, it will be helpful to make it clear that "stones" are involved; for example, "Do not move the stones set up to mark the property lines." However, the form of the boundary marker is not important here. So if a culture uses some other kind of moveable boundary marker, the translator may use that marker in this context, if it is more meaningful.

The men of old have set: the original conquerors of the land divided the territory and determined the exact boundaries of each person's property. Something like "previous generations" (NJPSV) or "former generations" (NRSV) is better; or else "your ancestors."

An alternative translation model for this verse is:

● In the land the LORD is giving you, your ancestors set up stones to mark the property lines between fields. Do not move these stones.

2B-23. Concerning witnesses (19.15-21)

RSV	TEV
	Concerning Witnesses
15 "A single witness shall not prevail against a man for any crime or for any wrong in connection with any offense that he has committed; only on the evidence of two witnesses, or of three witnesses, shall a charge be sustained. 16 If a malicious witness rises against any man to accuse him of wrongdoing, 17 then both parties to the dispute shall appear before the LORD, before the priests and the judges who are in office in those days; 18 the judges shall inquire diligently, and if the witness is a false witness and has accused his brother falsely, 19 then you shall do to him as he had meant to do to his brother; so you shall purge the evil from the midst of you. 20 And the rest shall hear, and fear, and shall never again commit any such evil among you. 21 Your eye shall not pity; it shall be life for life, eye for eye, tooth for tooth, hand for hand, foot for foot.	15 "One witness is not enough to convict someone of a crime; at least two witnesses are necessary to prove that someone is guilty. 16 If any of you try to harm another by false accusations, 17 both of you are to go to the one place of worship and be judged by the priests and judges who are then in office. 18 The judges will investigate the case thoroughly; and if you have made a false accusation, 19 you are to receive the punishment the accused would have received. In this way your nation will get rid of this evil. 20 Then everyone else will hear what happened; they will be afraid, and no one will ever again do such an evil thing. 21 In such cases show no mercy; the punishment is to be a life for a life, an eye for an eye, a tooth for a tooth, a hand for a hand, and a foot for a foot.

The main purpose of this section is to protect people from people who give false witness in a trial.

Section heading: instead of the simple "Concerning Witnesses" of TEV, something more elaborate may be better, like "What to do with people who give false witness," or "Witnesses Must Tell the Truth" (CEV).

19.15 RSV	TEV
"A single witness shall not prevail against a man for any crime or for any wrong in connection with any offense that he has committed; only on the evidence of two witnesses, or of three witnesses, shall a charge be sustained.	"One witness is not enough to convict someone of a crime; at least two witnesses are necessary to prove that someone is guilty.

With the beginning of this new section, translators are urged to reintroduce Moses as the speaker.

This verse is very similar to 17.6.

Any crime or . . . any wrong . . . any offense that he has committed: this is somewhat wordy. After the first noun in Hebrew (translated **crime**), the next two are closely related forms of the same noun, usually translated "sin," followed by the verb "to sin." NIV is a good model to follow: "any crime or offense he may have committed."

In connection with: in English at least, this is a rather wordy and an unnecessary way of stating the matter. NIV's English is much more natural and meaningful, as seen in the previous comment.

For **two witnesses, or of three**, see 17.6. The meaning is the same: "at least two witnesses," or "two or more witnesses."

Shall a charge be sustained: that is, an accusation will be upheld, be judged to be true.

An alternative translation model for this verse is:

• 	Before you convict a person of a crime, at least two witnesses
	must be able to testify that the person did it [or, is guilty].

19.16   RSV   TEV

**If a malicious witness rises against   If any of you try to harm another by
any man to accuse him of wrong-   false accusations,
doing,**

Verses 16-19 deal with a case in which there is only one witness. This person is called **a malicious witness**, that is, a hostile witness, someone who violates the truth (the same phrase occurs in Exo 23.1; Psa 35.11).

Wrongdoing: the Hebrew word is used in 13.5 to mean apostasy (RSV "rebellion against God"). It means the same thing in Isa 1.5; 31.6; Jer 28.16; 29.32 (its precise meaning in Isa 59.13 is in doubt). On the basis of the meaning of the word in these other passages, some commentators believe the charge here is not simply of wrongdoing in general but of apostasy in particular. The Septuagint here uses the word "ungodliness," which means apostasy; and TOB has "accuse him of rebellion" (which, in the context, is rebellion against God, not against the king). The whole paragraph indicates clearly that the crime is punishable by death, and the false witness himself shall be put to death (verse 19). It is recommended that the word or expression for "apostasy" be used here (using the same expression used in 13.5), namely "rebellion against God." So we may translate:

• 	If a person tries to harm another by falsely accusing that person
	of rebelling against God, ...

19.17   RSV   TEV

then both parties to the dispute shall appear before the LORD, before the priests and the judges who are in office in those days;	both of you are to go to the one place of worship and be judged by the priests and judges who are then in office.

Both parties to the dispute: that is, both the accuser and the accused.

Appear before the LORD: at the central sanctuary.

Before the priests and the judges who are in office in those days: see 17.8-12, where the same procedure is followed.

19.18   RSV   TEV

the judges shall inquire diligently, and if the witness is a false witness and has accused his brother falsely,	The judges will investigate the case thoroughly; and if you have made a false accusation,

The judges shall inquire diligently: the judges are to investigate the matter thoroughly; they are to interrogate the two people closely.

Accused his brother falsely: again, **brother** here is simply the other Israelite, without any indication of family relationship. NRSV "testified falsely against another," or TEV "and if the man has made a false accusation against his fellow Israelite."

19.19   RSV   TEV

then you shall do to him as he had meant to do to his brother; so you shall purge the evil from the midst of you.	you are to receive the punishment the accused would have received. In this way your nation will get rid of this evil.

Do to him as he meant to do to his brother: this is what is called the *lex talionis*, the law of equal retaliation. An alternative way of expressing this is "You must punish him in the same way you would have punished the accused person [or, the person he accused of doing wrong]."

Purge the evil from the midst of you: see verse 13; 17.7, 12.

19.20   RSV   TEV

And the rest shall hear, and fear, and shall never again commit any such evil among you.	Then everyone else will hear what happened; they will be afraid, and no one will ever again do such an evil thing.

This verse is almost exactly the same as 17.13; see also 13.1.

Never again commit any such evil: here the standard Hebrew word for "crime" or "wrongdoing" is used. So we may say "and no one will ever again commit this crime."

19.21   RSV   TEV

Your eye shall not pity; it shall be life for life, eye for eye, tooth for tooth, hand for hand, foot for foot.

In such cases show no mercy; the punishment is to be a life for a life, an eye for an eye, a tooth for a tooth, a hand for a hand, and a foot for a foot.

Your eye shall not pity: see verse 13, and 13.8.

Life for life, eye for eye, tooth for tooth, hand for hand, foot for foot: this should be expressed as concisely as possible, but the meaning should be quite clear. It should be stated generally and impersonally, in the manner of laws; for example, "One life shall be taken to pay for another life, one eye for another eye . . . ," and so forth. This legislation appears also in Exo 21.23-25; Lev 24.19-20.

2B-24. Concerning war (20.1-20)

RSV

TEV
Concerning War

1 "When you go forth to war against your enemies, and see horses and chariots and an army larger than your own, you shall not be afraid of them; for the LORD your God is with you, who brought you up out of the land of Egypt. 2 And when you draw near to the battle, the priest shall come forward and speak to the people, 3 and shall say to them, 'Hear, O Israel, you draw near this day to battle against your enemies: let not your heart faint; do not fear, or tremble, or be in dread of them; 4 for the LORD your God is he that goes with you, to fight for you against your enemies, to give you the victory.' 5 Then the officers shall speak to the people, saying, 'What man is there that has built a new house and has not dedicated it? Let him go back to his house, lest he die in the battle and another man dedicate it. 6 And what man is there that has planted a vineyard and has not enjoyed its fruit? Let him go back to his house, lest he die in the battle and another man enjoy its fruit. 7 And what man is there that has betrothed a wife and has not taken her? Let him go back to his house, lest he die in the battle and another man take her.'

1 "When you go out to fight against your enemies and you see chariots and horses and an army that outnumbers yours, do not be afraid of them. The LORD your God, who rescued you from Egypt, will be with you. 2 Before you start fighting, a priest is to come forward and say to the army, 3 'Men of Israel, listen! Today you are going into battle. Do not be afraid of your enemies or lose courage or panic. 4 The LORD your God is going with you, and he will give you victory.'

5 "Then the officers will address the men and say, 'Is there any man here who has just built a house, but has not yet dedicated it? If so, he is to go home. Otherwise, if he is killed in battle, someone else will dedicate his house. 6 Is there any man here who has just planted a vineyard, but has not yet had the chance to harvest its grapes? If so, he is to go home. Otherwise, if he is killed in battle, someone else will enjoy the wine. 7 Is there anyone here who is engaged to be married? If so, he is to go home. Otherwise, if he is killed in battle, someone else will marry the woman he is engaged to.'

8 And the officers shall speak further to the people, and say, 'What man is there that is fearful and fainthearted? Let him go back to his house, lest the heart of his fellows melt as his heart.' 9 And when the officers have made an end of speaking to the people, then commanders shall be appointed at the head of the people.

10 "When you draw near to a city to fight against it, offer terms of peace to it. 11 And if its answer to you is peace and it opens to you, then all the people who are found in it shall do forced labor for you and shall serve you. 12 But if it makes no peace with you, but makes war against you, then you shall besiege it; 13 and when the LORD your God gives it into your hand you shall put all its males to the sword, 14 but the women and the little ones, the cattle, and everything else in the city, all its spoil, you shall take as booty for yourselves; and you shall enjoy the spoil of your enemies, which the LORD your God has given you. 15 Thus you shall do to all the cities which are very far from you, which are not cities of the nations here. 16 But in the cities of these peoples that the LORD your God gives you for an inheritance, you shall save alive nothing that breathes, 17 but you shall utterly destroy them, the Hittites and the Amorites, the Canaanites and the Perizzites, the Hivites and the Jebusites, as the LORD your God has commanded; 18 that they may not teach you to do according to all their abominable practices which they have done in the service of their gods, and so to sin against the LORD your God.

19 "When you besiege a city for a long time, making war against it in order to take it, you shall not destroy its trees by wielding an axe against them; for you may eat of them, but you shall not cut them down. Are the trees in the field men that they should be besieged by you? 20 Only the trees which you know are not trees for food you may destroy and cut down that you may build siegeworks against the city that makes war with you, until it falls.

8 "The officers will also say to the men, 'Is there any man here who has lost his nerve and is afraid? If so, he is to go home. Otherwise, he will destroy the morale of the others.' 9 When the officers have finished speaking to the army, leaders are to be chosen for each unit.

10 "When you go to attack a city, first give its people a chance to surrender. 11 If they open the gates and surrender, they are all to become your slaves and do forced labor for you. 12 But if the people of that city will not surrender, but choose to fight, surround it with your army. 13 Then, when the LORD your God lets you capture the city, kill every man in it. 14 You may, however, take for yourselves the women, the children, the livestock, and everything else in the city. You may use everything that belongs to your enemies. The LORD has given it to you. 15 That is how you are to deal with those cities that are far away from the land you will settle in.

16 "But when you capture cities in the land that the LORD your God is giving you, kill everyone. 17 Completely destroy all the people: the Hittites, the Amorites, the Canaanites, the Perizzites, the Hivites, and the Jebusites, as the LORD ordered you to do. 18 Kill them, so that they will not make you sin against the LORD by teaching you to do all the disgusting things that they do in the worship of their gods.

19 "When you are trying to capture a city, do not cut down its fruit trees, even though the siege lasts a long time. Eat the fruit, but do not destroy the trees; the trees are not your enemies. 20 You may cut down the other trees and use them in the siege mounds until the city is captured.

As they invaded the land of Canaan, the Israelites would be fighting all the peoples there in order to wipe them out and take possession of the land, together with its cities and towns. Instructions about how they are to proceed are clear and detailed. Their fighting force was not a standing army, composed of professional soldiers, as most armies are today. Rather it was more like a militia, a citizens' army, that is, citizens who would enlist or be enlisted for fighting the enemy. Theirs was a "holy" war, a war led by God and fought to fulfil God's purposes for his chosen people. In the pursuit of these purposes, the Israelites would completely destroy the Canaanites (see verse 17, "utterly destroy"). If the Canaanites were not eliminated, they might lead the people away from worshiping Yahweh to the worship of their gods (verses 12-15).

Section heading: the TEV title "Concerning War" may not be satisfactory in some languages; something like "Conduct of Warfare" (NRSV), "Going to War" (NIV), or "Laws for Going to War" (CEV) may be better, or else "Instructions for war against the peoples of Canaan."

20.1   RSV   TEV

"When you go forth to war against   "When you go out to fight against
your enemies, and see horses and   your enemies and you see chariots
chariots and an army larger than   and horses and an army that out-
your own, you shall not be afraid of   numbers yours, do not be afraid of
them; for the LORD your God is with   them. The LORD your God, who res-
you, who brought you up out of the   cued you from Egypt, will be with
land of Egypt.   you.

With the beginning of this new chapter and section, it will be helpful to have something like "Moses said to the Israelites: . . ." or "Moses continued to speak to the Israelites: . . . ."

When you go forth to war against your enemies: this indicates that the Israelites would take the initiative, since they were the aggressors who were trying to destroy the native peoples of the land. A more natural way of saying this is "When you go out to fight your enemies" (see TEV). For **enemies** see 1.42.

Horses and chariots and an army larger than your own: for **horses and chariots** see Josh 11.4; 1 Kgs 20.25; Isa 31.1. **Horses and chariots** is a way of speaking of horse-drawn vehicles carrying the driver and one or two other fighters. Both the Assyrians and the Egyptians had chariots (see 11.4); the Israelite army was composed of men on foot, that is, foot soldiers, infantry troops. **Chariots** in some languages will be expressed as "war wagons" or "war wagons pulled by horses." For **horses** see 17.16.

You shall not be afraid of them: the reason the Israelites need not fear a superior enemy force is that Yahweh, their God, will fight for them (see 7.17-19; 8.14).

Who brought you up out of the land of Egypt: the verb in 8.14 is "brought you out," but it means exactly the same. If they recall how God destroyed the Egyptians when they, the Israelites, did not even have an army to fight them, this will give them courage.

20.2   RSV   TEV

And when you draw near to the bat-   Before you start fighting, a priest is
tle, the priest shall come forward and to come forward and say to the
speak to the people,   army,

When you draw near to battle: this continues from the beginning of verse 1, giving the people instructions on what to do just before they got ready to fight

338

the enemy. "Before you start fighting" (TEV), or even "Before you start fighting your enemies" are also possible models.

The priest: for **priest** see 10.6. There is no way of determining precisely who this priest was. Apparently his task was to determine whether Yahweh would give victory to the Israelites (see Judges 20.18-24; 1 Sam 14.36-42; 2 Chr 20.13-22).

The people: this is the normal Hebrew word for "people"; here, however, it means the fighters, "the troops" (NRSV, NJPSV); it is the same Hebrew word that in verse 1 is translated "an army." In English the word "soldiers" is not satisfactory, since this means professional military men (and women), paid to fight. An alternative expression is "fighting men."

20.3	RSV	TEV

and shall say to them, 'Hear, O Israel, you draw near this day to battle against your enemies: let not your heart faint; do not fear, or tremble, or be in dread of them;	'Men of Israel, listen! Today you are going into battle. Do not be afraid of your enemies or lose courage or panic.

The priest exhorts the Israelites not to be afraid.

Hear, O Israel: as in 6.3 and 4.

To battle against your enemies: that is, "to fight your enemies" (as in verse 1).

Let not your heart faint, do not fear, or tremble, or be in dread: the exhortation is quite wordy, with four different expressions for not to be afraid. This repetition is for emphasis. Translators should not feel compelled to find four different expressions, if this turns out to be unnatural in their language; TEV reduces the four expressions to three. In most languages there are good idiomatic expressions for fear and panic, and translators should make use of them; for example, "heart falls," "heart turns over [or, flops]," or "have a swollen heart." For **be in dread of them**, see 1.29.

20.4	RSV	TEV

for the LORD your God is he that goes with you, to fight for you against your enemies, to give you the victory.'	The LORD your God is going with you, and he will give you victory.'

There are no particular problems in translating this verse. The vivid language used of God should be preserved, if possible: Yahweh **goes** with them, Yahweh **fights** on their behalf and gives them **the victory** (see 3.22). If it is natural in the language, the full expression should be kept and not abbreviated as TEV has done (see Exo 14.14).

The LORD your God is he that goes with you: this is quite emphatic; the Hebrew is "the LORD your God is the one going with you." NJPSV "marches with you" may be a bit too much.

To give you the victory: or "to cause you to be victorious over your enemies," or "cause you to conquer . . . ."

20.5   RSV   TEV

Then the officers shall speak to the   "Then the officers will address the
people, saying, 'What man is there   men and say, 'Is there any man here
that has built a new house and has   who has just built a house, but has
not dedicated it? Let him go back to   not yet dedicated it? If so, he is to go
his house, lest he die in the battle   home. Otherwise, if he is killed in
and another man dedicate it.   battle, someone else will dedicate
                                             his house.

Then the officers shall speak to the people: these are the officers in charge of all the troops; they are not the same as the "commanders" in verse 9. For **officers** see 1.15; 16.18, where the meaning seems to be "overseers."

What man is there that . . . ? There is a series of questions in verses 5-8 which all begin the same way. This beginning can be translated in a number of ways: NJPSV has "Is there anyone who . . . ?" and TEV "Is there any man here"; however, NRSV "Has anyone . . . ?" is a bit too vague. Here it is all right to use the masculine "man" and not a more general "anyone," because only men were enlisted to fight. Instead of a question, a statement can be used, "Any man who . . ." (REB), or a conditional, "If any man [or, any of you]."

Has not dedicated it: this is the only Old Testament reference to the dedication of a private house; nothing is known about what would have been done. But the word **dedicated** (used of the Temple, 1 Kgs 8.63) indicates a religious ceremony, requesting God's protection and blessing, and promising God that he will be honored and obeyed by those who live in the house. It is not enough simply to say "and has not begun to live in it," as some translations do. In some languages it will be necessary to make clear who is the one to whom the house is **dedicated**; for example, "has not yet dedicated it to God."

Let him go back . . . lest he die in battle and another man . . . : the second part of the officers' statement is similar in all four instances, and a translation should reflect this. It may be better to modify this part of the verse somewhat: "If there is, you may go back home, because you may die in battle and another man will dedicate your house." TEV and REB "Otherwise" is a fairly high-level construction in English which translators may not be able to use in other languages. Possible alternatives are "It is possible that" or "It may happen that."

An alternative translation model for this verse is:

●   Then the officers will say to the fighting men, "If any man has
         built a new house, but hasn't yet dedicated it to God, he may go

home. It is possible that he may die in battle and someone else will dedicate his house."

20.6

RSV	TEV
And what man is there that has planted a vineyard and has not enjoyed its fruit? Let him go back to his house, lest he die in the battle and another man enjoy its fruit.	Is there any man here who has just planted a vineyard, but has not yet had the chance to harvest its grapes? If so, he is to go home. Otherwise, if he is killed in battle, someone else will enjoy the wine.

Planted a vineyard and has not enjoyed its fruit: Lev 19.23-25 makes it clear that no fruit was to be harvested in the first three years; the fourth year's harvest was to be offered to God, and only in the fifth year would the owner keep the fruit. In the case of a **vineyard**, the fruit is not the grapes as such but the wine that would be made from the grapes. The Hebrew verb translated **enjoyed** means "to appropriate for common use," meaning that the first harvest had already been presented to the LORD; however, the Greek verb of the Septuagint means "to be happy," "to rejoice." Both TEV and NJPSV have "harvest the grapes." We may say something like "planted a vineyard and has not yet had a chance to enjoy eating the grapes [or, drinking the wine]." For **vineyard** see 6.11.

The rest of the verse follows the same order as verse 5b.

Enjoy its fruit: or "enjoy drinking the wine."

20.7

RSV	TEV
And what man is there that has betrothed a wife and has not taken her? Let him go back to his house, lest he die in the battle and another man take her.'	Is there anyone here who is engaged to be married? If so, he is to go home. Otherwise, if he is killed in battle, someone else will marry the woman he is engaged to.'

Betrothed a wife: this means, in modern terms, to become engaged to a woman. In Hebrew culture at that time, once a man had "betrothed" a woman, she was considered to be his wife, even before they started living together (see Deut 22.23-24). And such a relationship could be broken only by a formal divorce. So **betrothed** was more than "engagement" is in most modern societies. The Greek verb in the Septuagint used to translate the Hebrew verb here is the one that is used in Luke 2.5 of Joseph and Mary. Deut 24.5 states that a newly-married man would be given one year's exemption from military duty. Other ways to express this are "agreed to marry a woman" or even "Has promised to marry a woman."

Taken: this could almost sound like forcible intercourse. It is better to say something like "married her." NJPSV translates "paid the bride-price for a wife, but has not yet married her," with a footnote to explain "the bride-price": "Thereby making her his wife legally, even though the marriage had not yet taken place."

This verse ends in the same way as verses 5 and 6.

20.8   RSV   TEV

And the officers shall speak further to the people, and say, 'What man is there that is fearful and fainthearted? Let him go back to his house, lest the heart of his fellows melt as his heart.'

"The officers will also say to the men, 'Is there any man here who has lost his nerve and is afraid? If so, he is to go home. Otherwise, he will destroy the morale of the others.'"

This last question seems to have been added to the original three. It is of a general nature, and the introduction to the question is fuller. Those who are afraid are told to go back home, because their fear might spread and infect the others.

Will speak further to the people: that is, they are to ask one more question of the men [or, troops].

Fearful: this is the common word "to be afraid."

Fainthearted: as in verse 9.

Melt as his heart: this is a fairly common idiom, meaning to become afraid. Having a heart that "melts" means that a person loses courage, or nerve.

20.9   RSV   TEV

And when the officers have made an end of speaking to the people, then commanders shall be appointed at the head of the people.

When the officers have finished speaking to the army, leaders are to be chosen for each unit.

The commanders in this verse are not the same as the **officers**; they are men who would be appointed to be in charge of the various units that would be formed after some men had gone back home, for the different reasons given above. For the size of the units, see 1.15, where the same Hebrew word for **commanders** is used.

Shall be appointed: the Hebrew verb is the third person plural of the active voice, literally "they shall appoint." In this context the subject or agent may be **the officers** (so NIV, CEV); for example, "they will appoint commanders." Alternatively the third plural may be used impersonally, which is often done, with the meaning "they [the commanders] shall assume command" (so NJPSV, NRSV). Or even the passive sense, as in RSV and TEV, may be intended. The meaning expressed by NJPSV and NRSV is to be preferred.

20.10   RSV   TEV

"When you draw near to a city to fight against it, offer terms of peace to it.	"When you go to attack a city, first give its people a chance to surrender.

When you draw near to a city to fight against it: verses 10-18 give instructions on laying siege to fortified towns, that is, towns that had walls around them. Verse 15 reveals that these instructions apply only to towns that are outside of Israel.

Offer terms of peace to it: before mounting a siege against a town, the Israelites are to lay down the conditions under which they will not attack it. So TEV says "first give its people a chance to surrender," and FRCL "first propose to the inhabitants that they surrender without fighting." CEV puts verse 15 first, with "Before you attack a town that is far from your land, offer peace . . . ." This is a good alternative solution.

20.11   RSV   TEV

And if its answer to you is peace and it opens to you, then all the people who are found in it shall do forced labor for you and shall serve you.	If they open the gates and surrender, they are all to become your slaves and do forced labor for you.

If the people accept the Israelites' offer, there will be no fighting and no bloodshed; but they will become the Israelites' slaves.

If its answer to you is peace: that is, "if the people of that town agree to what you demand."

It opens to you: this seems to mean that the people open the gates of the town so that the Israelites can enter and occupy the town. Or it may mean, as NRSV translates, "surrenders to you." In some languages it will be necessary to place this clause at the beginning; for example, " If the people of that town open the gates and surrender."

All the people who are found in it: a way of saying "all the inhabitants of the town," "all the people who live there."

Shall do forced labor for you and shall serve you: this is simply one statement, expressed by two verbs that have the same meaning. For the use of **forced labor**, see Judges 1.27-36. TEV has "they are all to become your slaves and do forced labor for you." Another way to express this is ". . . and you will force them to work for you."

20.12   RSV   TEV

But if it makes no peace with you, but makes war against you, then you shall besiege it;	But if the people of that city will not surrender, but choose to fight, surround it with your army.

But if it makes no peace . . . but makes war: these are the negative and the
positive aspects of the same action. If it is not unnatural to use both forms in
a given language, they should be used, for emphasis. An alternative way of
expressing these two clauses is "But if the people of that city will not accept
your offer of peace, but decide to fight you . . . . " Instead of **it**, the town, it may
be better to say "the inhabitants," or "the people who live there."

Besiege it: this means to put troops around the walls of the town, and to use
devices to break through the walls, or to climb over them, so that the attackers
can enter the town (see further at verse 19). In some languages translators will
need to use a descriptive phrase; for example, "then have your fighting men
surround the town and attack it."

20.13   RSV   TEV

| and when the LORD your God gives it into your hand you shall put all its males to the sword, | Then, when the LORD your God lets you capture the city, kill every man in it. |

The LORD your God gives it into your hand: the surrender of the Canaanites
is God's doing. TEV has "Then, when the LORD your God lets you capture the
city, . . ." (similarly CEV).

Put all the males to the sword: put . . . to the sword is an idiom that means
"kill." All adult males who might fight are to be killed at once. In many
languages "kill all the males" or "kill every man in the town" will be natural
ways to render this (see 13.15).

20.14   RSV   TEV

| but the women and the little ones, the cattle, and everything else in the city, all its spoil, you shall take as booty for yourselves; and you shall enjoy the spoil of your enemies, which the LORD your God has given you. | You may, however, take for yourselves the women, the children, the livestock, and everything else in the city. You may use everything that belongs to your enemies. The LORD has given it to you. |

All the other people are allowed to live, but they become the slaves of the
Israelites.

But the women and the little ones: the **little ones** were children, presumably
including adolescent boys not yet old enough to fight. "Take the women and
children as slaves" (CEV) is a good model.

All its spoil: this includes everything in the town that the conquerors can
make use of. The same holds true for **booty**, all the belongings of the inhabitants, which the Israelites will keep. For **spoil** and **booty** see 2.35.

Enjoy the spoil of your enemies: the verb **enjoy** is literally "to eat," used in
a figurative sense but easily understood. In a number of languages **and**

344

everything else . . . the spoil of your enemies may be shortened to something like "Take everything else that belongs to your enemies and use it."

Which the LORD your God has given you: the people are constantly reminded that it is God who wins the victory for them.

20.15   RSV   TEV

Thus you shall do to all the cities which are very far from you, which are not cities of the nations here.

That is how you are to deal with those cities that are far away from the land you will settle in.

This clause, which makes the instructions apply to towns beyond the borders of the land of Canaan, comes at the end of the passage. See the comment at verse 10, where it was suggested that verse 15 may be placed there.

Cities which are very far from you, which are not cities of the nations here: again a twofold statement, for emphasis. Notice the force of the word **here**; the point of view is that of someone who lives in Canaan.

For an account of what the Israelites actually did in besieging towns, see 2.33-35 and 3.6-7.

20.16   RSV   TEV

But in the cities of these peoples that the LORD your God gives you for an inheritance, you shall save alive nothing that breathes,

"But when you capture cities in the land that the LORD your God is giving you, kill everyone.

The cities of these peoples that the LORD your God gives you for an inheritance: this is the familiar language, the way of speaking of the land of Canaan, which was the **inheritance** (see "inherit" in 1.38), that is, the Promised Land that Yahweh gave the Israelites. Another way of rendering this clause is "But whenever you capture towns in that land that the LORD your God is giving you, ..."

You shall save alive nothing that breathes: the Hebrew is literally "You shall not allow to live all [or, every] breathing being." It seems clear that this includes all living beings, not simply human beings, and this is the meaning that should be expressed; so "anything that breathes" (NRSV), or "all the people and animals" (CEV). See Josh 10.40; 11.11, 14.

20.17-18   RSV   TEV

17 but you shall utterly destroy them, the Hittites and the Amorites, the Canaanites and the Perizzites, the Hivites and the Jebusites, as the

17 Completely destroy all the people: the Hittites, the Amorites, the Canaanites, the Perizzites, the Hivites, and the Jebusites, as the LORD

LORD your God has commanded;
18 that they may not teach you to do
according to all their abominable
practices which they have done in
the service of their gods, and so to
sin against the LORD your God.

ordered you to do. 18 Kill them, so
that they will not make you sin
against the LORD by teaching you to
do all the disgusting things that they
do in the worship of their gods.

You shall utterly destroy them: the Hebrew is emphatic, using the expression which is literally "destroying, you shall destroy them." See 2.34.

For the list of the peoples living in Canaan, see 7.1, where seven groups are listed (here the "Girgashites" are not included).

The single sentence of verses 17 and 18 may be too long. It may be a good idea to begin a new sentence at verse 18, as TEV does, by repeating the verb of the previous verse: "Kill them so that . . ." or "If you allow them to live [or, don't kill them], they will cause you to . . . ."

As the LORD your God has commanded: see 9.3.

They may not teach you . . . their abominable practices: see the same reason in 7.25; 8.18-19; 18.9.

In the service of their gods: the Hebrew is simply "for their gods," meaning "in the worship of their gods" (TEV).

And so to sin: it should be clear that the subject here is the Israelites, not the Canaanites: "And so you will sin against the LORD your God." Here, not as elsewhere, **your** is plural, not singular.

20.19	RSV	TEV

"When you besiege a city for a long time, making war against it in order to take it, you shall not destroy its trees by wielding an axe against them; for you may eat of them, but you shall not cut them down. Are the trees in the field men that they should be besieged by you?

"When you are trying to capture a city, do not cut down its fruit trees, even though the siege lasts a long time. Eat the fruit, but do not destroy the trees; the trees are not your enemies.

Verses 19-20 add another instruction with regard to the siege of a city (verses 10-15).

The Hebrew text of verse 19 is not altogether clear, but the meaning given by RSV, TEV, and CEV represents the most common interpretation of the text.

When you besiege a city for a long time: or "When your fighting men surround a town for a long time." For **besiege** see verse 12.

You shall not destroy its trees by wielding an axe against them: these are fruit trees that grow outside the city, and they are not to be cut down. TEV reduces the number of words considerably, with "do not cut down its fruit trees." The model of RSV is not recommended, as it gives the idea that as long as you don't use an **axe**, you may cut the trees down. The sentence means that under no condition may anyone cut down the trees.

It is also possible to reorder the first clauses of the verse as follows: "When you are attacking a town, even though you surround the town for a long time, don't chop down its fruit trees."

You may eat of them, but you shall not cut them down: the Israelites were allowed to eat the fruits of the trees, but they were not to destroy the trees. NRSV "Although you may take food from them . . ." is not much better than RSV, since in English people hardly speak of taking "food" from a tree. TEV is more natural with "Eat the fruit, but do not destroy the trees."

Are the trees in the field men that they should be besieged by you? The rhetorical question is a way of saying vividly that the trees are not human beings and so pose no threat to the Israelites. If the rhetorical question (expecting the answer "No") will be understood by the reader, it may be retained. Otherwise a negative statement should be used: "Trees are not men . . ." or "Fruit trees aren't your enemies" (TEV, CEV).

20.20 RSV	TEV
Only the trees which you know are not trees for food you may destroy and cut down that you may build siegeworks against the city that makes war with you, until it falls.	You may cut down the other trees and use them in the siege mounds until the city is captured.

Only the trees which . . . are not trees for food: trees that don't bear fruit may be cut down and the wood used to **build siegeworks** against the town. **Siegeworks** included ladders, battering rams, platforms, or towers. In some languages there will not be a single word available like **siegeworks,** but translators will need to list the objects used to capture the town; for example, "You may cut down other trees and make ladders and towers [or, platforms] to help you get over the walls of the town and capture it" (similarly CEV). TEV "siege mounds," namely mounds made from earth, is misleading because there were also all the other wooden objects listed above that were included in **siegeworks**.

You may destroy and cut down: one verb will be enough; the most natural way is to say "You may cut them down" or "You may cut down the trees that aren't fruit trees."

The city that makes war with you: it should be clear that the Israelites are the aggressors, so something like "the town you are fighting [or, besieging]."

Falls: this verb is used of a town that surrenders to the enemy; see the same verb used in the same context in 28.52. In some languages it will be necessary to talk about the people of the city surrendering, rather than a city "falling." So alternative models for translation may be "the people of the town you are fighting surrender to you," or "you capture the people of the town you are fighting."

2B-25. Concerning unsolved murders (21.1-9)

<table>
<tr><td align="center">RSV</td><td align="center">TEV
Concerning Unsolved Murders</td></tr>
</table>

1 "If in the land which the LORD your God gives you to possess, any one is found slain, lying in the open country, and it is not known who killed him, 2 then your elders and your judges shall come forth, and they shall measure the distance to the cities which are around him that is slain; 3 and the elders of the city which is nearest to the slain man shall take a heifer which has never been worked and which has not pulled in the yoke. 4 And the elders of that city shall bring the heifer down to a valley with running water, which is neither plowed nor sown, and shall break the heifer's neck there in the valley. 5 And the priests the sons of Levi shall come forward, for the LORD your God has chosen them to minister to him and to bless in the name of the LORD, and by their word every dispute and every assault shall be settled. 6 And all the elders of that city nearest to the slain man shall wash their hands over the heifer whose neck was broken in the valley; 7 and they shall testify, 'Our hands did not shed this blood, neither did our eyes see it shed. 8 Forgive, O LORD, thy people Israel, whom thou hast redeemed, and set not the guilt of innocent blood in the midst of thy people Israel; but let the guilt of blood be forgiven them.' 9 So you shall purge the guilt of innocent blood from your midst, when you do what is right in the sight of the LORD.

1 "Suppose someone is found murdered in a field in the land that the LORD your God is going to give you, and you do not know who killed him. 2 Your leaders and judges are to go out and measure the distance from the place where the body was found to each of the nearby towns. 3 Then the leaders of the town nearest to where the body was found are to select a young cow that has never been used for work. 4 They are to take it down to a spot near a stream that never runs dry and where the ground has never been plowed or planted, and there they are to break its neck. 5 The levitical priests are to go there also, because they are to decide every legal case involving violence. The LORD your God has chosen them to serve him and to pronounce blessings in his name. 6 Then all the leaders from the town nearest the place where the murdered person was found are to wash their hands over the cow 7 and say, 'We did not murder this one, and we do not know who did it. 8 LORD, forgive your people Israel, whom you rescued from Egypt. Forgive us and do not hold us responsible for the murder of an innocent person.' 9 And so, by doing what the LORD requires, you will not be held responsible for the murder.

This and the next three sections are each structured as follows: "If such and such happens, this is what you are to do: . . . ." If possible, a uniform structure and wording should be used for all these sections. Each separate section also begins with a very long sentence covering three or more verses. This is much too long for most translations, and the material should be divided up into smaller units.

In this section the Israelites are told what they are to do when a dead body is discovered and the murderer is unknown.

Section heading: the TEV title "Concerning Unsolved Murders" may give the impression that the section deals with how to discover the murderer; but it may be difficult to find a short phrase that adequately covers the subject. REB uses rather technical language: "Expiation for an unsolved murder." In nontechnical language this may be "How to remove from the people the guilt of an unsolved murder," or "What to do when no one knows who killed someone."

21.1   RSV   TEV

"If in the land which the LORD your   "Suppose someone is found mur-
God gives you to possess, any one   dered in a field in the land that the
is found slain, lying in the open   LORD your God is going to give you,
country, and it is not known who   and you do not know who killed him.
killed him,

With the beginning of a new section, translators should reintroduce Moses
as the speaker.

The land which the LORD your God gives you to possess: a phrase recurring
throughout the book (see 3.18).

Any one is found slain: this is most probably a case of murder; but it could
be manslaughter (19.4-6), since the circumstances of the slaying are unknown.
In many languages the passive clause must be transformed into an active one;
for example, "and someone happens to find [or, comes upon] the body of a
person whom they [persons unknown] have killed."

Lying in the open country: that is, outside the town. In a village, or even a
city, it would be unusual for a murder to take place undetected. Both TEV and
CEV have "in a field," but a more general translation such as "away from where
people live" is probably more accurate.

It is not known who killed him: the killer is unknown. The Hebrew uses the
masculine pronoun **him**, but obviously the same instructions apply if the
murdered person is a woman. CEV and NRSV are able to avoid exclusive language; CEV has "Suppose the body of a murder victim is found . . . and no one
knows who the murderer is," and NRSV "If . . . a body is found . . . and it is not
known who struck the person down . . . ."

21.2   RSV   TEV

then your elders and your judges   Your leaders and judges are to go
shall come forth, and they shall mea-   out and measure the distance from
sure the distance to the cities which   the place where the body was found
are around him that is slain;   to each of the nearby towns.

Your elders and your judges: see 5.23 and 1.16. The possessive **your** refers
to the people of Israel as a whole.

Come forth: translators need to pay attention to the point of view; what this
means is that the **elders** and **judges** are to "go out" (TEV) to the place where the
body was discovered. In certain languages it will be necessary to state where
they go or come out from. It is evident that the passage means that they would
come from all the nearby towns. So we may translate "Your leaders and judges
must go out [or, come out] from the nearby towns and measure . . . ."

Measure the distance: the purpose of this is to determine which is the closest
town to the dead body. Instead of RSV **cities** it is better to say "towns" (TEV, CEV;
also NRSV). It is assumed here that the early Hebrews did have practical means
for measuring long distances such as this. However, the term used by a

translator should be a general one and not refer to a measuring stick or tape that would be employed today. If a general term cannot be found, we may say something like "estimate" or "find out," and **measure the distance** may be expressed as "estimate the distance from the place where the body was found to each of the nearby towns."

Which are around him that is slain: this is a literal rendering of the Hebrew text. NRSV has "the towns that are near the body"; more natural translations in English are NIV "the neighboring towns" or NJB "the surrounding towns."

21.3   RSV   TEV

and the elders of the city which is nearest to the slain man shall take a heifer which has never been worked and which has not pulled in the yoke.	**Then the leaders of the town nearest to where the body was found are to select a young cow that has never been used for work.**

The elders of the city which is nearest: once it has been determined which is the closest town, **the elders** of that town are to handle the matter.

A heifer which has never been worked and which has not pulled in the yoke: this is a typical case of repetition, in which the general statement about work is followed by a statement referring to the particular type of work.

In the yoke: in English, the preposition **in** here means that the "young cow" (TEV) has not had a yoke placed around its neck so that it could pull the plow (see Num 19.2). TEV has "select a young cow that has never been used for work." In languages that do not use the passive voice, we may say "select a young cow that they have never used for work."

21.4   RSV   TEV

And the elders of that city shall bring the heifer down to a valley with running water, which is neither plowed nor sown, and shall break the heifer's neck there in the valley.	**They are to take it down to a spot near a stream that never runs dry and where the ground has never been plowed or planted, and there they are to break its neck.**

Bring the heifer down: the place where the **heifer** is to be killed is, like the animal itself, a place that has not been used for any purpose. It is still wild, it has never been farmed, **neither plowed nor sown**, or "where they [people in general] have never plowed the ground or sown crops."

A valley with running water: this is not a stream that appears and disappears with the seasonal rains, but an ever flowing stream fed by a spring. TEV has "a stream that never runs dry." We may also express this as "a stream that flows all year."

Break the heifer's neck: presumably by means of a blow with a pole, or an ax. This animal is not being sacrificed to God (see Exo 13.13; 34.20). This is not a sacrifice to take away sin.

21.5   RSV   TEV

And the priests the sons of Levi shall come forward, for the LORD your God has chosen them to minister to him and to bless in the name of the LORD, and by their word every dispute and every assault shall be settled.	The levitical priests are to go there also, because they are to decide every legal case involving violence. The LORD your God has chosen them to serve him and to pronounce blessings in his name.

The priests . . . shall come forward: once they have been notified of the case, they are to be in charge of the proceedings.

For the LORD your God has chosen them: **for** introduces the reason why the priests are to have a role in the case.

To minister to him: that is, they are in charge of worship (see 10.8). TEV has "chosen them to serve him," but CEV is better, with "chosen them to be his special servants at the place of worship."

To bless in the name of the LORD: the priests, the authorized representatives of the LORD, invoke his blessings upon the people. This may also be expressed as "to ask Yahweh to give them prosperity and well-being." Translators should look for the most natural way of expressing the idea of "well-being."

By their word every dispute and every assault shall be settled: again a repetition, the general class (**every dispute**, that is, "quarrels," "arguments," "controversies") and the particular type of case (**every assault**, that is, arguments that result in "violence" or "bodily harm"). See also 17.8-13. FRCL translates "matters of blows and wounds." TEV has "every legal case involving violence." We may also translate "every legal case where people hurt each other."

For the statement **by their word . . . shall be settled**, SPCL has "their decision will be final." This final clause may also be translated as "they are to decide every legal case involving violence."

A possible alternative translation model reordering the clauses of the verse is:

- The priests the descendants of Levi are to go there also, because they are to decide every legal case where people hurt each other. The LORD your God has chosen them to serve him and to ask him to give the people prosperity and well-being.

21.6   RSV   TEV

And all the elders of that city nearest to the slain man shall wash their hands over the heifer whose neck was broken in the valley;	Then all the leaders from the town nearest the place where the murdered person was found are to wash their hands over the cow

All the elders: as in verse 4.

Shall wash their hands over the heifer whose neck was broken in the valley: this repeats old information, which in some languages may not be very good style. It may be enough to say "shall wash their hands over the dead heifer" or "over the body of the dead cow." By this means the town leaders are transferring to the dead animal any guilt that may have been laid on the people of Israel as a whole (see similar proceedings in Lev 16.20-22).

21.7	RSV	TEV

and they shall testify, 'Our hands did not shed this blood, neither did our eyes see it shed.	and say, 'We did not murder this one, and we do not know who did it.

They shall testify: this translates two Hebrew verbs, "declare and say," giving the sense of a solemn declaration, a formal statement. They speak as representatives of the people. Translators need to find a term in their language that is similar to "solemnly declare" or "state emphatically."

Our hands did not shed this blood: they are speaking for the people of Israel. **Our hands** are those of the people as a whole, not just the hands of the elders. "We did not kill [or, 'murder,' TEV] this person," or even "We had no part in this murder" (CEV).

Neither did our eyes see it shed: that is, "nor did we see who committed the murder," or "we did not witness this bloodshed" (REB).

21.8	RSV	TEV

Forgive, O LORD, thy people Israel, whom thou hast redeemed, and set not the guilt of innocent blood in the midst of thy people Israel; but let the guilt of blood be forgiven them.'	LORD, forgive your people Israel, whom you rescued from Egypt. Forgive us and do not hold us responsible for the murder of an innocent person.'

Then the elders will pray, asking Yahweh to forgive the people. In some languages it will be helpful to begin this verse as follows: "Then the elders will pray to Yahweh, saying, '. . . .'" But it is possible also to understand everything the elders say (beginning with "Our hands did not shed this blood" in verse 7) as a prayer. In this case verse 8 will follow without any break, as in RSV and TEV.

Forgive: or "Absolve" (NRSV, NJPSV), or even "Expiate" (see REB "Accept expiation"; NIV "Accept this atonement"). But it seems best to use the more common and understandable term, **Forgive** (TEV, NJB, SPCL, BRCL, FRCL). **Forgive** is a difficult term to translate in many languages. Examples from a variety of languages that may be helpful to translators are "throw away sin," "cover over sin," "forget sin," and so on. *A Handbook on the Gospel of Mark*, page 13, gives many more useful examples. Other ways to translate **Forgive, O LORD**,

thy people Israel are "Yahweh, please forgive your people, Israel," or "Yahweh, please forget the sin of the people of Israel. We are your people."

Whom thou hast redeemed: this refers back to the liberation from Egypt (the Septuagint includes "from the land of Egypt" in its translation). So TEV has "rescued from Egypt."

Set not . . . in the midst of thy people Israel: "do not hold your people Israel responsible," or "please don't hold us responsible."

The guilt of innocent blood: that is, "the responsibility for the death [or, murder] of an innocent person."

Let the guilt of blood be forgiven them: using the same verb used at the beginning of the prayer. Translators need to decide whether this repetition is good style in their language or not. TEV doesn't repeat this sentence, but CEV makes a separate sentence, with "Please don't hold this crime against us." We may also make the meaning of **guilt of blood** or "crime" clear with "Please don't hold us responsible for murdering [or, killing] this person."

An alternative translation model for this verse is:

- Then the elders will pray to Yahweh, saying, "Please forgive the people of Israel. We are your people, and you rescued us from Egypt. Please don't hold us responsible for killing this innocent person."

21.9	RSV	TEV
	So you shall purge the guilt of innocent blood from your midst, when you do what is right in the sight of the LORD.	And so, by doing what the LORD requires, you will not be held responsible for the murder.

You shall purge . . . from your midst: see 13.5, and especially 19.13. However, the reference in these two passages is to purging the land of a killer by executing him. Since the killer is not known in this case, the people purge their guilt by doing what Yahweh requires, namely killing a young cow. So the translation may be "Yahweh will not hold you responsible for the murder of this person."

You do what is right: here, **what is right** is what God tells them to do. The Septuagint has the compound phrase "good and proper," which is what the Hebrew text in 6.18 has.

In the sight of the LORD: this goes with **what is right**, not with **when you do**. This is what Yahweh considers the right thing to do.

In many languages it will be better to place the second clause at the beginning, as TEV has done.

2B-26. How to treat a woman taken as a prisoner of war (21.10-14)

RSV

TEV
Concerning Women Prisoners of War

10 "When you go forth to war against your enemies, and the LORD your God gives them into your hands, and you take them captive, 11 and see among the captives a beautiful woman, and you have desire for her and would take her for yourself as wife, 12 then you shall bring her home to your house, and she shall shave her head and pare her nails. 13 And she shall put off her captive's garb, and shall remain in your house and bewail her father and her mother a full month; after that you may go in to her, and be her husband, and she shall be your wife. 14 Then, if you have no delight in her, you shall let her go where she will; but you shall not sell her for money, you shall not treat her as a slave, since you have humiliated her.

10 "When the LORD your God gives you victory in battle and you take prisoners, 11 you may see among them a beautiful woman that you like and want to marry. 12 Take her to your home, where she will shave her head, cut her fingernails, 13 and change her clothes. She is to stay in your home and mourn for her parents for a month; after that, you may marry her. 14 Later, if you no longer want her, you are to let her go free. Since you forced her to have intercourse with you, you cannot treat her as a slave and sell her.

The form and structure of this section are like those of the previous one.

Section heading: the title for this section should not be difficult to formulate: "How to treat a woman taken as a prisoner of war," or even "How to treat a woman whom you capture when you fight your enemies."

21.10   RSV   TEV

"When you go forth to war against your enemies, and the LORD your God gives them into your hands, and you take them captive,

"When the LORD your God gives you victory in battle and you take prisoners,

With the beginning of a new section, it will be helpful to begin with something like "Moses said to the Israelites, '. . . .'"

When you go forth to war against your enemies: this does not necessarily mean that the Israelites are taking the offensive; it means simply "when you are fighting your enemies." For **enemies** see 1.42.

The LORD your God gives them into your hands: this is a way of saying ". . . gives you the victory over them," or "helps you defeat your enemies [or, those that hate you]."

You take them captive: this does not mean taking all of them as captives; "when you take some prisoners [of war]" or "when you capture some of them."

354

21.11 RSV TEV

and see among the captives a beau-   you may see among them a beautiful
tiful woman, and you have desire for   woman that you like and want to
her and would take her for yourself   marry.
as wife,

A problem now arises in the switch from the plural forms of the verbs
referring to the Israelites (actually, in Hebrew, the singular is used for the
people as a whole) to the singular masculine form in verse 11. To display this
switch in English we would have to say, "And one [masculine] of you sees . . .
and you [masculine] want . . . ."

Sees among the captives a beautiful woman: except for **captives**, this offers
no difficulty. The more current form in English is "prisoners of war"; and, as the
rest of the section makes clear (see verse 13), the woman is unmarried.
However, if the term **captives** ("prisoners of war") was used at the end of the
previous verse, it will not be necessary to repeat it here. We may say "And one
of you sees a beautiful woman among them [the captives]."

You have desire for her: this means sexual desire, and a clear, but not
vulgar, term should be used. If a suitable expression cannot be found, it is
possible to combine it with the following clause and say, for example, "and want
to take her to be your wife."

And would take her for yourself as wife: in some languages this will be
expressed just like the Hebrew, while in others it will be rendered, for example,
as "you want to marry her" (NRSV; similarly CEV).

21.12 RSV TEV

then you shall bring her home to   Take her to your home, where she
your house, and she shall shave her   will shave her head,^{t} cut her finger-
head and pare her nails.   nails,

                                   ^{t} shave her head; *or* trim her hair.

You shall bring her home to your house: again the point of view is important; some languages will prefer "bring her," but in others it will be better to
say "you will take her home with you."

She shall shave her head and pare her nails: as the TEV footnote shows, the
Hebrew phrase translated **shave her head** can mean "trim her hair." The
Hebrew text has the third person feminine singular, as translated; the
Septuagint has the second singular, "you will shave . . . ." It is recommended
that translators follow the Hebrew. Another way to express this is "You shall
have her shave her head and pare her nails." These are signs of a new identity:
she is breaking her relationship with her own people and becoming a member
of the people of Israel.

21.13   RSV   TEV

And she shall put off her captive's   and change her clothes. She is to
garb, and shall remain in your house   stay in your home and mourn for her
and bewail her father and her mother   parents for a month; after that, you
a full month; after that you may go in   may marry her.
to her, and be her husband, and she
shall be your wife.

She shall put off her captive's garb: or "discard the clothes she had when she
was captured" (REB). Again, instead of "captured," "taken prisoner [of war]" is
better. So we may translate "She shall take off [or, get rid of] the clothes she
was wearing when they took her captive."

**Shall remain in your house and bewail her father and her mother a full
month**: this indicates that she is unmarried. **Bewail** here may be understood as
a ritual mourning or weeping over the death or loss of her parents.

**After that you may go in to her, and be her husband, and she shall be your
wife**: this is a very wordy way of saying, "After the month is up, you are free to
marry her." REB "you may have intercourse with her" is actually closer to the
Hebrew text, but since the act of intercourse, in this context, assumes
marriage, it is better to use the verb "to marry." The initiative is his, and the
woman's feelings are not relevant. The Hebrew for "be her husband" is "be her
baal," which, depending on the context, can mean either "lord" or "husband" (in
Hebrew society the husband was the lord).

21.14   RSV   TEV

Then, if you have no delight in her,   Later, if you no longer want her, you
you shall let her go where she will;   are to let her go free. Since you
but you shall not sell her for money,   forced her to have intercourse with
you shall not treat her as a slave,   you, you cannot treat her as a slave
since you have humiliated her.   and sell her.

If you have no delight in her: that is, "if she doesn't please you any longer,"
"if you lose your desire for her," or "if you no longer want to have sex with her."

You shall let her go: the Hebrew verb is used in the context of divorce in
22.19, 29 (CEV "you can divorce her"). Other ways to express "divorce her" are
"send her away," or perhaps "return her to her own people."

Where she will: this is important; she's a free (Israelite) woman, and no
restrictions are placed on her freedom to go anywhere she wants to.

You shall not sell her for money: in Hebrew the verb form is emphatic.

You shall not treat her as a slave: the Hebrew verb is used only here and in
24.7, and its precise meaning is disputed. REB has "treat her harshly," NJPSV
"enslave her," and BRCL "mistreat her." Some commentators take the meaning
to be "treat her as merchandise." It seems best to follow RSV and TEV here. For
slave see 5.6.

You have humiliated her: as TEV makes clear, this refers to his having had intercourse with her; she had no choice in the matter and was forced to have sex with him. CEV has "But you have slept with her as your wife."

2B-27. Concerning the first son's inheritance (21.15-17)

RSV	TEV
	Concerning the First Son's Inheritance
15 "If a man has two wives, the one loved and the other disliked, and they have borne him children, both the loved and the disliked, and if the first-born son is hers that is disliked, 16 then on the day when he assigns his possessions as an inheritance to his sons, he may not treat the son of the loved as the first-born in preference to the son of the disliked, who is the first-born, 17 but he shall acknowledge the first-born, the son of the disliked, by giving him a double portion of all that he has, for he is the first issue of his strength; the right of the first-born is his.	15 "Suppose a man has two wives and they both bear him sons, but the first son is not the child of his favorite wife. 16 When the man decides how he is going to divide his property among his children, he is not to show partiality to the son of his favorite wife by giving him the share that belongs to the first-born son. 17 He is to give a double share of his possessions to his first son, even though he is not the son of his favorite wife. A man must acknowledge his first son and give him the share he is legally entitled to.

Again the same structure and form are used, in one long sentence.

Section heading: in many languages there will be a widely used term for "firstborn [or, first] son," and that term should be used in the title of the section. Possible titles are "Concerning the First Son's Inheritance" (TEV), "Rights of a First-born Son" (CEV), and so on.

21.15 RSV	TEV
"If a man has two wives, the one loved and the other disliked, and they have borne him children, both the loved and the disliked, and if the first-born son is hers that is disliked,	"Suppose a man has two wives and they both bear him sons, but the first son is not the child of his favorite wife.

With the beginning of a new section, translators are urged to reintroduce Moses as the speaker.

The one loved and the other disliked: this is usually taken to mean that the man loves one wife more than the other, not that he actively dislikes (or, hates) one of his two wives. But it may be that the two terms are meant literally; in Mal 1.2-3, as the context shows, "hate" really means "hate" (see the use of this passage in Rom 9.13). It is recommended by this Handbook, however, that translators follow the interpretation taken by TEV and CEV, that the man loves one of the wives more than the other. TEV has "his favorite wife," and CEV translates "loves one more than the other."

They have borne him children: in the context "sons" is meant; daughters are not included. So TEV: "and they both bear him sons."

The first-born son is hers that is disliked: this is not natural English. The sense is "the wife he dislikes [or, likes less] bore his first son." The matter was of great importance to the women, since they would be supported by their sons after their husband's death.

TEV has a helpful translation model for this verse.

21.16   RSV   TEV

| then on the day when he assigns his possessions as an inheritance to his sons, he may not treat the son of the loved as the first-born in preference to the son of the disliked, who is the first-born, | When the man decides how he is going to divide his property among his children, he is not to show partiality to the son of his favorite wife by giving him the share that belongs to the first-born son. |

Then on the day may also be expressed as "when," or even "later, when . . ." (CEV).

When he assigns his possessions as an inheritance to his sons: here the TEV translation "children" for **sons** is not exact. The daughters play no role in the distribution of the man's estate; the assumption is that daughters get married and so will be taken care of by their husbands. An alternative model for this first sentence is "Later, when the man divides the property among his sons, ..."

In preference to: this translates a Hebrew idiomatic phrase, "over the face of," which indicates preference (also in 5.7). This final sentence may also be expressed as "he is not to show partiality to the son of his favorite wife by giving him the share that belongs to the first-born son."

21.17   RSV   TEV

| but he shall acknowledge the first-born, the son of the disliked, by giving him a double portion of all that he has, for he is the first issue of his strength; the right of the first-born is his. | He is to give a double share of his possessions to his first son, even though he is not the son of his favorite wife. A man must acknowledge his first son and give him the share he is legally entitled to. |

He shall acknowledge the first-born: in Hebrew this is the main clause. To keep the meaning of the whole verse clear, TEV has reordered the clauses and made them into separate sentences. In this context **acknowledge** means to show that the son of the wife who is not his favorite is indeed the first-born, and his rights will be respected.

By giving him a double portion of all that he has: the oldest son was given two-thirds of his father's property; the remaining one-third went to the younger brothers (or, brother).

He is the first issue of his strength: there may be some cultures in which there is an appropriate way to express this (as in the Hebrew culture), but this is not the case in those cultures whose language is English. All English language translations are artificial and awkward: NIV "That son is the first sign of his father's strength"; REB "the firstfruits of his manhood"; NJB, NJPSV "the first fruits of his vigor." Both TEV and CEV omit this clause as too repetitive, and other translators should do this, unless their language has an idiom similar to the Hebrew.

An alternative translation model combining verses 16 and 17 is the following:

- [16-17] Later, when the man divides the property among his sons, he must give a double share to his first-born son, even though he is not the son of his favorite wife.

2B-28. Concerning a disobedient son (21.18-21)

RSV	TEV
	Concerning a Disobedient Son
18 "If a man has a stubborn and rebellious son, who will not obey the voice of his father or the voice of his mother, and, though they chastise him, will not give heed to them, 19 then his father and his mother shall take hold of him and bring him out to the elders of his city at the gate of the place where he lives, 20 and they shall say to the elders of his city, 'This our son is stubborn and rebellious, he will not obey our voice; he is a glutton and a drunkard.' 21 Then all the men of the city shall stone him to death with stones; so you shall purge the evil from your midst; and all Israel shall hear, and fear.	18 "Suppose someone has a son who is stubborn and rebellious, a son who will not obey his parents, even though they punish him. 19 His parents are to take him before the leaders of the town where he lives and make him stand trial. 20 They are to say to them, 'Our son is stubborn and rebellious and refuses to obey us; he wastes money and is a drunkard.' 21 Then the men of the city are to stone him to death, and so you will get rid of this evil. Everyone in Israel will hear what has happened and be afraid.

Again the same form and structure, with verses 18-20 as one sentence. As the context shows, the son is a young adult (see 5.16; Exo 21.15).

Section heading: possible headings are "Concerning a Disobedient Son" (TEV), "A Son who Rebels" (CEV), or "How to treat a son who rebels against his parents."

21.18	RSV	TEV

"If a man has a stubborn and rebellious son, who will not obey the voice of his father or the voice of his mother, and, though they chastise him, will not give heed to them,	**"Suppose someone has a son who is stubborn and rebellious, a son who will not obey his parents, even though they punish him.**

With the beginning of a new section, translators should reintroduce Moses as the speaker.

A man: this is what the Hebrew says. TEV "someone" is not good, since in this context the father is in focus. So translators may use either **man** or "father."

A stubborn and rebellious son: so RSV, TEV, CEV, NRSV, NEB (see verse 26; Psa 78.8; Jer 5.23). This is the best way to translate the two adjectives. NJPSV has "wayward and defiant." For **stubborn** see 9.6, and for **rebellious** see 9.7.

Who will not obey the voice of his father or the voice of his mother: this represents the rather wordy Hebrew text, which is reinforced by the last clause, **will not give heed to them**. TEV has simply "who will not obey his parents."

They chastise him: this most likely involves physical punishment (see 22.18; Pro 13.24; 22.14; 23.13-14; 29.15), although the verb may mean simply "to discipline" or "punish" (see 8.5).

21.19   RSV   TEV

| then his father and his mother shall take hold of him and bring him out to the elders of his city at the gate of the place where he lives, | His parents are to take him before the leaders of the town where he lives and make him stand trial. |

Take hold of: this does not necessarily mean to conduct him as a prisoner to the place of judgment, but simply to take him there (TEV "take him before").

The elders of his city: see verse 6. As in other passages in Deuteronomy, **city** should be "town" (see 1.1, 28).

At the gate of the place where he lives: this refers to the open space in the town, near the gate in the town wall, where legal and commercial matters were settled (see 22.15; 25.7; Ruth 4.1-2, 15; Amos 5.10, 12, 15).

21.20   RSV   TEV

| and they shall say to the elders of his city, 'This our son is stubborn and rebellious, he will not obey our voice; he is a glutton and a drunkard.' | They are to say to them, 'Our son is stubborn and rebellious and refuses to obey us; he wastes money and is a drunkard.' |

Is stubborn and rebellious: the same words used in verse 18.

He will not obey our voice: as in verse 18.

A glutton and a drunkard: see the same phrase in Pro 23.20-21. Some take the Hebrew noun translated **glutton** to mean "spendthrift" (NJB) or "wastrel" (REB); NIV has "profligate"; TEV has "wastes money and is a drunkard." There is no way to be sure which is better; a term like **glutton** fits in nicely with **drunkard**; a **glutton** is someone who eats too much food, while a **drunkard** is someone who drinks too much wine. If there aren't exact technical terms available, we may translate "He eats too much food and drinks too much wine."

21.21   RSV   TEV

Then all the men of the city shall stone him to death with stones; so you shall purge the evil from your midst; and all Israel shall hear, and fear.	Then the men of the city are to stone him to death, and so you will get rid of this evil. Everyone in Israel will hear what has happened and be afraid.

Stone him to death: this is the action commanded (see 13.10).
Purge the evil from your midst: the effect of taking the action (see verse 9).
All Israel shall hear, and fear: the result (see 13.11).

2B-29. Laws concerning moral purity and personal cleanliness (21.22–23.14)

In this section eleven matters are dealt with. There is no apparent main topic around which the individual regulations revolve. One commentator proposes "Enhancing Solidarity," which is certainly broad enough to include about everything. The modern reader has trouble understanding the basis for some of these laws (for example, those laws listed in verses 5, 9-12); but, as commentators point out, it must have been obvious to the original readers. Other commentators point out that all the rules, with the exception of the last one, deal with respecting different forms of life, of God's created order.

Section heading: the Handbook heading attempts to cover the whole section. TEV and NIV have the title "Various Laws" for 21.22–22.12, and this can also just as well apply to the whole section to 23.14. However, it is also possible to make 21.22-23 a separate section with the title "The Body of a Criminal" (CEV) or "How to treat the dead body [or, corpse] of a criminal" (similarly FRCL and NRSV).

(a) How to treat a dead body (21.22-23)

RSV   TEV
                                      Various Laws

22 "And if a man has committed a crime punishable by death and he is put to death, and you hang him on a tree, 23 his body shall not remain all night upon the tree, but you shall bury him the same day, for a hanged man is accursed by God; you shall not defile your land which the LORD your God gives you for an inheritance.	22 "If someone has been put to death for a crime and the body is hung on a post, 23 it is not to remain there overnight. It must be buried the same day, because a dead body hanging on a post brings God's curse on the land. Bury the body, so that you will not defile the land that the LORD your God is giving you.

The reason for this law is that the body of a criminal impaled on a stake is a great disgrace; it "defiles the land" (verse 23).

Section heading: the suggested heading, "How to treat a dead body," should present no difficulty for translators.

21.22   RSV   TEV

"And if a man has committed a   "If someone has been put to death
crime punishable by death and he is   for a crime and the body is hung on
put to death, and you hang him on a   a post,
tree,

It will be helpful as at the beginning of other sections to begin with "Moses
said to the people of Israel" or something similar.

A crime punishable by death: in today's English jargon this is styled "a
capital offense" (NJB, NJPSV, REB).

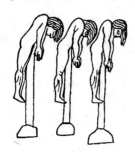

He is put to death: the text does not say how.
Presumably it is by stoning. In languages that do not
use the passive voice, we may translate "they [people
not named] put him to death." However, in some
languages the passive may be avoided through the
use of a verb similar to "suffer"; for example, "If a
man suffers death for . . . ." It is possible to avoid the
repetition in the Hebrew of this first sentence, with
something like "If they have put to death [or, exe-
cuted] a man who has committed a crime" (see TEV).

ANCIENT DRAWING OF   **Hang him on a tree**: this can mean that he is hung
VICTIMS ON STAKES   by his neck to a tree. The Hebrew word may mean
                            either "tree" or "wood" (that is, a stake, or a pole); see
Josh 8.29; 10.26-27; 2 Sam 4.12. Probably impalement is meant; the dead body
was fixed to a stake, or pole, driven into the ground. TEV here is quite
unsatisfactory.

21.23   RSV   TEV

his body shall not remain all night   it is not to remain there overnight. It
upon the tree, but you shall bury him   must be buried the same day, be-
the same day, for a hanged man is   cause a dead body hanging on a
accursed by God; you shall not de-   post brings God's curse on the land.
file your land which the LORD your   Bury the body, so that you will not
God gives you for an inheritance.   defile the land that the LORD your
                                        God is giving you.

Shall not remain all night: that is, the body is to be removed before sunset of
that same day (see Josh 8.29; 10.27); "Be sure to bury him that same day" (NIV).
TEV has "it [the body] is not to remain there overnight," and CEV "you must not
let it hang there overnight."

You shall bury him the same day: the Hebrew is emphatic, using the
compound form of the verb. Another way of emphasizing this is "He must be
buried the same day."

Accursed by God: not because the body is impaled on a stake, but because it is the body of a criminal put to death for his (or her) crime. The translation should not suggest that God curses the corpse; rather, this is a strong expression for something that is an offense or abomination to God. TEV has "because a dead body hanging on a post brings God's curse on the land" (similarly CEV). "Brings God's curse upon" may be transformed to "causes God to curse the land," or even "makes God say, 'May the land become cursed [or, unclean].' " (In Gal 3.13 Paul applies this verse to Christ's crucifixion.)

Defile the land: that is, render it unfit for the worship of the God of Israel.

Your land which the LORD your God gives you for an inheritance: see verse 1.

(b) Some other laws (22.1-12)

RSV

1 "You shall not see your brother's ox or his sheep go astray, and withhold your help from them; you shall take them back to your brother. 2 And if he is not near you, or if you do not know him, you shall bring it home to your house, and it shall be with you until your brother seeks it; then you shall restore it to him. 3 And so you shall do with his ass; so you shall do with his garment; so you shall do with any lost thing of your brother's, which he loses and you find; you may not withhold your help. 4 You shall not see your brother's ass or his ox fallen down by the way, and withhold your help from them; you shall help him to lift them up again.

5 "A woman shall not wear anything that pertains to a man, nor shall a man put on a woman's garment; for whoever does these things is an abomination to the LORD your God.

6 "If you chance to come upon a bird's nest, in any tree or on the ground, with young ones or eggs and the mother sitting upon the young or upon the eggs, you shall not take the mother with the young; 7 you shall let the mother go, but the young you may take to yourself; that it may go well with you, and that you may live long.

8 "When you build a new house, you shall make a parapet for your roof, that you may not bring the guilt of blood upon your house, if any one fall from it.

9 "You shall not sow your vineyard with two kinds of seed, lest the whole yield be forfeited to the sanctuary, the crop which you have sown and the yield of the vineyard. 10 You shall not plow with an ox and an ass together. 11 You shall not wear a mingled stuff, wool and linen together.

TEV

1 "If you see an Israelite's cow or sheep running loose, do not ignore it; take it back. 2 But if its owner lives a long way off or if you don't know who owns it, then take it home with you. When its owner comes looking for it, give it to him. 3 Do the same thing if you find a donkey, a piece of clothing, or anything else that an Israelite may have lost.

4 "If an Israelite's donkey or cow has fallen down, don't ignore it; help him get the animal to its feet again.

5 "Women are not to wear men's clothing, and men are not to wear women's clothing; the LORD your God hates people who do such things.

6 "If you happen to find a bird's nest in a tree or on the ground with the mother bird sitting either on the eggs or with her young, you are not to take the mother bird. 7 You may take the young birds, but you must let the mother bird go, so that you will live a long and prosperous life.

8 "When you build a new house, be sure to put a railing around the edge of the roof. Then you will not be responsible if someone falls off and is killed.

9 "Do not plant any crop in the same field with your grapevines; if you do, you are forbidden to use either the grapes or the produce of the other crop.

10 "Do not hitch an ox and a donkey together for plowing.

11 "Do not wear cloth made by weaving wool and linen together.

12 "Sew tassels on the four corners of your clothes.

363

12 "You shall make yourself tassels on the four corners of your cloak with which you cover yourself.

Section heading: the suggested heading is "Some other laws."

22.1	RSV	TEV

"**You shall not see your brother's ox or his sheep go astray, and withhold your help**ᵖ **from them; you shall take them back to your brother.**

"**If you see an Israelite's cow or sheep running loose, do not ignore it; take it back.**

ᵖ Heb *hide yourself*

Verses 1-4 deal with a single theme: providing help to a fellow-Israelite in case his animals wander off or lie helpless on the ground (see Exo 23.4-5, where the same kind of help is to be given to an enemy). In all these verses **brother** (also NEB, NJB) is a "fellow Israelite" (TEV, BRCL), or "fellow countryman" (REB, POCL, SPCL, FRCL); NJPSV "your fellow" is not natural, and NRSV "your neighbor" carries the wrong meaning.

If this is the beginning of a new section, Moses should be reintroduced as the speaker.

You shall not see . . . and withhold: it is better to structure as TEV does, "If you see . . . do not ignore it."

You: in the nature of the case, this is singular; so SPCL has "one of you."

Ox: TEV "cow" seems better in referring to cattle as a class (bovines). For "cow" see 5.14.

Sheep: the Hebrew term may apply to the young of sheep or goats; so FRCL has "goat or sheep." For **sheep** see 17.1.

Go astray: that is, the animal has wandered off. CEV has "wandering around lost."

Withhold your help: as the RSV footnote indicates, this translates the Hebrew "hide yourself." In English other ways to say this are "do not ignore it" (TEV, NJPSV, NIV) and "you must not disregard it" (NJB); other possible translations are "don't act as though you didn't see it" (BRCL); "don't pass by unconcernedly" (POCL).

Take them back: since the likelihood is that it is one animal or the other, not both an **ox** and a **sheep**, it is better to use the singular "it."

22.2	RSV	TEV

And if he is not near you, or if you do not know him, you shall bring it home to your house, and it shall be

But if its owner lives a long way off or if you don't know who owns it, then take it home with you. When its

with you until your brother seeks it; then you shall restore it to him.

owner comes looking for it, give it to him.

And if . . . or if . . . : here the people are told what to do if the owner of the animal lives a long way off or is unknown. The directions are quite clear, and there are no particular problems with the structure of the discourse or the meaning of the words. By saying "its owner," TEV (also FRCL, SPCL) neatly handles the problem of trying to translate **your brother**. In languages like English, that differentiate between the neuter **it** (the animal) and the masculine **he** (the owner), there is no problem in making it clear which is referred to. But where there is no neuter form, a translator must make sure that there is no confusion in determining who or what the pronouns refer to.

An alternative translation model for this verse is:

- If the owner of the animal lives too far away, or if you [singular] don't know who owns it, take the animal home with you. When its owner comes looking for it, give it back to him.

22.3 RSV TEV

And so you shall do with his ass; so you shall do with his garment; so you shall do with any lost thing of your brother's, which he loses and you find; you may not withhold your help.

Do the same thing if you find a donkey, a piece of clothing, or anything else that an Israelite may have lost.

And so you shall do: this verse expands the instructions to apply to a fellow Israelite's **ass**, **garment**, or anything else he may have lost (**any lost thing of your brother's**). For **ass** or "donkey" see 5.14.

You may not withhold your help: using the same verb used in verse 1. TEV expresses this clause at the beginning of the verse, with "Do the same thing," referring back to **help** in verse 1. CEV has "Do whatever you can to help."

22.4 RSV TEV

You shall not see your brother's ass or his ox fallen down by the way, and withhold your help[p] from them; you shall help him to lift them up again.

"If an Israelite's donkey or cow has fallen down, don't ignore it; help him get the animal to its feet again.

[p] Heb *hide yourself*

By the way: meaning "along the road" (CEV). The animal's owner is there, trying to lift it up.

You shall help him to lift them up again: The Hebrew is emphatic, with the double use of the verb, "helping lift up ... you shall help." TEV has "help him get the animal to its feet again." We may also translate in a way similar to the Hebrew, with "You shall help him lift the animal up so that it stands on its feet again."

22.5	RSV	TEV

"A woman shall not wear anything that pertains to a man, nor shall a man put on a woman's garment; for whoever does these things is an abomination to the LORD your God. | "Women are not to wear men's clothing, and men are not to wear women's clothing; the LORD your God hates people who do such things.

This law deals with transvestism, that is, using clothes normally worn by members of the other sex. It is called an **abomination**, which seems to link it up with customs associated with pagan cults. For the word **abomination** itself see 7.24; 18.12. In Lev 18.22 and 20.13 the same word is applied to homosexual behavior.

Anything that pertains to a man: this seems to include other things besides clothes, such as adornments and weapons. But in parallel with **a woman's garment**, it probably means simply a man's clothes.

22.6-7	RSV	TEV

6 "If you chance to come upon a bird's nest, in any tree or on the ground, with young ones or eggs and the mother sitting upon the young or upon the eggs, you shall not take the mother with the young; 7 you shall let the mother go, but the young you may take to yourself; that it may go well with you, and that you may live long. | 6 "If you happen to find a bird's nest in a tree or on the ground with the mother bird sitting either on the eggs or with her young, you are not to take the mother bird. 7 You may take the young birds, but you must let the mother bird go, so that you will live a long and prosperous life.

The underlying purpose in these instructions is not just humanitarian concern for other forms of life, but the preservation of a food source. A mother bird will lay more eggs and produce more young.

That it may go well with you, and that you may live long: this probably means more than a long life as such. It means the people will live for many generations in the Promised Land (see discussion at 6.2). TEV gives a helpful model for this verse; so also does CEV: ". . . Let her go free, and the LORD will bless you with a long and successful life."

22.8 RSV TEV

"When you build a new house, you shall make a parapet for your roof, that you may not bring the guilt of blood upon your house, if any one fall from it.

"When you build a new house, be sure to put a railing around the edge of the roof. Then you will not be responsible if someone falls off and is killed.

A parapet for your roof: a **parapet** is a railing placed at the edges of the flat roof. The roof was reached by outside steps, and people would gather there to relax and visit; see Josh 2.6; 2 Kgs 4.10. In some languages **a parapet** will be expressed as "a low wall."

The guilt of blood: responsibility for someone's death (see 19.10; 21.8). TEV has "then you will not be responsible if . . . ."

A ROOFTOP WITH A PARAPET

If any one fall from it: that is, ". . . fall to his or her death"; in this context the word **blood** carries the sense of a violent death. The last part of the verse may also be expressed as "Then if someone falls off the roof and is killed, it won't be your fault" (CEV).

22.9 RSV TEV

"You shall not sow your vineyard with two kinds of seed, lest the whole yield be forfeited to the sanctuary,[q] the crop which you have sown and the yield of the vineyard.

"Do not plant any crop in the same field with your grapevines; if you do, you are forbidden to use either the grapes or the produce of the other crop.

[q] Heb *become holy*

The three instructions in verses 9-11 have to do with what is regarded as an unnatural mixing of two different forms of creation (see the parallel in Lev 19.19).

Sow your vineyard with two kinds of seeds: this means sowing some sort of crop in the rows between the grapevines. So TEV has "Do not plant any crop in the same field with your grapevines." For **vineyard** see 6.11.

Lest the whole yield be forfeited to the sanctuary: as the RSV footnote indicates, this translates the causative form of the Hebrew verb "be holy." The meaning is that in this case both the crops and the wine belong to the LORD and will go to the Temple. There are various translations possible: ". . . may not be used" (NJPSV), "everything would be dedicated to the LORD" (FRCL, POCL), "you will not be allowed to use . . ." (SPCL), or even "you must bring to the place of worship everything you harvest from the vineyard" (CEV).

22.10   RSV   TEV

You shall not plow with an ox and an   **"Do not hitch an ox and a donkey**
ass together.   **together for plowing.**

The reason for the law prohibiting plowing with **an ox and an ass** yoked
together is not clear. The **ox** was considered to be a "clean" animal, the **ass**
"unclean" (14.1-8). Another way to express this is "Do not hitch an ox and a
donkey together when you plow the ground."

22.11   RSV   TEV

You shall not wear a mingled stuff,   **"Do not wear cloth made by weav-**
wool and linen together.   **ing wool and linen together.**

Wear a mingled stuff, wool and linen together: this old English means to
wear clothing made of wool and linen woven together. Where weaving is
unknown, or where **wool** and **linen** are also unknown, it is possible to say
simply "clothes made of two different kinds of thread."

22.12   RSV   TEV

"You shall make yourself tassels   **"Sew tassels on the four corners**
on the four corners of your cloak   **of your clothes.**
with which you cover yourself.

For a fuller statement of this law, see Num 15.37-41.
A tassel is an ornament made of threads or cords bound
at one end.

The **cloak** was the long outer garment.

TASSELS HANGING
FROM CLOAK

(c) The accused bride (22.13-21)

RSV

13 "If any man takes a wife, and goes in to her, and then spurns her, 14 and charges her with shameful conduct, and brings an evil name upon her, saying, 'I took this woman, and when I came near her, I did not find in her the tokens of virginity,' 15 then the father of the young woman and her mother shall take and bring out the tokens of her virginity to the elders of the city in the gate; 16 and the father of the young woman shall say to the elders, 'I gave my daughter to this man to wife, and he spurns her; 17 and lo, he has made shameful charges against her, saying, "I did not find in your daughter the tokens of virginity." And yet these are the tokens of my daughter's virginity.' And they shall spread the garment before the elders of the city. 18 Then the elders of that city shall take the man and whip him; 19 and they shall fine him a hundred shekels of silver, and give them to the father of the young woman, because he has brought an evil name upon a virgin of Israel; and she shall be his wife; he may not put her away all his days. 20 But if the thing is true, that the tokens of virginity were not found in the young woman, 21 then they shall bring out the young woman to the door of her father's house, and the men of her city shall stone her to death with stones, because she has wrought folly in Israel by playing the harlot in her father's house; so you shall purge the evil from the midst of you.

TEV
Laws concerning Sexual Purity

13 "Suppose a man marries a young woman and later he decides he doesn't want her. 14 So he makes up false charges against her, accusing her of not being a virgin when they got married.

15 "If this happens, the young woman's parents are to take the blood-stained wedding sheet that proves she was a virgin, and they are to show it in court to the town leaders. 16 Her father will say to them, 'I gave my daughter to this man in marriage, and now he doesn't want her. 17 He has made false charges against her, saying that she was not a virgin when he married her. But here is the proof that my daughter was a virgin; look at the bloodstains on the wedding sheet!' 18 Then the town leaders are to take the husband and beat him. 19 They are also to fine him a hundred pieces of silver and give the money to the young woman's father, because the man has brought disgrace on an Israelite woman. Moreover, she will continue to be his wife, and he can never divorce her as long as he lives.

20 "But if the charge is true and there is no proof that she was a virgin, 21 then they are to take her out to the entrance of her father's house, where the men of her city are to stone her to death. She has done a shameful thing among our people by having intercourse before she was married, while she was still living in her father's house. In this way you will get rid of this evil.

This case begins with one very long sentence (in RSV, verses 13-17), which in most languages should be broken up into smaller units. TEV offers a good model.

Section heading: if a heading is desired for this section, it may be entitled "The Accused Bride" (NRSV), or "When a Husband Accuses His Wife" (CEV).

22.13   RSV   TEV

"If any man takes a wife, and goes in to her, and then spurns her,

"Suppose a man marries a young woman and later he decides he doesn't want her.

With the beginning of a new section, Moses should be reintroduced as the speaker.

Takes a wife, and goes in to her: this is the literal Hebrew text; it is not standard English. It is assumed that a man will have sexual intercourse with his wife as soon as they are married, so something like the following may be better: "A man marries and, after making love to [or, sleeping with] his wife, decides that he doesn't like [or, love] her."

Spurns: this translates the verb normally rendered "to hate." NIV and NRSV have "dislikes her," NJPSV "takes an aversion to her," REB "turns against her," FRCL "stops loving her."

22.14   RSV   TEV

and charges her with shameful con-   So he makes up false charges
duct, and brings an evil name upon   against her, accusing her of not be-
her, saying, 'I took this woman, and   ing a virgin when they got married.
when I came near her, I did not find
in her the tokens of virginity,'

The verse begins with two complete statements that are to be understood together, and not as separate actions: **charges her with shameful conduct, and brings an evil name upon her**. This may be expressed as "He defames her, falsely accusing her of sexual immorality." The context shows that the accusation is false. NIV has "slanders her and gives her a bad name."

I took this woman: that is, "I took this woman as my wife" or "I married this woman."

When I came near her: this refers to the first time he made love to his wife. CEV has "when we slept together."

The tokens of virginity: as the following context shows, this is the bleeding caused by the rupture of the hymen of a virgin. (The hymen is the membrane that partly closes the opening of the vagina.) The blood would stain the bed sheet, and the bloodstained bed sheet served as proof that she was a virgin. This can be difficult, if not impossible, to describe in some languages, but the general "I discovered [or, found out] she wasn't a virgin" may be enough, in view of the details given in verses 15 and 17. TEV may serve as a model on how to handle this. If translators feel that a further explanation is needed, this may be placed in a footnote or glossary item. Many languages will have a term for "virgin," but in some languages translators will need to use a phrase; for example, "young woman [or, girl] who has never been with a man" or ". . . who has not slept with a man."

22.15   RSV   TEV

then the father of the young woman   "If this happens, the young wo-
and her mother shall take and bring   man's parents are to take the blood-
out the tokens of her virginity to the   stained wedding sheet that proves
elders of the city in the gate;   she was a virgin, and they are to
                                             show it in court to the town leaders.

The young woman's father and mother take the bloodstained sheet to **the elders of the city in the gate** (see 21.19).

Alternative translation models for this verse are:

●   If this happens, the girl's father and mother must go to the town gate and show the town leaders the blood-stained bed sheet to prove that the girl was a virgin.

●   If this happens, the girl's father and mother must take the bed sheet with the blood stains on it to the town gate to show to the town leaders. This will prove that the girl was a virgin.

22.16   RSV   TEV

and the father of the young woman shall say to the elders, 'I gave my daughter to this man to wife, and he spurns her;

Her father will say to them, 'I gave my daughter to this man in marriage, and now he doesn't want her.

The father . . . shall say: he reports to **the elders** what happened (see verse 14).

To wife means "to marry," "to be his wife."

And he spurns her: see verse 13.

22.17   RSV   TEV

and lo, he has made shameful charges against her, saying, "I did not find in your daughter the tokens of virginity." And yet these are the tokens of my daughter's virginity.' And they shall spread the garment before the elders of the city.

He has made false charges against her, saying that she was not a virgin when he married her. But here is the proof that my daughter was a virgin; look at the bloodstains on the wedding sheet!'

The father then quotes the very words the young man used, **I did not find in your daughter the tokens of virginity**. This can be stated in an indirect way, ". . . saying that he did not find in my daughter the tokens of virginity" or ". . . saying that he discovered that my daughter was not a virgin."

Yet these are the tokens of my daughter's virginity: or "this bloodstained bed cloth [or, sheet] proves that my daughter was a virgin," or "Look at the bloodstains on the wedding sheet" (TEV).

They shall spread the garment: it is better to say "cloth" or "bed sheet," and in some way the reader must be told that that bed sheet is stained with the young woman's blood. TEV expresses this much more clearly.

22.18   RSV   TEV

Then the elders of that city shall take   Then the town leaders are to take the
the man and whip him;   husband and beat him.

Whip him: probably with leather straps. But the verb is the same one used
in 21.18, and it may mean simply "to punish" or "to discipline," with the fine
(verse 19) being the punishment itself, not something in addition to the flog-
ging. However, most translations take the verb to mean **whip**, with the fine
being an additional punishment, and the Handbook recommends this approach.

22.19   RSV   TEV

and they shall fine him a hundred   They are also to fine him a hundred
shekels of silver, and give them to   pieces of silver and give the money
the father of the young woman, be-   to the young woman's father, because he has brought an evil name   cause the man has brought disgrace
upon a virgin of Israel; and she shall   on an Israelite woman. Moreover,
be his wife; he may not put her away   she will continue to be his wife, and
all his days.   he can never divorce her as long as
                                                 he lives.

A hundred shekels of silver: this is twice the amount of the standard bride
price a groom paid the father (see 22.29). So the young man would have to pay
the bride price again, plus an additional fifty shekels. A hundred shekels was
worth quite a lot. Translators should avoid transliterating the word "shekel,"
as it will be meaningless to the reader. A better model is "a hundred pieces of
silver" (TEV, CEV).
    A virgin of Israel: this is a solemn title, indicating the seriousness of the
man's conduct. However, if the use of a technical term meaning **virgin** sounds
strange in this context, we may say, for example, "because the man has
disgraced an Israelite girl [or, young woman]" or ". . . has caused an Israelite
young woman to receive shame [or, lose face]." The CEV rendering "accused his
bride of not being a virgin" doesn't really bring out the idea of disgrace within
the community of Israel.
    She shall be his wife; he may not put her away all his days: this is taken to
be a good ruling; the young woman's wishes are of no importance. A good
alternative model is "she shall continue to be his wife, and he can never divorce
her as long as he lives" (TEV).

22.20-21   RSV   TEV

20 But if the thing is true, that the   20 "But if the charge is true and
tokens of virginity were not found in   there is no proof that she was a vir-
the young woman, 21 then they shall   gin, 21 then they are to take her out
bring out the young woman to the   to the entrance of her father's house,

door of her father's house, and the men of her city shall stone her to death with stones, because she has wrought folly in Israel by playing the harlot in her father's house; so you shall purge the evil from the midst of you.

where the men of her city are to stone her to death. She has done a shameful thing among our people by having intercourse before she was married, while she was still living in her father's house. In this way you will get rid of this evil.

But if the thing is true: if, however, the father cannot prove that his daughter was a virgin when she was married, she must be put to death.

The door of her father's house: because she belongs to her father.

The men of her city shall stone her to death: this was the punishment for adultery. For **stone . . . to death**, see 13.10.

Wrought folly in Israel: **folly** is not simply a foolish thing but an immoral action. The fool is someone who disregards God's commands. TEV has "She has done a shameful thing among our people"; or we may say "She has caused all of our people to be disgraced [or, lose face]."

By playing the harlot: meaning "being promiscuous" (NIV). NJPSV has "committing fornication," NRSV "prostituting herself," TEV "having intercourse before she was married," CEV "sleeping with someone before she got married."

In her father's house: this does not necessarily mean that she was at home when she had sexual intercourse with a man. Rather, she was still under her father's care when she did this; she was still his daughter. TEV expresses this well.

You shall purge the evil from the midst of you: see 13.5.

(d) Adultery and related offenses (22.22-30) [22.22–23.1]

RSV

22 "If a man is found lying with the wife of another man, both of them shall die, the man who lay with the woman, and the woman; so you shall purge the evil from Israel.
23 "If there is a betrothed virgin, and a man meets her in the city and lies with her, 24 then you shall bring them both out to the gate of that city, and you shall stone them to death with stones, the young woman because she did not cry for help though she was in the city, and the man because he violated his neighbor's wife; so you shall purge the evil from the midst of you.
25 "But if in the open country a man meets a young woman who is betrothed, and the man seizes her and lies with her, then only the man who lay with her shall die. 26 But to the young woman you shall do nothing; in the young woman there is no offense punishable by death, for this case is like that of a man attacking and murdering his neighbor; 27 because he

TEV

22 "If a man is caught having intercourse with another man's wife, both of them are to be put to death. In this way you will get rid of this evil.
23 "Suppose a man is caught in a town having intercourse with a young woman who is engaged to someone else. 24 You are to take them outside the town and stone them to death. She is to die because she did not cry out for help, although she was in a town, where she could have been heard. And the man is to die because he had intercourse with someone who was engaged. In this way you will get rid of this evil.
25 "Suppose a man out in the countryside rapes a young woman who is engaged to someone else. Then only the man is to be put to death; 26 nothing is to be done to the woman, because she has not committed a sin worthy of death. This case is the same as when one man attacks another man and murders him. 27 The

373

came upon her in the open country, and though the betrothed young woman cried for help there was no one to rescue her.

28 "If a man meets a virgin who is not betrothed, and seizes her and lies with her, and they are found, 29 then the man who lay with her shall give to the father of the young woman fifty shekels of silver, and she shall be his wife, because he has violated her; he may not put her away all his days.

30 "A man shall not take his father's wife, nor shall he uncover her who is his father's.

man raped the engaged woman in the countryside, and although she cried for help, there was no one to help her.

28 "Suppose a man is caught raping a young woman who is not engaged. 29 He is to pay her father the bride price of fifty pieces of silver, and she is to become his wife, because he forced her to have intercourse with him. He can never divorce her as long as he lives.

30 "No man is to disgrace his father by having intercourse with any of his father's wives.

In this section five different cases of sexual misconduct are dealt with. In form and structure these regulations are like those in chapter 21.

Section heading: if a heading is desired for this section, a general title such as "Laws Concerning Sexual Misconduct" can be used; or TEV (22.12-30) "Laws concerning Sexual Purity" may be satisfactory. Other possibilities are "Adultery and Related Offenses" (NRSV) or "Laws about Illegal Sex" (CEV).

22.22	RSV	TEV

"If a man is found lying with the wife of another man, both of them shall die, the man who lay with the woman, and the woman; so you shall purge the evil from Israel.

"If a man is caught having intercourse with another man's wife, both of them are to be put to death. In this way you will get rid of this evil.

This is the first case dealing with adultery. Both the man and the woman are to be put to death, presumably by stoning (as in verses 21 and 24).

With the beginning of a new section, Moses should be reintroduced as the speaker.

Lying with the wife of another man means "having intercourse with [or, sleeping with] the wife of . . . ."

For **purge the evil**, see 13.5; 19.13.

22.23	RSV	TEV

"If there is a betrothed virgin, and a man meets her in the city and lies with her,

"Suppose a man is caught in a town having intercourse with a young woman who is engaged to someone else.

Verses 23-24 deal with another case, this one involving a woman who is engaged.

A betrothed virgin: to be **betrothed** meant that the marriage had already been agreed upon, and a bride-price had been paid by the groom to the woman's parents. In Israel such people were regarded as already married. So in some

374

languages this first sentence will be expressed as "Suppose a man is caught sleeping with a girl [or, young woman] for whom the bride-price has been paid by another man."

Lies with her: that is, "Has intercourse with her." As the next case shows (verses 25-27), it is assumed that she was a willing partner; she was not forced to have sex with the man.

22.24 RSV	TEV
then you shall bring them both out to the gate of that city, and you shall stone them to death with stones, the young woman because she did not cry for help though she was in the city, and the man because he violated his neighbor's wife; so you shall purge the evil from the midst of you.	You are to take them outside the town and stone them to death. She is to die because she did not cry out for help, although she was in a town, where she could have been heard. And the man is to die because he had intercourse with someone who was engaged. In this way you will get rid of this evil.

The long first sentence in RSV may be broken up into at least three shorter ones (see TEV).

You shall bring them both out to the gate of the city: this is where the sentence of death will be pronounced on them by the town's elders (see 22.15).

You shall stone them to death with stones: the plural **you** seems to include all the citizens of the town. In actual practice it appears that only the men carried out the death sentence.

TEV takes the text to mean that the actual execution took place outside the town (see also 17.5), not **at the gate of the city** (RSV, CEV). We should notice, however, that the execution in verse 21 above takes place inside the town. However, in this verse translators are urged to have either "outside the gates of the town" or simply "outside the town."

Because she did not cry for help: the reasoning here is that, since this took place in town, the woman would have cried out for help and been rescued if she didn't agree to have sex with the man. The fact that she didn't cry out is proof that she agreed to have sex with him.

Violated: the same verb used in 21.14 (see also 22.29).

You shall purge the evil: see 13.5.

22.25 RSV	TEV
"But if in the open country a man meets a young woman who is betrothed, and the man seizes her and lies with her, then only the man who lay with her shall die.	"Suppose a man out in the countryside rapes a young woman who is engaged to someone else. Then only the man is to be put to death;

375

Verses 25-29 deal with another case: rape. This case assumes that the woman did cry out but was not heard (see verse 27).

In the open country: meaning that it was at a distance from any town. We may express this as "in the fields outside a town" or "away from where people live."

Who is betrothed: see verse 23.

Seizes her and lies with her: both TEV and CEV combine the two actions with the term "rape," meaning sex by force. In languages that do not have a single term for "rape," we may say, for example, "forces her to have sex with him."

Then only the man is to be put to death: in languages that do not use the passive voice, this may be transformed to "they [people not named] shall kill only the man."

22.26 RSV	TEV
But to the young woman you shall do nothing; in the young woman there is no offense punishable by death, for this case is like that of a man attacking and murdering his neighbor;	nothing is to be done to the woman, because she has not committed a sin worthy of death. This case is the same as when one man attacks another man and murders him.

To the young woman you shall do nothing: TEV has "nothing is to be done to the girl," and CEV is more direct, with "Do not punish the woman at all."

No offense punishable by death: not a capital offense (see 21.22).

This case is like that of a man attacking and murdering his neighbor: the raped woman is like the murdered man; she is the innocent party, she is the victim.

Neighbor: a fellow Israelite. TEV and NJPSV have "another man [or, person]."

22.27 RSV	TEV
because he came upon her in the open country, and though the betrothed young woman cried for help there was no one to rescue her.	The man raped the engaged woman in the countryside, and although she cried for help, there was no one to help her.

This verse explains why the woman is presumed innocent. A woman promised in marriage would not willingly have sex with another man.

Because he came upon her in the open country: other ways to express this are "The man raped the engaged girl in the countryside," or even "the woman was alone out in the countryside when the man found her and raped her."

Though the . . . woman cried for help: see verse 24.

22.28 RSV TEV

"If a man meets a virgin who is not betrothed, and seizes her and lies with her, and they are found,

"Suppose a man is caught raping a young woman who is not engaged.

This is another case: a young woman (**a virgin**) not promised in marriage is raped (verse 29 "violated"). See Exo 22.16-17.

22.29 RSV TEV

then the man who lay with her shall give to the father of the young woman fifty shekels of silver, and she shall be his wife, because he has violated her; he may not put her away all his days.

He is to pay her father the bride price of fifty pieces of silver, and she is to become his wife, because he forced her to have intercourse with him. He can never divorce her as long as he lives.

Fifty shekels of silver: see verse 19.
Violated: see 21.14.
May not put her away all his days: see verse 19.

22.30 RSV TEV
[23.1]

ʳ"A man shall not take his father's wife, nor shall he uncover her who is his father's.ˢ

"No man is to disgrace his father by having intercourse with any of his father's wives.

ʳ Ch 23.1 in Heb
ˢ Heb *uncover his father's skirt*

In the Hebrew text this verse is 23.1, which means that the verse numbers of chapter 23 in RSV and TEV are one ahead of the numbers in the Hebrew text. The Hebrew chapter and verse numbers will be written within square brackets as a reminder to those who need to use this system.

For this case see 27.20; Lev 18.7-8; 20.11.

His father's wife: not his mother, but his stepmother, most likely one of his father's several wives.

Uncover her who is his father's: this translates the Hebrew "uncover his father's skirt," meaning to invade the privacy of the father's marriage. "To cover with the skirt" means to get married (Ruth 3.9; Ezek 16.8). This is not in addition to the first rule, as RSV **nor** suggests; rather it is an explanation of it, as TEV renders it. See also NRSV: "A man shall not marry his father's wife, thereby violating his father's rights." TEV is a good alternative model for the verse.

(e) Exclusion from the LORD's people (23.1-8) [23.2-9]

RSV

1 "He whose testicles are crushed or whose male member is cut off shall not enter the assembly of the LORD.
2 "No bastard shall enter the assembly of the LORD; even to the tenth generation none of his descendants shall enter the assembly of the LORD.
3 "No Ammonite or Moabite shall enter the assembly of the LORD; even to the tenth generation none belonging to them shall enter the assembly of the LORD for ever; 4 because they did not meet you with bread and with water on the way, when you came forth out of Egypt, and because they hired against you Balaam the son of Beor from Pethor of Mesopotamia, to curse you. 5 Nevertheless the LORD your God would not hearken to Balaam; but the LORD your God turned the curse into a blessing for you, because the LORD your God loved you. 6 You shall not seek their peace or their prosperity all your days for ever.
7 "You shall not abhor an Edomite, for he is your brother; you shall not abhor an Egyptian, because you were a sojourner in his land. 8 The children of the third generation that are born to them may enter the assembly of the LORD.

TEV
Exclusion from the LORD's People

1 "No man who has been castrated or whose penis has been cut off may be included among the LORD's people.
2 "No one born out of wedlock or any descendant of such a person, even in the tenth generation, may be included among the LORD's people.
3 "No Ammonite or Moabite—or any of their descendants, even in the tenth generation— may be included among the LORD's people. 4 They refused to provide you with food and water when you were on your way out of Egypt, and they hired Balaam son of Beor, from the city of Pethor in Mesopotamia, to curse you. 5 But the LORD your God would not listen to Balaam; instead he turned the curse into a blessing, because he loved you. 6 As long as you are a nation, never do anything to help these nations or to make them prosperous.
7 "Do not despise the Edomites; they are your relatives. And do not despise the Egyptians; you once lived in their land. 8 From the third generation onward their descendants may be included among the LORD's people.

This section deals with conditions that would prevent an Israelite from belonging to **the assembly of the LORD**, which was composed of adult males and was religious, political, and military in nature (see Judges 20.2). Men thus excluded could not take part in religious ceremonies and rites in the Temple or elsewhere, and were also excluded from military duty.

Section heading: the TEV heading "Exclusion from the LORD's People" may not be altogether satisfactory in some languages; NRSV has "Membership in the Assembly"; CEV has "Who Cannot Become One of the LORD's People."

23.1   RSV   TEV
[23.2]
   "**He whose testicles are crushed or whose male member is cut off shall not enter the assembly of the LORD.**

   "**No man who has been castrated or whose penis has been cut off may be included among the LORD's people.**

With the beginning of a new section, Moses should be reintroduced as the speaker.

Testicles are crushed: this could have happened either by an accident or in battle. TEV "has been castrated" is possible (Septuagint, Vulgate, also GECL,

POCL); most translations, however, are like RSV, and translators should follow this interpretation.

Male member is cut off: NRSV reflects modern American usage, "whose penis is cut off" (see also TEV). CEV uses the euphemism "private parts": "If a man's private parts have been crushed or cut off." Translators should employ language that will not be offensive to the reader or hearer. Such men could not be priests (Lev 21.20).

Shall not enter the assembly of the LORD: this sounds like going into an assembly hall. But what it means is "shall not belong to the assembly" or ". . . the LORD's people" (TEV, CEV). The Hebrew word *qahal* is translated in the Septuagint by *ekklesia*, which is the Greek word in the New Testament translated "church."

23.2 RSV	TEV
[23.3]	
"No bastard shall enter the assembly of the LORD; even to the tenth generation none of his descendants shall enter the assembly of the LORD.	"No one born out of wedlock or any descendant of such a person, even in the tenth generation, may be included among the LORD's people.

Bastard: in English this means someone born of parents not legally married to each other. TEV has "No one born out of wedlock," and CEV has "no one born outside of a legal marriage." The Hebrew word appears only here and in Zech 9.6, and its precise meaning is disputed. Here it can refer to a man born of an incestuous union (see Lev 18.6-18), or even a Jewish male whose mother was a Gentile (see Neh 13.23-25). Translators are advised to follow the interpretation taken by TEV and CEV.

Shall enter the assembly of the LORD: see verse 1.

Even to the tenth generation: this probably means "forever" (see "for ever" at the end of the next verse). It is not certain that a man belonging to the eleventh generation would be admitted.

23.3 RSV	TEV
[23.4]	
"No Ammonite or Moabite shall enter the assembly of the LORD; even to the tenth generation none belonging to them shall enter the assembly of the LORD for ever;	"No Ammonite or Moabite—or any of their descendants, even in the tenth generation—may be included among the LORD's people.

Ammonite . . . Moabite: these two peoples were said to be descendants of the two sons produced by the incestuous union between Lot and his two daughters. "Moab" was the son of the older daughter and "Benammi" the son of the younger daughter (Gen 19.30-38). It is not certain, however, that this regulation reflects that story. In a number of languages **No Ammonite or Moabite** will be expressed as "No person from the nation of Ammon or of Moab."

The tenth generation . . . for ever: this seems to indicate that "to the tenth generation" means for all time to come.

None belonging to them means "none of their descendants" (TEV, CEV).

Shall enter the assembly of the LORD: see verse 1.

23.4   RSV   TEV
[23.5]

| because they did not meet you with bread and with water on the way, when you came forth out of Egypt, and because they hired against you Balaam the son of Beor from Pethor of Mesopotamia, to curse you. | They refused to provide you with food and water when you were on your way out of Egypt, and they hired Balaam son of Beor, from the city of Pethor in Mesopotamia, to curse you. |

This verse gives two reasons for excluding Moabites and Ammonites from the assembly of the LORD (see the reference to this in Neh 13.1-2): (1) They did not supply the Israelites with provisions as they were on their way from Egypt to Canaan. Nothing is said about this in the account in Num 21–22; and in Deut 2.9, 19 the Israelites are given orders not to harass the Moabites or Ammonites. (2) They hired Balaam to put a curse on the Israelites. For this story see Num 22.4–24.25.

They hired Balaam: or "they paid money to Balaam."

Pethor of Mesopotamia: that is, the city of Pethor in the country, or region, of Mesopotamia ("between the rivers" Tigris and Euphrates).

To curse you means "to speak evil [or, hurting] words against you." See also 11.26.

An alternative translation model for this verse is:

● This is because, when you came out of Egypt, they refused to provide you with food and water. They also hired Balaam son of Beor, from the city of Pethor in the region of Mesopotamia, to put a curse on you.

23.5   RSV   TEV
[23,6]

| Nevertheless the LORD your God would not hearken to Balaam; but the LORD your God turned the curse into a blessing for you, because the LORD your God loved you. | But the LORD your God would not listen to Balaam; instead he turned the curse into a blessing, because he loved you. |

For this action see Num 23.7–24.9. It is noteworthy that in this short verse the full title **the LORD your God** is used three times.

Turned the curse into a blessing for you: this may be expressed as "instead of cursing you, the LORD blessed you" or "instead of letting evil [or, hurtful] things happen to you, the LORD caused you to become prosperous."

It will be helpful in some languages to put the final clause first, as follows:

- But Yahweh your [plural] God [or, the God you serve] loves you, so he would not listen to Balaam. Instead of letting evil things happen to you, he caused you to become prosperous.

23.6   RSV   TEV
[23.7]
You shall not seek their peace or | **As long as you are a nation, never do**
their prosperity all your days for | **anything to help these nations or to**
ever. | **make them prosperous.**

The RSV literal rendition of the Hebrew makes for a poor English sentence. The meaning is that the Israelites should never do anything, for all time to come, to contribute to the welfare and prosperity of the Ammonites and Moabites. So TEV has "As long as you are a nation, never do anything . . . ."

Their peace or their prosperity: the two nouns mean the same; **peace** stands here for welfare in general. TOB translates "prosperity or welfare," while NRSV has "welfare or prosperity." The CEV rendering "Don't even think of signing a peace treaty with" is too limited. TEV is better, with "never do anything to help these nations or to make them prosperous."

23.7   RSV   TEV
[23.8]
"You shall not abhor an Edomite, | **"Do not despise the Edomites;**
for he is your brother; you shall not | **they are your relatives. And do not**
abhor an Egyptian, because you | **despise the Egyptians; you once**
were a sojourner in his land. | **lived in their land.**

Abhor: this verb is related to the noun which in 22.5 is translated "abomination" (see the verb and the noun in 7.25-26). TEV has "Do not despise." We may also say "Do not look down on [or, treat with contempt]." CEV has the positive command, "You must be kind to . . . ."

An Edomite . . . is your brother: the Edomites were descended from Esau, also called Edom (Gen 36.1), the brother of Jacob, who was the ancestor of the Israelites. **Brother** here means "relative." In most languages "they are your relatives" (TEV) will be natural style.

An Egyptian, because you were a sojourner in his land: until the time of Moses, when the ruling king made them do hard labor, the Israelites were resident aliens in Egypt and were well treated. The CEV translation "you lived as foreigners in the country of Egypt" is a helpful model.

23.8   RSV   TEV
[23.9]

The children of the third generation   **From the third generation onward**
that are born to them may enter the   **their descendants may be included**
assembly of the LORD.   **among the LORD's people.**

The children of the third generation: this means the children who belong to
the third generation. These are the grandchildren of any Edomite or Egyptian
living in the land of Israel. So we may translate "and let their grandchildren be
included . . . ." The rendering "great-grandchildren" (CEV) is not followed by
other interpreters.

(f) Keeping the military camp clean (23.9-14) [23.10-15]

RSV   TEV
                                             Keeping the Military Camp Clean

9 "When you go forth against your enemies   9 "When you are in camp in time of war, you
and are in camp, then you shall keep yourself   are to avoid anything that would make you
from every evil thing.   ritually unclean. 10 If a man becomes unclean
10 "If there is among you any man who is   because he has had a wet dream during the
not clean by reason of what chances to him by   night, he is to go outside the camp and stay
night, then he shall go outside the camp, he   there. 11 Toward evening he is to wash him-
shall not come within the camp; 11 but when   self, and at sunset he may come back into
evening comes on, he shall bathe himself in   camp.
water, and when the sun is down, he may come   12 "You are to have a place outside the
within the camp.   camp where you can go when you need to
12 "You shall have a place outside the camp   relieve yourselves. 13 Carry a stick as part of
and you shall go out to it; 13 and you shall   your equipment, so that when you have a
have a stick with your weapons; and when you   bowel movement you can dig a hole and cover
sit down outside, you shall dig a hole with it, it up. 14 Keep your camp ritually clean, be-
and turn back and cover up your excrement.   cause the LORD your God is with you in your
14 Because the LORD your God walks in the   camp to protect you and to give you victory
midst of your camp, to save you and to give up over your enemies. Do not do anything inde-
your enemies before you, therefore your camp   cent that would cause the LORD to turn his
must be holy, that he may not see anything   back on you.
indecent among you, and turn away from you.

This section is not concerned simply with hygiene but with the sanctity, the
holiness, of the Israelites' camp. The wars they fight are holy wars, against the
enemies of Yahweh, the God of Israel, and the fighting men must keep themselves holy (see other instructions for warfare in chapter 26).

Section heading: two titles for this section in English versions are "Keeping
the Military Camp Clean" (TEV) and "Keep the Army Camp Acceptable" (CEV).
Other ways to render this title are "Don't do anything to make the army camp
unclean" or "Keep acceptable to Yahweh the place where the soldiers stay."

23.9 RSV TEV
[23.10]

"When you go forth against your enemies and are in camp, then you shall keep yourself from every evil thing.

"When you are in camp in time of war, you are to avoid anything that would make you ritually unclean.

With the beginning of a new section, Moses should be reintroduced as the speaker.

You go forth . . . and are in camp: this translates one Hebrew verb, "encamped [for battle]." So NIV, NRSV, REB say "you are encamped against your enemies," and NJB "When you are in camp, at war with your enemies." However, in some languages it will be helpful to put **in camp** in a separate clause or sentence; for example, "when you go to fight your enemies, make sure that your camp is . . . ." **Camp** may also be expressed as "the place where you set up your tents."

You shall keep yourself from every evil thing: as throughout all these rules and regulations, the singular "you" is for the people of Israel as a whole; but in many languages the plural will be more natural. The phrase **evil thing** is the same one that was used in 17.1, where it means "any defect." NRSV has "keep yourself from any impropriety," REB "avoid any foulness," NJPSV "anything untoward," and SPCL "any indecent act." TEV has translated correctly in the context, "avoid anything that would make you ritually unclean." However, a positive command, "make sure that your camp is acceptable to the LORD" (CEV), is also possible.

23.10 RSV TEV
[23.11]

"If there is among you any man who is not clean by reason of what chances to him by night, then he shall go outside the camp, he shall not come within the camp;

If a man becomes unclean because he has had a wet dream during the night, he is to go outside the camp and stay there.

Is not clean: this does not refer to being physically unclean but to ritual impurity, which would prevent the Israelite man from fulfilling his duties as a member of "the assembly of the LORD." In languages where the idea of ritual impurity will be difficult to express, we may say something like "he is unfit to worship [or, have fellowship with] Yahweh." CEV has a similar rendering: "makes a man unclean and unfit for worship."

By reason of what chances to him by night: this refers to "a wet dream," that is, an emission of semen (NRSV "a nocturnal emission"). This is dealt with also in Lev 15.16-17. Every language has its own way of referring to this; but translators should be careful not to use language that is offensive to the reader or hearer.

He shall go outside the camp, he shall not come within the camp: that is, "He must leave the camp and stay away from it the whole day" (as the next verse makes clear).

23.11 RSV	TEV
[23.12]	
but when evening comes on, he shall bathe himself in water, and when the sun is down, he may come within the camp.	Toward evening he is to wash himself, and at sunset he may come back into camp.

When evening comes on: that is, "in the late afternoon," "before sunset."

When the sun is down: meaning after sunset, when the next day begins, according to the Hebrew reckoning.

23.12 RSV	TEV
[23.13]	
"You shall have a place outside the camp and you shall go out to it;	"You are to have a place outside the camp where you can go when you need to relieve yourselves.

Verses 12-14 deal with defecating (going to the latrine, or toilet) while in camp.

The Hebrew text does not state the purpose for which the encamped Israelites are to **have a place outside the camp**. It is only understood from the context; and it may be necessary to say something like TEV, "where you can go when you need to relieve yourselves," or NIV "where you can go to relieve yourself."

You shall have a place outside the camp: this means to choose a place or "designate a place" (NIV). The CEV translation "Set up a place outside the camp to be used as a toilet area" is acceptable. Some languages have euphemisms, which are not offensive; Portuguese, for example, says *fazer necessidade* ("to do what is necessary," so POCL, BRCL). In languages where direct reference to defecation or urination is not offensive, we may say "designate a place outside the camp where people may go to defecate or urinate."

23.13 RSV	TEV
[23.14]	
and you shall have a stick with your weapons; and when you sit down outside, you shall dig a hole with it, and turn back and cover up your excrement.	Carry a stick as part of your equipment, so that when you have a bowel movement you can dig a hole and cover it up.

The instructions are clear, the vocabulary is simple.

A stick: the Hebrew word is used in this sense only here; elsewhere it means a pin or a tentpeg. For this kind of task a stick would be used. NIV "something to dig with" is satisfactory.

Your weapons: or, more generally, "your equipment" (TEV, NIV, REB); NRSV has "your utensils." NJPSV "gear" is the proper military term in English.

You sit down . . . dig a hole . . . turn back and cover up your excrement: in the nature of the case, first the man would dig a hole and then squat over it and relieve himself, after which he would cover up the excrement.

23.14	RSV	TEV
[23.15]		

	RSV	TEV
	Because the LORD your God walks in the midst of your camp, to save you and to give up your enemies before you, therefore your camp must be holy, that he may not see anything indecent among you, and turn away from you.	Keep your camp ritually clean, because the LORD your God is with you in your camp to protect you and to give you victory over your enemies. Do not do anything indecent that would cause the LORD to turn his back on you.

This verse gives the reason for the instructions in the previous two verses: the uncovered excrement would defile the camp, which was a holy place because of the presence of Yahweh.

The LORD your God walks in the midst of the camp: if possible this vivid language should be retained in translation. If this is not possible we may say "the LORD your God is with you" (TEV) or "the LORD is always present" (CEV).

To save you: that is, from the enemy; TEV "protect" is better in this context.

To give up your enemies before you: this means to give the Israelites victory over their enemies (TEV, CEV).

Your camp must be holy: TEV has "ritually clean," but in this case it seems advisable to retain a word for **holy**, whose primary meaning is "completely dedicated to the service of God." In some instances an explanatory footnote to the word may be helpful.

Anything indecent: the same word is used in 24.1. Here it means "offensive to God" (REB); NJPSV "unseemly" and FRCL "repugnant" are not quite as good. CEV has "filthy and disgusting things."

And turn away from you means "turn around and leave you," "turn his back on you" (TEV), or even "abandon you."

2C. Other laws for life in Canaan (23.15–26.19) [23.16–26.19]

This part of the book continues setting forth laws, rules, and regulations that will govern different aspects of life, private and collective, once the people are settled in the land of Canaan. There often does not seem to be a common theme in the various laws; each one stands on its own, independent of what comes before it or what follows.

Section heading: translators should have a general title for this collection of laws, like the Handbook heading. Each section will then have its own heading related to its particular theme.

2C-1. Runaway slaves (23.15-16) [23.16-17]

RSV	TEV
	Various Laws
15 "You shall not give up to his master a slave who has escaped from his master to you; 16 he shall dwell with you, in your midst, in the place which he shall choose within one of your towns, where it pleases him best; you shall not oppress him.	15 "If slaves run away from their owners and come to you for protection, do not send them back. 16 They may live in any of your towns that they choose, and you are not to treat them harshly.

The first subject in this group of laws is how to deal with a fugitive slave. The standard procedure in other countries was to punish, even to kill, anyone who harbored a fugitive slave.

The language used makes it certain that the slave's owner lives in another country, and the slave has fled to the land of Israel. CEV makes this clear with "When runaway slaves from other countries . . . ."

Section heading: the TEV heading "Various Laws" covers 23.15-25, which deals with five different matters. This section, verses 15-16, would have the title "Runaway slaves," or "How to treat slaves who run away from other countries."

23.15   RSV   TEV
[23.16]

"You shall not give up to his master a slave who has escaped from his master to you;

"If slaves run away from their owners and come to you for protection, do not send them back.

With the beginning of a new section, translators should reintroduce Moses as the speaker; for example, "Moses said, ..."

386

Give up to his master: that is, "return him to his master [or, owner]."

A slave: both TEV (second edition) and NRSV use the plural, which is an option. But it seems that the writer has the male slave in mind, so the masculine form is a faithful translation of the text; for example, "If a male slave runs away . . . ."

To you: that is, "to the land of Israel," "to an Israelite community."

An alternative model for verse 15 is:

- If a slave runs away from his owner in a foreign country, and comes to Israel for protection, you must not return him to his owner.

23.16 RSV	TEV
[23.17]	
he shall dwell with you, in your midst, in the place which he shall choose within one of your towns, where it pleases him best; you shall not oppress him.	They may live in any of your towns that they choose, and you are not to treat them harshly.

He shall dwell: this verse repeats in a positive way the negative command of the previous verse. But the whole statement is quite wordy, and a translation may choose to abbreviate it somewhat. TEV, however, seems too brief.

You shall not oppress him: the verb means "to treat harshly," "to mistreat," "to be cruel to."

The first part of this verse may be alternatively rendered as "Instead, you must let him choose which one of your towns he wants to live in . . . ."

2C-2. Male and female prostitutes (23.17-18) [23.18-19]

RSV	TEV
17 "There shall be no cult prostitute of the daughters of Israel, neither shall there be a cult prostitute of the sons of Israel. 18 You shall not bring the hire of a harlot, or the wages of a dog, into the house of the LORD your God in payment for any vow; for both of these are an abomination to the LORD your God.	17 "No Israelite, man or woman, is to become a temple prostitute. 18 Also, no money earned in this way may be brought into the house of the LORD your God in fulfillment of a vow. The LORD hates temple prostitutes.

Section heading: a possible title for this section is "Male and female prostitutes in the Temple" (on the translation of "prostitute" see the comments below).

23.17   RSV   TEV

[23.18]

"There shall be no cult prostitute   "No Israelite, man or woman, is to
of the daughters of Israel, neither   become a temple prostitute.
shall there be a cult prostitute of the
sons of Israel.

With the beginning of a new section, Moses should be reintroduced as the
speaker.

Cult prostitute: see also Lev 19.29. In Canaanite religions temple prostitutes
had intercourse with the worshipers in order to make sure that their fields and
flocks would be fertile.

It is clear from such passages as 1 Kgs 14.24; Hos 4.14; Amos 2.7 that temple
prostitution was a problem in Israel. It may be a good idea to use the expression "temple [or, cult] prostitutes," and provide an explanatory footnote, as
follows: "Such a person was found in Canaanite temples, where fertility gods
were worshiped. It was believed that intercourse with such a prostitute would
make fields and herds fertile." Many languages will have terms for male and
female prostitutes. But in languages where such words are not available, we
may say something like "men or women who sell their bodies [or, have sex] in
the temple for money."

Daughters of Israel . . . sons of Israel: that is, Israelite women or men.

CEV has a helpful model for this verse:

- *Moses said:*
  People of Israel, don't any of you ever be temple prostitutes. [Or one
  can say ". . . be prostitutes in the place where Yahweh is worshiped."]

It gives the following explanatory footnote:

- *temple prostitutes*: Some Canaanites worshiped by going to their
  temples and having sex with prostitutes that represented their
  gods.

23.18   RSV   TEV

[23.19]

You shall not bring the hire of a har-   Also, no money earned in this way
lot, or the wages of a dog,ᵗ into the   may be brought into the house of the
house of the LORD your God in pay-   LORD your God in fulfillment of a
ment for any vow; for both of these   vow. The LORD hates temple prosti-
are an abomination to the LORD your   tutes.
God.

ᵗ Or *sodomite*

The hire of a harlot: this refers to money earned by a female temple
prostitute.

The wages of a dog: money earned by a male temple prostitute. RSV footnote provides "sodomite" as an alternative rendering of **dog**. The context is that of temple prostitution. If a language does not have a term for a male prostitute, we may say, for example, "male who sells his body for money" (see verse 17).

Into the house of the LORD your God in payment for any vow: the money could not be given to the Temple as an offering that the man or woman had promised to make to Yahweh (see verse 21).

Both of them: that is, female and male prostitutes.

An abomination: see 7.25.

Alternative translation models for this verse are:

- The LORD your God is disgusted with [or, hates] men or women who sell their bodies for money. No money earned in this way may be brought into the house of the LORD, even if it was promised to him.

(The following for languages that do not use the passive)

- The LORD your God .... You may not bring money into the house of the LORD that you earned in this way, even if you have promised to give it to the LORD.

2C-3. Interest on loans (23.19-20) [23.20-21]

RSV	TEV
19 "You shall not lend upon interest to your brother, interest on money, interest on victuals, interest on anything that is lent for interest. 20 To a foreigner you may lend upon interest, but to your brother you shall not lend upon interest; that the LORD your God may bless you in all that you undertake in the land which you are entering to take possession of it.	19 "When you lend money or food or anything else to Israelites, do not charge them interest. 20 You may charge interest on what you lend to foreigners, but not on what you lend to Israelites. Obey this rule, and the LORD your God will bless everything you do in the land that you are going to occupy.

The subject of this section, interest on loans, is dealt with extensively in other places; see Exo 22.25; Lev 25.36-37; Deut 15.7-11.

Section heading: CEV has "Interest on Loans." Alternative models are "Do not require interest for loans" or "Do not ask people to pay back more than they borrow."

23.19 [23.20]	RSV	TEV
	"You shall not lend upon interest to your brother, interest on money, interest on victuals, interest on anything that is lent for interest.	**"When you lend money or food or anything else to Israelites, do not charge them interest.**

To your brother: your brother means "your fellow Israelite." Israelites were absolutely forbidden to charge any **interest** (literally "bite") on loans to fellow Israelites.

In cultures where the custom of paying interest is unknown, translators may say something like "When you lend money to another Israelite, do not make him pay back more than he borrowed" or ". . . pay additional money for the use of the money he has borrowed."

Money . . . victuals . . . anything: victuals means "food" or "provisions."

23.20   RSV   TEV
[23,21]

To a foreigner you may lend upon   You may charge interest on what
interest, but to your brother you   you lend to foreigners, but not on
shall not lend upon interest; that the   what you lend to Israelites. Obey this
LORD your God may bless you in all   rule, and the LORD your God will
that you undertake in the land which   bless everything you do in the land
you are entering to take possession   that you are going to occupy.
of it.

To a foreigner: interest could be charged on loans made to non-Israelites, (and they did not have to be released from debt in the seventh year; see 15.3). The **interest** was paid in advance of the loan.

That the LORD your God may bless you in all you undertake: see 12.7 and 15.10.

The land which you are entering to take possession of it: see 7.1.

2C-4. Promises to the LORD (23.21-23) [23.22-24]

RSV   TEV

21 "When you make a vow to the LORD your   21 "When you make a vow to the LORD your
God, you shall not be slack to pay it; for the   God, do not put off doing what you promised;
LORD your God will surely require it of you,   the LORD will hold you to your vow, and it is a
and it would be sin in you. 22 But if you re-   sin not to keep it. 22 It is no sin not to make a
frain from vowing, it shall be no sin in you.   vow to the LORD, 23 but if you make one volun-
23 You shall be careful to perform what has   tarily, be sure that you keep it.
passed your lips, for you have voluntarily
vowed to the LORD your God what you have
promised with your mouth.

A promise made to God must be kept promptly; see Eccl 5.4-6. See also the extensive treatment in Num 30.1-16.

Section heading: a possible heading for this section is "Promises to the LORD."

23.21-22 RSV	TEV
[23.22-23]	
21 "When you make a vow to the LORD your God, you shall not be slack to pay it; for the LORD your God will surely require it of you, and it would be sin in you. 22 But if you refrain from vowing, it shall be no sin in you.	21 "When you make a vow to the LORD your God, do not put off doing what you promised; the LORD will hold you to your vow, and it is a sin not to keep it. 22 It is no sin not to make a vow to the LORD,

With the beginning of a new section, Moses should be reintroduced as the speaker.

A vow: a promise to Yahweh to do something.

Not be slack to pay it: that is, "Do not put off fulfilling it." The verb **pay** makes it appear that it is a promise to give money to Yahweh, but the sense is broader; it is a promise to do something, and the thing must be done promptly. So NRSV has "do not postpone fulfilling it," and CEV has "do it as soon as you can."

Will surely require it of you: this translates the emphatic compound verbal phrase in Hebrew. The text does not say what God will do to make the man keep his promise. TEV has "the LORD will hold you to your vow." Another model is "the LORD will expect you to do what you promised."

It would be sin in you: this means "you would be guilty of sin" or ". . . of breaking the promise."

But if you refrain from vowing: the whole verse 22 may be expressed as follows:

- But if you don't make a promise to Yahweh, you won't be guilty of breaking a promise.

23.23 RSV	TEV
[23.24]	
You shall be careful to perform what has passed your lips, for you have voluntarily vowed to the LORD your God what you have promised with your mouth.	but if you make one voluntarily, be sure that you keep it.

What has passed your lips . . . what you have promised with your mouth: this repetition, as elsewhere, is for emphasis.

You have voluntarily vowed to the LORD your God: there was no obligation. The person who made the promise was not forced to do it. An alternative model may be "the LORD didn't force you to make a promise."

For the whole verse, many translators will find the TEV model simpler than RSV, which follows the Hebrew structure.

2C-5. The right to eat some of other people's crops (23.24-25) [23.25-26]

RSV	TEV
24 "When you go into your neighbor's vineyard, you may eat your fill of grapes, as many as you wish, but you shall not put any in your vessel. 25 When you go into your neighbor's standing grain, you may pluck the ears with your hand, but you shall not put a sickle to your neighbor's standing grain.	24 "When you walk along a path in someone else's vineyard, you may eat all the grapes you want, but you must not carry any away in a container. 25 When you walk along a path in someone else's grainfield, you may eat all the grain you can pull off with your hands, but you must not cut any grain with a sickle.

Two similar laws make up this section. (In the Septuagint the two verses are reversed.)

Section heading: as a title for this section, FRCL has "The right to gather certain crops"; NRSV "Limitations on Forage"; TOB "Nourishment for a passerby." CEV has "Eating Someone Else's Produce."

23.24 [23.25] RSV	TEV
"**When you go into your neighbor's vineyard, you may eat your fill of grapes, as many as you wish, but you shall not put any in your vessel.**	"**When you walk along a path in someone else's vineyard, you may eat all the grapes you want, but you must not carry any away in a container.**

Your neighbor's vineyard: the **neighbor** here, as usual, is a fellow Israelite, not necessarily someone who lives next door.

For **vineyard** see 6.11.

Your vessel: this is a container of some sort; it could be a bowl, or a basket, or a bag—anything that would hold grapes.

23.25 [23.26] RSV	TEV
When you go into your neighbor's standing grain, you may pluck the ears with your hand, but you shall not put a sickle to your neighbor's standing grain.	**When you walk along a path in someone else's grainfield, you may eat all the grain you can pull off with your hands, but you must not cut any grain with a sickle.**

Go into your neighbor's standing grain: there were paths that led through the grainfields. So TEV has "when you walk along a path in someone else's grainfield." Instead of **standing grain** TEV and NIV have "grainfield." The **grain** could be wheat or barley; BRCL gives this information in the text.

Pluck the ears with your hands: that is, pluck and eat them. This is what Jesus' disciples did (Mark 2.23).

Put a sickle to your neighbor's standing grain: they were not to cut the heads of grain and take them home. In cultures where sickles are not known, we may use a general translation as follows: "But don't cut down the stalks of grain and take them with you" (CEV).

2C-6. Divorce and remarriage (24.1-4)

RSV	TEV
	Divorce and Remarriage

1 "When a man takes a wife and marries her, if then she finds no favor in his eyes because he has found some indecency in her, and he writes her a bill of divorce and puts it in her hand and sends her out of his house, and she departs out of his house, 2 and if she goes and becomes another man's wife, 3 and the latter husband dislikes her and writes her a bill of divorce and puts it in her hand and sends her out of his house, or if the latter husband dies, who took her to be his wife, 4 then her former husband, who sent her away, may not take her again to be his wife, after she has been defiled; for that is an abomination before the LORD, and you shall not bring guilt upon the land which the LORD your God gives you for an inheritance.

1 "Suppose a man marries a woman and later decides that he doesn't want her, because he finds something about her that he doesn't like. So he writes out divorce papers, gives them to her, and sends her away from his home. 2 Then suppose she marries another man, 3 and he also decides that he doesn't want her, so he also writes out divorce papers, gives them to her, and sends her away from his home. Or suppose her second husband dies. 4 In either case, her first husband is not to marry her again; he is to consider her defiled. If he married her again, it would be offensive to the LORD. You are not to commit such a terrible sin in the land that the LORD your God is giving you.

This ruling regarding remarriage after divorce is one long sentence in Hebrew. In translation the material must be rearranged into smaller units, as in most modern translations. TEV offers a good model.

This section does not deal with divorce as such; it prohibits a divorced woman from remarrying her first husband after having married another man.

Section heading: a title cannot give the complete content of this section. TEV has "Divorce and Remarriage," and CEV has "A Law about Divorce." For ways to translate "divorce" see below.

24.1   RSV   TEV

"When a man takes a wife and marries her, if then she finds no favor in his eyes because he has found some indecency in her, and he writes her a bill of divorce and puts it in her hand and sends her out of his house, and she departs out of his house,

"Suppose a man marries a woman and later decides that he doesn't want her, because he finds something about her that he doesn't like.ᵘ So he writes out divorce papers, gives them to her, and sends her away from his home.

ᵘ something . . . like; *or* that she is guilty of some shameful conduct.

With the beginning of a new section, Moses should be reintroduced as the speaker.

When a man: this kind of legislation chooses one particular matter and says what must be done in that case—"If such and such happens . . ."; "Suppose that . . ." is a good way to express the meaning in English (TEV, CEV, NJB, NRSV).

A man takes a wife and marries her: this is rather wordy; in many languages it will be enough to say something like "a man takes a wife," "a man marries" or "a man gets married." In the culture of that day, it was the man who took the initiative.

She finds no favor in his eyes: again, it is the man's point of view that is maintained. This may be expressed as "if she doesn't please him" or "if he isn't pleased with her." It is difficult to determine the time element here; this may be something that happened on the wedding night, or it may refer to some physical defect of which the husband was ignorant. Or else it may refer to some moral fault or defect that becomes apparent only with the passing of time. In any case, the text does not mean a serious moral flaw such as adultery, which would be punishable by death, not by divorce. It may be best to imitate POCL, "later on he stops liking [or, loving] her" or TEV, "later he decides he doesn't want her."

He has found some indecency in her: the Hebrew word translated **indecency** is literally "nakedness." TEV "something about her that he doesn't like" is a possibility; the alternative rendering in the footnote offers another possibility: "later she is guilty of some shameful conduct." NRSV has "something objectionable," REB "something offensive," NJPSV "something obnoxious," CEV "something disgraceful about her"; these are all possible models.

He writes her a bill of divorce: a formal statement, presumably stating why he was sending her away. Some suppose that this included some sort of payment, but this cannot be proven. All the text says is that the husband gave his wife a document in which he stated that he was divorcing her. Many languages will have technical terms for the breaking of the marriage relationship. In other languages figurative language will be used, such as "driven out," "sent away," "returned to her parents," and so on. **A bill of divorce** may be alternatively rendered as "write her a paper to put her out," or " write a paper concerning sending her away," and so on.

Puts it in her hand: this is part of the procedure. The man must deliver it to his wife personally.

Sends her out of his house: this is the final step; he orders her to leave. There seems to be no sense of physical force in this action.

And she departs out of his house: in the Hebrew text this is the beginning of verse 2, not the end of verse 1 (NRSV repeats the RSV mistake). The Septuagint omits this clause. TEV, CEV, and NIV also omit it as redundant.

24.2	RSV	TEV
	and if she goes and becomes another man's wife,	Then suppose she marries another man,

And if she goes and becomes another man's wife: the text does not say how this happened. It only states that it has happened: "and gets married again." In certain languages this will be stated as "If some other man takes her as his wife."

24.3	RSV	TEV
	and the latter husband dislikes her and writes her a bill of divorce and puts it in her hand and sends her out of his house, or if the latter husband dies, who took her to be his wife,	and he also decides that he doesn't want her, so he also writes out divorce papers, gives them to her, and sends her away from his home. Or suppose her second husband dies.

The latter husband dislikes her: this is a most unnatural construction in English; something like "the second husband" or "this husband" is better. The same thing happens as in the first case: there is something about her that the second husband also doesn't like. The Hebrew verb is often translated "hates"; but here the more moderate **dislikes** is better in English. NJB has "takes a dislike to her."

Writes a bill of divorce . . . : the second husband follows the same three-step procedure followed by the first husband.

Or if the latter husband dies, who took her to be his wife: NRSV is better, "(or the second man who married her dies)." The point being made is that the woman may not remarry her first husband, so the possibility arises not only that the second husband may divorce her, but also that he may die. The clause **who took her to be his wife** is redundant information and will be unnatural style in a number of languages.

24.4	RSV	TEV
	then her former husband, who sent her away, may not take her again to be his wife, after she has been defiled; for that is an abomination before the LORD, and you shall not bring guilt upon the land which the LORD your God gives you for an inheritance.	In either case, her first husband is not to marry her again; he is to consider her defiled. If he married her again, it would be offensive to the LORD. You are not to commit such a terrible sin in the land that the LORD your God is giving you.

Her former husband, who sent her away, may not take her again to be his wife: this is the conclusion and the essential part of the whole regulation. Again, the Hebrew is quite redundant; the information **who sent her away** is not needed, although there is no harm in including it if it is not poor style. Both TEV and CEV have "her first husband." We may also say "the first man who took her as his wife."

After she has been defiled: this "defilement" is the result of her having married another man in addition to her first husband. So far as the first husband is concerned, she is **defiled,** that is, ritually impure. It is almost as if she had committed adultery. TEV takes it that this is from the husband's point of view; note also REB "for him she has become unclean." This is a possible model, but the absolute way of stating it as in RSV and NJPSV ("she has been defiled") may be better.

An abomination before the LORD: or "the LORD hates this." See 7.25.

You shall not bring guilt upon the land: instead of **guilt** a word like "sin" may be better (see TEV). But it may be better to try to express the idea of the effect this sin would have on the land itself. The land, that is, the country of Israel, is seen as having a moral quality that can be polluted by sin. So something like "you will cause the land to be contaminated [or, be made impure] by sin" may be better (so CEV "their marriage would pollute the land").

The land which the LORD your God gives you for an inheritance: the standard reminder; see 4.21.

2C-7. A newly married man (24.5)

RSV	TEV
	Various Laws
"When a man is newly married, he shall not go out with the army or be charged with any business; he shall be free at home one year, to be happy with his wife whom he has taken.	"When a man is newly married, he is not to be drafted into military service or any other public duty; he is to be excused from duty for one year, so that he can stay at home and make his wife happy.

TEV takes 24.5–25.4 as a single section with the general title, "Various Laws." There are eleven different units in this long passage, and instead of making one long section, it is recommended by this Handbook that each individual law be regarded as a section and given its own title.

This law reflects the situation described in 20.7. Here, besides being excused from active military service for a year, the newly-married man is also excused from being responsible for **any business**, which probably refers to other public duties (so commentators; also TEV and REB).

Section heading: this first section, verse 5, may have the heading "A newly married man," or more precisely, "Law concerning a man who has just taken a wife."

24.5 RSV	TEV
"When a man is newly married, he shall not go out with the army or be charged with any business; he shall be free at home one year, to be	"When a man is newly married, he is not to be drafted into military service or any other public duty; he is to be excused from duty for one year,

happy with his wife whom he has taken.	so that he can stay at home and make his wife happy.[v]

[v] make his wife happy; *or* be happy with his wife.

It will be helpful to reintroduce Moses as the speaker at the beginning of this new section.

He shall not . . . be charged with any business: it is impossible to think that the man would not have to work for a living for a whole year. CEV interprets "public duties" as only "forced labor," but other types of work are also possible. So "do any other work for the government [or, town]" is another possible rendering. Alternative translation models for the first part of this verse may be:

- Moses said to the people of Israel, "If a man has been married less than a year, they cannot send him off to war or make him do other work for the government."

- . . . "If a man has just taken a wife, he cannot be sent off to fight Israel's enemies or be forced to work for the town."

He shall be free at home one year: that is, exempt from all public responsibilities.

To be happy with his wife: the Masoretic form of the Hebrew text has the causative form of the verb, "to make his wife happy" (Septuagint, TEV, FRCL, NIV, NJB and others). The Hebrew consonants, however, may be given other vowels, making the verb mean "be happy with his wife," as RSV and REB translate. It seems better to stay with the Masoretic text; a translation may give the alternative in a footnote, as TEV does.

Whom he has taken: this information is redundant, and may be omitted.

2C-8. Loans (24.6)

RSV	TEV
"No man shall take a mill or an upper millstone in pledge; for he would be taking a life in pledge.	"When you lend someone something, you are not to take as security his millstones used for grinding his grain. This would take away the family's means of preparing food to stay alive.

Section heading: CEV has "Loans"; another possible heading is "Law about lending money to other people."

24.6

RSV	TEV
"No man shall take a mill or an upper millstone in pledge; for he would be taking a life in pledge.	"When you lend someone something, you are not to take as security his millstones used for grinding his grain. This would take away the family's means of preparing food to stay alive.

Take . . . in pledge: an Israelite could not charge a fellow-Israelite any interest on a loan. In order to make sure that the loan would be repaid, however, the lender would take an object of value from the borrower and keep it until the loan had been repaid. This item would serve as a **pledge**, that is, a promise on the part of the borrower that the loan would be repaid.

A mill: this refers to the small mill in every household with which the housewife would grind the grain every day in order to make bread. It consisted of two stones; it was enough to take away the **upper millstone** to render the mill ineffective.

An alternative translation model for the first part of this verse is:

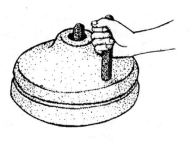

A PAIR OF MILLSTONES

- When you lend money to a fellow Israelite, you are allowed to keep something of his as a guarantee that he will pay back the money. But don't take either of the two stones used for grinding grain.

He would be taking a life in pledge: without the mill the family's health would be in danger. CEV has a helpful model: "they need those millstones for grinding grain into flour to make bread." However, if the information about grinding grain has been put into the previous sentence, we may say something like "they [he] use that flour for making bread to eat."

2C-9. Kidnaping (24.7)

RSV	TEV
"If a man is found stealing one of his brethren, the people of Israel, and if he treats him as a slave or sells him, then that thief shall die; so you shall purge the evil from the midst of you.	"If any of you kidnap Israelites and make them your slaves or sell them into slavery, you are to be put to death. In this way your nation will get rid of this evil.

Section heading: CEV has "Kidnaping," but in certain languages it will be better to use a full sentence, such as "Law against kidnaping fellow Israelites."

24.7   RSV   TEV

"If a man is found stealing one of his brethren, the people of Israel, and if he treats him as a slave or sells him, then that thief shall die; so you shall purge the evil from the midst of you.

"If any of you kidnap Israelites and make them your slaves or sell them into slavery, you are to be put to death. In this way your nation will get rid of this evil.

Is found stealing one of his brethren: as elsewhere, **brethren** means fellow-Israelites. To **steal** here means to "abduct by force" or "kidnap," and translators should use a term that clearly shows that the person has been abducted or taken away against his or her will. See the parallel passage in Exo 21.16.

The people of Israel are the same people as the **brethren** in the previous phrase, and in many languages the RSV literal rendering of the Hebrew will be unnatural style. It will be simpler to translate as "to kidnap a fellow-Israelite" (see also TEV).

Treats him as a slave: the same verb is used here that appears in 21.14 and nowhere else in the Old Testament. Here it seems to mean to keep him as his own slave. For **slave** see 5.6.

Or sells him: this is the other possibility. The kidnapper may try to sell his fellow-Israelite to someone else who will keep him as a slave.

That thief should die: such a person is to be executed.

So you shall purge the evil from the midst of you: see 13.5.

2C-10. Law about skin disease (24.8-9)

                    RSV   TEV

8 "Take heed, in an attack of leprosy, to be very careful to do according to all that the Levitical priests shall direct you; as I commanded them, so you shall be careful to do. 9 Remember what the LORD your God did to Miriam on the way as you came forth out of Egypt.

8 "When you are suffering from a dreaded skin disease, be sure to do exactly what the levitical priests tell you; follow the instructions that I have given them. 9 Remember what the LORD your God did to Miriam as you were coming from Egypt.

Section heading: a possible heading is "Law about skin disease."

24.8   RSV   TEV

"Take heed, in an attack of leprosy, to be very careful to do according to all that the Levitical priests shall direct you; as I commanded them, so you shall be careful to do.

"When you are suffering from a dreaded skin disease, be sure to do exactly what the levitical priests tell you; follow the instructions that I have given them.

Leprosy: it is known that the disease referred to by the Hebrew word is not what is called leprosy today. It was some kind of unsightly skin disease, such as "modern psoriasis or favus" (Mayes); few modern translations use the word "leprosy." Something like "a dreaded skin disease" (TEV) can be used, or else a footnote, such as NIV gives for "leprous disease": "The Hebrew word was used for various diseases affecting the skin—not necessarily leprosy." In Lev 13.47-59 the word is used for mildew, or mold, on clothing or leather objects, and in Lev 14.33-53 it is used of mildew on houses. It was considered to make the clothing, the leather objects, or the houses ritually impure, and they would have to be made clean (see Lev 13–14).

All that the Levitical priests shall direct you: for **Levitical priests** see 17.9. Here **direct** means "teach," "instruct."

As I commanded them: Moses is speaking, and the text makes it appear that he is talking about the kind of instructions found in Leviticus 13–14.

24.9   RSV   TEV

Remember what the LORD your God did to Miriam on the way as you came forth out of Egypt.

Remember what the LORD your God did to Miriam as you were coming from Egypt.

Remember what the LORD your God did to Miriam: see Num 12.10-15. For **the LORD your God** see 1.6.

As you came forth: Again the translator is reminded of the fact that Moses is the speaker, and the second person **you** could be read to mean that Moses was not with them. If that is what the reader will understand, then the translation should read "as we came out of Egypt."

2C-11. Loans (24.10-13)

RSV   TEV

10 "When you make your neighbor a loan of any sort, you shall not go into his house to fetch his pledge. 11 You shall stand outside, and the man to whom you make the loan shall bring the pledge out to you. 12 And if he is a poor man, you shall not sleep in his pledge; 13 when the sun goes down, you shall restore to him the pledge that he may sleep in his cloak and bless you; and it shall be righteousness to you before the LORD your God.

10 "When you lend someone something, do not go into his house to get the garment he is going to give you as security; 11 wait outside and let him bring it to you himself. 12 If he is poor, do not keep it overnight; 13 return it to him each evening, so that he can have it to sleep in. Then he will be grateful, and the LORD your God will be pleased with you.

In this section further instructions are given on the matter of lending money to a fellow-Israelite and how the **pledge** is to be handled.

Section heading: see the identical heading at verse 6.

24.10-11 RSV TEV

10 "When you make your neighbor a loan of any sort, you shall not go into his house to fetch his pledge. 11 You shall stand outside, and the man to whom you make the loan shall bring the pledge out to you.	10 "When you lend someone something, do not go into his house to get the garment he is going to give you as security; 11 wait outside and let him bring it to you himself.

You shall not go into his house: in this case the lender is not to intimidate the borrower—who would be a poorer person—by forcing his way into his house and demanding the object to be given as a pledge. Rather he is to wait at the door for his fellow-Israelite (**your neighbor**) to bring the object out to him.

Fetch his pledge: in many languages it will be necessary to make it clear here that what is pledged is a piece of clothing (verse 13); for example, "Don't go into the house to get the garment he is going to give you as security" (TEV) or ". . . to give you to guarantee that he will pay the money back."

Bring the pledge out to you: or "bring it [the garment] out to you."

An alternative translation model for verses 10 and 11 may be:

- [10]Moses said to the people of Israel, "When you lend a fellow Israelite some money, do not go into his house to get the garment that he is going to give to you as a guarantee that he will pay back the money. [11]Instead, wait outside and he will bring out the garment you have agreed on.

24.12 RSV TEV

And if he is a poor man, you shall not sleep in his pledge;	If he is poor, do not keep it overnight;

You shall not sleep in his pledge: as the context makes clear (verse 13), the object given in pledge is the poor man's cloak, that is, the long outer garment with which he covered himself as he slept. Without it he would be cold. The lender, therefore, is not to keep the man's garment after sundown, but is to return it to its owner. CEV makes it clear that the man is so poor that the long outer garment (cloak, or coat) is the only thing he can give as a guarantee: "Suppose someone is so poor that a coat is the only thing that can be offered as a guarantee on a loan."

The literal translation of RSV does not make it immediately clear that, in this context, the object given in pledge is the man's garment. It is better to supply that information immediately in verse 10, as TEV does: "the garment he is going to give you as security." NRSV translates verse 12 as follows: "you shall not sleep in the garment given you as[f] the pledge," with the following footnote: "Heb lacks *the garment given you as.*"

24.13   RSV   TEV

when the sun goes down, you shall restore to him the pledge that he may sleep in his cloak and bless you; and it shall be righteousness to you before the LORD your God.	return it to him each evening, so that he can have it to sleep in. Then he will be grateful, and the LORD your God will be pleased with you.

When the sun goes down: "at nightfall," the time to go to bed. In this context the sense is "each evening" (TEV).

You shall restore: the Hebrew is an emphatic form.

Bless you: this can mean "thank you," but more probably it means "ask God to bless you," or "ask God to make you prosperous."

Shall be righteousness to you before the LORD your God: God will consider such an act as the right conduct, the proper behavior. TEV "will be pleased with you" departs unnecessarily from the clear meaning of the Hebrew text. NJPSV has "it will be to your merit before the LORD your God," BRCL "what the LORD your God considers right," and CEV "Then the LORD your God will notice that you have done the right thing."

2C-12. Poor people's wages (24.14-15)

RSV   TEV

14 "You shall not oppress a hired servant who is poor and needy, whether he is one of your brethren or one of the sojourners who are in your land within your towns; 15 you shall give him his hire on the day he earns it, before the sun goes down (for he is poor, and sets his heart upon it); lest he cry against you to the LORD, and it be sin in you.	14 "Do not cheat poor and needy hired servants, whether they are Israelites or foreigners living in one of your towns. 15 Each day before sunset pay them for that day's work; they need the money and have counted on getting it. If you do not pay them, they will cry out against you to the LORD, and you will be guilty of sin.

Section heading: another possible heading is "The wages you pay to poor people."

24.14   RSV   TEV

"You shall not oppress a hired servant who is poor and needy, whether he is one of your brethren or one of the sojourners who are in your land within your towns;	"Do not cheat poor and needy hired servants, whether they are Israelites or foreigners living in one of your towns.

Oppress: the ordinary meaning is "mistreat," "treat harshly," "abuse," "exploit." Here, however, HOTTP understands the Masoretic Hebrew text to mean "you shall not exert any pressure [by means of] the wages of a poor man." REB translates this meaning with "keep back the wages of a poor man," and CEV "don't hold back their pay." SPCL gives both meanings: "exploit or keep back the wages." Should a translator decide to follow the recommendation of HOTTP, REB and CEV offer good models to follow.

A hired servant: a person who works for pay, usually on a daily basis (as the next verse makes clear).

Your brethren: that is, your fellow-Israelites (TEV, CEV).

The sojourners who are in your land within your towns: for **sojourners**, "alien residents," see 1.16. It is enough to say simply "the foreigners [or, non-Israelites] who live in your land."

24.15	RSV	TEV

you shall give him his hire on the day he earns it, before the sun goes down (for he is poor, and sets his heart upon it); lest he cry against you to the LORD, and it be sin in you.	**Each day before sunset pay them for that day's work; they need the money and have counted on getting it. If you do not pay them, they will cry out against you to the LORD, and you will be guilty of sin.**

His hire: that is, his pay, wages, salary.

Before the sun goes down: so he will have money as he goes home. He would be working until dark.

He is poor and sets his heart upon it: that is, he depends on the money he will be paid every day. NIV has "is counting on it," the Septuagint "places his hope on it" (similarly TEV), CEV "need the money to survive."

Lest he cry against you to the LORD: that is, "so that he will not ask the LORD to punish you." It will be helpful to add "If you do not pay him on time" to the clause "ask the LORD to punish you" (see below).

It be sin in you: this is the opposite of "righteousness" at the end of verse 13.

An alternative translation model for this verse may be:

- Each day before sunset you must pay him for the work he has done. He is a poor person and needs that money to survive. If you do not pay him on time, he will complain about you to Yahweh, who will punish you for your sin.

2C-13. The death penalty (24.16)

RSV	TEV
"The fathers shall not be put to death for the children, nor shall the children be put to death for the fathers; every man shall be put to death for his own sin.	"Parents are not to be put to death for crimes committed by their children, and children are not to be put to death for crimes committed by their parents; people are to be put to death only for a crime they themselves have committed.

The individual responsibility of each sinner (see Jer 31.29) contrasts sharply with the statement in 5.9 (see also the regulation in 13.12-18).

Section heading: possible headings are "The death penalty" or "The law about putting people to death."

24.16 RSV	TEV
"The fathers shall not be put to death for the children, nor shall the children be put to death for the fathers; every man shall be put to death for his own sin.	**"Parents are not to be put to death for crimes committed by their children, and children are not to be put to death for crimes committed by their parents; people are to be put to death only for a crime they themselves have committed.**

The fathers shall not be . . . . : instead of **fathers** the language used should include both sexes (see TEV). NRSV has at the end "only for their own crimes may persons be put to death." In languages that do not use the passive voice, we may say, for example, "You must not put parents to death for crimes that their children have committed, and you must not put children to death for crimes that . . . ."

In this context **sin** has the sense of some crime that calls for the death penalty. So we may say "Don't put anyone to death for someone else's crime" (CEV; similarly TEV).

2C-14. Don't mistreat the powerless (24.17-18)

RSV	TEV
17 "You shall not pervert the justice due to the sojourner or to the fatherless, or take a widow's garment in pledge; 18 but you shall remember that you were a slave in Egypt and the LORD your God redeemed you from there; therefore I command you to do this.	17 "Do not deprive foreigners and orphans of their rights; and do not take a widow's garment as security for a loan. 18 Remember that you were slaves in Egypt and that the LORD your God set you free; that is why I have given you this command.

Again the Israelites are reminded that they were slaves in Egypt, and so they must deal in a kindly and compassionate manner with those who have no power in their society, the **sojourner**, the **fatherless**, and the **widow**.

Section heading: another possible heading is "Don't mistreat people who have no power."

24.17 RSV	TEV
"You shall not pervert the justice due to the sojourner or to the father-	**"Do not deprive foreigners and orphans of their rights; and do not**

| less, or take a widow's garment in pledge; | take a widow's garment as security for a loan. |

Pervert the justice due: see 16.19. Here the sense is "deprive of their rights," or "deny justice." The command may also be stated in a positive manner: "Make sure they get their rights," or ". . . they are treated fairly" (CEV).

Sojourner: see 1.16.

In **to the sojourner or to the fatherless**, the Masoretic form of the Hebrew text has no "and" before the second noun. HOTTP recommends "the fatherless sojourner"; but this is a very strange phrase and occurs nowhere else in the Old Testament. NJB and TOB have "the sojourner or the fatherless," stating that instead of the Hebrew text they are following ancient versions. NJPSV has a note, and all other major translations consulted (NIV, NRSV, REB, SPCL, BRCL, POCL, FRCL) follow the same text, but without a footnote. This will make the verse agree with the following verses, where the three categories "foreigners, orphans, and widows" are mentioned in that order in each verse. Translators are urged to do the same. For **orphans** see 10.18.

Take a widow's garment in pledge: as in the parallel case in verse 6. She needs her clothes.

24.18 RSV	TEV
but you shall remember that you were a slave in Egypt and the LORD your God redeemed you from there; therefore I command you to do this.	Remember that you were slaves in Egypt and that the LORD your God set you free; that is why I have given you this command.

You shall remember: see 15.15.

For **redeemed** see 7.8.

2C-15. Leave some of your harvest for the poor (24.19-22)

RSV	TEV
19 "When you reap your harvest in your field, and have forgotten a sheaf in the field, you shall not go back to get it; it shall be for the sojourner, the fatherless, and the widow; that the LORD your God may bless you in all the work of your hands. 20 When you beat your olive trees, you shall not go over the boughs again; it shall be for the sojourner, the fatherless, and the widow. 21 When you gather the grapes of your vineyard, you shall not glean it afterward; it shall be for the sojourner, the fatherless, and the widow. 22 You shall remember that you were a slave in the land of Egypt; therefore I command you to do this.	19 "When you gather your crops and fail to bring in some of the grain that you have cut, do not go back for it; it is to be left for the foreigners, orphans, and widows, so that the LORD your God will bless you in everything you do. 20 When you have picked your olives once, do not go back and get those that are left; they are for the foreigners, orphans, and widows. 21 When you have gathered your grapes once, do not go back over the vines a second time; the grapes that are left are for the foreigners, orphans, and widows. 22 Never forget that you were slaves in Egypt; that is why I have given you this command.

At the time of harvest the Israelites are always to leave some for the resident aliens, the orphans, and the widows (see all three in 10.19; 14.29). See the same kind of legislation in Lev 19.9-10, 23.22.

Section heading: another possible heading is "Leave some of your crops for poor people."

24.19   RSV   TEV

"When you reap your harvest in your field, and have forgotten a sheaf in the field, you shall not go back to get it; it shall be for the sojourner, the fatherless, and the widow; that the LORD your God may bless you in all the work of your hands.

"When you gather your crops and fail to bring in some of the grain that you have cut, do not go back for it; it is to be left for the foreigners, orphans, and widows, so that the LORD your God will bless you in everything you do.

When you reap: this would be done with a scythe or sickle. We may say simply "cut down your grain."

Your harvest: in verses 19-21 the main agricultural products are cited. These are grain (wheat or barley), olive trees (for the production of olive oil), and vineyard (for the production of wine). For comments on these crops see 7.13.

A sheaf consists of stalks of ripe grain that have been cut and tied into a bundle, with the heads of grain at one end.

SHEAVES OF GRAIN

For the sojourner, . . .: the Septuagint adds "the poor" at the beginning of the list here. For **sojourner** see 1.16.

The LORD your God may bless you in all the work of your hands: see 14.29.

24.20   RSV   TEV

When you beat your olive trees, you shall not go over the boughs again; it shall be for the sojourner, the fatherless, and the widow.

When you have picked your olives once, do not go back and get those that are left; they are for the foreigners, orphans, and widows.

Beat: this would be done with a stick, to knock down the olives.

You shall not go over the boughs again: they were not to go back and knock down the olives that did not fall off the first time.

At the end of this verse the Septuagint adds the command that is given in verse 22.

24.21-22 RSV TEV

21 When you gather the grapes of your vineyard, you shall not glean it afterward; it shall be for the sojourner, the fatherless, and the widow. 22 You shall remember that you were a slave in the land of Egypt; therefore I command you to do this.

21 When you have gathered your grapes once, do not go back over the vines a second time; the grapes that are left are for the foreigners, orphans, and widows. 22 Never forget that you were slaves in Egypt; that is why I have given you this command.

Gather: this would be by hand.

You shall not glean it afterwards: they were not to go back and pick the clusters that had been left.

For **You shall remember . . .** , see verse 18.

2C-16. Whipping as punishment for a crime (25.1-3)

RSV TEV

1 "If there is a dispute between men, and they come into court, and the judges decide between them, acquitting the innocent and condemning the guilty, 2 then if the guilty man deserves to be beaten, the judge shall cause him to lie down and be beaten in his presence with a number of stripes in proportion to his offense. 3 Forty stripes may be given him, but not more; lest, if one should go on to beat him with more stripes than these, your brother be degraded in your sight.

1 "Suppose two Israelites go to court to settle a dispute, and one is declared innocent and the other guilty. 2 If the guilty one is sentenced to be beaten, the judge is to make him lie face downward and have him whipped. The number of lashes will depend on the crime he has committed. 3 He may be given as many as forty lashes, but no more; more than that would humiliate him publicly.

This law limits the number of lashes that may be given to a person found guilty of some crime.

Section heading: CEV has "Whipping as Punishment for a Crime." It is also possible to say "The law about whipping a criminal."

25.1 RSV TEV

"If there is a dispute between men, and they come into court, and the judges decide between them, acquitting the innocent and condemning the guilty,

"Suppose two Israelites go to court to settle a dispute, and one is declared innocent and the other guilty.

407

With the beginning of a new section, Moses should be reintroduced as the speaker.

The occasion for this law is a **dispute**, that is, a legal controversy between two Israelites that must be settled in **court** by **the judges** (see 1.16).

Between men: it is better to say "two Israelites" (TEV) or "two Israelite men."

Decide between them: for the procedure to be followed, see similar cases in 17.8-13; 19.17-18. A more natural way of stating this is "the judges decide that one [of the two men] is guilty." It should be understood from this that the other one is innocent.

Acquitting the innocent and condemning the guilty: the Hebrew text uses two pairs of cognate phrases, that is, phrases consisting of a verb and an adjective formed from the same Hebrew root. TEV combines the final two clauses as follows: "one is declared innocent and the other guilty." We may also translate "the judges decide that one [of the two men] is guilty and the other is innocent."

25.2   RSV   TEV

| then if the guilty man deserves to be beaten, the judge shall cause him to lie down and be beaten in his presence with a number of stripes in proportion to his offense. | If the guilty one is sentenced to be beaten, the judge is to make him lie face downward and have him whipped. The number of lashes will depend on the crime he has committed. |

If the guilty man deserves to be beaten: this is a serious offense, and the guilty person is to be flogged, that is, beaten with a whip made of leather thongs, or perhaps with a rod. In languages that do not use the passive voice, we may say, for example, "If the judges order them to beat [or, whip] the guilty man."

The judge shall cause him to lie down: the judge will have the man lie prone, that is, face down on the ground. The Septuagint keeps the plural "the judges" from the previous verse (so also CEV).

In his presence: to make sure the punishment is carried out exactly as he ordered. Another way to express this is "in front of him."

A number of stripes in proportion to his offense: this would be according to the judge's decision. **Stripes** may be also expressed as "lashes," "strokes," or "blows," or even "times," as in "the number of times that he is to be hit with the whip."

25.3   RSV   TEV

| Forty stripes may be given him, but not more; lest, if one should go on to beat him with more stripes than | He may be given as many as forty lashes, but no more; more than that would humiliate him publicly. |

**these, your brother be degraded in
your sight.**

Forty stripes may be given him: in no case could the judge order more than
forty lashes to be given to the guilty person. In later times the maximum was
reduced to thirty-nine lashes (see 2 Cor 11.24) to make sure that the limit in
this law was not exceeded. Another way to express this is "They may not hit
him more than forty times with the whip."

Your brother: that is, your fellow-Israelite. REB "your neighbor" is not correct
in this context.

Degraded in your sight: the sense is that a fellow-Israelite should not be
publicly humiliated or "made to lose face in front of the other Israelites."

2C-17. Don't muzzle an ox (25.4)

RSV	TEV
"You shall not muzzle an ox when it treads out the grain.	"Do not muzzle an ox when you are using it to thresh grain.

This law is cited in 1 Cor 9.9 and 1 Tim 5.18; in both passages it is interpreted figuratively, not literally.

Section heading: CEV has "Don't Muzzle an Ox." Another way to express this
is "Don't put something over the mouth of an ox to keep it from eating."

25.4	RSV	TEV
	"You shall not muzzle an ox when it treads out the grain.	**"Do not muzzle an ox when you are using it to thresh grain.**

You shall not muzzle an ox: the **muzzle** was an object placed over the mouth
of the ox to prevent it from eating the grain as it was treading on it. In cultures
where muzzles are unknown, we may translate, for example, "You must not put
anything over the mouth of an ox while . . . ." For a comment on **ox** see 5.14.

Treads out the grain: the ox would either be walked across the threshing
floor, thus separating the grains from the ears, or else it would pull a threshing
sledge across the floor (or, platform). According to this law the ox should be
allowed to eat some of the ears of grain as it worked. In cultures where other
methods are used for threshing grain, a cultural note in the glossary describing
the Hebrew method will be helpful.

Alternative ways of expressing this verse are:

- You shall not put anything on the mouth of an ox to prevent it
from eating while it is treading out the grain.

- You must not prevent an ox from eating while . . . .

2C-18. Duty to a dead brother (25.5-10)

RSV	TEV
	Duty to a Dead Brother

5 "If brothers dwell together, and one of them dies and has no son, the wife of the dead shall not be married outside the family to a stranger; her husband's brother shall go in to her, and take her as his wife, and perform the duty of a husband's brother to her. 6 And the first son whom she bears shall succeed to the name of his brother who is dead, that his name may not be blotted out of Israel. 7 And if the man does not wish to take his brother's wife, then his brother's wife shall go up to the gate to the elders, and say, 'My husband's brother refuses to perpetuate his brother's name in Israel; he will not perform the duty of a husband's brother to me.' 8 Then the elders of his city shall call him, and speak to him: and if he persists, saying, 'I do not wish to take her,' 9 then his brother's wife shall go up to him in the presence of the elders, and pull his sandal off his foot, and spit in his face; and she shall answer and say, 'So shall it be done to the man who does not build up his brother's house.' 10 And the name of his house shall be called in Israel, The house of him that had his sandal pulled off.

5 "If two brothers live on the same property and one of them dies, leaving no son, then his widow is not to be married to someone outside the family; it is the duty of the dead man's brother to marry her. 6 The first son that they have will be considered the son of the dead man, so that his family line will continue in Israel. 7 But if the dead man's brother does not want to marry her, she is to go before the town leaders and say, 'My husband's brother will not do his duty; he refuses to give his brother a descendant among the people of Israel.' 8 Then the town leaders are to summon him and speak to him. If he still refuses to marry her, 9 his brother's widow is to go up to him in the presence of the town leaders, take off one of his sandals, spit in his face, and say, 'This is what happens to the man who refuses to give his brother a descendant.' 10 His family will be known in Israel as 'the family of the man who had his sandal pulled off.'

This law is the basis for the custom of "levirate marriage," which was practiced in ancient Israel. The purpose of the custom was to ensure that a man who died before he had produced a male heir might nevertheless have an heir.

Section heading: the TEV title "Duty to a Dead Brother" or "Son for a Dead Brother" (CEV) may be satisfactory in some, if not most, languages. FRCL has "The Childless Widow," which is much too general. Some translations use the technical term "levirate," but this word is familiar only to specialists and is quite unsatisfactory in a translation for general use.

25.5   RSV   TEV

"If brothers dwell together, and one of them dies and has no son, the wife of the dead shall not be married outside the family to a stranger; her husband's brother shall go in to her, and take her as his wife, and perform the duty of a husband's brother to her.

"If two brothers live on the same property and one of them dies, leaving no son, then his widow is not to be married to someone outside the family; it is the duty of the dead man's brother to marry her.

Brothers dwell together: not necessarily in the same house, but on the same family property. TEV makes this clear, with "live on the same property." In this instance **brothers** means blood brothers.

One of them dies and has no son: the Hebrew word is the normal one for **son**; but the Septuagint has "seed" (meaning descendants, of either sex). As quoted in the Gospels, Mark 13.19 has "has no child," Matt 22.24 "has no children," and Luke 20.28 "is childless." It seems from the context that the meaning here is a male descendant, a **son** (so also TEV, CEV, NIV).

The wife of the dead: many languages will have a technical term such as "widow" for this woman, and say for example, "his widow," or "the widow of the man"; but in other languages "the wife of the dead man" may be preferable.

Shall not be married outside the family to a stranger: the woman was not to be married off to a man belonging to a clan different from the one her dead husband belonged to. The main reason for this, it seems, was to keep property from passing on to another family. **Shall not be married** suggests that the woman would not take the initiative to choose a partner, but that her family would find a new husband for her. TEV follows this interpretation with "then his widow is not to be married to." CEV "his widow must not marry" appears to clash with Hebrew custom.

Go in to her, and take her as his wife: this is a normal way in Hebrew of speaking of possessing a woman sexually; in most languages there are more appropriate ways of saying this. In many languages "and take her as his wife" will be sufficient.

In the Hebrew text the noun "brother-in-law," the verb **perform the duty of a husband's brother**, and the noun **brother's wife** in verse 7 are all cognates, that is, they come from the same Hebrew root; they appear only here and in Gen 38.8. For **perform the duty of a husband's brother**, NJPSV has "perform the *levir*'s duty." TEV combines both sentences with "it is the duty of the dead man's brother to marry her." This will be a helpful model for many translators.

25.6	RSV	TEV

And the first son whom she bears shall succeed to the name of his brother who is dead, that his name may not be blotted out of Israel.	The first son that they have will be considered the son of the dead man, so that his family line will continue in Israel.

The first son whom she bears: even though the Septuagint has "the first child," translators should make it clear that this is a male child.

Shall succeed to the name of his brother who is dead: here, of course, **his brother** is the father's brother. The meaning is that the baby boy will be given his (dead) uncle's name, not the name of his actual father. CEV has "and their first son will be the legal son of the dead man."

His name may not be blotted out: that is, the family line or name of the dead man will not cease to exist (so TEV), but continue in a normal way.

25.7   RSV   TEV

And if the man does not wish to take his brother's wife, then his brother's wife shall go up to the gate to the elders, and say, 'My husband's brother refuses to perpetuate his brother's name in Israel; he will not perform the duty of a husband's brother to me.'	But if the dead man's brother does not want to marry her, she is to go before the town leaders and say, 'My husband's brother will not do his duty; he refuses to give his brother a descendant among the people of Israel.'

Verses 7-10 describe the procedure to be followed if the dead man's brother does not wish to fulfil his duty as a brother-in-law.

Go up to the gate to the elders: see similar language in 21.19. For **elders** see 5.23.

Does not wish to take his brother's wife: or "refuses to marry the widow" (CEV).

Refuses to perpetuate his brother's name: **perpetuate** is the same Hebrew verb "make stand" that is used in verse 6 ("succeed to"). TEV has "he refuses to give his brother a descendant among the people of Israel."

Not perform the duty of a husband's brother: the same language as used in verse 5.

25.8   RSV   TEV

Then the elders of his city shall call him, and speak to him: and if he persists, saying, 'I do not wish to take her,'	Then the town leaders are to summon him and speak to him. If he still refuses to marry her,

Then the elders of his city shall call him: in this way the actions of the man and their consequences for the family are made public.

25.9   RSV   TEV

then his brother's wife shall go up to him in the presence of the elders, and pull his sandal off his foot, and spit in his face; and she shall answer and say, 'So shall it be done to the man who does not build up his brother's house.'	his brother's widow is to go up to him in the presence of the town leaders, take off one of his sandals, spit in his face, and say, 'This is what happens to the man who refuses to give his brother a descendant.'

This sets the procedure to be followed if the dead man's brother tells the town's elders that he will not perform his duty.

In the presence of the elders: or "while the town leaders watch" (CEV).

Pull his sandal off his foot: the symbolic meaning of this act is not clear. If we need to say which foot, we can say "his right foot." See the procedure described in Ruth 4.7-9. The Hebrew **sandal** refers to footwear tied with straps.

Spit in his face: this, of course, is a highly insulting act.

Shall answer: this is a formal statement. In English it may be expressed as "shall declare" or "shall state."

So shall it be done: this does not refer to some future happening; it is the public humiliating insult which has just been inflicted on the man. Other ways of expressing this are "This is what happens" (TEV) or "That's what happens" (CEV).

The man who does not build up his brother's house: here **house** means "family," and the meaning is that, by refusing to produce a son for his brother, the man is allowing the brother's family name to disappear. Both TEV and CEV are good models for translation.

25.10 RSV	TEV
And the name of his house[u] shall be called in Israel, The house of him that had his sandal pulled off.	His family will be known in Israel as 'the family of the man who had his sandal pulled off.'

[u] Heb *its name*

This repeats what is said in verse 9.

House again means "family."

Shall be called in Israel: that is, "will be known from that time on among the people of Israel"; or we may say "the people of Israel will call his family . . . ."

The house of him that had his sandal pulled off: or "the family of the man who had his sandal pulled off" (TEV; similarly CEV).

2C-19. When two men fight (25.11-12)

RSV	TEV *Other Laws*
11 "When men fight with one another, and the wife of the one draws near to rescue her husband from the hand of him who is beating him, and puts out her hand and seizes him by the private parts, 12 then you shall cut off her hand; your eye shall have no pity.	11 "If two men are having a fight and the wife of one tries to help her husband by grabbing hold of the other man's genitals, 12 show her no mercy; cut off her hand.

Section heading: for this law NRSV has the title "Immodest Assault." This may not be a good model for some languages. CEV is better, with "When Two Men Fight."

25.11 RSV	TEV
"When men fight with one another, and the wife of the one draws near to rescue her husband from the hand of him who is beating him, and puts out her hand and seizes him by the private parts,	"If two men are having a fight and the wife of one tries to help her husband by grabbing hold of the other man's genitals,

With the beginning of a new section, Moses should be reintroduced as the speaker.

Men fight with one another: the context makes it clear that this is a case of two men having a fight. So we may say "If two men are fighting with each other."

To rescue her husband from the hand of him who is beating him: that is, "from his assailant's attack." It is clear that it is the wife of the man who is losing the fight who rushes in to help her husband.

The private parts: in translation an appropriate word or expression that can be read aloud in mixed company must be used to refer to the male genitals.

25.12 RSV	TEV
then you shall cut off her hand; your eye shall have no pity.	show her no mercy; cut off her hand.

You shall cut off her hand: the proper authorities are to make the decision. It is pointed out that only here (besides the "law of retaliation" ruling in 19.21) is mutilation prescribed as appropriate punishment.

Your eye shall have no pity: the same phrase used in 19.21.

2C-20. Be honest in business (25.13-16)

RSV	TEV
13 "You shall not have in your bag two kinds of weights, a large and a small. 14 You shall not have in your house two kinds of measures, a large and a small. 15 A full and just weight you shall have, a full and just measure you shall have; that your days may be prolonged in the land which the LORD your God gives you. 16 For all who do such things, all who act dishonestly, are an abomination to the LORD your God.	13-14 "Do not cheat when you use weights and measures. 15 Use true and honest weights and measures, so that you may live a long time in the land that the LORD your God is giving you. 16 The LORD hates people who cheat.

This regulation about honest weights and measures is an important one and appears quite frequently (Lev 19.35-36; Pro 16.11, 20.23; Ezek 45.10-12; see also the prophets' denunciations in Hos 12.7 and Micah 6.10-11).

Section heading: a good model for a heading is "Be Honest in Business" (CEV).

25.13-14	RSV	TEV

13 "You shall not have in your bag two kinds of weights, a large and a small. 14 You shall not have in your house two kinds of measures, a large and a small.

13-14 "Do not cheat when you use weights and measures.

With the beginning of a new section, Moses should be reintroduced as the speaker.

As a comparison with RSV shows, the TEV has given a summary of the two verses without losing any essential information. But most translations will prefer to follow the wordier form of the Hebrew.

Your bag: where the **weights** were kept. In buying, the dishonest merchant would put a heavier weight in one of the plates of the scales, so as to get more produce on the other plate; in selling, he would use a lighter weight, thereby decreasing the amount of produce the buyer was getting. Where the Hebrew system of weights and balances is unknown, translators should attempt to adapt the translation to the system used in their culture.

Your house: this can be translated simply "in your possession" (see TEV). Again, a dishonest person would use two different **measures** (baskets or some other containers for measuring volume), one larger than the other, for his own benefit.

25.15	RSV	TEV

A full and just weight you shall have, a full and just measure you shall have; that your days may be prolonged in the land which the LORD your God gives you.

Use true and honest weights and measures, so that you may live a long time in the land that the LORD your God is giving you.

This is the positive command that matches the negative commands in the previous verses. For buying and for selling, everyone should use the same set of accurate weights and measures, in conformity with the official standard.

Full and just: REB has "true and correct," TEV "true and honest," and CEV "weigh and measure things honestly."

That your days may be prolonged in the land: see 5.16; 22.6.

The land which the LORD your God gives you: see 7.1.

25.16   RSV   TEV

For all who do such things, all who act dishonestly, are an abomination to the LORD your God.   **The LORD hates people who cheat.**

All who do such things, all who act dishonestly: the second clause refers to the same set of people as the first clause. The two may be brought together as follows: "all who do such dishonest things," or "all who cheat or are dishonest."

An abomination to the LORD your God: see 7.25; 18.12; 22.5.

2C-21. The command to kill the Amalekites (25.17-19)

RSV   TEV
The Command to Kill the Amalekites

17 "Remember what Amalek did to you on the way as you came out of Egypt, 18 how he attacked you on the way, when you were faint and weary, and cut off at your rear all who lagged behind you; and he did not fear God. 19 Therefore when the LORD your God has given you rest from all your enemies round about, in the land which the LORD your God gives you for an inheritance to possess, you shall blot out the remembrance of Amalek from under heaven; you shall not forget.

17 "Remember what the Amalekites did to you as you were coming from Egypt. 18 They had no fear of God, and so they attacked you from the rear when you were tired and exhausted, and killed all who were straggling behind. 19 So then, when the LORD your God has given you the land and made you safe from all your enemies who live around you, be sure to kill all the Amalekites, so that no one will remember them any longer. Do not forget!

For the hostility that existed between the Israelites and the Amalekites, see Exo 17.8-16; and in 1 Sam 15.1-9 see the incident between King Saul and the Amalekites, and how he treated King Agag. Agag appears again in the book of Esther (3.1-2) as the ancestor of the evil Haman.

Section heading: for this section the TEV title seems adequate: "The Command to Kill the Amalekites." If a fuller statement is needed, something like the following will do: "Moses commands the Israelites to kill the Amalekites."

25.17   RSV   TEV

"Remember what Amalek did to you on the way as you came out of Egypt,   **"Remember what the Amalekites did to you as you were coming from Egypt.**

With the beginning of a new section, Moses should be reintroduced as the speaker.

Amalek was a region to the south of the land of Israel, south and west of the Dead Sea. Here **Amalek** is not a man's name but the name of a people; it is better to say "the Amalekites" or "the people of the Amalek region" (see 7.1).

As you came out of Egypt: see in 24.9 the remarks made about this use of the second person plural, **you**.

25.18	RSV	TEV

how he attacked you on the way, when you were faint and weary, and cut off at your rear all who lagged behind you; and he did not fear God.	They had no fear of God, and so they attacked you from the rear when you were tired and exhausted, and killed all who were straggling behind.

He attacked you on the way: the Amalekites attacked the Israelites as they made their way from Egypt to the Promised Land. If a pronoun is used it should agree with the noun in the previous verse; note TEV "They."

You were faint and weary; or, as in TEV, "tired and exhausted." The long trek had left the Israelites weak and tired.

Cut off at your rear all who lagged behind you: the Amalekites attacked from the rear and killed the stragglers, who were unable to keep up with the main body of Israelites.

He did not fear God: they were a pagan people, without any concern for God. In many languages it will be helpful to put this clause at the beginning of the verse as follows: "they were not afraid of God, so they attacked . . ."; or if we keep the clause at the end of the verse, we may say "this showed that the Amalekites were not afraid of [or, did not respect] God."

25.19	RSV	TEV

Therefore when the LORD your God has given you rest from all your enemies round about, in the land which the LORD your God gives you for an inheritance to possess, you shall blot out the remembrance of Amalek from under heaven; you shall not forget.	So then, when the LORD your God has given you the land and made you safe from all your enemies who live around you, be sure to kill all the Amalekites, so that no one will remember them any longer. Do not forget!

When the LORD your God has given you rest from all your enemies round about: see 3.20; 12.9.

The land which the LORD your God gives you for an inheritance to possess: for this oft-repeated statement see 3.18; 7.1. Here is one of the few passages where the two Hebrew words for "inherit" and "inheritance" are used (see the double use also in 15.4).

Blot out the remembrance of Amalek: see 9.14; 25.6. The meaning here is that the Amalekites are to be destroyed so completely that they will no longer be remembered. 1 Chr 4.43 tells of the destruction of the last surviving Amalekites by King Hezekiah of Judah (ruled 716-657 B.C.). TEV has "be sure to kill all the Amalekites, so that no one will remember them any longer," or "... so completely that no one will remember they ever lived" (CEV).

From under heaven: this is simply a way of saying "in the whole world."

You shall not forget: this is more in the nature of a command than a statement. We may say "Do not forget!" (TEV) or "Remember this!"

2C-22. The first part of the harvest (26.1-11)

RSV

1 "When you come into the land which the LORD your God gives you for an inheritance, and have taken possession of it, and live in it, 2 you shall take some of the first of all the fruit of the ground, which you harvest from your land that the LORD your God gives you, and you shall put it in a basket, and you shall go to the place which the LORD your God will choose, to make his name to dwell there. 3 And you shall go to the priest who is in office at that time, and say to him, 'I declare this day to the LORD your God that I have come into the land which the LORD swore to our fathers to give us.' 4 Then the priest shall take the basket from your hand, and set it down before the altar of the LORD your God.

5 "And you shall make response before the LORD your God, 'A wandering Aramean was my father; and he went down into Egypt and sojourned there, few in number; and there he became a nation, great, mighty, and populous. 6 And the Egyptians treated us harshly, and afflicted us, and laid upon us hard bondage. 7 Then we cried to the LORD the God of our fathers, and the LORD heard our voice, and saw our affliction, our toil, and our oppression; 8 and the LORD brought us out of Egypt with a mighty hand and an outstretched arm, with great terror, with signs and wonders; 9 and he brought us into this place and gave us this land, a land flowing with milk and honey. 10 And behold, now I bring the first of the fruit of the ground, which thou, O LORD, hast given me.' And you shall set it down before the LORD your God, and worship before the LORD your God; 11 and you shall rejoice in all the good which the LORD your God has given to you and to your house, you, and the Levite, and the sojourner who is among you.

TEV
Harvest Offerings

1 "After you have occupied the land that the LORD your God is giving you and have settled there, 2 each of you must place in a basket the first part of each crop that you harvest and you must take it with you to the one place of worship. 3 Go to the priest in charge at that time and say to him, 'I now acknowledge to the LORD my God that I have entered the land that he promised our ancestors to give us.'

4 "The priest will take the basket from you and place it before the altar of the LORD your God. 5 Then, in the LORD's presence you will recite these words: 'My ancestor was a wandering Aramean, who took his family to Egypt to live. They were few in number when they went there, but they became a large and powerful nation. 6 The Egyptians treated us harshly and forced us to work as slaves. 7 Then we cried out for help to the LORD, the God of our ancestors. He heard us and saw our suffering, hardship, and misery. 8 By his great power and strength he rescued us from Egypt. He worked miracles and wonders, and caused terrifying things to happen. 9 He brought us here and gave us this rich and fertile land. 10 So now I bring to the LORD the first part of the harvest that he has given me.'

"Then set the basket down in the LORD's presence and worship there. 11 Be grateful for the good things that the LORD your God has given you and your family; and let the Levites and the foreigners who live among you join in the celebration.

In TEV the general title "Harvest Offerings" heads a section (26.1-15) that gives information on two different offerings. The first part of this section (verses 1-11) refers to the offering of a part of the first crops grown after the Israelites have settled in the land of Canaan. This first share belonged to God

(18.4; see also Exo 22.28; 23.19; 34.26; Lev 2.12, 14; 23.10-17), as did also the first-born male of the domestic animals (Exo 13.11-15). This offering was accompanied by the recital of a confession and the promise to obey God's laws (verses 5-10). The produce was taken to the central sanctuary (verse 2) and given to the priest, who set it down in front of the altar (verses 3-4).

Section heading: this section, verses 1-11, may be entitled "The first part of the harvest," or even "Give the LORD the First Part of Your Harvest" (CEV).

26.1 RSV	TEV
"When you come into the land which the LORD your God gives you for an inheritance, and have taken possession of it, and live in it,	"After you have occupied the land that the LORD your God is giving you and have settled there,

With the beginning of a new chapter and section, Moses should be reintroduced as the speaker.

The land which the LORD your God gives you for an inheritance and have taken possession of it: for the double use of **inheritance** and **take possession**, see 3.18 and 25.19.

And live in it: this refers to a time when the Israelites have settled down and have had time to grow their first crops.

26.2 RSV	TEV
you shall take some of the first of all the fruit of the ground, which you harvest from your land that the LORD your God gives you, and you shall put it in a basket, and you shall go to the place which the LORD your God will choose, to make his name to dwell there.	each of you must place in a basket the first part of each crop that you harvest and you must take it with you to the one place of worship.

Take some of the first of all the fruit of the ground: this means crops, of course, and the word **fruit** (also NRSV) should be understood in the general sense of "crops" or "produce," not just what grew on fruit trees. Other ways to express this are "the first part of each crop that you harvest" (TEV) or "when you begin harvesting each of your crops, the first things you pick . . ." (CEV).

And you shall put it in a basket: the amount offered was a token amount (**some**), which could be carried in **a basket**. In cultures where many types of baskets are used, a translator should find a term for **basket** that foodstuffs such as grain or fruit are generally stored or carried in.

The place which the LORD your God will choose, to make his name to dwell there: the central sanctuary; see 12.11.

CEV has a helpful model for verses 1 and 2:

● ¹ *Moses said to Israel:*

The LORD is giving you the land, and soon you will conquer it, settle down, ² and plant crops. And when you begin harvesting each of your crops, the very first things you pick must be put in a basket. Take them to the place where the LORD your God chooses to be worshiped.

26.3   RSV   TEV

And you shall go to the priest who is in office at that time, and say to him, 'I declare this day to the LORD your God that I have come into the land which the LORD swore to our fathers to give us.'

Go to the priest in charge at that time and say to him, 'I now acknowledge to the LORD my God that I have entered the land that he promised our ancestors to give us.'

The priest who is in office at that time: see the same statement of priests and judges in 17.9; 19.17.

I declare this day to the LORD your God: it is somewhat strange that the man refers to Yahweh as the God of the priest; it may seem that **your** (singular) is exclusive, meaning that Yahweh is not the God of the man himself; but this is not the case. Ways to avoid this problem are "the LORD my God" (TEV, as in some Septuagint manuscripts) or "the LORD our God" (CEV). Some languages, however, may wish to follow the Hebrew text quite literally and say "the LORD [or, Yahweh], the God you serve" (and see "your God" in the next verse). The verb **declare** introduces a formal statement, a solemn confession.

I have come into this land: the sense is that he is now living in Canaan.

The LORD swore to our fathers to give us: see 1.8.

26.4   RSV   TEV

Then the priest shall take the basket from your hand, and set it down before the altar of the LORD your God.

"The priest will take the basket from you and place it before the altar of the LORD your God.

Set it down before the altar of the LORD your God: here **your** is singular again, but this time it refers to the man who is making the offering.

In verse 10 it is the man himself, and not **the priest**, as here, who places the basket in front of the altar. For **altar** see 7.5.

26.5   RSV   TEV

"And you shall make response before the LORD your God, 'A wandering Aramean was my father; and he went down into Egypt and sojourned

Then, in the LORD's presence you will recite these words: 'My ancestor was a wandering Aramean, who took his family to Egypt to live. They were

there, few in number; and there he became a nation, great, mighty, and populous.	few in number when they went there, but they became a large and powerful nation.

You shall make response: a compound verbal phrase is used, "you will declare and say"; see 21.7. This is a formal statement. Another way to render this is "you will recite these words."

Before the LORD your God: see 1.6.

A wandering Aramean: here **Aramean** means a native of Aram, modern Syria. Most take it to mean Jacob, but some others think it is Abraham. Jacob, however, seems to be more likely. This is the only place in the Old Testament where the noun **Aramean** appears. Instead of **wandering** (so most translations), some take the Hebrew to mean "ailing" or "perishing." It seems better to take the sense as **wandering**, which means not having a fixed place to live, or "moving from place to place." "Homeless" (CEV) is misleading, since that means "not having a house or place to live in"; but Jacob lived in a tent, which was considered to be his home.

My father: "my ancestor," that is, Jacob. But Jacob's name should not appear in the text. For **father** or "ancestor" see 1.8.

He went down into Egypt: from Canaan, or possibly from Haran if the reference is to Abraham. The phrase **went down** is the conventional way of speaking in Hebrew about going from Canaan to Egypt; it does not mean descending from the mountains to the plains (although it is true that Egypt was lower in altitude than Canaan). An alternative model for this clause and the previous one is "My ancestor was an Aramean who moved from place to place. Eventually he and his family went to Egypt to live."

Sojourned: that is, he lived in Egypt as a foreigner, a resident alien (see 1.16).

Few in number: that is, he and his family were few. In Gen 46.8-27 it is recorded that Jacob and his family numbered seventy in all when they went to Egypt. The RSV translation **and he went down into Egypt . . . few in number** does not clearly state that Jacob had his family with him. CEV keeps the same clause order but is somewhat clearer, with "who went to live in Egypt. There were only a few in his family then . . . ." TEV has a better model, "who took his family to Egypt to live. They were few in number . . . ."

He became a nation: that is, he and his family, who were few at first, eventually became a large ethnic community in Egypt (see Exo 1.7).

Great, mighty, and populous: these are very similar in meaning, and it is not necessary to find three different adjectives in order to represent faithfully the meaning of the text. **Great** and **mighty** may be combined in a number of languages; they refer to the corporate strength of a large group of people rather than the physical strength of an individual. Instead of **populous** something like "numerous" (so REB), or even "a large number of people," is better.

26.6   RSV   TEV

And the Egyptians treated us harsh-   The Egyptians treated us harshly
ly, and afflicted us, and laid upon us   and forced us to work as slaves.
hard bondage.

The Egyptians treated us harshly: CEV has "were cruel and had no pity on
us." By a dramatic shift to the first person plural **us**, the Israelite becomes part
of the events that had taken place centuries before.

Treated us harshly, and afflicted us, and laid upon us hard bondage: again
three terms that are similar in meaning are used to stress the cruel oppression
they suffered in Egypt (see Exo 1.8-14). CEV uses four verbs: "The Egyptians
were cruel and had no pity on us. They abused our people and forced us into
slavery." TEV uses two verbs, combining the last two. An alternative model is:

● The Egyptians treated us harshly and made us do hard labor [or,
  work very hard] until our spirits [or hearts, or livers] were sore
  [or, broken].

26.7   RSV   TEV

Then we cried to the LORD the God of   Then we cried out for help to the
our fathers, and the LORD heard our   LORD, the God of our ancestors. He
voice, and saw our affliction, our toil, heard us and saw our suffering,
and our oppression;   hardship, and misery.

We cried to the LORD: the sense is that they protested, they prayed in
anguish and pain to the LORD to rescue them.

The God of our fathers: again the sense is "our ancestors." This is usually a
reference to Abraham, Isaac, and Jacob. In some languages direct speech will
be used for the first part of this verse: "We called out to Yahweh the God our
ancestors worshiped, saying, 'Please help us!' "

The LORD heard our voice: that is, the LORD heard our prayers, our cries, our
protests.

Saw our affliction . . . toil . . . oppression: again three terms that are similar
in meaning are used to stress the desperate nature of their situation. Here TEV
uses three terms: "our suffering, hardship, and misery." CEV has only two: "we
were in trouble and abused." Another possible model for the final part of this
verse is "He heard our cries for help, and saw how miserable we were as the
Egyptians oppressed us and made us work hard."

26.8   RSV   TEV

and the LORD brought us out of   By his great power and strength he
Egypt with a mighty hand and an   rescued us from Egypt. He worked

| outstretched arm, with great terror, with signs and wonders; | miracles and wonders, and caused terrifying things to happen. |

Brought us out of Egypt: or "led us out"; the verb should not have the overtone of transporting or carrying.

A mighty hand and an outstretched arm: see 4.34.

Great terror, with signs and wonders: these are the means by which Yahweh made the Egyptian king agree to let the Israelites leave Egypt. The word **terror** here refers to the effect the **signs and wonders**, that is, the plagues, had on the Egyptians. The word **signs** generally means "miracles," and **wonders** often functions as a term that emphasizes this same meaning (see 4.34). The **signs and wonders** were done by Yahweh before he led them out of Egypt, so we may reorder the text as follows: "Then you made the Egyptians very afraid [or, terrified] with your powerful miracles, and led us out of Egypt."

26.9	RSV	TEV

| and he brought us into this place and gave us this land, a land flowing with milk and honey. | He brought us here and gave us this rich and fertile land. |

Brought us into this place: this is parallel to "brought us out of" in verse 8.

Gave us this land: once more the belief of the people of Israel is stated, that the "conquest" of the land of Canaan was not their achievement but God's gift.

A land flowing with milk and honey: see 6.3.

26.10	RSV	TEV

| And behold, now I bring the first of the fruit of the ground, which thou, O LORD, hast given me.' And you shall set it down before the LORD your God, and worship before the LORD your God; | So now I bring to the LORD the first part of the harvest that he has given me.'

"Then set the basket down in the LORD's presence and worship there. |

Behold: a stylistic feature, without much meaning in this context. In some languages an attention-getting word like "Look, LORD, I bring" may be used. Most modern translations such as NRSV have "So now I bring . . . ." CEV has "Now, LORD, I bring . . . ."

The first of the fruit of the ground: see verse 2.

Which thou, O LORD, hast given me: the second person of direct address should be retained in translation (unlike TEV). And it will be good to begin the verse as follows, "So now, LORD, I bring to you the first share of the crops that you have given me."

We should notice that here the single quotation mark in RSV and TEV closes the man's confession, which began in verse 5.

You shall set it down before the LORD your God: here the offerer himself does it, not the priest (as in verse 4); **before the LORD your God** probably means "in front of the LORD's altar" (CEV).

Worship before the LORD your God: here also, the sense is to worship in front of the altar, or simply "bow down before the LORD your God" (NIV, NRSV). NJB has "prostrate yourself in the presence of Yahweh your God." We can say either "bow down" or "worship"; perhaps "worship" is to be preferred.

26.11 RSV	TEV
and you shall rejoice in all the good which the LORD your God has given to you and to your house, you, and the Levite, and the sojourner who is among you.	Be grateful for the good things that the LORD your God has given you and your family; and let the Levites and the foreigners who live among you join in the celebration.

You shall rejoice . . . you, and the Levite, and the sojourner who is among you: this appears to suggest a festive meal in the sanctuary (see 12.18; 14.23). CEV makes this clear, with "Then you and your family must celebrate by eating a meal at the place of worship to thank the LORD your God for giving you such a good harvest."

The Levite: rather "the Levites." For a comment on **Levite** see 12.12.

The sojourner: see 1.16.

Among you is an impossible phrase in English, since **you** is singular, referring to the man who is making the offering. It means, of course, "[the resident aliens] who live in your [plural] towns, villages, or communities."

2C-23. Give ten-percent of your harvest to the LORD (26.12-15)

RSV	TEV
12 "When you have finished paying all the tithe of your produce in the third year, which is the year of tithing, giving it to the Levite, the sojourner, the fatherless, and the widow, that they may eat within your towns and be filled, 13 then you shall say before the LORD your God, 'I have removed the sacred portion out of my house, and moreover I have given it to the Levite, the sojourner, the fatherless, and the widow, according to all thy commandment which thou hast commanded me; I have not transgressed any of thy commandments, neither have I forgotten them; 14 I have not eaten of the tithe while I was mourning, or removed any of it while I was unclean, or offered any of it to the dead; I have obeyed the voice of the LORD my God, I have done according to all that thou hast commanded me. 15 Look down from	12 "Every third year give the tithe—a tenth of your crops—to the Levites, the foreigners, the orphans, and the widows, so that in every community they will have all they need to eat. When you have done this, 13 say to the LORD, 'None of the sacred tithe is left in my house; I have given it to the Levites, the foreigners, the orphans, and the widows, as you commanded me to do. I have not disobeyed or forgotten any of your commands concerning the tithe. 14 I have not eaten any of it when I was mourning; I have not taken any of it out of my house when I was ritually unclean; and I have not given any of it as an offering for the dead. I have obeyed you, O LORD; I have done everything you commanded concerning the tithe. 15 Look down from your holy place in heaven and bless your people Israel; bless also the rich

thy holy habitation, from heaven, and bless
thy people Israel and the ground which thou
hast given us, as thou didst swear to our
fathers, a land flowing with milk and honey.'

and fertile land that you have given us, as you
promised our ancestors.'

These verses deal with another offering, the one-tenth of the crops that was
given away every three years to the poor and needy.

Section heading: as a separate section these verses may have a title such as
"Give one-tenth of your harvest to Yahweh."

26.12 RSV TEV

"When you have finished paying
all the tithe of your produce in the
third year, which is the year of tithing, giving it to the Levite, the sojourner, the fatherless, and the widow, that they may eat within your
towns and be filled,

"Every third year give the tithe—a
tenth of your crops—to the Levites,
the foreigners, the orphans, and the
widows, so that in every community
they will have all they need to eat.
When you have done this,

There must be a rearrangement of this verse to provide the needed information (see TEV); REB has "In the third year, the tithe-year, ..." And the very long
sentence (verses 12-14) must be broken up as in TEV. One way to do this is to
begin a new sentence at verse 13, "Then say in the presence of the LORD your
God . . . ." This will require restructuring verse 12, for which TEV also offers a
good model.

With the beginning of a new section here, Moses should be reintroduced as
the speaker.

Paying all the tithe of your produce: this is not a voluntary offering; it is
required by the Law (see 14.28-29). The **tithe** is one-tenth of the whole amount.
FRCL provides a good model for retaining the technical term "tithe" and
explaining it: "After you have finished paying the tithe, that is, one-tenth of
your crops, ..." In some languages, however, there will not be a technical term
for **tithe**, so we may simply say "give ten percent" or "give one part out of every
ten parts." In 14.22 the Israelites were commanded to give a tithe, or ten
percent, every year to the LORD. It will therefore be helpful to make that clear
here as CEV does: "Every year you are to give ten percent of your harvest to the
LORD, but every third year, this ten percent must be given to the poor . . . ."

The third year, which is the year of tithing: every three years the Israelite
farmer was obliged to give away one-tenth of all his crops to feed the poor and
needy. The text does not say how the produce would be distributed.

The Levite, the sojourner, the fatherless, and the widow: see 14.29.

Eat within your towns and be filled: they may eat as much as they wish, until
they are satisfied. **Your towns** may also be expressed as "your towns and
villages" or "every community" (TEV).

26.13 RSV	TEV
then you shall say before the LORD your God, 'I have removed the sacred portion out of my house, and moreover I have given it to the Levite, the sojourner, the fatherless, and the widow, according to all thy commandment which thou hast commanded me; I have not transgressed any of thy commandments, neither have I forgotten them;	say to the LORD, 'None of the sacred tithe is left in my house; I have given it to the Levites, the foreigners, the orphans, and the widows, as you commanded me to do. I have not disobeyed or forgotten any of your commands concerning the tithe.

You shall say before the LORD your God: as in verses 5 and 10. The context makes it quite certain that this does not take place at the central sanctuary. So this should be expressed as "Then you shall say to the LORD," or even "Then you must pray, 'Our Lord and our God, . . .' " (CEV).

I have removed . . . : the Israelite declares that he has taken the full amount from his house and has given it to **the Levite, the sojourner, the fatherless, and the widow**.

The sacred portion: that is, the one-tenth to be given to the poor and needy. Another way to express this is "none of your [Yahweh's] portion that has been set apart for the poor is left in my house," or "none of the ten percent of my harvest that is yours and has been set apart for the poor . . . ."

According to all thy commandments which thou hast commanded me: this is emphatic and very personal. For **commandment** see 4.2.

I have not transgressed . . . neither have I forgotten them: he has not disobeyed any of the commandments, either intentionally (**transgressed**) or unintentionally (**forgotten**). These **commandments** are not just the Ten Commandments but all of God's rules and laws. We may also translate this final sentence as "I have not disobeyed or forgotten any of your commandments concerning this ten percent."

26.14 RSV	TEV
I have not eaten of the tithe while I was mourning, or removed any of it while I was unclean, or offered any of it to the dead; I have obeyed the voice of the LORD my God, I have done according to all that thou hast commanded me.	I have not eaten any of it when I was mourning; I have not taken any of it out of my house when I was ritually unclean; and I have not given any of it as an offering for the dead.^w I have obeyed you, O LORD; I have done everything you commanded concerning the tithe.
	^w for the dead; *or* to the dead.

The vow the offerer makes shows that the tithe is actually offered to Yahweh, though he gives it to the poor and needy.

I have not eaten of the tithe while I was mourning: in some cultures there are terms for **mourning** for the dead and for the periods of mourning that follow the death of a relative. In others, descriptive phrases will be used; for example, "weep showing sorrow for the death of a person."

Or removed any of it while I was unclean: an Israelite might accidentally come in contact with a corpse and thus become ritually **unclean** (Num 19.11, 14). If the man became unclean for this reason or for any other reason, handling the produce would make it unfit to be offered to God.

Removed any of it means "taken it out of the house" for whatever reason, perhaps to give it to someone other than a needy person. An alternative translation model for the first part of this verse is:

- I have not eaten any of it when I was weeping to show my sorrow for the death of a person; in fact I never took any of it out of the house when I was ritually unclean.

Offered any of it to the dead: see the related passage in 14.1. There are various interpretations of this rite:
(1) Placing food and drink on the tomb for the dead person to have while on his or her way to the world of the dead.
(2) Making an offering to the god of the dead, or the vegetation god Baal, as the Canaanites did.
(3) Having a festive meal in honor of the dead person.
There is no way to decide which of these three (or some other explanation) is correct. Most translations make their interpretation known by translating "offer *for* the dead" or else "offer *to* the dead" (see TEV text and the alternate translation in its footnote).

To complicate the matter, in English **the dead** is a collective noun, meaning "dead people"; if a translation wants to make the phrase singular, it will have to say "a dead person." FRCL has "an offering for a dead person"; TOB has "offering to a dead person," with a footnote explaining that the meaning of this ritual is not known. The *Pléiade* translation also has "to a dead person" and explains in footnote that this is a sacrificial feast in honor of the dead person. It is impossible to be dogmatic; if the phrase "offering for [or, on behalf of] a dead person" makes sense, this may be used. But where it is possible to do it, an explanatory footnote would be useful.

I have obeyed the voice of the LORD **my God**: the offerer now repeats his vow of complete obedience to God. He has obeyed God's laws. TEV says clearly "I have obeyed you, O LORD."

I have done according to all that thou hast commanded me: or "I have done everything exactly as you commanded concerning the tithe [or, ten percent]." Again this is very emphatic and personal (as in verse 13).

26.15　　　RSV	TEV
Look down from thy holy habitation, from heaven, and bless thy people Israel and the ground which thou hast given us, as thou didst swear to our fathers, a land flowing with milk and honey.'	**Look down from your holy place in heaven and bless your people Israel; bless also the rich and fertile land that you have given us, as you promised our ancestors.'**

This prayer is addressed to God, who lives in his **holy habitation** in **heaven**; this may indicate that the worshiper is not in the central sanctuary (see verse 13). The translation of **holy habitation** should not mean a temple or a church; an expression like "your house" should be used. Here **holy** can be translated "your own home": it is **holy** because God lives there (see 5.12; 14.2).

Bless thy people Israel: or "cause your people Israel to be prosperous."

Bless . . . the ground which thou hast given us: that is, the land of Canaan. Another way to express this is "cause this land that you have given us to produce many crops [or, much fruit]."

As thou didst swear to our fathers: see 1.8.

A land flowing with milk and honey: see 6.3 and verse 9.

An alternative translation model for this verse is:

- Look down from your home in heaven [or, from heaven, where you live] and cause your people Israel to prosper. You promised our ancestors that you would give us a land full of cattle and produce [or crops, or fruit]. You have done what you promised.

2C-24. The Lord's own people (26.16-19)

RSV	TEV
	The Lord's Own People
16 "This day the Lord your God commands you to do these statutes and ordinances; you shall therefore be careful to do them with all your heart and with all your soul. 17 You have declared this day concerning the Lord that he is your God, and that you will walk in his ways, and keep his statutes and his commandments and his ordinances, and will obey his voice; 18 and the Lord has declared this day concerning you that you are a people for his own possession, as he has promised you, and that you are to keep all his commandments, 19 that he will set you high above all nations that he has made, in praise and in fame and in honor, and that you shall be a people holy to the Lord your God, as he has spoken."	16 "Today the Lord your God commands you to obey all his laws; so obey them faithfully with all your heart. 17 Today you have acknowledged the Lord as your God; you have promised to obey him, to keep all his laws, and to do all that he commands. 18 Today the Lord has accepted you as his own people, as he promised you; and he commands you to obey all his laws. 19 He will make you greater than any other nation that he has created, and you will bring praise and honor to his name. You will be his own people, as he promised."

This section brings to an end the major division that began at 5.1, "Moses' second discourse." The covenant with God is reaffirmed, and the people are enjoined to obey all the laws that Moses has transmitted to them.

Section heading: besides the TEV title "The LORD's own people," other titles are available as models: NRSV "Ratification of the Covenant"; NIV "Follow the LORD's Commands"; CEV "The LORD Is Your God and You Are His People."

26.16 RSV	TEV
"This day the LORD your God commands you to do these statutes and ordinances; you shall therefore be careful to do them with all your heart and with all your soul.	"Today the LORD your God commands you to obey all his laws; so obey them faithfully with all your heart.

With the beginning of a new section, Moses should be reintroduced as the speaker.

This day: or, as in TEV, "Today." Appearing also in verses 17 and 18, this phrase emphasizes the fact that all the contents of this long speech (section 2 of the book, 5.1–26.19, or possibly even all of Moses' discourses to the people of Israel in Moab) were given on one day (see 5.1; 11.2, 8, 26, 32; 27.9).

Statutes and ordinances: see 4.1.

With all your heart and with all your soul: see 4.29; 6.5.

26.17 RSV	TEV
You have declared this day concerning the LORD that he is your God, and that you will walk in his ways, and keep his statutes and his commandments and his ordinances, and will obey his voice;	Today you have acknowledged the LORD as your God; you have promised to obey him, to keep all his laws, and to do all that he commands.

You have declared this day concerning the LORD: this is a formal statement; some think it may be a technical term used in ratifying a covenant. It is balanced by the parallel in the next verse, "the LORD has declared this day concerning you." Unlike TEV, the verbal parallel should be maintained in translation, if possible.

You will walk in his ways: this is the life of obedience to God's laws (see 9.6; 10.12; 11.22). In a number of languages figurative expressions similar to **walk in his ways** will be used; for example, "walk along his paths," or "follow his paths."

His statutes and his commandments: see 4.1, 2.

Obey his voice: as in verse 14.

26.18   RSV   TEV

and the LORD has declared this day   Today the LORD has accepted you as
concerning you that you are a people   his own people, as he promised you;
for his own possession, as he has   and he commands you to obey all
promised you, and that you are to   his laws.
keep all his commandments,

   You are a people for his own possession: see the same expression in 7.6;
14.2.
   You are to keep all his commandments: there is a lot of repetition in this
section, emphasizing the importance of these instructions.
   An alternative translation model combining verses 17 and 18 may be:

●   ¹⁷⁻¹⁸ Today you have acknowledged [or, confessed] that Yahweh
           will be your God. You have promised to walk in his paths, to keep
           all his laws, and do all he commands you. Since you have agreed
           to keep all his commands, on his part Yahweh has agreed that
           you will be his own people.

26.19   RSV   TEV

that he will set you high above all na-   He will make you greater than any
tions that he has made, in praise and   other nation that he has created, and
in fame and in honor, and that you   you will bring praise and honor to
shall be a people holy to the LORD   his name.ˣ You will be his own peo-
your God, as he has spoken."   ple, as he promised."

                                         ˣ bring praise . . . name; *or* receive
                                         praise and honor.

   He will set you high above all nations: God promises that, if the people obey
his commands, Israel will be the most powerful nation on earth. This promise
is repeated in 28.1. TEV has "He will make you greater than any other nation
that he has created"; or we may say "The LORD created all nations, but he will
make you greater than any of them" (similarly CEV).
   All nations that he has made: God is the Creator of all peoples, not just of
Israel.
   In praise and in fame and in honor: again there are three terms similar in
meaning, emphasizing the high status that God will give Israel. This phrase,
however, can also be understood to refer to the "praise, fame, and honor" that
people will give God because of Israel's power: "to bring him praise and fame
and glory" (NEB, REB, also Mayes). Those who favor this interpretation refer to
the same expression in Jer 13.11; but no other major translation agrees with
NEB and REB. It is recommended that the meaning given by RSV and TEV be
followed. Another model may be "People will praise and honor you."
   A people holy to the LORD your God: see 7.6; 14.2, 21.

3. Instructions for entering Canaan

(27.1–28.68)

This section contains instructions about things the people must do once they have entered the land of Canaan. Most of these instructions consist of God's curses on acts of disobedience and rebellion (27.11-26), God's blessings on a faithful and obedient people (28.1-14), and a very long list of disasters that will come if the people are disobedient (28.15-68).

3A. God's laws written on stones (27.1-10)

RSV

1 Now Moses and the elders of Israel commanded the people, saying, "Keep all the commandment which I command you this day. 2 And on the day you pass over the Jordan to the land which the LORD your God gives you, you shall set up large stones, and plaster them with plaster; 3 and you shall write upon them all the words of this law, when you pass over to enter the land which the LORD your God gives you, a land flowing with milk and honey, as the LORD, the God of your fathers, has promised you. 4 And when you have passed over the Jordan, you shall set up these stones, concerning which I command you this day, on Mount Ebal, and you shall plaster them with plaster. 5 And there you shall build an altar to the LORD your God, an altar of stones; you shall lift up no iron tool upon them. 6 You shall build an altar to the LORD your God of unhewn stones; and you shall offer burnt offerings on it to the LORD your God; 7 and you shall sacrifice peace offerings, and shall eat there; and you shall rejoice before the LORD your God. 8 And you shall write upon the stones all the words of this law very plainly."

9 And Moses and the Levitical priests said to all Israel, "Keep silence and hear, O Israel: this day you have become the people of the LORD your God. 10 You shall therefore obey the voice of the LORD your God, keeping his commandments and his statutes, which I command you this day."

TEV

God's Laws Written on Stones

1 Then Moses, together with the leaders of Israel, said to the people, "Obey all the instructions that I am giving you today. 2 On the day you cross the Jordan River and enter the land that the LORD your God is giving you, you are to set up some large stones, cover them with plaster, 3 and write on them all these laws and teachings. When you have entered the rich and fertile land that the LORD, the God of your ancestors, promised you, 4 and you are on the other side of the Jordan, set up these stones on Mount Ebal, as I am instructing you today, and cover them with plaster. 5 Build an altar there made of stones that have had no iron tools used on them, 6 because any altar you build for the LORD your God must be made of uncut stones. There you are to offer the sacrifices that are to be burned, 7 and there you are to sacrifice and eat your fellowship offerings and be grateful in the presence of the LORD your God. 8 On the stones covered with plaster write clearly every word of God's laws."

9 Then Moses, together with the levitical priests, said to all the people of Israel, "Give me your attention, people of Israel, and listen to me. Today you have become the people of the LORD your God; 10 so obey him and keep all his laws that I am giving you today."

431

Section heading: the main heading, "Instructions for entering Canaan," may be also rendered as "Moses gives instructions to the people before they enter Canaan." The subheading, "God's laws written on stones," will be a good model for many translators; but some translators will prefer to have a complete sentence, "Moses tells the people to write God's laws on stones."

27.1   RSV   TEV

Now Moses and the elders of Israel commanded the people, saying, "Keep all the commandment which I command you this day.

Then Moses, together with the leaders of Israel, said to the people, "Obey all the instructions that I am giving you today.

And the elders of Israel: see 5.23. Moses associates **the elders** with him, although he speaks on his own authority in the first person.

All the commandment: for **commandment** see 4.2; and for **all the commandment** see 5.31.

I command: Moses speaks in his own name.

This day: as often throughout these discourses. See 26.16.

27.2   RSV   TEV

And on the day you pass over the Jordan to the land which the LORD your God gives you, you shall set up large stones, and plaster them with plaster;

On the day you cross the Jordan River and enter the land that the LORD your God is giving you, you are to set up some large stones, cover them with plaster,

Pass over the Jordan: that is, cross the river from the east side to the west side.

The land which the LORD your God gives you: a recurring statement (see 26.1).

Set up large stones: the text does not say how many **stones**; since **all the words of this law** (verse 3) were to be written on them, many would be required. TEV has "some large stones."

Plaster them with plaster: this would make it possible to write the laws on the stones, instead of having to carve them. Some suggest that this **plaster** was more in the nature of what is now called "whitewash" (NIV). Whitewashing seems to have been practiced in Egypt. CEV has "white plaster." Other ways to express **plaster them with plaster** are "take lime and daub [or, cover] it over the stones," or in cultures where lime or plaster are unknown, we may say "cover them with a white substance."

27.3   RSV   TEV

and you shall write upon them all the
words of this law, when you pass
over to enter the land which the LORD
your God gives you, a land flowing
with milk and honey, as the LORD, the
God of your fathers, has promised
you.

and write on them all these laws and
teachings. When you have entered
the rich and fertile land that the
LORD, the God of your ancestors,
promised you,

All the words of this law: notice that TEV has "all these laws and teachings"
(see 1.5). This assumes that all the laws given in Deuteronomy have been
recorded and assembled.

When you pass over: there is considerable repetition in verses 1-4; the
crossing of the Jordan is mentioned three times, and in a number of languages
this information may need be supplied only once (see the alternative translation model for verses 2-4 below).

A land flowing with milk and honey: see 6.3.

As the LORD, the God of your fathers, has promised you: that is, as the LORD
promised their ancestors that he would give them and their descendants the
land of Canaan (see 1.8; 26.15).

27.4   RSV   TEV

And when you have passed over the
Jordan, you shall set up these
stones, concerning which I command you this day, on Mount Ebal,
and you shall plaster them with plaster.

and you are on the other side of the
Jordan, set up these stones on
Mount Ebal, as I am instructing you
today, and cover them with plaster.

When you have passed over the Jordan: as in verses 2 and 3.

This day: as in verse 1.

Mount Ebal: in the hill country of Israel, some forty-eight kilometers (thirty
miles) north of Jerusalem, near the city of Shechem. This verse appears to say
that the people are to plaster the stones after setting them up on Mount Ebal.
Since it would take several days for them to get to Mount Ebal, this verse does
not agree with verse 1, in which the Israelites are told to set up the stones the
day they cross the Jordan. Two different traditions have been brought together
in this narrative.

Instead of **Ebal** HOTTP prefers "Gerizim," citing as justification the factor
which it calls "interpretive modifications." The Samaritan text has "Mount
Gerizim," which was the holy mountain of the Samaritans after the split
between Samaritans and Jews in the fourth century B.C. HOTTP gives its
decision only a {D} rating, and the argument can go either way: it could be that
the Samaritan text made the change, or the Masoretic text (the Hebrew text
that has come down to us) may have made the change in the interests of the

Jews. While several English translations have "Gerizim" in their footnotes, none of the most commonly used versions have it in the text. It is recommended that translators follow the Hebrew (Masoretic) Text.

The repetition in verses 2-4 will be unnatural in a number of languages. In such cases it will be better to combine these verses in a way similar to the following:

- [2-4] Soon you will cross the Jordan River and enter the land that the LORD your God has promised to give you. He is the God your ancestors worshiped. It is a land full of cattle and crops [or, produce]. As soon as you enter the land, go to Mount Ebal. Set up some large stones there and cover them with lime [or plaster]. Then write on them all these laws and teachings.

27.5   RSV   TEV

And there you shall build an altar to the LORD your God, an altar of stones; you shall lift up no iron tool upon them.	Build an altar there made of stones that have had no iron tools used on them,

There you shall build: the important thing about Mount Ebal is the **altar**, not the stones.

An altar of stones . . . lift up no iron tool on them: the **altar** is to be built with **stones** as they are found, without any work being done on them with iron tools to shape them. Another way to express this is "But don't use stones that you have cut with iron tools." For **altar** see 7.5.

27.6   RSV   TEV

You shall build an altar to the LORD your God of unhewn[v] stones; and you shall offer burnt offerings on it to the LORD your God;	because any altar you build for the LORD your God must be made of uncut stones. There you are to offer the sacrifices that are to be burned,

[v] Heb *whole*

An altar . . . of unhewn stones: this repeats verse 5 concerning the stones. To avoid unnecessary repetition we may follow TEV, "because any altar you build for the LORD your God must be made of uncut stones," or CEV, "Look for stones that can be used without being cut."

Burnt offerings: see 12.6.

27.7   RSV   TEV

and you shall sacrifice peace offer-   and there you are to sacrifice and eat
ings, and shall eat there; and you   your fellowship offerings and be
shall rejoice before the LORD your   grateful in the presence of the LORD
God.   your God.

Sacrifice peace offerings: these are sacrifices in which only part of the
animal was burned on the altar; the rest was eaten by the worshipers. This
sacrifice is not mentioned by name elsewhere in Deuteronomy (but see the
comments on 12.27; also see Exo 20.34 and Lev 3.1-17). The purpose of the
offering was to restore *shalom* or fellowship with someone else. Modern
translations use different terms for it: REB "shared-offering"; NRSV "sacrifice of
well-being"; TEV "fellowship offering"; or we may say "offer sacrifices to restore
fellowship with each other," or even "kill animals before Yahweh to restore
. . . ."
For **eat** and **rejoice** see 26.11; Exo 32.6.

27.8   RSV   TEV

And you shall write upon the stones   On the stones covered with plaster
all the words of this law very plain-   write clearly every word of God's
ly."   laws."

This verse is a repetition of the first part of verse 3, with **very plainly** added.
In order to avoid the appearance of unnecessary repetition, translators may use
the following model:

●   Don't forget to write out a copy of these laws on the stones that
       you are going to set up. Make sure that the writing is easy to
       read.

27.9   RSV   TEV

And Moses and the Levitical   Then Moses, together with the
priests said to all Israel, "Keep si-   levitical priests, said to all the people
lence and hear, O Israel: this day you   of Israel, "Give me your attention,
have become the people of the LORD   people of Israel, and listen to me.
your God.   Today you have become the people
                                          of the LORD your God;

The Levitical priests: see 17.9.
All Israel: that is, the people mentioned in verse 1.
Keep silence and hear: or "Be quiet and listen to me" (CEV), or even "Give me
your attention . . . and listen to me" (TEV).

This day you have become the people of the LORD your God: this is the day on which Moses (and the elders) were speaking to the people in preparation for the crossing of the Jordan. This is covenant language (see 26.18).

27.10   RSV   TEV

You shall therefore obey the voice of the LORD your God, keeping his commandments and his statutes, which I command you this day."

so obey him and keep all his laws that I am giving you today."

This verse repeats what was stated at length in 26.16-19.
Commandments and statutes: see 4.1, 2.
I command you this day: as in verse 1.

3B. The curses on disobedience (27.11-26)

RSV

TEV
The Curses on Disobedience

11 And Moses charged the people the same day, saying, 12 "When you have passed over the Jordan, these shall stand upon Mount Gerizim to bless the people: Simeon, Levi, Judah, Issachar, Joseph, and Benjamin. 13 And these shall stand upon Mount Ebal for the curse: Reuben, Gad, Asher, Zebulun, Dan, and Naphtali. 14 And the Levites shall declare to all the men of Israel with a loud voice:

15 " 'Cursed be the man who makes a graven or molten image, an abomination to the LORD, a thing made by the hands of a craftsman, and sets it up in secret.' And all the people shall answer and say, 'Amen.'

16 " 'Cursed be he who dishonors his father or his mother.' And all the people shall say, 'Amen.'

17 " 'Cursed be he who removes his neighbor's landmark.' And all the people shall say, 'Amen.'

18 " 'Cursed be he who misleads a blind man on the road.' And all the people shall say, 'Amen.'

19 " 'Cursed be he who perverts the justice due to the sojourner, the fatherless, and the widow.' And all the people shall say, 'Amen.'

20 " 'Cursed be he who lies with his father's wife, because he has uncovered her who is his father's.' And all the people shall say, 'Amen.'

21 " 'Cursed be he who lies with any kind of beast.' And all the people shall say, 'Amen.'

22 " 'Cursed be he who lies with his sister, whether the daughter of his father or the

11 Then Moses said to the people of Israel, 12 "After you have crossed the Jordan, the following tribes are to stand on Mount Gerizim when the blessings are pronounced on the people: Simeon, Levi, Judah, Issachar, Joseph, and Benjamin. 13 And the following tribes will stand on Mount Ebal when the curses are pronounced: Reuben, Gad, Asher, Zebulun, Dan, and Naphtali. 14 The Levites will speak these words in a loud voice:

15 " 'God's curse on anyone who makes an idol of stone, wood, or metal and secretly worships it; the LORD hates idolatry.'

"And all the people will answer, 'Amen!'

16 " 'God's curse on anyone who dishonors his father or mother.'

"And all the people will answer, 'Amen!'

17 " 'God's curse on anyone who moves a neighbor's property line.'

"And all the people will answer, 'Amen!'

18 " 'God's curse on anyone who leads a blind person in the wrong direction.'

"And all the people will answer, 'Amen!'

19 " 'God's curse on anyone who deprives foreigners, orphans, and widows of their rights.'

"And all the people will answer, 'Amen!'

20 " 'God's curse on anyone who disgraces his father by having intercourse with any of his father's wives.'

"And all the people will answer, 'Amen!'

21 " 'God's curse on anyone who has sexual relations with an animal.'

daughter of his mother.' And all the people shall say, 'Amen.'

23 " 'Cursed be he who lies with his mother-in-law.' And all the people shall say, 'Amen.'

24 " 'Cursed be he who slays his neighbor in secret.' And all the people shall say, 'Amen.'

25 " 'Cursed be he who takes a bribe to slay an innocent person.' And all the people shall say, 'Amen.'

26 " 'Cursed be he who does not confirm the words of this law by doing them.' And all the people shall say, 'Amen.'

"And all the people will answer, 'Amen!'

22 " 'God's curse on anyone who has intercourse with his sister or half sister.'

"And all the people will answer, 'Amen!'

23 " 'God's curse on anyone who has intercourse with his mother-in-law.'

"And all the people will answer, 'Amen!'

24 " 'God's curse on anyone who secretly commits murder.'

"And all the people will answer, 'Amen!'

25 " 'God's curse on anyone who accepts money to murder an innocent person.'

"And all the people will answer, 'Amen!'

26 " 'God's curse on anyone who does not obey all of God's laws and teachings.'

"And all the people will answer, 'Amen!'

In this section there are twelve curses. In the context the meaning of the repeated expression **Cursed be** is that God is called upon to punish the Israelite who disobeys these rules.

Section heading: in TEV this section has the heading "The Curses on Disobedience." For both the heading and the text, the translator must decide on the most appropriate way to express the meaning of **Cursed be** (RSV, NRSV, NJPSV) or "God's curse on" (TEV) in verses 15-26. Other ways of saying this are "Cursed is" (NIV), "Accursed be" (NJB), "A curse on" (REB), or "We ask the Lord to put a curse on" (CEV). Examples of other headings for the section are "Twelve Curses" (NRSV) and "Curses on Those who Disobey" (CEV). In a number of languages the best way to translate this will be to use a complete sentence, "May God punish those who disobey" or "God will punish . . . ."

27.11-12   RSV   TEV

11 And Moses charged the people the same day, saying, 12 "When you have passed over the Jordan, these shall stand upon Mount Gerizim to bless the people: Simeon, Levi, Judah, Issachar, Joseph, and Benjamin.

11 Then Moses said to the people of Israel, 12 "After you have crossed the Jordan, the following tribes are to stand on Mount Gerizim when the blessings are pronounced on the people: Simeon, Levi, Judah, Issachar, Joseph, and Benjamin.

Moses charged the people: that is, he ordered, commanded, gave instructions to them (see 21.7).

The same day: repeated for emphasis (verse 10).

Mount Gerizim: just north of Mount Ebal (verse 4). See 11.29-30 for the two mountains.

Bless in this context means "ask Yahweh to do good things for" (see also 1.11).

The six tribes on Mount Gerizim, **Simeon, Levi, Judah, Issachar, Joseph**, and **Benjamin,** have the names of six of the sons Jacob had by his wives Leah and Rachel. Here the tribe of **Levi** is included, although they were not provided with a large area of land as were the others, and so they were often not included in the lists of the twelve tribes. The use of **Joseph** as one of the tribes is also rare but does occur (see Gen 49.22-26). In the division of the land, the tribe of Levi was not given its own territory, and the total of twelve tribes was reached by having Manasseh and Ephraim, the two sons of Joseph, counted as two separate tribes. For a comment on "tribes" see 1.13.

For the record of this ceremony, see Josh 8.30-35.

27.13   RSV   TEV

And these shall stand upon Mount   And the following tribes will stand on
Ebal for the curse: Reuben, Gad,   Mount Ebal when the curses are pro-
Asher, Zebulun, Dan, and Naphtali.   nounced: Reuben, Gad, Asher, Zebu-
                                       lun, Dan, and Naphtali.

For the curse: this may be rendered as "to listen to the curses" or "to hear how Yahweh will punish people." BRCL rearranges the verse: "The curses will be pronounced from Mount Ebal, and there the following tribes will stand: . . . ." For a comment on **curse** see 11.26. Or the full sentence may be alternatively rendered as "The tribes of . . . will go up and stand on Mount Ebal, where they will listen to the curses [or, hear how Yahweh will punish people]."

The six tribes on Mount Ebal, **Reuben**, **Gad**, **Asher**, **Zebulun**, **Dan**, and **Naphtali**, have the names of sons of Leah (Reuben and Zebulun), of Bilhah, Rachel's slave (Dan and Naphtali), and of Zilpah, Leah's slave (Gad and Asher); see Gen 35.22-26. All of these tribes had their territory in the north of Israel or on the east side of the Jordan.

An alternative translation model for this verse is:

●   The tribes of Reuben, Gad, Asher, Zebulun, Dan, and Naphtali will go up on Mount Ebal, where they will hear how Yahweh will punish people.

27.14   RSV   TEV

And the Levites shall declare to all   The Levites will speak these words
the men of Israel with a loud voice: in a loud voice:

The Levites: see 12.12. These are the men from the tribe of Levi who served in the tabernacle, not the whole tribe of Levi.

All the men of Israel: the Septuagint has "all Israel," and NRSV translates "all the Israelites." CEV has "all the rest of the people," while TEV omits the phrase altogether. To be consistent with verses 11 and 12, this should refer to all the people, not just to the males.

With a loud voice: because of the distances at that location, it would have to be a very loud voice! In some languages this will be made very clear with "will shout loudly."

27.15   RSV   TEV

" 'Cursed be the man who makes a graven or molten image, an abomination to the LORD, a thing made by the hands of a craftsman, and sets it up in secret.' And all the people shall answer and say, 'Amen.'

" 'God's curse on anyone who makes an idol of stone, wood, or metal and secretly worships it; the LORD hates idolatry.'
"And all the people will answer, 'Amen!'

Cursed be the man: or "God will punish the person." See also the comment on "curse" at 11.26.

A graven or molten image: see 4.16 and 9.12, 16; also 5.8; Exo 20.4. NIV "carves an image or casts an idol" better represents the meaning than RSV; TEV also makes it quite clear: "makes an idol of stone, wood, or metal." We may also say "makes a likeness of a false god out of stone, ..."

An abomination to the LORD: TEV has "The LORD hates idolatry," and CEV has "The LORD is disgusted with idols." See also 7.25.

Made by the hands of a craftsman: unless the language requires it, "the hands of" can be dispensed with in translation, since the maker (**the man**, or "anyone") has been mentioned in the first sentence (see TEV, CEV).

Sets it up in secret: this does not mean that God's **curse** will not apply if this is done in public. It is simply a way of stating the obvious: very few Israelites would worship idols publicly. TEV "worships" emphasizes the reason why an Israelite would make an idol, and is a legitimate translation of the text.

All the people: this means the people of all twelve tribes, not only the six tribes on Mount Ebal.

Amen: a way of affirming the truth of the statement. Its sense is "So be it," "It is so," or "We agree!"

27.16   RSV   TEV

" 'Cursed be he who dishonors his father or his mother.' And all the people shall say, 'Amen.'

" 'God's curse on anyone who dishonors his father or mother.'
"And all the people will answer, 'Amen!'

For this curse, see 5.16; 21.18-21.

Dishonors is the exact opposite of "honor" in 5.16.

The Hebrew has the masculine **he . . . his**, but in this verse the general "person," or the plural "persons," or "all" (CEV) may be used in translation. We should note, however, that in some of the other similar curses, the male Israelite is the subject (see verses 20, 22, 23).

27.17   RSV   TEV

" 'Cursed be he who removes his   " 'God's curse on anyone who
neighbor's landmark.' And all the   moves a neighbor's property line.'
people shall say, 'Amen.'   "And all the people will answer,
                                     'Amen!'

For this prohibition, see 19.14.

27.18   RSV   TEV

" 'Cursed be he who misleads a   " 'God's curse on anyone who
blind man on the road.' And all the leads a blind person in the wrong
people shall say, 'Amen.'   direction.'
                                     "And all the people will answer,
                                     'Amen!'

This rule is not mentioned elsewhere in Deuteronomy; see Lev 19.14.

The sense of **misleads** in this context is quite plain: it means to give wrong directions to, or to provide false information. So CEV has "anyone who tells blind people to go the wrong way."

27.19   RSV   TEV

" 'Cursed be he who perverts the   " 'God's curse on anyone who de-
justice due to the sojourner, the   prives foreigners, orphans, and wid-
fatherless, and the widow.' And all ows of their rights.'
the people shall say, 'Amen.'   "And all the people will answer,
                                     'Amen!'

For other references to this behavior, see 24.17; 26.12.

27.20   RSV   TEV

" 'Cursed be he who lies with his   " 'God's curse on anyone who dis-
father's wife, because he has uncov- graces his father by having inter-
ered her who is his father's.'ʷ And all course with any of his father's
the people shall say, 'Amen.'   wives.'
                                     "And all the people will answer,
ʷ Heb *uncovered his father's skirt*   'Amen!'

For this curse see 22.30; Lev 18.8.

The added words, **her who is his father's,** emphasize that this is a grave sin because the man is violating **his father's** rights. The RSV footnote gives the literal Hebrew text. This information is of little help, if any, to the reader, and may be ignored.

27.21   RSV   TEV

" 'Cursed be he who lies with any kind of beast.' And all the people shall say, 'Amen.'

" 'God's curse on anyone who has sexual relations with an animal.'
"And all the people will answer, 'Amen!'

This rule does not appear elsewhere in Deuteronomy; see Lev 18.23; 20.15. In cultures where people may occasionally lie with animals to keep warm, a literal translation of **lies with** will convey the wrong meaning. The curse in this verse is directed against "sexual relations with an animal."

27.22   RSV   TEV

" 'Cursed be he who lies with his sister, whether the daughter of his father or the daughter of his mother.' And all the people shall say, 'Amen.'

" 'God's curse on anyone who has intercourse with his sister or half sister.'
"And all the people will answer, 'Amen!'

Sister: as the following words suggest, this can include both full- and half-sisters. No matter that the woman is only the man's half-sister (TEV, CEV), either by his father or by his mother, such behavior is prohibited. See Lev 18.9; 20.17.

27.23   RSV   TEV

" 'Cursed be he who lies with his mother-in-law.' And all the people shall say, 'Amen.'

23 " 'God's curse on anyone who has intercourse with his mother-in-law.'
"And all the people will answer, 'Amen!'

This prohibition is not found elsewhere in Deuteronomy; see Lev 18.8; 20.14.

27.24   RSV   TEV

" 'Cursed be he who slays his neighbor in secret.' And all the people shall say, 'Amen.'

" 'God's curse on anyone who secretly commits murder.'
"And all the people will answer, 'Amen!'

Slays his neighbor in secret: the **secret** nature of the crime is made clear here, since no such curse is needed when the murderer is known. See the procedure laid out in 21.1-9. CEV has "anyone who commits murder, even when there are no witnesses to the crime." For "murder" see 5.17.

27.25 RSV	TEV
" 'Cursed be he who takes a bribe to slay an innocent person.' And all the people shall say, 'Amen.'	" 'God's curse on anyone who accepts money to murder an innocent person.' "And all the people will answer, 'Amen!'

This is not stated directly elsewhere in Deuteronomy; but see in 16.19 the prohibition against taking bribes; see also Exo 23.6-8. TEV has "anyone who accepts money to murder an innocent person" (similarly CEV).

27.26 RSV	TEV
" 'Cursed be he who does not confirm the words of this law by doing them.' And all the people shall say, 'Amen.'	" 'God's curse on anyone who does not obey all of God's laws and teachings.' "And all the people will answer, 'Amen!'

This is a summary statement, bringing the twelve curses to a close.

Confirm . . . by doing them: a better expression of the sense is NRSV: "uphold . . . by obeying them." By obeying these regulations the Israelite would prove that he upheld or obeyed the laws. The substance of this verse is quoted by Paul in Gal 3.10.

The words of this law: see verse 3.

3C. The blessings of obedience (28.1-14)

RSV	TEV
	The Blessings of Obedience
1 "And if you obey the voice of the LORD your God, being careful to do all his commandments which I command you this day, the LORD your God will set you high above all the nations of the earth. 2 And all these blessings shall come upon you and overtake you, if you obey the voice of the LORD your God. 3 Blessed shall you be in the city, and blessed shall you	1 "If you obey the LORD your God and faithfully keep all his commands that I am giving you today, he will make you greater than any other nation on earth. 2 Obey the LORD your God and all these blessings will be yours: 3 "The LORD will bless your towns and your fields.

be in the field. 4 Blessed shall be the fruit of your body, and the fruit of your ground, and the fruit of your beasts, the increase of your cattle, and the young of your flock. 5 Blessed shall be your basket and your kneading-trough. 6 Blessed shall you be when you come in, and blessed shall you be when you go out.

7 "The LORD will cause your enemies who rise against you to be defeated before you; they shall come out against you one way, and flee before you seven ways. 8 The LORD will command the blessing upon you in your barns, and in all that you undertake; and he will bless you in the land which the LORD your God gives you. 9 The LORD will establish you as a people holy to himself, as he has sworn to you, if you keep the commandments of the LORD your God, and walk in his ways. 10 And all the peoples of the earth shall see that you are called by the name of the LORD; and they shall be afraid of you. 11 And the LORD will make you abound in prosperity, in the fruit of your body, and in the fruit of your cattle, and in the fruit of your ground, within the land which the LORD swore to your fathers to give you. 12 The LORD will open to you his good treasury the heavens, to give the rain of your land in its season and to bless all the work of your hands; and you shall lend to many nations, but you shall not borrow. 13 And the LORD will make you the head, and not the tail; and you shall tend upward only, and not downward; if you obey the commandments of the LORD your God, which I command you this day, being careful to do them, 14 and if you do not turn aside from any of the words which I command you this day, to the right hand or to the left, to go after other gods to serve them.

4 "The LORD will bless you with many children, with abundant crops, and with many cattle and sheep.

5 "The LORD will bless your grain crops and the food you prepare from them.

6 "The LORD will bless everything you do.

7 "The LORD will defeat your enemies when they attack you. They will attack from one direction, but they will run from you in all directions.

8 "The LORD your God will bless your work and fill your barns with grain. He will bless you in the land that he is giving you.

9 "If you obey the LORD your God and do everything he commands, he will make you his own people, as he has promised. 10 Then all the peoples on earth will see that the LORD has chosen you to be his own people, and they will be afraid of you. 11 The LORD will give you many children, many cattle, and abundant crops in the land that he promised your ancestors to give you. 12 He will send rain in season from his rich storehouse in the sky and bless all your work, so that you will lend to many nations, but you will not have to borrow from any. 13 The LORD your God will make you the leader among the nations and not a follower; you will always prosper and never fail if you obey faithfully all his commands that I am giving you today. 14 But you must never disobey them in any way, or worship and serve other gods.

Chapter 28 brings to a close Moses' instructions to the people for entering Canaan (chapters 27–28). In two sections of blessings (verses 1-14) and curses (verses 15-68) Moses impresses upon the people the need to obey Yahweh their God if they wish to become a prosperous and powerful nation in the land they are about to enter.

For other passages like this one, see 7.12-24; 11.13-17.

Section heading: the Handbook and TEV title "The Blessings of Obedience" may not be adequate for some languages. Perhaps "The blessings the people will receive if they obey God" or "The LORD will make you prosper if you obey" will be more satisfactory.

28.1 RSV TEV

"And if you obey the voice of the LORD your God, being careful to do

"If you obey the LORD your God and faithfully keep all his commands

all his commandments which I command you this day, the LORD your God will set you high above all the nations of the earth.

that I am giving you today, he will make you greater than any other nation on earth.

It will be helpful at this point to introduce Moses again as the speaker; for example, "Moses said to the people . . . ."

If you obey the voice of the LORD your God: Hebrew has the compound "[if] obeying you obey," to make the statement more emphatic; this is expressed in POCL as "If you really obey," and in CEV as "If you completely obey."

Being careful to do: an expression often used (see 27.16).

All his commandments which I command you this day: see 27.1.

Set you high above all the nations of the earth: see 26.19.

28.2 RSV TEV

And all these blessings shall come upon you and overtake you, if you obey the voice of the LORD your God.

Obey the LORD your God and all these blessings will be yours:

All these blessings: in this context a blessing is something good that is given by God. So we may also translate as "Yahweh your God will give you all these good things."

Come upon you and overtake you: this vivid language portrays the blessings as living and active; for the second verb NJPSV has "and take effect," and REB "and light on you." Perhaps something like "come and remain with you" or "will always be yours" will be satisfactory in many languages. The first sentence may then be expressed as "Yahweh your God will give you all these good things, and they will always be yours."

If you obey: it may be better to place this clause at the beginning of the verse, as TEV does, or even combine the two instances of **if you obey** in verses 1 and 2 as follows:

- 1-2 Moses said to the people of Israel: "Today I am giving you the commands of Yahweh, the God you worship. If you completely obey them, he will make you greater than any of the other nations on earth. He will also give you all these good things, and they will always be yours.

28.3 RSV TEV

Blessed shall you be in the city, and blessed shall you be in the field.

"The LORD will bless your towns and your fields.

Blessed shall you be: in Hebrew the participle "blessed [be]" appears six times in verses 3-6; this is balanced in verses 16-19, in which the participle

444

"cursed [be]" also appears six times. This is more apparent in RSV than in TEV, and it is recommended that a translation preserve this stylistic feature if it reads naturally. Other ways of saying **Blessed shall you be** are "A blessing on" (REB), "You will be blessed" (NJPSV, NIV), "The LORD will bless you" (TEV), or "The LORD will make you prosper [or, be successful]."

In the city . . . in the field: these were the places where the Israelites worked; so something like "wherever you work" or "everywhere you work," or even "in your businesses and farms," may be more satisfactory than the literal rendering of the Hebrew idiom (see a similar idiom in 6.7).

The CEV model is a good alternative one:

• The LORD will make your businesses and your farms successful.

28.4	RSV	TEV
Blessed shall be the fruit of your body, and the fruit of your ground, and the fruit of your beasts, the increase of your cattle, and the young of your flock.		**"The LORD will bless you with many children, with abundant crops, and with many cattle and sheep.**

Blessed shall be: or "The LORD will cause you to have [or, give you] many . . . ."

The fruit of your body: meaning children, descendants, offspring.

The fruit of your ground: that is "abundant crops" (TEV).

The fruit of your beasts: this refers to cattle and other domesticated animals. So TEV has "many cattle and sheep."

The increase of your cattle, and the young of your flock: this double phrase is an explanation of **the fruit of your beasts**; so NRSV has "the fruit of your livestock, both the increase of your cattle and the issue of your flock." The use of **fruit** as the offspring of animals is not natural English, but in a number of other languages it will be natural style. In English NIV is better: ". . . the calves of your herds and the lambs of your flocks." For the whole expression CEV has "and your herds of cattle and flocks of sheep and goats will produce many young."

28.5	RSV	TEV
Blessed shall be your basket and your kneading-trough.		**"The LORD will bless your grain crops and the food you prepare from them.**

Your basket: this was a utensil for storing grain at home (see "basket" in 26.4).

Your kneading-trough: a wide, shallow bowl in which the housewife mixed the flour and other ingredients to make bread (see Exo 12.34).

Both objects in this verse are ways of referring to their contents: grain and bread, with bread representing food in general.

An alternative translation model for this verse is:

• The LORD will cause you to have abundant grain and much food to eat.

28.6   RSV   TEV

Blessed shall you be when you come in, and blessed shall you be when you go out.

"The LORD will bless everything you do.

When you come in ... when you go out: this means "in all your activities [or, ventures]," "at home and at work," or even "through the whole of life" (see this idiom in verse 19; 31.2; Psa 121.8; Isa 37.28). So CEV says "The LORD will make you successful in everything you do."

28.7   RSV   TEV

"The LORD will cause your enemies who rise against you to be defeated before you; they shall come out against you one way, and flee before you seven ways.

"The LORD will defeat your enemies when they attack you. They will attack from one direction, but they will run from you in all directions.

Your enemies who rise up against you: this seems to indicate that the enemies are attacking; so NJB has "The enemies who attack you . . . ." For a comment on **enemies** see 1.42.

The LORD will cause . . . to be defeated before you: that is, Yahweh will defeat them. FRCL says "the LORD will give you victory over them," and NJB "Yahweh will defeat before your eyes." The text may mean either that Yahweh will defeat the enemy by himself, or else that Yahweh will give the Israelites victory over them; the second meaning seems preferable.

They shall come . . . one way, and flee . . . seven ways: the enemy will attack as a disciplined body of troops marching together, but then will flee in disarray in all directions. **Seven** represents totality: "in all directions" (TEV).

28.8   RSV   TEV

The LORD will command the blessing upon you in your barns, and in all that you undertake; and he will bless you in the land which the LORD your God gives you.

"The LORD your God will bless your work and fill your barns with grain. He will bless you in the land that he is giving you.

Command the blessing upon you in your barns: this refers to the contents of the barns, that is, grain and other crops. Another way to express this is "give you so much grain that your barns [or, storage places] will be full."

In all that you undertake: that is, in all the work the Israelites do.

In the land which the LORD your God gives you: a repetition of this familiar refrain in Deuteronomy.

An alternative translation model for this verse may be:

- Yahweh will make you prosper in the land that he is giving you. You will be successful in everything you do. You will have so much grain that your barns will be full.

28.9	RSV	TEV
The LORD will establish you as a people holy to himself, as he has sworn to you, if you keep the commandments of the LORD your God, and walk in his ways.	"If you obey the LORD your God and do everything he commands, he will make you his own people, as he has promised.

Establish you: this gives the idea of firmness, permanence, endurance (also in 29.13).

A people holy to himself: that is, "a people completely dedicated to him" (7.6; 14.2; see Exo 19.6), namely, "his own special people" (CEV).

As he has sworn to you: the LORD's solemn promise (see 1.8).

Keep the commandments of the LORD your God, and walk in his ways: these are two ways of saying the same thing, for emphasis; for **walk in his ways** see 8.6; 10.12.

28.10	RSV	TEV
And all the peoples of the earth shall see that you are called by the name of the LORD; and they shall be afraid of you.	Then all the peoples on earth will see that the LORD has chosen you to be his own people, and they will be afraid of you.

All the peoples of the earth: CEV renders this as "everyone on earth." This exaggerated language should be preserved in translation.

You are called by the name of the LORD: in essence this means that Yahweh has chosen the Israelites to be his own people; it indicates ownership. In 12.5 the place of worship is where Yahweh will "put his name" and live there—it will be his house, his home, with his people (also Jer 7.10-11). And Jer 14.9 has the same use of the idiom: the people of Israel are called by Yahweh's name, meaning they are Yahweh's people, they belong to him. Here REB has "the LORD has named you as his very own," and TEV "that the LORD has chosen you to be his own people." See also Num 6.27: "They [the priests] shall put my name on

447

the people of Israel." In 1 Kgs 8.43 Solomon says, in his prayer dedicating the Temple to Yahweh, "this house which I have built is called by thy name." The CEV translation "that you belong to the LORD" is a good model.

They will be afraid: for **afraid** see 1.29.

28.11   RSV   TEV

And the LORD will make you abound in prosperity, in the fruit of your body, and in the fruit of your cattle, and in the fruit of your ground, within the land which the LORD swore to your fathers to give you.	The LORD will give you many children, many cattle, and abundant crops in the land that he promised your ancestors to give you.

In verses 11-14 the promise of prosperity is renewed.

Make you abound in prosperity: or "make you prosper very much." TEV and CEV omit this as unnecessary, since the following clauses reveal in detail how the Israelites will prosper.

The fruit of your body . . . of your cattle . . . of your ground: as in verse 4.

The land which the LORD swore to your fathers to give you: see 1.8. As always, **fathers** means ancestors.

28.12   RSV   TEV

The LORD will open to you his good treasury the heavens, to give the rain of your land in its season and to bless all the work of your hands; and you shall lend to many nations, but you shall not borrow.	He will send rain in season from his rich storehouse in the sky and bless all your work, so that you will lend to many nations, but you will not have to borrow from any.

Open to you his good treasury the heavens: people thought of **the heavens** in physical terms as the place where the winds and the rains were stored (see Gen 7.11 and 8.2, the beginning and end of the Flood; see also Job 38.37; Psa 135.7). Translators are urged to keep the figurative language of **treasury** or "storehouse" if possible; for example, "He will send rain . . . from his rich storehouse in the sky" (TEV), or "The LORD will open the storehouses in the sky, where he keeps the rain."

The rain . . . in its season: that is, at the right time, when the crops needed it. It may be that this emphasis on Yahweh's power to give rain reflects the belief among the Canaanites that their god Baal was the giver of rain. CEV has a helpful model: "he will send rain on your land at just the right times."

Bless all the work of your hands: see 2.7.

You shall lend . . . but you shall not borrow: this is not a command but a promise of prosperity. The Israelites will be prosperous enough to lend to other peoples, and never needy enough to have to borrow from them. For **lend** and **borrow** see 15.6.

28.13   RSV   TEV

And the LORD will make you the head, and not the tail; and you shall tend upward only, and not downward; if you obey the commandments of the LORD your God, which I command you this day, being careful to do them,	The LORD your God will make you the leader among the nations and not a follower; you will always prosper and never fail if you obey faithfully all his commands that I am giving you today.

The vivid language in this verse should be preserved in translation, if it makes sense.

The head . . . the tail: that is, "in first place . . . in last place," in terms of prosperity, power, and prestige. So TEV has "will make you the leader among the nations and not the follower" (similarly CEV).

Tend upward only, and not downward: this means to increase, to go forward, to become even more prosperous, and never the contrary. So "you will always prosper and never fail" (TEV), and "Israel will be wealthy and powerful, not poor and weak" (CEV).

For the rest of the verse, see the same language in verse 1.

28.14   RSV   TEV

and if you do not turn aside from any of the words which I command you this day, to the right hand or to the left, to go after other gods to serve them.	But you must never disobey them in any way, or worship and serve other gods.

If you do not turn aside . . . to the right hand or to the left: this is a figure of complete obedience, without any deviation (see 5.32). So TEV has "you must never disobey."

The words which I command you this day: as often stated in the book, this refers to all of Moses' words delivered on the same day in one long discourse.

To go after other gods to serve them: there is a constant indication in Deuteronomy of rivalry between Yahweh and the gods of Canaan; to serve other gods is to be guilty of idolatry (see 8.19).

3D. The consequence of disobedience (28.15-35)

RSV

TEV

The Consequences of Disobedience

15 "But if you will not obey the voice of the LORD your God or be careful to do all his commandments and his statutes which I command you this day, then all these curses shall come upon you and overtake you. 16 Cursed shall you be in the city, and cursed shall you be in the field. 17 Cursed shall be your basket and your kneading-trough. 18 Cursed shall be the fruit of your body, and the fruit of your ground, the increase of your cattle, and the young of your flock. 19 Cursed shall you be when you come in, and cursed shall you be when you go out.

20 "The LORD will send upon you curses, confusion, and frustration, in all that you undertake to do, until you are destroyed and perish quickly, on account of the evil of your doings, because you have forsaken me. 21 The LORD will make the pestilence cleave to you until he has consumed you off the land which you are entering to take possession of it. 22 The LORD will smite you with consumption, and with fever, inflammation, and fiery heat, and with drought, and with blasting, and with mildew; they shall pursue you until you perish. 23 And the heavens over your head shall be brass, and the earth under you shall be iron. 24 The LORD will make the rain of your land powder and dust; from heaven it shall come down upon you until you are destroyed.

25 "The LORD will cause you to be defeated before your enemies; you shall go out one way against them, and flee seven ways before them; and you shall be a horror to all the kingdoms of the earth. 26 And your dead body shall be food for all birds of the air, and for the beasts of the earth; and there shall be no one to frighten them away. 27 The LORD will smite you with the boils of Egypt, and with the ulcers and the scurvy and the itch, of which you cannot be healed. 28 The LORD will smite you with madness and blindness and confusion of mind; 29 and you shall grope at noonday, as the blind grope in darkness, and you shall not prosper in your ways; and you shall be only oppressed and robbed continually, and there shall be no one to help you. 30 You shall betroth a wife, and another man shall lie with her; you shall build a house, and you shall not dwell in it; you shall plant a vineyard, and you shall not use the fruit of it. 31 Your ox shall be slain before your eyes, and you shall not eat of it; your ass shall be violently taken away before your face, and shall not be restored to

15 "But if you disobey the LORD your God and do not faithfully keep all his commands and laws that I am giving you today, all these evil things will happen to you:

16 "The LORD will curse your towns and your fields.

17 "The LORD will curse your grain crops and the food you prepare from them.

18 "The LORD will curse you by giving you only a few children, poor crops, and few cattle and sheep.

19 "The LORD will curse everything you do.

20 "If you do evil and reject the LORD, he will bring on you disaster, confusion, and trouble in everything you do, until you are quickly and completely destroyed. 21 He will send disease after disease on you until there is not one of you left in the land that you are about to occupy. 22 The LORD will strike you with infectious diseases, with swelling and fever; he will send drought and scorching winds to destroy your crops. These disasters will be with you until you die. 23 No rain will fall, and your ground will become as hard as iron. 24 Instead of rain, the LORD will send down duststorms and sandstorms until you are destroyed.

25 "The LORD will give your enemies victory over you. You will attack them from one direction, but you will run from them in all directions, and all the people on earth will be terrified when they see what happens to you. 26 When you die, birds and wild animals will come and eat your bodies, and there will be no one to scare them off. 27 The LORD will send boils on you, as he did on the Egyptians. He will make your bodies break out with sores. You will be covered with scabs, and you will itch, but there will be no cure. 28 The LORD will make you lose your mind; he will strike you with blindness and confusion. 29 You will grope about in broad daylight like someone blind, and you will not be able to find your way. You will not prosper in anything you do. You will be constantly oppressed and robbed, and there will be no one to help you.

30 "You will be engaged to a young woman—but someone else will marry her. You will build a house—but never live in it. You will plant a vineyard—but never eat its grapes. 31 Your cattle will be butchered before your very eyes, but you will not eat any of the meat. Your donkeys will be dragged away while you look on, and they will not be given back to you.

you; your sheep shall be given to your enemies, and there shall be no one to help you. 32 Your sons and your daughters shall be given to another people, while your eyes look on and fail with longing for them all the day; and it shall not be in the power of your hand to prevent it. 33 A nation which you have not known shall eat up the fruit of your ground and of all your labors; and you shall be only oppressed and crushed continually; 34 so that you shall be driven mad by the sight which your eyes shall see. 35 The LORD will smite you on the knees and on the legs with grievous boils of which you cannot be healed, from the sole of your foot to the crown of your head.

Your sheep will be given to your enemies, and there will be no one to help you. 32 Your sons and daughters will be given as slaves to foreigners while you look on. Every day you will strain your eyes, looking in vain for your children to return. 33 A foreign nation will take all the crops that you have worked so hard to grow, while you receive nothing but constant oppression and harsh treatment. 34 Your sufferings will make you lose your mind. 35 The LORD will cover your legs with incurable, painful sores; boils will cover you from head to foot.

These verses begin the long section which sets out the consequences of disobedience, balancing the blessings which are the consequence of obedience in verses 1-14. An important matter here is to be consistent in translating the noun **curse** and the verbal phrase **cursed be** (see 27.16-26).

Section heading: the whole long section (verses 15-68) is entitled by TEV "The Consequences of Disobedience." Other titles are "Curses" (NJB, verses 16-46); "Threats of Misfortune" (FRCL); "Punishments for the Disobedient"; or "The LORD will put curses on you if you disobey."

28.15   RSV   TEV

"But if you will not obey the voice of the LORD your God or be careful to do all his commandments and his statutes which I command you this day, then all these curses shall come upon you and overtake you.

"But if you disobey the LORD your God and do not faithfully keep all his commands and laws that I am giving you today, all these evil things will happen to you:

With the beginning of a new section, Moses should be reintroduced as the speaker.

Obey the voice . . . be careful to do: these are parallel and have the same meaning (see verse 13).

His commandments and his statutes: see 4.1-2. For the language see verse 1.

These curses shall come upon you and overtake you: see verse 2. For a comment on "curse" see 11.26.

28.16-17   RSV   TEV

16 Cursed shall you be in the city, and cursed shall you be in the field.

16 "The LORD will curse your towns and your fields.

451

17 Cursed shall be your basket and your kneading-trough.	17 "The LORD will curse your grain crops and the food you prepare from them.

These verses are the opposites of verses 3 and 5. Here **cursed** means "will fail," and the two verses may be alternatively translated as:

- ^16-17^ Yahweh will cause your businesses and farms to fail. You won't have enough grain and there will not be enough food to eat.

28.18-19   RSV   TEV

18 Cursed shall be the fruit of your body, and the fruit of your ground, the increase of your cattle, and the young of your flock. 19 Cursed shall you be when you come in, and cursed shall you be when you go out.	18 "The LORD will curse you by giving you only a few children, poor crops, and few cattle and sheep. 19 "The LORD will curse everything you do.

These verses are the opposites of verses 4 and 6. Verse 18 is not quite as full as verse 4; it does not include "and the fruit of your beasts."

A possible alternative translation model for these verses is:

- ^18^ Yahweh will punish you by giving you few children and poor crops. Your cattle and sheep won't produce many young. ^19^ He will make you fail [or, be unsuccessful] in everything you do.

28.20   RSV   TEV

"The LORD will send upon you curses, confusion, and frustration, in all that you undertake to do, until you are destroyed and perish quickly, on account of the evil of your doings, because you have forsaken me.	"If you do evil and reject the LORD, he will bring on you disaster, confusion, and trouble in everything you do, until you are quickly and completely destroyed.

In many languages the repetition will be perfectly acceptable and should be used. But in some languages translators will need to restructure the parts that are wordy and repetitious, and where groups of different terms have the same meaning and are used freely.

Curses, confusion, and frustration: other verses in this section will also have three or more terms that mean the same thing, which are used for effect. It is not always necessary to try to match word for word, especially if the total effect in the translation will create needless and boring repetition. The word translated **curses** here is different from the word in verse 15; it appears only here and in Pro 3.33; Mal 2.3; 3.9. Both TEV and CEV interpret **curses** as "disasters," namely calamitous events such as floods, earthquakes, or pestilence that happen suddenly with a huge loss of life. The plagues described in verse 27 are an example of the kind of disaster that Yahweh will send. **Confusion** is used also in 7.23, indicating panic in war; and **frustration** appears only here in the Old Testament; it seems to indicate "menace" or "threat," that is, the dangers posed by their enemies.

You are destroyed and perish quickly: more repetition. TEV has "quickly and completely destroyed," or we may say "Your enemies will destroy you quickly and completely."

On account of the evil of your doings: their sins will cause their downfall.

Because you have forsaken me: this is the underlying cause for their punishment. **Me** refers to God, not to Moses (see the same in 7.4).

In some languages it will be helpful to put the final two clauses at the beginning of the verse; for example, "If you do evil and reject the LORD" (TEV).

A possible alternative translation model for this verse is:

- If you do evil and reject Yahweh, no matter what you try to do [or, accomplish], he will cause terrible things to happen to you and confuse you. You will meet only trouble, and your enemies will destroy you quickly and completely.

28.21 RSV	TEV
The LORD will make the pestilence cleave to you until he has consumed you off the land which you are entering to take possession of it.	He will send disease after disease on you until there is not one of you left in the land that you are about to occupy.

The pestilence: if a particular disease is intended, it is probably the (bubonic) plague; the Septuagint translates the Hebrew noun *dever* by "death." Other ways to render **pestilence** are "disease after disease" (TEV), or "terrible diseases" (CEV).

Cleave to you until he has consumed you: Yahweh will send this plague on the rebellious Israelites until he has killed them all, and not one Israelite is left in the Promised Land. The vivid language should be retained if possible. **Cleave to you** may also be rendered as "stay with you" or "make you so sick that you will all . . . ." **Until he has consumed you** means "until all of you are dead," or "not one of you is left" (TEV). This first sentence may be alternatively rendered "He will send terrible diseases upon you that will make you so sick that not one of you will stay alive."

The land you are entering to take possession of it: see 1.8.

28.22   RSV   TEV

The LORD will smite you with con-   The LORD will strike you with infec-
sumption, and with fever, inflamma-   tious diseases, with swelling and
tion, and fiery heat, and with   fever; he will send drought and
drought,ˣ and with blasting, and with   scorching winds to destroy your
mildew; they shall pursue you until   crops. These disasters will be with
you perish.   you until you die.

ˣ Another reading is *sword*

This verse lists seven afflictions in all. There is no complete agreement on the
meaning of each one of them. TEV represents all seven by five different terms.

Smite: TEV renders this as "strike." This is again the use of vivid language;
God will attack them.

You throughout this verse and the rest of the chapter means all the
Israelites. So in many languages a plural pronoun should be used.

Consumption . . . fever . . . inflammation: these are wasting diseases and
plagues that will kill them all; there is considerable redundancy in the list. The
first affliction appears only here and in Lev 26.16; in English "consumption"
means wasting of tissue; it used to refer to the disease called tuberculosis but
is no longer used in that sense. REB has "wasting disease"; TEV "infectious
diseases." **Fever** should present no problem in translation. **Inflammation**
appears only here in the Old Testament; REB has "ague," which means an
attack of fever or a recurring chill or fit of shivering. CEV combines **fever** and
inflammation as "burning fever." Another way to say this is "very hot fever like
a fire."

Fiery heat . . . drought: these two may refer to diseases or to weather
conditions. NJPSV has a footnote: "The exact nature of these afflictions
uncertain." For the first one NJPSV has "scorching heat," NJB "burning fever,"
BRCL "fevers," POCL "epidemics." As an alternative for **drought** the RSV footnote
has "sword," which is the word as spelled in the Hebrew text as we have it; TOB,
NJPSV, and HOTTP ({C} rating) all prefer "drought," but POCL follows the Hebrew
with "wars." **Drought** is probably the preferred interpretation and is
recommended by this Handbook (so RSV, TEV, CEV). It is very likely that **fiery
heat** goes with **fever** and **inflammation**. TEV seems to agree with this interpretation and has "swelling and fever," while CEV has "burning fever and swelling
and pain." Another way to express this is "swelling and burning fever."

Blasting: NRSV "blight" is better; this is an extremely hot wind, so BRCL has
"scorching winds."

Mildew: there is general agreement that this is what the Hebrew word
means. This disease is caused by a type of fungus that grows on plants after
they are hurt by destructive scorching east winds. It was considered a tool of
Yahweh's judgment (Hag 2.17; Amos 4.9). Another way to express **mildew** is
"cause your crops to rot." The translator should keep in mind that this is not
after the harvest, but before the harvest. So if "crops" is understood to mean
"harvested grain," we may say "cause your plants to rot."

They shall pursue you: more vivid language; the afflictions are pictured as wild animals or relentless enemies. TEV has "These disasters will be with you until you die."

28.23   RSV   TEV

And the heavens over your head   No rain will fall, and your ground will
shall be brass, and the earth under   become as hard as iron.
you shall be iron.

The heavens . . . shall be brass: the sense of this is that "No rain shall fall" (TEV). If the Hebrew figurative language is retained, NRSV "sky" is better than **heavens**. It is also possible to keep the figurative language and also give the meaning of "drought," as CEV does with "The LORD will make the sky overhead seem like a bronze roof that keeps out the rain."

The earth . . . shall be iron: because of the prolonged drought the soil will dry out and become hard as iron (see Lev 26.19). CEV is even clearer, with "the ground under your feet will become hard as iron."

Some translators will find it useful to combine verses 21-23 in order to eliminate the repetition. The following is a model which does this:

- [21-23] The LORD will send terrible diseases to attack you until all of you die in the land that he is giving you. You will suffer from contagious diseases and burning fevers of various kinds. The LORD will make the sky overhead seem like a bronze roof that keeps the rain out. And the ground under your feet will become hard as iron. He will send scorching winds to ruin your crops and cause them to rot.

28.24   RSV   TEV

The LORD will make the rain of your   Instead of rain, the LORD will send
land powder and dust; from heaven   down duststorms and sandstorms
it shall come down upon you until   until you are destroyed.
you are destroyed.

The LORD will make the rain of your land powder and dust: in a vivid figure of speech, instead of rain from the sky, dust and sand will come down on the earth beneath. TEV "duststorms and sandstorms" sacrifices the beauty of the original for clarity of meaning.

Until you are destroyed: the picture that has been given is of total destruction, wiping out the Israelite people (see verses 20, 21).

28.25 RSV	TEV

"The LORD will cause you to be defeated before your enemies; you
shall go out one way against them,
and flee seven ways before them;
and you shall be a horror to all the
kingdoms of the earth.

"The LORD will give your enemies
victory over you. You will attack
them from one direction, but you will
run from them in all directions, and
all the people on earth will be terrified when they see what happens to
you.

The first part of this verse states the opposite of verse 7; the Israelites will
be defeated by their enemies, and not the other way round.

Go out . . . against them: that is, march out from their towns and go to war
against their enemies.

You shall be a horror to all the kingdoms of the earth: that is, all the people
of the world will be horrified at what will happen to the Israelites (see verse 37;
see also Jer 15.4; 24.9). NJB has "a terrifying object lesson," TEV "will be
terrified when they see what happens to you," and CEV "a horrible sight for . . .
"; or we may say "when the other nations on earth see what happens to you,
they will be terrified."

All the kingdoms of the earth: a way of saying "all the people in the world."

28.26 RSV	TEV

And your dead body shall be food for
all birds of the air, and for the beasts
of the earth; and there shall be no
one to frighten them away.

When you die, birds and wild animals will come and eat your bodies,
and there will be no one to scare
them off.

Your dead body: a collective expression; all the Israelites will have been
killed. Therefore many translations have "your dead bodies [or, corpses]" or
something similar.

Birds of the air . . . the beasts of the earth: scavenger birds such as vultures
and buzzards, and meat-eating animals. Another way to express this is "the
scavenger birds and the wild [or, forest] animals."

No one to frighten them away: because everyone has been killed (see Jer 7.35;
34.20). This final sentence may be placed at the beginning of the verse as
follows:

●   There will be no one left to scare away [or, frighten] the scavenger birds and wild animals while they are eating your dead
bodies.

28.27   RSV   TEV

The LORD will smite you with the   The LORD will send boils on you, as
boils of Egypt, and with the ulcers   he did on the Egyptians. He will
and the scurvy and the itch, of which   make your bodies break out with
you cannot be healed.   sores. You will be covered with
                                        scabs, and you will itch, but there
                                        will be no cure.

Smite: the same Hebrew verb that in 1.44 is translated "beat . . . down." Here
smite means "to make you suffer" (CEV), "afflict you with," or "cause you to
have."

The boils of Egypt: that is, the plague of boils that God sent on the Egyptians
(Exo 9.9-11). This contradicts what is promised in 7.15; see also 28.60. **Boils** are
a hot and inflammatory swelling of the skin.

Ulcers, scurvy, itch: again, three different diseases; the meaning of each one
is disputed. REB has "tumors, scabs, and itch," NJPSV "hemorrhoids, boil-scars,
and itch," NIV "tumors, festering sores, and itch."

For **ulcers** see Job 2.7-8. Some make the suggestion that this may be
elephantiasis (a parasitic disease carried by mosquitoes), or a skin infection in
that part of the world that produces ulcerous boils that leave scars. In many
languages we may say, for example, "open sores," "infected [or, ulcerated] boils,"
or even "tropical ulcers," meaning boils or sores that have pus in them.

Scurvy is a disease caused by deficiency of vitamin C, characterized by soft
and bleeding gums, bleeding under the skin, and extreme weakness (*American
Heritage Dictionary*, third edition, 1992). This is the only time this term appears in the Bible. In some cultures this may be a common disease, and there
will be satisfactory terms or expressions to describe it. However, in cultures
where the disease is unknown, translators may transliterate the word **scurvy**
and include a note in the Glossary describing the disease.

The itch: TEV has "and you will itch," while CEV has "crusty itchy patches on
your skin."

Of which you cannot be healed: these are incurable diseases. Formally this
curse is incompatible with the previous ones, which state that every person will
be killed. But logic does not always rule in such lists of curses.

A possible alternative translation model for this verse is:

- The LORD will make you suffer with the same diseases that he
  inflicted on the Egyptians. He will give you boils and ulcerated
  sores. You will have scurvy and your skin will itch all over. There
  will be no one to cure you.

28.28   RSV   TEV

The LORD will smite you with mad-   The LORD will make you lose your
ness and blindness and confusion of   mind; he will strike you with blind-
mind;   ness and confusion.

Madness, blindness, and confusion of mind: all three of these terms are
found also in Zech 12.4, where they are the consequences of war. Here they may
refer more to mental and psychological disorders. **Madness** means "to become
insane," "lose your mind," or "have a twisted mind." Most languages will have
suitable terms for this condition.

Blindness is loss of sight.

Confusion of mind is literally "numbness of heart" (it occurs only here and
in Zech 12.4). NJPSV translates "dismay," while TEV has "confusion" (similarly
CEV). In many languages an expression similar to the Hebrew will be appropriate; for example, "make your minds [or, hearts] numb [or without feeling]."

BRCL may prove useful as a model: "The LORD will punish you, causing you
to become insane, blind, and confused."

An alternative translation model for this verse may be:

- Yahweh will cause you to lose your minds. He will make you
  become blind and cause your hearts to be numb [or, confused].

28.29	RSV	TEV

and you shall grope at noonday, as the blind grope in darkness, and you shall not prosper in your ways; and you shall be only oppressed and robbed continually, and there shall be no one to help you.	You will grope about in broad daylight like someone blind, and you will not be able to find your way. You will not prosper in anything you do. You will be constantly oppressed and robbed, and there will be no one to help you.

Grope at noonday: that is, "try to find their way in broad daylight." CEV has
"even in bright sunshine you will have to feel your way around."

The blind grope in darkness: this is not logical, since to a blind person it's all
the same, whether it's daytime or nighttime. Therefore some translations have
taken the "darkness" here to mean the blindness itself, that is, the interior
darkness, not the exterior darkness (so TEV, FRCL, POCL, BRCL). But even if it is
not logical (see Job 5.14; Isa 59.10), it may be that RSV is how the Hebrew text
should be translated. CEV provides an ingenious solution: "like a blind person
who cannot tell day from night."

You shall not prosper in your ways: this is a general statement of total
failure; see NIV "unsuccessful in everything you do," or we may say "You will not
prosper [or, succeed] in anything you do." Some translations, however, relate
this to what comes before it: NRSV "you shall be unable to find your way"
similarly TOB); NJB "your steps will lead you nowhere"; REB "you will fail to find
your way." It is better for the translator to follow the first interpretation,
although the second interpretation is also possible.

Oppressed and robbed continually: they will be the target of attack by all
evil people. In a number of languages translators will use the active voice here;
for example, "People will constantly oppress [or, abuse] you and rob you."

No one to help you: as in verse 26.

An alternative translation model for this verse may be:

- Even in broad daylight [or, bright sunshine] you will feel your way around like a blind person who cannot tell day from night. You will fail in everything you do. People will continually oppress you and rob you, and there will be no one to help you.

28.30 RSV	TEV
You shall betroth a wife, and another man shall lie with her; you shall build a house, and you shall not dwell in it; you shall plant a vineyard, and you shall not use the fruit of it.	"You will be engaged to a young woman—but someone else will marry her. You will build a house—but never live in it. You will plant a vineyard—but never eat its grapes.

All three possibilities in this verse are dealt with in 20.5-7, which lists reasons for exempting a man from active military duty.

Betroth a wife: other ways to express this are "get engaged to a woman," "marry a woman," or "take a woman as wife." The language reflects male dominance; the text addresses men, not women.

Another man shall lie with her: TEV has "marry her"; however, the Hebrew verb is not the usual one for having sexual intercourse with a woman. It appears only here and in Isa 13.16; Jer 3.2; Zech 14.2, and seems to mean forcible intercourse, rape. This verb was considered obscene by the Masoretes (the scribes who copied and passed on the Hebrew text) and was regularly substituted by another verb, less offensive, that means "to lie with." So it is probably truer to the meaning of the text to say "take her and ravish her" (NIV), or "will enjoy her" (NJPSV), or "will ravish her" (REB), or even "raped by enemy soldiers" (CEV).

You shall build a house, and you shall not dwell in it: this would happen because of either death or exile.

You shall plant a vineyard, and you shall not use the fruit of it: because someone else will take possession of it.

28.31 RSV	TEV
Your ox shall be slain before your eyes, and you shall not eat of it; your ass shall be violently taken away before your face, and shall not be restored to you; your sheep shall be given to your enemies, and there shall be no one to help you.	Your cattle will be butchered before your very eyes, but you will not eat any of the meat. Your donkeys will be dragged away while you look on, and they will not be given back to you. Your sheep will be given to your enemies, and there will be no one to help you.

All the violent acts that will be inflicted on the Israelites are clearly stated and should offer no problems for the translator.

The singular general terms **your ox . . . your ass . . . your sheep** are better translated as plurals: "your cattle, your donkeys, and your flocks [of sheep]." We should not think, as NIV seems to suggest, that the text is talking about the one and only ox, and one donkey (but many sheep!). The Hebrew word translated **sheep** applies both to sheep and goats; but most translations have only "sheep." For **ox**, **ass**, and **sheep** see 5.14.

Before your eyes . . . before your face: that is, "in your presence," "as you look on."

Shall be given to your enemies: by strict grammatical rules, this says in English that someone other than **your enemies** will take possession of the sheep and give them to the enemies; it seems more likely, however, that this is simply a way of saying that the enemies will take away the sheep.

There shall be no one to help you: as in verse 29. The Hebrew is simply "and none to you [singular] a helper." Some translations take this to refer to the sheep, "to rescue them" (so NIV, REB). It seems better, however, to translate as RSV and TEV have done.

An alternative translation model in languages that do not use the passive is the following:

- They shall kill your cattle as you watch, but you will not eat any of the meat. As you are watching they will drag away your donkeys and will not return them to you. Your enemies will steal your sheep, and there will be no one to help you.

28.32	RSV	TEV

Your sons and your daughters shall be given to another people, while your eyes look on and fail with longing for them all the day; and it shall not be in the power of your hand to prevent it.	Your sons and daughters will be given as slaves to foreigners while you look on. Every day you will strain your eyes, looking in vain for your children to return.

In this statement there is the same passive construction used in the previous verse: **shall be given**.

Your sons and daughters shall be given to another people: that is, they will be taken as prisoners of war to some foreign country. TEV adds "as slaves," which is permissible; they certainly wouldn't be taken to foreign countries to become citizens! In languages that do not use the passive, we may say, for example, "I will give your sons and daughters to foreigners while you watch."

Your eyes look on: "in your presence," or "as you watch."

Fail with longing for them all the day: an expressive figure of speech (see Lam 4.17). They will look and look, in vain, for the return of their children. NIV has "you will wear out your eyes watching for them day after day"; a better way of rendering this may be ". . . as you watch, day after day, for them to return home."

It shall not be in the power of your hand to prevent it: that is, you won't be able to prevent them from being taken into exile to a foreign country. Or, as FRCL translates, "you won't be able to effect their return," or BRCL "you won't be able to do anything to bring them back." This seems to be the better choice.

28.33 RSV	TEV
A nation which you have not known shall eat up the fruit of your ground and of all your labors; and you shall be only oppressed and crushed continually;	A foreign nation will take all the crops that you have worked so hard to grow, while you receive nothing but constant oppression and harsh treatment.

A nation which you have not known: as in Jer 22.15-17, this means a foreign people the Israelites have never had any dealings with (TEV "a foreign nation").

Eat up the fruit of your ground and of all your labors: that is, they will either take possession of or destroy all the crops that the Israelites had worked so hard to grow. "Take possession of," or even "eaten," is the preferred meaning. TEV has "will take all the crops that you have worked so hard to grow," and CEV "everything you harvest will be eaten by foreigners."

You shall be only oppressed and crushed continually: the word **only** modifies the whole curse; the sense is "all you will get is ceaseless oppression"; NIV "cruel oppression" expresses the sense well. In a number of languages the active voice will be the preferred style; for example, "they will constantly oppress you and treat you harshly."

28.34 RSV	TEV
so that you shall be driven mad by the sight which your eyes shall see.	Your sufferings will make you lose your mind.

So that you shall be driven mad by the sight which your eyes shall see: the cruel actions of their enemies will make them go crazy. NJB has "you will be driven mad by the sights you see," SPCL "when you see these things you will go crazy"; or we may say "when you [plural] see all these terrible things, you will go insane [or, lose your minds]."

28.35 RSV	TEV
The LORD will smite you on the knees and on the legs with grievous boils of which you cannot be healed, from	The LORD will cover your legs with incurable, painful sores; boils will cover you from head to foot.

the sole of your foot to the crown of your head.

The LORD will smite you: see verse 27.
Grievous boils: see verse 27.
From the sole of your foot to the crown of your head: that is, "all over you." The boils will spread from **knees** and **legs** to the whole body, "from head to foot" (TEV; similarly CEV).

3D. The LORD will take you to a foreign country (28.36-37)

RSV	TEV
36 "The LORD will bring you, and your king whom you set over you, to a nation that neither you nor your fathers have known; and there you shall serve other gods, of wood and stone. 37 And you shall become a horror, a proverb, and a byword, among all the peoples where the LORD will lead you away.	36 "The LORD will take you and your king away to a foreign land, where neither you nor your ancestors ever lived before; there you will serve gods made of wood and stone. 37 In the countries to which the LORD will scatter you, the people will be shocked at what has happened to you; they will make fun of you and ridicule you.

The theme of the consequences of disobedience continues to the end of chapter 28; however, it is recommended by this Handbook that translators divide verses 36-68 into four sections. The first one, verses 36-37, gives a warning about the punishment of exile, which is the loss of the greatest of Yahweh's blessings, life in the Promised Land.

Section heading: this section may have the title "The LORD will make you go to a foreign country."

28.36 RSV	TEV
"The LORD will bring you, and your king whom you set over you, to a nation that neither you nor your fathers have known; and there you shall serve other gods, of wood and stone.	**"The LORD will take you and your king away to a foreign land, where neither you nor your ancestors ever lived before; there you will serve gods made of wood and stone.**

With the beginning of a new section, Moses should be reintroduced as the speaker.

The LORD will bring . . . to a nation: in some languages this will be expressed as "will take." The verb "bring" or "take" should not suggest that Yahweh will transport them by supernatural means; the idea is that he will bring a foreign king and his army to fight against the Israelites, who will take them into exile as prisoners of war.

You, and your king: that is, the whole nation of Israel. This foresees a time when the Israelites will have kings as their rulers. For **king** see the comment at 1.5.

Your king whom you set over you: the point of reference here is their future defeat and exile, after they have become a nation and have chosen a king to rule over them. The Septuagint has "your rulers, whoever you appoint over you." Unlike TEV and CEV, translators are encouraged to include this clause. Other ways to express it are "the king you choose" or "the man whom you choose to be your king." This clause reflects an anti-monarchy bias—the selection of a king was your doing, not Yahweh's.

A nation that neither you nor your fathers have known: see verse 33; as usual, **fathers** means ancestors.

You shall serve other gods, of wood and stone: see 4.28.

28.37	RSV	TEV
	And you shall become a horror, a proverb, and a byword, among all the peoples where the LORD will lead you away.	In the countries to which the LORD will scatter you, the people will be shocked at what has happened to you; they will make fun of you and ridicule you.

A horror, a proverb, and a byword: again, three terms that mean almost the same thing are used for emphasis (see verse 25). **Horror** here, as in verse 25, is something that horrifies others (NRSV "object of horror"). So TEV has "the people will be shocked at what has happened to you," and CEV "people . . . will shudder when they see." **A proverb** means that the Israelites will become examples of victims of cruel treatment by enemies. The tragic fate of the Israelites will be remembered, and people will refer to it when the subject of national defeat arises. **Byword** means almost the same as **proverb**; the Hebrew word appears here, in 1 Kgs 9.7; 2 Chr 7.20; Jer 24.9, and nowhere else in the Old Testament. It has the basic meaning of "taunt," that is, to ridicule, to make fun of someone. NJB "laughingstock" is a good idiom in English. REB has "a horror, a byword, and an object-lesson." BRCL translates "They will be horrified at what happened to you; they will malign you and make fun of you."

Where the LORD will lead you away: defeat in war and the exile are the doings of Yahweh. As Yahweh had led them out of slavery in Egypt, he will lead them back into slavery. This final sentence may be placed at the beginning of the verse as follows:

• The people of countries to which Yahweh scatters you will be shocked at what has happened to you.

3F. Poor crops (28.38-42)

RSV	TEV
38 You shall carry much seed into the field, and shall gather little in; for the locust shall consume it. 39 You shall plant vineyards and dress them, but you shall neither drink of the wine nor gather the grapes; for the worm shall eat them. 40 You shall have olive trees throughout all your territory, but you shall not anoint yourself with the oil; for your olives shall drop off.	38 "You will plant plenty of seed, but reap only a small harvest, because the locusts will eat your crops. 39 You will plant vineyards and take care of them, but you will not gather their grapes or drink wine from them, because worms will eat the vines. 40 Olive trees will grow everywhere in your land, but you will not have any olive oil, because the olives will drop off.

In this section the consequence of disobedience is the opposite of the blessing of prosperity referred to in verses 4 and 11. These verses deal with the three main crops of the Israelites in Canaan: grain (wheat and barley), vineyards, and olive trees. All will fail, due to natural causes: locusts will eat the standing crops, worms will destroy the grapevines, and the olives will fall off before maturing.

Section heading: possible titles for this section are "Poor crops" or "Yahweh will give you [plural] few crops [or, fruit]."

28.38

RSV	TEV
You shall carry much seed into the field, and shall gather little in; for the locust shall consume it.	**"You will plant plenty of seed, but reap only a small harvest, because the locusts will eat your crops.**

Carry much seed into the field: that is, sow much seed in their fields.

Shall gather little in: meaning that they will "reap only a small harvest" (TEV; similarly CEV), or "they will reap very little grain."

The locust: that is, "locusts"; see Exo 10.1-20 for the plague of locusts in Egypt. **The locust** here was the desert type of winged

LOCUSTS EATING LEAVES

hopping insect that swarmed in the air. Locusts destroy all plant life when they move in large swarms. For further information see FFB, pages 53-54. It may be helpful for translators to include a picture of this insect.

28.39

RSV	TEV
You shall plant vineyards and dress them, but you shall neither drink of the wine nor gather the grapes; for the worm shall eat them.	**You will plant vineyards and take care of them, but you will not gather their grapes or drink wine from them, because worms will eat the vines.**

Plant vineyards and dress them: the verb **dress** here means to do all that is needed to make sure that the vines will grow strong and healthy; this includes cutting them back at the right time. REB "cultivate" is better English for nonspecialists. For **vineyards** see the comment at 6.11.

Neither drink of the wine nor gather the grapes: curiously enough, this is in reverse order to what actually takes place, and the translator must decide whether this will cause difficulty for the reader. TEV reverses the order with "you will not gather their grapes or drink wine from them" (similarly CEV).

The worm: an appropriate word must be found in the language, to speak of crop-eating worms or grubs ("the grub," NJB, REB). **Them** in many languages will be expressed as "the grape vines."

28.40 RSV	TEV
You shall have olive trees throughout all your territory, but you shall not anoint yourself with the oil; for your olives shall drop off.	Olive trees will grow everywhere in your land, but you will not have any olive oil, because the olives will drop off.

You shall have olive trees throughout all your territory: or "Olive trees will grow everywhere in your land" (TEV).

You shall not anoint yourself with the oil: this is the use of olive oil in normal daily body care (see Ruth 3.3; 2 Sam 12.20; 14.2); it does not refer to its use in the ordination of kings or priests. Another way to express this is "You shall not have any of the oil to put on your bodies."

Your olives shall drop off: because the olive trees are not healthy, and the olives drop off before they mature.

28.41 RSV	TEV
You shall beget sons and daughters, but they shall not be yours; for they shall go into captivity.	You will have sons and daughters, but you will lose them, because they will be taken away as prisoners of war.

They shall not be yours . . . they shall go into captivity: the meaning is clear; while still young and living at home, their sons and daughters will be snatched from them by the enemy and taken away as prisoners of war.

An alternative translation model for this verse is:

- You will have sons and daughters, but your enemies will take them away as prisoners.

28.42   RSV   TEV

All your trees and the fruit of your ground the locust shall possess.

All your trees and crops will be devoured by insects.

This verse repeats, in a briefer form, the warning of verse 38.
The fruit of your ground: "the crops" (see verse 11).
The locust shall possess: that is, "the locusts will destroy."

3G. More curses for disobedience (28.43-57)

RSV   TEV

43 The sojourner who is among you shall mount above you higher and higher; and you shall come down lower and lower. 44 He shall lend to you, and you shall not lend to him; he shall be the head, and you shall be the tail. 45 All these curses shall come upon you and pursue you and overtake you, till you are destroyed, because you did not obey the voice of the LORD your God, to keep his commandments and his statutes which he commanded you. 46 They shall be upon you as a sign and a wonder, and upon your descendants for ever.

47 "Because you did not serve the LORD your God with joyfulness and gladness of heart, by reason of the abundance of all things, 48 therefore you shall serve your enemies whom the LORD will send against you, in hunger and thirst, in nakedness, and in want of all things; and he will put a yoke of iron upon your neck, until he has destroyed you. 49 The LORD will bring a nation against you from afar, from the end of the earth, as swift as the eagle flies, a nation whose language you do not understand, 50 a nation of stern countenance, who shall not regard the person of the old or show favor to the young, 51 and shall eat the offspring of your cattle and the fruit of your ground, until you are destroyed; who also shall not leave you grain, wine, or oil, the increase of your cattle or the young of your flock, until they have caused you to perish. 52 They shall besiege you in all your towns, until your high and fortified walls, in which you trusted, come down throughout all your land; and they shall besiege you in all your towns throughout all your land, which the LORD your God has given you. 53 And you shall eat the offspring of your own body, the flesh of your sons and daughters, whom the LORD your God has given you, in the siege and in the distress with which your enemies shall distress you. 54 The man who is the most

43 "Foreigners who live in your land will gain more and more power, while you gradually lose yours. 44 They will have money to lend you, but you will have none to lend them. In the end they will be your rulers.

45 "All these disasters will come on you, and they will be with you until you are destroyed, because you did not obey the LORD your God and keep all the laws that he gave you. 46 They will be the evidence of God's judgment on you and your descendants forever. 47 The LORD blessed you in every way, but you would not serve him with glad and joyful hearts. 48 So then, you will serve the enemies that the LORD is going to send against you. You will be hungry, thirsty, and naked—in need of everything. The LORD will oppress you harshly until you are destroyed. 49 The LORD will bring against you a nation from the ends of the earth, a nation whose language you do not know. They will swoop down on you like an eagle. 50 They will be ruthless and show no mercy to anyone, young or old. 51 They will eat your livestock and your crops, and you will starve to death. They will not leave you any grain, wine, olive oil, cattle, or sheep; and you will die. 52 They will attack every town in the land that the LORD your God is giving you, and the high, fortified walls in which you trust will fall.

53 "When your enemies are besieging your towns, you will become so desperate for food that you will even eat the children that the LORD your God has given you. 54-55 Even the most refined man of noble birth will become so desperate during the siege that he will eat some of his own children because he has no other food. He will not even give any to his brother or to the wife he loves or to any of his children who are left. 56-57 Even the most refined woman of noble birth, so rich that she has never had to walk anywhere, will behave

tender and delicately bred among you will grudge food to his brother, to the wife of his bosom, and to the last of the children who remain to him; 55 so that he will not give to any of them any of the flesh of his children whom he is eating, because he has nothing left him, in the siege and in the distress with which your enemy shall distress you in all your towns. 56 The most tender and delicately bred woman among you, who would not venture to set the sole of her foot upon the ground because she is so delicate and tender, will grudge to the husband of her bosom, to her son and to her daughter, 57 her afterbirth that comes out from between her feet and her children whom she bears, because she will eat them secretly, for want of all things, in the siege and in the distress with which your enemy shall distress you in your towns.

in the same way. When the enemy besieges her town, she will become so desperate for food that she will secretly eat her newborn child and the afterbirth as well. She will not share them with the husband she loves or with any of her children.

This section warns of a reversal of national fortunes in terms that make it the opposite of blessings promised for obedience in verses 1, 7, 12, and 13.

Section heading: CEV has "More Curses for Disobedience." Another possible heading is "Other ways that Yahweh will punish you [plural]."

28.43-44 RSV	TEV
43 The sojourner who is among you shall mount above you higher and higher; and you shall come down lower and lower. 44 He shall lend to you, and you shall not lend to him; he shall be the head, and you shall be the tail.	**43 "Foreigners who live in your land will gain more and more power, while you gradually lose yours. 44 They will have money to lend you, but you will have none to lend them. In the end they will be your rulers.**

Natural conditions will be reversed: the resident aliens (see 1.16) will become more prosperous and powerful than the Israelites.

Shall mount above you higher and higher: they will become ever richer and more powerful. We may also express this as "foreigners who live in your land will become richer and more powerful."

You shall come down lower and lower: this verse presents a picture that is the opposite of verses 12b-13; the Israelites will decline in power and wealth. CEV has "while you become poor and powerless."

28.45 RSV	TEV
All these curses shall come upon you and pursue you and overtake you, till you are destroyed, because you did not obey the voice of the LORD your God, to keep his com-	**"All these disasters will come on you, and they will be with you until you are destroyed, because you did not obey the LORD your God and keep all the laws that he gave you.**

**mandments and his statutes which
he commanded you.**

This verse is a summarizing statement; see verse 15.

All these curses: this refers to all the disasters foretold in verses 15-44.

Shall come upon you . . . pursue . . . overtake: again the use of vivid
language, portraying these disasters as wild animals or merciless enemies.

Till you are destroyed: in the context, this is total destruction, extinction of
the Israelites as a people.

Did not obey the voice of the LORD your God: see verse 1.

His commandments and his statutes: see 4.1-2. This clause and the previous
one may be placed at the beginning of the verse, as follows:

- Moses said to the Israelites: "If you [plural] don't obey the laws
  and teachings that the LORD your God is giving you, he will send
  all these disasters on you. They will follow you until they completely destroy you.

28.46　　　　RSV　　　　　　　　　　　　　　　TEV

They shall be upon you as a sign and a wonder, and upon your descendants for ever.	They will be the evidence of God's judgment on you and your descendants forever.

They shall be upon you: that is, they will befall you, come down on you.

A sign and a wonder: see the two words in 4.34. Here they mean a solemn
warning, a powerful reminder, to other people, as TEV makes clear. Some,
however, take this to be a solemn warning to the Israelites themselves; but the
Hebrew preposition translated **upon** seems to require the other meaning. NJPSV
has "They shall serve as signs and proofs against you and your offspring . . .";
or we may say ". . . that God is punishing you."

You and your descendants for ever: formally this contradicts the passages
that foretell the total destruction of the Israelites.

28.47　　　　RSV　　　　　　　　　　　　　　　TEV

"Because you did not serve the LORD your God with joyfulness and gladness of heart, by reason of the abundance of all things,	The LORD blessed you in every way, but you would not serve him with glad and joyful hearts.

You did not serve the LORD your God with joyfulness and gladness of heart:
here a new note is added, that of gratitude and joy.

By reason of the abundance of all things: this translation does not convey
the meaning of the text very clearly. The sense is that the Israelites had been
blessed with prosperity and peace, and for this reason they should have served

God joyfully and gladly. NRSV is somewhat better: "Because you did not serve the LORD your God joyfully and with gladness of heart for all the abundance of everything . . ."; or we may say ". . . even though he has made you prosper in every way."

28.48 RSV	TEV
therefore you shall serve your enemies whom the LORD will send against you, in hunger and thirst, in nakedness, and in want of all things; and he will put a yoke of iron upon your neck, until he has destroyed you.	So then, you will serve the enemies that the LORD is going to send against you. You will be hungry, thirsty, and naked—in need of everything. The LORD[y] will oppress you harshly until you are destroyed.
	[y] The LORD; *or* Your enemies.

You shall serve your enemies: they will work as slaves for their enemies.

Whom the LORD will send against you: all the disasters are Yahweh's doing. It will be good to make this clear in translation; for example, "you shall serve your enemies as slaves," "you will serve the enemies that the LORD is going to send against you" (TEV), or even "he [Yahweh] will send enemies to attack you and make you their slaves" (CEV). However, it is also possible to say something like "Yahweh will let your enemies . . . ," as Yahweh will not actually be the one oppressing them. For a comment on **enemies** see 1.42.

In hunger and thirst, in nakedness, and in want of all things: this is a vivid description of the absolute misery to which they will be reduced. CEV has "Then you will live in poverty with nothing to eat, drink, or wear."

He will put a yoke of iron upon your neck: this is a picture of total and degrading slavery, and God will cause it to happen. See Jer 28.13-14 for the same figure of speech. Notice that TEV, in a footnote, gives "Your enemies" as a possible rendering of the Hebrew text, instead of "The LORD."

Until he has destroyed you: see the same kind of statements in verses 20, 22, 24.

An alternative translation model for verses 47 and 48 is:

- [47] The LORD caused you to prosper in every way, but you would not serve him with glad and joyful hearts. [48] For this reason he will send enemies to attack you, and you will serve them as slaves. You will be hungry, thirsty, and have nothing to wear. You will live in poverty. The LORD will let your enemies treat you harshly until you die.

28.49 RSV	TEV
The LORD will bring a nation against you from afar, from the end of the	The LORD will bring against you a nation from the ends of the earth, a

earth, as swift as the eagle flies, a
nation whose language you do not
understand,

nation whose language you do not
know. They will swoop down on you
like an eagle.

In RSV verses 49-51 are one sentence, which must be broken into several
smaller units.

A nation . . . from afar, from the end of the earth: this is a normal way of
speaking of a country a great distance from Israel.

As swift as the eagle flies: it does not appear that the swiftness is the main
point of comparison, but rather the manner in which an **eagle** swoops down on
its prey. TEV has "will swoop down on you like an eagle," and NRSV, NIV, REB,
and NJPSV have the same kind of statement. See a similar use of the figure in
Jer 48.40; Hos 8.1. In cultures where eagles are unknown, we may use a similar
bird if that is available, or say something like "just like a large bird of prey
swoops down."

A nation whose language you do not understand: this is natural, since these
people would come from a far off land, and the Israelites would never have had
any dealings with them. CEV has a helpful model: "foreigners who speak a
strange language."

28.50	RSV	TEV

a nation of stern countenance, who
shall not regard the person of the old
or show favor to the young,

They will be ruthless and show no
mercy to anyone, young or old.

A nation of stern countenance: these foreigners are fierce-looking (NRSV
"grim-faced," NJB "grim of face"). In other words "They are merciless,"
"ruthless" (TEV), or "won't show mercy" (CEV).

Not regard the person of the old or show favor to the young: they show no
respect for anyone; they have pity on no one.

28.51	RSV	TEV

and shall eat the offspring of your
cattle and the fruit of your ground,
until you are destroyed; who also
shall not leave you grain, wine, or oil,
the increase of your cattle or the
young of your flock, until they have
caused you to perish.

They will eat your livestock and your
crops, and you will starve to death.
They will not leave you any grain,
wine, olive oil, cattle, or sheep; and
you will die.

Shall eat: this doesn't mean just to "eat" (TEV) or "take" (CEV), as such, but
take possession of, and possibly destroy all the livestock (see the same verb in
verse 35).

The offspring of your cattle and the fruit of your ground: see verse 11.

Until you are destroyed: see verses 20, 24.

Not leave you grain, wine, or oil: see verses 38-40. They will do away with all the property of the Israelites.

The increase of your cattle or the young of your flock: see verses 4, 18.

Until they have caused you to perish: all the things the enemy will do will completely wipe out the Israelites; they will disappear.

28.52	RSV	TEV

They shall besiege you in all your towns, until your high and fortified walls, in which you trusted, come down throughout all your land; and they shall besiege you in all your towns throughout all your land, which the LORD your God has given you.	They will attack every town in the land that the LORD your God is giving you, and the high, fortified walls in which you trust will fall.

Verses 52-57 speak of how the enemy will besiege the **fortified** towns and all other settlements in Israel, and what will happen when the people are under siege.

They shall besiege you: to **besiege** is to surround a town with enemy troops, thus preventing anyone from leaving or entering, in an attempt to get the people in the town to surrender. For a comment on the translation of **besiege**, see 20.12.

Your high and fortified walls: high walls surrounded fortified towns, with parapets on top from which the defending forces could shoot arrows at the enemy. Other ways to say this are "high and well-protected walls" or "high and strong walls, inside of which you feel safe."

In which you trusted: but to no avail; the enemy will break through the walls.

Come down: this is the same verb translated as "fall" in 20.20. CEV has "the enemy will tear them down."

They shall besiege you: repeating the thought of the first part of the verse; this is now expanded to include **all your towns throughout all your land**.

Which the LORD your God has given you: as often stated in this book.

A possible alternative translation model for this verse is:

• All over the land that the LORD your God gave you, your enemies will surround all your towns. You may feel safe inside your high and strong walls, but your enemies will tear them down.

28.53	RSV	TEV

And you shall eat the offspring of your own body, the flesh of your sons and daughters, whom the LORD	"When your enemies are besieging your towns, you will become so desperate for food that you will even eat

your God has given you, in the siege and in the distress with which your enemies shall distress you.

the children that the LORD your God has given you.

This is a grim description of siege conditions, with emphasis on cannibalism (see Lev 26.29; 2 Kgs 6.28-29; Jer 19.9; Lam 2.24; 4.10; Ezek 5.10).

You shall eat the offspring of your own body, the flesh of your sons and daughters: the emphatic form should be reproduced in translation if possible. But if it sounds unnatural in a translator's language, we may say, for example, "you will even eat the children" (TEV).

Whom the LORD your God has given you: for this reason they are all the more precious.

In the siege and in the distress with which your enemies shall distress you: this describes the general situation, and it is better to place it at the beginning of the verse (see TEV). This full statement is repeated, with slight variations, in verses 55 and 57. More natural ways of stating this should be used: "the desperate straits to which your enemies will reduce you during the siege," or "while your [plural] enemies are surrounding your towns, you will become so desperate that you will even eat . . . ." "Desperate" may be also expressed as "without hope," "hopeless," "feel that there is nothing else to do," "feel there is no way out," "feel that there is no other path to follow."

28.54-55   RSV   TEV

54 The man who is the most tender and delicately bred among you will grudge food to his brother, to the wife of his bosom, and to the last of the children who remain to him; 55 so that he will not give to any of them any of the flesh of his children whom he is eating, because he has nothing left him, in the siege and in the distress with which your enemy shall distress you in all your towns.

54-55 Even the most refined man of noble birth will become so desperate during the siege that he will eat some of his own children because he has no other food. He will not even give any to his brother or to the wife he loves or to any of his children who are left.

Notice how TEV and CEV have combined verses 54-55, for a more natural and clearer statement.

The man who is the most tender and delicately bred among you: something like "most refined and sensitive" represents well the meaning of the text. This is expressed as "most gentle and sensitive" (NIV); "The gentlest and tenderest man among you" (NJB); "most refined and gentle" (REB); "a man who had been gentle and kind" (CEV). TEV "most refined man of noble birth" appears to miss the point.

Will grudge food: that is, "will not share any of his food," which, in this context, consists of the flesh of some of his own children (verse 55). The Hebrew expression translated **grudge** is "make the eye hostile" (see 15.9); here it means to look at his family with indifference and hostility. So we may translate as "he will viciously [or, nastily] refuse to share his food with . . . ," or even "he will look at them with a vicious look and refuse to share . . . ."

Brother: in a number of languages translators will need to indicate the relative age of a **brother**, whether older or younger. In such a case we may say, for example, "to his older or younger brother."

The wife of his bosom: that is, his dear, or beloved, wife.

To the last of the children who remain to him: or "any of his children who are left," or even ". . . who are still alive."

He will not give any of them: this repeats information from verse 54 and may be omitted in a number of languages.

Because he has nothing left him: TEV says "because he had no other food." That is the reason why he is eating the flesh of some of his own children.

In the siege and in the distress: as in verse 53.

A possible translation model combining verses 54 and 55 is the following:

- ⁵⁴⁻⁵⁵ Because the enemies are surrounding his town, a man who had been gentle and kind will become so desperate that he will eat his own children. He will do this because he feels that there is nothing else he can do; he has no food left. He will viciously refuse to share any of the meat with his brother or his beloved wife or any of his children that are left.

28.56-57 RSV	TEV
56 The most tender and delicately bred woman among you, who would not venture to set the sole of her foot upon the ground because she is so delicate and tender, will grudge to the husband of her bosom, to her son and to her daughter, 57 her afterbirth that comes out from between her feet and her children whom she bears, because she will eat them secretly, for want of all things, in the siege and in the distress with which your enemy shall distress you in your towns.	56-57 Even the most refined woman of noble birth, so rich that she has never had to walk anywhere, will behave in the same way. When the enemy besieges her town, she will become so desperate for food that she will secretly eat her newborn child and the afterbirth as well. She will not share them with the husband she loves or with any of her children.

TEV and CEV have combined verses 56 and 57 to make a clearer and less repetitive translation.

The most tender and delicately bred woman: exactly the same language used of the man in verse 54. In some cultures the same terms cannot be applied to both men and women.

Would not venture to set the sole of her foot upon the ground: this seems to mean that she is so delicately bred and has lived in such luxury that she never would walk barefoot on the ground; some, however (see TEV), take it to mean that she is so wealthy that she has never had to walk anywhere, but was transported either in a litter or in a carriage. It seems better to take it in the first sense. In any case this is an obvious exaggeration; it seems very unlikely that an adult woman could live all her life, especially raising children, without once setting her foot on the ground.

Will grudge: as in verse 56. TEV has "will behave in the same way," meaning she will refuse to share the flesh of the child with others.

The husband of her bosom: like **the wife of his bosom** in verse 54.

To her son and to her daughter: that is, "to her children."

Her afterbirth . . . and her children whom she bears: **afterbirth** is the soft tissue that surrounds the baby before birth and comes out from the womb after childbirth. It is hardly possible that the writer was thinking of a siege that would last long enough for a woman to give birth several times. It is better to follow TEV, "the child" (see POCL "the son"; similarly NJB, BRCL). FRCL cites the Septuagint for the singular. REB "or any boy or girl that she may bear," and CEV "eat both her new-born baby and the afterbirth" are commendable ways of handling the matter.

For want of all things: because she has no food left and has become desperate with hunger.

3H. Disobedience brings destruction (28.58-68)

RSV	TEV
58 "If you are not careful to do all the words of this law which are written in this book, that you may fear this glorious and awful name, the LORD your God, 59 then the LORD will bring on you and your offspring extraordinary afflictions, afflictions severe and lasting, and sicknesses grievous and lasting. 60 And he will bring upon you again all the diseases of Egypt, which you were afraid of; and they shall cleave to you. 61 Every sickness also, and every affliction which is not recorded in the book of this law, the LORD will bring upon you, until you are destroyed. 62 Whereas you were as the stars of heaven for multitude, you shall be left few in number; because you did not obey the voice of the LORD your God. 63 And as the LORD took delight in doing you good and multiplying you, so the LORD will take delight in bringing ruin upon you and destroying you; and you shall be plucked off the land which you are entering to take possession of it. 64 And the LORD will scatter you among all peoples, from one end of the earth to the other; and there you shall serve other gods, of wood and stone, which neither you nor your fathers have known. 65 And among these nations you shall find no ease, and there shall be no rest	58 "If you do not obey faithfully all of God's teachings that are written in this book and if you do not honor the wonderful and awesome name of the LORD your God, 59 he will send on you and on your descendants incurable diseases and horrible epidemics that can never be stopped. 60 He will bring on you once again all the dreadful diseases you experienced in Egypt, and you will never recover. 61 He will also send all kinds of diseases and epidemics that are not mentioned in this book of God's laws and teachings, and you will be destroyed. 62 Although you become as numerous as the stars in the sky, only a few of you will survive, because you did not obey the LORD your God. 63 Just as the LORD took delight in making you prosper and in making you increase in number, so he will take delight in destroying you and in bringing ruin on you. You will be uprooted from the land that you are about to occupy. 64 "The LORD will scatter you among all the nations, from one end of the earth to the other, and there you will serve gods made of wood and stone, gods that neither you nor your ancestors have ever worshiped before. 65 You will find no peace anywhere, no place to call

for the sole of your foot; but the LORD will give you there a trembling heart, and failing eyes, and a languishing soul; 66 your life shall hang in doubt before you; night and day you shall be in dread, and have no assurance of your life. 67 In the morning you shall say, 'Would it were evening!' and at evening you shall say, 'Would it were morning!' because of the dread which your heart shall fear, and the sights which your eyes shall see. 68 And the LORD will bring you back in ships to Egypt, a journey which I promised that you should never make again; and there you shall offer yourselves for sale to your enemies as male and female slaves, but no man will buy you."

your own; the LORD will overwhelm you with anxiety, hopelessness, and despair. 66 Your life will always be in danger. Day and night you will be filled with terror, and you will live in constant fear of death. 67 Your hearts will pound with fear at everything you see. Every morning you will wish for evening; every evening you will wish for morning. 68 The LORD will send you back to Egypt in ships, even though he said that you would never have to go there again. There you will try to sell yourselves to your enemies as slaves, but no one will want to buy you."

These verses are a climax to the long list of consequences or punishments that will come upon the Israelites if they are disobedient to the commands of Yahweh, their God.

Section heading: CEV has the heading "Disobedience Brings Destruction"; this may also be expressed as "If you disobey Yahweh, he will destroy you."

28.58 RSV TEV

"If you are not careful to do all the words of this law which are written in this book, that you may fear this glorious and awful name, the LORD your God,

"If you do not obey faithfully all of God's teachings that are written in this book and if you do not honor the wonderful and awesome name of the LORD your God,

With the beginning of a new section, Moses should be reintroduced as the speaker.

If you are not careful to do all the words of this law which are written in this book: here the writer abandons the point of view that all these words were spoken by Moses in Moab; Moses could hardly refer to **this book**, that is, the book we call Deuteronomy, as though it were already in existence. For **this law** see also 1.5.

That you may fear this glorious and awful name: NRSV is better English, "fearing this glorious and awesome name." TEV expresses the verse more clearly: "If you do not obey . . . and if you do not honor . . . ." To **fear** here means to "respect," "honor," "revere" (see 4.10).

Glorious and awful: or "majestic and awesome." In some languages we may say something like "the great name that inspires [or, causes] fear."

The LORD your God: this is the very name they must honor and respect.

28.59 RSV TEV

then the LORD will bring on you and your offspring extraordinary afflic-

he will send on you and on your descendants incurable diseases and

tions, afflictions severe and lasting, and sicknesses grievous and lasting.

horrible epidemics that can never be stopped.

Here again adjectives and a series of terms which all mean the same thing are used for emphasis.

Will bring on you: or "will punish you . . . with" (CEV), or even "will cause you to become sick with . . . ."

On you and your offspring: "on you and on your descendants" (TEV).

Extraordinary afflictions, afflictions severe and lasting: for **afflictions** NIV, NJB, and NJPSV have "plagues," which is better in English.

Sicknesses grievous and lasting: TEV "horrible epidemics" may serve as a good model to follow.

28.60   RSV   TEV

And he will bring upon you again all the diseases of Egypt, which you were afraid of; and they shall cleave to you.

He will bring on you once again all the dreadful diseases you experienced in Egypt, and you will never recover.

All the diseases of Egypt: this means all the plagues God sent on the Egyptians; see verse 27; 7.15.

They shall cleave to you: a vivid way of saying that the Israelites will not be healed; these illnesses are incurable.

28.61   RSV   TEV

Every sickness also, and every affliction which is not recorded in the book of this law, the LORD will bring upon you, until you are destroyed.

He will also send all kinds of diseases and epidemics that are not mentioned in this book of God's laws and teachings, and you will be destroyed.

Every sickness also, and every affliction: NJB has "all the plagues and all the diseases," REB "sickness and plague of every kind." NJB "other diseases and plagues" best fits the context.

Not recorded in the book of this law: see the similar statement in verse 58; see also 29.21; 30.10; 31.26.

Until you are destroyed: see verses 10, 14, 51.

28.62   RSV   TEV

Whereas you were as the stars of heaven for multitude, you shall be left few in number; because you did not obey the voice of the LORD your God.

Although you become as numerous as the stars in the sky, only a few of you will survive, because you did not obey the LORD your God.

You were as the stars of heaven for multitude: for parallel statements of growth in size and number, see 1.10; 10.22; 26.5.

You shall be left few in number: or "only a few of you will survive" (TEV), or "... will stay alive."

You did not obey the voice of the LORD your God: see verse 1.

28.63 RSV	TEV
And as the LORD took delight in doing you good and multiplying you, so the LORD will take delight in bringing ruin upon you and destroying you; and you shall be plucked off the land which you are entering to take possession of it.	Just as the LORD took delight in making you prosper and in making you increase in number, so he will take delight in destroying you and in bringing ruin on you. You will be uprooted from the land that you are about to occupy.

This verse is clear and unambiguous, as it makes the most depressing statement in the whole book about Yahweh, who will **take delight** in punishing, destroying, wiping out his people.

Take delight means "is very happy to" or "his heart is glad."

Doing you good: or "making you prosper [or, be successful]."

Multiplying you: other ways to express this are "making you increase in number" (TEV) or "help your nation grow" (CEV).

Be plucked off the land: this is good, vivid language and should be retained unless it becomes ridiculous. TEV, NIV, and REB have "uprooted," and CEV has "pull you up by the roots."

The land which you are entering to take possession of it: repeating a statement often made (see 1.8).

28.64 RSV	TEV
And the LORD will scatter you among all peoples, from one end of the earth to the other; and there you shall serve other gods, of wood and stone, which neither you nor your fathers have known.	"The LORD will scatter you among all the nations, from one end of the earth to the other, and there you will serve gods made of wood and stone, gods that neither you nor your ancestors have ever worshiped before.

This verse predicts the same disasters and uses the same vocabulary as in verse 36.

Will scatter you may also be rendered as "will cause you to scatter," or even "will cause your enemies to take you away to every nation on earth."

All peoples, from one end of the earth to the other: the exaggerated language should not be softened in translation.

Gods, of wood and stone: see the comment at 4.28.

477

Which neither you nor your fathers have known: this may also be expressed as "neither you nor your ancestors have ever worshiped before" (TEV).

28.65   RSV   TEV

| **And among these nations you shall find no ease, and there shall be no rest for the sole of your foot; but the LORD will give you there a trembling heart, and failing eyes, and a languishing soul;** | **You will find no peace anywhere, no place to call your own; the LORD will overwhelm you with anxiety, hopelessness, and despair.** |

No ease: that is, no peace or security, no safety (see 3.20; 12.9).

No rest for the sole of your foot: no permanent residence, no place to call their own.

A trembling heart: fear or anxiety.

Failing eyes: this seems to mean blindness, which does not fit in with the other two expressions in this group; perhaps it means a loss of hope and cheerfulness (TEV has "hopelessness").

A languishing soul: despair, discouragement (see 6.9).

TEV offers a good model for all three expressions: "anxiety, hopelessness, and despair."

28.66   RSV   TEV

| **your life shall hang in doubt before you; night and day you shall be in dread, and have no assurance of your life.** | **Your life will always be in danger. Day and night you will be filled with terror, and you will live in constant fear of death.** |

Your life shall hang in doubt before you: the following statements clarify the meaning of this. Things will be so bad that there is no assurance of a return to normal conditions in the future. So TEV has "Your life will always be in danger"; or we may say "You will always be in danger of people killing you."

Night and day you shall be in dread: fear will be their constant companion. Other ways to express this are "All the time you will be terribly afraid," or ". . . your hearts [or, liver] will fall completely."

No assurance of your life: they will have absolute despair as they look to the future. This repeats the information in the first sentence. TEV omits the repetition, and some translators will find that model helpful.

28.67   RSV   TEV

| **In the morning you shall say, 'Would it were evening!' and at evening you** | **Your hearts will pound with fear at everything you see. Every morning** |

478

shall say, 'Would it were morning!' because of the dread which your heart shall fear, and the sights which your eyes shall see.

you will wish for evening; every evening you will wish for morning.

Would it were evening! . . . Would it were morning! Or "I wish it were day . . . I wish it were night" (CEV). See similar statements in Job 7.4.

The dread which your heart shall fear: they will be filled with fear, with no relief as they look to the future. The vivid language in TEV, "Your hearts will pound with fear," will be a good model for many translators.

The sights which your eyes shall see: all about them they will see the terrible conditions to which all the Israelites have been subjected.

Translators are urged to examine TEV as a possible model. CEV also has a good model:

- Every morning you will wake up to such terrible sights that you will say, "I wish it were night!" And at night you will be terrified and say, "I wish it were day!"

28.68 RSV	TEV
And the LORD will bring you back in ships to Egypt, a journey which I promised that you should never make again; and there you shall offer yourselves for sale to your enemies as male and female slaves, but no man will buy you."	The LORD will send you back to Egypt in ships, even though he*ᶻ* said that you would never have to go there again. There you will try to sell yourselves to your enemies as slaves, but no one will want to buy you."

ᶻ he; *or* I.

This verse speaks of the great reversal of fortune, when Yahweh will take his people back to Egypt as slaves.

Bring you back: "take you back" is better in English.

In ships to Egypt: a word that means "sailing ships" or "ships with sails" must be used. The phrase is strange, since people living in Canaan could travel to Egypt by land.

A journey which I promised that you should never make again: this promise is referred to also in 17.16, but the promise itself is not recorded. Here **I promised** refers to God, not to Moses; see TEV "he said" and "I said" in the footnote as an alternative rendering.

You shall offer yourselves for sale to your enemies as male and female slaves: this is the ultimate degradation. The Israelites will ask the Egyptians to buy them as slaves, but no one will want them.

4. Moses' third speech

(29.1–30.20)

4A. The agreement in Moab (29.1-29)

1 These are the words of the covenant which the LORD commanded Moses to make with the people of Israel in the land of Moab, besides the covenant which he had made with them at Horeb.

2 And Moses summoned all Israel and said to them: "You have seen all that the LORD did before your eyes in the land of Egypt, to Pharaoh and to all his servants and to all his land, 3 the great trials which your eyes saw, the signs, and those great wonders; 4 but to this day the LORD has not given you a mind to understand, or eyes to see, or ears to hear. 5 I have led you forty years in the wilderness; your clothes have not worn out upon you, and your sandals have not worn off your feet; 6 you have not eaten bread, and you have not drunk wine or strong drink; that you may know that I am the LORD your God. 7 And when you came to this place, Sihon the king of Heshbon and Og the king of Bashan came out against us to battle, but we defeated them; 8 we took their land, and gave it for an inheritance to the Reubenites, the Gadites, and the half-tribe of the Manassites. 9 Therefore be careful to do the words of this covenant, that you may prosper in all that you do.

10 "You stand this day all of you before the LORD your God; the heads of your tribes, your elders, and your officers, all the men of Israel, 11 your little ones, your wives, and the sojourner who is in your camp, both he who hews your wood and he who draws your water, 12 that you may enter into the sworn covenant of the LORD your God, which the LORD your God makes with you this day; 13 that he may establish you this day as his people, and that he may be your God, as he promised you, and as he swore to your fathers, to Abraham, to Isaac, and to Jacob. 14 Nor is it with you only

1 These are the terms of the covenant that the LORD commanded Moses to make with the people of Israel in the land of Moab; all this was in addition to the covenant which the LORD had made with them at Mount Sinai.

2 Moses called together all the people of Israel and said to them, "You saw for yourselves what the LORD did to the king of Egypt, to his officials, and to his entire country. 3 You saw the terrible plagues, the miracles, and the great wonders that the LORD performed. 4 But to this very day he has not let you understand what you have experienced. 5 For forty years the LORD led you through the desert, and your clothes and sandals never wore out. 6 You did not have bread to eat or wine or beer to drink, but the LORD provided for your needs in order to teach you that he is your God. 7 And when we came to this place, King Sihon of Heshbon and King Og of Bashan came out to fight against us. But we defeated them, 8 took their land, and divided it among the tribes of Reuben and Gad, and half the tribe of Manasseh. 9 Obey faithfully all the terms of this covenant, so that you will be successful in everything you do.

10 "Today you are standing in the presence of the LORD your God, all of you—your leaders and officials, your men, 11 women, and children, and the foreigners who live among you and cut wood and carry water for you. 12 You are here today to enter into this covenant that the LORD your God is making with you and to accept its obligations, 13 so that the LORD may now confirm you as his people and be your God, as he promised you and your ancestors, Abraham, Isaac, and Jacob. 14 You are not the only ones with whom the LORD is making this covenant with its obligations. 15 He is making it with all of us who stand here in his presence

that I make this sworn covenant, 15 but with him who is not here with us this day as well as with him who stands here with us this day before the LORD our God.

16 "You know how we dwelt in the land of Egypt, and how we came through the midst of the nations through which you passed; 17 and you have seen their detestable things, their idols of wood and stone, of silver and gold, which were among them. 18 Beware lest there be among you a man or woman or family or tribe, whose heart turns away this day from the LORD our God to go and serve the gods of those nations; lest there be among you a root bearing poisonous and bitter fruit, 19 one who, when he hears the words of this sworn covenant, blesses himself in his heart, saying, 'I shall be safe, though I walk in the stubbornness of my heart.' This would lead to the sweeping away of moist and dry alike. 20 The LORD would not pardon him, but rather the anger of the LORD and his jealousy would smoke against that man, and the curses written in this book would settle upon him, and the LORD would blot out his name from under heaven. 21 And the LORD would single him out from all the tribes of Israel for calamity, in accordance with all the curses of the covenant written in this book of the law. 22 And the generation to come, your children who rise up after you, and the foreigner who comes from a far land, would say, when they see the afflictions of that land and the sicknesses with which the LORD has made it sick—23 the whole land brimstone and salt, and a burntout waste, unsown, and growing nothing, where no grass can sprout, an overthrow like that of Sodom and Gomorrah, Admah and Zeboiim, which the LORD overthrew in his anger and wrath—24 yea, all the nations would say, 'Why has the LORD done thus to this land? What means the heat of this great anger?' 25 Then men would say, 'It is because they forsook the covenant of the LORD, the God of their fathers, which he made with them when he brought them out of the land of Egypt, 26 and went and served other gods and worshiped them, gods whom they had not known and whom he had not allotted to them; 27 therefore the anger of the LORD was kindled against this land, bringing upon it all the curses written in this book; 28 and the LORD uprooted them from their land in anger and fury and great wrath, and cast them into another land, as at this day.'

29 "The secret things belong to the LORD our God; but the things that are revealed belong to us and to our children for ever, that we may do all the words of this law.

today and also with our descendants who are not yet born.

16 "You remember what life was like in Egypt and what it was like to travel through the territory of other nations. 17 You saw their disgusting idols made of wood, stone, silver, and gold. 18 Make sure that no man, woman, family, or tribe standing here today turns from the LORD our God to worship the gods of other nations. This would be like a root that grows to be a bitter and poisonous plant. 19 Make sure that there is no one here today who hears these solemn demands and yet convinces himself that all will be well with him, even if he stubbornly goes his own way. That would destroy all of you, good and evil alike. 20 The LORD will not forgive such a man. Instead, the LORD's burning anger will flame up against him, and all the disasters written in this book will fall on him until the LORD has destroyed him completely. 21 The LORD will make an example of him before all the tribes of Israel and will bring disaster on him in accordance with all the curses listed in the covenant that is written in this book of the LORD's teachings.

22 "In future generations your descendants and foreigners from distant lands will see the disasters and sufferings that the LORD has brought on your land. 23 The fields will be a barren waste, covered with sulfur and salt; nothing will be planted, and not even weeds will grow there. Your land will be like the cities of Sodom and Gomorrah, of Admah and Zeboiim, which the LORD destroyed when he was furiously angry. 24 Then the whole world will ask, 'Why did the LORD do this to their land? What was the reason for his fierce anger?' 25 And the answer will be, 'It is because the LORD's people broke the covenant they had made with him, the God of their ancestors, when he brought them out of Egypt. 26 They served other gods that they had never worshiped before, gods that the LORD had forbidden them to worship. 27 And so the LORD became angry with his people and brought on their land all the disasters written in this book. 28 The LORD became furiously angry, and in his great anger he uprooted them from their land and threw them into a foreign land, and there they are today.'

29 "There are some things that the LORD our God has kept secret; but he has revealed his Law, and we and our descendants are to obey it forever.

In his third speech (chapters 29–30) Moses calls the people together and briefly recounts their departure from Egypt, their forty-year trek through the wilderness, and their arrival in the plains of Moab, where they are now. As they prepare to enter Canaan, Moses calls on them to accept the new covenant that God is making with them, and warns them of the terrible consequences if they disobey God's laws. He gives them a choice between life and death, and urges them, "Choose life!"

This Handbook will follow TEV in considering chapter 29 as one section.

Section heading: translators should have a major heading, "Moses' third speech," which may also be expressed as "Moses talks to the Israelites again." There should also be a subheading for 29.1-29, "The agreement in Moab," "The Lord's Covenant with Israel in the Land of Moab" (TEV), or "The Agreement in Moab" (CEV); NRSV is similar, "The Covenant Enacted in Moab," while NIV has "Renewal of the Covenant." For translators who prefer to use a complete sentence, something like the following may be appropriate: "The LORD makes another covenant [or agreement] with the people of Israel in the Land of Moab."

29.1 RSV	TEV
[28.69]	
ʸThese are the words of the covenant which the LORD commanded Moses to make with the people of Israel in the land of Moab, besides the covenant which he had made with them at Horeb.	These are the terms of the covenant that the LORD commanded Moses to make with the people of Israel in the land of Moab; all this was in addition to the covenant which the LORD had made with them at Mount Sinai.

ʸ Ch 28.69 in Heb

In the Hebrew text this is verse 69 of chapter 28; consequently RSV and TEV have 29 verses in chapter 29, whereas the Hebrew text has 28 verses; some modern translations, such as FRCL, NJB, NJPSV, and TOB, follow the Hebrew text (see the same thing at 12.32 and 22.30). A translator must weigh various options before deciding whether to follow the verse numbering of the Hebrew text or the numbering of RSV and TEV.

The most important factor will be whether there is already a tradition with which the readers are familiar, or which is commonly followed in the region where the translation is to be used. If the translation is the first one in that region or in that language, it seems better to follow the verse numbering of RSV. This Handbook will follow the RSV and TEV numbering. Whatever is done about the numbering, this verse begins a new section of the book.

These are the words of the covenant: **words** is not simply the text (whether oral or written) of the covenant, but "the terms" (TEV, NIV, REB, NJPSV), "the conditions" (BRCL), or "the things they had to do in order to keep the covenant [or, agreement]." FRCL has "This is how Moses drew up a covenant with the Israelites"; or we may say "The following are the things that the Israelites had to do in order to keep the agreement that Yahweh was making with them." For **covenant** see 4.13.

The land of Moab: see 1.5.

Besides the covenant which he had made with them at Horeb: the subject **he** is not Moses but Yahweh. **Besides the covenant** means "This was in addition to the covenant" (TEV). FRCL puts this whole comment within parentheses: "(This covenant is different from the one that was drawn up at Mount Horeb.)" Other possible models are "This agreement is distinct from [or, in addition to] the one that Yahweh made with them at Mount Sinai," or even "These terms [or, conditions] were added to those that were in the agreement that Yahweh made . . . ." For **Horeb** see 1.6. The translator should be careful not to say "This agreement *replaces* the one . . . ."

29.2 RSV	TEV
[29.1]	
ᶻAnd Moses summoned all Israel and said to them: "You have seen all that the LORD did before your eyes in the land of Egypt, to Pharaoh and to all his servants and to all his land,	Moses called together all the people of Israel and said to them, "You saw for yourselves what the LORD did to the king of Egypt, to his officials, and to his entire country.

ᶻ Ch 29.1 in Heb

Moses summoned all Israel: Moses called all the people to gather to listen to him. In Deuteronomy statements like this typically indicate the opening of a new discourse or speech.

And said: at this point Moses is clearly identified as the speaker. But whether Yahweh or Moses is speaking needs to be kept quite clear as the chapter progresses.

You have seen all that the LORD did before your eyes: this means "You saw all the things that Yahweh did in your presence" or ". . . as you were watching." In some languages this will be rendered as "You saw with your own eyes all the things that the LORD did . . . ," while in other languages we may simply say "You saw the LORD perform all . . . ," as the phrase **before your eyes** repeats the information already given in the clause **you have seen**. As a matter of fact, most of the Israelites standing in front of Moses hadn't really seen all these things, but Moses is including them with their parents (see also 4.34, where Moses uses the inclusive pronoun "we").

Pharaoh: this is a title, not a name; however, in 7.8 and 11.3 it appears as a proper name (so TEV and CEV there).

His servants: this means his officials, especially the court officers.

All his land: not simply the country as such, but all the people of Egypt. So CEV has "everyone else in the country."

29.3   RSV   TEV
[29.2]

the great trials which your eyes saw,   **You saw the terrible plagues, the**
the signs, and those great wonders;   **miracles, and the great wonders that**
                                             the LORD performed.

Great trials . . . signs . . . great wonders: see 4.34; 7.19. These three similar
terms are used together for emphasis. They refer primarily to the ten plagues
that Yahweh sent on Egypt.
   The information in this verse refers back to the clause "all that the LORD did"
in the previous verse. So it is possible to combine verses 2 and 3 as follows:

•   2-3 Moses called together the people of Israel and said to them:
           "You saw with your own eyes the terrible plagues, the miracles,
           and the great wonders that Yahweh did to punish the king of
           Egypt, his officers, and everyone else in the land."

29.4   RSV   TEV
[29.3]

but to this day the LORD has not   **But to this very day he has not let**
given you a mind to understand, or   **you understand what you have ex-**
eyes to see, or ears to hear.   **perienced.**

   Yahweh has kept hidden the meaning of all those miracles, primarily their
basic significance, which was that they were the means whereby Yahweh was
making the Israelites his own people. This is a theme found elsewhere in the
Old Testament, most notably in Isa 6.9-10 (and see its use in Matt 13.14-15;
Mark 4.12; Luke 8.10; John 12.40; Acts 28.26-27).
   The LORD has not given you: the translation should not make it appear that
the Israelites did not have minds, or eyes, or ears. The meaning is that God had
not allowed them to understand fully the significance of those events. In some
languages translators will be able to retain language similar to the Hebrew; for
example, "The LORD didn't let your hearts [or, minds] understand what your
eyes saw and your ears heard." In other languages the TEV rendering, "he has
not let you understand what you have experienced," expresses the meaning
quite clearly, if not with so much emphasis as the Hebrew text has.
   To this day: this means "until today" (NJB). There is no clear hint that things
will change and the people will finally understand the meaning of those events.

29.5   RSV   TEV
[29.4]

I have led you forty years in the   **For forty years the LORD led you**
wilderness; your clothes have not   **through the desert, and your clothes**
worn out upon you, and your san-   **and sandals never wore out.**
dals have not worn off your feet;

I have led you: this could be Moses speaking, but this is unlikely when we consider the clause "that I am the LORD your God" at the end of the following verse. CEV solves this problem by saying "He has even told you, 'For forty years, I, the LORD led you through the desert.' "

For **wilderness** see 1.1.

Clothes have not worn out upon you: this means that, after the forty years that had elapsed since leaving Egypt, they were still wearing the same clothes. The same applies to their sandals, which **have not worn off your feet**. In Hebrew the same verb "grow old" or "wear out" is used both for the clothes and the sandals; the Septuagint uses two different verbs, and in some languages two verbs will be necessary. However, in many modern translations we find only one verb; for example, " your clothes and sandals never wore out" (TEV, similarly CEV).

29.6	RSV	TEV
[29.5]		
	you have not eaten bread, and you have not drunk wine or strong drink; that you may know that I am the LORD your God.	You did not have bread to eat or wine or beer to drink, but the LORD provided for your needs in order to teach you that he is your God.

You have not eaten bread: that is, during the forty years the Israelites had not eaten bread but only the manna that God sent them every day (see 8.2-5). It may be necessary to make this clear, either in the text, for example, "I gave you special food instead of bread, wine, or beer," or by means of an explanatory footnote.

Wine or strong drink: this **strong drink** is not distilled liquor, but something more like "beer" (TEV, FRCL, POCL, BRCL). NJPSV has "or other intoxicant," NIV "other fermented drink," NJB "fermented liquor."

That you may know that I am the LORD your God: that is, all the trials and difficulties they had experienced throughout the forty years were intended to teach them to acknowledge Yahweh as their God, to confess that he is their God. FRCL has "The LORD took care of you so that you might understand that he is your God." In translation it should be made clear that the speaker here is Yahweh, not Moses (see the note in the previous verse).

A possible alternative translation model combining verses 5 and 6 is the following:

- 5-6 The LORD has told you, "For forty years, I, the LORD, led you through the wilderness, but your clothes and sandals didn't wear out, and I gave you special food instead of bread, wine, and beer. I did these things so that you would know that I am the God you serve."

29.7   RSV   TEV
[29.6]

And when you came to this place, Sihon the king of Heshbon and Og the king of Bashan came out against us to battle, but we defeated them;	And when we came to this place, King Sihon of Heshbon and King Og of Bashan came out to fight against us. But we defeated them,

Notice the change from **you came** to **against us** and **we defeated them**. In most languages the translation will be less confusing to the reader if the first person (inclusive plural) pronoun is used throughout the verse (see TEV and CEV). There is a change in speaker here from Yahweh to Moses.

This place: Moab in particular and the whole Transjordan region in general. "Here" (CEV) is a more neutral word.

For the battles against **Sihon** and **Og**, see 2.26–3.11; Num 21.21-35.

29.8   RSV   TEV
[29.7]

we took their land, and gave it for an inheritance to the Reubenites, the Gadites, and the half-tribe of the Manassites.	took their land, and divided it among the tribes of Reuben and Gad, and half the tribe of Manasseh.

Gave it for an inheritance: that is, "gave it to them to possess" (see 4.21).

The Reubenites, the Gadites, and the half-tribe of the Manassites: see 3.12-17. It is better to have "the people of the tribes of Reuben, of Gad, and half the tribe of Manasseh."

29.9   RSV   TEV
[29.8]

Therefore be careful to do the words of this covenant, that you may prosper[a] in all that you do.	Obey faithfully all the terms of this covenant, so that you will be successful in everything you do.

[a] Or *deal wisely*

For **be careful to do** see 28.1, 56; for **the words of this covenant**, see 29.1.

You may prosper: nearly all modern translations understand the Hebrew verb to mean **prosper**, or "be successful"; see NRSV "succeed in everything that you do." There is no need to provide an alternative translation, as RSV does.

29.10   RSV   TEV
[29.9]

"You stand this day all of you before the LORD your God; the heads of	"Today you are standing in the presence of the LORD your God, all of

your tribes,^b your elders, and your officers, all the men of Israel,	you—your leaders and officials, your men,

^b Gk Syr: Heb *your heads, your tribes*

In RSV verses 10-13 are one long sentence. As elsewhere, in many languages the text should be broken up into several sentences.

This day means "Today," as often in the book.

You stand . . . all of you before the LORD your God: the sense is as in TEV, "you are standing in the presence of the LORD your God." This is the general statement; then, for emphasis, the various groups of people are named. **Before the LORD your God** means "in this place where Yahweh is present," or "in the LORD's presence" (CEV).

The heads of your tribes: the leaders of the twelve tribes. RSV's textual footnote is unnecessary. The Hebrew "your heads your tribes" means simply "your tribal leaders," as NJPSV translates it.

For **elders** see 5.23; for **officers** see 1.15.

All the men of Israel: they are mentioned first, and the women and children are listed in the next verse as belonging to them or being related to them. A possible alternative model for this verse for this verse may be:

- Today all of you are standing here in the LORD's presence, including your leaders and officials . . . .

29.11	RSV	TEV
[29.10]		
your little ones, your wives, and the sojourner who is in your camp, both he who hews your wood and he who draws your water,		women, and children, and the foreigners who live among you and cut wood and carry water for you.

Your little ones: a term should be used that indicates children still living with their parents; the Hebrew does not mean just babies or toddlers.

For **sojourner** see 1.16. The people who performed the menial tasks were often foreigners; see especially the story about the Gibeonites in Joshua 9.

Hews your wood: TEV has the more common English, "cut wood"; this was primarily to use as firewood. **Draws your water** (TEV "carry water for you") refers primarily to water to be drunk.

29.12	RSV	TEV
[29.11]		
that you may enter into the sworn covenant of the LORD your God, which the LORD your God makes with you this day;		You are here today to enter into this covenant that the LORD your God is making with you and to accept its obligations,

That you may enter: the purpose, as stated, connects with the beginning of verse 10, "You stand this day all . . . ."

Enter into the sworn covenant: to "enter" a covenant means to become party to it, to agree to abide by its terms and conditions. The Hebrew expression translated **sworn covenant** is expressed in various ways. For example: NJPSV "with its sanctions"; TEV "and accept its obligations"; REB "accept the oath and enter the covenant"; NIV "a covenant the LORD is making with you this day and sealing with an oath"; FRCL "and invites you to seal it with a solemn vow"; NRSV "the covenant of the LORD your God, sworn by an oath."

There are two things to consider in interpreting **sworn covenant**:

(1) the nature of the additional Hebrew word *'alah*, whether it refers to an oath, a curse, a stipulation, or a sanction; and

(2) whether this proceeds from Yahweh or from the Israelites.

As the various translations demonstrate, there is no agreement on these two matters. In the context, with the various blessings and curses playing such a prominent role, it seems that (1) these are conditions, or stipulations, or penalties, or sanctions; and (2) they are imposed by Yahweh; the very wording **the sworn covenant of the LORD your God** affirms this.

The translations of TEV, CEV, and NJPSV most closely follow this interpretation, and translators are advised to take TEV as a model. TEV has "You are here today to enter into this covenant that the LORD your God is making with you, and to accept its obligations"; or we may say ". . . to promise that you will keep your part of the agreement with the LORD our God."

This day means "today."

29.13	RSV	TEV
[29.12]	that he may establish you this day as his people, and that he may be your God, as he promised you, and as he swore to your fathers, to Abraham, to Isaac, and to Jacob.	so that the LORD may now confirm you as his people and be your God, as he promised you and your ancestors, Abraham, Isaac, and Jacob.

Establish you this day as his people: this is the main purpose, which is dependent upon the first, "that you may enter" at the beginning of verse 12. Through the covenant Yahweh confirms, acknowledges, and confesses that they are, in theory and in fact, a people who belong to him, and they will be seen as such by others.

That he may be your God: the covenant affects the status both of Yahweh and of the people of Israel. **Your God** means "the God you [will] serve."

As he swore to your fathers, to Abraham, to Isaac, and to Jacob: see 1.8.

29.14-15	RSV	TEV
[29.13-14]	14 Nor is it with you only that I make this sworn covenant, 15 but with him	14 You are not the only ones with whom the LORD is making this cove-

who is not here with us this day as well as with him who stands here with us this day before the LORD our God.

nant with its obligations. 15 He is making it with all of us who stand here in his presence today and also with our descendants who are not yet born.

Nor is it with you only: this covenant affects others besides those present that day in the plains of Moab.

The pronoun **I** refers to Yahweh, not Moses. In this verse Yahweh replaces Moses as the speaker. Another way to render the first sentence is "You are not the only ones I am making this agreement with." Or it may be better to use the third person reference to God, as TEV does, with Moses as speaker.

With him who is not here: this does not mean those Israelites who happened to be away from camp that day, but the people yet to be born, the children and descendants of those present.

Stands here with us . . . before the LORD our God: this **with us** seems to mean Moses and the leaders (verse 10). The phrase **the LORD our God** is most unusual and should be faithfully translated. **Our** is inclusive, that is, it includes the hearers as well as the speaker.

Notice that **this day** appears twice in verse 15. A possible alternative translation model eliminating this and other repetitions in the Hebrew is the following (Yahweh speaking):

- ¹⁴⁻¹⁵ You who are standing here in my presence today are not the only ones with whom I am making this agreement with all its conditions. I, the LORD your God, am also making it with your descendants.

29.16 RSV TEV
[29.15]

"You know how we dwelt in the land of Egypt, and how we came through the midst of the nations through which you passed;

"You remember what life was like in Egypt and what it was like to travel through the territory of other nations.

In verses 16-17 Moses is the speaker again, and he gives a brief review of the situation of the Israelites as slaves in Egypt. This serves as an introduction to the long warning that follows (verses 18-28).

The translator will notice the switch from the first person plural **we dwelt** and **we came** to the second person plural **you passed** (verse 16) and **you have seen** (verse 17). Translators should study the TEV to see one way to handle this problem. NIV and others are also able to eliminate such inconsistencies.

We dwelt in the land of Egypt: according to the historical account in Deuteronomy, the adult generation that left Egypt had already died (see 2.14-15; 5.3), and it is the succeeding generation that is ready to enter the Promised Land. The verb translated **dwelt** is itself neutral, indicating neither prosperity nor hardship; but the modifying **how** was understood by the original readers of this account to indicate the condition of the Hebrews as slaves, in the latter part of their stay in Egypt; TEV refers indirectly to this with "what life was like in Egypt."

We came through the midst of the nations: as reported in chapters 1–3.

Through which you passed: this is as repetitive and illogical in Hebrew as it is in English. An alternative translation is "and [you know] what it was like to travel through the lands of other nations."

29.17   RSV   TEV
[29.16]

and you have seen their detestable   You saw their disgusting idols made
things, their idols of wood and stone,   of wood, stone, silver, and gold.
of silver and gold, which were
among them.

Their detestable things: that is, **their idols**. The pronoun **their** very likely refers back to both **Egypt** and **the nations** in verse 16, so it is possible to combine the two verses as CEV does (and see also the alternative model below). The Hebrew word translated **detestable** carries a sense of thoroughly disgusting, completely revolting. NRSV has "their . . . detestable things, the filthy idols," somewhat like TEV "their disgusting idols."

Idols of wood and stone, of silver and gold: see a similar statement in 4.28. For a comment on **idols** see 4.16.

Which were among them: this will be repetitive in many languages and may be deleted, as TEV and CEV have done.

An alternative translation model combining verses 16 and 17 is the following:

- 16-17 You know that when we lived in Egypt, you saw the Egyptians worship disgusting idols made of wood, stone, silver and gold. Then as you traveled through the lands of other nations, you saw those people worship other disgusting idols.

29.18   RSV   TEV
[29.17]

Beware lest there be among you a   Make sure that no man, woman,
man or woman or family or tribe,   family, or tribe standing here today
whose heart turns away this day   turns from the LORD our God to wor-
from the LORD our God to go and   ship the gods of other nations. This
serve the gods of those nations; lest   would be like a root that grows to be
there be among you a root bearing   a bitter and poisonous plant.
poisonous and bitter fruit,

In RSV verses 18-19 are a very long and complex sentence, which must be broken down into smaller units that will be easier to understand.

Beware lest there be among you: this is fairly unnatural English. Something like "Make sure that none of you" is better.

490

Man . . . woman . . . family . . . tribe: the various units of the nation. For **tribes** see 1.13.

Whose heart turns away . . . to go and serve the gods of those nations: this indicates a loss of loyalty and love, a betrayal or defection. See similar passages in 11.28; 13.6-7; 27.15. For **gods** see 4.28.

It is possible to state the first part of this verse positively as follows (Moses speaking):

- Make sure that every man, woman, family, and tribe here today remains faithful to Yahweh and never starts worshiping the gods of other nations.

The LORD our God: once more the first person plural; again the Septuagint has the second person plural.

Lest there be a root bearing poisonous and bitter fruit: this metaphor is fairly clear in meaning; TEV has changed it to the simile "This would be like a root." This refers to concealed betrayal, secret apostasy, whose results will become highly visible. Heb 12.15 makes reference to this passage. In some languages it will be helpful to begin the sentence with "If you do this you will be like . . . ." CEV translates "If even one of you worships idols, you will be like . . . ."

29.19 RSV	TEV
[29.18]	
one who, when he hears the words of this sworn covenant, blesses himself in his heart, saying, 'I shall be safe, though I walk in the stubbornness of my heart.' This would lead to the sweeping away of moist and dry alike.	Make sure that there is no one here today who hears these solemn demands and yet convinces himself that all will be well with him, even if he stubbornly goes his own way. That would destroy all of you, good and evil alike.

One who, when he hears the words of this sworn covenant: that is, someone who hears the terms and conditions of the covenant—especially the curses (28.15-68). Another way to express this clause is "You may be a person who hears the solemn conditions of the LORD's covenant [or, agreement] with you . . . ."

One who . . . blesses himself in his heart, saying: that is, he reassures himself or comforts himself. Other renderings are TEV "convinces himself," REB "flatters himself," SPCL "believes himself to be too good," TOB "believes himself blessed," BRCL "tells himself that all will be well." All of these are good.

Sworn covenant: as in verse 12.

I shall be safe: this translates the Hebrew "I will have peace [or, safety]" (*shalom*). In some languages direct speech (see RSV) will be natural style, whereas translators in other languages will prefer to follow TEV and CEV and use indirect speech.

Though I walk in the stubbornness of my heart: he recognizes that he is stubbornly following his own desires and not the terms of the covenant. TEV has "even if he stubbornly goes his own way." However, if a translator uses direct speech, the following is a possible alternative: "even if I am stubborn and go my own way."

This would lead to the sweeping away of moist and dry alike: this is not something the person speaking says, but is a comment by Moses or by the writer of the account. The meaning of the saying seems clear enough, though its origin is unknown. It means that all will be swept away, that is, punished or destroyed. The word **would** in this construction in English indicates that what the sentence refers to has not actually happened (and it may not happen); it will only apply if some person does what the first part of the verse warns against. NJPSV translates this sentence literally and has a footnote explaining the figure: "[that is] everything." The Septuagint translates "the sinner will be destroyed together with the sinless," and TEV has "That would destroy all of you, good and evil alike." The CEV translation is more general, with "cause the rest of Israel to be punished along with you." In languages that do not use the passive, we may say "that will cause them [unknown people] to destroy all of you, good and evil people alike."

29.20   RSV   TEV
[29.19]

The LORD would not pardon him, but rather the anger of the LORD and his jealousy would smoke against that man, and the curses written in this book would settle upon him, and the LORD would blot out his name from under heaven.

The LORD will not forgive such a man. Instead, the LORD's burning anger will flame up against him, and all the disasters written in this book will fall on him until the LORD has destroyed him completely.

Verses 20-21 state the punishment that Yahweh will send on such a person. It is described in vivid and repetitious detail. Moses is still the speaker.

The LORD would not pardon him: as long as he continues in his stubborn ways, he cannot be forgiven. **Him** refers to anyone who acts like this. So we may say "Yahweh will not pardon that person." For a comment on **pardon** or "forgive," see 21.8.

The anger of the LORD and his jealousy: for **jealousy** see 4.24; 6.15. Here, as often, the two nouns **anger** and **jealousy** can be translated as one phrase, a noun modified by an adjective: "the intense [or, furious] anger" (see in 1.27, where there are more than two terms).

Would smoke against that man: God's anger is compared to a fire that flames out and burns and destroys. NJPSV translates "[the LORD's] anger and passion [will] rage against that man." TEV has "will flame up against." It is also possible to use a simile; for example, "The LORD will become furiously angry with that person, just like a flame that leaps up and burns him."

492

The curses written in this book: see 28.58. The Septuagint expands considerably: "all the curses of this covenant written in this book of the law." CEV is similar, with "all the curses in *The Book of God's Law*."

Would settle upon him: that is, they would be applied to him, be laid upon him, or "fall upon him" (TEV); or we may say "piling on him all the curses in . . . ."

The LORD would blot out his name from under heaven: God will destroy the man and his family, so that there are no descendants left to carry on the family name (see 9.14; 25.19).

29.21   RSV   TEV
[29.20]

And the LORD would single him out   The LORD will make an example of
from all the tribes of Israel for ca-   him before all the tribes of Israel and
lamity, in accordance with all the   will bring disaster on him in accor-
curses of the covenant written in this   dance with all the curses listed in the
book of the law.   covenant that is written in this book
          of the LORD's teachings.

Single him out from all the tribes of Israel: the LORD will concentrate all his punishments on that one person. TEV has "The LORD will make an example of him before all . . . ."

Calamity: from what follows, this is total and irreversible destruction. So we may say "and will destroy him [or, that person] completely."

In accordance with all the curses of the covenant written in this book of the law: in Hebrew the passive participle **written** modifies **the covenant**; the Septuagint has "all the curses of the covenant that are written . . . ." See a similar expression in verse 20. For **law** see 1.5.

29.22   RSV   TEV
[29.21]

And the generation to come, your   "In future generations your de-
children who rise up after you, and   scendants and foreigners from dis-
the foreigner who comes from a far   tant lands will see the disasters and
land, would say, when they see the   sufferings that the LORD has brought
afflictions of that land and the sick-   on your land.
nesses with which the LORD has
made it sick—

A sentence begins here that ends at verse 24, with verse 23 inserted as a vivid description of the ravaged land. The structure of RSV should not be imitated here; see TEV for a good model.

The generation to come, your children who rise up after you: this is repetitious, the two phrases saying the same thing, that is, "your descendants." For a comment on **descendants** see 1.8.

The foreigner who comes from a far land: as in other similar instances, the plural should be used, "the foreigners who come . . . ." It is also possible to render this as "people from all lands [or, countries]." Care should be taken not to give the impression that "your descendants" (TEV) are also from "distant lands," as TEV seems to suggest (so also CEV).

Would say: this is picked up at the beginning of verse 24, where their statement appears. In Hebrew **say** here in verse 22 is third person singular, agreeing with the singular **generation**; in verse 24 it is plural, agreeing with "all the nations."

When they see the afflictions of that land: beginning here and extending to the end of verse 23, there is the description of the ravages inflicted on the land of Israel. The Hebrew noun translated **afflictions** is the same one that in 25.3 is used of the blows of a whip; see also 28.61. NRSV translates "the devastation of that land."

The sicknesses with which the LORD has made it sick: this clause is parallel to the previous expression and has the same meaning. TEV has "the disasters and sufferings"; CEV has "diseases and disasters"; NJPSV translates "the plagues and diseases," NIV "calamities and diseases."

Translators should be careful that **that land** is understood by the reader to mean the land of Canaan ("your land" TEV, CEV), which at the time of these terrible events had been the land of Israel for many years.

It is possible to reorder the clauses of this verse, putting the final sentence at the beginning as a preface to verses 22-24 as follows (Moses speaking):

- 22 The LORD will cause your land to have all sorts of diseases and calamities. Your descendants and the foreigners who will later come from faraway countries will see that your land 23 has become . . . .

29.23
[29.22]

RSV	TEV
the whole land brimstone and salt, and a burnt-out waste, unsown, and growing nothing, where no grass can sprout, an overthrow like that of Sodom and Gomorrah, Admah and Zeboiim, which the LORD overthrew in his anger and wrath—	The fields will be a barren waste, covered with sulfur and salt; nothing will be planted, and not even weeds will grow there. Your land will be like the cities of Sodom and Gomorrah, of Admah and Zeboiim, which the LORD destroyed when he was furiously angry.

The description is detailed and vivid. For the devastation that befell Sodom and Gomorrah, Admah and Zeboiim, see Gen 19.24-25.

The whole land brimstone and salt, and a burnt-out waste: **brimstone** is an obsolete term; the proper word in modern English is "sulfur." Sulfur is a yellow substance that burns with great heat. It was sometimes sprinkled on fields along with salt to make them infertile and thus unable to produce crops. Sulfur was often thought of as accompanied by fire when biblical writers described God's punishment. In cultures where sulfur is unknown, a translator may say, for example, "yellow rocks called sulfur," or "yellow rocks that burn hot called sulfur." As a translation NRSV is more natural English: "all its soil burned out by sulfur and salt." NIV has "a burning waste of sulfur and salt," NJPSV "all its soil devastated by sulfur and salt." The idea of **burnt-out [waste]** is that the soil has been completely denuded of all vegetation, and nothing will ever grow there again (**unsown, and growing nothing**). NRSV is good: "nothing planted, nothing sprouting."

If translators follow the model in verse 22, reordering the clauses, they may begin this verse as follows: "²² . . . that your land ²³ has become a scorching desert, covered by sulfur and salt" (CEV).

No grass can sprout: no plants can grow there. NRSV has "unable to support any vegetation." TEV has "nothing will be planted, and not even weeds will grow there"; CEV translates "nothing is planted, nothing sprouts, and nothing grows."

An overthrow: the object of **overthrow** is **that land** (verse 22), **the whole land** (verse 23). The verb that is chosen must match the object; to "overthrow" a land or country is not a natural way to speak in English; something like "devastate" or "destroy" is better. In the case of the four cities, however, **overthrow** is alright. NIV has handled this well: "It will be like the destruction of Sodom and Gomorrah, of Admah and Zeboiim, which the LORD overthrew . . . ." CEV is even better, with "It will be as lifeless as the land around the cities of . . . ." This catches the idea of land made "lifeless" by sulfur and salt.

His anger and wrath: two similar terms again, which may be rendered "his furious anger."

29.24   RSV   TEV
[29.23]
yea, all the nations would say, 'Why   Then the whole world will ask, 'Why
has the LORD done thus to this land?   did the LORD do this to their land?
What means the heat of this great   What was the reason for his fierce
anger?'   anger?'

Yea, all the nations would say: this picks up from verse 22.

Why has the LORD done thus to this land? This presents a picture of **all the nations**, that is, people everywhere in the world, hearing about the total destruction of the land of Israel.

What means the heat of this great anger? This may be expressed as in BRCL, "Why did he get so angry and furious?" or simply "Why was he so furious?" Translators need to find a term that describes extreme or fierce anger. Some languages will have figurative expressions like the Hebrew, and talk about God's heart being hot with anger, or his nostrils flaring with anger.

29.25   RSV   TEV
[29.24]
Then men would say, 'It is because   And the answer will be, 'It is because
they forsook the covenant of the   the LORD's people broke the cove-
LORD, the God of their fathers, which   nant they had made with him, the

| he made with them when he brought them out of the land of Egypt, | God of their ancestors, when he brought them out of Egypt. |

Then men would say: the conditional **would** construction continues, because of its use at the beginning, from verse 19 on. For **men** say "people," or else say "And the answer will be" (as in TEV, NIV, and REB); or we may say "Then people will answer like this." Or in some languages a translator may use the passive, "And they will be told" (NJPSV), or "They will be given the answer" (CEV).

They forsook the covenant: some suggest that here **covenant** refers to the Ten Commandments (see 4.13); but such a limitation of the word should not appear in the text itself. It is better to have a general statement such as "broke the covenant that he had made with them" or "they rejected the agreement Yahweh had made with them." TEV "the covenant they had made with him" is wrong; it was Yahweh who made the covenant.

The LORD, the God of their fathers: as always, **fathers** means ancestors.

Which he made with them: that is, "with the Israelites."

29.26 RSV	TEV
[29.25]	
and went and served other gods and worshiped them, gods whom they had not known and whom he had not allotted to them;	They served other gods that they had never worshiped before, gods that the LORD had forbidden them to worship.

Went . . . served . . . worshiped: this does not mean that they went to another country in order to worship idols; **went** here serves simply as an auxiliary, introducing an action that follows. See a similar statement in 28.14. In some languages one expression will cover the idea of **served** and **worshiped** (see TEV). However, in other languages the sentence may be expressed by something like "they served other gods and bowed down before them."

Gods whom they had not known: see 11.28; 28.64. These were gods "that they had never worshiped before" (TEV).

Whom he had not allotted to them: the idea behind this is that Yahweh, the high God, had allotted each people their own god (see 4.19; 32.8-9). BRCL expresses the idea well: ". . . gods that God had not chosen to be worshiped by his people."

29.27 RSV	TEV
[29.26]	
therefore the anger of the LORD was kindled against this land, bringing upon it all the curses written in this book;	And so the LORD became angry with his people and brought on their land all the disasters written in this book.

The anger of the LORD was kindled: this is a common figure of speech; anger is spoken of as fire. In a number of languages it will be possible to use similar figurative expressions to describe God's anger becoming hot. An example is "Yahweh's heart [or, liver] became hot with anger, just like burning with fire."

Against this land: in RSV the foreigners who are saying all this are pictured as being on or near the devastated land of Israel. But the Hebrew does not necessarily mean that, and NRSV renders it "against that land," as does REB.

All the curses: in Hebrew this is the same noun used in 27.13; 28.15.

Written in this book: this is strange, because the foreigners are talking about **this book**, that is, Deuteronomy (see 28.58), which they could hardly be expected to know about. CEV attempts to deal with the difficulty by saying *"The Book of God's Law."*

29.28 RSV TEV
[29.27]

and the LORD uprooted them from their land in anger and fury and great wrath, and cast them into another land, as at this day.'	The LORD became furiously angry, and in his great anger he uprooted them from their land and threw them into a foreign land, and there they are today.'

The LORD uprooted them from their land . . . and cast them into another land: the verb translated "uproot" is not used elsewhere in Deuteronomy or the other "books of Moses" (Genesis, Exodus, Leviticus, Numbers). This is a vivid way of describing the people of Israel being taken as prisoners of war to a foreign country. The background of this was probably the period of the Babylonian captivity. The picture of **uprooted** may be also expressed as "pulled them up by the roots." However, if the figure sounds strange, a translator may say something like "then the LORD became furiously angry [or, his anger burned hotly], and he removed the Israelites from their land, just like someone pulls up a plant by its roots."

In anger and fury and great wrath: here three similar terms are used together for emphasis.

And cast them into another land: the picture is of someone pulling weeds out of the ground and tossing or throwing them aside.

As at this day: the day or time when those foreigners are talking about the terrible disasters that have fallen on the Israelites.

The speech of the foreigners, which began at verse 25, ends here.

29.29 RSV TEV
[29.28]

"The secret things belong to the LORD our God; but the things that are revealed belong to us and to our children for ever, that we may do all the words of this law.	"There are some things that the LORD our God has kept secret; but he has revealed his Law, and we and our descendants are to obey it forever.

This verse sounds like a proverbial saying that the writer did not intend to be part of what Moses said. But there is no way, other than placing it within parentheses, to indicate this. It is better to translate it as part of Moses' discourse. It combines with 30.11-14 as a frame for 30.1-10. It will be helpful to begin this verse with "Moses said" or "Then Moses continued to speak."

The secret things belong to the LORD our God: this pertains primarily to future events, but in a general way it states that there are matters that human beings cannot know; God alone knows. So TEV has "there are some things that the LORD our God has kept secret."

The things that are revealed: that is, God has made some things known, primarily, in this context, the covenant and its conditions. In many languages it will be helpful to make the subject or agent of the action clear; for example, "but he [God] has revealed his law to us and our descendants."

Belong to us and to our children for ever: here **us** are the people of Israel; **our children** are their descendants.

We may do all the words of this law: see 1.5; 4.2; 6.25.

A possible alternative translation model for this verse is:

- The LORD our [inclusive] God has not revealed certain things to us and our descendants; but he has revealed his law to us. We and our descendants must obey it forever.

4B. Israel will return to the LORD (30.1-10)

RSV

1 "And when all these things come upon you, the blessing and the curse, which I have set before you, and you call them to mind among all the nations where the LORD your God has driven you, 2 and return to the LORD your God, you and your children, and obey his voice in all that I command you this day, with all your heart and with all your soul; 3 then the LORD your God will restore your fortunes, and have compassion upon you, and he will gather you again from all the peoples where the LORD your God has scattered you. 4 If your outcasts are in the uttermost parts of heaven, from there the LORD your God will gather you, and from there he will fetch you; 5 and the LORD your God will bring you into the land which your fathers possessed, that you may possess it; and he will make you more prosperous and numerous than your fathers. 6 And the LORD your God will circumcise your heart and the heart of your offspring, so that you will love the LORD your God with all your heart and with all your soul, that you may live. 7 And the LORD your God will put all these curses upon your foes and enemies who perse-

TEV
Conditions for Restoration and Blessing

1 "I have now given you a choice between a blessing and a curse. When all these things have happened to you, and you are living among the nations where the LORD your God has scattered you, you will remember the choice I gave you. 2 If you and your descendants will turn back to the LORD and with all your heart obey his commands that I am giving you today, 3 then the LORD your God will have mercy on you. He will bring you back from the nations where he has scattered you, and he will make you prosperous again. 4 Even if you are scattered to the farthest corners of the earth, the LORD your God will gather you together and bring you back, 5 so that you may again take possession of the land where your ancestors once lived. And he will make you more prosperous and more numerous than your ancestors ever were. 6 The LORD your God will give you and your descendants obedient hearts, so that you will love him with all your heart, and you will continue to live in that land. 7 He will turn all these curses against your enemies, who hated you and oppressed you, 8 and you will again obey him

cuted you. 8 And you shall again obey the voice of the LORD, and keep all his commandments which I command you this day. 9 The LORD your God will make you abundantly prosperous in all the work of your hand, in the fruit of your body, and in the fruit of your cattle, and in the fruit of your ground; for the LORD will again take delight in prospering you, as he took delight in your fathers, 10 if you obey the voice of the LORD your God, to keep his commandments and his statutes which are written in this book of the law, if you turn to the LORD your God with all your heart and with all your soul.

and keep all his commands that I am giving you today. 9 The LORD will make you prosperous in all that you do; you will have many children and a lot of livestock, and your fields will produce abundant crops. He will be as glad to make you prosperous as he was to make your ancestors prosperous, 10 but you will have to obey him and keep all his laws that are written in this book of his teachings. You will have to turn to him with all your heart.

This chapter can be treated as one section, as it is in TEV ("Conditions for Restoration and Blessing") or NRSV ("Preparations for Renewal of Covenant"). Some, like BRCL, divide it into two sections. It seems better, however, to have three sections: verses 1-10; 11-14; 15-20. A number of translations do this, and the Handbook will also follow this approach.

Section heading: verses 1-10 may have the title "Israel will return to the LORD" (TOB, FRCL), or "The people of Israel repent and serve Yahweh again," or even "The LORD will Bring You Back" (CEV).

30.1	RSV	TEV

"And when all these things come upon you, the blessing and the curse, which I have set before you, and you call them to mind among all the nations where the LORD your God has driven you,

"I have now given you a choice between a blessing and a curse. When all these things have happened to you, and you are living among the nations where the LORD your God has scattered you, you will remember the choice I gave you.

With the beginning of a new section, Moses should be reintroduced as the speaker.

Verses 1-3 are one long sentence in RSV, which must be broken into smaller units. See TEV for a helpful model.

When all these things come upon you, the blessing and the curse: Moses looks to the future, when the people of Israel will have experienced all the blessings and curses promised in chapter 28. **The blessing** may be translated as "the good things he will do for you." **The curse** may be rendered as "how he will punish you if you reject him," or "the punishments he will bring upon you if . . . ." But see the comments on **curse** at 11.26.

Which I have set before you: throughout this chapter Moses is the speaker. Moses has listed the blessings and the curses, and the Israelites are to choose between them. It will be helpful in a number of languages to reorder the first part of the verse, as shown in the alternative translation model given at the end.

And you call them to mind: TEV has restructured the sentence for greater clarity, placing this clause at the end of the verse and rendering "you will remember the choice I gave you."

Among all the nations where the LORD your God has driven you: this is a reference to exile, here spoken of as exile in various foreign countries. The verb "drive" is used in this sense only here in Deuteronomy; it appears quite frequently in Jeremiah. It means "to scatter," as in "He will scatter you in faraway countries" (CEV). For "scattered" see 4.27.

An alternative translation model for this verse is:

- Moses said to the Israelites: "I am now letting you choose between two things: the good things that Yahweh will do for you or the punishments that he will bring upon you if you reject him. When all these things that I have told you about happen to you, and you are living in faraway countries where the LORD your God has scattered you, you will remember the choice I gave you.

30.2	RSV	TEV
	and return to the LORD your God, you and your children, and obey his voice in all that I command you this day, with all your heart and with all your soul;	If you and your descendants will turn back to the LORD and with all your heart obey his commands that I am giving you today,

Return to the LORD your God: see 4.30.

You and your children: not only the next generation but all succeeding generations; in other words "your descendants" (TEV).

Obey . . . with all your heart and with all your soul: see 4.29-30; 6.5.

Again **this day** ("today") is emphasized.

30.3	RSV	TEV
	then the LORD your God will restore your fortunes, and have compassion upon you, and he will gather you again from all the peoples where the LORD your God has scattered you.	then the LORD your God will have mercy on you. He will bring you back from the nations where he has scattered you, and he will make you prosperous again.

Restore your fortunes: this expression may be translated "bring you back from captivity" (NIV alternative rendering, in footnote). But the majority of translations give the sense it has in RSV, that is, deliver them from their misery and humiliation and make them a prosperous people again. In essence the two variant translations mean the same thing. CEV has "Then he will stop punishing you"; but another possible translation is "He will make you prosperous again" (TEV).

500

Have compassion: see 13.17.

Gather you again from all the peoples: this presupposes that the Israelites will be scattered among many nations.

Scattered: see 4.27.

30.4 RSV	TEV
If your outcasts are in the uttermost parts of heaven, from there the LORD your God will gather you, and from there he will fetch you;	Even if you are scattered to the farthest corners of the earth, the LORD your God will gather you together and bring you back,

Your outcasts: the Hebrew noun here is related to the verb "has driven" in verse 1. NRSV is much better here: "Even if you are exiled." TEV translates "Even if you are scattered." Another way to express this is "Even if you live in other countries."

In the uttermost parts of heaven: obviously this is "to the ends of the earth" as NRSV has it, or "the ends of the world" (NJPSV); see a similar phrase in 4.32. NIV has "the most distant lands under the heavens."

Will gather you . . . will fetch you: two very similar expressions, for emphasis.

30.5 RSV	TEV
and the LORD your God will bring you into the land which your fathers possessed, that you may possess it; and he will make you more prosperous and numerous than your fathers.	so that you may again take possession of the land where your ancestors once lived. And he will make you more prosperous and more numerous than your ancestors ever were.

This verse tells how the fortunes of the Israelites will be reversed.

Bring you into the land which your fathers possessed: **bring** is repetitive and redundant; TEV and CEV omit it. **You** here refers not to the people being addressed that day in Moab, but to their descendants in the distant future who will be taken into exile; and **your fathers** are the ancestors of those distant descendants, not the ancestors of the people listening to Moses. If readers of the translation are likely to understand that "you" and "your ancestors" mean the people present there that day and their own ancestors, some means must be found to eliminate this misunderstanding, either in the text or else by means of a footnote. See the alternative translation model at the end of the verse for a way to put this in the text.

Possess: see 1.8.

Make you more prosperous and numerous than your fathers: that is, the people who return from exile will become more prosperous and numerous than their ancestors who had lived in the land of Israel before the exile. Again **you** may be translated as "your descendants."

An alternative translation model for this verse is:

- . . . so that your descendants may again take possession of the land where their ancestors once lived. He will make your descendants more prosperous and numerous than their ancestors ever were.

30.6   RSV   TEV

And the LORD your God will circum-   The LORD your God will give you and
cise your heart and the heart of your   your descendants obedient hearts,
offspring, so that you will love the   so that you will love him with all your
LORD your God with all your heart   heart, and you will continue to live in
and with all your soul, that you may   that land.
live.

Here Moses is talking about the people present with him there in the plains of Moab.

Will circumcise your heart and the heart of your offspring: circumcision was the sign of belonging to the people of Yahweh, the people of the covenant; an uncircumcised man was, by definition, a Gentile, a pagan. In effect this clause means that God will make these stubborn and disobedient Israelites his obedient people once more (see 10.16; Jer 4.4). CEV begins the verse with the statement "You and your descendants are stubborn, but the LORD will make you willing to obey him." We may also say "but the LORD will make your hearts and the hearts of your descendants obedient to him."

Love the LORD your God with all your heart and with all your soul: see 6.5.

That you may live: this might be quite literally true; but primarily it means to have a long and prosperous existence as a nation in the land of Canaan. So TEV has "and you will continue to live in that land."

30.7   RSV   TEV

And the LORD your God will put all   He will turn all these curses against
these curses upon your foes and   your enemies, who hated you and
enemies who persecuted you.   oppressed you,

All these curses: that is, all the disasters or punishments listed in 28.15-68; see 29.20. Another way to express this first sentence is "Then the LORD will stop punishing you; instead he will bring these disasters upon your enemies."

Put . . . upon your foes and enemies: see 7.15. The two nouns "foes and enemies" mean exactly the same thing; see NIV "on your enemies who hate you and persecute you" (similarly TEV). For **enemies** see 1.42.

Persecuted you: or this may be expressed as "oppressed you" (TEV), "took advantage of you" (NRSV), or even "attack you" (CEV).

30.8   RSV   TEV

And you shall again obey the voice   and you will again obey him and
of the LORD, and keep all his com-   keep all his commands that I am
mandments which I command you   giving you today.
this day.

This verse repeats statements made elsewhere, using the same language; see
28.1 for the whole verse.

Obey the voice of the LORD, **and keep all his commandments**: these two
clauses mean the same.

I command you this day: Moses is the speaker.

30.9   RSV   TEV

The LORD your God will make you   The LORD will make you prosperous
abundantly prosperous in all the   in all that you do; you will have many
work of your hand, in the fruit of   children and a lot of livestock, and
your body, and in the fruit of your   your fields will produce abundant
cattle, and in the fruit of your   crops. He will be as glad to make
ground; for the LORD will again take   you prosperous as he was to make
delight in prospering you, as he took   your ancestors prosperous,
delight in your fathers,

Make you abundantly prosperous: this is emphatic language, and the
exaggerated style should be respected. In certain languages the picture of **fruit**
may be used; for example, "cause you to be very fruitful in everything you do:
having many children [the fruit of your body]" and so on.

The work of your hand: see 28.12.

The fruit of your body . . . your cattle . . . your ground: see 28.4, 11.

Will again take delight in prospering you: or "will be happy to do good things
for you" (CEV). See 28.63 for the opposite.

Your fathers: "your ancestors."

30.10   RSV   TEV

if you obey the voice of the LORD   but you will have to obey him and
your God, to keep his command-   keep all his laws that are written in
ments and his statutes which are   this book of his teachings. You will
written in this book of the law, if you   have to turn to him with all your
turn to the LORD your God with all   heart.
your heart and with all your soul.

This verse repeats the essence of verse 8. Like TEV and CEV it will be helpful
in a number of languages to begin with the equivalent of the adversative "but":
"But you must . . . ."

Obey the voice of the LORD your God may be shortened to "Obey him [Yahweh]."

For **commandments** see 4.2; for **statutes** see 4.1.

Written in this book of the law: see 28.58.

Turn to the LORD your God with all your heart and with all your soul: see 4.29.

4C. God's word is very near (30.11-14)

RSV	TEV
11 "For this commandment which I command you this day is not too hard for you, neither is it far off. 12 It is not in heaven, that you should say, 'Who will go up for us to heaven, and bring it to us, that we may hear it and do it?' 13 Neither is it beyond the sea, that you should say, 'Who will go over the sea for us, and bring it to us, that we may hear it and do it?' 14 But the word is very near you; it is in your mouth and in your heart, so that you can do it.	11 "The command that I am giving you today is not too difficult or beyond your reach. 12 It is not up in the sky. You do not have to ask, 'Who will go up and bring it down for us, so that we can hear it and obey it?' 13 Nor is it on the other side of the ocean. You do not have to ask, 'Who will go across the ocean and bring it to us, so that we may hear it and obey it?' 14 No, it is here with you. You know it and can quote it, so now obey it.

In this section Moses declares that Yahweh's commands are not difficult to understand or obey. Verses 12-14 are cited by Paul in Rom 10.6-8.

Section heading: TOB and FRCL have the title "God's Word is very near." Another possible heading is "God's commandments are not too difficult."

30.11 RSV	TEV
"For this commandment which I command you this day is not too hard for you, neither is it far off.	"The command that I am giving you today is not too difficult or beyond your reach.

This commandment which I command you this day: Moses is speaking, and with the beginning of a new section, he should be reintroduced as the speaker. **This commandment** means all the laws and teachings that he has given that day (see verse 16, below; see also "all the commandment" in Moses' second speech, at 5.31). So translators may express this as "These commandments" rather than "This commandment."

Not too hard for you: not difficult to obey.

Neither is it far off: not hard to understand, since it is right there with them, and not in some distant land. That is what TEV "is not . . . beyond your reach" intends to say. See Psa 139.6 for a similar use of the idiom.

An alternative translation model for this verse is:

● Moses said to the people of Israel: "These commandments that I am giving you today are not too difficult to understand or obey.

30.12   RSV   TEV

It is not in heaven, that you should   **It is not up in the sky. You do not**
say, 'Who will go up for us to heav-   **have to ask, 'Who will go up and**
en, and bring it to us, that we may   **bring it down for us, so that we can**
hear it and do it?'   **hear it and obey it?'**

Not in heaven: that is, not beyond normal human capacity to acquire and
understand. In many languages **heaven** will be expressed as "the sky."

The rhetorical question **Who will go up for us to heaven?** is a vivid way of
saying that such an idea is foolish. The CEV model is a good one: "How can we
obey the LORD's commands? They are in heaven and no one can go up to them."

That we may hear it and do it: the opposite of this is an unreal possibility. We
may also say "So that we may hear them and obey them."

30.13   RSV   TEV

Neither is it beyond the sea, that you   **Nor is it on the other side of the**
should say, 'Who will go over the sea   **ocean. You do not have to ask, 'Who**
for us, and bring it to us, that we may   **will go across the ocean and bring it**
hear it and do it?'   **to us, so that we may hear it and**
                                           obey it?'

Beyond the sea: or "on the other side of the ocean" (TEV), or "across the sea"
(CEV). This is another way of referring to some distant land.

The question here is similar to that in the previous verses and is used for the
same purpose.

30.14   RSV   TEV

But the word is very near you; it is in   **No, it is here with you. You know it**
your mouth and in your heart, so that   **and can quote it, so now obey it.**
you can do it.

Is very near you: that is, it is accessible, it is understandable. CEV has "No,
these commands are nearby."

In your mouth: that is, in language you understand and speak; so we may say
"you quote them."

In your heart: that is, you already know it. TEV reverses the order of the two
verbs: "You know it and can quote it."

So that you can do it: or "so now obey it" (TEV); CEV has "All you have to do
is obey."

For similar language to this, see in 6.6-7; 11.18.

4D. Choose life (30.15-20)

RSV   TEV

15 "See, I have set before you this day life
and good, death and evil. 16 If you obey the
commandments of the LORD your God which I
command you this day, by loving the LORD
your God, by walking in his ways, and by
keeping his commandments and his statutes
and his ordinances, then you shall live and
multiply, and the LORD your God will bless you
in the land which you are entering to take
possession of it. 17 But if your heart turns
away, and you will not hear, but are drawn
away to worship other gods and serve them,
18 I declare to you this day, that you shall
perish; you shall not live long in the land
which you are going over the Jordan to enter
and possess. 19 I call heaven and earth to
witness against you this day, that I have set
before you life and death, blessing and curse;
therefore choose life, that you and your descendants may live, 20 loving the LORD your God,
obeying his voice, and cleaving to him; for that
means life to you and length of days, that you
may dwell in the land which the LORD swore to
your fathers, to Abraham, to Isaac, and to
Jacob, to give them."

15 "Today I am giving you a choice between
good and evil, between life and death. 16 If you
obey the commands of the LORD your God,
which I give you today, if you love him, obey
him, and keep all his laws, then you will prosper and become a nation of many people. The
LORD your God will bless you in the land that
you are about to occupy. 17 But if you disobey
and refuse to listen, and are led away to worship other gods, 18 you will be destroyed—I
warn you here and now. You will not live long
in that land across the Jordan that you are
about to occupy. 19 I am now giving you the
choice between life and death, between God's
blessing and God's curse, and I call heaven
and earth to witness the choice you make.
Choose life. 20 Love the LORD your God, obey
him and be faithful to him, and then you and
your descendants will live long in the land that
he promised to give your ancestors, Abraham,
Isaac, and Jacob."

Verses 15-20 are the final exhortation, the end of Moses' third speech. Some
translations make this a separate section, with its own heading.

Section heading: a suitable title is "Choose life" (TOB, FRCL).

30.15   RSV   TEV

"See, I have set before you this
day life and good, death and evil.

"Today I am giving you a choice
between good and evil, between life
and death.

In this section Moses is still the speaker.

See, I have set before you this day means "Today I am giving you the choice
between," or "Today I am letting you choose between."

Life and good, death and evil: notice that TEV has rearranged the four into
two contrasting pairs, "good and evil . . . life and death."

Life and good: this is the option for **life**, a long existence as a people in the
Promised Land (verse 18). **Good** here is prosperity, success, wealth; NIV, NJPSV,
NRSV, NJB have "prosperity," POCL "happiness," CEV "success." Its opposite, **evil**,
is "disaster" (CEV, NJB), "adversity" (NRSV, NJPSV), "destruction" (NIV). For the
two options FRCL has "success and failure."

30.16   RSV   TEV

If you obey the commandments of   If you obey the commands of the
the LORD your God^c which I com-   LORD your God,ᵃ which I give you
mand you this day, by loving the   today, if you love him, obey him, and
LORD your God, by walking in his   keep all his laws, then you will pros-
ways, and by keeping his command-   per and become a nation of many
ments and his statutes and his ordi-   people. The LORD your God will bless
nances, then you shall live and multi-   you in the land that you are about to
ply, and the LORD your God will bless   occupy.
you in the land which you are enter-
ing to take possession of it.   ᵃ *One ancient translation* If you obey
          the commands of the LORD your God;
ᶜ Gk: Heb lacks *If you obey the com-*   *Hebrew does not have these words.*
mandments of the LORD *your God*

If you obey the commandments of the LORD your God: as the RSV footnote
indicates, this is not in the Hebrew text but in the Septuagint; it is endorsed by
HOTTP ({B} rating, stating that the omission is due to a scribal error), and is
followed by TEV, NRSV, REB, NJB. Some translations, like NIV, NJPSV, TOB, follow
the Hebrew text in not including the clause. It is recommended that translators
follow the Septuagint with a textual footnote as RSV and TEV do.

Which I command you this day: as in other parts of the book, the day when
Moses was giving that discourse (his third speech) in the plains of Moab.

By loving . . . walking . . . keeping: this is how the Israelites were to obey
God's law.

Loving the LORD your God: in 6.5 it was stressed that this kind of "love"
contains not only the elements of liking and affection, but also devotion and
loyalty. If translators cannot find a term that contains all these elements, an
expression such as "Love and be loyal [or, faithful] to the LORD" may be
required.

The two participial phrases, **by walking in his ways** and **by keeping his
commandments and his statutes and his ordinances**, are parallel and have a
similar meaning. However, if at all possible translators should retain both
expressions. In a number of languages a figurative expression similar to **by
walking in his ways** may be used. An example is "walking along his paths,"
meaning "to live your life the way he has told you." **By keeping his commandments** means "obeying all his laws and teachings." For **commandments, statutes**, and **ordinances** see 4.1, 2.

You shall live and multiply: that is, they will increase in number. TEV offers
a good model: "you will prosper and become a nation of many people."

30.17   RSV   TEV

But if your heart turns away, and you   But if you disobey and refuse to
will not hear, but are drawn away to   listen, and are led away to worship
worship other gods and serve them,   other gods,

If your heart turns away, and you will not hear: that is, if they defect, or they abandon their loyalty and devotion. To **hear** is to obey. TEV translates "If you disobey and refuse to listen," while CEV has "you might choose to disobey and reject the LORD."

Are drawn away to worship other gods and serve them: see 4.19. In languages that do not have the passive voice, translators may say, for example, "and they [other people, foreigners] entice you into bowing down to other gods [or, false gods] and worshiping them."

30.18   RSV   TEV

| I declare to you this day, that you shall perish; you shall not live long in the land which you are going over the Jordan to enter and possess. | you will be destroyed—I warn you here and now. You will not live long in that land across the Jordan that you are about to occupy. |

I declare to you this day: these words introduce a formal, important statement. They may also be rendered as "I am warning you today."

You shall perish; you shall not live long in the land: this means that they as individuals and as a nation will soon disappear; see 8.19. The phrase **you shall perish** is emphatic in Hebrew and may also be expressed as "you will be destroyed"; but in languages that do not use the passive, we may say, for example, "your enemies [or, those that hate you] will destroy you."

Going over the Jordan: from east to west.

CEV has an excellent model, combining and restructuring the clauses in verses 16-18 as follows:

- 16-18 I am commanding you to be loyal to the LORD, to live the way he has told you, and to obey his laws and teachings. You are about to cross the Jordan River and take the land that he is giving you. If you obey him, you will live and become successful and powerful. On the other hand, you might choose to disobey the LORD and reject him. So I'm warning you that if you bow down and worship other gods, you won't have long to live.

30.19   RSV   TEV

| I call heaven and earth to witness against you this day, that I have set before you life and death, blessing and curse; therefore choose life, that you and your descendants may live, | I am now giving you the choice between life and death, between God's blessing and God's curse, and I call heaven and earth to witness the choice you make. Choose life. |

I call heaven and earth to witness against you: see 4.26.

Life and death, blessing and curse: see verse 15; the choice is theirs.

Choose life, that you and your descendants may live: nothing less than continued existence as a people is at stake; they will be a prosperous and powerful people, or else they will disappear. Both TEV and CEV (see below) have excellent alternative models. CEV keeps the clauses in the same order as RSV, but TEV places the first clause at the end of the verse. Either model is possible.

- Right now I call the sky and the earth to be witnesses that I am offering you this choice. Will you choose for the LORD to make you prosperous and give you a long life? Or will he put you under a curse and kill you? Choose life! (CEV)

30.20 RSV	TEV
loving the LORD your God, obeying his voice, and cleaving to him; for that means life to you and length of days, that you may dwell in the land which the LORD swore to your fathers, to Abraham, to Isaac, and to Jacob, to give them."	Love the LORD your God, obey him and be faithful to him, and then you and your descendants will live long in the land that he promised to give your ancestors, Abraham, Isaac, and Jacob."

RSV has this verse as a continuation of verse 19, with the verbal phrases **loving . . . obeying . . . cleaving** as the means by which the people will **choose life**. But in many languages it is better to follow TEV and others and begin a new sentence here, with the verbs in the imperative.

Loving the LORD your God: see the comment in verse 16.

Cleaving to him: see 10.20; this is "loyalty," "love," "faithful obedience." This is part of what **loving** means, and CEV combines the first and third commands as "Be completely faithful to the LORD . . . ."

Means life to you and length of days: that is, "this is how you will have a long and prosperous existence as a nation." CEV begins a new sentence here: "The LORD is the only one who can give life, and he will let you live a long time in the land."

The LORD swore to your fathers, to Abraham, to Isaac, and to Jacob, to give them: see 1.8.

5. Moses' last actions

(31.1–33.29)

Chapter 31 begins the final part of Deuteronomy. Some treat chapters 31–34 as a single section; for example, NJB entitles these chapters "Last Actions and Death of Moses," and FRCL has "Farewells and death of Moses." It seems better to have chapter 34 as a separate section as TEV does. The TEV title is "Moses' Last Words"; but, since chapters 31–33 report some things that Moses did, a better title may be something like "Moses' Last Actions and Instructions." There will, however, be subsections in each chapter.

5A. Joshua becomes Moses' successor (31.1-8)

RSV	TEV
	Joshua Becomes Moses' Successor

RSV	TEV
1 So Moses continued to speak these words to all Israel. 2 And he said to them, "I am a hundred and twenty years old this day; I am no longer able to go out and come in. The LORD has said to me, 'You shall not go over this Jordan.' 3 The LORD your God himself will go over before you; he will destroy these nations before you, so that you shall dispossess them; and Joshua will go over at your head, as the LORD has spoken. 4 And the LORD will do to them as he did to Sihon and Og, the kings of the Amorites, and to their land, when he destroyed them. 5 And the LORD will give them over to you, and you shall do to them according to all the commandment which I have commanded you. 6 Be strong and of good courage, do not fear or be in dread of them: for it is the LORD your God who goes with you; he will not fail you or forsake you." 7 Then Moses summoned Joshua, and said to him in the sight of all Israel, "Be strong and of good courage; for you shall go with this people into the land which the LORD has sworn to their fathers to give them; and you shall put them in possession of it. 8 It is the LORD who goes before you; he will be with you, he will not fail you or forsake you; do not fear or be dismayed."	1 Moses continued speaking to the people of Israel, 2 and said, "I am now a hundred and twenty years old and am no longer able to be your leader. And besides this, the LORD has told me that I will not cross the Jordan. 3 The LORD your God himself will go before you and destroy the nations living there, so that you can occupy their land; and Joshua will be your leader, as the LORD has said. 4 The LORD will destroy those people, just as he defeated Sihon and Og, kings of the Amorites, and destroyed their country. 5 The LORD will give you victory over them, and you are to treat them exactly as I have told you. 6 Be determined and confident. Do not be afraid of them. Your God, the LORD himself, will be with you. He will not fail you or abandon you." 7 Then Moses called Joshua and said to him in the presence of all the people of Israel, "Be determined and confident; you are the one who will lead these people to occupy the land that the LORD promised to their ancestors. 8 The LORD himself will lead you and be with you. He will not fail you or abandon you, so do not lose courage or be afraid."

Section heading: for this first section in chapter 31, we may use the title "Joshua Becomes Moses' Successor" (TEV), or "Moses appoints Joshua as leader of Israel."

31.1	RSV	TEV

So Moses continued to speak these words to all Israel.

Moses continued speaking to the people of Israel,

Moses continued to speak: this translates the Masoretic version of the Hebrew text, which says literally "Moses went and spoke"; the Qumran Hebrew manuscript and the Septuagint have "Moses finished speaking." There are several factors that must be considered in deciding which one to follow. HOTTP (decision {C}) prefers the Masoretic text, citing factors 5 (assimilation to parallel passages) and 4 (easier reading). If the Masoretic text is followed, it can be understood in two different ways: (1) "Moses went and spoke," indicating movement on Moses' part (so NJB, NJPSV, NIV); or (2) "Moses continued to speak" (RSV, TEV, FRCL, SPCL, BRCL, POCL). If the translator wishes to follow the other text, as do NRSV and REB, a footnote should be added, indicating the source of this wording. This Handbook recommends that translators follow RSV and TEV.

All Israel: that is, "all the people of Israel."

31.2	RSV	TEV

And he said to them, "I am a hundred and twenty years old this day; I am no longer able to go out and come in. The LORD has said to me, 'You shall not go over this Jordan.'

and said, "I am now a hundred and twenty years old and am no longer able to be your leader. And besides this, the LORD has told me that I will not cross the Jordan.

A hundred and twenty years old: the text states that Moses is 120 years old; it is not saying that this is his 120th birthday. In the book itself this is the day when Moses was giving this speech to the Israelites in the plains of Moab. Moses began the first of his addresses on the first day of the eleventh month of the fortieth year after the Israelites left Egypt (1.3 ,5).

I am no longer able to go out and come in: that is, "to lead an active life" or "to get about" (NRSV). Some, like TEV and CEV, take it in the more restricted sense of "to lead," but the broader sense seems preferable (see 28.6, 19).

You shall not go over this Jordan: **this Jordan** is natural style in Hebrew, but in many other languages translators will prefer something like "the Jordan River" or even "the Jordan River here in front of you." This decision by the LORD is referred to in 1.37; 3.27; 4.21-22; and see Num 20.12 for the occasion when the LORD took this decision.

31.3   RSV   TEV

The LORD your God himself will go   The LORD your God himself will go
over before you; he will destroy   before you and destroy the nations
these nations before you, so that you   living there, so that you can occupy
shall dispossess them; and Joshua   their land; and Joshua will be your
will go over at your head, as the   leader, as the LORD has said.
LORD has spoken.

The LORD your God himself will go over: it is God who will lead the people
across the river and into the land of Canaan. It will be helpful in many
languages to make it clear that **go over** means "go over the Jordan River"; so
we may say "The LORD your God himself will go before you across the Jordan
River."

Before you means that Yahweh will lead them as they conquer the land.

He will destroy these nations before you: for this declaration see 1.23; 2.12.
These nations are the peoples that the Israelites will encounter in the land of
Canaan, namely, "the nations that live on the other side of the Jordan" (CEV).

You shall dispossess them: for this verb see 9.1; 11.23; 12.2, 29.

Joshua will go over at your head: indeed it will be Yahweh who will take
them into the Promised Land, but **Joshua** will go in front of them and lead
them there.

As the LORD has spoken: in certain languages that do not use indirect
speech, it is possible to begin the verse with this clause; for example,

• For Yahweh said, "I will go before you across the Jordan River,
  and will destroy the nations on the other side so that you can
  occupy their land. Joshua will be your leader, as I have said."

31.4   RSV   TEV

And the LORD will do to them as he   The LORD will destroy those people,
did to Sihon and Og, the kings of the   just as he defeated Sihon and Og,
Amorites, and to their land, when he   kings of the Amorites, and destroyed
destroyed them.   their country.

For the defeat of **Sihon and Og**, see 29.7-8; Num 21.21-35.

He destroyed them: not only the two kings as such, but their armies as well.
Some translators will prefer to continue using direct speech with Yahweh as
the speaker through verse 6. In such cases it will be helpful to begin this verse
with "The LORD went on to say, 'I will destroy those people . . . .' "

31.5 RSV TEV

And the LORD will give them over to you, and you shall do to them according to all the commandment which I have commanded you.

The LORD will give you victory over them, and you are to treat them exactly as I have told you.

This verse contains two parallel and complementary statements.

The LORD will give them over to you means that God makes it possible for the Israelites to defeat their enemies; **them** are the peoples they will fight in the land of Canaan.

You shall do to them according to all the commandment which I have commanded you means that the Israelites will destroy their enemies, as the LORD had commanded. So we may render this statement "As I have commanded you, 'Kill them all!'"

All the commandment: see the detailed instructions in 7.1-5.

31.6 RSV TEV

Be strong and of good courage, do not fear or be in dread of them: for it is the LORD your God who goes with you; he will not fail you or forsake you."

Be determined and confident. Do not be afraid of them. Your God, the LORD himself, will be with you. He will not fail you or abandon you."

This verse contains three pairs of terms that mean the same thing, making for an effective and attractive style in Hebrew. If they are natural and effective, a translation should try to match them.

Be strong and of good courage: see 3.28. This is expressed in NRSV as "Be strong and bold"; NJB has "Be strong, stand firm," NJPSV "Be strong and resolute," TEV "Be determined and confident"; or we may say something like "Keep your heart strong and don't let it waver."

Do not fear or be in dread: **fear** and **dread** mean exactly the same thing, and there may be difficulty in finding two words that will fit naturally. See 1.21, 29. A different way of saying this may be useful in some languages: "Don't let them frighten you or terrify you."

It is the LORD your God who goes with you: the idea is not simply to accompany the Israelites, but to provide them leadership and help; God is on their side. So CEV has "will always be at your side." However, in languages where translators are using direct speech, we may say, for example, "I, Yahweh your God, will always be at your side."

He will not fail you or forsake you: see a similar promise in 4.31. To **fail** someone is to not keep a promise, not to do what you have promised to do. In this context Yahweh would **not fail** the Israelites by not helping them, as he said he would, or by deserting (**forsake**) them. Another way to express this sentence is "I will always help you and will never abandon you."

31.7 RSV	TEV
Then Moses summoned Joshua, and said to him in the sight of all Israel, "Be strong and of good courage; for you shall go with this people into the land which the LORD has sworn to their fathers to give them; and you shall put them in possession of it.	Then Moses called Joshua and said to him in the presence of all the people of Israel, "Be determined and confident; you are the one who will lead these people to occupy the land that the LORD promised to their ancestors.

In his charge to Joshua (verses 7-8) Moses repeats in part what God had said to him, using the same expressions.

Summoned: this word in English is used of a person of high rank ordering someone of lower rank to come to him; in this situation that sense fits, since Moses is superior in rank to Joshua. In most contexts, however, the verb also has the sense that the person who is being summoned is going to be reprimanded. This other sense, of course, should be avoided in translation. Both TEV and CEV use "called."

Be strong and of good courage: see verse 6.

You shall go with this people: as is said of Yahweh in verse 6.

The land which the LORD has sworn to their fathers to give them: see 1.8.

You shall put them in possession of it: the verb "take possession of" (see 1.38) is here used as a causative, meaning "you shall cause [or, enable] them to take possession of the land."

31.8 RSV	TEV
It is the LORD who goes before you; he will be with you, he will not fail you or forsake you; do not fear or be dismayed."	The LORD himself will lead you and be with you. He will not fail you or abandon you, so do not lose courage or be afraid."

It is the LORD who goes before you; he will be with you: again two statements that mean the same. Yahweh will lead them as they advance into Canaan.

He will not fail you or forsake you: as in verse 6.

Do not fear or be dismayed: here the second verb is different from the one in verse 6, but it has a very similar meaning.

5B. The Law is to be read every seven years (31.9-13)

RSV

TEV

*The Law Is to Be Read Every
Seven Years*

9 And Moses wrote this law, and gave it to the priests the sons of Levi, who carried the ark of the covenant of the LORD, and to all the elders of Israel. 10 And Moses commanded them, "At the end of every seven years, at the set time of the year of release, at the feast of booths, 11 when all Israel comes to appear before the LORD your God at the place which he will choose, you shall read this law before all Israel in their hearing. 12 Assemble the people, men, women, and little ones, and the sojourner within your towns, that they may hear and learn to fear the LORD your God, and be careful to do all the words of this law, 13 and that their children, who have not known it, may hear and learn to fear the LORD your God, as long as you live in the land which you are going over the Jordan to possess."

9 So Moses wrote down God's Law and gave it to the levitical priests, who were in charge of the LORD's Covenant Box, and to the leaders of Israel. 10 He commanded them, "At the end of every seven years, when the year that debts are canceled comes around, read this aloud at the Festival of Shelters. 11 Read it to the people of Israel when they come to worship the LORD your God at the one place of worship. 12 Call together all the men, women, and children, and the foreigners who live in your towns, so that everyone may hear it and learn to honor the LORD your God and to obey his teachings faithfully. 13 In this way your descendants who have never heard the Law of the LORD your God will hear it. And so they will learn to obey him as long as they live in the land that you are about to occupy across the Jordan."

Section heading: for this section TEV has the heading "The Law Is to Be Read Every Seven Years." In some languages the passive form may not be suitable; and the title should make clear that the section is talking about a public reading of the Law. FRCL has "Public reading of the Law every seven years." Other ways to express this are "Read these laws aloud for the Israelites to hear every seven years" or "Read these laws in the hearing of the Israelites every seven years."

31.9 RSV

TEV

And Moses wrote this law, and gave it to the priests the sons of Levi, who carried the ark of the covenant of the LORD, and to all the elders of Israel.

So Moses wrote down God's Law and gave it to the levitical priests, who were in charge of the LORD's Covenant Box, and to the leaders of Israel.

Moses wrote this law: see 1.5. This means the book of Deuteronomy; thus CEV translates "Moses wrote down all of these laws and teachings," or we may say "Moses wrote down all these laws and teachings in *The Book of God's Law* and gave it to the . . . ."

Gave it: he gave the written record, that is, the book in which he had written the Law.

The priests the sons of Levi: see 18.1.

Who carried the ark of the covenant of the LORD: see 10.8.

Elders: see 5.23.

31.10   RSV   TEV

And Moses commanded them, "At   He commanded them, "At the end of
the end of every seven years, at the   every seven years, when the year
set time of the year of release, at the   that debts are canceled comes
feast of booths,   around, read this aloud at the Festi-
          val of Shelters.

Moses commanded them: in the context **them** refers to the Levites and the
elders, so translators should have something like "Moses commanded these
priests and leaders" or "gave them to the priests and the leaders" (CEV).

At the end of every seven years: as the statements in 14.28 and 15.1 show,
this means "every seventh year" (NJB). FRCL has "Every seven years, the year
of the forgiveness of debts," BRCL "Every seven years, in the year set for
forgiveness of debts," CEV "the year when loans do not need to be repaid."

The set time of the year of release: this is the year when all debts were
forgiven; see 15.1-3. In a number of languages those two clauses may be
combined (see TEV).

The feast of booths: known also as Sukkoth (TEV, CEV "Festival of Shelters"),
this seven-day festival began on the date 15 Tishri, which corresponds more or
less to the beginning of October (see 16.13-15).

31.11   RSV   TEV

when all Israel comes to appear be-   Read it to the people of Israel when
fore the LORD your God at the place   they come to worship the LORD your
which he will choose, you shall read   God at the one place of worship.
this law before all Israel in their hear-
ing.

When all Israel comes to appear before the LORD: this was one of the three
annual festivals when all Israelite males twenty-one years and older were
required to be present (see 16.1-17; Exo 23.14-17).

Here **all Israel** (twice) should be translated "all Israelites," as the next verse
makes clear.

The place which he shall choose: see 12.5; 16.16.

You shall read this law . . . in their hearing: a public reading of the Law
during the Festival of Shelters. **In their hearing** may be expressed as "for them
to hear." The whole sentence may also be rendered as "read these laws and
teachings aloud so that all the people of Israel may hear."

31.12   RSV   TEV

Assemble the people, men, women,   Call together all the men, women,
and little ones, and the sojourner   and children, and the foreigners who

within your towns, that they may hear and learn to fear the LORD your God, and be careful to do all the words of this law,	live in your towns, so that everyone may hear it and learn to honor the LORD your God and to obey his teachings faithfully.

All the Israelites, men, women, and children are to be present; also all "the foreigners who live in your towns" (TEV); see 1.8.

Assemble: or "call together" (TEV), or even "call all the men, women, . . . to come together."

May hear and learn to fear the LORD your God: see 4.10.

Be careful to do all the words of this law: see 26.16; 28.58.

31.13   RSV   TEV

and that their children, who have not known it, may hear and learn to fear the LORD your God, as long as you live in the land which you are going over the Jordan to possess."	In this way your descendants who have never heard the Law of the LORD your God will hear it. And so they will learn to obey him as long as they live in the land that you are about to occupy across the Jordan."

Their children, who have not known it: this means their descendants, yet to be born. The regular reading of the Law must never cease. TEV has a good model: "In this way your descendants who have never heard the law of the LORD your God"; or we may say "In this way each new generation of your descendants will hear the law . . . ."

As long as you live: this applies not only to the people there who are listening to Moses, but to all Israelites in the future. The Septuagint has "they live," and this is how TEV translates it, in order to apply the saying to the Israelites yet to be born.

To possess: see 1.8.

5C. The LORD's last instructions to Moses (31.14-29)

RSV   TEV
                                              The LORD's Last Instructions to Moses

14 And the LORD said to Moses, "Behold, the days approach when you must die; call Joshua, and present yourselves in the tent of meeting, that I may commission him." And Moses and Joshua went and presented themselves in the tent of meeting. 15 And the LORD appeared in the tent in a pillar of cloud; and the pillar of cloud stood by the door of the tent.

16 And the LORD said to Moses, "Behold, you are about to sleep with your fathers; then this people will rise and play the harlot after

14 Then the LORD said to Moses, "You do not have much longer to live. Call Joshua and bring him to the Tent, so that I may give him his instructions." Moses and Joshua went to the Tent, 15 and the LORD appeared to them there in a pillar of cloud that stood by the door of the Tent.

16 The LORD said to Moses, "You will soon die, and after your death the people will become unfaithful to me and break the covenant that I made with them. They will abandon me

the strange gods of the land, where they go to be among them, and they will forsake me and break my covenant which I have made with them. 17 Then my anger will be kindled against them in that day, and I will forsake them and hide my face from them, and they will be devoured; and many evils and troubles will come upon them, so that they will say in that day, 'Have not these evils come upon us because our God is not among us?' 18 And I will surely hide my face in that day on account of all the evil which they have done, because they have turned to other gods. 19 Now therefore write this song, and teach it to the people of Israel; put it in their mouths, that this song may be a witness for me against the people of Israel. 20 For when I have brought them into the land flowing with milk and honey, which I swore to give to their fathers, and they have eaten and are full and grown fat, they will turn to other gods and serve them, and despise me and break my covenant. 21 And when many evils and troubles have come upon them, this song shall confront them as a witness (for it will live unforgotten in the mouths of their descendants); for I know the purposes which they are already forming, before I have brought them into the land that I swore to give." 22 So Moses wrote this song the same day, and taught it to the people of Israel.

23 And the LORD commissioned Joshua the son of Nun and said, "Be strong and of good courage; for you shall bring the children of Israel into the land which I swore to give them: I will be with you."

24 When Moses had finished writing the words of this law in a book, to the very end, 25 Moses commanded the Levites who carried the ark of the covenant of the LORD, 26 "Take this book of the law, and put it by the side of the ark of the covenant of the LORD your God, that it may be there for a witness against you. 27 For I know how rebellious and stubborn you are; behold, while I am yet alive with you, today you have been rebellious against the LORD; how much more after my death! 28 Assemble to me all the elders of your tribes, and your officers, that I may speak these words in their ears and call heaven and earth to witness against them. 29 For I know that after my death you will surely act corruptly, and turn aside from the way which I have commanded you; and in the days to come evil will befall you, because you will do what is evil in the sight of the LORD, provoking him to anger through the work of your hands."

and worship the pagan gods of the land they are about to enter. 17 When that happens, I will become angry with them; I will abandon them, and they will be destroyed. Many terrible disasters will come upon them, and then they will realize that these things are happening to them because I, their God, am no longer with them. 18 And I will refuse to help them then, because they have done evil and worshiped other gods.

19 "Now, write down this song. Teach it to the people of Israel, so that it will stand as evidence against them. 20 I will take them into this rich and fertile land, as I promised their ancestors. There they will have all the food they want, and they will live comfortably. But they will turn away and worship other gods. They will reject me and break my covenant, 21 and many terrible disasters will come on them. But this song will still be sung, and it will stand as evidence against them. Even now, before I take them into the land that I promised to give them, I know what they are thinking."

22 That same day Moses wrote down the song and taught it to the people of Israel.

23 Then the LORD spoke to Joshua son of Nun and told him, "Be confident and determined. You will lead the people of Israel into the land that I promised them, and I will be with you."

24 Moses wrote God's Law in a book, taking care not to leave out anything. 25 When he finished, he said to the levitical priests, who were in charge of the LORD's Covenant Box, 26 "Take this book of God's Law and place it beside the Covenant Box of the LORD your God, so that it will remain there as a witness against his people. 27 I know how stubborn and rebellious they are. They have rebelled against the LORD during my lifetime, and they will rebel even more after I am dead. 28 Assemble all your tribal leaders and officials before me, so that I can tell them these things; I will call heaven and earth to be my witnesses against them. 29 I know that after my death the people will become wicked and reject what I have taught them. And in time to come they will meet with disaster, because they will have made the LORD angry by doing what he has forbidden."

Section heading: the TEV heading for this section is "The LORD's Last Instructions to Moses." FRCL is different, "Israel will be unfaithful to the Lord," and CEV has "Israel Will Reject the LORD."

31.14 RSV TEV

And the LORD said to Moses, "Behold, the days approach when you must die; call Joshua, and present yourselves in the tent of meeting, that I may commission him." And Moses and Joshua went and presented themselves in the tent of meeting.

Then the LORD said to Moses, "You do not have much longer to live. Call Joshua and bring him to the Tent, so that I may give him his instructions." Moses and Joshua went to the Tent,

The days approach when you must die: some different ways of expressing this are "You will soon die" (CEV), "the day of your death is near" (NIV), "your time to die is near" (NRSV), "The time is drawing near for you to die" (NJPSV), "the time is near when you must die" (NJB). This is meant as a statement of fact; it is neither a promise nor a threat as such.

Call Joshua, and present yourselves in the tent of meeting: **present yourselves** applies to Moses and Joshua. The **tent of meeting** (the "tabernacle") was the place where God "met" his people, that is, where he was present with them (see Exo 27.21; 33.7-11; Lev 25.22; 29.42-45; 33.7-11; Num 27.19). **The tent of meeting** may also be expressed as "the tent where I meet with you" or "the sacred tent" (CEV). Translators should avoid following the model of TEV, which simply capitalizes "Tent." People listening to the text read aloud will not hear this special marking device. These two clauses may be more simply expressed as "Call Joshua, and bring him with you to the sacred tent."

I may commission him: that is, "install him in office." In Num 27.8-19 Yahweh orders Moses to commission Joshua. Another way to express this is "appoint him as leader of Israel" (CEV). TEV "give him his instructions" is misleading.

31.15 RSV TEV

And the LORD appeared in the tent in a pillar of cloud; and the pillar of cloud stood by the door of the tent.

and the LORD appeared to them there in a pillar of cloud that stood by the door of the Tent.

Appeared . . . in a pillar of cloud: this means a cloud the size and shape of a pillar, but not a solid object. An alternative translation may be "in a cloud in the form of a pillar [or, column]." In cultures where "pillars" or "columns" are unknown, something like "in a thick cloud" is possible. Here the text does not mean that the cloud was God's means of transportation. A possible alternative model is the following: "And the Lord descended in a cloud in the form of a pillar and stood by the door of the tent of meeting; and the cloud stood by the door of the tent."

Stood by the door: presumably on the outside of the tent. An alternative way to render this is "outside the entrance to the tent."

31.16   RSV   TEV

And the LORD said to Moses, "Be-   The LORD said to Moses, "You will
hold, you are about to sleep with   soon die, and after your death the
your fathers; then this people will   people will become unfaithful to me
rise and play the harlot after the   and break the covenant that I made
strange gods of the land, where they with them. They will abandon me and
go to be among them, and they will   worship the pagan gods of the land
forsake me and break my covenant   they are about to enter.
which I have made with them.

The accusations and denunciations in verses 16-21 reveal that that very same generation, the very people Moses will teach the song to (verse 19), will forsake Yahweh, break the covenant, and will be punished by Yahweh as soon as they cross the Jordan and settle in Canaan.

You are about to sleep with your fathers: this is a Hebrew idiom for dying, the thought being that the dead person will join his or her ancestors in Sheol. There may be some languages in which this idea will sound natural, but English is not one of them. REB is probably the best attempt in English: "you are about to die and join your forefathers." But even this will not sound natural to many readers. POCL does the same: "You are going to die, you are going to join your ancestors." In many languages the best translation will be one in which the normal term or expression for dying is used. TEV and CEV have done a good job of restructuring, with all the information included: "You will soon die . . . ."

Will rise and play the harlot after strange gods: again the idiom **play the harlot** is not a natural one; the meaning is to forsake God, likening this act to a married person who leaves his or her spouse and goes off after lovers (see 4.25-28; Exo 34.15-16). So TEV has "the people will become unfaithful to me," and CEV translates "the people will reject me."

Strange gods of the land, where they go to be among them: **strange gods** are foreign gods, the gods of pagans. The Canaanites had their own gods, and for the Israelites to live in Canaan meant to live with the Canaanite gods. For **gods** see 4.28.

Forsake me and break my covenant which I have made with them: see verse 6 for **forsake**.

It will be helpful for many translators to restructure this verse. The following is a possible alternative model:

•   The LORD said to Moses, "You will soon die, and the Israelites will be going into a land where the inhabitants worship other gods. So after you die they will reject [or, be unfaithful to] me and will start worshiping these false gods. In this way they will break the agreement I made with them.

31.17 RSV   TEV

Then my anger will be kindled against them in that day, and I will forsake them and hide my face from them, and they will be devoured; and many evils and troubles will come upon them, so that they will say in that day, 'Have not these evils come upon us because our God is not among us?'	When that happens, I will become angry with them; I will abandon them, and they will be destroyed. Many terrible disasters will come upon them, and then they will realize that these things are happening to them because I, their God, am no longer with them.

My anger will be kindled against them: see 29.20, 23, 27-28.

Hide my face from them: that is, God will not look on them with love and concern; he will, in effect, withdraw his help from them (see the figure in Psa 13.1; 27.9).

They will be devoured: this means they will be destroyed by God's anger, which will "eat" them up.

Many evils and troubles will come upon them: such as famines, droughts, epidemics, and hostile enemies. Translators should use a general statement; for example, "Many terrible disasters will come upon them" (TEV), or "I will send disasters and sufferings that . . ." (CEV).

In that day: the day God starts punishing them (see the phrase at the beginning of the verse). The more general statement "When that happens" (TEV) is not as good as "on that day."

Have not these evils come upon us because our God is not among us? This is not a question for information; it is a way of stating that they know their troubles are God's punishment for their sins: God has abandoned them. So we may translate "On that day they will realize that they are suffering because I [God] have abandoned them."

31.18 RSV   TEV

And I will surely hide my face in that day on account of all the evil which they have done, because they have turned to other gods.	And I will refuse to help them then, because they have done evil and worshiped other gods.

This verse is a summarizing conclusion, using terms and expressions of the previous verses.

I will surely hide: this translates the emphatic Hebrew phrase, the double use of the verb, meaning "I will refuse to help them" (TEV), or "I will pay no attention to them."

Because they have turned to other gods: this is precisely the evil that they have done; so NRSV says "by turning to other gods." To "turn" to other gods is to abandon Yahweh in order to worship and serve them. So it is possible to express this as "Because they have abandoned me and started worshiping other [or, false] gods."

31.19   RSV   TEV

Now therefore write this song, and teach it to the people of Israel; put it in their mouths, that this song may be a witness for me against the people of Israel.	"Now, write down this song. Teach it to the people of Israel, so that it will stand as evidence against them.

Now therefore write this song: for **this song** see verse 30 and 32.1-43. In Hebrew **write** is the second person plural, meaning that Moses and Joshua are to write down the song; but the other two verbs are singular. This makes for an awkward sentence, and only Osty, TOB, and the French edition of *The Jerusalem Bible* (*Bible de Jérusalem*) follow the Hebrew. (In languages like English, that have no different endings to distinguish between the second person singular and the second person plural, a translation such as NJPSV "write" will be read as second person singular.) FRCL uses an impersonal form: "And now, the words of this song that I am going to dictate to you are to be written down." NIV attempts to preserve the Hebrew by translating "write down for yourselves this song and teach it"—but this is not natural, and "teach" will read as a plural form also. BRCL uses the singular "write," with a footnote indicating that the Hebrew text has the plural; this is one way to handle the matter. Another possible alternative is "I want you and Joshua to write down this song. Then you, Moses, are to teach it to . . . ."

Teach it to the people of Israel; put it in their mouths: these two commands say almost the same thing. A literal translation of the second command may sound funny in a number of languages. A possible alternative is "have them learn it by heart" or ". . . memorize it."

That this song may be a witness for me against the people of Israel: the song (32.1-43) is a recital of God's dealings with the people of Israel, how he led them, provided for them, and protected them. So the song was a **witness** on God's behalf whenever he would have to judge and punish the Israelites for forsaking him. See the same statement about **the book of the law** in verse 24. The TEV translation "so that it will stand as evidence against them" may be difficult to translate in some languages. The longer version of CEV may be a good alternative: "they will know what I warn them to do, and so they will have no excuse for not obeying me."

31.20   RSV   TEV

For when I have brought them into the land flowing with milk and honey, which I swore to give to their fathers, and they have eaten and are full and grown fat, they will turn to other gods and serve them, and despise me and break my covenant.	I will take them into this rich and fertile land, as I promised their ancestors. There they will have all the food they want, and they will live comfortably. But they will turn away and worship other gods. They will reject me and break my covenant,

When I have brought them: or better, "After I have taken them."
Land flowing with milk and honey: see 6.3.
Which I swore to give to their fathers: see 1.8.
They have eaten and are full and grown fat: these are metaphors for becoming prosperous, wealthy, and complacent. See 6.10-11; 8.12.
They will turn to other gods and serve them: see verses 16, 18.
Despise me: to "reject" (TEV), or "turn their backs on me" (CEV); see Num 14.11, 23.
Break my covenant: as in verse 16, the fuller form is better: "break the covenant [or, agreement] I made with them."

31.21   RSV   TEV

And when many evils and troubles have come upon them, this song shall confront them as a witness (for it will live unforgotten in the mouths of their descendants); for I know the purposes which they are already forming, before I have brought them into the land that I swore to give."	and many terrible disasters will come on them. But this song will still be sung, and it will stand as evidence against them. Even now, before I take them into the land that I promised to give them, I know what they are thinking."

Many evils and troubles have come upon them: see verse 17.
This song shall confront them as a witness: this is a court setting; the Israelites are being judged and the song is a hostile witness (see verse 18). In many languages it will be possible to retain the vivid imagery of a song standing "as evidence" (TEV). But in some languages it will be difficult to talk about a song confronting someone as a witness. In such cases translators may follow CEV: "I will remind them that they know the words of this song"; but even better may be "they will remember the words of this song and will realize that I am punishing them."
(For it will live unforgotten in the mouths of their descendants): this means that the song will have been taught to the descendants of the generation that will occupy the land, and they will know why God is punishing his people.
I know the purposes which they are already forming: the noun translated **purposes** is often used of an instinct, mostly evil, which leads people to do evil things (see Gen 6.5; 8.21). This is expressed in NIV as "I know what they are

disposed to do"; NJPSV has "I know what plans they are devising even now," and REB "I know which way their thoughts incline." Something like "I know what their [evil] impulses are" will be satisfactory in some languages.

31.22   RSV   TEV

So Moses wrote this song the same   **That same day Moses wrote down**
day, and taught it to the people of   **the song and taught it to the people**
Israel.   **of Israel.**

Moses wrote this song . . . and taught it to the people: see verses 30, 44.
The same day: or "that same day" (TEV). This means the same day when the Lord spoke to Moses and told him to do this.

31.23   RSV   TEV

And the LORD commissioned Jo-   **Then the LORD spoke to Joshua**
shua the son of Nun and said, "Be   **son of Nun and told him, "Be confi-**
strong and of good courage; for you   **dent and determined. You will lead**
shall bring the children of Israel into   **the people of Israel into the land that**
the land which I swore to give them: **I promised them, and I will be with**
I will be with you."   **you."**

The LORD commissioned Joshua the son of Nun: see verse 14. For a detailed account see Num 27.15-23. Translators should find a strong term such as "gave authority to Joshua," to indicate the importance of Moses' action.
Be strong and of good courage: see verse 6.
You shall bring the children of Israel into the land which I swore to give them: instead of **children of Israel**, "Israelites" (NRSV) or "the people of Israel" should be used. And instead of **bring** many languages will prefer "take."
I will be with you: see verse 8.

31.24   RSV   TEV

When Moses had finished writing   **Moses wrote God's Law in a book,**
the words of this law in a book, to   **taking care not to leave out anything.**
the very end,

In RSV verses 24-26 are one sentence. It is not complex nor overly long; but a translation may wish to follow TEV and make verse 24 one sentence and verses 25-26 another sentence, or follow CEV, which has two sentences in verses 25-26.
The words of this law: see 28.58.

A book: many readers will assume that **a book** at that time was like books at the present time, in the form of a volume of pages called a codex. But at that time it was a scroll made of sheets of animal hide or papyrus, sewn together. In some languages it may be necessary to make this clear; but since the nature and function of a scroll, at that time, and of a book, in the present time, are one and the same, it seems acceptable to use the word "book"

SCROLLS, PEN, AND INKWELL

and its equivalents in other languages. Such a thing is done for other artifacts, such as clothing and containers, which were quite different in biblical times from what they are today.

To the very end: in the context this means to the end of the book we have now. FRCL offers a good model for this verse: "Moses wrote in a book the complete text of the law of God. When he had finished . . . ."

31.25-26   RSV   TEV

25 Moses commanded the Levites who carried the ark of the covenant of the LORD, 26 "Take this book of the law, and put it by the side of the ark of the covenant of the LORD your God, that it may be there for a witness against you.

25 When he finished, he said to the levitical priests, who were in charge of the LORD's Covenant Box, 26 "Take this book of God's Law and place it beside the Covenant Box of the LORD your God, so that it will remain there as a witness against his people.

The Levites who carried the ark of the covenant of the LORD: see verse 9; 10.8.

Put it by the side of the ark: the ark or "sacred box" itself was in the Most Holy Place in the "tent of meeting," which was separated by a curtain from the larger Holy Place (Exo 26.33-34; 40.16-21). While this book was to be placed by the side of the ark, the two stone tablets containing the Ten Commandments were placed inside the ark (10.2, 5; Exo 40.20).

A witness against you: as it stands in Hebrew and translated literally in RSV, Moses is talking to the Levites, and what he says in verses 26-27 and 29 is directed at them. But this seems hard to believe. Moses is speaking about all the Israelites, as Yahweh had done in verses 16-22. TEV makes the appropriate changes by having at the end of verse 26 ". . . as a witness against his people," then using the third plural in verse 27 and introducing "the people" as the subject in verse 29. FRCL and BRCL do the same, and translators may wish to follow their example. GECL has done it differently by adding at the end of verse 26, after the closing quotation marks of Moses' statement, the following words: "And turning to the people, he went on to say, ..." This is also a good model.

In any case it should be clear that the denunciations in verses 26-27 and 29 are directed not only at the Levites but at all the Israelites.

31.27   RSV   TEV

For I know how rebellious and stub-   I know how stubborn and rebellious
born you are; behold, while I am yet   they are. They have rebelled against
alive with you, today you have been   the LORD during my lifetime, and
rebellious against the LORD; how   they will rebel even more after I am
much more after my death!   dead.

   Rebellious and stubborn: see the two adjectives in 9.6-7.
   While I am yet alive with you, today: this does not make good sense in English. TEV and REB have "during my lifetime," NIV "while I am alive and with you," NJPSV "even now, while I am still alive in your midst."
   You have been rebellious against the LORD: see 1.26; 9.23-24.
   How much more after my death! This can be expressed more clearly as, for example, "I am sure [or, I know] that after I die you [plural] will be even more rebellious."

31.28   RSV   TEV

Assemble to me all the elders of   Assemble all your tribal leaders and
your tribes, and your officers, that I   officials before me, so that I can tell
may speak these words in their ears   them these things; I will call heaven
and call heaven and earth to witness   and earth to be my witnesses against
against them.   them.

   Assemble: here Moses is talking to the Levites (verse 25). It will be helpful for readers to put this information in the text; for example, "Then he said to the Levites, 'Assemble . . . .' "
   The elders of your tribes: for **elders** see 5.23; this is the only place in the Old Testament where this phrase occurs.
   Your officers: see 1.15.
   I may speak these words in their ears: Moses is going to speak directly to them.
   Call heaven and earth to witness against them: see 4.26 and 30.19. In the present verse the sky and the earth will be witnesses that the people of Israel know what they are supposed to do but haven't done it.

31.29   RSV   TEV

For I know that after my death you   I know that after my death the people
will surely act corruptly, and turn   will become wicked and reject what

aside from the way which I have commanded you; and in the days to come evil will befall you, because you will do what is evil in the sight of the LORD, provoking him to anger through the work of your hands."

I have taught them. And in time to come they will meet with disaster, because they will have made the LORD angry by doing what he has forbidden."

After my death you will surely act corruptly: as in 4.16, 25, this refers to idolatry (see the context of the phrase in verses 9, 12, 16). The general expression "become wicked" of TEV is not satisfactory. The rendering of CEV, "You will stop caring about what is right and what is wrong," is better.

Turn aside from the way which I have commanded you: see 11.28.

The days to come: see 4.30.

Evil will befall you, because you will do what is evil: the first use of **evil** is in the sense of "disaster," "punishment," "ruin," or "terrible things will happen to you" (CEV). In the second case **evil** is "sin," or "doing what he [God] has forbidden" (TEV). In very few languages will the same word be a satisfactory translation for the same Hebrew word, used with two different meanings.

Provoking him to anger: see 4.25.

The work of your hands: this can be taken in the limited sense of "what you have made," that is, idols, as in 4.28; so NIV has "what your hands have made." But it seems more likely that this is a general way of speaking about their wicked behavior or deeds, as a whole.

CEV has an excellent alternative translation model for this verse:

- I am going to die soon, and I know that in the future you will stop caring about what is right and what is wrong, and so you will disobey the LORD and stop living the way I told you to live. The LORD will be angry, and terrible things will happen to you.

5D. The song of Moses (31.30–32.44)

RSV

30 Then Moses spoke the words of this song until they were finished, in the ears of all the assembly of Israel:

Chapter 32

1 "Give ear, O heavens, and I will speak;
   and let the earth hear the words of my mouth.
2 May my teaching drop as the rain,
   my speech distil as the dew,
   as the gentle rain upon the tender grass,
   and as the showers upon the herb.
3 For I will proclaim the name of the LORD.
   Ascribe greatness to our God!

TEV

The Song of Moses

30 Then Moses recited the entire song while all the people of Israel listened.

Chapter 32

1 "Earth and sky, hear my words,
   listen closely to what I say.
2 My teaching will fall like drops of rain
   and form on the earth like dew.
   My words will fall like showers on young plants,
   like gentle rain on tender grass.
3 I will praise the name of the LORD,
   and his people will tell of his greatness.

527

4 "The Rock, his work is perfect;
    for all his ways are justice.
  A God of faithfulness and without iniquity,
    just and right is he.
5 They have dealt corruptly with him,
    they are no longer his children because of their blemish;
  they are a perverse and crooked generation.
6 Do you thus requite the LORD,
    you foolish and senseless people?
  Is not he your father, who created you,
    who made you and established you?
7 Remember the days of old,
    consider the years of many generations;
  ask your father, and he will show you;
    your elders, and they will tell you.
8 When the Most High gave to the nations
    their inheritance,
  when he separated the sons of men,
  he fixed the bounds of the peoples
    according to the number of the sons of God.
9 For the LORD's portion is his people,
    Jacob his allotted heritage.

10 "He found him in a desert land,
    and in the howling waste of the wilderness;
  he encircled him, he cared for him,
    he kept him as the apple of his eye.
11 Like an eagle that stirs up its nest,
    that flutters over its young,
  spreading out its wings, catching them,
    bearing them on its pinions,
12 the LORD alone did lead him,
    and there was no foreign god with him.
13 He made him ride on the high places of
    the earth,
  and he ate the produce of the field;
  and he made him suck honey out of the
    rock,
    and oil out of the flinty rock.
14 Curds from the herd, and milk from the
    flock,
  with fat of lambs and rams,
    herds of Bashan and goats,
  with the finest of the wheat—
    and of the blood of the grape you
      drank wine.
15 "But Jeshurun waxed fat, and kicked;
    you waxed fat, you grew thick, you became sleek;
  then he forsook God who made him,
    and scoffed at the Rock of his salvation.

4 "The LORD is your mighty defender,
    perfect and just in all his ways;
  Your God is faithful and true;
    he does what is right and fair.
5 But you are unfaithful, unworthy to be
    his people,
    a sinful and deceitful nation.
6 Is this the way you should treat the
    LORD,
    you foolish, senseless people?
  He is your father, your Creator,
    he made you into a nation.

7 "Think of the past, of the time long ago;
    ask your parents to tell you what happened,
    ask the old people to tell of the past.
8 The Most High assigned nations their
    lands;
    he determined where peoples should
    live.
  He assigned to each nation a heavenly
    being,
9   but Jacob's descendants he chose for
    himself.

10 "He found them wandering through the
    desert,
    a desolate, wind-swept wilderness.
  He protected them and cared for them,
    as he would protect himself.
11 Like an eagle teaching its young to fly,
    catching them safely on its spreading
    wings,
    the LORD kept Israel from falling.
12 The LORD alone led his people
    without the help of a foreign god.

13 "He let them rule the highlands,
    and they ate what grew in the fields.
  They found wild honey among the rocks;
    their olive trees flourished in stony
    ground.
14 Their cows and goats gave plenty of milk;
    they had the best sheep, goats, and
    cattle,
    the finest wheat, and the choicest
    wine.

15 "The LORD's people grew rich, but rebellious;
    they were fat and stuffed with food.
  They abandoned God their Creator
    and rejected their mighty savior.
16 Their idolatry made the LORD jealous;
    the evil they did made him angry.
17 They sacrificed to gods that are not real,
    new gods their ancestors had never
    known,
    gods that Israel had never obeyed.

16 They stirred him to jealousy with strange
    gods;
    with abominable practices they pro-
       voked him to anger.
17 They sacrificed to demons which were no
    gods,
    to gods they had never known,
    to new gods that had come in of late,
    whom your fathers had never dreaded.
18 You were unmindful of the Rock that
    begot you,
    and you forgot the God who gave you
       birth.

19 "The LORD saw it, and spurned them,
    because of the provocation of his sons
       and his daughters.
20 And he said, 'I will hide my face from
    them,
    I will see what their end will be,
    for they are a perverse generation,
    children in whom is no faithfulness.
21 They have stirred me to jealousy with
       what is no god;
    they have provoked me with their
       idols.
    So I will stir them to jealousy with those
       who are no people;
    I will provoke them with a foolish na-
       tion.
22 For a fire is kindled by my anger,
    and it burns to the depths of Sheol,
    devours the earth and its increase,
    and sets on fire the foundations of the
       mountains.

23 " 'And I will heap evils upon them;
    I will spend my arrows upon them;
24 they shall be wasted with hunger,
    and devoured with burning heat
    and poisonous pestilence;
    and I will send the teeth of beasts against
    them,
    with venom of crawling things of the
       dust.
25 In the open the sword shall bereave,
    and in the chambers shall be terror,
    destroying both young man and virgin,
    the sucking child with the man of gray
       hairs.
26 I would have said, "I will scatter them
    afar,
    I will make the remembrance of them
       cease from among men,"
27 had I not feared provocation by the ene-
    my,
    lest their adversaries should judge
       amiss,
    lest they should say, "Our hand is trium-
       phant,

18 They forgot their God, their mighty sav-
    ior,
    the one who had given them life.
19 "When the LORD saw this, he was angry
    and rejected his sons and daughters.
20 'I will no longer help them,' he said;
    'then I will see what happens to them,
    those stubborn, unfaithful people.
21 With their idols they have made me an-
    gry,
    jealous with their so-called gods,
    gods that are really not gods.
    So I will use a so-called nation to make
       them angry;
    I will make them jealous with a nation
       of fools.
22 My anger will flame up like fire
    and burn everything on earth.
    It will reach to the world below
    and consume the roots of the moun-
       tains.

23 " 'I will bring on them endless disasters
    and use all my arrows against them.
24 They will die from hunger and fever;
    they will die from terrible diseases.
    I will send wild animals to attack them,
    and poisonous snakes to bite them.
25 War will bring death in the streets;
    terrors will strike in the homes.
    Young men and young women will die;
    neither babies nor old people will be
       spared.
26 I would have destroyed them completely,
    so that no one would remember them.
27 But I could not let their enemies boast
    that they had defeated my people,
    when it was I myself who had crushed
       them.'

28 "Israel is a nation without sense;
    they have no wisdom at all.
29 They fail to see why they were defeated;
    they cannot understand what
       happened.
30 Why were a thousand defeated by one,
    and ten thousand by only two?
    The LORD, their God, had abandoned
       them;
    their mighty God had given them up.
31 Their enemies know that their own gods
    are weak,
    not mighty like Israel's God.
32 Their enemies, corrupt as Sodom and Go-
    morrah,
    are like vines that bear bitter and poi-
       sonous grapes,
33 like wine made from the venom of
    snakes.

the LORD has not wrought all this.' "

28 "For they are a nation void of counsel,
    and there is no understanding in
        them.
29 If they were wise, they would understand
        this,
    they would discern their latter end!
30 How should one chase a thousand,
    and two put ten thousand to flight,
unless their Rock had sold them,
    and the LORD had given them up?
31 For their rock is not as our Rock,
    even our enemies themselves being
        judges.
32 For their vine comes from the vine of Sod-
        om,
    and from the fields of Gomorrah;
their grapes are grapes of poison,
    their clusters are bitter;
33 their wine is the poison of serpents,
    and the cruel venom of asps.

34 "Is not this laid up in store with me,
    sealed up in my treasuries?
35 Vengeance is mine, and recompense,
    for the time when their foot shall slip;
for the day of their calamity is at hand,
    and their doom comes swiftly.
36 For the LORD will vindicate his people
    and have compassion on his servants,
when he sees that their power is gone,
    and there is none remaining, bond or
        free.
37 Then he will say, 'Where are their gods,
    the rock in which they took refuge,
38 who ate the fat of their sacrifices,
    and drank the wine of their drink
        offering?
Let them rise up and help you,
    let them be your protection!

39 " 'See now that I, even I, am he,
    and there is no god beside me;
I kill and I make alive;
    I wound and I heal;
    and there is none that can deliver out
        of my hand.
40 For I lift up my hand to heaven,
    and swear, As I live for ever,
41 if I whet my glittering sword,
    and my hand takes hold on judgment,
I will take vengeance on my adversaries,
    and will requite those who hate me.
42 I will make my arrows drunk with blood,
    and my sword shall devour flesh—
with the blood of the slain and the cap-
        tives,
    from the long-haired heads of the ene-
        my.'

34 "The LORD remembers what their ene-
        mies have done;
    he waits for the right time to punish
        them.
35 The LORD will take revenge and punish
        them;
    the time will come when they will fall;
    the day of their doom is near.
36 The LORD will rescue his people
    when he sees that their strength is
        gone.
He will have mercy on those who serve
        him,
    when he sees how helpless they are.
37 Then the LORD will ask his people,
    'Where are those mighty gods you
        trusted?
38 You fed them the fat of your sacrifices
    and offered them wine to drink.
Let them come and help you now;
    let them run to your rescue.

39 " 'I, and I alone, am God;
    no other god is real.
I kill and I give life, I wound and I heal,
    and no one can oppose what I do.
40 As surely as I am the living God,
    I raise my hand and I vow
41   that I will sharpen my flashing sword
    and see that justice is done.
I will take revenge on my enemies
    and punish those who hate me.
42 My arrows will drip with their blood,
    and my sword will kill all who oppose
        me.
I will spare no one who fights against me;
    even the wounded and prisoners will
        die.'

43 "Nations, you must praise the LORD's
        people—
    he punishes all who kill them.
He takes revenge on his enemies
    and forgives the sins of his people."

44 Moses and Joshua son of Nun recited
this song, so that the people of Israel could
hear it.

43 "Praise his people, O you nations;
　　for he avenges the blood of his ser-
　　　vants,
　and takes vengeance on his adversaries,
　　and makes expiation for the land of his
　　　people."
44 Moses came and recited all the words of
this song in the hearing of the people, he and
Joshua the son of Nun.

This long poetic section is often referred to as "The song of Moses." For a discussion of translating Hebrew poetry, with illustrations from this section and chapter 33, please refer to the section "Translating poetry" in "Translating Deuteronomy," pages 7 and following.

Section heading: the TEV title for this section is "The Song of Moses." This will be satisfactory in some languages, while in others, perhaps, a fuller form will be better: "The song that God ordered Moses to recite to the people," or "God orders Moses to write a song in a book."

31.30　　　　RSV　　　　　　　　　　　　TEV

Then Moses spoke the words of this song until they were finished, in the ears of all the assembly of Israel:　　**Then Moses recited the entire song while all the people of Israel listened.**

Spoke the words of this song until they were finished: TEV "recited the entire song" is today's English and contains all the information present in the Hebrew text. NRSV "recited the words of this song to the very end" is somewhat more formal.

In the ears of all the assembly of Israel: this indicates that the people were all gathered together to hear Moses recite the song. Besides the TEV text, a possible translation is "as all the people of Israel listened attentively"; but the term **assembly** really includes the sense that Moses called everyone together for a special meeting where he recited the words of this song. CEV follows this interpretation, with:

● 　　Moses called a meeting of all the people of Israel so he could
　　　teach them the words to the song that the LORD had given to him.
　　　And here are the words . . . .

32.1　　　　　　　　　　RSV

**"Give ear, O heavens, and I will speak;
　　and let the earth hear the words of my mouth.**

TEV

"Earth and sky, hear my words,
listen closely to what I say.

A.D. Mayes sees verses 1-25 of the song as a charge that God brings against his people in a court of law, and finds the following structure:

(1) Introduction: witnesses are summoned (verses 1-3);
(2) Introductory statement of the issue at hand (verses 4-6);
(3) Presentation speech, recalling Yahweh's good actions on behalf of the people (verses 7-14);
(4) Indictment: Israel is charged with apostasy (verses 15-18);
(5) Declaration of guilt and threat of punishment (verses 19-25).

Translators should be aware of this and should divide the text into paragraphs in such a way as to reflect this structure.

Give ear, O heavens . . . and let the earth hear: both **heavens** and **earth** are addressed as living beings and are summoned as witnesses (see 30.19). Unless absolutely necessary, the simple "heaven" and "earth" should be used; to say "inhabitants of heaven" and "inhabitants of earth" diminishes considerably the force and beauty of the text. Instead of **heavens** many languages will prefer "sky" (so TEV and CEV).

I will speak . . . the words of my mouth: these expressions mean exactly the same thing. The translator must determine in every instance whether the use of pairs of expressions like this makes for an effective style; in some languages the constant use of this device sounds unnatural and makes the text less appealing. TEV and CEV put **heavens** and **earth** together in the first line, and CEV combines the two lines as follows:

●   Earth and sky,
                    listen to what I say!

32.2   RSV

May my teaching drop as the rain,
my speech distil as the dew,
as the gentle rain upon the tender grass,
and as the showers upon the herb.

TEV

My teaching will fall like drops of rain
and form on the earth like dew.
My words will fall like showers on young plants,
like gentle rain on tender grass.

The first two lines are parallel, having approximately the same meaning, and the last two are also in parallel lines and modify the verbs of the first two lines. A translator should determine whether a restructuring of the verse would make it easier to understand. See two different types of restructuring in TEV and in the CEV model given at the end of the comments on this verse.

May . . . : this comes as a wish, an effective way to begin a speech, especially one that is going to charge the accused party of evil conduct. The speaker promises that he will not be threatening or blustering, but he hopes to convince his hearers by means of a gentle and mild statement of facts. Where the equivalent of the English verb form for expressing a wish, "may," is not natural or available in a language, a translator should find the most natural way of expressing a desire. Examples are "I want [or, wish] that my teaching will . . ." or "I pray that . . . ."

Drop as rain . . . distil as the dew: TEV "will fall" fails to express the poetic quality of the Hebrew **drop**. CEV softens the effect by combining lines b and c of the verse as follows:

- My words will be like gentle rain
  on tender young plants.

For the figure of **rain** dropping, see 33.28; Job 29.22-23. As for **dew**, the verb **distil** in English is a correct rendering of the Hebrew, but not natural; to distil a liquid is to vaporize it and then allow it to condense so as to remove impurities. People more naturally speak of dew "forming" or "condensing" (TEV, NIV), and in some languages the word for **dew** will be something like "water that clings." And even though dew does not actually fall, as rain does, in some languages this will be the most natural way to speak of dew. The point of this figure of speech is the speaker's hope that his audience will listen with sympathy to what he is about to say; see the NJPSV footnote: "(that is), may my words be received eagerly."

Gentle rain . . . showers: these two have almost the same meaning; the Hebrew term for the first one appears only here in the Old Testament.

The tender grass . . . the herb: again, two nouns that are close in meaning. In these and similar instances the translator should not be too concerned to match the original text with two very similar terms in his or her language, especially if one of the two happens to be a very specialized term not used by the majority of speakers. TEV has a good model: "young plants . . . tender grass."

The CEV translation of the whole verse is a good model:

- Israel, I will teach you.
  My words will be like gentle rain
  on tender young plants,
  or like dew on the grass.

32.3   RSV

> For I will proclaim the name of the LORD.
> Ascribe greatness to our God!

TEV

> I will praise the name of the LORD,
> and his people will tell of his greatness.

These two lines are not parallel; the first one is a declaration, the second a command for the people to tell about Yahweh's greatness. REB joins the two lines: "When I proclaim the name of the LORD, you will respond . . . ." This is a possibility.

Proclaim the name of the LORD: this does not mean only that he will utter it, or tell people what the name is, but he will "praise" it (TEV), "exalt" it; **the name** usually stands for the person. Mayes comments that the expression means "to make open declaration of his character as shown in his actions with his people and with individuals also." One possible translation is "I will tell how great the LORD is."

Ascribe greatness: the Hebrew has "Give greatness," as though **greatness** were an object that can be given to God. This can be handled in different ways. For example, NIV has "Oh, praise the greatness," NJB "Oh, tell the greatness," and NJPSV "Give glory to our God." It means to recognize and confess the greatness of God. We may also express this as "All you people should tell Yahweh how great he is," or "All you people should say, 'Yahweh is wonderful!'"

32.4   RSV

> "The Rock, his work is perfect;
>   for all his ways are justice.
> A God of faithfulness and without iniquity,
>   just and right is he.

TEV

> "The LORD is your mighty defender,
>   perfect and just in all his ways;
> Your God is faithful and true;
>   he does what is right and fair.

In verses 4-6 Moses makes a brief statement of the reason for this charge against the people of Israel.

The Rock: a title for God; the Septuagint, in all places where this title appears in this song (also verses 15, 18, 30), translates "God." The main idea of the metaphor (as in Psa 18.2) is that of defense, protection. FRCL has "The Lord is a protecting rock," CEV "The LORD is a mighty rock"; but in some languages it may not be satisfactory to use simply a word for "rock." BRCL, SPCL translate the meaning of the metaphor: "He is our protector"; POCL has "He is our refuge," while REB has "the Creator," drawing from verse 18, where God is spoken of as Creator. TEV has "your mighty defender," using the second person plural pronoun as required by what is coming in verse 5. It is recommended that the meaning be expressed by "strong defender," "mighty protector," or the like.

His work is perfect . . . all his ways are justice: the first two lines of the verse have almost the same meaning; one refers to Yahweh's actions, the other to his manner of doing things. TEV has "perfect and just in all his ways."

A God of faithfulness and without iniquity: these final two lines expand on what was said about God in line two. The first quality, **faithfulness**, describes God as someone who does what he says he will do, who keeps his promise: "a trustworthy God" (NJB). We may also say "You can always trust what he promises," or even "He always does what he promises to do." The second quality, **without iniquity**, describes him as never doing anything wrong; in this context, however, it may be that NJPSV "A faithful God, never false," is closer to the meaning, the second term being the negative way of stating what the first one says. Another way to express this is "and never breaks his promises [or, words]."

Just and right: these are very close in meaning, with the sense of "true," "upright," "honest," "fair."

32.5   RSV

> They have dealt corruptly with him,
>   they are no longer his children because of their blemish;
>   they are a perverse and crooked generation.

TEV

> But you are unfaithful, unworthy to be his people,[b]
>   a sinful and deceitful nation.

[b] *Probable text* But you . . . people; *Hebrew unclear.*

Except for the line **they are a perverse and crooked generation**, this verse in Hebrew is very difficult. Moses is talking about the people of Israel. NRSV translates the first line in Hebrew as "yet his degenerate children have dealt falsely with him," with a footnote stating that the meaning of the Hebrew is uncertain; NJPSV and NIV have alternative renderings in footnotes.

HOTTP ({B} rating) proposes the following:

> it [that is, the generation of the last line] has dealt perversely with him, they are no longer his children (that is their blemish).

HOTTP also suggests that a note should be added: " '(that is their blemish)' perhaps a gloss." This may be a good model for those translations in which the

note "perhaps a gloss" is helpful; but in many translations a note like this will
hinder rather than help. In such cases a translator can use the TEV as a model,
with the footnote "Hebrew unclear."

The first thing to do when translating is to clearly establish who RSV **They**
are. TEV and CEV do well by introducing at once "You," that is, the people of
Israel; but we may also say "You people of Israel . . . ."

The following is proposed as a model, translating along the lines suggested
by HOTTP:

●   But you have sinned against the LORD,
             and because of your faults
             you are no longer his children;
             you are a wicked and deceitful people.

It is important that readers should understand this verse as an accusation
and not just as a statement of fact. See similar language in 9.12.

32.6   RSV

        Do you thus requite the LORD,
            you foolish and senseless people?
        Is not he your father, who created you,
            who made you and established you?

                                     TEV

        Is this the way you should treat the LORD,
            you foolish, senseless people?
        He is your father, your Creator,
            he made you into a nation.

Requite the LORD: the verb **requite** means to repay or to pay back; so REB says
"is this how you repay the LORD?" In a more general sense "how you treat the
LORD" is a possibility (similarly TEV).

Foolish and senseless: two terms almost the same in meaning; other
possibilities are "stupid," "dull," "witless." The sense of "ignorant" is not
primary; it is not a lack of information but a lack of good judgment—even being
stupid. So BRCL has "a people without any good sense or wisdom." The first two
lines may be reversed as follows:

●   You are foolish and stupid people,
             Is this the way you repay the LORD?

The second question is also an accusation.

Your father, who created you: the verb **created** means to "bring into being,"
to "give life." It is different from the verb used in Gen 1.1, but it is the same
verb used in Gen 4.1, where it is said to be the origin of the name "Cain" (see

also Exo 15.16); so NRSV has "the people whom you have acquired." But if the equivalent of the verb "acquire" is used, care must be taken that it is not understood as a purchase, with a price paid to someone, as the NIV footnote "who bought you" suggests. This Handbook recommends that translators use the word "create" or "Creator" in the text (with TEV, CEV, and NIV), with a footnote saying, for example, "Or *Father, who acquired you.*"

Who made you and established you: the verb "make" is the one most generally used of making something; to "establish" means to make secure or strong. The text is talking about how God **made** the people of Israel into a nation, a people of his own; this happened when he brought them out of Egypt. So TEV has "he made you into a nation." Translators are advised to follow TEV as a model for this verse.

32.7 RSV

> Remember the days of old,
> consider the years of many generations;
> ask your father, and he will show you;
> your elders, and they will tell you.

TEV

> "Think of the past, of the time long ago;
> ask your parents to tell you what happened,
> ask the old people to tell of the past.

Here begins the presentation or prosecution speech (verses 7-14), in which Yahweh's good actions on behalf of the people are described.

Remember . . . consider: two verbs that are close in meaning; **remember** means to "think back," to "recall,"; to **consider** is to "ponder," or "reflect."

The days of old . . . the years of many generations: again two expressions that are very close in meaning. See similar language in 4.32. Once more the translator is reminded that if two similar expressions like this seem artificial and unnatural, one will do. TEV has "think of the past, of the time long ago"; but CEV combines the two lines, with "Think about past generations."

Ask your father . . . your elders: two terms for older people; **elders** here is used in the sense of "older people." And **father** is not necessarily only the male parent; see CEV "your parents or any of your elders."

Show you . . . tell you: again two verbs that mean exactly the same thing. We may combine the two lines as follows: "They will tell you." However, in some languages it will be necessary to give the content of "tell"; for example, "They will tell you about those days long ago." The final part of the verse may then be translated as:

- Ask your parents or any of the older people.
  They will tell you about those days long ago.

32.8   RSV

> **When the Most High gave to the nations their inheritance,**
>   **when he separated the sons of men,**
> **he fixed the bounds of the peoples**
>   **according to the number of the sons of God.**[d]

   [d] Compare Gk: Heb *Israel*

TEV

> **The Most High assigned nations their lands;**
>   **he determined where peoples should live.**
> **He assigned to each nation a heavenly being,**

The Most High: a title for Yahweh as the greatest of all gods (see Psa 47.2). Another way to express this is "God, who is above [or, greater than] all other gods."

Gave to the nations their inheritance: Yahweh "gave" (CEV) or assigned land, territory, for each nation to possess as its own. For **inheritance** see 4.21.

When he separated the sons of men: NRSV "divided humankind" is a better expression of the meaning. This states that Yahweh divided the human race into distinct and separate ethnic groups or nations. This line and the previous line have practically the same meaning, and in a number of languages they may be combined; for example, "When God, who is greater than all other gods, gave land to every nation."

He fixed the bounds of the peoples: Yahweh divided the surface of the earth among the different peoples, and for each nation he set the boundaries of its territory. TEV has a good model: "he determined where peoples should live."

According to the number of the sons of God: the RSV footnote says "Compare Greek; Heb *Israel*." The Hebrew text is literally "the number of the sons of Israel," meaning "the number of Israelites"; the Septuagint has "according to the number of angels." The NRSV text is more accurate: "according to the number of gods." Its footnote explains that this is based on some Qumran manuscripts as well as the Septuagint, and gives the rendering of the Hebrew as "the Israelites." HOTTP ({A} rating) takes "number of gods" to be the correct text, and it should be translated. The sense is that, in accordance with the number of gods, Yahweh divided humankind into separate peoples, so that each people would have its own god; and Yahweh reserved Israel to be his own people (see 4.19-20). An alternative model, then, is "He determined where each nation should live, each with its own god, which he chose."

32.9   RSV

> **For the LORD's portion is his people,**
>   **Jacob his allotted heritage.**

TEV

but Jacob's descendants he chose for himself.

The LORD's portion . . . his allotted heritage: two expressions that mean the same; see a similar thought in 7.6; 10.15. The passage must not be read as though someone else had allotted Yahweh the people of Israel as his own possession; it is Yahweh himself who does this, who decides that Israel will be his own people. The following verses 10-14 show how Yahweh did this.

His people . . . Jacob: these terms have the same sense; **Jacob** here is a way of talking about the people of Israel.

Another possible model for this verse is:

●   but the LORD himself
          is the God of the people of Israel
          [or, is the God of Jacob's descendants].

32.10   RSV

"He found him in a desert land,
    and in the howling waste of the wilderness;
he encircled him, he cared for him,
    he kept him as the apple of his eye.

TEV

"He found them wandering through the desert,
    a desolate, wind-swept wilderness.
He protected them and cared for them,
    as he would protect himself.

He found him in a desert land: this is a picturesque way of talking about Yahweh and the people of Israel during the Israelites' forty-year trek through the wilderness on their way to the land of Canaan. The language should be retained, meaning that God happened to find the people on their way to Canaan. In many languages **him** should be changed to "them." However, it is also possible to change **him** to "you [plural]" and say "Israel, Yahweh found you [plural] wandering in the desert," or even "People of Israel, Yahweh found you . . . ."

The howling waste of the wilderness: see a description of the wilderness in 8.15. **The howling waste** is an expression meaning uninhabited, desolate, dreary territory. It is possible to take **howling waste** to refer to a desolate wilderness with howling winds sweeping through it. So TEV has "a desolate, wind-swept wilderness, " and CEV translates "a barren desert, filled with howling winds."

He encircled . . . he cared: the verb **encircled** does not indicate a threatening move to capture, but a gesture of love. POCL has "surrounded with care," NRSV "shielded," TEV "protected," SPCL "embraced him in his arms." **Cared** translates a form of the verb which appears only here in the Old Testament; some, like SPCL, understand it in the light of the Septuagint, "he instructed him." The more general term "care for," however, seems preferable.

He kept him as the apple of his eye: indicating the worth of Israel to God. The phrase **the apple of his eye** (also Pro 7.2; Psa 17.8) is literally "the little man" in the eye. Different languages have their own expression for this; Spanish and Portuguese say "the girl of the eyes." The English word "pupil" (of the eye) comes from Latin *pupilla*, "little doll." A more general translation is "just as he takes care of his own eyes," or "just as though you were his own eyes."

A possible alternative translation model for this verse is:

●   People of Israel, Yahweh found you [plural]
            wandering through a desolate wilderness,
            filled with howling winds.
        He protected you, and cared for you
            just like he takes care of his own eyes.

32.11   RSV

    Like an eagle that stirs up its nest,
        that flutters over its young,
    spreading out its wings, catching them,
        bearing them on its pinions,

                TEV

    Like an eagle teaching its young to fly,[c]
    catching them safely on its spreading wings,
    the LORD kept Israel from falling.

[c] teaching its young to fly; *or* watching over its young.

Like an eagle that stirs up its nest: of the four lines in this verse, the meaning of this line is the most difficult to determine. NRSV is the same as RSV; other renderings are NJPSV "Like an eagle who rouses his nestlings," POCL "like an eagle keeping watch over its young who are in the nest," NJB "Like an eagle watching its nest," REB "As an eagle watches over its young." The Hebrew verb usually means to "disturb" or "stir up"; but the meaning "watch" found in the Septuagint is defended by some and is the meaning given by REB and NJB, and it is an alternative rendering given in the TEV footnote. This meaning is the one recommended here. So we may also say something like "Yahweh is like an eagle watching over its young in the nest."

An eagle: in cultures where eagles are unknown, some other large bird of prey may be used. See a picture of an eagle at 14.12, and see FFB, pages 82-85.

That flutters over its young: the verb in this line is the same one used in Gen 1.2 of the spirit (or, wind) of God hovering over the abyss. TEV "teaching its young to fly" (also CEV) follows the Vulgate, *provocans ad volandum*, "enticing [its young] to fly." This, however, is most unlikely, and it is recommended that the RSV rendering be followed.

Spreading out its wings, catching them: RSV and other translations take this line and the next one to apply to the eagle and its young. But a number of commentaries and translations take this line and the next one to apply to Yahweh and his people, not to the eagle and its young. So NJPSV says "so did he spread his wings and take them" (also Osty, *Pléiade*).

The last line, **bearing them on its pinions**, therefore refers also to God, not to the eagle. So God "carries them on his wings"; the Hebrew word for "wings" here is different from the one used in the previous line. For the figure of God doing this for his people, see Exo 19.4.

A possible alternative translation model for this verse is:

•
> The LORD is like an eagle guarding its nest,
>   and hovering over its young.
> The LORD is always ready to spread his wings
>   and catch his people when they are falling.

32.12   RSV

> the LORD alone did lead him,
>   and there was no foreign god with him.

TEV

> The LORD alone led his people
>   without the help of a foreign god.

The LORD alone did lead him: here the figure changes from the LORD carrying his people on his wings to leading them on their way; **him** refers to the people of Israel. So we may translate "The LORD alone led his people" (TEV), or "Israel, the LORD led you" CEV).

There was no foreign god with him: this verse emphasizes that Yahweh did this alone, without help from any pagan god—thereby proving that Israel belongs to him alone (see TEV).

32.13   RSV

> He made him ride on the high places of the earth,
>   and he ate the produce of the field;
> and he made him suck honey out of the rock,
>   and oil out of the flinty rock.

TEV

"He let them rule the highlands,
  and they ate what grew in the fields.
They found wild honey among the rocks;
  their olive trees flourished in stony ground.

Here the song begins to tell the story of the Israelites in the land of Canaan, after they settled down and became a strong, prosperous people.

He made him ride on the high places of the earth: the exact origin of the verbal phrase **He made him ride** (also Isa 58.14) is unknown. It seems to imply riding on an animal, perhaps a horse, but this cannot be proven. The usual phrase is "to walk [or, stride] on the high places" (see 33.29; Psa 18.33; Amos 4.13; Micah 1.3). But the meaning of this figure is quite clear; it means to be given possession of, to conquer, to own, to rule. Yahweh gave Israel the highlands of Canaan; so NJPSV says "He set him atop the highlands" (see 8.7-9; Exo 15.17). This is not steep, mountainous country as such, but the highlands, as compared with the seacoast and lowland plains. The verbal phrase **made him ride on** is a poetic figure that means to give possession of or dominion over. Another way to express this sentence is "He let them [or, you] rule in the high country of Canaan."

He ate the produce of the field: here the valleys and plains are joined to the highlands. Following the Samaritan text, the Septuagint, Syriac, and Targum, NRSV has "and fed him" (that is, God fed Israel). HOTTP prefers the Hebrew Text, however ({A} rating), and this should be followed. **He** here, of course, refers to the Israelites. So in many languages something like "they [or, you] ate what grew in the fields" will be more satisfactory.

He made him suck honey out of the rock: the verb **made him suck** is figurative language in which to "suckle" a child is a picture of God tenderly feeding his people (see Gen 21.7). The text is talking about wild beehives found among clefts of rocks and crags, where the Israelites would get honey (see the figure in Isa 7.18-19). So TEV has "they found wild honey among the rocks."

And oil out of the flinty rock: this is olive oil, and the meaning is that olive trees were growing on rocky hillsides. TEV offers a good model for the translation of the last part of the verse.

32.14   RSV

Curds from the herd, and milk from the flock,
  with fat of lambs and rams,
  herds of Bashan and goats,
with the finest of the wheat—
  and of the blood of the grape you drank wine.

TEV

Their cows and goats gave plenty of milk;
 they had the best sheep, goats, and cattle,
 the finest wheat, and the choicest wine.

RSV begins a new sentence that is not a true sentence but a series of noun phrases. In most languages it is better to begin a new sentence with a subject and verb: "He fed them with," "He sustained them with," or "He provided them with."

Curds from the herd, and milk from the flock: the first expression refers to sour milk, or **curds** (something like cottage cheese) or yogurt from cows' milk (see Gen 18.5), and the second expression refers to goats' **milk**. An alternative model for these first lines is:

● He [Yahweh] fed them [or, you] with curds [or, yogurt] from their [or, your] cows, and milk from their [or, your] goats.

Fat of lambs and rams, herds of Bashan and goats: **rams** are male sheep, and **herds of Bashan** are cows and bulls. The word **fat** here means, in a general way, well-fed, fat animals.

Besides herds and flocks of animals, the Israelites had good crops (**the finest of the wheat**), and fine wine from their vineyards (**of the blood of the grape you drank wine**). Notice the shift to the second person **you**; it is better to stay with the third person and not change, if a translator has been using the third person throughout; but some translators will have been using the second person pronoun since verse 10. So we may translate "He gave you the finest wheat and the best wine."

At the end of this verse, the Samaritan text and the Septuagint add "Jacob ate and was well fed." HOTTP supports this ({C} rating) and recommends that it be included. Among major modern translations, REB and NJB do so. If a translator decides to include it, he or she can say something like the following: "They [or, You] had all they [or, you] needed, and grew prosperous."

32.15 RSV

"But Jeshurun waxed fat, and kicked;
 you waxed fat, you grew thick, you became sleek;
 then he forsook God who made him,
 and scoffed at the Rock of his salvation.

TEV

"The LORD's people grew rich, but rebellious;
 they were fat and stuffed with food.
 They abandoned God their Creator
 and rejected their mighty savior.

Jeshurun: this is an affectionate name for the people of Israel, and it appears also in 33.5, 26: Isa 44.2; in all instances the Septuagint translates "Jacob." **Jeshurun** means "the upright one." If the name is used in the text, a footnote like the one in NIV should be used: "*Jeshurun* means *the upright one*, that is, Israel." In most languages it will be better to use "Israel" or "Yahweh's people" in the text.

Kicked: that is, "rebelled." For a description of rebellion see 8.12-17.

You waxed fat . . . grew thick . . . became sleek: these are successive stages in the process of becoming fat and prosperous (see 31.20). In this context **sleek** means well-fed, healthy, even prosperous. Notice the change from the third person of narration to the second person of address. The second line of the verse expands what is said in the first line; see point 2 in the section about "Translation of Poetry" in "Translating Deuteronomy" at the beginning of the Handbook (page 8). It is thus possible to combine the two lines as follows:

● People of Israel, you grew rich and revolted against God . . . .

He forsook: another change of person; see 31.16. However, "you [plural]" may be kept by translators who have been using the second person pronoun throughout.

Scoffed: NIV and TEV take it to mean "rejected," as a closer parallel to **forsook**. NJPSV translates "spurned" (see its use in Jer 14.21; but the meaning "treat with contempt" is to be found in Micah 7.6; Nahum 3.6). See below for a way to combine these two verbs.

The Rock of his salvation: that is, the Rock (see verse 4) who saved them. Translators should be careful that the translation of the final two lines doesn't seem to refer to two separate deities, one who is **the God who made him** and the other **the Rock of his salvation**. Since **scoffed at** and **forsook** in the previous line are so close in meaning, it is possible to combine the information in the final two lines as follows:

● They [or, You] rejected God their [or, your] Creator,
   the one who is their [or, your] mighty savior.

32.16   RSV

They stirred him to jealousy with strange gods;
with abominable practices they provoked him to anger.

                                           TEV

Their idolatry made the LORD jealous;
the evil they did made him angry.

Stirred him to jealousy: see 4.24. God is spoken of in very human terms, as though he were a husband made jealous by the adulterous (extramarital) affairs of his wife.

Strange gods: the Hebrew is simply "strangers"; the meaning here is "pagan gods," "gods of other nations." Another way to express this is "They [or, You] caused Yahweh to be jealous when you worshiped foreign gods."

Abominable practices: the poetic form places this Hebrew term in parallel with the idols of the first line; therefore this term refers, not the rites of worship of pagan gods as such, but to the idols themselves, as in verse 21 (see 7.25). So NRSV has "abhorrent things," and CEV "disgusting idols."

Provoked him to anger: see 4.25; 31.17.

CEV restructures the verse in a helpful way:

•   You made God jealous and angry
                     by worshiping disgusting idols
                         and foreign gods.

32.17   RSV

They sacrificed to demons which were no gods,
    to gods they had never known,
to new gods that had come in of late,
    whom your fathers had never dreaded.

TEV

They sacrificed to gods that are not real,
    new gods their ancestors had never known,
    gods that Israel had never obeyed.

This verse is one sentence in Hebrew, but in some languages more than one sentence may be needed. Translators should use a style that is appropriate and natural in their language.

They sacrificed to demons: "to sacrifice" means to offer sacrifices, usually of animals. Only here and in Psa 106.37 does this noun occur. **Demons** refers to the "foreign gods," who were thought of as representing demons. Some translators may wish to keep the word **demons** ("dirty or evil spirits") and translate similarly to CEV:

•   You offered sacrifices
                     to demons, those useless gods

Which were no gods: that is, they were not really divine, but demonic; so TEV says "gods that are not real." But the Hebrew text may be translated "not to God" (NRSV), and this seems preferable. See 1 Cor 10.20. So "rather than offering them [the sacrifices or animals] to God" will be a good model.

Gods they had never known: see 9.24.

New gods that had come in of late: that is, gods they got to know after they had settled in Canaan. This does not mean that those gods had arrived recently in Canaan, but that they had recently become known to the Israelites. So we may say "gods they [or, you] had just come to know."

Whom your fathers had never dreaded: the verb is more or less parallel with **never known** of two lines above. It is used of religious awe, reverence, or respect. As elsewhere, **fathers** means ancestors.

An alternative translation model for this verse is:

- They [or, You] offered sacrifices to foreign gods
  rather than offering them to God.
  These were gods that they [or, you] had just come to know,
  gods that your ancestors had never worshiped

32.18   RSV

> **You were unmindful of the Rock that begot you,ᵉ**
> **and you forgot the God who gave you birth.**

ᵉ Or *bore*

TEV

> **They forgot their God, their mighty savior,**
> **the one who had given them life.**

You were unmindful . . . you forgot: the two verbs mean the same thing and indicate a gradual apostasy on the part of the Israelites; they neglected and finally abandoned their own God.

The Rock: see verse 4; here REB translates "the Creator."

That begot you . . . who gave you birth: as the RSV footnote indicates, the first verb may mean "who bore you," which is the text of NRSV. In Gen 4.18 it means "beget"; but most often it means "bear," as a mother. The second verb is that of a mother giving birth, using a female figure for God. The first verb may be of a father (**begot**) or of a mother ("bore"). It is not really possible to decide this one way or the other. Some suggest that the writer deliberately used a male figure and a female figure; but it seems more reasonable to suppose that the two parallel lines have the same meaning, in both of them God being compared to a mother. It is recommended that this interpretation be followed. See similar sayings in Isa 49.15; 66.13.

The CEV translation is a good model for translators to follow:

- You turned away
  from God, your Creator;
  you forgot the Mighty Rock,
  the source of your life.

But it is important to retain the image of God as mother, so it is preferable to translate:

●   You rejected the mighty Savior,
            the one who bore you.
         You turned away from the God
            who gave you birth.

32.19   RSV

**"The LORD saw it, and spurned them,
     because of the provocation of his sons and his daughters.**

                                  TEV

**"When the LORD saw this, he was angry
     and rejected his sons and daughters.**

In verses 19-25 the sentence is passed: Israel is guilty and will be punished.

The LORD saw it: he **saw** or noticed that the Israelites had turned away from him. In some languages it will be good to supply this information; for example, "When the LORD saw that they [or, you] had turned away from him."

Spurned: this means he rejected them; no longer would they be his people.

The provocation of his sons and his daughters: that is, they provoked him, or made him angry; see the verb in verse 21. TEV rearranges the text for greater ease of understanding, as does NJPSV: "The LORD saw this and was vexed, and spurned His sons and His daughters."

We may reorder the clauses of this verse as follows:

●   You were the LORD's children,
            but you made him angry
            when he saw that you had turned away from him.
         So he rejected you, [20] and said,

32.20   RSV

**And he said, 'I will hide my face from them,
     I will see what their end will be,
 for they are a perverse generation,
     children in whom is no faithfulness.**

                                  TEV

**'I will no longer help them,' he said;
     'then I will see what happens to them,
     those stubborn, unfaithful people.**

And he said: this marks the beginning of Yahweh's words, which continue almost to the end of the song; from this point to the end of verse 42, "I" and "me" refer to Yahweh. But see comments below about problems in translating third person references to Yahweh within this direct speech.

I will hide my face from them: see 31.17-18.

I will see what their end will be: that is, "I will see what will happen to them." God speaks here as a spectator; he does not affirm that he himself will be responsible for what becomes of them. CEV translates "I'll just watch and see what happens to you" (similarly TEV).

A perverse generation: see verse 5.

Children in whom is no faithfulness: that is, "unfaithful children," who do not respect or obey God their Father.

We may restructure this verse as follows:

- You are unfaithful people
    and I can't trust you.
  So I won't help you any longer;
  I'll just watch
    and see what happens to you.

32.21   RSV

  They have stirred me to jealousy with what is no god;
    they have provoked me with their idols.
  So I will stir them to jealousy with those who are no people;
    I will provoke them with a foolish nation.

                            TEV

  With their idols they have made me angry,
    jealous with their so-called gods,
    gods that are really not gods.
  So I will use a so-called nation to make them angry;
    I will make them jealous with a nation of fools.

Stirred me to jealousy: see verse 16; this is parallel with **they have provoked me**, or "made me angry" (see 31.29).

What is no god: see verse 17; this is parallel with **their idols** in the next line. The TEV rendering "so-called gods" is difficult to translate. Something like "worthless and false gods" will be easier.

I will stir them to jealousy . . . I will provoke them: God will do to his people exactly what they have done to him—a perfect payback. Two alternative ways of combining these first two lines are:

- You worshiped worthless idols
    and made me jealous and angry.

- You made me jealous and angry
  because you worshiped worthless idols
  which are not gods at all.

Those who are no people: this is the counterpart of **what is no god**. God will use nations and peoples who are inferior and who do not merit the name "people"; instead they are **a foolish nation** (see verse 6). See Paul's use of this verse in Rom 10.19. **Those who are no people** and **a foolish nation** refer to the same nation, not to two different nations. It will be helpful in some languages to combine the two lines as follows:

- Now I will send a nation of worthless and stupid people to make you jealous and angry.

32.22   RSV

For a fire is kindled by my anger,
  and it burns to the depths of Sheol,
devours the earth and its increase,
  and sets on fire the foundations of the mountains.

TEV

My anger will flame up like fire
  and burn everything on earth.
It will reach to the world below[d]
  and consume the roots of the mountains.

[d] THE WORLD BELOW: *This refers to the world of the dead.*

A fire is kindled by my anger: God's anger is compared to a fire that destroys everything before it (see 4.24). TEV uses a simile: "My anger will flame up like fire." We may also say "I will be very angry, and just like fire flares up, my anger will burn." CEV uses another picture: "I will breathe out fire that . . . ."

It burns to the depths of Sheol: God's fire burns all the way through the surface of the earth to the very bottom of the world of the dead.

Devours the earth and its increase: that is, the earth and everything that grows on it; NIV translates "the earth and its harvests."

Notice that TEV, logically enough, reverses the order of these two lines, beginning with the earth, and then going down to the roots of the mountains and the world of the dead.

The foundations of the mountains: in the Hebrew concept of the universe, the sky was a flat disk supported by the mountains, whose roots reached down to the depths of Sheol (see Psa 18.7-8; Amos 7.4). TEV may serve as a model for this verse.

32.23   RSV

" 'And I will heap evils upon them;
    I will spend my arrows upon them;

TEV

" 'I will bring on them endless disasters
    and use all my arrows against them.

I will heap evils on them: this means misfortunes, "endless disasters" (TEV), or "disaster after disaster" (CEV).

I will spend my arrows upon them: see verse 42. Here **spend** means to use or to use up; God will shoot all his arrows at his people. He will use up all possible disasters or calamities that are available to him. This is a vivid figure for disasters, epidemics, famines, and other misfortunes. The figure may not make sense in a culture that does not know of bows and arrows; but it would not be proper to say "shoot my bullets" as a cultural equivalent. Since **arrows** here refers back to **evils** in the first line, we may simply say "I will bring on you one disaster after another to strike you," or "I will cause all kinds of disasters to come upon you," or "I will cause you to experience one disaster after another," or even "I will use up all the disasters available to me to strike you with."

32.24   RSV

they shall be wasted with hunger,
    and devoured with burning heat
    and poisonous pestilence;
and I will send the teeth of beasts against them,
    with venom of crawling things of the dust.

TEV

They will die from hunger and fever;
    they will die from terrible diseases.
I will send wild animals to attack them,
    and poisonous snakes to bite them.

They shall be wasted . . . and devoured: the two verbs have the same meaning, complete destruction; the first verb is found only here in the Old Testament. Other ways to translate this are "They [or, You] will die from . . ." (TEV) or "They [or, You] will be destroyed by . . . ."

Hunger . . . burning heat . . . poisonous pestilence: it is not at once apparent what **burning heat** and **poisonous pestilence** stand for; they may be ways of speaking of droughts and poisonous snakes, or of fevers and deadly plagues.

550

There is no way to be sure (see 28.21-22; Psa 78.49). TEV is a good model to follow.

The teeth of beasts . . . the venom of crawling things in the dust: these are wild animals that will devour them, and poisonous snakes that will kill them. Again TEV has a good alternative model.

32.25   RSV

> **In the open the sword shall bereave,**
>   **and in the chambers shall be terror,**
> **destroying both young man and virgin,**
>   **the sucking child with the man of gray hairs.**

                TEV

> **War will bring death in the streets;**
>   **terrors will strike in the homes.**
> **Young men and young women will die;**
>   **neither babies nor old people will be spared.**

In the open in the first line is balanced by **in the chambers** in the second. The meaning is "both outdoors, in the streets of the towns, and indoors, in their houses."

The sword shall bereave: that is, enemy warriors will kill them. There is no indication what the term **terror** refers to here (see Isa 24.17). But as a parallel to **the sword**, **terror** probably refers to the enemies as they invade the homes and strike terror in the hearts of their victims. But the word may refer to the terror the people feel, and which would cause them to die (so FRCL, BRCL, CEV). So we may say "Outdoors your enemies will kill you, and indoors you will be so frightened that you will die."

The overall meaning is that everyone will be killed: young men and women, children and old people. The translator need not try to find the exact equivalent of **virgin** or **the man of gray hairs**; these are ways of speaking of young women and old people.

The clauses of the verse may be reordered as follows:

●
> Young men and women,
> babies and old people
>   will be killed in the streets,
>   and die from fright in their homes.

32.26   RSV

> **I would have said, "I will scatter them afar,**
>   **I will make the remembrance of them cease from among men,"**

TEV

I would have destroyed them completely,
so that no one would remember them.

Verses 26-27 are a turning point in the song; from his threats to destroy the people, the LORD turns to a promise to forgive and restore them.

Here Yahweh quotes himself, and this is in a song that Moses is reciting. In verse 20 Moses starts quoting Yahweh—a quotation that goes to the end of verse 42. Here in verse 26 it may be awkward and most unnatural to try to imitate the Hebrew structure, and the translator may choose to bypass the quotation, as TEV and CEV do; see also NRSV. So verse 26 can begin, with Yahweh as speaker, "I thought I would scatter them . . . , 27 but I feared provocation . . . ." NJPSV has "I might have . . . ." CEV has "I wanted to scatter you."

I would have said: as the context shows, the consequence of his possible declaration keeps Yahweh from saying this; so the meaning is, "I could have said . . . but I didn't, because . . . ." See in 9.25-29, where Moses makes the same kind of plea to God. In some languages it will be necessary to state clearly that Yahweh is speaking; for example: Yahweh says, "I might have said, 'I will scatter . . . ,' " or "Yahweh says, 'I might have scattered . . . .' "

I will scatter them afar: there is some doubt about the form of the Hebrew text, but the sense of dispersion is what the Septuagint has (see the same verb in 4.27), and this is what most translations say. NJPSV has "reduced them to naught," NJB has "crush them to dust," and TEV "destroyed them completely," the sense of which more closely parallels the next line. It is recommended that translators follow this model.

I will make the remembrance of them cease from among men: see the similar statement in 25.19; see also Num 14.12. God would have destroyed them so completely that in the future people would not even remember that they had existed.

32.27   RSV

had I not feared provocation by the enemy,
lest their adversaries should judge amiss,
lest they should say, "Our hand is triumphant,
the LORD has not wrought all this." '

TEV

But I could not let their enemies boast
that they had defeated my people,
when it was I myself who had crushed them.'

Had I not feared provocation from the enemy: this verse explains why Yahweh did not destroy his people as he had considered doing. The **provocation** here, as the rest of the verse shows, would be the enemy's boast that they, not

Yahweh, had defeated the Israelites. So NIV "but I dreaded the taunt of the enemy" is good, as is NJPSV ". . . the taunts." The expression **feared**, as Yahweh speaks about himself, should not be disregarded (as TEV does). **Provocation** or "taunt" may also be expressed by something like "the sound of your enemies saying" (CEV), or ". . . your enemies jeering at you, saying."

Lest their adversaries should judge amiss: the two nouns **enemy** and **adversaries** mean exactly the same thing. **Lest** is rarely used in modern English; the meaning of the construction is that Israel's enemies would not understand correctly what had happened; so NRSV has "for their adversaries might misunderstand." The first two lines may be combined as follows:

- But I was afraid that your enemies would misunderstand and boast,

Lest they should say: here Yahweh quotes what the enemies of Israel would have said if he had destroyed his people. It is not necessary in translation to keep direct speech, and indirect speech may be better: "and say [or, boast] that they had defeated my people, and not I, the LORD." But the direct speech is more vivid.

Our hand is triumphant: that is, "we defeated them."

The LORD has not wrought all this: it was not Yahweh who caused their total destruction—this is what Israel's enemies would have said. CEV has a good model for the final two lines:

- 'We defeated Israel
  with no help from the LORD.'

32.28 RSV

"For they are a nation void of counsel,
and there is no understanding in them.

TEV

"Israel is a nation without sense;
they have no wisdom at all.

In verses 28-33 it is not at once clear whom Yahweh is speaking about. It may be the people of Israel, or their enemies (so NRSV, REB). Or it is possible that verses 28-31 are about Israel, and verses 32-33 about their enemies (TEV, FRCL, BRCL, POCL, *Pléiade*). There is no way to be sure, but it seems best to follow the lead of TEV, CEV, and others; and this is what the following comments will do. Again, it is possible that in verses 28-31 the speaker is Moses, and God resumes as speaker in verse 32 (NJPSV introduces Yahweh as speaker in verse 34). It is recommended that translators who must identify the speaker should pick Moses; for example, "Moses said," or "Moses continued to speak, saying, ' . . . ' "

They are a nation: Moses is speaking about the people of Israel, and the translation should make this clear.

There is no understanding in them: or "they have no wisdom at all," "they don't think very clearly." The whole verse may be also expressed as "The people of Israel are a nation that have no wisdom at all. They don't think very clearly."

32.29   RSV

> If they were wise, they would understand this,
>   they would discern their latter end!

TEV

> They fail to see why they were defeated;
>   they cannot understand what happened.

If they were wise, they would understand this: **this** refers to the punishment that their evil behavior brought upon them, as described in verses 20-25 (see TEV). See the similar passage in 5.20.

Discern their latter end: they would see beforehand what was going to happen to them; see verse 20.

32.30   RSV

> How should one chase a thousand,
>   and two put ten thousand to flight,
> unless their Rock had sold them,
>   and the LORD had given them up?

TEV

> Why were a thousand defeated by one,
>   and ten thousand by only two?
> The LORD, their God, had abandoned them;
>   their mighty God had given them up.

The Israelites had been defeated in war by an enemy army much smaller than theirs; so the ironic question points out that this incredible defeat—one enemy soldier routing a thousand Israelites—could happen only because the LORD was no longer fighting for them.

The verse is in the form of a rhetorical question, which may be effective in some languages; in many, however, if not in most, a rhetorical question may be misunderstood and should thus be translated as a strong statement.

How should one chase a thousand: that is, "How could one [enemy] soldier put to rout [or chase, or put to flight] one thousand [Israelite] soldiers?" or, as

554

a statement, "The only reason why one enemy soldier defeated one thousand Israelite soldiers was . . . ." TEV offers another good model.

Two put ten thousand to flight: or "two enemies defeated ten thousand." This is parallel, but it heightens the sheer absurdity of the matter.

Their Rock had sold them: see verse 4; **sold** means that Yahweh sold (or, abandoned) them to the enemy (see Judges 2.14; 3.8; 4.2; 10.7).

The LORD had given them up: that is, he had abandoned them (see 23.15). An alternative translation model for this verse is:

• One enemy soldier defeated a thousand Israelite soldiers,
  and ten thousand Israelites were defeated by two of their enemies.
  This is because Yahweh, their mighty protector [or, Rock],
  has abandoned them to their enemies,
  and has let their enemies defeat them.

However, in some languages it may be better to reverse the order of the lines as follows:

• The Mighty God sent his people away,
  the LORD abandoned them.
  That is why one enemy [soldier] routed a thousand [Israelites],
  two enemy soldiers put ten thousand Israelites to flight.

32.31 RSV

For their rock is not as our Rock,
  even our enemies themselves being judges.

TEV

Their enemies know that their own gods are weak,
  not mighty like Israel's God.

The defeat of the Israelites can be understood only on the assumption that Yahweh had deliberately abandoned them; the gods of the enemies could not have defeated the God of Israel.

Their rock is not as our Rock: it seems clear that here Moses must be the speaker. The abrupt change to the first plural (**our Rock . . . our enemies**) may be difficult in some languages; see how TEV has handled this. The comparison is between the power of the gods and the power of Yahweh; so it will be good to say "their rock is [or, their gods are] not as powerful as our Rock [or, our God]."

Even our enemies themselves being judges: this is unintelligible English; presumably it means "as even our enemies themselves admit." See NIV "as even our enemies concede." NRSV and REB follow the Septuagint, "our enemies are fools"; but this is not recommended.

Alternative translation models for this verse are:

- Even our enemies know [or, admit]
   that their gods are not as powerful as our [inclusive] God.

   . . . their gods are not as powerful a rock as our [inclusive] God.

32.32-33   RSV

> ³²For their vine comes from the vine of Sodom,
>   and from the fields of Gomorrah;
> their grapes are grapes of poison,
>   their clusters are bitter;
> ³³their wine is the poison of serpents,
>   and the cruel venom of asps.

TEV

> ³²Their enemies, corrupt as Sodom and Gomorrah,
>   are like vines that bear bitter and poisonous grapes,
> ³³like wine made from the venom of snakes.

Verses 32-33 describe how worthless are the pagan enemies, how corrupt and sinful they are. Notice the careful progression: **their vine . . . their grapes . . . their clusters . . . their wine**.

Some background information on **Sodom** and **Gomorrah** may be supplied in a footnote (see below), to make the text clear to the reader.

TEV has shifted slightly and made the enemies themselves the term of comparison, not their actions; FRCL does this also, "As for them, they are no better than the people of Sodom and Gomorrah . . . ," with a footnote, "*The people of Sodom and Gomorrah* were well known for their immorality; see Gen 18.20-21; 19.4-11." This is a good alternative model to follow. However, we may also keep the picture of a vine and translate as follows:

- Their enemies are like a grapevine
   planted in the fields of Sodom and Gomorrah.^x

Their grapes are grapes of poison, their clusters are bitter: these two lines have the same meaning. It is unlikely that a literal translation will make sense in any language. BRCL provides a good model to follow: "They are like grape-vines that bear worthless grapes, bitter and poisonous grapes," or following on from the first two lines:

- They [the vines] produce grapes [or, fruit]
   that are bitter and poisonous [or, full of bitter poison].

Verse 33 should continue without a break, if possible. Its two lines also have the same meaning. Again BRCL is a good model: "they are like wine made of snake's poison, the deadly poison of serpents."

Serpents . . . asps: in this context these nouns mean the same. In modern English **serpents** (RSV, NIV, NRSV, REB) no longer makes much sense. NJPSV has "asps . . . vipers," NJB "snakes . . . vipers."

32.34 RSV

> **"Is not this laid up in store with me,**
> **sealed up in my treasuries?**

TEV

> **"The LORD remembers what their enemies have done;**
> **he waits for the right time to punish them.**

In verses 34-35 God is the speaker; then in verses 36-38 Moses is probably the speaker, although Yahweh often refers to himself in the third person, and it is possible that these verses are an instance of that. In many languages it will be good to introduce Yahweh as the speaker in this verse; for example, "The LORD says, 'Don't I . . . .' " Notice, however, that TEV and CEV keep "the LORD" in the third person; that is also possible.

Is not this: that is, his plans to punish Israel's enemies (verse 35) and vindicate his people (verse 36). So we may translate "Yahweh says, 'What I have planned to do to the Israelites and their enemies, I am keeping . . . .' "

Laid up in store . . . sealed up in my treasuries: this is a way of saying that God's plan is safe and secure, and cannot be taken from him. Instead of a rhetorical question, a declaration may be better. So NJPSV says "Lo, I have it all put away, sealed up in my storehouses," and SPCL has "All of this I am keeping for myself, I am guarding it as a treasure." The emphasis is not on the worth of it but on Yahweh's determination to keep all his plans strictly to himself, not sharing them with anyone. In this verse TEV departs too far from the focus of the original.

A possible alternative translation model for this verse is:

> Yahweh says,
> "What I have planned to do to the Israelites and their enemies
>   I am keeping for myself.
>   I am guarding it as I would a treasure."

32.35 RSV

> **Vengeance is mine, and recompense,**
> **for the time when their foot shall slip;**
> **for the day of their calamity is at hand,**
> **and their doom comes swiftly.**

**The LORD will take revenge and punish them;
the time will come when they will fall;
the day of their doom is near.**

Vengeance is mine: this renders the Hebrew text, "to me vengeance." The
Samaritan text and the Septuagint have "the day [of vengeance]" as a runover
from verse 34. HOTTP favors this ({C} rating), although of the modern versions
only REB, GECL, and SPCL agree. The Handbook recommends that translators
follow this. So verse 35 should begin "For the day of recompense and vengeance
. . ." or "For the day [or, time] when I will take revenge and punish them will
soon come."

And recompense: though the enemies are God's instrument in punishing his
people, still they are responsible for what they have done, and they will be
punished. The RSV text (if followed) can be rendered "I will take revenge, I will
punish."

For the time when their foot shall slip: this can follow on from the previous
line, but it seems better to make this an independent statement, as NIV has
done, "In due time their foot will slip," or FRCL "when the day of their fall ar-
rives," or we may even say "Suddenly they will fall!"

The day of their calamity . . . their doom: the next two lines have the same
sense, pointing to the punishment that God will send on the enemies in the
form of disasters and destruction. For **calamity** see 29.21.

At hand . . . comes swiftly: these two expressions also have the same meaning, emphasizing that the enemies will be punished very soon.

An alternative translation model for this verse is:

●
   For the day when I will take revenge
   and punish them will soon come!
   Suddenly their foot will slip,
   and all sorts of disasters will quickly follow.

32.36   RSV

**For the LORD will vindicate his people
and have compassion on his servants,
when he sees that their power is gone,
and there is none remaining, bond or free.**

**The LORD will rescue his people
when he sees that their strength is gone.
He will have mercy on those who serve him,
when he sees how helpless they are.**

Will vindicate . . . have compassion: these two verbs do not have the same meaning; one indicates action, the other speaks of the emotion that prompts the action. A translation may wish to reverse the two statements. To **vindicate** is a term from the law court, meaning that the judge gives judgment in favor of an accused person, thereby demonstrating that that person is innocent of wrongdoing.

His people . . . his servants: again, these are exact parallels. **His servants** should not be taken to indicate only those who serve God in priestly functions; it means all the Israelites. An alternative model reversing the order of the two lines is the following:

●   The LORD will have mercy on [or feel sorry for] his servants the Israelites and will declare them innocent.

When he sees that their power is gone: the literal meaning should be expressed; God will act when he becomes aware of his people's pitiful situation.

There is none remaining, bond or free: the text as translated seems to say that all the Israelites will have disappeared. The exaggerated language of poetry allows for this, and the translator should keep this meaning. A possible alternative translation model is:

●   And no Israelite, whether slave or free person, remains alive.

32.37   RSV

> **Then he will say, 'Where are their gods,**
> **the rock in which they took refuge,**

TEV

> **Then the LORD will ask his people,**
> **'Where are those mighty gods you trusted?**

In verses 37-38 there is another shift in the pronouns referring to the people of Israel, from the third plural in verse 37 and the first part of verse 38 to the second person of direct address in the last part of verse 38.

Then he will say: it will be helpful for translators to show who Yahweh is speaking to here; for example, "Then Yahweh will ask his people" (see TEV).

Their gods: the gods of the pagans, that Israel had gone to for help; so TEV, SPCL, FRCL, BRCL. This makes sense (see verses 16-17) and is recommended to translators.

Where are their gods . . . ? This is not a question for information about their whereabouts, but rather a mocking question. "What happened to those gods of yours in whom you trusted?" God tells the Israelites (end of verse 38) that they should go to them for help.

The rock in which they took refuge: for **rock** see verse 31. We may also express this as "The powerful gods they went to for protection?" (See also TEV.)

32.38   RSV

> **who ate the fat of their sacrifices,**
>   **and drank the wine of their drink offering?**
> **Let them rise up and help you,**
>   **let them be your protection!**

TEV

> **You fed them the fat of your sacrifices**
>   **and offered them wine to drink.**
> **Let them come and help you now;**
>   **let them run to your rescue.**

The RSV text carries on this verse as a continuation of the question that starts in verse 37. In some languages this may be difficult to do, and it will be better to start this verse as a new sentence.

Who ate the fat of their sacrifices: the fat was considered the choicest part of the animal offered in sacrifice. Instead of "who ate the fat of your sacrifices," TEV and FRCL have "You fed them the fat of your sacrifices," which may be easier to follow.

Drank the wine of their offerings: this means they drank the wine of the drink offerings; these also are sacrifices. TEV has "and offered them wine to drink."

Let them rise up and help you: this is a sarcastic suggestion, not a request. It may be expressed as "They ought to get up and help you now." As elsewhere **rise up** functions as an auxiliary verb indicating the beginning of the action expressed in the main verb: "Let them help you now!"

Let them be your protectors: this is parallel to the previous line; the Hebrew word translated **protectors** appears only here in the Old Testament. So the final two lines may be translated:

- > They ought to get up and help you now
  >   or come and protect you.

32.39   RSV

> " 'See now that I, even I, am he,
>   and there is no god beside me;
> I kill and I make alive;
>   I wound and I heal;
>   and there is none that can deliver out of my hand.

TEV

" 'I, and I alone, am God;
no other god is real.
I kill and I give life, I wound and I heal,
and no one can oppose what I do.

Verses 39-42 are a single unit of poetry in which God vows to punish the enemies of the Israelites; they are his enemies, too.

See now that I, even I, am he: see 4.35, 39. The Hebrew text says "I, I [am]
he," which the Septuagint translates by "I am." This is a reference to the name
of God, emphasizing the fact that only Yahweh is God. So FRCL translates
"Recognize, therefore, I alone am able to save. There is no other god but me."
POCL has "Pay attention! I am the only God, and there is no other God like me";
and SPCL has "I am the only God; there are no other gods besides me." CEV has
"Don't you understand? I am the only God; there are no others."

I kill and I make alive; I wound and I heal: his power for hurting and for
helping is absolute, and none can stop him when he decides to act.

There is none that can deliver out of my hand: God says that there is no one
who can save someone he has decided to punish. The absolute **none** would
include not only human beings but angelic and divine beings as well; so TEV has
"no one can oppose what I do," and CEV "and nothing can stop me."

32.40   RSV

For I lift up my hand to heaven,
and swear, As I live for ever,

TEV

As surely as I am the living God,
I raise my hand and I vow

God speaks as a human being, lifting up his hand to heaven and taking a
solemn vow to exterminate his enemies (verses 40-42).

I lift up my hand to heaven: this is the normal way of taking a vow (see Psa
106.26; Rev 10.5-6); in Dan 12.7 both hands are lifted. In Gen 14.22; Exo 6.8;
Num 14.30; Neh 9.15; Ezek 20.5 the Hebrew text says simply "I raise my hand,"
meaning "I take a vow." If the idea of God raising his hand **to heaven** seems
ridiculous, it is all right to say only "I raise my hand" (TEV).

Swear: this means to take a solemn vow (see 1.8).

As I live for ever: this may be translated in different ways. TEV says "As
surely as I am the living God," FRCL "As surely as I live forever," BRCL "I swear
by my eternal life." It must be clear to readers that verses 41 and 42 are the
content of God's promise. TEV will serve as a good alternative model.

32.41   RSV

> **if I whet my glittering sword,[f]**
> **and my hand takes hold on judgment,**
> **I will take vengeance on my adversaries,**
> **and will requite those who hate me.**

[f] Heb *the lightning of my sword*

TEV

> **that I will sharpen my flashing sword**
> **and see that justice is done.**
> **I will take revenge on my enemies**
> **and punish those who hate me.**

If I whet my glittering sword: this makes for an awkward statement. It is better to say, as NRSV does, "When I whet . . . ," or to follow NIV, "When I sharpen my flashing sword." Or it is possible to make this a statement, as FRCL does: "I sharpen and polish my sword." In cultures where swords are unknown, but other kinds of knives are used, there are many ways to express **sword**; for example, "a

A SWORD

large long knife," "a large knife like a machete," or "a weapon called a 'sword.' "

My hand takes hold on judgment: this can mean "when I get ready to judge [or, punish]," or else "When I seize the instrument of judgment," that is, **my . . . sword**.

Everything considered, it seems best to take this verse as the very oath, or vow, that God makes:

•
> I will sharpen [and polish] my sword,
> I will grasp [or, seize] it to enforce justice.
> I will take revenge on my enemies,
> I will repay those who hate me.

For **vengeance** see verse 35.

Requite: in this context the verb means to pay back, to punish the enemies as they deserve.

32.42   RSV

> **I will make my arrows drunk with blood,**
> **and my sword shall devour flesh—**
> **with the blood of the slain and the captives,**
> **from the long-haired heads of the enemy.'**

TEV

**My arrows will drip with their blood,
and my sword will kill all who oppose me.
I will spare no one who fights against me;
even the wounded and prisoners will die.'**

The vivid figure of making his **arrows** drunk and of his **sword** eating flesh may be kept in certain languages. CEV offers an alternative model using such a figure:

● My arrows will get drunk
on enemy blood

In a number of languages, however, this figure and the following one may be too strange to translate literally (see the same figures in Jer 46.10). TEV offers a good model. SPCL has "I will drench my arrows with blood, and my sword will kill them [his enemies] off."

The blood of the slain and the captives: this means that even the captives will be slain; the Hebrew text says "all the slain . . . ." FRCL offers a good model: "None of the enemy warriors will escape; wounded or captive, they will all be victims."

The long-haired heads of the enemy: see Judges 5.2. When consecrated for military service, warriors would not cut their hair while at war; this is the long hair of dedicated warriors. Num 6.5 and Ezek 44.20 speak of the long hair of dedicated priests. It will be good to keep "long-haired heads" in the translation, with a footnote explaining this custom, and the last two lines may be alternatively rendered as:

● I will kill all the captives
and cut off the long-haired heads of the enemy.

32.43 RSV

**"Praise his people, O you nations;
for he avenges the blood of his servants,
and takes vengeance on his adversaries,
and makes expiation for the land of his people."**[g]

[g] Gk Vg: Heb *his land his people*

TEV

**"Nations, you must praise the LORD's people—
he punishes all who kill them.
He takes revenge on his enemies
and forgives the sins of his people."**

The song ends with Moses exhorting the nations to praise Israel for what God has done on their behalf, and translators should reintroduce Moses as the speaker here.

Praise his people, O you nations: that is, "All peoples everywhere, you are urged to praise the LORD's people," or "All peoples everywhere, you must say to the LORD's people, 'You are wonderful [or, great].' "

But NRSV and REB translate the Qumran manuscript and the Septuagint, as follows:

> Praise, O heavens, his people,
>   worship him, all you gods (NRSV).

> Rejoice with him, you heavens,
>   bow down, all you gods, before him (REB).

HOTTP recommends the following modified form of the text of Qumran manuscript and Septuagint ({B} rating):

> Cry out for joy with him, you heavens,
>   Bow down before him, all you gods.

It is recommended that translators follow HOTTP as translated by REB. In the first line "him" refers to the Israelites, the LORD's people; in the second line "him" is the LORD. A possible rendering is:

- > Heavens, you must cry out for joy
  >   with the LORD's people,
  > and all you gods bow down
  >   before the LORD.

He avenges the blood of his servants: here, as elsewhere, **the blood** means violent death; and **his servants** are his people, the Israelites (verse 36). Here the Qumran manuscript and Septuagint have "his children," which HOTTP prefers ({B} rating); it is followed by NRSV. It is recommended that "his children" be adopted as the text to be translated; "his children" means the same as **his servants**, that is, the Israelites, the LORD's people.

Takes vengeance on his adversaries: see verse 41.

Makes expiation for the land of his people: the verb **makes expiation** means to do what is needed to remove the result of the sins of the people. In effect the sins made the land unclean, and it must be purified—which God does. The text does not say how God does this. TEV "forgives the sins of his people" expresses an important element of the text, but it does not focus on the land (of Israel), as the text itself does. So it is better, with NJB "purify" and NJPSV "cleanse," to make the land the object of the verb. We may say something like the following: "He cleanses the land of his people from the impurities caused by their sins."

There is a further textual problem here; the Hebrew text as we have it has "his land his people"; but the Qumran manuscript and the Septuagint have "the land of his people," which HOTTP ({B} rating) and this Handbook recommend.

32.44 RSV TEV

Moses came and recited all the words of this song in the hearing of the people, he and Joshua[h] the son of Nun.

Moses and Joshua son of Nun recited this song, so that the people of Israel could hear it.

[h] Gk Syr Vg: Heb *Hoshea*

See the close parallel to this verse at 31.30, at the beginning of Moses' recital.

Moses came and recited all the words of this song: here **came** indicates movement; **recited** translates the verb normally meaning "to say, to speak."

In the hearing of the people: see 31.30.

He and Joshua the son of Nun: the verbs **came** and **recited** are both in the third singular, meaning Moses only. It is possible to say something like the following: "Moses went with Joshua before the people, and [he] recited the entire song as the people listened."

5E. Moses' final instructions (32.45-47)

RSV

TEV

Moses' Final Instructions

45 And when Moses had finished speaking all these words to all Israel, 46 he said to them, "Lay to heart all the words which I enjoin upon you this day, that you may command them to your children, that they may be careful to do all the words of this law. 47 For it is no trifle for you, but it is your life, and thereby shall live long in the land which you are going over the Jordan to possess."

45 When Moses had finished giving God's teachings to the people, 46 he said, "Be sure to obey all these commands that I have given you today. Repeat them to your children, so that they may faithfully obey all of God's teachings. 47 These teachings are not empty words; they are your very life. Obey them and you will live long in that land across the Jordan that you are about to occupy."

Verses 45-52 are considered to be one section by TEV, with the title "Moses' Final Instructions." But since the greater part of verses 45-52 has to do with Yahweh's instructions to Moses, it is better to limit the section to verses 45-47.

Section heading: the TEV title "Moses' final instructions" can serve for this short section. NJB has the title "The Law, the Source of Life." Another possible title is "The Law can give long life."

32.45-46 RSV TEV

45 And when Moses had finished speaking all these words to all Israel, 46 he said to them, "Lay to heart all the words which I enjoin upon you this day, that you may command

45 When Moses had finished giving God's teachings to the people, 46 he said, "Be sure to obey all these commands that I have given you today. Repeat them to your children,

them to your children, that they may be careful to do all the words of this law.	so that they may faithfully obey all of God's teachings.

Had finished speaking all these words to all Israel: see 31.36; 32.44.

Lay to heart: that is, "cherish," "memorize," "remember," "meditate on." BRCL has "Think seriously," and CEV has "Always remember."

All the words which I enjoin upon you this day: it is difficult to say whether **all the words** here means the words of the song that Moses has just recited, or some or all of the earlier part of the book of Deuteronomy. To **enjoin** means to direct, order, command; it is more than to advise or recommend.

In keeping with the parallel passages 4.26; 30.19; 31.28, NRSV translates "Take to heart all the words that I am giving in witness against you this day" (see REB "all the warnings"). It is recommended that translators follow this interpretation of the text; otherwise they should feel free to follow the TEV translation, "Be sure to obey all these commands that I have given you today."

You may command them to your children: see 4.9.

That they may be careful to do all the words of this law: this means all the teachings in the book of Deuteronomy (see **this law** in 1.5); so CEV has "everything written in *The Book of God's Law*."

32.47   RSV   TEV

For it is no trifle for you, but it is your life, and thereby you shall live long in the land which you are going over the Jordan to possess."	These teachings are not empty words; they are your very life. Obey them and you will live long in that land across the Jordan that you are about to occupy."

It is no trifle for you, but it is your life: see 30.20. This emphasizes the seriousness of the matter; what Moses has taught the people is not something insignificant that they can take or leave. Their very existence as a people depends on their obedience to the Law. CEV has a helpful model: "The Law isn't empty words. It can give you long life . . . ."

Thereby you shall live long in the land: see 30.20. **Thereby** means "by means of it" and refers to obeying the Law, and TEV has "Obey them [the teachings] and you will live . . . ."

Possess: see 1.8. For parallels see 4.26, 40.

5F. God allows Moses to see the Promised Land (32.48-52)

          RSV   TEV

48 And the LORD said to Moses that very day, 49 "Ascend this mountain of the Abarim, Mount Nebo, which is in the land of Moab, opposite Jericho; and view the land of Canaan,	48 That same day the LORD said to Moses, 49 "Go to the Abarim Mountains in the land of Moab opposite the city of Jericho; climb Mount Nebo and look at the land of Canaan that I am

which I give to the people of Israel for a possession; 50 and die on the mountain which you ascend, and be gathered to your people, as Aaron your brother died in Mount Hor and was gathered to his people; 51 because you broke faith with me in the midst of the people of Israel at the waters of Meribath-kadesh, in the wilderness of Zin; because you did not revere me as holy in the midst of the people of Israel. 52 For you shall see the land before you; but you shall not go there, into the land which I give to the people of Israel."

about to give the people of Israel. 50 You will die on that mountain as your brother Aaron died on Mount Hor, 51 because both of you were unfaithful to me in the presence of the people of Israel. When you were at the waters of Meribah, near the town of Kadesh in the wilderness of Zin, you dishonored me in the presence of the people. 52 You will look at the land from a distance, but you will not enter the land that I am giving the people of Israel."

Section heading: SPCL has "God Allows Moses to See the Promised Land"; NIV has "Moses to Die on Mount Nebo"; NJB has "Moses' Death Foretold." We may also say "God tells Moses that he will die."

32.48-49 RSV	TEV
48 And the LORD said to Moses that very day, 49 "Ascend this mountain of the Abarim, Mount Nebo, which is in the land of Moab, opposite Jericho; and view the land of Canaan, which I give to the people of Israel for a possession;	**48 That same day the LORD said to Moses, 49 "Go to the Abarim Mountains in the land of Moab opposite the city of Jericho; climb Mount Nebo and look at the land of Canaan that I am about to give the people of Israel.**

Verses 48-49 are one sentence; it may be better to break it up into two or more sentences.

That very day: the "same day" (TEV) in which everything related in this part of Deuteronomy took place.

Ascend this mountain of the Abarim, Mount Nebo: see 3.23-27. **Abarim** is a plural form and means the Abarim range of mountains, east of the Dead Sea. So TEV has "Abarim Mountains," and CEV has "Abarim Mountain range." Another possible translation is "group of mountains named Abarim." It is possible to translate the first sentence by using two verbs instead of the single one **ascend**; for example, "Go up into the group of mountains named Abarim . . . climb to the top of Mount Nebo." **Nebo** was one of the mountains of that range (see Num 27.12).

In the land of Moab, opposite Jericho: that is, the city of Jericho lay on the other side (the west side) of the Jordan River. It will be helpful in many languages to restructure the beginning of verse 49 in a similar way to TEV and CEV: "Go up into the group of mountains named Abarim here in the land of Moab across the Jordan River from the city of Jericho. Climb to the top of Mount Nebo . . . ."

View the land of Canaan: Moses is ordered to take a good look at it, since he will not be allowed to go there. We may begin a new sentence here: "When you reach the top [of Mount Nebo], look at the land."

Which I give to the people of Israel for a possession: see Josh 22.19. Here the word translated **possession** is different from the two words normally used (see 1.8, 38). It means "landed property," but in this context it has the same meaning as the two other words.

32.50	RSV	TEV
	and die on the mountain which you ascend, and be gathered to your people, as Aaron your brother died in Mount Hor and was gathered to his people;	You will die on that mountain as your brother Aaron died on Mount Hor,

And die: in the context this is a command. But we may say something like "you shall die" (NRSV, NJPSV).

On the mountain which you ascend: this will be needless repetition in some languages; in others it will be normal style.

Be gathered to your people: that is, Moses will go to Sheol, where the other dead Israelites are. This is a common way of speaking of dying; see Gen 25.3; 27.13; 35.29; Num 27.13 (and see the similar expression in 31.16). In some cultures this will be a normal way of talking about death; where it is not, this phrase should not be used. The translation should say simply "you will die."

As Aaron your brother: for Aaron's death see 10.6; Num 20.22-29; 33.38-39. TEV is a good model for this verse.

32.51	RSV	TEV
	because you broke faith with me in the midst of the people of Israel at the waters of Meribath-kadesh, in the wilderness of Zin; because you did not revere me as holy in the midst of the people of Israel.	because both of you were unfaithful to me in the presence of the people of Israel. When you were at the waters of Meribah, near the town of Kadesh in the wilderness of Zin, you dishonored me in the presence of the people.

For the parallel to this passage, see Num 27.12-14.

You broke faith with me: the verb is plural, and the meaning is that both Moses and Aaron broke faith with God. NJB takes the plural to mean Moses and the other Israelites; it seems better, however, to understand it to mean the two brothers. See the account of this in Num 20.1-13. To "break faith" means to be disloyal, unfaithful, disobedient.

The waters of Meribath-Kadesh: TEV expands this to say "the waters of Meribath, near the town of Kadesh." In this context **waters** means springs of water. So CEV has "Meribah Spring." We may also say "at Meribah where the water pours out of a rock."

The wilderness of Zin: on the southern border of Judah, toward the Dead Sea. For **wilderness** see 1.1.

You did not revere me as holy: again the verb is plural, referring to Moses and Aaron. God's holiness is his way of being God, separated from all that is morally and spiritually unclean. To revere God as holy is to show him the respect and honor due to him. The two men did not respect the holiness of the God of Israel when they disobeyed him. CEV translates **holy** as "I am God," and renders the final sentence as follows: "I am God, but there in front of the Israelites, you did not treat me with the honor and respect that I deserve."

32.52   RSV   TEV

For you shall see the land before   You will look at the land from a dis-
you; but you shall not go there, into   tance, but you will not enter the land
the land which I give to the people of   that I am giving the people of Israel."
Israel."

You shall see the land before you: **you** is singular; God is speaking only to Moses. The particular sense here is brought out by TEV, CEV, REB, NIV: "you will see from a distance."

The land which I give to the people of Israel: once more emphasizing the fact that the Promised Land was a gift from God.

5G. Moses blesses the tribes of Israel (33.1-29)

RSV   TEV
                                             Moses Blesses the Tribes of Israel

1 This is the blessing with which Moses the   1 These are the blessings that Moses, the
man of God blessed the children of Israel   man of God, pronounced on the people of Israel
before his death. 2 He said,   before he died.
"The LORD came from Sinai,
    and dawned from Seir upon us;   2   The LORD came from Mount Sinai;
    he shone forth from Mount Paran,   he rose like the sun over Edom
he came from the ten thousands of holy   and shone on his people from Mount
    ones,   Paran.
    with flaming fire at his right hand.   Ten thousand angels were with him,
3   Yea, he loved his people;   a flaming fire at his right hand.
    all those consecrated to him were in   3   The LORD loves his people
        his hand;   and protects those who belong to him.
so they followed in thy steps,   So we bow at his feet
    receiving direction from thee,   and obey his commands.
4   when Moses commanded us a law,   4   We obey the Law that Moses gave us,
    as a possession for the assembly of Ja-   our nation's most treasured posses-
        cob.   sion.
5   Thus the LORD became king in Jeshurun, 5   The LORD became king of his people Is-
    when the heads of the people were   rael
        gathered,   when their tribes and leaders were
    all the tribes of Israel together.   gathered together.

6 "Let Reuben live, and not die,
  nor let his men be few."

7 And this he said of Judah:
"Hear, O LORD, the voice of Judah,
  and bring him in to his people.
With thy hands contend for him,
  and be a help against his adversaries."

8 And of Levi he said,
"Give to Levi thy Thummim,
  and thy Urim to thy godly one,
whom thou didst test at Massah,
  with whom thou didst strive at the waters of Meribah;
9 who said of his father and mother,
  'I regard them not';
he disowned his brothers,
  and ignored his children.
For they observed thy word,
  and kept thy covenant.
10 They shall teach Jacob thy ordinances,
  and Israel thy law;
they shall put incense before thee,
  and whole burnt offering upon thy
  altar.
11 Bless, O LORD, his substance,
  and accept the work of his hands;
crush the loins of his adversaries,
  of those that hate him, that they rise
  not again."

12 Of Benjamin he said,
"The beloved of the LORD,
  he dwells in safety by him;
he encompasses him all the day long,
  and makes his dwelling between his
  shoulders."

13 And of Joseph he said,
"Blessed by the LORD be his land,
  with the choicest gifts of heaven above,
  and of the deep that couches beneath,
14 with the choicest fruits of the sun,
  and the rich yield of the months,
15 with the finest produce of the ancient
  mountains,
  and the abundance of the everlasting
  hills,
16 with the best gifts of the earth and its
  fulness,
  and the favor of him that dwelt in the
  bush.
Let these come upon the head of Joseph,
  and upon the crown of the head of him
  that is prince among his brothers.
17 His firstling bull has majesty,
  and his horns are the horns of a wild
  ox;

6 Moses said about the tribe of Reuben:
"May Reuben never die out,
Although their people are few."

7 About the tribe of Judah he said:
"LORD, listen to their cry for help;
Unite them again with the other tribes.
Fight for them, LORD,
And help them against their enemies."

8 About the tribe of Levi he said:
"You, LORD, reveal your will by the Urim
  and Thummim
Through your faithful servants, the Le-
  vites;
You put them to the test at Massah
And proved them true at the waters of
  Meribah.
9 They showed greater loyalty to you
Than to parents, brothers, or children.
They obeyed your commands
And were faithful to your covenant.
10 They will teach your people to obey your
  Law;
They will offer sacrifices on your altar.
11 LORD, help their tribe to grow strong;
Be pleased with what they do.
Crush all their enemies;
Let them never rise again."

12 About the tribe of Benjamin he said:
"This is the tribe the LORD loves and pro-
  tects;
He guards them all the day long,
And he dwells in their midst."

13 About the tribe of Joseph he said:
"May the LORD bless their land with rain
And with water from under the earth.
14 May their land be blessed with sun-rip-
  ened fruit,
Rich with the best fruits of each season.
15 May their ancient hills be covered with
  choice fruit.
16 May their land be filled with all that is
  good,
Blessed by the goodness of the LORD,
Who spoke from the burning bush.
May these blessings come to the tribe of
  Joseph,
Because he was the leader among his
  brothers.
17 Joseph has the strength of a bull,
The horns of a wild ox.
His horns are Manasseh's thousands
And Ephraim's ten thousands.
With them he gores the nations
And pushes them to the ends of the
  earth."

with them he shall push the peoples,
 all of them, to the ends of the earth;
such are the ten thousands of Ephraim,
 and such are the thousands of Manasseh."

18 And of Zebulun he said,
"Rejoice, Zebulun, in your going out;
 and Issachar, in your tents.
19 They shall call peoples to their mountain;
 there they offer right sacrifices;
for they suck the affluence of the seas
 and the hidden treasures of the sand."

20 And of Gad he said,
"Blessed be he who enlarges Gad!
Gad couches like a lion,
 he tears the arm, and the crown of the
  head.
21 He chose the best of the land for himself,
 for there a commander's portion was
  reserved;
and he came to the heads of the people,
 with Israel he executed the commands
 and just decrees of the LORD."

22 And of Dan he said,
"Dan is a lion's whelp,
 that leaps forth from Bashan."

23 And of Naphtali he said,
"O Naphtali, satisfied with favor,
 and full of the blessing of the LORD,
possess the lake and the south."

24 And of Asher he said,
"Blessed above sons be Asher;
 let him be the favorite of his brothers,
 and let him dip his foot in oil.
25 Your bars shall be iron and bronze;
 and as your days, so shall your
  strength be.

26 "There is none like God, O Jeshurun,
 who rides through the heavens to your
  help,
 and in his majesty through the skies.
27 The eternal God is your dwelling place,
 and underneath are the everlasting
  arms.
And he thrust out the enemy before you,
 and said, Destroy.
28 So Israel dwelt in safety,
 the fountain of Jacob alone,
in a land of grain and wine;
 yea, his heavens drop down dew.
29 Happy are you, O Israel! Who is like you,
 a people saved by the LORD,
the shield of your help,
 and the sword of your triumph!

18 About the tribes of Zebulun and Issa-
char he said:
"May Zebulun be prosperous in their
 trade on the sea,
And may Issachar's wealth increase at
 home.
19 They invite foreigners to their mountain
And offer the right sacrifices there.
They get their wealth from the sea
And from the sand along the shore."

20 About the tribe of Gad he said:
"Praise God, who made their territory
 large.
Gad waits like a lion
To tear off an arm or a scalp.
21 They took the best of the land for them-
 selves;
A leader's share was assigned to them.
They obeyed the LORD's commands and
 laws
When the leaders of Israel were gathered
 together."

22 About the tribe of Dan he said:
"Dan is a young lion;
He leaps out from Bashan."

23 About the tribe of Naphtali he said:
"Naphtali is richly blessed by the LORD's
 good favor;
Their land reaches to the south from
 Lake Galilee."

24 About the tribe of Asher he said:
"Asher is blessed more than the other
 tribes.
May he be the favorite of his brothers,
And may his land be rich with olive trees.
25 May his towns be protected with iron
 gates,
And may he always live secure."

26 People of Israel, no god is like your God,
 riding in splendor across the sky,
 riding through the clouds to come to
  your aid.
27 God has always been your defense;
 his eternal arms are your support.
He drove out your enemies as you ad-
  vanced,
 and told you to destroy them all.
28 So Jacob's descendants live in peace,
 secure in a land full of grain and wine,
 where dew from the sky waters the
  ground.
29 Israel, how happy you are!
There is no one like you,
 a nation saved by the LORD.

Your enemies shall come fawning to you;
and you shall tread upon their high
places."

The LORD himself is your shield and your
sword,
to defend you and give you victory.
Your enemies will come begging for mercy,
and you will trample them down.

REB makes a single section of chapters 33–34, which it calls "Moses' final words and death." It seems preferable, however, to divide the two chapters into two sections, as many translations and commentators do.

Section heading: the TEV and CEV title for this section is "Moses Blesses the Tribes of Israel" (also POCL, SPCL); FRCL has "Moses Blesses the Twelve Tribes of Israel," and a title such as this is adequate for most translations. The main problem will be the way in which the verb "blesses" is translated, since God is the one who actually blesses people; so another way to translate this title is "Moses tells the people how God will take care of [or, be good to] them."

33.1	RSV	TEV

This is the blessing with which Moses the man of God blessed the children of Israel before his death.

These are the blessings that Moses, the man of God, pronounced on the people of Israel before he died.

This is the blessing with which Moses . . . blessed: TEV "that Moses . . . pronounced" is the normal way in English of referring to the act of speaking a blessing (also REB, NIV, NJPSV). A **blessing** is a gift from God (see 1.11). Moses prays for, or invokes, God's blessings on the people. TEV has the plural "the blessings," but it is better to keep the singular form if this is natural in the language of the translation.

The man of God: see also Josh 14.6. In English the meaning of **man of God** is in the expression as a whole rather than in its individual words. It is used of Samuel in 1 Kgs 9.6, of the prophet Shemaiah in 1 Kgs 12.22, of Elijah in 2 Kgs 1.9-13, of Elisha in 2 Kgs 5.8, of the prophet Igdaliah in Jer 35.4, and of unnamed prophets in 1 Sam 2.27 and 1 Kgs 13.1. If the phrase "the man who belonged to God" or "the man who obeyed God" is much too general, the best solution will probably be "the prophet of God," or "the man who spoke for God"; and the first part of the verse may also be expressed as "Moses spoke for God, and before he died, he asked God to do good things for the people of Israel, saying, '. . . .' "

The children of Israel: as elsewhere, "the Israelites."

Before his death: or "before he died."

33.2		RSV

He said,

    "**The LORD came from Sinai,
     and dawned from Seir upon us;[i]
     he shone forth from Mount Paran,**

he came from the ten thousands of holy ones,
with flaming fire^j at his right hand.

ⁱ Gk Syr Vg: Heb *them*
^j The meaning of the Hebrew word is uncertain

TEV

The LORD came from Mount Sinai;
he rose like the sun over Edom
and shone on his people from Mount Paran.
Ten thousand angels were with him,
a flaming fire at his right hand.^e

^e *Probable text* Ten thousand . . . right hand; *Hebrew unclear.*

The LORD came from Sinai: it was at Mount Sinai that the LORD came to the people of Israel. The destination is **upon us**, that is, to "us" or "them," depending on how the next line is translated.

Dawned . . . shone forth: these mean exactly the same thing; they compare the LORD's coming to the rising of the sun.

Seir: that is, "Edom" (TEV); see "hill country of Edom" in 1.2.

Upon us: this is the text of the Septuagint, Syriac, and Vulgate; the Hebrew text has "upon them," which HOTTP prefers ({B} rating). The choice of "us" or "them" will depend on how the Israelites will be referred to in translation of the poem. It is possible that the meaning is rather "to them," that is, on behalf of the Israelites. Both TEV and CEV have "to his people." This interpretation is recommended.

Mount Paran: see Num 10.12. This was the first place where the Israelites stopped after leaving Mount Sinai; the wilderness of Paran was to the south of the land of Canaan. A possible alternative model for these first three lines is:

- From Mount Sinai Yahweh came down to help us;
  he rose like the sun and shone from Edom,
  and his light shone from Mount Paran.

He came from the ten thousands of holy ones: NRSV has "With him were myriads of holy ones," following the Septuagint, the Samaritan, Syriac, and Vulgate texts. HOTTP ({C} rating) prefers "and with him" over "and he came," a text that represents different vowels for the same consonants of the Hebrew text. And in the following "from the ten thousands of holy ones," HOTTP ({B} rating) states that "from" functions as a partitive, a form that refers to a part or quantity of something—in this instance "some," as in "[and with him] some of the ten thousands . . . ." But the text is handled differently by others; NJPSV has "And approached from Ribeboth-kodesh," and NJB "From them he came after the meeting at Kodesh." It is recommended that translators follow NRSV's model above. The **holy ones** are angels. TEV follows this interpretation, with "Ten thousand angels were with him." In languages where "angels" will be

translated as "heavenly messengers," it will be better to say something like "his
heavenly helpers," or even "his soldiers [or, warriors]" (CEV).

With flaming fire at his right hand: RSV adds the footnote "Heb uncertain";
NJPSV has a similar note and translates "Lightning flashing at them from his
right." It is difficult to envisage "flaming fire" **at** Yahweh's **right hand**; it seems
to be a way of speaking of lightning, which Yahweh carries as a weapon. The
language of this verse pictures Yahweh as a warrior.

An alternative translation model for this verse is:

●   Yahweh came down from Mount Sinai to help us;
            he rose like the sun and shone on his people from Edom.
            And his light shone from Mount Paran.
        Thousands of his angels were with him,
            and fire flamed from his hand.

33.3   RSV

>   Yea, he loved his people;^k
>   all those consecrated to him were in his^x hand;
>   so they followed^j in thy steps,
>   receiving direction from thee,

>   ^k Gk: Heb *peoples*
>   ^x Heb *thy*
>   ^j The meaning of the Hebrew word is uncertain

                                    TEV

>   The LORD loves his people^f
>   and protects those who belong to him.
>   So we bow at^g his feet
>   and obey his commands.

>   ^f *One ancient translation* his people; *Hebrew* the peoples.
>   ^g *Probable text* bow at; *Hebrew unclear.*

Verses 3-5 are difficult to understand.

Yea, he loved his people: this is the Septuagint; the Hebrew text has "the
peoples." NRSV restructures and translates "Indeed, O favorite among peoples."
The Hebrew verb, a participle translated **he loved**, appears only here in the Old
Testament. A possible alternative rendering is "Indeed [or, Truly], Yahweh
loves his people the Israelites."

All those consecrated to him: this means the people of Israel; they "belong
to him" (TEV); see 7.6; 14.2, 21.

In his hand: the Hebrew text has "your hand," which HOTTP prefers ({A}
rating). The personal pronouns and adjectives should be used consistently of
God and the people of Israel in such a way that the readers will know who is

being referred to in each instance. This is a translational problem, not a textual one. The phrase **in his hand** means that the LORD "protects his people" (CEV, see TEV), he guards them, keeps them safe.

They followed in thy steps: the Hebrew verb, as Mayes says, "is quite unknown." Mayes recommends joining two Hebrew words of the Hebrew text into one (a verb attested also in Job 24.24; Psa 106.43; Eccl 10.18), meaning "be low." The meaning then will be "and they prostrated themselves," which is what TEV, CEV, NIV, and NJB have. It is recommended that translators take this approach. Other possible models are "So they bow at his feet," or ". . . prostrate themselves before him," or even "worship at his feet" (CEV).

Receiving direction from thee: this refers to the laws that God gave his people; NIV translates "instruction." REB translates the whole line "They sit at his feet and receive his instructions." This is a possibility.

33.4 RSV

> when Moses commanded us a law,
>   as a possession for the assembly of Jacob.

TEV

> We obey the Law that Moses gave us,
>   our nation's most treasured possession.

When Moses commanded us a law: Moses is still speaking, and in many languages it will be helpful to indicate this by saying, for example, "I gave you God's law." For the verb **commanded** see 2.37. It is better to start a new sentence here, as NRSV does: "Moses charged us with the law." It is possible to join verse 4 to verse 3, as RSV, NJPSV and NIV do; however, this Handbook recommends that a new sentence begin here and that verse 4 be joined to verse 5. If this is done it is possible to begin by including information from verse 5b and c with 4a as follows: "⁴⁻⁵ When all the tribes of Israel gathered together, I gave you God's Law. . . ."

A possession for the assembly of Jacob: the assembly of Jacob (see 9.10) is the people of Israel. For **possession** see the verb in 1.8; TEV has "our nation's most treasured possession"; or we may say "the most precious thing that our nation has."

33.5 RSV

> Thus the LORD became king in Jeshurun,
>   when the heads of the people were gathered,
>   all the tribes of Israel together.

575

TEV

The LORD became king of his people Israel
when their tribes and leaders were gathered together.

Then the LORD became king in Jeshurun: for **Jeshurun** see 32.15. The Hebrew text says only "and there was a king in Jeshurun." This could refer to Yahweh or to Moses; or it could refer to some other person, as NRSV translates, "There arose a king in Jeshurun" (also REB, and NJB). It is recommended that RSV and TEV be followed.

The heads of the people were gathered: this means the chiefs, the leaders of the Israelites, perhaps the tribal leaders.

All the tribes of Israel together: this is parallel with the previous line. The two lines together can be translated "all the tribes and their leaders assembled [together]."

Verses 4 and 5 may be combined as follows:

● ⁴⁻⁵ When all the people of Israel gathered together,
I gave you God's Law,
the most treasured thing our nation has.
Then the LORD became king of the Israelites.

33.6 RSV

"Let Reuben live, and not die,
nor let his men be few."

TEV

Moses said about the tribe of Reuben:
"May Reuben never die out,
Although their people are few."

From this verse to the end of verse 25, the words of blessing are addressed to each of the tribes of Israel in turn. We notice that the tribe of Simeon is missing. Levi is listed as a tribe, and in the case of Joseph (verses 13-17), his two sons are named (verse 17), thus making a total of twelve.

The translator must choose, in each instance, between the name only (such as "Judah," "Levi," "Benjamin," and so on) and the phrase "the tribe of Judah," and so on. In most cases it will be better to say "the tribe of . . . ," since that is what the text means. FRCL has "the descendants of," which in some cases may be better. So we may say here "Tribe of Reuben, you will . . ." or "People of the tribe of Reuben . . . ."

TEV opens the verse with "Moses said about the tribe of Reuben"; this is translational, providing this blessing with the same kind of introduction that appears in all the other blessings; FRCL has "And Moses continued." It is recommended that TEV be followed.

Let Reuben live, and not die: the prayer, or wish, is that the tribe of Reuben will always continue to exist and never disappear. In English "not die out" (NRSV, REB, NJB) carries the idea of a group not disappearing.

Nor let his men be few: as some commentators say, this is a wrong translation. The Hebrew text has "and his people be few"; the negative of "and not die" in the previous line does not modify this line. NJPSV, TEV, and NJB have "although his people are few." It is better to follow REB, "but may he be few in number" (also TOB, Osty). This is actually a request that the tribe of Reuben will never become strong and dominant; see Gen 49.3-4.

A possible alternative translation model for this verse is:

- Moses said about the people of the tribe of Reuben:
    "May you never die out;
        but may you always be few in number."

33.7 RSV

> **And this he said of Judah:**
> **"Hear, O LORD, the voice of Judah,**
> **and bring him in to his people.**
> **With thy hands contendⁱ for him,**
> **and be a help against his adversaries."**

ⁱ Cn: Heb *with his hands he contended*

TEV

> **About the tribe of Judah he said:**
> **"LORD, listen to their cry for help;**
> **Unite them again with the other tribes.**
> **Fight for them, LORD,**
> **And help them against their enemies."^h**

^h *Probable text* Fight for . . . enemies; *Hebrew* The tribe of Judah will fight for itself, and the LORD will help it against its enemies.

And this he said of Judah: TEV says "About the tribe of Judah he said." Translators may follow these models, or introduce the name of Judah into the first line:

- People of the tribe of Judah, the LORD will listen to you, as . . . .

Hear, O LORD, the voice of Judah: this is a request, or prayer, that the LORD will answer the prayer for help made by the people of Judah.

Bring him in to his people: this is a prayer that the LORD will make the tribe of Judah a part of the people of Israel again. When the northern tribes rebelled and became a separate nation, Judah was left alone as a separate nation, the

Kingdom of Judah (see 1 Kgs 12.16-17). Alternative translation models are "and bring them [or, you] back to the other tribes," or "unite you with the other tribes."

With thy hands contend for him: the RSV footnote indicates that this is a conjecture; the Hebrew is literally "with his hands he contended." HOTTP ({B} rating) prefers "with his hands he contends for him," meaning that he, Judah, fights for (or, defends) himself (see also TEV footnote). NJPSV has "Though his own hands strive for him," but in a footnote says *"better* 'Make his hands strong for him.' " This is how REB and NRSV translate: "strengthen his hands for him"; SPCL has "Defend him with your power." It is recommended that translators follow NRSV, perhaps with a footnote indicating that the Hebrew text has "with his hands he contended." The translation can be "Make them [that is, the people of the tribe of Judah] strong," or "May the LORD make you strong."

Be a help against his adversaries: this request complements the previous one; it asks God to help the people of Judah as they fight their enemies. CEV has "now the LORD will help you."

33.8   RSV

    And of Levi he said,
       "Give to Levi[m] thy Thummim,
         and thy Urim to thy godly one,
       whom thou didst test at Massah,
         with whom thou didst strive at the waters of Meribah;

   [m] Gk: Heb lacks *Give to Levi*

                    TEV

    About the tribe of Levi he said:
       "You, LORD, reveal your will by the Urim and Thummim[i]
       Through your faithful servants, the Levites;
       You put them to the test at Massah
       And proved them true at the waters of Meribah.

   [i] URIM AND THUMMIM: *Two objects used by the priest to determine God's will; it is not known precisely how they were used.*

And of Levi he said: again it is better to say something like "About the tribe of Levi he said" (TEV) or "About the people of the tribe of Levi . . . ."

Give to Levi: as the RSV footnote states, this is from the Septuagint; it is not found in the Hebrew text as we have it. NRSV follows RSV but adds a Qumran manuscript in support of this addition. It is recommended that it be kept in translation. HOTTP ({C} rating) prefers the following text:

        to Levi your Thummim were given,
        and your Urim (to a man, your holy one).

Levi . . . thy godly one: the name **Levi** and the expression **thy godly one** are parallel; **thy godly one** may be translated "the one who is dedicated to God," or "you people who are God's priests."

The **Thummim** and **Urim** were two objects (perhaps stones) used by the priest to determine God's will (see Exo 28.30; Lev 8.8; 1 Sam 14.41-42). It is not known precisely how they were used. It may be good to give this information in a footnote, as TEV does: "URIM AND THUMMIM: *Two objects used by the priest to determine God's will.*" CEV leaves out the reference to **Urim** and **Thummim**; but it is recommended that translators retain it.

Thou didst test . . . thou didst strive: these are parallel and close in meaning. To **test** someone is to subject that person to hardships and difficulties in order to reveal that person's character. Another way to express this is "You caused them to endure hardships at Massah, to see what kind of people they were" (see also 8.2). To **strive** is to fight against. TEV "proved them true" seems too far wide of the mark.

For **Massah** see 6.16; 9.22; Exo 17.7; for **Meribah** see 32.51; Exo 17.7.

33.9   RSV

> who said of his father and mother,
>   'I regard them not';
> he disowned his brothers,
>   and ignored his children.
> For they observed thy word,
>   and kept thy covenant.

                                 TEV

> They showed greater loyalty to you
> Than to parents, brothers, or children.
> They obeyed your commands
> And were faithful to your covenant.

TEV shows how the first and second parts of this verse hang together; the Levites showed greater loyalty and dedication to Yahweh than to their parents, siblings, and children. Simply to translate all lines as complete, independent statements fails to bring out the meaning of the verse.

Who said of his father and mother, 'I regard them not': in many languages there is no need to reproduce the direct speech of the Hebrew text; in a number of cases it will be better to use indirect discourse (see TEV). In all cases the plural forms should be used: "fathers and mothers [or, parents], brothers and sisters [or, siblings], sons and daughters [or, children]." The background for this appears to be the incident narrated in Exo 32.35-39, in which the Levites slaughtered their own people at the command of Yahweh. To **regard** is to have feeling for, or to be concerned with. In idiomatic English this may be expressed as "They mean nothing to me." SPCL preserves the same structure for all three, to good effect:

> Who said to his parents: "I have never seen you,"
> and to his brothers: "I don't know you,"
> and to his children: "I don't know who you are."

Either this or TEV can serve as a good model for the translator. In English **brothers** is exclusive, so "brothers and sisters" should be used. NRSV "his kin" includes all relatives, and not simply blood brothers and sisters.

Disowned . . . ignored: these terms have the same meaning.

They observed thy word: a reader of RSV does not know who **they** are. It refers, of course, to the Levites.

Observed . . . kept: these terms have the same meaning.

Thy word . . . thy covenant: these are parallel but not identical; **word** is a general term for God's message, God's laws and commands, and **covenant** refers to the special relationship between Yahweh and the people of Israel.

We may reverse the order of the clauses in this verse and translate as follows:

● Obeying the LORD's commands and keeping the agreement that he made with Israel was more important to you than the life of your father or mother, or brothers or sisters, or your own children.

33.10   RSV

> **They shall teach Jacob thy ordinances,**
> **and Israel thy law;**
> **they shall put incense before thee,**
> **and whole burnt offering upon thy altar.**

TEV

> **They will teach your people to obey your Law;**
> **They will offer sacrifices on your altar.**

They shall teach: it is better to use the present tense, "They teach" (NRSV; also NIV); see 17.9-10.

Thy ordinances: see 4.1. For **thy law** see 1.5. The two terms are equivalent.

Jacob . . . Israel: these are identical in this context.

They shall put: again the present tense is better, "They place" (NRSV).

Before thee . . . upon thy altar: in this context these are the same; the altar was the place where sacrifices were offered to God.

Incense: see Exo 30.7; Lev 16.12-13. It is an aromatic substance that was used with sacrifices. In cultures where incense or other spices are unknown, translators may use a general term; for example, "sweet smelling things." For **whole burnt offering** see 13.16.

33.11   RSV

> Bless, O LORD, his substance,
> and accept the work of his hands;
> crush the loins of his adversaries,
> of those that hate him, that they rise not again."

TEV

> Lord, help their tribe to grow strong;
> Be pleased with what they do.
> Crush all their enemies;
> Let them never rise again."

Bless ... his substance: the noun **substance** can be used of skill or strength (TEV, and also NIV "all his skills"); most often it means wealth or property (see 8.18), which is the meaning here. So we may also translate "LORD give the people of this tribe the power to become rich," or "I pray that the LORD will give you the power to . . . ."

Accept the work of his hands: this does not seem to refer to a single thing, but to everything the Levites do (so TEV, CEV).

Crush the loins of his adversaries: it may be that in some languages the equivalent of **loins** (the sexual organs of a man) in this context is still part of current speech; it certainly is not in English. It is better to use a verb like "defeat" or "destroy," with the direct object "his [or their, or your] enemies."

That they rise not again: the enemies are to be defeated and remain powerless forever, never a threat to the people of Israel again. Another way to express this is "so that they [the enemies] will never be able to fight you again."

33.12   RSV

> Of Benjamin he said,
> "The beloved of the LORD,
> he dwells in safety by him;
> he encompasses him all the day long,
> and makes his dwelling between his shoulders."

TEV

> About the tribe of Benjamin he said:
> "This is the tribe the LORD loves and protects;
> He guards them all the day long,
> And he dwells in their midst."[j]

[j] And he . . . midst; *or* They live under his protection.

Of Benjamin he said: see the models for other tribes in previous verses.

The beloved of the LORD: see in Gen 44.20; Benjamin was Jacob's favorite son. It is better to make this a statement with a finite verb: "The tribe that the LORD loves" (similarly TEV), or "Yahweh loves you, people of the tribe of Benjamin."

He dwells in safety by him: see 12.10; 33.28. **He** is Benjamin; **him** is Yahweh. NJPSV has "He rests securely beside Him." Another way to render this is "You [the people of the tribe of Benjamin] rest securely beside Yahweh."

NRSV renders the first two lines of this blessing as "The beloved of the LORD rests in safety—the High God[m] surrounds him all day long—." The footnote says "Heb *above him*." There is a textual problem here. HOTTP ({B} rating) favors this alternative rendering adopted by NRSV, and translators should feel free to follow it as the text to be translated. But instead of "the High God," the more usual "the Most High" should be used. CEV follows this interpretation, with "The LORD most High loves you, tribe of Benjamin." The adoption of this text results in a change in the first line, as set forth by NRSV; instead of four lines (RSV) there will be three lines.

He encompasses him all the day long: this is like the NRSV text; **he** is Yahweh and **him** is the tribe of Benjamin. The verb **encompasses** means to surround with care, to protect.

Makes his dwelling between his shoulders: this can be understood in two ways:

(1) Benjamin lies safely between the shoulders (meaning, "in the arms") of Yahweh;

(2) Yahweh lives in "the shoulders," that is, the hills, of the tribe of Benjamin. The verb "to dwell" is the one used in 12.11 (see also Isa 8.18). This is a reference to a sanctuary in the territory of the tribe of Benjamin; it may be Shiloh, or Bethel, but it is most probably Jerusalem itself, which was at one time regarded as being in the territory of Benjamin (see Josh 15.8; 18.28). The first interpretation is favored by NRSV, NIV, NJPSV, REB, SPCL, BRCL; the second one is adopted by NJB, TEV, CEV, TOB, FRCL, POCL, Osty. It is impossible to rule out either alternative, but on the whole the second interpretation seems more probable. CEV reverses the order of the final two lines as follows:

-                                He will live among your hills
                               and protect you.

33.13   RSV

    And of Joseph he said,
        "Blessed by the LORD be his land,
        with the choicest gifts of heaven above,[n]
        and of the deep that couches beneath,

[n] Two Heb Mss and Tg: Heb *with the dew*

TEV

About the tribe of Joseph he said:
"May the LORD bless their land with rain
And with water from under the earth.

Verses 13-16b are one sentence in Hebrew; it does flow smoothly in English, and in some languages this structure may be kept. But see TEV as a model for breaking it down into smaller units.

Of Joseph: TEV begins, "About the tribe of Joseph." At no time was there a geographical entity called "The tribe of Joseph." Two of the tribes, Manasseh and Ephraim, were named after the two sons of Joseph, and they appear in verse 17. "Descendants of Joseph" (CEV) is a good alternative model.

Blessed by the LORD be his land: an active verb may be better; for example, "May the LORD bless . . ." (TEV, NIV), or "I ask the LORD to be kind to you and cause rain to fall on your land."

With the choicest gifts of heavens above: the RSV footnote says this translation is based on two Hebrew manuscripts and a Targum. The Hebrew text as we have it is literally "with the dew." HOTTP ({A} rating) follows the Hebrew text and recommends a note: "see similar passages in Gen 27.28, 39; 49.25." The Hebrew noun is "dew," and translators should stay with this word and not change to "rain" (TEV). So we may translate in the following way: "I ask the LORD to cause dew to come from the sky." For a comment on **dew** see 32.2.

The deep that couches beneath: this refers to the vast body of underground water which, according to the Hebrew concept of the world, was the source of springs and rivers (see Gen 49.25). See the description of the land of Canaan in 8.7. The verb **couches** is used of animals lying down to rest or else lying in wait for prey (in Gen 49.9 it is used of a lion; in Deut 22.6 it is used of a mother bird spreading her wings over her young chicks). If possible, a translation should reproduce the meaning of the Hebrew verb.

An alternative translation model for this verse is:

- Descendants of Joseph,
  may the LORD be kind to you
    and cause dew to come from the sky
    and water to come up from deep beneath the ground.

33.14   RSV

with the choicest fruits of the sun,
and the rich yield of the months,

TEV

May their land be blessed with sun-ripened fruit,
Rich with the best fruits of each season.

This verse continues without a break from verse 13; it is the object of **Blessed . . . be**. Expressed in the active voice the connection is "May the LORD be kind to you [bless] and cause . . . ."

Choicest fruits . . . rich yield: these are two similar expressions for good crops.

Of the sun: that is, the sun as the agent in the growing of good crops. NJB has "the best of what the sun makes grow," and NIV "the best the sun brings forth." In some languages this may not be a familiar concept, and certain adaptations will have to be made. One possibility is ". . . will ripen in the sunshine" (CEV; similarly TEV).

The rich yield of the months: the Hebrew word for "month" is "moon" (as it is in many other languages); so NJPSV has "the bounteous crop of the moons," and NIV "the finest the moon can yield." This makes for better parallelism with the previous line; but the idea that the moon helps crops to grow may appear very odd in some cultures. It seems better to translate as **months**, referring to the crops as they mature during different seasons of the year (see TEV). However, we may retain the idea of **months** with "Month by month, your fruit will ripen . . ." (CEV).

33.15   RSV

> **with the finest produce of the ancient mountains,**
> **and the abundance of the everlasting hills,**

TEV

> **May their ancient hills be covered with choice fruit.**

The finest produce . . . the abundance: these are parallel terms, indicating quality and quantity. So we may say "choice fruits" (CEV).

The ancient mountains . . . the everlasting hills: these are parallel expressions and mean the same thing. See Gen 49.26, also of Joseph. The TEV translation will serve as a good alternative model.

33.16   RSV

> **with the best gifts of the earth and its fulness,**
> **and the favor of him that dwelt in the bush.**
> **Let these come upon the head of Joseph,**
> **and upon the crown of the head of him that is prince among**
> **his brothers.**

TEV

> **May their land be filled with all that is good,**
> **Blessed by the goodness of the LORD,**

> **Who spoke from the burning bush.**
> **May these blessings come to the tribe of Joseph,**
> **Because he was the leader among his brothers.**

The best gifts of the earth and its fulness: this is a summary statement; it means everything that grows—crops, vineyards, fruit trees. The phrase **the earth and its fulness** means the ability of the earth to bring forth bumper crops: "this rich [or, fertile] land." POCL translates "the rich yield of the land and everything it produces"; or we may say "all the best things that the land can produce."

The favor of him that dwelt in the bush: this is a reference to the events narrated in Exo 3.1-6. The idea of God living in the bush is a bit strange; the Septuagint translates "who was seen in the bush." TEV is justified, in terms of what actually happened, in translating "who spoke from the burning bush." NJPSV translates "the Presence in the bush," and FRCL "the favor of the God present in the bush." Another possibility is BRCL, "the God who appeared in the burning bush" (similarly CEV). Either this, or ". . . of God, who appeared . . ." is recommended as a model for translators.

Let these come upon the head . . . upon the crown of the head: these have the same meaning. NRSV "on the brow" for the second expression (also NIV) may be better than "the crown," which is the top of the head, not a king's or queen's headwear.

Joseph is described as **prince among his brothers**, that is, the leader or the most outstanding one. The Hebrew word translated **prince** may in some contexts mean "Nazirite," that is, someone who is dedicated to God (see the story of Samson in Judges 13.5, 7); so NJB has "the consecrated one." However, it is better to say "leader" (TEV). An alternative rendering for the second part of this verse is:

- I ask that all these things happen
    to the people of the tribe of Joseph,
  because he [Joseph] was the leader
    among his brothers.

33.17 RSV

> **His firstling bull has majesty,**
> **and his horns are the horns of a wild ox;**
> **with them he shall push the peoples,**
> **all of them, to the ends of the earth;**
> **such are the ten thousands of Ephraim,**
> **and such are the thousands of Manasseh."**

TEV

> **Joseph has the strength of a bull,**
> **The horns of a wild ox.**

> **His horns are Manasseh's thousands**
> **And Ephraim's ten thousands.**
> **With them he gores the nations**
> **And pushes them to the ends of the earth."**

Notice that here TEV has switched from the tribe of Joseph (verses 13-16) to Joseph himself. However, it is also possible to bring the reference to Ephraim and Manasseh forward from the end of this verse to the beginning and say "Ephraim and Manasseh, your thousands of soldiers are big and strong like . . . ."

His firstling bull: there is a textual problem here. HOTTP ({B} rating) judges the text to be "the first-born of his bull," in which the "first-born" is Joseph; "bull" is God and "his" refers to Joseph, meaning "Joseph is the first-born of his God." This does not seem very likely and is not recommended to the translator. A Qumran manuscript, plus the Samaritan, Septuagint, Syriac, and Vulgate omit "his," and this is the text that should be followed.

It is better to translate the verse as a simile, not as metaphor. So NIV says "In majesty he is like a firstborn bull"; likewise NJPSV has "Like a firstling bull in majesty." Some translations (TEV, FRCL) omit "firstborn," but this is not recommended. In this passage **majesty** refers primarily to size and strength.

His horns are the horns of a wild ox: **wild ox** and **bull** have the same meaning here and may be represented by one animal, as in FRCL: "Like the wild buffalo he is armed with two powerful horns." Instead of **horns** POCL has "strong" and "strength": "He is beautiful, like the firstborn of a bull, and strong as a buffalo; with his strength he will attack all peoples." It is also possible to say "and as a wild ox uses its horns to gore its enemies, they [Ephraim and Manasseh] will gore . . . ." CEV changes the simile of "gore" to the weapons that the Israelites will use to kill their enemies: "they will run their spears through . . . ."

With them he shall push the peoples, all of them, to the ends of the earth: this is standard exaggerated language, proper to this kind of poetry. The tribe of Joseph would be powerful and would drive back all the surrounding peoples. The Hebrew verb means "to gore," and NRSV offers a better text to follow: "with them he gores the peoples, driving them to the ends of the earth" (see also TEV).

Notice that TEV has placed the last two lines of this verse before the previous two lines in order to make clear the relationship between them. This may be a good thing for other translations to do.

Such are the ten thousands of Ephraim, and such are the thousands of Manasseh: as NJPSV makes clear, the meaning here is that one horn is **Ephraim**, the other **Manasseh**; TEV is a good model. Here these two sons of Joseph are cited in order to make the total number of tribes come to twelve. It may be a good idea, with POCL and BRCL, to have a footnote identifying Ephraim and Manasseh as sons of Joseph and two tribes of Israel.

FRCL maintains the order of the Hebrew text, ending the verse as follows: "One of the horns is the multitude of Ephraim, the other, the many troops of Manasseh." In both cases, as the context makes clear, **the ten thousands** and **the thousands** are men available as warriors. It is also possible, as indicated above, to drastically restructure the verse as follows:

●   The thousands of soldiers
        of the tribes of Ephraim and Manasseh
        are big and strong like bulls.
      As a wild ox uses its horns to gore its enemies,
        so they will gore their enemies
        and push them to the ends of the earth.

33.18   RSV

And of Zebulun he said,
      "Rejoice, Zebulun, in your going out;
      and Issachar, in your tents.

TEV

About the tribes of Zebulun and Issachar he said:
      "May Zebulun be prosperous in their trade on the sea,
      And may Issachar's wealth increase at home.

In verses 18-19 two tribes are mentioned together, Zebulun and Issachar. **In your going out . . . in your tents: your going out** talks about travels abroad, in this context maritime commerce and trade (see Gen 49.13). **In your tents** refers to the home life of a pastoral or nomadic people. TEV has a good model for this verse.

33.19   RSV

They shall call peoples to their mountain;
      there they offer right sacrifices;
      for they suck the affluence of the seas
      and the hidden treasures of the sand."

TEV

They invite foreigners to their mountain
And offer the right sacrifices there.
They get their wealth from the sea
And from the sand along the shore."

They shall call peoples to their mountain: as the context shows, this refers to a place of worship; a hill or high place was the usual spot where altars and worship places were built. If a particular mountain is meant, this could be Mount Carmel or, more probably, Mount Tabor. The people of these two tribes invite **peoples** to come and worship with them. Some take this to refer to their fellow Israelites; CEV makes this clear with "So invite the other tribes." In English **peoples** will be taken by readers to mean other groups or nations (RSV,

NRSV, NIV, REB); so TEV has "invite foreigners." The meaning "other tribes," "fellow-Israelites," is to be preferred.

Offer right sacrifices: these are the appropriate sacrifices, the ones required by the Law.

They suck the affluence of the seas: some languages may have a verb that expresses the meaning of **suck** in a natural fashion. For **suck** see the same verb in 32.13. TEV is here a good model to follow. The plural **seas** can be a reference to the Mediterranean Sea and Lake Galilee, or else it is used in a general sense and may be translated "the sea" (FRCL, TEV, CEV, REB).

The hidden treasures of the sand: this is not a good translation, since it suggests treasures along the seashore that have been hidden by others. The meaning is still that of trade carried on by ships sailing the seas. Some commentators mention the increasing use of sand in making pottery. Again TEV has a good alternative model.

33.20   RSV

> And of Gad he said,
>> "Blessed be he who enlarges Gad!
>> Gad couches like a lion,
>> he tears the arm, and the crown of the head.

TEV

> About the tribe of Gad he said:
>> "Praise God, who made their territory large.
>> Gad waits like a lion
>> To tear off an arm or a scalp.

Blessed be he who enlarges Gad! here God is the one referred to as **blessed**, and in this kind of statement the meaning is to "give thanks for God," "give praise to God." In most languages God cannot be the object of the verb "to bless," as though a human being were blessing God. **Enlarges Gad** means that God will give them more land. A possible alternative model for these first two lines is:

●
> People of the tribe of Gad,
>> the LORD will be kind to you
>> and give you more land.
> So you must praise him.

Gad is compared to a **lion**, who lies in wait for its prey. The verb **couches** here normally means to "live," "dwell in," so the meaning "Gad lives there like a lion" (NIV) is also possible (in verse 13 a different Hebrew verb is used).

Tears the arm, and the crown of the head: that is, attacking and tearing off an arm or the scalp of the victim. On the people of Gad as fighters, see Gen 49.19.

33.21 RSV

> He chose the best of the land for himself,
> for there a commander's portion was reserved;
> and he came to the heads of the people,
> with Israel he executed the commands
> and just decrees of the LORD."

TEV

> They took the best of the land for themselves;
> A leader's share was assigned to them.
> They obeyed the LORD's commands and laws
> When the leaders of Israel were gathered together."ᵏ

ᵏ *One ancient translation* When the leaders . . . together; *Hebrew unclear.*

He chose the best of the land for himself: that is, in the division of the land of Canaan among the twelve tribes. Another way to express this is "You chose the best of the land for yourselves."

A commander's portion: this means "a larger share," which would be given to a leader.

And he came to the heads of the people: NRSV has "he came at the head of the people." However, TEV and others follow the text of old translations and take the meaning as "the leaders of Israel" (see the TEV footnote). This gives the sense that, when the tribal leaders came together to divide the land, they decided that the tribe of Gad should have "a ruler's portion."

RSV indicates no textual problems here; NJPSV, however, notes that the meaning of the whole of verse 21 is uncertain. A change to the way the text of the first three lines is read is proposed by HOTTP ({C} rating), resulting in the following: "He chose the best portion for himself, for (where) the portion of the commander (was) there the chiefs of the people gathered together." In this restructured text the second line is joined to the third, not to the first. There seem to be as many solutions to this problem as there are translations.

Out of the many possibilities it is recommended that REB serve as the basic text:

- He chose the best for himself,
  for to him was allotted a ruler's portion,
  when the chiefs of the people were gathered together.

We may reorder the first three lines of the verse as follows:

- When the tribal leaders met together
  they assigned the best of the land to you;
  it was a ruler's portion.

589

RSV has reversed the order of the last two lines, translating **with Israel he executed the commands and just decrees of the LORD**. It is recommended that this rendition be ignored completely. NRSV "he executed the justice of the LORD, and his ordinances for Israel" is better. For "ordinances" see 4.1.

The last two parallel lines may be translated as follows:

●   When the leaders of Israel were gathered together,
        he [Gad] carried out the LORD's righteous will
        and his ordinances [or, laws] for the people of Israel.

If translators choose to follow the radical restructuring of the first three lines of the verse suggested above, a possible model for the whole verse is:

●   When the leaders of the tribes met together,
        they assigned the best of the land to you—
        the ruler's portion.
      You also carried out the LORD's righteous will
        and his ordinances for the people of Israel.

The following is offered as another possible model:

●   He chose the best of the land for himself;
      When the leaders of the tribes gathered together
      They assigned a leader's share to him.
      He carried out the LORD's righteous will,
      He obeyed the laws that the LORD gave to the people of Israel.

33.22   RSV

     And of Dan he said,
          "Dan is a lion's whelp,
             that leaps forth from Bashan."

                    TEV

     About the tribe of Dan he said:
          "Dan is a young lion;
          He leaps out from Bashan."

Dan is a lion's whelp: this is said of Judah in Gen 49.9. The figure can be expressed as a metaphor, "Dan is a young lion," or as a simile, "Dan is like a young lion." In most instances a simile will probably be better.

Leaps forth from Bashan: Bashan was a region east of the Jordan River, south of Lake Galilee (see 3.1). The text is talking about military raids against neighboring peoples. It does not mean Dan "leaps out of Bashan"; it means that from his lair in Bashan Dan assaults his enemies, and in a number of languages something like the following will be a possible translation:

- From your lair [or, cave] in Bashan
  you leap out on [or, attack] your enemies.

33.23 RSV

And of Naphtali he said,
"O Naphtali, satisfied with favor,
and full of the blessing of the LORD,
possess the lake and the south."

TEV

About the tribe of Naphtali he said:
"Naphtali is richly blessed by the LORD's good favor;
Their land reaches to the south from Lake Galilee."

Satisfied with and **full of** mean exactly the same thing, as do **favor** and **the blessing of the LORD**. NIV does a good job of combining the various elements: "Naphtali is abounding with the favor of the LORD, and is full of his blessing."

In some cases it will be better to change and make Naphtali the object of Yahweh's action: "The LORD has been good to [the tribe of] Naphtali, and has poured out his blessings on him [or, them]." However, in a number of languages translators will need to make the meaning of **blessing** clear; for example:

- About the people of the tribe of Naphtali he said,
  "Yahweh has been very kind to you
  and given you many good things. . . ."

Possess the lake and the south: some translations use the indicative mood (TEV "their land reaches to"; also REB, SPCL, BRCL), but it seems better to retain the imperative.

The lake translates the Hebrew word "the sea," which also bears the meaning "west." Since the territory of the tribe of Naphtali was west of Lake Galilee, "the sea" would be Lake Galilee itself. It is recommended that the following serve as a model: "Take possession of territory to the west and to the south of your land" (so FRCL).

33.24 RSV

And of Asher he said,
"Blessed above sons be Asher;
let him be the favorite of his brothers,
and let him dip his foot in oil.

591

TEV

About the tribe of Asher he said:
"Asher is blessed more than the other tribes.
May he be the favorite of his brothers,
And may his land be rich with olive trees.

Blessed above sons be Asher: or "May God bless the tribe of Asher more than all the other tribes." **Sons** here are the twelve sons of Jacob, that is, the twelve tribes. Another way to express this is "People of the tribe of Asher, may the LORD love you and be kinder to you than to the other tribes."

Be the favorite of his brothers: that is, God's favorite among the twelve brothers—not his brothers' favorite.

Let him dip his foot in oil: this is a picture of prosperity; it is talking about olive oil, not petroleum, and means an abundance of productive olive trees. The tribe of Asher occupied rich land along the Mediterranean coastline. A possible model for this line is "May your olive trees bear abundantly [or, have many olives]"; but some translators will wish to keep the poetic picture: "May your olive trees bear so many olives that you will have enough oil even to dip your feet in."

33.25   RSV

Your bars shall be iron and bronze;
and as your days, so shall your strength be.

TEV

May his towns be protected with iron gates,
And may he always live secure."

Your bars shall be iron and bronze: this is quite unintelligible. It speaks of a strong defense. A "bar" is a long and strong piece of wood or iron that is used to keep a door or a gate closed against anyone who wants to enter to do harm. NIV has "The bolts of your gates will be iron and bronze." FRCL offers a better model: "He is secure behind his doors with bars of iron and bronze."

As your days, so shall your strength be: in the context **strength** is security, not might. So NJB has "and your security [be] as lasting as your days," that is, "may you be secure all your life," and NJPSV "and [may] your security last all your days." See also TEV. As commentators point out, the Hebrew word translated **strength** is otherwise unknown in Hebrew; but the context seems clear enough, and the Septuagint translates "your strength."

33.26   RSV

> "There is none like God, O Jeshurun,
>   who rides through the heavens to your help,
>   and in his majesty through the skies.

                                                 TEV

> People of Israel, no god is like your God,
>   riding in splendor across the sky,
>   riding through the clouds to come to your aid.

In verses 26-29 Moses addresses the people of Israel with a final outburst of praise to God.

For **Jeshurun** as a name for Israel, see 32.15.

There is none like God: the comparison is not with human beings but with the gods of other peoples, "There is no god like your God" (see TEV). If "your" will be understood as not including Moses, it will be better to say "our."

Who rides through the heavens to your help: the verb "to ride" suggests a vehicle of some sort; in this context it's the clouds, or a cloud, on which God rides (see Psa 18.9-10; 68.4; 104.3; Isa 19.1). If needed this may be stated in the translation: "who rides the clouds across the sky like a chariot."

Through the heavens . . . through the skies: these are parallel and the same in meaning; but instead of **skies** the Hebrew word means "clouds" (so TEV, REB; see 2 Sam 22.12).

In his majesty: here we should understand **majesty** in terms of strength, power. See Exo 15.7.

TEV makes a slight rearrangement of the last two lines, to good effect. CEV also rearranges the lines:

>   the clouds are his chariot
>   as he rides across the skies
>   to come and help us.

33.27   RSV

> The eternal God is your dwelling place,
>   and underneath are the everlasting arms.
> And he thrust out the enemy before you,
>   and said, Destroy.

                                                 TEV

> God has always been your defense;
>   his eternal arms are your support.
> He drove out your enemies as you advanced,
>   and told you to destroy them all.

The eternal God is your dwelling place: this is a picture of safety and security; so NIV, NJB, NJPSV have "your refuge." **The eternal God** may also be expressed as "God who never dies [or, who lives forever]."

Underneath are the everlasting arms: that is, God's arms are placed to maintain, support, save his people. POCL "his power is your support forever" is clear but loses the beauty of the metaphor. CEV has "he carries us in his arms."

He thrust out the enemy before you: as the people of Israel invaded the land of Canaan, Yahweh drove out their enemies.

And said, Destroy: see 1.27. God commanded the Israelites to kill their enemies (see 7.2, 24).

33.28   RSV

> So Israel dwelt in safety,
>   the fountain of Jacob alone,
> in a land of grain and wine;
>   yea, his heavens drop down dew.

                                TEV

> So Jacob's descendants live in peace,
>   secure in a land full of grain and wine,
>   where dew from the sky waters the ground.

So Israel dwelt in safety: it may be better to use the present tense. NJPSV, for example, says "Thus Israel dwells in safety" (see also TEV).

The fountain of Jacob: **Israel** and **Jacob** are parallel and refer to the same group. But the Hebrew word translated **fountain** is written the same as one meaning "abode" (see Isa 13.22), and NRSV, NJPSV, and REB make the change: "Untroubled is Jacob's abode." It is recommended that this be followed. Should the translator decide to stay with the Hebrew text, **fountain** is a figure of speech meaning "descendants" (TEV).

Alone: here this means "undisturbed," not bothered or threatened by anyone, since the Israelites had expelled all the inhabitants of Canaan.

A land of grain and wine: this speaks of bumper crops of wheat and barley, and productive vineyards. So CEV has "and you will have plenty of grain and wine."

His heavens drop down dew: the verb occurs only here and at 32.2. It may be better to say "the heavens" (so NJPSV, NRSV, NIV and others), or "sky" (TEV, CEV).

33.29   RSV

> Happy are you, O Israel! Who is like you,
>   a people saved by the LORD,

> the shield of your help,
>   and the sword of your triumph!
> Your enemies shall come fawning to you;
>   and you shall tread upon their high places."

TEV

> Israel, how happy you are!
>   There is no one like you,
>   a nation saved by the LORD.
> The LORD himself is your shield and your sword,
>   to defend you and give you victory.
> Your enemies will come begging for mercy,
>   and you will trample them down.

Here end Moses' words to the people of Israel.

Happy are you, O Israel! The translator must decide whether it is better to say "Israel" or "people of Israel." Here **happy** has the meaning of "fortunate." So "People of Israel, you are so fortunate" is a good alternative model.

Grammatically RSV **Who is like you . . .** is a question, demanding a question mark at the end of the sentence. This is a rhetorical question whose answer is "No one." It is better to render it as an emphatic declaration, "There is no other people like you . . . ," followed by the reasons for this affirmation. See a similar kind of statement in 4.7.

A people saved by the LORD: this can be a reference to their deliverance from slavery in Egypt, or more generally to their being protected and guarded by Yahweh during their forty years' trek through the wilderness. If it is the latter we may say "Yahweh has continually protected you."

The shield . . . the sword: a **shield** is a defensive weapon, a **sword** an offensive weapon. God both defended the Israelites and attacked their enemies. Some translators will prefer to use similes; for example, "Like a shield he protects you, and like a sword he kills your enemies."

Your help: or "to help you," that is, "to defend you."

Your triumph: or "to win the victory for you."

Shall come fawning to you: the form of this verb occurs only here in the Old Testament. It means to act submissively, or else to try to gain favor by flattery. NJPSV and REB translate "cringing." TEV has "begging for mercy," and CEV has "will bow in fear."

Tread upon their high places: this can mean to walk triumphantly over their land (see "high places" in 32.13). The phrase can be understood to mean the pagan shrines of those people. But the opinion of most is that "their backs" is meant (NJPSV, NRSV, REB, NJB; the Septuagint translates "their neck").

An alternative translation model for this verse is:

- People of Israel,
    how fortunate you are!
  The LORD has continually guarded you.

Like a shield he protects you,
   and like a sword he kills your enemies.
Your enemies will come and beg you not to kill them,
   but you will trample on their backs.

6. The death of Moses

(34.1-12)

1 And Moses went up from the plains of Moab to Mount Nebo, to the top of Pisgah, which is opposite Jericho. And the LORD showed him all the land, Gilead as far as Dan, 2 all Naphtali, the land of Ephraim and Manasseh, all the land of Judah as far as the Western Sea, 3 the Negeb, and the Plain, that is, the valley of Jericho the city of palm trees, as far as Zoar. 4 And the LORD said to him, "This is the land of which I swore to Abraham, to Isaac, and to Jacob, 'I will give it to your descendants.' I have let you see it with your eyes, but you shall not go over there." 5 So Moses the servant of the LORD died there in the land of Moab, according to the word of the LORD, 6 and he buried him in the valley in the land of Moab opposite Beth-peor; but no man knows the place of his burial to this day. 7 Moses was a hundred and twenty years old when he died; his eye was not dim, nor his natural force abated. 8 And the people of Israel wept for Moses in the plains of Moab thirty days; then the days of weeping and mourning for Moses were ended.

9 And Joshua the son of Nun was full of the spirit of wisdom, for Moses had laid his hands upon him; so the people of Israel obeyed him, and did as the LORD had commanded Moses. 10 And there has not arisen a prophet since in Israel like Moses, whom the LORD knew face to face, 11 none like him for all the signs and the wonders which the LORD sent him to do in the land of Egypt, to Pharaoh and to all his servants and to all his land, 12 and for all the mighty power and all the great and terrible deeds which Moses wrought in the sight of all Israel.

1 Moses went up from the plains of Moab to Mount Nebo, to the top of Mount Pisgah east of Jericho, and there the LORD showed him the whole land: the territory of Gilead as far north as the town of Dan; 2 the entire territory of Naphtali; the territories of Ephraim and Manasseh; the territory of Judah as far west as the Mediterranean Sea; 3 the southern part of Judah; and the plain that reaches from Zoar to Jericho, the city of palm trees. 4 Then the LORD said to Moses, "This is the land that I promised Abraham, Isaac, and Jacob I would give to their descendants. I have let you see it, but I will not let you go there."

5 So Moses, the LORD's servant, died there in the land of Moab, as the LORD had said he would. 6 The LORD buried him in a valley in Moab, opposite the town of Bethpeor, but to this day no one knows the exact place of his burial. 7 Moses was a hundred and twenty years old when he died; he was as strong as ever, and his eyesight was still good. 8 The people of Israel mourned for him for thirty days in the plains of Moab.

9 Joshua son of Nun was filled with wisdom, because Moses had appointed him to be his successor. The people of Israel obeyed Joshua and kept the commands that the LORD had given them through Moses.

10 There has never been a prophet in Israel like Moses; the LORD spoke with him face-to-face. 11 No other prophet has ever done miracles and wonders like those that the LORD sent Moses to perform against the king of Egypt, his officials, and the entire country. 12 No other prophet has been able to do the great and terrifying things that Moses did in the sight of all Israel.

This final section of the book gives a record of the death of Moses and his burial by the LORD (verses 1-8), and concludes with a tribute to Moses, the greatest of all the prophets of Israel (verses 10-12).

Section heading: the TEV and CEV title "The Death of Moses" is quite sufficient. NRSV has the rather wordy "Moses' Departure and Epitaph."

34.1   RSV   TEV

And Moses went up from the   Moses went up from the plains of
plains of Moab to Mount Nebo, to the   Moab to Mount Nebo, to the top of
top of Pisgah, which is opposite   Mount Pisgah east of Jericho, and
Jericho. And the LORD showed him   there the LORD showed him the
all the land, Gilead as far as Dan,   whole land: the territory of Gilead as
                                         far north as the town of Dan;

The plains of Moab: see 1.5; Num 36.13.

To Mount Nebo: see 32.45. This is on the east side of the Jordan River, opposite the city of Jericho.

To the top of Pisgah: see 3.17. Either two traditions have been joined together here, or else **Pisgah** is taken to be the highest peak of **Nebo**. TEV follows the second interpretation, understanding Pisgah to be a separate peak of Mount Nebo, whereas CEV understands Mount Nebo to be a separate peak on Mount Pisgah. Translators may follow either TEV or CEV.

Opposite Jericho: see 32.49.

Showed him all the land: on both sides of the Jordan River.

Gilead: a territory on the east side of the Jordan River (see 2.36), its south end reaching the northern tip of the Dead Sea.

As far as Dan: the town of **Dan** was the northernmost town in the territory of the tribe of Dan, north of Lake Galilee.

34.2   RSV   TEV

all Naphtali, the land of Ephraim and   the entire territory of Naphtali; the
Manasseh, all the land of Judah as   territories of Ephraim and Manasseh;
far as the Western Sea,   the territory of Judah as far west as
                                          the Mediterranean Sea;

CEV introduces the verse with the following: "He let Moses see the territories that would soon belong to . . . ." For the location of the regions and places mentioned in verses 1-3, see the map on page xii.

Naphtali: the northern region west of the Jordan River.

Ephraim and Manasseh: south of Naphtali.

Judah: the southernmost region on the west side of the Jordan.

The Western Sea: that is, the Mediterranean (see 11.24).

RSV   TEV

the Negeb, and the Plain, that is, the   the southern part of Judah; and the
valley of Jericho the city of palm   plain that reaches from Zoar to
trees, as far as Zoar.   Jericho, the city of palm trees.

The Negeb: the desert region south of Judah (see 1.7). It will be good to begin
a new sentence here with, for example, "The LORD showed Moses the land
called the Negeb that lay to the south of Judah." Some traditions transliterate
the name as "the Negev."

The Plain, that is, the valley of Jericho . . . as far as Zoar: see TEV for the
translation of this region. This is a reference to the basin of the Dead Sea;
Jericho was in the northwest, and Zoar in the southeast, south of the Dead Sea.

The city of palm trees: a familiar description of Jericho (see Judges 1.16;
3.13).

34.4   RSV   TEV

And the LORD said to him, "This is   Then the LORD said to Moses, "This
the land of which I swore to Abra-   is the land that I promised Abraham,
ham, to Isaac, and to Jacob, 'I will   Isaac, and Jacob I would give to their
give it to your descendants.' I have   descendants. I have let you see it,
let you see it with your eyes, but you   but I will not let you go there."
shall not go over there."

**The land of which I swore to Abraham, Isaac, and Jacob, 'I will give it to your
descendants'**: among other passages, see 1.8; 6.10; 9.5; 30.20.

I have let you see it with your eyes, but you shall not go over there: see 3.27.

34.5   RSV   TEV

So Moses the servant of the LORD   So Moses, the LORD's servant, died
died there in the land of Moab, ac-   there in the land of Moab, as the
cording to the word of the LORD,   LORD had said he would.

The servant of the LORD: this is a title of honor (see Josh 1.1); there is no idea
of servility or hard labor. In some languages this will be rendered as "The
LORD's man" or even "The LORD's right hand person." Translators need to find
a term that shows that in Yahweh's eyes Moses had dignity and status.

There in the land of Moab: this is included for emphasis; Moses did not die
in Canaan.

According to the word of the LORD: that is, "as the LORD had said he would."
But in light of 32.50, it is possible to translate "at the command of the LORD"
(NJPSV), or "as the LORD decreed" (NJB).

34.6   RSV   TEV

and he buried him in the valley in the land of Moab opposite Beth-peor; but no man knows the place of his burial to this day.	The LORD buried him in a valley in Moab, opposite the town of Beth-peor, but to this day no one knows the exact place of his burial.

He buried him: that is, Yahweh buried Moses.

In the valley in the land of Moab opposite Beth-peor: see 3.29. This is where the people of Israel have been all this time; RSV indicates this by using the definite article **the** rather than the indefinite "a" (TEV, CEV). Translators are urged to follow the interpretation of RSV.

No man knows: meaning "no person," or "no one" (TEV, CEV).

To this day: that is, to the day this account was written (see 2.22).

34.7   RSV   TEV

Moses was a hundred and twenty years old when he died; his eye was not dim, nor his natural force abated.	Moses was a hundred and twenty years old when he died; he was as strong as ever, and his eyesight was still good.

One hundred and twenty years old: see 31.2.

His eye was not dim, nor his natural force abated: the noun translated "natural force" occurs only here in the Old Testament; perhaps it refers to sexual power. NRSV translates "his sight was unimpaired, and his vigor had not abated." If the idea of **natural force** or "vigor" is hard to translate, we may follow TEV, with "was as strong as ever," or CEV "his body was still strong."

34.8   RSV   TEV

And the people of Israel wept for Moses in the plains of Moab thirty days; then the days of weeping and mourning for Moses were ended.	The people of Israel mourned for him for thirty days in the plains of Moab.

See the similar account of Aaron's death in Num 20.20. **Thirty days** seems to have been the normal length of time of mourning for a leader.

Then the days of weeping and mourning . . . were ended: this is quite redundant information. To make the text less repetitive, it may be placed at the beginning of the next paragraph (as in NJPSV). CEV has a good model for this verse:

- The people of Israel stayed in the lowlands of Moab, where they mourned and grieved thirty days for Moses, as was their custom.

34.9 RSV TEV

And Joshua the son of Nun was full of the spirit of wisdom, for Moses had laid his hands upon him; so the people of Israel obeyed him, and did as the LORD had commanded Moses.

Joshua son of Nun was filled with wisdom, because Moses had appointed him to be his successor. The people of Israel obeyed Joshua and kept the commands that the LORD had given them through Moses.

This verse is somewhat of a shift; it is not a recital of what happened next, as we might expect, but a general statement about Joshua, successor of Moses. For the commissioning of Joshua, see 31.1-8; Num 27.12-23.

Full of the spirit of wisdom: this is God-given wisdom.

Moses had laid his hands on him: see Num 27.22-23. It will be helpful to place this information at the beginning of the verse as follows: "Before Moses died, he placed his hands on Joshua and appointed him to be his successor. Yahweh filled him with wisdom [or, made him a very wise person]."

The people of Israel obeyed him: this goes quite naturally with what follows; they did **as the LORD had commanded Moses** and obeyed Joshua (see TEV).

34.10 RSV TEV

And there has not arisen a prophet since in Israel like Moses, whom the LORD knew face to face,

There has never been a prophet in Israel like Moses; the LORD spoke with him face-to-face.

Verses 10-12 are a final statement from the perspective on an editor or editors after the time of Moses. They summarize the life and work of Moses and express the regard the people of Israel have held for him throughout their history. It will be helpful to begin a anew paragraph here, and some translators will need to introduce a discourse marker or a change in verbal form that will indicate that this was written at a later period than that of Moses.

Has not arisen a prophet since in Israel like Moses: see 18.15, 18. The verb "arise" here means to "appear," or "be."

The LORD knew face to face: in most instances the phrase is "to speak face to face" (5.4; Exo 33.11); Num 12.8 has "speak mouth to mouth." If the verb "know" is retained, the idea must be conveyed of intimate knowledge, close friendship (see Exo 33.11). So we may say "He was Yahweh's friend."

34.11 RSV TEV

none like him for all the signs and the wonders which the LORD sent him to do in the land of Egypt, to Pharaoh and to all his servants and to all his land,

No other prophet has ever done miracles and wonders like those that the LORD sent Moses to perform against the king of Egypt, his officials, and the entire country.

The sentence structure of RSV is not good; the translator should follow TEV, using two or more complete sentences for verses 11 and 12.

None like him for all the signs and the wonders: that is, there was no one who performed **the signs and the wonders** he performed. See 4.34; 26.8.

The LORD sent him to do in the land of Egypt: this is a reference to the ten plagues (Exo 7.14–12.26).

To Pharaoh and to all his servants and to all his land: see 29.2.

34.12   RSV   TEV

and for all the mighty power and all the great and terrible deeds which Moses wrought in the sight of all Israel.	No other prophet has been able to do the great and terrifying things that Moses did in the sight of all Israel.

All the mighty power and all the great and terrible deeds: the first expression refers to Moses' **power** to perform signs and wonders; the second describes the **deeds** themselves. Translators may say something like the following:

• How great was his power, how mighty [or, awesome] and terrifying the deeds that Moses performed in the presence of the Israelites!

Selected Bibliography

Bible Texts, Versions, and Helps

Ancient Texts

Biblia Hebraica Stuttgartensia 1967/77. Edited by K. Elliger and W. Rudolph. Stuttgart: Deutsche Bibelstiftung.

Septuaginta: id est Vetus Testamentum graece iuxta LXX interpretes. 1950. Edited by Alfred Rahlfs. Stuttgart: Württembergische Bibelanstalt. (Cited as the Septuagint.)

Modern Versions

Die Bibel in heutigem Deutsch: Die Gute Nachricht des Alten und Neuen Testaments. 1982. Stuttgart: Deutsche Bibelgesellschaft. (Cited as GECL, German common language version.)

La Bible. 1973. Traduction française sur les textes originaux par Émile Osty avec la collaboration de Joseph Trinquet. Paris: Éditions du Seuil. (Cited as Osty.)

The Bible: A New Translation. 1926. James Moffatt, translator. London: Hodder and Stoughton. (Cited as Mft.)

La Bible: L'ancien Testament, tome 1. 1956. Paris: Bibliothèque de la Pléiade. (Cited as Pléiade.)

La Bible de Jérusalem. 1984. Paris: Éditions du Cerf.

La Bible en français courant. 1982. Paris: Société biblique française. (Cited as FRCL, French common language version.)

A Bíblia Sagrada: Tradução na Linguagem de Hoje. 1988. São Paulo: Sociedade Bíblica do Brasil. (Cited as BRCL, Brazilian common language version.)

Bíblia Sagrada: Tradução em português corrente. 1993. Lisboa: Sociedade Bíblica de Portugal. (Cited as POCL, Portuguese common language version.)

Dios Habla Hoy: La Biblia, Versión Popular. 1979. New York: Sociedades Biblicas Unidas. (Cited as SPCL, Spanish common language version.)

Good News Bible: The Bible in Today's English. 1992. New York: American Bible Society. (Cited as TEV.)

The Holy Bible. 1955. Translated by Ronald A. Knox. London: Burns & Oates. (Cited as Knox.)

The Holy Bible: Contemporary English Version. 1995. New York: American bible society. (Cited as CEV.)

The Holy Bible: New International Version. 1987. New York: New York International Bible Society. (Cited as NIV.)

The Holy Bible: Revised Standard Version. 1973. New York: Division of Christian Education of the National Council of the Churches of Christ in the United States of America. (Cited as RSV.)

The Jerusalem Bible. 1966. London: Darton, Longman, & Todd; and New York: Doubleday. (Cited as JB.)

New Revised Standard Version Bible. 1989. New York: Division of Christian Education of the National Council of the Churches of Christ in the United States of America. (Cited as NRSV.)

The New English Bible. 1970. London: Oxford University Press. (Cited as NEB.)

Revised English Bible. 1992. London: Oxford University Press. (Cited as REB.)

The New Jerusalem Bible. 1985. Garden City, New York: Doubleday. (Cited as NJB.)

La Sainte Bible: Traduite d'apres les textes originaux hébreu et grec. 1978. Nouvelle version Segond révisée. 2ᵉ édition. Paris: Alliance Biblique Universelle. (Cited as Segond.)

TANAKH: A New Translation of the Holy Scriptures According to the Traditional Hebrew Text. 1985. Philadelphia: Jewish Publication Society. (Cited as NJPSV, New Jewish Publication Society version.)

[Thai Common Language Bible.] 1985. Bangkok: Bible Society of Thailand. (Cited as Thai.)

Traduction œcuménique de la Bible. 1977. Paris: Société Biblique française et Éditions du Cerf. (Cited as TOB.)

Lexicons, Concordances, and Other Reference Works

Preliminary and Interim Report on the Hebrew Old Testament Text Project. 1973. London: United Bible Societies. (Cited as HOTTP.)

Fauna and Flora of the Bible. 1972. London: United Bible Societies. (Cited as FFB.)

Holladay, William L., editor. 1971. *A Concise Hebrew and Aramaic Lexicon of the Old Testament.* Grand Rapids, Michigan: Eerdmans.

Hulst, A.R. 1960. *Old Testament Translation Problems.* Leiden: E.J. Brill.

Nelson's Complete Concordance of the Revised Standard Version. 1957. New York: Thomas Nelson.

Robinson, David, editor. 1983. *Concordance to the Good News Bible.* Swindon: The British and Foreign Society.

Commentaries

Blenkinsopp, Joseph. 1990. "Deuteronomy," *The New Jerusalem Biblical Commentary* (pages 94-109). Englewood Cliffs, New Jersey: Prentice Hall.

Bratcher, R.G., and Nida, E.A. 1961. *A Handbook on the Gospel of Mark.* London: United Bible Societies.

Bratcher, R.G., and Reyburn, W.D. 1991. *A Handbook on the Book of Psalms.* New York: United Bible Societies.

Clark, D.J., and Hatton, H.A. 1989. *A Handbook on the Books of Nahum, Habakkuk, and Zephaniah.* New York: United Bible Societies.

Clements, R.E. 1989. *Deuteronomy.* Sheffield: Sheffield Academic Press.

Craigie, Peter C. 1976. *The Book of Deuteronomy.* Grand Rapids: Eerdmans.

Driver, S.L. 1902. *A Critical and Exegetical Commentary on Deuteronomy* (third edition). Edinburgh: T & T Clark.

Mayes, A.D.H. 1979. *The New Century Bible Commentary: Deuteronomy.* Grand Rapids: Eerdmans. Nelson, Richard. 1988. "Deuteronomy," *Harper's Bible Commentary* (pages 209-234). San Francisco: Harper & Row.

Péter-Contesse, R., and Ellington, J. 1990. *A Handbook on Leviticus.* New York: United Bible Societies.

BIBLIOGRAPHY

von Rad, G. 1962. "Deuteronomy," *The Interpreter's Dictionary of the Bible* (volume I, pages 831-838). New York: Abingdon Press.

Reyburn, W.D. 1992. *A Handbook on the Book of Job.* New York: United Bible Societies.

de Waard, J., and Smalley, W.A. 1979, *A Handbook on the Book of Amos.* New York: United Bible Societies.

Weinfeld, Moshe. 1992. "Deuteronomy, Book of," *The Anchor Bible Dictionary* (volume II, pages 168-183). New York: Doubleday.

Glossary

This Glossary contains terms that are technical from an exegetical or a linguistic viewpoint. Other terms not defined here may be referred to in a Bible dictionary.

ABSTRACT NOUN is one that refers to a quality or characteristic, such as "beauty" or "darkness."

ACTIVE. See **VOICE.**

ACTOR is the one who accomplishes the action in a sentence or clause, regardless of whether the grammatical construction is active or passive. In "John struck Bill" (active) and "Bill was struck by John" (passive), the actor in either case is John.

ADJECTIVE is a word that limits, describes, or qualifies a noun. In English, "red," "tall," "beautiful," and "important" are adjectives.

ADVERB is a word that limits, describes, or qualifies a verb, an adjective, or another adverb. In English, "quickly," "soon," "primarily," and "very" are adverbs.

ADVERSATIVE describes something opposed to or in contrast with something already stated. "But" and "however" are adversative conjunctions.

AGENT is one who does the action in a sentence or clause, regardless of whether the grammatical construction is active or passive. In "John hit Bill" (active) and "Bill was hit by John" (passive), the agent in both cases is "John."

AMBIGUITY refers to words or sentences that have more than one possible meaning in a given context. For example, in the sentence "Mike said that if Joe comes, he will speak to the president," "he" could refer to Mike or to Joe. Thus this sentence is **AMBIGUOUS.** Often what is ambiguous in written form is not ambiguous when actually spoken, since intonation and other features of speech help to make the meaning clear. In written discourse, context also helps to indicate which meaning is intended by the author.

ANCIENT VERSIONS. See **VERSIONS.**

AUXILIARY is a word that combines closely with another word and that serves to specify certain important aspects of meaning. **AUXILIARY** verbs often express tense, aspect, mood, person, or number; for example, "shall," "will," "may," or "ought."

BORROWING is the process of using a foreign word in another language. For example, "matador" is a Spanish word that has been **BORROWED** by English speakers for "bullfighter."

CAUSATIVE relates to events and indicates that someone or something caused something to happen, rather than that the person or thing did it directly. In "The child grew flowers," the verb "grew" is a causative, since it was not the child who grew, but rather the child caused the flowers to grow.

CIRCUMSTANTIAL is an adjective that refers to any kind of circumstance that modifies an event. In grammatical terms, for example, "When the sun rose, the boy woke up," the temporal clause "When the sun rose" is a **CIRCUMSTANTIAL CLAUSE**, modifying the main action "the boy woke up."

CLAUSE is a grammatical construction, normally consisting of a subject and a predicate. The **MAIN CLAUSE** is that clause in a sentence that can stand alone as a complete sentence, but which has one or more dependent or subordinate clauses related to it. A **SUBORDINATE CLAUSE** is dependent on the main clause, but it does not form a complete sentence. See also **COMPLEX SENTENCE**.

CLIMAX is the point in a discourse, such as a story or speech, which is the most important, or the turning point, or the point of decision.

COGNATES are related words derived from a common source. The English words "love," "loving," "lovable," "lovely," and "lovingly" are cognates.

COLLECTIVE describes a group of things (or persons) considered as a whole, such as "rice" or "crowd." In English a collective noun is considered to be singular or plural, more or less on the basis of traditional usage; for example, "The crowd is [The people are] becoming angry."

COMMAND. See **IMPERATIVE**.

COMMON LANGUAGE TRANSLATION uses language that is widely understood and accepted by most speakers. In such a translation, substandard speech, dialect peculiarities, and highly literary or technical terms are avoided.

COMPLEX SENTENCE contains at least one modifying clause in addition to the main clause.

COMPOUND refers to forms of words or phrases consisting of two or more parts.

CONDITION is that which shows the circumstance under which something may be true. In English a **CONDITIONAL** phrase or clause is usually introduced by "if." For example, *"If you dig a pit,* you may fall into it," or "The story, *if true,* will cause much joy."

CONJUNCTIONS are words that serve as connectors between words, phrases, clauses, and sentences. "And," "but," "if," "because," and "or" are typical conjunctions in English.

CONSEQUENCE is that which shows the result of a condition or event. In the sentence "If you dig a pit, you may fall into it," falling is the consequence of the first action, digging.

CONSONANTS are speech sounds that are produced by blocking or restricting the passage of air as it comes from the lungs through the mouth. The written letters representing those sounds are also called **CONSONANTS**; for example, "b," "c," "d," or "f" in English. **CONSONANTS** were originally the only spoken sounds written in the Hebrew alphabet. Marks for **VOWELS** were added later above or below the **CONSONANTS**. See also **VOWELS**.

CONSTRUCTION. See **STRUCTURE**.

CONTEXT is that which precedes or follows any part of a discourse. For example, the context of a word or phrase in Scripture would be the other words and phrases associated with it in the sentence, paragraph, section, and even the entire book in which it occurs. The context of a term often affects its meaning, so that a word may not mean exactly the same thing in one context that it does in another. Context is also the set of circumstances or facts surrounding an event or situation. See also **IMMEDIATE CONTEXT**.

CULTURE (CULTURAL) is the combination of beliefs, values, social institutions, customs, and material objects (such as tools or ornaments) of any group of people. A culture is passed on from one generation to another but undergoes development or gradual change.

DEPENDENT CLAUSE is a grammatical construction consisting normally of a subject and predicate, which is dependent upon or embedded within some other construction. For example, "if he comes" is a dependent clause in the sentence "If he comes, we'll have to leave." See also **CLAUSE**.

DESCRIPTIVE is said of a word or phrase that characterizes or describes another term.

DIRECT ADDRESS, DIRECT DISCOURSE, DIRECT QUOTATION, DIRECT SPEECH. See **DISCOURSE**.

DIRECT OBJECT is the goal of an event or action specified by a verb. In "John hit the ball," the direct object of "hit" is "ball."

609

DISCOURSE is the connected and continuous communication of thought by means of language, whether spoken or written. The way in which the elements of a discourse are arranged is called **DISCOURSE STRUCTURE**. **DIRECT DISCOURSE** (or, **DIRECT ADDRESS, DIRECT QUOTATION, DIRECT SPEECH**) is the reproduction of the actual words of one person quoted and included in the discourse of another person; for example, "He declared 'I will have nothing to do with this man.'" **INDIRECT DISCOURSE** (or, **INDIRECT QUOTATION, INDIRECT SPEECH**) is the reporting of the words of one person within the discourse of another person, but in an altered grammatical form rather than as an exact quotation; for example, "He said he would have nothing to do with that man."

DUAL is a grammatical form, in Hebrew and some other languages, involving two paired objects such as "eyes," "hands," or "horns." Sometimes words fall into the dual category, even though they do not exist in pairs. This is true, for example, of the word "Egypt" in Hebrew.

DYNAMIC EQUIVALENCE TRANSLATION refers to a translation that tries to give the intended meaning of the **SOURCE TEXT** in a natural and meaningful way so that it produces a response in today's reader that is essentially equivalent to that of the original reader. **LITERAL** translations pay more attention to reproducing the forms found in the **SOURCE** text. For example, RSV follows the Hebrew wording of Psa 104.29 and says: "they die and return to their dust." CEV tries to give a **DYNAMIC EQUIVALENT TRANSLATION**: "they die and rot."

EMPHASIS (EMPHATIC) is the relative importance given to an element in a discourse. **EMPHASIS** is conveyed by many different devices, depending on the language; for example, positioning of words, emphatic **PARTICLES**, intensifiers, or **IDEOPHONES**. In "Oh, that you had heeded my commandments!" (Isa 48.18, the New KJV), the particle "Oh" marks this statement as **EMPHATIC**.

EQUIVALENCE (EQUIVALENT) is a very close similarity in meaning, as opposed to similarity in form.

EUPHEMISM is a mild or indirect term used in the place of another term that is felt to be impolite, distasteful, or vulgar; for example, "to pass away" is a euphemism for "to die."

EXAGGERATION is stating more than the speaker or writer knows to be true. **EXAGGERATION** may be used to express humor, to say something **IRONICAL** or **SARCASTIC**, or to make a particular point. For example, "Everyone is doing it" can mean "Many people are doing it" (implying "and I want to do it, too"). See also **HYPERBOLE**.

EXCLUSIVE and **INCLUSIVE** describe words or expressions that exclude or include certain people. For example:
The **EXCLUSIVE** or **INCLUSIVE** first person plural pronouns for "we" in some languages appear as two distinct pronouns, one excluding and the other including the person(s) spoken to. For example, "*We* were married yesterday"

excludes the friend to whom one may be speaking, but includes the wife if the husband is speaking to her.

EXCLUSIVE terms such as "brothers" exclude "sisters" in many languages while some languages use **INCLUSIVE** terms that refer to both, such as "siblings." In translating, it is often better to use **INCLUSIVE** language, depending upon the meaning to be conveyed. For example, "believers" can be used instead of "brothers," and "human beings" can be used for "men" when both men and women are the intended meaning in the original text.

EXEGESIS (EXEGETICAL) is the process of determining the meaning of a text (or the result of this process), normally in terms of "who said what to whom under what circumstances and with what intent." A correct exegesis is indispensable before a passage can be translated correctly.

EXHORTATION is the verbal act of encouraging, attempting, or urging, to make someone change a course of action or a matter of belief. "Do your best to encourage one another!" is an **EXHORTATION**.

FEMININE is one of the categories of nouns and pronouns in many languages. In most of these languages this category may include terms that are not related to the female sex.

FIGURE, FIGURE OF SPEECH, FIGURATIVE EXPRESSION, or **FIGURATIVE LANGUAGE** involves the use of words in other than their literal or ordinary sense in order to bring out some aspect of meaning by comparison or association. For example, when the psalmist says "my cup overflows," he is not saying his cup is too full. He is rather using a **FIGURE OF SPEECH** to say that he is as content as someone who has been served a generous portion. **METAPHORS** and **SIMILES** are common figures of speech.

FINITE VERB is a verb form that distinguishes person, number, tense, mode, or aspect. It contrasts with an infinitive verb form, which does not indicate these features but only the action or state.

FIRST PERSON. See **PERSON**.

FOCUS is the center of attention in a discourse. It may be marked in a special way such as by word order, a special particle, or repetition.

FORMAL EQUIVALENCE is a type of translation in which many features of the source text, especially the form of the discourse, have been literally reproduced in the translation. This approach often results in an unnatural style in the receptor language, or sometimes in the lack of any meaning at all. See **LITERAL**.

FULL STOP is a punctuation mark indicating the end of a sentence; this mark is also called a "period."

FUNCTIONAL EQUIVALENCE is a type of translation that attempts to convey the same set of communicative functions as that of the original **SOURCE** text. Some important functions of communication are to convey information, to express or evoke emotions, to promote changes in thinking or behavior, or to maintain good interpersonal relations. See also **DYNAMIC EQUIVALENCE**, which has a similar meaning.

FUTURE TENSE. See **TENSE**.

GENERIC refers to a **GENERAL** class or kind of object. It contrasts with "specific." For example, the word "food" is a generic term, while "fruit" is more specific. However, the word "fruit" is a **GENERIC** term for the more specific word "orange."

GOAL is the object that receives or undergoes the action of a verb. Grammatically, the goal may be the subject of a passive construction ("John was hit," in which "John" is the goal of "hit"), or of certain intransitives ("the door shut"), or it may be the direct object of a transitive verb (as "John" in "the ball hit John").

GREEK is the language in which the New Testament was written. It belongs to the Indo-European family of languages and was the language spoken in Achaia, which is Greece in modern times. By the time of Christ Greek was used by many of the people living in the eastern part of the Roman empire, so that early Christians could speak and write to one another in Greek, even though they were born in different countries. By that time the entire Hebrew Old Testament had been translated into Greek, a version referred to as the **SEPTUAGINT**.

HEBREW is the language in which the Old Testament was written. It belongs to the Semitic family of languages. By the time of Christ many Jewish people no longer used Hebrew as their common language, but spoke Aramaic (a language related to Hebrew) or Greek.

The **HEBREWS** originally included people who did not belong to the twelve tribes of Israel, but after the Israelites settled in Canaan, the term generally was used to refer to the people of the twelve tribes, who had their own Hebrew language and culture.

HYPERBOLE is a figure of speech that makes use of **EXAGGERATION**. A deliberate overstatement is made to create a special effect. "He cries night and day" is an example of **HYPERBOLE**. The statement does not mean that the person cries every moment of the day and night, but that he cries a great deal.

IDEOPHONE is a form of expressive language that can describe anything that a person's senses may feel or observe. It can express an emotion, a sound (onomatopoeia), a smell, quality, texture, or movement. Ideophones use sounds and combinations of sounds that make them stand out from other words in a language. They are especially common in African languages. For example, in one language *prrrr!* expresses whiteness or brightness. In another language *yaa* indicates complete emptiness.

IDIOM, or **IDIOMATIC EXPRESSION,** is a combination of terms whose meanings cannot be understood by adding up the meanings of the parts. "To hang one's head" is an English idiom. "A drop in the bucket" is an idiom coming from Hebrew (Isa 40.15). Idiomatic expressions almost always lose their meaning or convey a wrong meaning when translated literally from one language to another.

IMMEDIATE CONTEXT refers to the words which immediately precede or follow a discourse or segment of discourse, and which often help one to interpret the meaning of the whole section. For example, Psalm 1.2 is a passage in the immediate context of Psalm 1.1 and helps to interpret it. See also **CONTEXT.**

IMPERATIVE refers to forms of a verb that indicate commands or requests. In Psa 34.11 there are two imperative forms, *"Come,* you children, *listen* to me." Imperatives are often used together with **VOCATIVE** expressions ("you children"). In some languages imperatives occur only in the second person; but in others imperatives also occur in the first and third persons. These are usually expressed in English by the use of "must" or "let"; for example, "They *must work* harder!" or *"Let us go* to the house of the LORD."

IMPERSONAL VERB is a usage of the verb that denotes an action by an unspecified agent. It may involve the use of the third person singular, as in "It is raining" or "One normally prefers cake," or in some languages the use of the third person plural, as in "They say . . . ." In still other languages the first person plural is used, as in "We cook this way," meaning "People cook this way." Such a pronoun is sometimes referred to as the **INDEFINITE PRONOUN.**

IMPLICIT (IMPLIED) refers to information which is conveyed by a text, but which is not expressed in words. The speaker assumes that the hearer understands the meaning. Often the meaning is clear from the **CONTEXT.** For example, when Hannah says in 1 Sam 2.6 "He brings down to Sheol and *raises up*," the **IMPLIED** or **IMPLICIT** meaning is *"raises up to life."* See **EXPLICIT.**

IMPLY. See **IMPLICIT, IMPLIED.**

INCLUSIVE. See **EXCLUSIVE AND INCLUSIVE.**

INDICATIVE refers to forms of a verb in which an act or condition is stated as an actual fact rather than as a potentiality, a hope, or an unrealized condition. The verb "won" in "The king won the battle" is in the indicative form.

INDIRECT ADDRESS, INDIRECT DISCOURSE, INDIRECT QUOTATION, INDIRECT SPEECH. See **DISCOURSE.**

INDIRECT OBJECT is the benefactive goal of the event or action specified by a verb. In "John threw Henry the ball," the direct object or goal of "threw" is "ball," and the indirect object is "Henry." See **DIRECT OBJECT**.

INTERPRETATION of a text is the exegesis of it. See **EXEGESIS**.

IRONY (IRONIC) is a sarcastic or humorous manner of discourse in which what is said is intended to express its opposite; for example, "That was a smart thing to do!" when intended to convey the meaning "That was a stupid thing to do!" See also **EXAGGERATION, HYPERBOLE**, and **SARCASM**.

LITERAL refers to the ordinary or primary meaning of a word, phrase, or clause. For example, the **LITERAL** meaning of "my cup overflows" is that liquid is streaming over the top of the speaker's cup. The **FIGURATIVE** meaning is that the person is happy or satisfied. A **LITERAL TRANSLATION** follows the **SOURCE** text very closely, trying to imitate the order of words or sentences, and translating expressions word-for-word. Such translations are frequently unnatural, meaningless, or even incorrect.

MAIN CLAUSE. See **CLAUSE**.

MANUSCRIPTS are books, documents, or letters written or copied by hand. A **SCRIBE** is one who copies a manuscript. Thousands of manuscript copies of various Old and New Testament books still exist, but none of the original manuscripts are known to exist. See **TEXT**.

MARKERS (MARKING) are features of words or of a discourse that signal some special meaning or some particular structure. For example, words for speaking may mark the onset of direct discourse, a phrase such as "Once upon a time" may mark the beginning of a fairy story, and various types of parallelism are the dominant markers of biblical poetry. The word "body" may require a marker to clarify whether a person, a group, or a corpse is meant.

MASCULINE is one of the categories of nouns and pronouns in many languages. In most of these languages this category may include terms that are not related to the male sex. See also **FEMININE** and **NEUTER**.

MASORETIC TEXT is the traditional written text of the Hebrew Old Testament established by Hebrew scholars during the eighth and ninth centuries A.D.

METAPHOR is likening one object, event, or state (the "topic") to another (the "image") to which it is not directly or closely related in meaning. For example, when a person says "I am a worm," he is describing his state as being lowly, miserable, or of no value. Biblical metaphors are often difficult to understand because the basis for the comparison is not always stated, as in the line "The LORD is my rock" (Psa 18.1). At other times either the image or the basis of comparison is unfamiliar or used differently in the receptor language. For example, when the psalmist says "He remembers that we are dust" (103.14), he is not referring to the dirt or dust on our bodies. Metaphors are the most commonly used figures of speech and are often so subtle that a speaker or writer is not conscious of the fact that he or she is using figurative language. See **SIMILE**.

MODIFY is to directly affect the meaning of another part of the sentence, as when an adjective modifies a noun or an adverb modifies a verb.

NOUN is a word that names a person, place, thing, quality, action or idea.

OBJECT of a verb is the goal of an event or action specified by the verb. In "John hit the ball," the object of "hit" is "ball." See **DIRECT OBJECT, INDIRECT OBJECT**.

OVERLAPPING is the way in which part of the meanings of two words cover the same general area of meaning, although the remainder of the meanings covered by the two words is not the same. For example, "love" and "like" overlap in referring to human affection.

PAPYRI (singular **PAPYRUS**) are, in the context of this Handbook, those texts of the Scriptures that were written originally on papyrus (an early form of paper) and that are representative of the earliest forms of the text.

PARAGRAPH is a distinct unit of prose discourse that usually deals with a single topic or theme. A **PARAGRAPH** is made up of **SENTENCES**.

PARALLEL, PARALLELISM, generally refers to some similarity in the content and/or form of two parts of a construction; for example, "The man was blind; he could not see." The structures that correspond to each other in the two statements are said to be parallel. **PARALLEL PASSAGES** are two separate biblical references that resemble each other in one or more ways.

In Hebrew poetry in particular, **PARALLELISM** refers to two or more poetic lines that are alike in some way and need to be interpreted together. They may be related in sound, meaning, or grammatical structure (or all three). In the following lines from Eccl 3.4, the lines are **PARALLEL** in meaning and structure. In Hebrew there are also similarities in sound:

> a time to weep and a time to laugh
> a time to mourn and a time to dance

PARTICIPIAL indicates that the phrase, clause, construction, or other expression described is marked by a **PARTICIPLE**. **PARTICIPIAL PHRASE** is a phrase marked by a participle. See **PARTICIPLE**.

PARTICIPLE is a verbal adjective, that is, a word that retains some of the characteristics of a verb while functioning as an adjective. In the phrase "land flowing with milk and honey," "flowing" is a participle. Participles are very common in Hebrew.

PARTICLE is a small word whose grammatical form does not change and which has a particular function. In English the most common particles are prepositions and conjunctions, such as "with," "into," or "and."

PASSIVE. See **VOICE**.

PENTATEUCH refers to the first five books of the Bible, sometimes called "the Torah," "the Law," or "the Books of Moses."

PERSON, as a grammatical term, refers to the speaker, the person spoken to, or the person or thing spoken about. **FIRST PERSON** is the person(s) speaking (such as "I," "me," "my," "mine," "we," "us," "our," or "ours"). **SECOND PERSON** is the person(s) or thing(s) spoken to (such as "thou," "thee," "thy," "thine," "ye," "you," "your," or "yours"). **THIRD PERSON** is the person(s) or thing(s) spoken about (such as "he," "she," "it," "his," "her," "them," or "their"). The examples given here are all pronouns, but in many languages the verb forms have affixes that mark first, second, or third person and also indicate whether they are **SINGULAR** or **PLURAL**.

PHRASE is a dependent grammatical construction of two or more words, but less than a complete clause or a sentence. A phrase is usually given a name according to its function in a sentence, such as that of a "noun phrase," "verb phrase," or "prepositional phrase." For example, "the boy in front" is a noun phrase, "in front of the house" is a prepositional phrase, and "carried a heavy load" is a verb phrase.

PLURAL refers to the form of a word that indicates more than one. See **SINGULAR**.

POETRY (**POETIC**) refers to a literary genre that differs from everyday speech and from **PROSE** because of its rhythmic and heightened style. Poets use special language to create a mood or image to be shared with the hearer or reader. Each language has special stylistic devices such as figurative language, word order variation, wordplay, repetition or rhyming that are especially frequent in **POETRY** (compare Judges 4 and 5). The boundary between beautiful, artistic **PROSE** and **POETRY** is sometimes difficult to determine, but speakers of a language can usually distinguish poetry from ordinary speech. **POETRY** is usually written or spoken in measured or balanced lines, while prose is not. See **PROSE**.

POINT OF VIEW. See **VIEWPOINT**.

POSSESSIVE refers to a grammatical relationship in which one noun or pronoun is said to "possess" another ("John's car," "his son," "their destruction"). See also **POSSESSIVE PRONOUNS** under **PRONOUNS**.

PREPOSITION is a word whose function is to indicate the relation of a noun or pronoun to another noun, pronoun, verb, or adjective within a clause. Some English prepositions are "for," "from," "in," "to," and "with."

PRESENT TENSE. See **TENSE.**

PRONOMINAL refers to **PRONOUNS.**

PRONOUNS are words that are used in place of nouns, such as "he," "him," "his," "she," "we," "them," "who," "which," "this," or "these." **POSSESSIVE PRONOUNS** are pronouns such as "my," "our," "your," or "his," which indicate possession.

PROPER NAME, by contrast with a common noun, is the name of a unique object, as "Jerusalem," "Joshua," "Jordan." However, the same name may be applied to more than one object; for example, "John" (the Baptist or the Apostle) and "Antioch" (of Syria or Pisidia).

PROSE is the ordinary form of spoken or written language, without a special style and structure such as elaborate imagery, meter, and rhythm that are often characteristic of poetry. However, literary **PROSE** may share some of the features of poetry such as figures of speech, wordplay, repetition, or even parallelism.

PURPOSE CLAUSE designates a construction that states the purpose involved in some other action; for example, "John came in order to help him." See also **CLAUSE.**

QUOTATION. See **DIRECT QUOTATION,** under **DISCOURSE.**

READ, READING. See **TEXT, TEXTUAL.**

RECEPTOR is the person(s) receiving a message. The **RECEPTOR LANGUAGE** is the language into which a translation is made. For example, in a translation from Hebrew into German, Hebrew is the source language and German is the receptor language. The receptor culture is the culture of the people who speak the receptor language.

REDUNDANT (REDUNDANCY) describes anything that is entirely predictable from the context. For example, in "John, he did it," the pronoun "he" is redundant. A feature may be redundant and yet may be important to retain in certain languages, perhaps for stylistic or for grammatical reasons.

REFLEXIVE has to do with verbs and pronouns where the one doing the action and the one on whom the action is performed are the same person. Sometimes the goal is explicit (as in "He dresses himself"); at other times it is implicit (as in "He dresses"). See also **VOICE, ACTIVE,** and **PASSIVE.**

RENDER means to translate or express in a language different from the original.

RENDERING is the manner in which a specific passage is translated from one language to another.

617

RESTRUCTURE. See **STRUCTURE.**

RHETORICAL QUESTION is an assertion or exhortation that is put in the form of a question, but one which is not intended to ask for information. Rhetorical questions are usually employed for emphasis and often express the mood, emotion, or attitude of the person asking them. When the prophet says "Have you not known? Have you not heard?" (Isa 40.21), he really means "You surely know and you have been told!"

ROOT refers to the smallest element of a word, from which other words may be derived. For example, "friend" is the root of "friendliness." In Hebrew most roots are made up of three consonants, and many words are formed on the basis of this root. For example, the root *b-r-k* is the basis for the noun "blessing," the adjective "blessed," and the verb "to bless."

SARCASM is a strong form of irony. **SARCASTIC** comments are always negative and intended to ridicule or reprove the person or subject to which they are directed. For example, "Some king you are!" really means "You are a worthless king!" **SARCASM**, like irony, is often marked by special intonation, but in written form **SARCASM** must be recognized from the context.

SCRIBE, SCRIBAL. See **MANUSCRIPT.**

SECOND PERSON. See **PERSON.**

SEMANTIC refers to meaning. **SEMANTICS** is the study of the meaning of any element of discourse, oral or written.

SENTENCE is a grammatical construction composed of one or more clauses and capable of standing alone. **SENTENCES** that have the same topic or theme combine to form a **PARAGRAPH.**

SEPTUAGINT is a Greek translation of the Hebrew Old Testament. This translation was completed about 200 years before the birth of Christ and was the Scripture used by many New Testament writers. It is often abbreviated as LXX.

SIMILE (pronounced SIM-i-lee) is a **FIGURE OF SPEECH** that describes one event or object (the "topic") by comparing it to another event or object (the "image"). **SIMILES** always use words of comparison such as "like" or "as." "Your lips [the topic] are like a scarlet thread [the image]" is a **SIMILE** from Song of Songs 4.3. Similes differ from metaphors in that metaphors do not mark the image with words that indicate comparison. See **METAPHOR.**

SINGULAR refers to the form of a word that indicates one thing or person, in contrast to **PLURAL**, which indicates more than one , or **DUAL**, which indicates a pair. See **DUAL, PLURAL.**

SOURCE LANGUAGE is the language in which an original message is produced. For the Old Testament the **SOURCE TEXT** is in Hebrew, while for the New Testament it is in Greek.

STRUCTURE is the systematic arrangement of the elements of language, including the ways in which words combine into phrases, phrases into clauses, clauses into sentences, and sentences into larger units of discourse. This process can be compared to constructing a building, so **STRUCTURES** are often spoken of as **CONSTRUCTIONS**. To separate and rearrange the various components of a sentence or some other unit of discourse in the translation process is to **RESTRUCTURE** it.

STYLE is the form or manner in which the content of a discourse is expressed. Each language has its own set of **STYLISTIC** devices that make a text pleasing to the reader or hearer. For example, in Hebrew, repetition is much appreciated, while in English, repetition is often avoided by the use of synonyms. Authors or storytellers may also have their own individual **STYLE**.

SUBJECT is one of the two major divisions of a clause, the other being the predicate. In "The small boy walked to school," "The small boy" is the subject. Typically the subject is a noun phrase. It should not be confused with the semantic **AGENT**, or **ACTOR**.

SUBORDINATE CLAUSE. See **CLAUSE**.

SUFFIX is a letter or one or more syllables added to the end of a word, to modify the meaning in some manner. For example, "-s" suffixed to "tree" changes the word from singular to plural, "trees," while "-ing" suffixed to "sing" changes the verb to a participle, "singing."

SUPERLATIVE refers to the form of an adjective or adverb that indicates that the object or event described possesses a certain quality to a degree greater than does any other object or event being considered. "Most happy" and "finest" are adjectives in the superlative degree.

SYMBOL (SYMBOLIC) is a form, whether linguistic or nonlinguistic, which is arbitrarily and conventionally associated with a particular meaning. For example, the word "cross" is a linguistic symbol, referring to a particular object. Similarly, within the Christian tradition, the cross as an object is a symbol for the death of Jesus.

SYNONYMS are words that are different in form but similar in meaning, such as "boy" and "lad." Expressions that have essentially the same meaning are said to be **SYNONYMOUS**. However, no two words are completely synonymous.

SYRIAC is the name of a Semitic language, a part of the Aramaic family, used in Western Asia, into which the Bible was translated at a very early date (the **SYRIAC VERSION**).

TABOO refers to something set apart as sacred by religious custom and is therefore forbidden to all but certain persons or uses (**POSITIVE TABOO**), or something that is regarded as evil and therefore forbidden to all by tradition or social usage (**NEGATIVE TABOO**).

TARGET (or **RECEPTOR**) **LANGUAGE** refers to the language into which the **SOURCE TEXT** is being translated. In the case of Today's English Version, the **TARGET LANGUAGE** is English. **TARGET CULTURE** refers to the cultural **CONTEXT** or life-setting of the people who speak the **TARGET LANGUAGE**.

TARGUM is an Aramaic translation or paraphrase of a section of the ancient Hebrew Scriptures.

TENSE refers to the time an event occurs, often in relation to other events in a discourse. The most common tenses are past, present, and future.

TEXT, TEXTUAL, refers to the various biblical manuscripts. A **TEXTUAL READING** is the form in which words occur in a particular manuscript (or group of manuscripts), especially where it differs from others. **TEXTUAL EVIDENCE** is any evidence from manuscripts that may support a particular reading. **TEXTUAL PROBLEMS** arise when manuscripts contain different readings.

THEME is the central idea or main point of a discourse. For example, we can say that "purification from sin" is the major **THEME** in Psalm 51.

THIRD PERSON. See **PERSON**.

TRANSITION in discourse involves passing from one thought to another or one literary unit to another. Most languages have special words such as "now" or "then" to mark these transitions.

TRANSLATION is the transfer of a message in a **SOURCE LANGUAGE** text into another language, the **RECEPTOR LANGUAGE**. A good translation aims at giving the closest natural equivalent in the **TARGET LANGUAGE** in terms of meaning (content and function) and, if possible, also form (style and structure).

TRANSLATIONAL refers to translation. A translator may seem to be following an inferior textual reading (see **TEXTUAL**) when he or she is simply adjusting the rendering to the requirements of the receptor language, that is, for a **TRANSLATIONAL REASON**.

TRANSLITERATE is to represent in the **TARGET LANGUAGE** the approximate sounds or letters of words occurring in the **SOURCE LANGUAGE**. **TRANSLITERATING** is different from **TRANSLATING**. For example, "Amen" in Hebrew may be **TRANSLITERATED** in one language as "*amin*," or it may be **TRANSLATED** as "So be it."

UNAMBIGUOUS indicates that a word or phrase is clearly understood in only one way. See **AMBIGUOUS**.

VERBS are a grammatical class of words that express existence, action, state, or occurrence, such as "be," "run," "become," or "think." In some languages ideas expressed by adjectives in English may be better expressed by verbs; for example, "to be hot" or "to be angry."

VERBAL refers to words being used in oral or written communication. It may also describe a word that is like a **VERB**.

VERSIONS are translations. The ancient versions are translations of the Bible, or of portions of the Bible, made in early times; for example, the Greek Septuagint, the ancient Syriac, or the Ethiopic versions.

VIEWPOINT (**POINT OF VIEW**) is the location or situation or circumstance from which a speaker or writer presents a message. If, for example, the **VIEWPOINT PLACE** is the top of a hill, movement in the area will be described differently from the way one would describe it from the bottom of a hill. If the **VIEWPOINT PERSON** is a priest, he will speak of the temple in a way that differs from that of a common person.

VOCATIVE describes a word or phrase used to address a person or group in direct speech. In "Save me, O God" (Psa 54.1), "O God" is a **VOCATIVE**. Some languages have a special grammatical form to show that a word is used in this way.

VOICE in grammar is the relation of the action expressed by a verb to the participants in the action. In English and many other languages, the **ACTIVE VOICE** indicates that the subject performs the action ("John hit the man"), while the **PASSIVE VOICE** indicates that the subject is being acted upon ("The man was hit").

VOWELS are speech sounds of the vocal cords, produced by unobstructed air passing from the lungs though the mouth. The written letters representing those sounds are also called **VOWELS**; for example, "a," "i," or "u," which are the most common vowels found in the world's languages. In Hebrew **VOWELS** were originally not written, but they were added later as small marks written under or above the consonants. See also **CONSONANTS**.

VULGATE is the Latin version of the Bible translated and/or edited originally by Saint Jerome near the end of the fourth century. It has been traditionally the official version of the Roman Catholic Church.

Index

This index includes concepts, key words, and terms for which this Handbook contains a discussion useful for translators. Hebrew terms have been transliterated and are found in English alphabetical order.